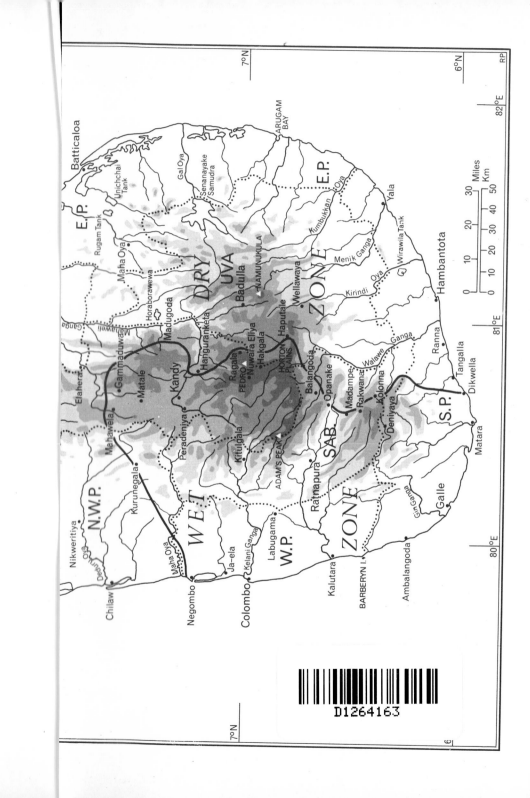

A GUIDE TO THE
BIRDS OF CEYLON

ILLUSTRATED BY THE AUTHOR
G. M. HENRY

WITH 30 HALF-TONE PLATES
OF WHICH 27 ARE COLOURED
AND 136 BLACK-AND-WHITE DRAWINGS

SECOND EDITION

K. V. G. DE SILVA & SONS
KANDY
SRI LANKA

This edition published 1978 by
K. V. G. De Silva & Sons (Kandy)
86, D. S. Senanayake Veediya
Kandy, Sri Lanka
44/9 Y.M.B.A. Building, Fort, Colombo
By arrangement with Oxford University Press

First published by Oxford University Press 1955
Second edition 1971

PRINTED IN GREAT BRITAIN BY HEADLEY BROTHERS LTD
109 KINGSWAY LONDON WC2B 6PX AND ASHFORD KENT

And God said . . .

> Let fowl fly above the earth
> In the open firmament of heaven.

And God created . . . every winged fowl after its kind:
And God saw that it was good.

Genesis i. 20-1

'Every beast of the forest is *Mine*,

> the cattle on a thousand hills.

I know all the birds of the air,

> and all that moves in the field
> is *Mine*.'

Psalm 50. 10–11
(Revised Standard Version)

DEDICATED

TO THE PRAISE AND GLORY OF GOD

AND HIS SON JESUS CHRIST

OF WHOM IT IS WRITTEN:

'ALL THINGS HAVE BEEN CREATED THROUGH HIM

AND UNTO HIM; AND HE IS BEFORE ALL THINGS,

AND IN HIM ALL THINGS CONSIST.'

St Paul, Colossians i. 16-17

PREFACE TO THE SECOND EDITION

WHEN I was a lad of 13, I received as a Sunday School prize a copy of a delightful book on Indian Natural History entitled *A Naturalist on the Prowl*, written by EHA (Edward Hamilton Aitken). In his first chapter, the author writes, concerning the book of nature: 'I speak of reading the book. There are many who busy themselves with it and do not read it. There is your doctor of nomenclature, who devotes his laborious life to the elucidation of such questions as whether you shall call the common crow *Corvus impudicus* or *Corvus splendens*. He is an index-maker. Then there is a host of commentators, and editors, who toil to shed such light as they may on the text, or, oftener, on each other. Lastly, there is your collector, who makes extracts. I esteem all these laborious men and feel grateful to them and rejoice that I am none of them, for I hold with Matthew Arnold, that the best use to which you can put a good book is to read and enjoy it.'

This well reflects my own attitude to the world of Nature.

Several reviewers of the first edition of this book criticized my failure to arrange the Orders and Families in accordance with the latest system of classification, or to use the most up-to-date scientific nomenclature for some of the birds. In extenuation of these grievous faults, I will here confess that my interest in birds is primarily aesthetic; their beauty of form, colour, texture and pattern of plumage; their flight, song, behaviour and elusiveness appeal to me far more than the —to my mind, utterly barren—attempts to achieve a uniform set of technical names or a universally acceptable scheme of classification.

However, in the Appendix to this edition (p. 435) an attempt has been made to satisfy the yearnings for up-to-dateness of the laborious people aforesaid, by providing parallel lists of *Families* of birds as arranged in this book and in Phillips's *A (1952) Revised Checklist of the Birds of Ceylon*, published by the National Museums of Ceylon in April 1953; the scientific names adopted by Phillips, where they differ from mine, are also given in the Appendix. It is, however, almost amusing to observe that not a few of the *Checklist* names have undergone further alterations in more recent works; and in several instances, scientific names of birds, after undergoing many vicissitudes at the hands of various authors have now returned to those first bestowed by the original describers!

What a merry game the classification and nomenclature experts indulge in (not to mention the 'subspecies-mongers') !

v

PREFACE

Since the first edition of this book was published, the list of recorded species of Ceylon birds has been augmented by the collection or sight-recording of several migrant species, mostly amongst the smaller waders, sandpipers, etc. These have been dealt with in the Appendix, which students are earnestly advised to consult.

It is hoped that the additional black-and-white illustrations on pages 437 ff., showing different types of nests, will prove to be an acceptable feature of this revised edition.

My grateful thanks are tendered to my Publishers, the Oxford University Press, and to the block-makers and printers, Messrs. Headley Brothers Ltd, Ashford, Kent, for the great care and patience they have bestowed to make the book a worthy one; and I have again to thank my friend Major W. W. A. Phillips for his generous kindness in supplying much of the additional material contained in the Appendix.

G.M.H.

Constantine, Falmouth
Cornwall

INTRODUCTION

THE serious study of Ceylon's abundant bird life may be said to have commenced about a century ago with the systematic collection of specimens by E. L. Layard, the naming and description of the results by Blyth, and the publication of lists of the birds of the Island by Layard, Kelaart and others. In 1872, Holdsworth published in the *Proceedings of the Zoological Society of London* a paper on the 'Birds of Ceylon', in which he described a number of species and figured some of them. These researches led to the foundational work of Captain W. Vincent Legge, R.A., a military officer stationed in Ceylon from 1868 to 1877. He amassed large collections and copious notes on distribution, habits, nesting, etc., and on his return to England, and after several years of most painstaking and thorough work, he published his magnificent monograph *A History of the Birds of Ceylon*. It contained a number of hand-coloured lithographs of the species of birds then considered to be peculiar to the Island. Legge's monumental work is still, though long out of print, a great mine of information, and all subsequent work on the subject is largely based upon it.

The publication of this splendid work had, however, one unfortunate effect. Its grand proportions and detailed descriptions seem to have created the impression in Ceylon that the last word had been said on its birds. A perusal of Legge shows that, during and before his time, not a few planters and others were keenly interested in collecting birds and studying their distribution and habits; but after Legge's book appeared, this enthusiasm seems to have died down to a great extent and, except for a few very useful papers by A. L. Butler and F. Lewis, little research appears to have been done for many years. Soon after his appointment, in 1910, as Director of the Colombo Museum, Dr Joseph Pearson set about remedying this state of affairs, with the result that Mr W. E. Wait, C.C.S., undertook the preparation of a handy and inexpensive *Manual of the Birds of Ceylon*, which appeared first in 1925, with a second edition in 1931. For the serious bird-student, Wait's *Manual* proved an invaluable aid giving, as it did, a convenient hand-list and a concise, yet accurate, account of the Ceylonese avifauna. To beginners and would-be students, however, it proved to be much less useful, mainly because of its inadequacy of illustration. The publication by the Ceylon Government, between 1927 and 1935, in four parts, of my *Coloured Plates of the Birds of Ceylon* was an attempt to remedy this deficiency in Wait's book; but, inasmuch as only 64 species were portrayed out of some 380, and the work was priced beyond the means of many, its success was limited.

In this work the general principle adopted has been to illustrate the more colourful birds in colour, those of duller plumage by black-and-white drawings in the text; but in following this principle I have allowed myself considerable latitude. Considerations of cost prohibit the figuring of all the species in colour, but it is hoped that the text-figures, in conjunction with the descriptions, will make recognition of the birds easy. In the accounts of species, no attempt has been made to give exhaustive information; the purpose of the book may be stated as the provision of a means of identifying birds in the field—mainly through the illustrations—and a framework of basic facts upon which students may build their own observations. In the case of a few exceptionally interesting birds somewhat fuller accounts are given.

A few hints upon methods of getting to know the birds may be acceptable; these make no pretence of being exhaustive, but they have proved useful in my own experience. In the first rank of bird-studying tools, I would place the note-book; this is absolutely essential for anything like serious study, and its use provides the surest and quickest means of 'learning the birds'. It should be carried everywhere and used constantly. While I feel bound to confess that my own note-taking and field-sketching have been done very unsystematically and often on exceedingly miscellaneous materials (backs of envelopes and the like) I strongly recommend any beginner to procure at the outset a strong, weatherproof form of loose-leaf note-book, such as admits of refills being inserted as soon as one is filled with notes; the loose-leaf system has obvious advantages for subsequent filing and indexing. In the note-book should be recorded any observation, of even the smallest interest, at the time it is seen; the mere fact of writing an observation on the spot compels attention to accuracy, and focuses the attention on details which would be overlooked or forgotten if left to be recorded later. As far as practicable, the rule in making notes should be 'one observation, one page'; if disconnected notes on several species or subjects are written on a single page, filing and indexing become impossible. Write on one side only of a leaf; too much economy in the use of paper leads to dreadful complications later on. Every observation should be dated, and its locality given; other circumstances, such as weather, wind force and direction, time of day, etc., often prove to be very valuable afterwards.

The habit of making 'transects' is very important. Every species seen and *certainly identified* during a country walk, or in a single area in a single day, should be noted in the book, with as close an approximation as may be to the number of individuals of each species observed. Such transects, if regularly made and carefully kept, provide in the course of a few years valuable information on many aspects of bird-life. Never forget that *accuracy* is the prime consideration in all note-making.

Nothing so enforces accuracy of observation as an attempt to draw the thing seen, and therefore it is well to cultivate the habit of making sketches in the note-book of any bird, or detail of its environment that strikes one. Elaborate or artistic drawings are not necessary; if desired, they may be made later at leisure; but their place is not in the field note-book, where simple sketches of line or mass, with accuracy as the only requirement, are what is wanted. Even the crudest of drawings is better than none.

A good working knowledge of a bird's external features is essential in studying birds and making notes about them. The beginner is strongly urged to give a little time to the task of learning the parts of a bird, as illustrated in the Glossary which follows this Introduction—preferably in conjunction with a dead bird, which can be pulled about and compared with the figures—so as to become familiar with the names and structure of the various parts.

Next to the note-book, in importance, come visual aids. Birds, in general, are shy of man; the great majority are small; and without some optical assistance our range of effective observation of them is severely restricted. Unfortunately, good field-glasses are expensive and cheap ones are not worth buying. However, the pleasure and usefulness given by a first-class instrument are so great that every bird-lover is strongly urged to obtain a pair at the earliest possible moment. In selecting them, the following points should be borne in mind: (*a*) They must be of the prismatic, adjustable-width type (ordinary opera glasses are practically useless for bird work). (*b*) The magnification should be ×6 or ×8 diameters (under ×6 give insufficient magnification, over ×8 give too small a field of view, and are impossible to hold steady enough for continuous observation—as every vibration of the hands is magnified in the same degree as the bird being watched). (*c*) The field of view must be as large as possible. Two kinds of focusing arrangement are available: the central focusing-screw; and independent eye-piece focusing; the former enables focusing to be done with one hand, the other requires both hands. I personally prefer the independent eye-piece focusing type for tropical conditions, because they keep the eye-pieces freer from dust and damp than the other form and, in any case, it is seldom that one can hold field-glasses with one hand steady enough for bird-work. Field-glasses are delicate instruments, and should be carefully used; they must always be carried, when not actually in use, in their case. In the tropics, their optical glass parts are readily attacked by fungi, which spread over the prisms and lenses, etching the glass and quickly ruining their polish and transparency; to avoid this, it is essential that they be kept, when not in use, either in some form of desiccator, or else in an air-tight receptacle containing a gaseous disinfectant such as carbolic acid, or formalin. I have had good results with the latter. If carefully looked after, a good pair of field-glasses will last a lifetime and give endless pleasure to their owner.

THE TOPOGRAPHY, CLIMATE, AND VEGETATION OF CEYLON, IN RELATION
TO BIRD LIFE

Geologically, Ceylon is a detached portion of the South-Indian peninsula; it appears highly probable that at one time it was part of the subcontinent and occupied a position to the west of where it now lies, with its present north-south axis in a more north-easterly direction. Then its great mountain massif would form the southern end of the Western Ghats, and its flat northern half would be in continuity with the Carnatic plain of South India. Through some vast stress developing in the earth's crust in this region, a split appeared across the Ghat, severing what is now Ceylon from Travancore; and, as the gap slowly widened, a mass of land drifted eastwards to form, first, a peninsula attached to the Carnatic, and eventually an island—Ceylon. On this hypothesis, it is evident that the southern, mountainous half of Ceylon will have been severed from the parent continent for a vastly longer period of time than the northern, 'Carnatic' portion. It is well known that forms of life (including birds), separated and isolated from their parent stock, tend to diverge from it, eventually forming distinct species; and the longer the period of separation, the more strongly marked the difference between the two stocks. This may serve to explain the fact that nearly all the peculiar species of Ceylon birds (in common with mammals, reptiles, insects, etc., as well) are confined to the southern, mountainous half of Ceylon. They have been severed so long from their parent-species in India that the 'family likeness' has been lost, and they have become distinct species; whereas the birds, etc., of the northern (and especially of the north-western) portion of the Island, having been separated from their parent stock in the Carnatic for a comparatively brief period, have had time to form, at most, only slightly distinct subspecies of their Indian counterparts.

This hypothetical explanation of the presence of so many peculiar forms in the southern portion of Ceylon is not, however, the whole story; for a good many of the endemics are quite distinct from their relatives in South India (e.g. the Green-billed Coucal, Ceylon Blue Magpie, Yellow-fronted Barbet, Legge's Flowerpecker, etc.). It seems probable that these represent a relic-fauna—surviving in Southern

Ceylon, but whose parent stocks have died out completely on the mainland.

The climate of Ceylon in relation to its topography has been frequently described of late years, and may be found ably discussed in the *Manual of the Mammals of Ceylon* by W. W. A. Phillips, p. xvi. Here it is only necessary to point out that, due mainly to the position of the great mountain massif of Ceylon in relation to the direction of the two annually-recurring winds (the south-west and north-east monsoons), the Island has two very distinct climatic zones correlated with the annual rainfall; these are known as the 'wet zone' and the 'dry zone' respectively. (A third zone, the 'central hill zone', is usually described, but inasmuch as the hills are in one or other of the two zones abovementioned, it appears to me that the central hill zone is an unnecessary complication.) The presence of the great mountain massif in the centre of the southern half of the Island has the effect of causing the moisture-laden south-west monsoon (blowing from about May to September), as it strikes the hills, to shed its moisture in the form of rain upon the south-western sector; while at the same time, the country to the north-west, north and east of the hills receives little or none of this rain. During the remaining months of the year the north-east monsoon blows, giving rainy conditions in these parts, and also producing frequent afternoon thunder-storms in the wet zone as well. It follows that the wet zone receives the full rainfall of the south-west monsoon and also a regular quota of rain during the north-east monsoon, with no extended period of the year free from rain; this gives to this part of the Island an annual, well-distributed rainfall of from 80 to 200 inches or more. In the dry zone, however, the great bulk of the annual rainfall, of from 25 to 75 inches, falls during three or four months of the year, mostly from November to February; and the remainder of the year is generally dry in spite of steady wind. The effect of this distribution of the rainfall upon both plant and animal life is obvious.

While no hard-and-fast line can be drawn between the wet and dry zones, the boundaries of the wet zone may roughly be defined by a line drawn as follows: from Negombo on the west coast, through Kurunegala, to Mahawela, Gammaduwa, Madugoda, Hanguranketa, Ragala, Haputale, Balangoda, Madampe, Kolonna, to Dikwella between Tangalla and Matara, on the southern coast; thence following the south-western coast-line to Negombo. All the Island outside this boundary is in the dry zone; and of this, the driest parts are the north-western coastal area from about Chilaw to Elephant Pass (including the Jaffna Peninsula); and the south-eastern coastal strip, from about Ranna to Arugam Bay. In these semi-arid areas, the vegetation takes on a more or less desert-flora character, and the bird life is correspondingly specialized; strangely, it is these very dry areas that show the greatest abundance and variety of birds usually associated with water—the ducks and wading-birds; which are but poorly represented in the high-rainfall areas.

A few remarks should be made concerning the effect of cultivation upon Ceylon's bird life. In the days of Layard and Kelaart, the greater part of the Island was clothed with more or less dense forest; in the low-country dry zone this forest was largely of a secondary type, caused by the reversion to jungle of extensive cultivation which existed in the heyday of the ancient kings; but in the wet zone and the mountains it was mainly indigenous, virgin forest. These vast, forested tracts naturally gave harbourage to an avifauna of a different general complexion from that of the present day. The forest-haunting types of birds were doubtless far more numerous and widely-distributed than they are today, but the commoner and more familiar, garden- and scrub-frequenting types of bird would be less numerous and widespread than they now are. In Legge's time, the mountain forests had already been drastically felled over enormous areas to make room for coffee; a process which has gone on ever since (though tea and rubber have taken the place of coffee), so that the montane and wet-zone forests are nowadays but a pitiful remnant of what they were. Even where remnants of these forests exist—on the highest hills, and here and there in the wet zone—they are being steadily and surely whittled away, both by clear-felling and, more insidiously still, by the ceaseless cutting of saplings within their borders by the neighbouring estate- and village-populations. These remnants of the once vast mountain and wet-zone forests of Ceylon are the sole remaining refuge of all the more interesting of the endemic bird species (not to mention mammals, reptiles, amphibians, insects and plants) of our Island; and unless drastic steps are taken now to preserve these relic-forests throughout the hills and the wet zone, it can only be a question of time before many of Ceylon's most interesting forms of wild life will be exterminated. Even small pockets of forest scattered through cultivated areas should be preserved intact from human interference. A particularly pernicious form of this interference, in the case of the mountain forests, is the replacement of native forest by plantations of exotic trees, such as conifers, acacias and eucalyptus. These plants—admirable, no doubt, in their own countries—have a ruinous effect on the fauna and flora, and on the scenery, wherever they are grown in Ceylon; their dismal plantations support none of the more interesting forms of wild life.

Besides the rapid disappearance of forests, the following factors have an important bearing on the future of Ceylon's avifauna. The opening up of the country by roads and modern means of transport; the ever-increasing availability of firearms; and the breaking down, through spreading materialism, of religious aversion to the taking of life—these things all have a deleterious influence on bird-life, operating first against the larger, edible species, such as peafowl, junglefowl, storks and ducks, etc., but sooner or later affecting all birds—sometimes tending towards the increase of numbers or distribution of some species, sometimes diminishing them—but nearly always working against the rarer, more specialized and interesting species.

As scientific names of animals are often a stumbling-block to those who lack scientific training, the following remarks may help to throw light on what is really a very simple matter. All living things, on being scientifically described, are given two names which are in Latin form (Latin being regarded as an 'international' language). The first name is that of the genus, the second that of the species. The species is the unit of classification, and consists of all members of a normally interbreeding population; a genus may comprise one or more of such units. For instance, the House Crow belongs to the species *splendens*, all members of which collectively form a normally breeding population; the Black Crow, while closely related to the House Crow, does not interbreed with it and is a different species, *macrorhynchos*; but the relationship of these two crows is expressed by placing both species in the same genus, *Corvus*. Thus, we have *Corvus splendens*, the House Crow, and *Corvus macrorhynchos*, the Black Crow. However, while all members of the widely-distributed House Crow would freely interbreed, and therefore all belong to the same species, House Crows from different parts of their range show slight, but constant, differences of size or coloration, etc.; the House Crows of north-west India are all paler-coloured, and those of Ceylon are smaller and darker, than those of peninsular India. Each such local race of a species, therefore, is given a third, or subspecific, name, to indicate this fact; the House Crow of north-west India is *Corvus splendens zugmayeri*, that of Ceylon is *Corvus splendens protegatus*, while that of peninsular India is *Corvus splendens splendens* (the typical, or first-described race is always indicated by repeating the specific name for the subspecies).

Because this book deals with the birds of a definite geographical area, I have felt obliged to use subspecific names; but in practically every case where such names occur in the succeeding pages it may be taken that a closely-related form, or forms, of the same bird dwells in the neighbouring continent of India. In the great majority of cases, the differences between the Island race and its Indian counterpart, or counterparts, are trifling matters of shades of colour, or the length of bill, wings, etc.; and if these are ignored, this book may be used as a guide to most of the common birds of India, as well as to those of Ceylon. About 358 out of the 397 species and subspecies herein dealt with are either the same as the Indian forms, or are so little different from them as to be, for practical purposes, identical.

To avoid misunderstanding, it may be well to point out that it is customary to place the name of the original describer of a species or subspecies immediately after the scientific name. If the genus remains unchanged the author's name is unbracketed, but where his species has subsequently been transferred (whether by himself or anybody else) to another genus, his name is enclosed in brackets, thus:

> *Molpastes cafer cafer* (Linnaeus)—*cafer* was originally placed by Linnaeus in the genus *Turdus,* and his name is therefore in brackets;

> *Copsychus saularis ceylonensis* Sclater—*ceylonensis* was placed in the genus *Copsychus* by Sclater; there has been no change of genus, so Sclater's name is unbracketed.

For the benefit of the uninitiated it may be well to point out that names of orders all terminate in *-iformes*—e.g. *Passeriformes*; family names terminate in *-idae,* and sub-family names in *-inae.* (The latter category is used very little in the present work.)

While this book was in the press a very important addition to the bird literature of Ceylon was published. It is *A (1952) Revised Checklist of the Birds. of Ceylon* by W. W. A. Phillips, published by the National Museums of Ceylon. This is a work which no serious student of the Island's avifauna can afford to be without; but readers who consult it will observe at once that the arrangement of Orders and families differs from that adopted here, and a brief explanation of this discrepancy is desirable. Phillips follows, in the main, the classification proposed by Wetmore, whereas I have followed, with some modifications, the older system used by Wait, Whistler and other authors. It must always be borne in mind that no linear arrangement of Orders and families could possibly express satisfactorily the lines of descent and inter-relationships of birds, even were these certainly known; any system of classification based on the supposed course of evolution must inevitably depend largely on intelligent guesswork, and only a very bold optimist would claim that finality had been reached in deciding on the least objectionable arrangement. As this book is not intended as a work on classification and nomenclature but as a help towards 'enjoying the birds', the precise arrangement is not of very grea⁺ importance, and I do not think that any student will find much diff.culty in correlating the *Guide* with the *Checklist.*

A further discrepancy between this book and the *Checklist* will be found in the names employed for some of the birds. So far as English names are concerned, where I have made changes I have tried to bring common sense to bear. Discrepancies in scientific names are mainly in those of genera. These are so much matters of individual opinion that it is rare to find any two works (even by the same author), on any particular avifauna, using identical sets of scientific names! This instability of scientific nomenclature is very puzzling to the lay reader, and is universally admitted to be a great hindrance to real progress in our knowledge of birds; but as no general agreement on the names to be used seems to be in sight, one must make the best of it. A little practice in the art of—shall we say 'intuition'—generally enables one to discover the identity of a bird in literature in spite of its numerous scientific aliases.

Regarding the Sinhalese and Tamil names employed here, I have in the main adopted those given by Wait, with a few modifications and additions from other sources; it is to be observed, however, that, except in the cases of well-known birds of distinctive characteristics in plumage or habits, vernacular names are by no means as specific or generally known as English names. It is much to be hoped that accurate and specific Sinhalese and Tamil names for all the birds will soon be discovered (or else invented) and put into general use in Ceylon. .

It remains for me to acknowledge my indebtedness, and to express my grateful thanks, to the many friends who, in one way and another, have helped in the preparation of this book. To Major W. W. A. Phillips I am indebted for much help, most generously rendered. Particularly in the sections on nesting, I have drawn freely on the mass of accurate information contained in his series of papers on the 'Nests and Eggs of Ceylon Birds', published in the *Ceylon Journal of Science*, Section B, commencing with vol. 21, 1939; and in his numerous other papers. To my friends Ralph and Mary West I owe thanks for much kind hospitality, helpful companionship, and encouragement. To all the members of the Ceylon Bird Club I am indebted for valuable notes and records. Mr J. D. Macdonald, Keeper of Birds at the British Museum (Natural History) and his assistants have been very cooperative in lending me skins for figuring, and I offer them my warm thanks. The Alexander Library of Ornithology, at the Edward Grey Institute in Oxford, has been most useful, and I thank Mr W. B. Alexander, its Librarian, for his ready help and advice on many occasions.

I should like, at this point, to pay a tribute to the memory of Dr Casey A. Wood, who, by commissioning me to paint the originals of the *Coloured Plates of the Birds of Ceylon*, and by using his influence to get them published by the Ceylon Government, gave me much encouragement and help at a time when these things were much needed.

Last, but by no means least, my grateful thanks are due to my wife, without whose constant help and patience this book would never have materialized.

G.M.H.

Church Enstone
Oxford

GLOSSARY OF TERMS

axillary: Belonging to the base of the wing, on the under side; the 'armpit' as it were; the axillaries are a small tuft of feathers situated in this position.

banyan: A wild fig-tree, *Ficus benghalensis*, well known for its aerial roots. Its figs are an important source of food to many birds.

bo: *Ficus religiosa*, the sacred fig-tree; the pipal of India. Its small figs are eagerly eaten by many birds.

cere: An area of bare, more or less swollen, and often waxy-looking skin at the base of the upper mandible in certain birds (hawks, parrots, pigeons, etc.). The nostrils are situated in it.

chena: A system of shifting cultivation, in which forest is felled and burnt, and a few seasons' crops raised on the soil, which is then abandoned to grow again into jungle. It results in the degradation of tall forest into poor scrub-land, and has a strong influence on bird life.

coverts: Name given to rows or groups of feathers which *cover* certain features of a bird. The principal sets of coverts are: *ear-coverts*; *wing-coverts* (rows of graded feathers on the upper and under surfaces of the wing, covering the bases of the flight- [or quill] feathers, and clothing the skin of the wing; they are graded into *greater*, *median*, and *lesser* series); *tail-coverts* (covering the bases of the tail feathers, above and below); *tibia-coverts* (feathers covering the tibia, or part of the exposed leg above the hock-joint). (See diagrams A and B.)

dadap: *Erythrina lithosperma*, a shade and green-manure tree much grown on tea and cocoa estates. Its scarlet flowers secrete nectar beloved of many birds, and its soft dead wood is often chosen by barbets and woodpeckers in which to excavate their nest-holes.

dihedral: The angle between the wings in soaring flight; 'strong dihedral' means that the wings are held in the shape of a very wide V.

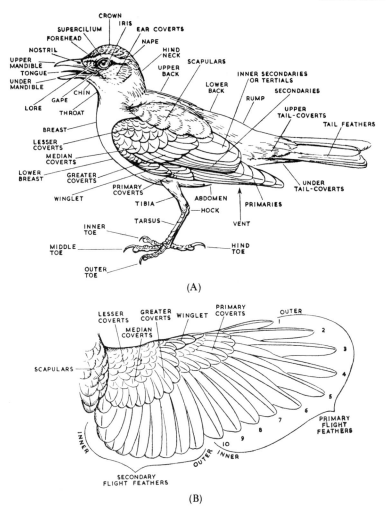

(A)

(B)

External features of a bird

dry zone: The portions of Ceylon which, owing to the distribution of the
mountain massifs, receive little rain during the south-west monsoon, and therefore undergo, annually, a long, dry period, from
about February to November; the dry zone comprises, roughly,
the entire northern half of the Island, and the low country to the
east and south-east of the mountain massifs. (See Introduction,
p. xi, and end-paper map.)

2

eclipse: The name given to a phase of plumage assumed by a moult, annually, by certain birds, particularly the males, when the breeding season is over. It usually consists in the male becoming more or less like the female for a time, until breeding plumage is reassumed by another moult. (Cf. male sunbirds, and many ducks.)

festoon: A rounded lobe on the cutting margin of the upper mandible of some hawks and eagles; to be distinguished from the 'tooth' in a *falcon's* beak, which has a bony core, whereas a 'festoon' is merely part of the horny covering of the beak.

flank: The side of a bird's body, covered by the closed wing; flank feathers often project over the edge of the closed wing.

gape: The corner of the mouth, or the angle where upper and lower mandibles meet.

gorget: A line curving from the gape around the throat or fore-neck, often enclosing a throat-patch of different colour from the surrounding parts. (Cf. Plate 25, fig. 4, facing p. 296.)

graduated: Becoming gradually narrower, away from the base; applied especially to tails where the outer feathers increase in length rapidly and progressively inwards towards the centre pair.

hock-joint: The backwardly-pointing joint in a bird's leg, where tibia and tarsus meet; it corresponds to our ankle and is often mis-called the 'knee'; but the true knee in a bird is higher up, points forwards, and is quite concealed beneath the feathers of the flank.

hora: *Dipterocarpus zeylanicus*, a lofty, straight-trunked tree which grows abundantly in the wet zone of Ceylon.

illuk: *Imperata cylindrica.* A grass which grows, more or less vertically, to a height of about three feet; it covers large areas of land in various parts of the Island.

iris (pl. irides): The area of a bird's eye surrounding the central pupil; its colouring gives much of the character of a bird's facial expression.

jak: *Artocarpus integrifolia*; a well-known fruit- and timber-tree.

kumbuk: *Terminalia arjuna*, a large, water-loving tree which flourishes on the banks of rivers or tanks, especially in the dry zone.

kurakkan: *Eleusine coracana*; a small grain, the ragi of India; it is a favourite chena crop.

lantana: *Lantana aculeata*; a prickly shrub, introduced into Ceylon and India many years ago, but now a widespread weed, forming dense, tangled thickets on waste land, abandoned chenas, etc. It produces masses of orange, or pink flowers, and small, purplish-black berries.

loiterer: Applied to migrant birds which fail to depart on the spring migration, remaining in their winter quarters; such loiterers are nearly always young birds, and they do not, as a rule, moult into breeding dress, but retain their non-breeding, or winter, plumage throughout the south-west monsoon.

lore: The small area on a bird's face lying between the eye and the base of the beak. In some birds (e.g. herons) the lore is bare but, usually, it is clothed with feathers. The lore is bounded above by the supercilium, and below, by the gape.

mā-dun: *Syzygium jambolana*, a tree which flourishes in the dry zone and parts of the wet zone; it bears large quantities of small purplish-black fruits.

māna: *Cymbopogon confertiflorus*; a coarse grass, with a pleasant, lemon-like scent when crushed, which grows in large tussocks to heights of up to six feet. It clothes large areas of hill-sides, and gives harbourage to many species of birds.

mandible: Strictly, the lower jaw-bone; but, in birds, the term is applied to both upper and lower portions of the beak.

mantle: The feathers of the upper back together with the scapulars; these form a cloak-like covering over the back and shoulders of a bird. Many birds sleep with the beak, or the entire head, concealed beneath the feathers of the mantle.

nape: The back of a bird's head, where the neck is attached.

nillu: Sinhalese name for plants of the genus *Strobilanthes*, which, in large variety, form a major item in the undergrowth of the hill forests of Ceylon. They flower simultaneously at intervals of several years, seed profusely, and die down to grow again from seed.

nuchal: To do with the nape, or back of the head; e.g. a nuchal crest is one growing on the back of the head.

nuga: A wild tree of the genus *Ficus*; it produces, at certain seasons, quantities of small figs, which are much liked by fruit-eating birds.

palu: *Mimusops hexandra*; a large timber tree which grows commonly in dry-zone jungles. About May and June it produces large quantities of small, sweet, yellow berries.

patana: Open grass-land on hill-sides and mountain plateaux. The custom of villagers of setting fire to the grass whenever dry weather prevails, in order to produce a crop of tender shoots for cattle to graze, causes immense destruction to patana-living birds.

primary: The nine to eleven long flight feathers which arise from the 'hand' portion of a bird's wing—i.e. those farthest from the body when the wing is spread—are called primaries; they are the most important feathers for flight. Primaries are numbered from the outermost inwards, towards the bird's body.

red cotton: *Bombax malabaricum*, a big, straight-trunked tree which flowers when its leaves have been shed, producing masses of fleshy-red blossoms which secrete large quantities of pale greenish, opalescent nectar; this is eagerly sought by many birds.

rictal bristles: A row of stiff bristles, more or less developed, arranged along the sides of the base of the upper mandible; they are very well developed in flycatchers and nightjars, and in some other birds.

scapulars: A definite group of feathers, separate from those of the upper back, which cover a bird's shoulders and base of the wing above (see diagram A). Together with the feathers of the upper back they constitute the 'mantle'.

sclerotic: The portion of the eyeball surrounding the transparent cornea, corresponding to the 'white of the eye' in man; in most birds it is quite hidden under the eyelids.

secondary: The row of long flight feathers which arise from the 'forearm' portion of a bird's wing are called secondaries; in a spread wing they extend from the elbow joint, near the body, to adjoin the inner primary near the middle of the wing. Their number varies in different orders of birds, from very few in swifts to many in, say, pelicans. In many birds (e.g. wagtails, sandpipers, some ducks, etc.), the four or five innermost (those nearest the body, attached to the forearm near the elbow) are very elongated; these are sometimes called the *tertials*, or *tertiaries*, but 'inner secondaries' is nowadays more commonly used.

shola: A patch of forest surrounded by grass-land or cultivation, on a mountain slope; generally occupying a sheltered valley.

speculum: A more or less rectangular patch of colour (often metallic green, purple, etc.) on the outer web of the secondaries in many species of ducks.

stoop: The swift, downward plunge of a falcon or other hawk upon its prey.

sub-song: Subdued warbling uttered by many passerine birds, usually when they are resting contentedly—say during the heat of the afternoon.

supercilium: A line of small feathers, often of a different colour from those near them, passing from the base of the beak near the nostril, over the lore, and above the eye—in the position of an eyebrow. (See diagram A.)

syndactyle: The foot structure in certain birds (e.g. kingfishers) in which the three front toes are more or less united for much of their length.

tank: A large, artificial lake; the term is applied in Ceylon to the immense reservoirs built by the ancient kings for impounding rain water for irrigation. In many of these reservoirs, the extent of water varies from a few acres, at the end of the dry season, to thousands of acres after the rains.

tarsus: The, usually, long and slender portion of a bird's leg between the hock-joint and the foot; the toes are attached to its lower extremity. It bears feathers in only a few birds (e.g. most owls and some eagles), but in most it is covered with horny scales or scutes.

tertial, tertiary: See *secondary*; a term sometimes applied to the four or five secondaries nearest to the body of a bird.

tibia: The upper portion of a bird's leg extending from the knee to the hock; it is generally fully clothed with feathers—the tibia-coverts—but wading-birds generally have its lower portion naked.

wedge-shaped: Applied to a bird's tail when the feathers proceeding outwards from the central pair are progressively a little shorter; it has much the same meaning as 'graduated', but a wedge-shaped tail is generally shorter and broader than a graduated one.

wet zone: The south-western portion of Ceylon, which receives its main rainfall during the south-west monsoon. The greater part of this area has a rainfall of upwards of a hundred inches annually. (See Introduction, p. xi, and end-paper map.)

wing-bar: A band of colour different from the surroundings, passing through the middle of a bird's wing; it may be formed by the tips (or more) of the greater and/or median coverts, or by the bases of the secondaries and inner primaries; or by a combination of these features. The presence or absence of a white or coloured wing-bar is a very useful means of identification in many birds, particularly shore-birds.

winglet: Also called the alula, or the bastard-wing; it is a small group of four or five stiff feathers, attached to the mobile 'thumb' of a bird's wing, on the leading edge, just beyond the wrist-bend. The winglet can be raised at will by a bird, and it has a very important function in maintaining stability in flight—particularly slow flight. (See diagram B.)

wrist-bend: The curved angle of the wing which projects forwards on the side of the breast when the wing is closed; it is often partly hidden by the breast feathers and the scapulars.

zygodactyle: A form of the foot found in certain orders of birds (e.g. parrots, woodpeckers, cuckoos, etc.), in which two toes point forwards and two backwards. In all zygodactyle birds, except the trogons, the second and third toes point forwards, the first and fourth point backwards—i.e. it is the outer (fourth) toe that is turned backwards. In trogons, the first and second point backwards, the third and fourth point forwards. (Note, the normal hind toe—corresponding to our great toe—is counted as the first.) (See diagram C.)

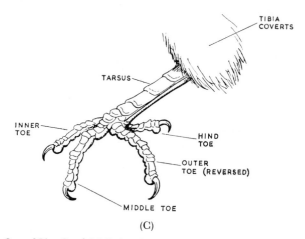

(C)

Leg of Blue-faced Malkoha, showing zygodactyle form of foot

SYSTEMATIC INDEX

Order PASSERIFORMES

Family CORVIDAE. Crows and Magpies (*page 1*)

Corvus macrorhynchos culminatus Sykes. Black Crow
Corvus splendens protegatus Madarasz. House Crow
Cissa ornata (Wagler). Ceylon Blue Magpie

Family PARIDAE. Tits (*page 5*)

Parus major mahrattarum Hartert. Ceylon Grey Tit

Family SITTIDAE. Nuthatches (*page 6*)

Sitta frontalis frontalis Swainson. Velvet-fronted Blue Nuthatch

Family TIMALIIDAE. Babblers (*page 7*)

Turdoides striatus striatus (Dumont). Common Babbler
Turdoides rufescens (Blyth). Ceylon Rufous Babbler
Turdoides cinereifrons (Blyth). Ashy-headed Babbler
Pomatorhinus horsfieldii melanurus Blyth. ⎫ Ceylon Scimitar Babbler
        ,,   ,,   *holdsworthi* Whistler. ⎭
Dumetia hyperythra phillipsi Whistler. Ceylon White-throated Babbler
Chrysomma sinensis nasalis (Legge). Ceylon Yellow-eyed Babbler
Pellorneum fuscocapillum fuscocapillum (Blyth). ⎫ Brown-capped Babbler
        ,,   ,,   *babaulti* (Wells). ⎭
Rhopocichla atriceps nigrifrons (Blyth). ⎫ Black-fronted Babbler
        ,,   ,,   *siccatus* Whistler. ⎭

Family PYCNONOTIDAE. Bulbuls (*page 16*)

Aegithina tiphia multicolor (Gmelin). Ceylon Iora
Chloropsis aurifrons insularis Whistler & Kinnear. Gold-fronted Chloropsis
Chloropsis jerdoni (Blyth). Jerdon's Chloropsis
Microscelis psaroides humii Whistler & Kinnear. Ceylon Black Bulbul
Molpastes cafer cafer (Linnaeus). Red-vented Bulbul
Iole icterica (Strickland). Yellow-browed Bulbul
Pycnonotus melanicterus (Gmelin). Black-capped Bulbul
Pycnonotus luteolus insulae Whistler & Kinnear. Ceylon White-browed Bulbul
Kelaartia penicillata (Blyth). Yellow-eared Bulbul

Family TURDIDAE. Chats, Robins, and Thrushes (*page 23*)

Luscinia brunnea brunnea (Hodgson). Indian Blue Chat
Saxicola caprata atrata (Blyth). Ceylon Pied Bush Chat
Oenanthe leucomela [leucomela (Pallas)]. Pied Wheatear
Cyanosylvia svecica (Linnaeus). Bluethroat
Saxicoloides fulicata leucoptera (Lesson). Ceylon Black Robin

xxiii

Copsychus saularis ceylonensis Sclater. Southern Magpie-Robin
Kittacincla malabarica leggei Whistler. Ceylon Shama
Turdus simillimus kinnisii (Blyth). Ceylon Blackbird
Geokichla wardii (Blyth). Pied Ground Thrush
Geokichla citrina citrina (Latham). Northern Orange-headed Ground Thrush
Oreocincla dauma imbricata (Layard). Ceylon Scaly Thrush
Oreocincla spiloptera Blyth. Spotted-winged Thrush
Monticola solitaria pandoo (Sykes). Indian Blue Rock Thrush
Arrenga blighi Holdsworth. Ceylon Arrenga

Family MUSCICAPIDAE. Flycatchers (*page 35*)

Siphia hyperythra Cabanis. Kashmir Red-breasted Flycatcher
Muscicapa rubeculoides rubeculoides (Vigors). Blue-throated Flycatcher
Muscicapa tickelliae nesaea (Oberholser). Ceylon Orange-breasted Blue Flycatcher
Muscicapa sordida (Walden). Dusky-blue Flycatcher
Muscicapa latirostris Raffles. Brown Flycatcher
Muscicapa muttui muttui (Layard). Layard's Flycatcher
Culicicapa ceylonensis ceylonensis (Swainson). Ceylon Grey-headed Flycatcher
Tchitrea paradisi paradisi (Linnaeus). Indian Paradise Flycatcher
    „   „   *ceylonensis* Zarudny & Härms. Ceylon Paradise Flycatcher
Hypothymis azurea ceylonensis Sharpe. Ceylon Azure Flycatcher
Leucocirca aureola compressirostris Blyth. White-browed Fantail Flycatcher

Family SYLVIIDAE. Warblers (*page 42*)

Locustella certhiola (Pallas). Pallas's Grasshopper Warbler
Schoenicola platyura (Jerdon). Broad-tailed Grass Warbler
Acrocephalus stentoreus meridionalis (Legge). Ceylon Great Reed Warbler
Acrocephalus dumetorum Blyth. Blyth's Reed Warbler
Hippolais caligata rama (Sykes). Sykes's Booted Warbler
    „   „   *scita* (Eversmann). Eversmann's Booted Warbler
Sylvia althaea Hume. Hume's Whitethroat
Sylvia curruca blythi Ticehurst & Whistler. Indian Lesser Whitethroat
Phylloscopus trochiloides nitidus Blyth. Green Tree Warbler
    „   „   *viridanus* Blyth. Greenish Tree Warbler
    „   „   *trochiloides* (Sundevall). Sundevall's Tree Warbler
Phylloscopus magnirostris Blyth. Large-billed Tree Warbler
Orthotomus sutorius sutorius (Pennant).   }
    „   „   *fernandonis* Whistler. } Ceylon Tailor-bird
Cisticola juncidis omalura Blyth. Ceylon Fantail Warbler
Prinia hodgsonii pectoralis Legge. Franklin's Prinia
Prinia socialis brevicauda Legge. Ceylon Ashy Prinia
Prinia polychroa valida (Blyth). Ceylon Large Prinia
Prinia inornata insularis (Legge). Ceylon White-browed Prinia
Bradypterus palliseri (Blyth). Ceylon Warbler

Family LANIIDAE. Shrikes (*page 56*)

Lanius schach caniceps Blyth. Southern Rufous-rumped Shrike
Lanius excubitor lahtora (Sykes). Indian Great Grey Shrike
Lanius cristatus cristatus Linnaeus. Brown Shrike
    „   „   *lucionensis* Linnaeus. Philippine Shrike

Hemipus picatus leggei Whistler. Ceylon Pied Shrike
Tephrodornis pondicerianus affinis Blyth. Ceylon Wood Shrike

Family CAMPEPHAGIDAE. Minivets and Cuckoo-Shrikes (*page 61*)

Pericrocotus flammeus Forster. Orange Minivet
Pericrocotus peregrinus ceylonensis Whistler & Kinnear. Ceylon Little Minivet
Coracina sykesi (Strickland). Black-headed Cuckoo-Shrike
Coracina novaehollandiae layardi (Blyth). Ceylon Large Cuckoo-Shrike

Family DICRURIDAE. Drongos (*page 65*)

Dicrurus macrocercus minor Blyth. Ceylon Black Drongo
Dicrurus longicaudatus longicaudatus Jerdon. Indian Grey Drongo
Dicrurus caerulescens leucopygialis Blyth. ⎫
   ,,   ,,   *insularis* (Sharpe). ⎬ Ceylon Common Drongo
Dissemurus paradiseus lophorhinus (Vieillot). Ceylon Crested Drongo
   ,,   ,,   *ceylonensis* Sharpe. Ceylon Racquet-tailed Drongo

Family ARTAMIDAE. Swallow-Shrikes (*page 71*)

Artamus fuscus Vieillot. Ashy Swallow-Shrike

Family IRENIDAE. Bluebirds (*page 72*)

Irena puella puella (Latham). Fairy Bluebird

Family ORIOLIDAE. Orioles (*page 73*)

Oriolus oriolus kundoo Sykes. Indian Golden Oriole
   ,,   ,,   *oriolus* (Linnaeus). European Golden Oriole
Oriolus chinensis diffusus Sharpe. Black-naped Oriole
Oriolus xanthornus ceylonensis Bonaparte. Ceylon Black-headed Oriole

Family EULABETIDAE. Grackles (*page 76*)

Eulabes religiosa indica Cuvier. Common Grackle
Eulabes ptilogenys (Blyth). Ceylon Grackle

Family STURNIDAE. Starlings and Mynahs (*page 78*)

Pastor roseus (Linnaeus). Rose-coloured Starling
Temenuchus pagodarum (Gmelin). Brahminy Mynah
Sturnia senex (Bonaparte). White-headed Starling
Acridotheres tristis melanosternus Legge. Ceylon Common Mynah

Family PLOCEIDAE. Weavers, Munias, and Sparrows (*page 82*)

Ploceus philippinus philippinus (Linnaeus). Baya Weaver
Ploceus manyar flaviceps Lesson. Striated Weaver
Munia malacca (Linnaeus). Black-headed Munia
Munia oryzivora (Linnaeus). Java Sparrow
Uroloncha striata striata (Linnaeus). White-backed Munia
Uroloncha kelaarti kelaarti (Jerdon). Ceylon Hill Munia

Uroloncha punctulata lineoventer (Hodgson). Spotted Munia
Uroloncha malabarica (Linnaeus). White-throated Munia
Gymnorhis xanthocollis (Burton). Yellow-throated Sparrow
Passer domesticus soror Ripley. Ceylon House Sparrow

Family ALAUDIDAE. Larks (*page 90*)

Alauda gulgula gulgula Franklin. ⎫ Indian Skylark
    ,,   ,,   *australis* Brooks. ⎭
Mirafra affinis ceylonensis Whistler. Ceylon Bush-Lark
Eremopterix grisea ceylonensis Whistler. Ceylon Finch-Lark

Family MOTACILLIDAE. Pipits and Wagtails (*page 94*)

Anthus richardi richardi Vieillot. Richard's Pipit
Anthus campestris thermophilus (Jerdon). Blyth's Pipit
Anthus rufulus malayensis Eyton. Indian Pipit
Motacilla alba dukhunensis Sykes. Indian White Wagtail
Motacilla maderaspatensis Gmelin. Large Pied Wagtail
Motacilla citreola (? subspecies). Yellow-headed Wagtail
Motacilla cinerea melanope Pallas. Grey Wagtail
Motacilla flava thunbergi Billberg. Grey-headed Yellow Wagtail
Dendronanthus indicus (Gmelin). Forest Wagtail

Family HIRUNDINIDAE. Swallows (*page 101*)

Hirundo rustica rustica Linnaeus. European Swallow
    ,,   ,,   *gutturalis* Scopoli. East Asian Swallow
Hirundo javanica domicola Jerdon. Hill Swallow
Hirundo daurica hyperythra Blyth. Ceylon Swallow
    ,,   ,,   *erythropygia* Sykes. Sykes's Striated Swallow
Hirundo fluvicola Jerdon. Indian Cliff Swallow

Family ZOSTEROPIDAE. White-eyes (*page 106*)

Zosterops palpebrosa egregia Madarasz. Ceylon Small White-eye
Zosterops ceylonensis Holdsworth. Ceylon Hill White-eye

Family NECTARINIIDAE. Sunbirds (*page 108*)

Cinnyris lotenia lotenia (Linnaeus). Loten's Sunbird
Cinnyris asiatica asiatica (Latham). Purple Sunbird
Cinnyris zeylonica zeylonica (Linnaeus). Purple-rumped Sunbird
Cinnyris minima Sykes. Small Sunbird

Family DICAEIDAE. Flowerpeckers (*page 113*)

Dicaeum erythrorhynchos ceylonensis Babault. Ceylon Small Flowerpecker
Dicaeum agile zeylonicum (Whistler). Ceylon Thick-billed Flowerpecker
Dicaeum vincens (Sclater). Legge's Flowerpecker

Family PITTIDAE. Pittas (*page 116*)

Pitta brachyura (Linnaeus). Indian Pitta

Order PICIFORMES

Family PICIDAE. Woodpeckers (*page 118*)

Picus xanthopygaeus (Gray). Small Scaly-bellied Green Woodpecker
Picus chlorolophus wellsi Meinertzhagen. Ceylon Yellow-naped Woodpecker
Dryobates mahrattensis mahrattensis (Latham). Yellow-fronted Pied Woodpecker
Dryobates hardwickii gymnophthalmos (Blyth). Ceylon Pygmy Woodpecker
Micropternus brachyurus jerdonii (Malherbe). Rufous Woodpecker
Brachypternus benghalensis jaffnensis Whistler. Ceylon Golden-backed Woodpecker
　　　　,,　　　　,, 　　*erithronotus* (Vieillot). Ceylon Red-backed Woodpecker
Chrysocolaptes festivus tantus Ripley. Black-backed Yellow Woodpecker
Chrysocolaptes guttacristatus stricklandi (Layard). Crimson-backed Woodpecker

Family CAPITONIDAE. Barbets (*page 126*)

Thereiceryx zeylanicus zeylanicus (Gmelin). Brown-headed Barbet
Cyanops flavifrons (Cuvier). Yellow-fronted Barbet
Xantholaema haemacephala indica (Latham). Crimson-breasted Barbet
Xantholaema rubricapilla rubricapilla (Gmelin). Ceylon Small Barbet

Order CORACIIFORMES

Family CORACIIDAE. Rollers (*page 131*)

Coracias benghalensis indica Linnaeus. Indian Roller
Eurystomus orientalis (Linnaeus). Broad-billed Roller

Family MEROPIDAE. Bee-eaters (*page 133*)

Merops orientalis ceylonicus Whistler. Ceylon Green Bee-eater
Merops superciliosus philippinus Linnaeus. Blue-tailed Bee-eater
Merops leschenaulti leschenaulti Vieillot. Chestnut-headed Bee-eater

Family ALCEDINIDAE. Kingfishers (*page 136*)

Ceryle rudis leucomelanura Reichenbach. Indian Pied Kingfisher
Alcedo atthis taprobana Kleinschmidt. Ceylon Common Kingfisher
Alcedo meninting phillipsi Stuart Baker. Ceylon Blue-eared Kingfisher
Ceyx erithacus (Linnaeus). Three-toed Kingfisher
Pelargopsis capensis gurial (Pearson). Stork-billed Kingfisher
Halcyon smyrnensis fusca (Boddaert). Ceylon White-breasted Kingfisher
Halcyon pileata (Boddaert). Black-capped Purple Kingfisher

Family BUCEROTIDAE. Hornbills (*page 143*)

Anthracoceros coronatus coronatus (Boddaert). Malabar Pied Hornbill
Tockus gingalensis (Shaw). Ceylon Grey Hornbill

Family UPUPIDAE. Hoopoes (*page 146*)

Upupa epops çeylonensis Reichenbach. Ceylon Hoopoe

Order APODIFORMES

Family APODIDAE. Swifts (*page 148*)

Apus melba bakeri Hartert. Ceylon White-bellied Swift
Apus affinis singalensis Madarasz. Ceylon White-rumped Swift
Cypsiurus parvus batassiensis (Griffith). Palm Swift
Chaetura gigantea indica Hume. Brown-throated Spinetail Swift
Collocalia fuciphaga unicolor (Jerdon). Indian Edible-nest Swift

Family HEMIPROCNIDAE. Tree Swifts (*page 148*)

Hemiprocne longipennis coronata (Tickell). Indian Crested Swift

Order CAPRIMULGIFORMES

Family CAPRIMULGIDAE. Nightjars (*page 158*)

Caprimulgus asiaticus eidos Peters. Southern Common Indian Nightjar
Caprimulgus macrurus aequabilis Ripley. Horsfield's Jungle Nightjar
Caprimulgus indicus kelaarti Blyth. Ceylon Highland Nightjar

Family PODARGIDAE. Frogmouths (*page 162*)

Batrachostomus moniliger Blyth. Ceylon Frogmouth

Order TROGONIFORMES

Family TROGONIDAE. Trogons (*page 164*)

Harpactes fasciatus fasciatus (Pennant). Ceylon Trogon

Order CUCULIFORMES

Family CUCULIDAE. Cuckoos, Malkohas, and Coucals (*page 166*)

Cuculus canorus telephonus Heine. Asiatic Common Cuckoo
Cuculus poliocephalus poliocephalus Latham. Small Cuckoo
Cuculus micropterus micropterus Gould. Indian Cuckoo
Hierococcyx varius ciceliae Phillips. Ceylon Hawk-Cuckoo
Cacomantis merulinus passerinus (Vahl). Indian Plaintive Cuckoo
Penthoceryx sonneratii waiti Stuart Baker. Ceylon Bay-banded Cuckoo
Chalcites maculatus (Gmelin). Emerald Cuckoo
Surniculus lugubris lugubris (Horsfield). Drongo-Cuckoo
Clamator jacobinus jacobinus (Boddaert). Pied Crested Cuckoo
Clamator coromandus (Linnaeus). Red-winged Crested Cuckoo
Eudynamys scolopaceus scolopaceus (Linnaeus). Koel
Rhopodytes viridirostris (Jerdon). Blue-faced Malkoha
Phaenicophaeus pyrrhocephalus (Pennant). Red-faced Malkoha
Taccocua leschenaultii leschenaultii Lesson. Southern Sirkeer
Centropus sinensis parroti Stresemann. Common Coucal
Centropus chlororhynchus Blyth. Green-billed Coucal

Order PSITTACIFORMES

Family PSITTACIDAE. Parakeets and the Lorikeet (*page 184*)

Psittacula eupatria eupatria (Linnaeus). Ceylon Large Parakeet
Psittacula krameri manillensis (Bechstein). Rose-ringed Parakeet
Psittacula cyanocephala cyanocephala (Linnaeus). Blossom-headed Parakeet
Psittacula calthorpae Blyth. Emerald-collared Parakeet
Loriculus beryllinus (Forster). Ceylon Lorikeet

Order STRIGIFORMES

Family STRIGIDAE. Owls (*page 192*)

Tyto alba stertens Hartert. Eastern Barn Owl
Phodilus badius assimilis Hume. Ceylon Bay Owl
Asio flammeus flammeus (Pontoppidan). Short-eared Owl
Strix leptogrammica ochrogenys (Hume). Brown Wood Owl
Ketupa zeylonensis zeylonensis (Gmelin). Ceylon Fish Owl
Bubo nipalensis blighi Legge. Forest Eagle-Owl
Otus scops leggei Ticehurst. Ceylon Little Scops Owl
Otus bakkamoena bakkamoena Pennant. Collared Scops Owl
Glaucidium radiatum radiatum (Tickell). Jungle Owlet
Glaucidium cuculoides castanonotum (Blyth). Chestnut-backed Owlet
Ninox scutulata hirsuta (Temminck). Brown Hawk-Owl

Order FALCONIFORMES

Family PANDIONIDAE. Osprey (*page 203*)

Pandion haliaetus haliaetus (Linnaeus). Osprey

Family ACCIPITRIDAE. Vultures, Eagles, Hawks,
and their allies (*page 205*)

Neophron percnopterus ginginianus (Latham). Smaller White Scavenger Vulture
Hieraaetus pennatus (Gmelin). Booted Eagle
Hieraaetus fasciatus (Vieillot). Bonelli's Eagle
Hieraaetus kienerii kienerii (Geoffroy). Rufous-bellied Hawk-Eagle
Ictinaetus malayensis perniger (Hodgson). Black Eagle
Spizaetus cirrhatus ceylanensis (Gmelin). Ceylon Hawk-Eagle
Spizaetus nipalensis kelaarti Legge. Mountain Hawk-Eagle
Spilornis cheela spilogaster (Blyth). Ceylon Serpent Eagle
Haliaeetus leucogaster (Gmelin). White-bellied Sea Eagle
Ichthyophaga ichthyaetus plumbeiceps Stuart Baker. Ceylon Grey-headed Fishing
    Eagle
Haliastur indus indus (Boddaert). Brahminy Kite
Milvus migrans govinda Sykes. Pariah Kite
Elanus caeruleus vociferus (Latham). Black-winged Kite
Circus macrourus (Gmelin). Pale Harrier
Circus pygargus (Linnaeus). Montagu's Harrier
Circus melanoleucos (Pennant). Pied Harrier

Order CHARADRIIFORMES

Family TURNICIDAE. Bustard-Quails (*page 266*)
Turnix suscitator leggei Stuart Baker. Ceylon Bustard-Quail

Family JACANIDAE. Jaçanas (*page 267*)
Hydrophasianus chirurgus (Scopoli). Pheasant-tailed Jaçana

Family BURHINIDAE. Stone Curlews and Stone Plovers (*page 269*)
Burhinus oedicnemus indicus (Salvadori). Indian Stone Curlew
Esacus recurvirostris (Cuvier). Great Stone Plover

Family GLAREOLIDAE. Coursers and Pratincoles (*page 272*)
Cursorius coromandelicus coromandelicus (Gmelin). Indian Courser
Glareola pratincola maldivarum Forster. Indian Large Pratincole
Glareola lactea Temminck. Indian Little Pratincole

Family DROMADIDAE. Crab Plover (*page 275*)
Dromas ardeola Paykull. Crab Plover

Family CHARADRIIDAE. Plovers, Lapwings, and their allies (*page 277*)
Haematopus ostralegus Linnaeus. Oyster-catcher
Lobivanellus indicus indicus (Boddaert). Red-wattled Lapwing
Lobipluvia malabarica (Boddaert). Yellow-wattled Lapwing
Chettusia gregaria (Pallas). Sociable Plover
Squatarola squatarola (Linnaeus). Grey Plover
Pluvialis dominica fulva (Gmelin). Asiatic Golden Plover
Charadrius leschenaultii leschenaultii Lesson. Large Sand Plover
Charadrius mongolus atrifrons Wagler. Lesser Sand Plover
Charadrius dubius curonicus Gmelin. European Little Ringed Plover
,,   ,,   *jerdoni* (Legge). Indian Little Ringed Plover
Charadrius hiaticula (*tundrae* Lowe). Ringed Plover
Eupoda asiatica (Pallas). Caspian Plover
Leucopolius alexandrinus seebohmi (Hartert & Jackson). Ceylon Kentish Plover
,,   ,,   *alexandrinus* (Linnaeus). Kentish Plover
Recurvirostra avosetta Linnaeus. Avocet
Himantopus himantopus ceylonensis Whistler. Ceylon Black-winged Stilt

Family SCOLOPACIDAE. Sandpipers, Snipes, and their allies (*page 294*)
Arenaria interpres interpres (Linnaeus). Turnstone
Phalaropus lobatus (Linnaeus). Red-necked Phalarope
Limosa lapponica lapponica (Linnaeus). Bar-tailed Godwit
Limosa limosa limosa (Linnaeus). Black-tailed Godwit
Numenius arquata orientalis Brehm. Eastern Curlew
Numenius phaeopus phaeopus (Linnaeus). Whimbrel
Xenus cinereus (Güldenstädt). Terek Sandpiper
Tringa ochropus Linnaeus. Green Sandpiper

xxxi

Tringa glareola Linnaeus. Wood Sandpiper
Tringa stagnatilis (Bechstein). Marsh Sandpiper
Tringa nebularia (Gunnerus). Greenshank
Tringa totanus eurhinus (Oberholser). Eastern Redshank
Tringa erythropus (Pallas). Spotted Redshank
Actitis hypoleucos (Linnaeus). Common Sandpiper
Philomachus pugnax (Linnaeus). Ruff and Reeve
Crocethia alba (Pallas). Sanderling
Calidris canutus canutus (Linnaeus). Knot
Calidris testacea (Pallas). Curlew-Sandpiper
Calidris minuta (Leisler). Little Stint
Calidris temminckii (Leisler). Temminck's Stint
Calidris subminuta (Middendorf). Long-toed Stint
Limicola falcinellus falcinellus (Pontoppidan). Broad billed Sandpiper
Scolopax rusticola Linnaeus. Woodcock
Capella nemoricola (Hodgson). Wood Snipe
Capella gallinago gallinago (Linnaeus). Fantail Snipe
Capella stenura (Bonaparte). Pintail Snipe
Capella megala (Swinhoe). Swinhoe's Snipe
Capella media (Latham). Great Snipe
Lymnocryptes minimus (Brünnich). Jack Snipe

Family ROSTRATULIDAE. Painted Snipes (*page 325*)

Rostratula benghalensis benghalensis (Linnaeus). Painted Snipe

Family LARIDAE. Terns and Gulls (*page 327*)

Chlidonias hybrida indica (Stephens). Indian Whiskered Tern
Chlidonias leucopterus (Temminck). White-winged Black Tern
Gelochelidon nilotica nilotica (Gmelin). Gull-billed Tern
Hydroprogne caspia (Pallas). Caspian Tern
Thalasseus bengalensis (Lesson). Smaller Crested Tern
Thalasseus bergii velox (Cretzschmar). Large Crested Tern
Sterna hirundo tibetana Saunders. Tibetan Common Tern
Sterna dougallii korustes (Hume). Eastern Roseate Tern
Sterna albifrons sinensis Gmelin. White-shafted Little Tern
     ,,   ,,   *saundersi* Hume. Black-shafted Little Tern
Sterna anaethetus anaethetus Scopoli. Brown-winged Tern
Sterna fuscata fuscata Linnaeus. Sooty Tern
Anous stolidus pileatus (Scopoli). Philippine Noddy
Larus ichthyaetus Pallas. Great Black-headed Gull
Larus brunneicephalus Jerdon. Brown-headed Gull
Larus fuscus (*taimyrensis* Buturlin). Lesser Black-backed Gull

Family STERCORARIIDAE. Skuas (*page 343*)

Stercorarius skua antarctica (Lesson). Antarctic Skua
     ,,   ,,   *mccormickii* Saunders. McCormick's Skua
Stercorarius pomarinus (Temminck). Pomatorhine Skua

Order RALLIFORMES

Family RALLIDAE. Rails, Crakes, Waterhens, and Coots (*page 346*)

Rallus aquaticus indicus Blyth. Indian Water Rail
Hypotaenidia striata gularis (Horsfield). Blue-breasted Banded Rail
Porzana pusilla pusilla (Pallas). Baillon's Crake
Rallina eurizonoides nigrolineata (Gray). Banded Crake
Amaurornis fuscus fuscus (Linnaeus). Ruddy Crake
Amaurornis phoenicurus phoenicurus (Pennant). White-breasted Waterhen
Gallinula chloropus indicus Blyth. Indian Waterhen
Gallicrex cinerea (Gmelin). Kora
Porphyrio poliocephalus poliocephalus (Latham). Purple Coot
Fulica atra atra Linnaeus. Common Coot

Order PELICANIFORMES

Family PELICANIDAE. Pelicans (*page 356*)

Pelicanus roseus Gmelin. Spotted-billed Pelican

Family PHALACROCORACIDAE. Cormorants and Darters (*page 356*)

Phalacrocorax carbo sinensis (Shaw). Southern Cormorant
Phalacrocorax fuscicollis Stephens. Indian Shag
Phalacrocorax niger (Vieillot). Little Cormorant
Anhinga melanogaster Pennant. Indian Darter

Family SULIDAE. Gannets (*page 357*)

Sula leucogaster plotus (Forster). Brown Gannet
Sula dactylatra personata Gould. Masked Gannet
Sula sula (*rubripes* Gould). Red-footed Booby

Family PHAETHONTIDAE. Tropic-birds (*page 357*)

Phaethon lepturus lepturus Daudin. Yellow-billed Tropic-bird

Family FREGATIDAE. Frigate-birds (*page 357*)

Fregata minor aldabrensis Mathews. Great Frigate-bird
Fregata ariel iredalei Mathews. Small Frigate-bird

Order PROCELLARIIFORMES

Family HYDROBATIDAE. Storm Petrels (*page 369*)

Oceanites oceanicus (Kuhl). Wilson's Storm Petrel
Oceanodroma monorhis monorhis (Swinhoe). Ashy Storm Petrel

Family PROCELLARIIDAE. Petrels and Shearwaters (*page 370*)

Puffinus leucomelas (Temminck). White-fronted Shearwater
Puffinus pacificus chlororhynchus Lesson. Green-billed Shearwater

3

Puffinus carneipes Gould. Flesh-footed Shearwater
Puffinus tenuirostris (Temminck). Slender-billed Shearwater
Daption capensis (Linnaeus). Cape Petrel

Order CICONIIFORMES

Family THRESKIORNITHIDAE. Ibises and Spoonbills (*page 375*)

Platalea leucorodia Linnaeus. Spoonbill
Threskiornis melanocephala (Latham). White Ibis
Plegadis falcinellus falcinellus (Linnaeus). Glossy Ibis

Family CICONIIDAE. Storks (*page 375*)

Dissoura episcopus episcopus (Boddaert). Indian White-necked Stork
Xenorhynchus asiaticus asiaticus (Latham). Black-necked Stork
Anastomus oscitans (Boddaert). Open-bill
Ibis leucocephalus (Pennant). Painted Stork
Ciconia ciconia (Linnaeus). White Stork
Ciconia nigra (Linnaeus). Black Stork
Leptoptilos javanicus (Horsfield). Lesser Adjutant

Family ARDEIDAE. Herons, Egrets, and Bitterns (*page 376*)

Ardea purpurea manilensis Meyen. Eastern Purple Heron
Ardea cinerea rectirostris Gould. Eastern Grey Heron
Ardea goliath Cretzschmar. Giant Heron
Egretta alba modesta (Gray). Eastern Large Egret
Egretta intermedia intermedia (Wagler). Median Egret
Egretta garzetta garzetta (Linnaeus). Little Egret
Demigretta asha (Sykes). Indian Reef Heron
Bubulcus ibis coromandus (Boddaert). Cattle Egret
Ardeola grayii (Sykes). Pond Heron
Butorides striatus javanicus (Horsfield). Little Green Heron
Nycticorax nycticorax nycticorax (Linnaeus). Night Heron
Gorsachius melanolophus melanolophus (Raffles). Malay Bittern
Ixobrychus sinensis sinensis (Gmelin). Yellow Bittern
Ixobrychus cinnamomeus (Gmelin). Chestnut Bittern
Dupetor flavicollis flavicollis (Latham). Black Bittern

Family PHOENICOPTERIDAE. Flamingos (*page 376*)

Phoenicopterus ruber roseus Pallas. Flamingo

Order ANSERIFORMES

Family ANATIDAE. Geese and Ducks (*page 407*)

Anser anser (Linnaeus). Grey-lag Goose
Sarkidiornis melanota (Pennant). Comb Duck
Nettapus coromandelianus coromandelianus (Gmelin). Cotton Teal
Dendrocygna javanica (Horsfield). Whistling Teal

Dendrocygna bicolor bicolor (Vieillot). Large Whistling Teal
Casarca ferruginea (Pallas). Ruddy Sheldrake
Anas poecilorhyncha poecilorhyncha Forster. Spotted-billed Duck
Anas strepera Linnaeus. Gadwall
Anas acuta acuta Linnaeus. Pintail
Anas querquedula Linnaeus. Garganey
Anas crecca crecca Linnaeus. Teal
Anas penelope Linnaeus. Wigeon
Spatula clypeata (Linnaeus). Shoveller
Aythya fuligula (Linnaeus). Tufted Duck

Order PODICIPITIFORMES

Family PODICIPITIDAE. Grebes (*page 422*)

Podiceps ruficollis capensis Salvadori. Little Grebe

APPENDIX

Additions and Amendments (*page 424*)
Order of Families Compared (*page 435*)

LIST OF PLATES

(Unless otherwise stated, the sexes are nearly alike, and the illustration shows
the adult male)

PLATE 1 (facing p. 24)

1. Velvet-fronted Blue Nuthatch
2. Gold-fronted Chloropsis
3. Jerdon's Chloropsis, male and female
4. Ceylon Blue Magpie
5. Indian Blue Chat, male and female
6. Ceylon Iora, male and female

PLATE 2 (facing p. 25)

1. Yellow-browed Bulbul
2. Black-capped Bulbul
3. Yellow-eared Bulbul
4. Ceylon White-browed Bulbul
5. Ceylon Black Bulbul
6. Red-vented Bulbul

PLATE 3 (facing p. 40)

1. Orange Minivet, male and female
2. Ceylon Little Minivet, male and female
3. Ceylon Shama
4. Ceylon Scimitar Babbler (race *holdsworthi*)
5. Indian Blue Rock Thrush, male
6. Pied Ground Thrush, male and female
7. Northern Orange-headed Ground Thrush, male
8. Spotted-winged Thrush

PERCHING BIRDS
ORDER PASSERIFORMES—SPARROW-LIKE BIRDS

THIS order is by far the largest, containing nearly half the birds of the world. In the Ceylon list, it includes all the birds from the crows to the pitta (p. 116). While its members are very diverse in many ways, they all have a kind of family likeness which enables them to be easily recognized. The legs and feet, in particular, show a common structure. They all have four toes, arranged three in front and one behind, the toes unwebbed and quite separate from one another to their bases, and the hind toe arising at the same level as the front ones and capable of moving independently of them. The young are blind and nearly naked on hatching.

The main features of each family in the order are given at the head of the families.

THE CROWS AND MAGPIES
Family CORVIDAE

These are the largest members of the *Passeriformes*. They are characterized by strong beaks, legs and feet; short lores; and the nostrils more or less covered by forwardly-directed, bristly feathers. They are omnivorous, adaptable birds of intelligent and resourceful nature, bold and predatory in seeking food. Ceylon species are non-migratory; appear to pair for life; and build open stick nests, usually in trees.

Ceylon possesses two species of crows, and one magpie.

THE BLACK CROW, or VILLAGE CROW
('Jungle Crow' in India)

Corvus macrorhynchos culminatus Sykes. Resident

Sinhalese: Kākā, Kaputā. Tamil: Kākā, Kākam

Larger than the House Crow, and with a much heavier beak. Sexes alike. The plumage is black throughout, without the smoky-grey tinge on the neck that marks the House Crow.

This crow is common almost throughout the Island, except in the highest hills; and it is steadily extending its range even there, being now not uncommon in Nuwara Eliya, where it was unknown a few years

I

ago. Although by no means averse from human society, it is much less dependent on man for its subsistence than the House Crow and may be found in jungle areas, remote from human habitations; however, it is commonest in villages and the outskirts of towns, finding the daily task

of food-getting easier there than in remote districts. It lives in pairs, apparently mating for life, but a number of pairs will gather where food is plentiful, and it associates quite freely with its smaller relative. It is a bolder bird than the House Crow and, although equally villainous, there is a robust independence about it that in some measure redeems it from the contempt that the House

× one-ninth

Crow inspires. In a mixed company of the two species it is amusing to observe the deference shown to it by the House Crows. Its food consists of most edible substances, animal or vegetable, but it prefers carrion. Almost any small animal will be attacked, and I have seen full-grown bulbuls and palm squirrels captured by it; eggs and nestlings are, of course, its delight. The usual note of this crow is a deep *caw*, but it also utters various croaks and conversational noises. When courting, the male expresses his feelings in amusing attitudinizings; raising his head feathers into a bushy crest, quivering the half-opened wings over the back, he gives voice to a series of squawks and croaks, interspersed with caws. The flight is powerful, and is often high in air, especially when the birds are flying to and from their roosting places, morning and evening.

The breeding season is from April to September, July being the favourite month. The nest is an untidy mass of sticks, with a fairly deep hollow, lined with fibres; it is placed, usually, in a tall tree, or in the crown of a palm. The three or four eggs are pale green or blue, speckled with brown and grey; they measure about 42 × 29 mm.

The Koel often victimizes this crow, by foisting its eggs upon it.

THE HOUSE CROW, or GREY-NECKED CROW

Corvus splendens protegatus Madarasz. Resident

Sinhalese: Kaputā, Kolamba Kākā. Tamil: Oor-kākam

Smaller than the Black Crow, with relatively smaller beak, smoky-grey neck, and more glossy wings. Sexes alike.

This is a coast crow in Ceylon, but it is steadily extending its range inland, following the roads and railway. A notorious parasite of man, it is seldom to be found at any distance from human habitations, and never in jungle districts. Every town and village around the coasts is now infested with this bird, whose raucous and incessant cawing is the very first bird-sound to greet a visitor arriving in the Island. A scavenger, and quite omnivorous, there are few items of human food that come amiss to its ravenous appetite; and its thieving propensities are too well known to need description. Where it is not sternly discouraged (preferably by shooting a couple once a month, regularly) it becomes a real pest. It is a cowardly bird, and any animal that can put

up a good defence against it, when attacked, stands a good chance of being left alone; but woe betide the fledgling bird, small chicken, or lizard that is found by the crows. It understands well the advantages of team-work, and it is amusing to watch the gangster methods that are adopted by two or more of these birds in tackling any animal too formidable to be destroyed by one alone. The flight is powerful and, in travelling to and from the roosting

× one-eighth

places, very long distances are covered daily. This crow habitually roosts in large flocks which assemble, in twos, threes, and larger parties, from all points of the compass to favourite groups of trees or palms— often those growing on small islands, e.g. Crow Island, in the mouth of the Kelani river, and Barberyn Island, half a mile off the west coast. At one of these roosts, as dusk descends, the babel of caws produced by the myriads of crows assembled to spend the night is deafening.

Almost the only good thing to be said for the 'Blackguard Crow' is that he is an excellent husband and father! The breeding season is from May to August or September, but June is the favourite month. Crows at this season look very dapper in their glossy breeding plumage; later in the year, they look scrawny and moth-eaten. This, too, is the season when they are particularly dangerous to chickens and young birds, for they have young of their own to feed. The nest is a mass of twigs, with the hollow lined with fibres; it is set in a tree—large or small—or in the crown of a palm, with no attempt at concealment. The three to five eggs are brighter green or blue than those of the Black Crow, and their markings are denser; they measure about 36 × 27 mm.

Like the last species, this crow is often tricked by the Koel into fostering its offspring.

3

THE CEYLON BLUE MAGPIE

Cissa ornata (Wagler). Species peculiar to Ceylon

Sinhalese: Kehibellā. No Tamil name recorded

Plate 1, facing p. 24 (×one-quarter)

Between the mynah and House Crow in size, but with a long, much graduated tail. Sexes similar. This beautiful bird cannot be mistaken for any other Ceylonese species.

It inhabits the heavy virgin forests of the mountains and wet-zone foot-hills, and is scarce and usually shy, but locally common and bolder. It associates in flocks up to six or seven, but pairs or solitary individuals are sometimes met with. A very energetic, agile bird, most of its time is spent in searching for food among foliage at all levels from the ground to the tops of tall trees. It hops from branch to branch, prying into every bunch of leaves and probing under shreds of bark, etc., and in doing so it adopts attitudes worthy of a tit—often hanging upside-down and sometimes clinging to a single, tough leaf: I have seen it capture and devour the following creatures: hairy caterpillars, green tree-crickets, various chafer beetles, tree-frogs, and lizards. The hairy caterpillars were carefully rubbed against mossy branches, presumably to divest them of their stinging hairs, before being swallowed; beetles, frogs, etc., were held firmly under one foot and picked to pieces by the powerful beak. I have also seen it eating the fruit of *Freycinetia*, the climbing screw-pine, but its main food is of an animal nature.

While satisfying its morning hunger it is generally silent except for low conversational squeaks and chirps, but at other times it is very noisy, uttering a great variety of loud notes, most of which have a rasping or raucous quality. A loud, jingling call uttered with the beak wide open, and audible for some hundreds of yards, may be rendered *chink chink*, or *cheek cheek*—in various repetitions and variations. Other notes are: a very rasping *crakrakrakrak*; a plain, loud *whee whee*, sometimes rendered as *tweewi-krāā*. Solitary birds indulge in a quaint sub-song of squeaks, chatterings and sucking noises, interspersed with imitations of the notes of other birds. A tame Blue Magpie—captured when fully adult—which I possessed, included in its repertoire a beautiful rendering of the *chok, chaw-choyik* of a distant junglecock.

Wet weather seems to have a tonic effect on this bird; at any rate, it is always more noisy in rainy weather. Flocks move about a good deal, but each adheres to a definite, though extensive, territory. Occasionally they leave the forest and visit estate gardens, etc., but normally the jungle is their home. The flight is rather weak and seldom long sustained. The moulting season is August to November.

The breeding season is in the first quarter of the year, so far as is known, but the nest has seldom been found. Ralph West found a pair building in January 1944, in the top of a small jungle tree growing in a strip of forest bordering a stream in a tea estate at about 5,000 feet elevation. The nest resembled a small crow's nest, but was lined with 'old man's beard' lichen; it was very well concealed among small twigs and foliage near the top of the tree. Unfortunately the birds deserted before eggs were laid. The eggs number three to five and are whitish, profusely spotted and speckled with various shades of brown. They measure about 30·5 × 22·1 mm.

THE TITS
Family PARIDAE

Tits are small perching birds, of very characteristic appearance and habits although they have few very pronounced anatomical features. The beak is very short, straight and conical, strong, yet not deep like the beak of a weaver or sparrow. The nostrils at the base of it are concealed beneath short, forwardly-directed feathers. The legs and feet, though rather short, are strong. The plumage is soft and abundant, that of the head full, giving the birds a big-headed, chubby look. They are very active, acrobatic little birds, usually seen on trees, though they visit the ground quite freely. They are inclined to be pugnacious towards other birds. They feed on both animal and vegetable substances, but generally prefer the former. They build bulky nests, generally in holes, and lay spotted eggs.

Ceylon has but one tit, a local race of the very widespread Great Tit of Europe.

THE CEYLON GREY TIT

Parus major mahrattarum Hartert. Resident

No Sinhalese name recorded. Tamil: Sittu-kuruvi

A sparrow-sized, grey, black and white bird, with a short beak, conspicuous white cheeks, and a white wing-bar.

It is always active, flitting in pairs or family parties from tree to tree, searching every bark-crevice or flake of lichen for its prey, which consists of small insects—beetles, moths, caterpillars, etc. It is very abundant in the hills and sparingly distributed over much of the low

5

country, and may be found both in deep forest and in the neighbourhood of human dwellings. Up-country Grey Tits are tame and familiar, but in the low country they are shy and vagrant. The notes consist of a loud call *cheewit*, a monotonous song, generally uttered from high in a tree, *waheechi waheechi waheechi* or *tisswee tisswee tisswee* (with other variations); and a chattering scold or alarm-note. The young solicit food from their parents in a reedy *dee-dee, dee-dee-dee.*

× one-third

The nest is a mass of moss, fibres, cow-hair, etc., placed in a hole or cavity, usually in a tree trunk or branch but not infrequently under bungalow eaves, etc. The four to six eggs are white, speckled, mainly around the larger end, with reddish spots; they measure about 17·5 × 12·6 mm. The principal breeding season is in the first half of the year, but many birds breed again in September–November.

THE NUTHATCHES
Family SITTIDAE

Nuthatches are small birds with something of the habits of woodpeckers, as they spend most of their time climbing about the trunks and larger branches of trees. Unlike woodpeckers, however, they generally begin near the top of a tree and work downwards, running jerkily about the bark in every direction—often back- or head-downwards. The tail is short and square, of normal feathers, and is not used as a prop, as woodpeckers use theirs. The beak is straight, pointed, and rather narrow; the legs short, the feet large and strong, with very strong, sharp claws, and long, stout hind toe. Nuthatches feed largely on the insects that hide in bark crevices, though some (non-Ceylonese) species also eat nuts, which they break open by hammering (or 'hatching') with the beak—first having wedged the nut into a crevice to hold it firm. They nest in natural holes, or those made by other birds, in trees, sometimes reducing the size of the entrance by building it up with mud. The eggs are spotted.

Ceylon has a single species which is also widely distributed in India.

6

THE VELVET-FRONTED BLUE NUTHATCH

Sitta frontalis frontalis Swainson. Resident

Sinhalese: Panu-kurullā. No recorded Tamil name

Plate 1, facing p. 24 (male; × one-third)

Sparrow-size. Sexes almost alike. A bird which cannot be mistaken for any other in Ceylon owing to the combination of its blue and pinkish-buff coloration and its tree-trunk climbing habits.

It is widely distributed in forested areas in Ceylon, but is much commoner in the hills than in the low country. A most active little bird, it spends most of its time running in rather a jerky fashion about the trunks and branches of trees, incessantly searching for the small insects that hide beneath flakes of bark, etc. Unlike the woodpecker tribe, it commonly alights near the *top* of a tree and works downwards, with its head, as often as not, in a downward direction. The voice is a shrill *chik, chik*, occasionally changing to a sharp chittering note. Except while feeding young, in a family party, it usually goes in pairs.

The nest is stated by W. W. A. Phillips to be somewhat like that of the Grey Tit, but smaller, and it is placed in a cavity in a tree—usually a natural one, but sometimes a barbet's abandoned nest-hole is used. The nest is rather hard to find, but the birds sometimes reveal its site by their excited behaviour in its neighbourhood. They commonly alight some distance above the nest-hole and run down into it. The three or four broadly-oval, glossless eggs are white, spotted with red, and measure about 17·2 × 13·2 mm.

THE BABBLERS
Family TIMALIIDAE

The babblers are a large family of tropical and sub-tropical birds found in Africa and the oriental region; in most parts of the latter they are very numerous, both in species and in individuals, and they form a large proportion of the 'small bird' fauna in India, Malaysia, etc. In Ceylon, however, they are not so strongly represented as in some other parts of the oriental region. They may be described as small to medium-sized perching birds, of usually dull colouring and largely terrestrial habits; their plumage is long, lax and soft; the wings are short and rounded, the flight feeble and never long-sustained; the legs and feet are strong, with the hind toe and its claw stout and powerful. Babblers are not migratory; for the most part, they frequent forest or scrub-land, and many forms are very gregarious, going about in troops up to a dozen or so. Most species are inclined to be noisy, uttering a great variety of more or less melodious calls or else squeaks, rattles and chatterings —hence their popular name. Their nests, which are placed in various situations, but usually within a yard or two of the ground (sometimes on it), are either open ones of typical 'bird's-nest' form, or are more or less domed over; they are placed in bushes or the like, or among low herbage or forest-floor rubbish, but not in holes. The eggs of the larger forms are unspotted, those of the smaller species are usually spotted. Babblers feed largely on insects and other small animals, but wild fruits are also eaten.

The familiar Common Babbler or 'Seven Sisters' may be taken as a typical member of this family.

THE COMMON BABBLER, or 'SEVEN SISTERS'

Turdoides striatus striatus (Dumont). Race peculiar to Ceylon

Sinhalese: Demalichchā. Tamil: Vēlaikkāra-kuruvi (Wait), Kalani-kuruvi or Puliny-kuruvi (Phillips)

Size, between the Red-vented Bulbul and Common Mynah. Sexes similar. A uniformly yellowish-grey, frumpish-looking bird, common everywhere except in the higher hills and in heavy forest, and always seen in flocks which often number more than seven but seldom fewer.

× two-fifths

Its pale orbital region and bluish-white eye give it a curiously anaemic look.

It feeds on both insects and vegetable substances, and is partial to waste rice and curry thrown out of houses, and to wild figs, such as banyan fruit. Most of its food is taken on the ground, and it has a habit of holding morsels, too large to swallow, in its outstretched foot while it picks off pieces. The troop keeps up a noisy conversation of squeaks, trilling and 'musical-chattering' notes, and occasionally its members indulge in a kind of dance—along a branch or a palm-frond—when they jerk and quiver their wings and tails most energetically, trilling the while. The flight is weak (the wings being very short and rounded) and, if any distance is to be covered, the birds prefer to hop to the top of a tree and take off from there; then they proceed in a series of rapid flutterings alternating with sailing on steady wings—usually following each other one at a time. They are not aggressive birds, but are courageous in defence of one another if attacked by hawks, cats, etc.

The nest, a fairly deep cup, neat inside but rather untidy outside, is well-concealed in a thick bush or hedge. The three to five eggs are beautiful, glossy turquoise blue, unmarked, and measure about 23·8 × 18·4 mm. The main breeding season is March–May, with a second brood in August–November, but breeding proceeds to some extent all the year round.

THE CEYLON RUFOUS BABBLER

Turdoides rufescens (Blyth). Peculiar to Ceylon

Sinhalese: Ratu-demalichchā. Tamil: Vēlaikkāra-kuruvi

Very similar in size and form to the last species, but distinguished from it by its rufous coloration and bright orange beak and legs. Sexes similar.

It is a forest bird, seldom seen away from deep jungle. It occurs in all forests of the wet zone and in the hills to the highest elevations, and is fairly common, living in flocks of seven to ten or more. It is a noisy bird, and the presence of a flock may generally be known at some distance by the continual chattering, squeaking and chirping with which its members converse together. It feeds mainly on insects, but doubtless eats also many jungle berries. The flight is weak and

× one-fifth

4

consists of little more than fluttering from tree to tree in the jungle, with an occasional glide across a ravine. This babbler and also the Common and Ashy-headed Babblers have a curious association with small squirrels of the palm squirrel group. Whenever a flock of these birds is on the feed, a squirrel is almost sure to be found in their near neighbourhood. In the case of the Common Babbler it will be a common palm squirrel, while in the case of either of the others it will be the little dusky-striped squirrel or, perhaps, Layard's squirrel.

The nest has very seldom been found as it is concealed in dense masses of foliage in thick forest. It resembles that of the last species, and the eggs, two or three in number, appear to be almost indistinguishable from those of the Common Babbler. They are described as deep greenish blue, and measure about 24·2 × 18 mm.

THE ASHY-HEADED BABBLER

Turdoides cinereifrons (Blyth). Species peculiar to Ceylon

Sinhalese: Alu-demalichchā. Tamil: Vēlaikkāra-kuruvi

Very slightly larger than the Common Babbler, and easily distinguished from both it and the Rufous Babbler by its mainly black beak, dark grey legs, grey head, and dark reddish-brown back, wings and tail. It is also a neater-looking bird.

× one-fifth

It is confined to the deep forests of the wet zone and the adjacent mountains where, on the southern and western aspects of the main range, it ascends to at least 5,000 feet. Like the two preceding babblers, it lives in flocks, and is a noisy bird keeping up a constant flow of 'babblings', squeaks, and chatterings, which can easily be mistaken for those of the Rufous Babbler—which inhabits the same jungles. The members of the troop work steadily through the damp undergrowth, fluttering from tree to tree in their constant search for the insects which form their main food. Each troop is generally accompanied by one or two little jungle squirrels, which probably find their company a useful insurance against being surprised by the numerous enemies that these little beasts have to contend with in their jungle home.

The nesting habits of this bird are still unknown, but the breeding season is probably in the first quarter of the year as I have several times met with young birds, little more than nestlings, in April.

THE CEYLON SCIMITAR BABBLER

Pomatorhinus horsfieldii melanurus Blyth. Race peculiar to the low-country wet zone of Ceylon

Pomatorhinus horsfieldii holdsworthi Whistler. Race peculiar to the hills and low-country dry zone of Ceylon

Sinhalese: Parandel-kurullā. No Tamil name recorded

Plate 3, facing p. 40 (race *holdsworthi*; ×one-quarter)

Rather smaller and more slenderly built than the Common Babbler. Its yellow scimitar-beak, long white eyebrow, snowy shirt-front, notes and habits all make it easy to recognize as one of the most attractive of the commoner birds of Ceylon.

It is found in jungle almost everywhere, low country and mountains alike, and it loves forests, large or small. It is not confined to them, however, and, provided sufficient cover is available, it will take up residence on estates or in well-wooded gardens. It lives in pairs or family parties which travel steadily through the forest, often in association with many other species of birds, all intently foraging for food. Scimitar Babblers pay much attention to bark-crevices, moss, bunches of dead leaves, etc., probing everywhere for their insect prey. Constantly they call to each other in the beautiful sonorous notes that are so delightful a feature of the Ceylon forests: *pawp-a-pawp* says one (probably the male), to be answered by a quiet *kā-krēe, kā-krēe* by its mate; other notes are *pop pop-prrr* and a deep guttural *wŏch wŏhorro*. Besides these loud calls there are various chirps and rattles, uttered while feeding or when suspicious.

The nest is commonly placed among dense herbage, ferns, etc., near the ground, but sometimes in a tree cavity or deep fork. It is an untidy mass of grass-blades and dead leaves, more or less domed over, and lined with fibres. Two or three pure white eggs are laid, which measure about 25·1 × 18·6 mm. There are two breeding seasons in the year, the main one about March–May, and a secondary one towards the end of the year.

The low-country wet-zone race (*melanurus*) of this bird differs from the hill and dry-zone race (*holdsworthi*) in being richly ferruginous on back, wings and tail, instead of olivaceous; but the two races do not differ in habits or notes.

THE CEYLON WHITE-THROATED BABBLER

Dumetia hyperythra phillipsi Whistler. Race peculiar to Ceylon

Sinhalese: Parandel-kurullā. No Tamil name recorded

Sparrow-sized. Sexes alike. An undistinguished-looking little bird of olive brown, white and pale rufous coloration, with a pale beak, face and eyes which give it an anaemic appearance, not unlike a miniature of the Common Babbler.

It is widely distributed, in both low country and hills, up to 5,000 feet or even higher in some districts, wherever the vegetation suits its habits. It is essentially a bird of scrub-land, and its favourite haunts are in māna-grass, etc., mingled with lantana or other scrub growth; but it is not averse to tea estates where jungly ravines occur. It lives in small flocks which skulk in the bushes, only exposing themselves to view when it becomes necessary to leave one patch of scrub for another. Then the birds flutter across one by one with squeaks of alarm, and chattering or churring notes with which they seem to warn each other to

× one-quarter

'beware'. The food consists mainly of insects, but no doubt berries form a proportion of its diet.

The main breeding season is March–May, with a secondary season in August–September, but odd nests may be found during most of the year. The nest is a ball of dry grass, bamboo leaves, etc., with an entrance-hole at one side, and it is set, usually, near the ground in a bush, tussock of māna-grass or the like. It is not easy to find unless the bird reveals its position by fluttering out when one approaches the site. The eggs are broad ovals; glossy white in ground-colour, and thickly speckled with brownish red. They number three, sometimes four, and measure about 18 × 13·7 mm.

THE CEYLON YELLOW-EYED BABBLER

Chrysomma sinensis nasalis (Legge). Race peculiar to Ceylon

Sinhalese: Hambu-kurullā. No Tamil name recorded

Nearly the size of the Red-vented Bulbul. Sexes similar. A plump, full-throated bird with a black beak and conspicuously orange-yellow iris and eyelid. The supercilium, lores, and entire underparts are pure white; forehead dark brown; crown, back, wings and tail light greyish brown.

It inhabits long grass and scrub, and is found in scattered colonies over much of the low country, and up to 5,000 feet in the hills on the

drier, eastern side; the Uva patanas seem to be its principal habitat. A skulking bird, it lives in pairs or small flocks which spend most of their time hiding in dense shrubbery; but towards evening they often become bolder and perch on twigs in full view, uttering a loud call *peer peer* or *peerpeer kowhihihihi*. The male's song sounds something like *cuttykra-weerko wiwiwiwiwi* whistled briskly. The alarm note is *krrrk, krrk, krrrr*. The flight is straight and

× two-sevenths

fluttering, and usually takes the bird only from one clump of scrub to the next. The Yellow-eyed Babbler feeds mainly on insects, but I have seen one eating lantana berries.

February to May are the usual breeding months, but odd nests may be seen at other times of the year. The nest is a very deep, neat cup composed of coarse grass-blades, etc., bound together with cobwebs, and fastened to several stems of māna-grass, lantana, bracken, etc., at a height of three or four feet in a clump of scrub. It is not well concealed as a rule. The three, or sometimes four, eggs are glossy and white, or pinkish, in ground-colour, profusely spotted and speckled with various shades of brownish red; they measure about 19·7 × 14·6 mm.

THE BROWN-CAPPED BABBLER

Pellorneum fuscocapillum fuscocapillum (Blyth). Peculiar to the low-country wet zone and hills of Ceylon

Pellorneum fuscocapillum babaulti (Wells). Peculiar to the low-country dry zone of Ceylon

Sinhalese: Parandel-kurullā, 'Redi diang' (='give me cloth'— onomatopoeic). No Tamil name recorded

About the size of the magpie-robin, but with a shorter tail. Sexes similar. It is a soberly coloured bird, brown with a darker brown cap, and the face, supercilium and all underparts pale rusty. Race *fusco-capillum* is a dark form found in the hills and damp south-western sector of the Island; *babaulti* being the dry-zone race.[1]

A shy jungle-loving bird, it lives in pairs and is found, wherever there is forest, throughout the Island except perhaps in the driest parts of the Northern and Southern Provinces. It ascends the hills to at least 5,000 feet on the drier, Uva side, less high on the western aspect. Though comparatively seldom seen, it is a common bird in most of its range as may easily be discovered if one can recognize its notes. The call-note is a monotonously repeated, clear whistle which sounds like *prit-tee dear*—the middle syllable being higher pitched than the others. In the breeding season, the male sings a quaint little lilting song, whistling up and down the scale in a manner very suggestive of a small boy expressing *joie de vivre*. Both call and song are very easily imitated by whistling, and thus the little per-

× two-sevenths

former may be decoyed within view. The alarm-note is a sharp *wit*, or *quit it it* (rapid), and the scolding-note is a low *chr chrr chrr*; while uttering this the throat feathers are raised. It spends most of its time on the ground, turning over dead leaves in its search for the insects that hide under them and, in dry weather, a pair may often be discovered by the rustling thus produced.

The nest is a domed, outwardly untidy structure composed of dead leaves, skeleton leaves, dry grass, etc., placed on the ground among the same kind of objects, among which it is practically impossible to distinguish unless, and until, the bird flies off at one's feet. It is often situated at the base of a tree or shrub and is always in deep forest. The two eggs are broad ovals, white or off-white, and thickly speckled with some shade of brown. They measure about 22·2 × 16·2 mm.

The South Indian representative of this bird is the Spotted Babbler, which has a rufous-brown cap and white underparts boldly spotted with black; in spite of its very different appearance, the fact that its call, song, habits and nidification are all almost indistinguishable from those of the Brown-capped Babbler indicate close relationship between the two species.

[1] A third race of this bird, *P. f. scortillum* Ripley has recently been described (*Spolia Zeylanica*, vol. 24, 1946, p. 226). It is darker than *P. f. fuscocapillum*, and inhabits the wettest parts of the wet zone.

THE BLACK-FRONTED BABBLER

Rhopocichla atriceps nigrifrons (Blyth). Race peculiar to the low-country wet zone of Ceylon

Rhopocichla atriceps siccatus Whistler. Race peculiar to the hills and low-country dry zone of Ceylon

Sinhalese: Parandel-kurullā, Battichchā. No Tamil name recorded

Sparrow-size. Sexes alike in plumage. A shy little bird, whose black forehead, pale eye, white breast, and brown back, wings and tail, make it easy to recognize.

It is found almost throughout the Island, but only where fairly heavy forest exists as it prefers dense shade with thick undergrowth such as bamboo or nillu. It is generally found in little troops, probably family parties. Though retiring it is inquisitive, and an observer who will enter its jungle haunts and *keep still* will have no difficulty in making its acquaintance. When alarmed, it warns its neighbours by a low rattling note, and it also utters sundry squeaks and an occasional *chak*. It feeds on insects, for which it searches diligently in the herbage.

× one-half

The nest is a ball, about six inches in diameter, composed of dead leaves, bamboo blades, etc., and placed, quite conspicuously, in a fork of a small sapling at a height of three to seven feet from the ground. The entrance is a wide opening in one side of the ball, and the egg-cavity, which is generally unlined, is very shallow. The two eggs are white, speckled with brownish red, and measure about 19 × 14 mm. While eggs may be found almost throughout the year, the main breeding season is from February to May, and a secondary one in October and November.

The wet-zone race (*nigrifrons*) is much richer, warmer brown on back, wings and tail than is *siccatus*.

THE BULBULS

Family Pycnonotidae

Bulbuls are a large family of smallish perching birds (up to mynah-size), found in Africa, south-eastern Europe, southern Asia, and the islands belonging to these regions. They are arboreal in habits, seldom descending to the ground. Their diet consists largely of small fruits, though they eat many insects as well. They live mostly in pairs, but these often unite to form small, loose flocks. The sexes are alike (except in a few forms belonging to the subfamily *Liotrichinae*); the young are unspotted and resemble their parents except for being duller in coloration. They are birds of gardens, scrub-land and forest, and do not migrate, though local movements sometimes take place in response to conditions of food-supply and climate. Their voices are cheerful and generally pleasant to hear though they do not 'sing' to any great extent.

In structure, bulbuls are not strikingly different from many other families of small birds; their principal characteristic is the shortness of the legs; the plumage is full and soft; the wings are rounded and rather short; the tail is either square or very slightly forked at the tip; the head is crested in many forms.

Their nests are open cups, sometimes of rather scanty construction, placed among foliage in bushes or trees—never in holes. The eggs are always speckled or spotted.

For the purposes of this work the family is divided into two sub-families: the *Liotrichinae*, which includes the Iora and two species of Chloropsis; and the *Pycnonotinae*, which includes all the rest of the bulbuls in Ceylon.

THE CEYLON IORA

Aegithina tiphia multicolor (Gmelin). Resident

Sinhalese: Panu-kurullā. Tamil: Sinna Māmpala-kuruvi

Plate 1, facing p. 24 (male lower, female upper; ×one-third)

Sparrow-size. This little bird, though common enough, escapes observation by its habit of hopping quietly about amongst the thick foliage of trees where its colours tend to conceal it. It is found everywhere in the Island up to about 3,000 feet and, as a visitor, ascending occasionally to 5,000 feet or higher; it prefers the dry zone, however, in most parts of which it is very common. It feeds on insects, especially caterpillars, for which it searches assiduously among the leaves of bushes and trees; it seldom voluntarily visits the ground. Gardens, scrub-jungle and forest margins are its normal haunts. It lives in pairs, which keep in touch with each other by frequently calling in a variety of sweet-toned whistles which have rather a 'drowsy' quality. Common calls are: a long drawn crescendo *whee-e-e-e-too*—the last syllable dropping suddenly in the scale; *weet we too* is a variation of this, and another is *whip-wee-bird-ee*—'*bird*' being dropped in pitch. The usual style of flight is a straight flutter from tree to tree but, when courting, the male gives a wonderful exhibition; he springs into the air, fluffs out all his very voluminous body plumage, and slowly descends in a spiral to the bush where his lady-love sits. In this display he suggests a black, white and yellow woolly ball.

The Iora breeds mainly in the first half of the year, April, May and June being the favourite months. The nest is a neat little cup, composed of fibres, bast, etc., bound together and fastened to a twig, or twigs, with strands of cobweb which give it a whitish appearance. The rim is neatly finished off with the same substance. It is set, as a rule, on the upper side of a stout twig, often with other twigs flanking and steadying it. The two—rarely three—eggs are matt white, with bold streaks and blotches of slate-grey and brown which tend to run longitudinally and to form a zone around the large end. They measure about 17·4 × 13·4 mm.

THE GOLD-FRONTED CHLOROPSIS

Chloropsis aurifrons insularis Whistler & Kinnear. Resident

Sinhalese: Nil-kurullā, Girā-kurullā. No Tamil name recorded

Plate 1, facing p. 24 (male; × one-third)

Size of the Red-vented Bulbul. Sexes nearly alike; young birds lack the orange forehead and black-and-mauve throat-patch, these parts being pale green. Unless a fairly close view is obtained this bird is not very easy to distinguish from Jerdon's Chloropsis, but the orange forehead may usually be detected if a pair of binoculars be used.

It lives among green foliage in trees, never descending to the ground, and would often escape observation were it not for its notes. Though rather local, it is widely distributed throughout the low country, except in the extreme north, and in the hills up to at least 3,000 feet, being commonest in the damper hill districts. Its food consists of insects especially caterpillars, some berries, and the nectar of loranthus, coral tree and silk cotton. It is usually seen in pairs. This bird keeps up a continual flow of sweet melody in which it includes clever imitations of the notes of many other birds. The flight is direct but seldom long sustained, usually merely from one clump of trees to the next.

The nest has seldom been found because it is well concealed among foliage near the end of a high branch. The two eggs are described as being pale cream, variously spotted or blotched with pale reddish or red-brown. They measure about 21 × 15 mm.

JERDON'S CHLOROPSIS

Chloropsis jerdoni (Blyth). Resident

Sinhalese: Nil-kurullā, Girā-kurullā. No Tamil name recorded

Plate 1, facing p. 24 (male lower, female upper; × one-third)

Size of the Red-vented Bulbul. The sexes differ as shown in the plate. This chloropsis is much commoner and more widely distributed than the preceding species, particularly in the low-country dry zone, where it occurs almost everywhere except, I believe, in the Jaffna Peninsula. It ascends the hills to at least 3,500 feet. Usually in pairs, it is not seldom found solitary, while family parties remain together for some time after the young are fledged. Like the Gold-fronted Chloropsis, it is more often heard than seen, its green plumage and undemonstrative way of hopping about among leafy trees making it very inconspicuous. Its marvellous power of mimicry is constantly exercised with imitations of the notes of all the small birds of the neighbourhood—magpie-robins, drongos, sunbirds, tailor-birds—all are cleverly mimicked; while every now and then the shrill *kikeeya kikeeya kikeeya* of the shikra is introduced to flavour the mixture. The food consists of insects, such as green tree-crickets, mantises and caterpillars; fruit; and nectar from flowers. It is a bird of the tree canopy, and seldom or never descends to ground level.

The breeding season is believed to last from November till May, but the nest is so well concealed among foliage, often at a considerable height, that it is not often found. It is a small hammock, composed of inner bark and fibres, slung between two twigs of a small forked branch. There are two eggs in a normal clutch; they are described as glossless ovals, cream-coloured or white, and sparingly marked with small spots and lines of brown or purplish black; they measure about 21·1 × 15·1 mm.

THE CEYLON BLACK BULBUL

Microscelis psaroides humii Whistler & Kinnear. Race peculiar to Ceylon

Sinhalese: Kalu Kondayā. Tamil: Karuppu Kondé-kuruvi

Plate 2, facing p. 25 (× one-quarter)

Somewhat larger than the Red-vented Bulbul; nearly as large as a mynah, but less stoutly built. Sexes similar. In spite of its name, only the short, rather ragged-looking crest is black, the rest of the plumage being dark grey, browner on wings and tail. The red beak and legs distinguish it from all other bulbuls, and the only bird it might be mistaken for is the Ceylon blackbird, which it somewhat resembles in coloration; but its short legs, and noisy and lively habits, should make such a mistake impossible.

It is found everywhere in the hills up to 5,500 feet, and in forested areas in the low-country wet zone; but it is scarce and local in the dry zone. A bird of the treetops, it loves forest sholas bordering mountain streams, patana woods and copses, forest margins and the like. In such places it lives in scattered flocks, whose members spend much of their time dashing from one fruiting tree to another, keeping up a continual noisy conversation of squeaks and raucous noises; some of these sound like: *squeek squeek, squēēdlee-ee* or *chēēk, crēēeorēr*. The scold-note is a cat-like mew, *mēēē*. Although these notes are loud and raucous, they sound by no means unpleasant when heard to the accompaniment of bright sunshine, rushing water and grand scenery. The Black Bulbul feeds largely on fruit, jungle berries, wild figs, etc., but it eats numbers of insects as well.

The nest is a small, untidy cup of rather coarse twiglets, leaf midribs, moss and the like, placed in a fork of a branch from ten to twenty feet from the ground. Usually the birds prefer trees somewhat detached from the main forest. The nest is not very well concealed as a rule. The two eggs are white or pinkish, speckled with brownish-red and purplish markings; they measure about 26 × 18 mm. The main breeding season is in March–May, with second broods often reared in July–September.

THE RED-VENTED BULBUL

Molpastes cafer cafer (Linnaeus). Resident

Sinhalese: Kondé-kurullā, Kondayā. Tamil: Kondé-kuruvi

Plate 2, facing p. 25 (× one-quarter)

Size of the magpie-robin. Sexes similar. The jaunty crest, black head, mottled brown body and bright vermilion under tail-coverts make this familiar bird quite unmistakable; in flight, the white rump-patch shows up conspicuously.

It is found everywhere, except in heavy forest, in the low country; and in the hills up to at least 6,000 feet. It feeds on berries (lantana berries being especially favoured) and insects of many kinds. The notes consist of sprightly calls, some of which suggest the words *ginger beer* and *sweet potatoes*; a loud shriek is uttered when a hawk suddenly appears, and the scolding-note, used when an owl, sneaking cat, or snake, is discovered, is a loud indignant chatter. A sweet, low sub-song is commonly uttered during the afternoon siesta.

In courtship, the male fluffs out his plumage and spreads the vermilion under tail-coverts laterally; the female reacts by depressing her crest, lowering head, wings and tail, and performing curious side-to-side motions with her beak while she utters inane chirps and quivers her wings. The nest is a compact cup composed of small twigs, stalks, etc., lined with fibres or fine rootlets, and bound together with cobwebs; it is placed in almost any bush, very little wisdom being shown by the birds in the selection of a site. To make up for this—and the resultant inevitable destruction of eggs and young—this bulbul is very prolific, laying several clutches of eggs yearly. Breeding proceeds to some extent throughout the year, but March–May, and again, August–September are the favourite seasons. The two or three eggs are very variable in colour, but usually the ground-colour is some shade of pink, profusely spotted and blotched with purplish or reddish brown. They measure about 21 × 15 mm. In defence of their young the parents will feign injury, fluttering before an enemy to entice him away from the babies.

THE YELLOW-BROWED BULBUL

Iole icterica (Strickland). Resident

Sinhalese: Kāhā Kondayā. No Tamil name recorded

Plate 2, facing p. 25 (× one-quarter)

Size of the Red-vented Bulbul, or magpie-robin. Sexes alike. A rich yellowish-green bird with bright yellow face and underparts, which is commonly found in forest throughout the low country, except the extreme north, and in the hills up to 4,000 feet. In the hills and wet zone it occurs wherever there is high forest, but in the dry zone it is mostly confined to the tall trees fringing streams or tanks, or growing about rocky hills. It goes in small troops and enlivens the forest by its noisy but musical calls. A note *zu-kink-up*—attributed by Legge to the Black Bulbul—really belongs to this species, and it has many notes besides. It appears to feed more on insects than fruit, but this point requires further investigation.

The nest is rather a scanty and untidy cup, composed of dead leaves bound together with strands of inner bark and some cobwebs, lined with fine rootlets. It is placed in a fork high up in a jungle sapling or, very often, suspended between two twigs among foliage at the end of a branch—often overhanging a stream, and so inaccessible. The two eggs are described as being white, or pinkish, thickly speckled with pale brownish red, or pink markings (Wait). They measure about 23 × 16·6 mm.

THE BLACK-CAPPED BULBUL

Pycnonotus melanicterus (Gmelin). Species peculiar to Ceylon

Sinhalese: Kāhā Kondayā. No Tamil name recorded

Plate 2, facing p. 25 (× one-quarter)

Rather smaller than the Red-vented Bulbul. In general coloration somewhat like the preceding species, but at once distinguished by its black cap and white-tipped, dark-brown tail.

It is found in pairs or small parties throughout the hills, up to at least 4,000 feet, and in scattered colonies in the dry zone except in the most arid parts. It prefers forest varied by open country, sholas and the like, to dense forest. As with most bulbuls, fruit (berries) and insects form its food. Its call-note is a plaintive, minor-key whistle on an ascending scale, something like *yor, yer ye*, or *wer wer we we*—each syllable higher than the last.

The nest is very similar to small ones of the Red-vented Bulbul. It is a cup, composed of small twigs, rootlets, etc., rather flimsily built, and lined scantily with fibres. It is well concealed among foliage, either in a low bush or in a small tree growing in a wooded ravine or on the out-skirts of forest, etc. The eggs normally number two, and they resemble small ones of the Red-vented Bulbul, being pinkish white, heavily spotted and speckled with reddish brown. They measure about 20·9 × 15·7 mm. The breeding season is in March and April, with a second period in August–September, but nests may be found in other months occasionally.

THE CEYLON WHITE-BROWED BULBUL

Pycnonotus luteolus insulae Whistler & Kinnear. Race peculiar to Ceylon

Sinhalese: Galu-guduwā. No Tamil name recorded

Plate 2, facing p. 25 (×one-quarter)

Size of the Red-vented Bulbul. Sexes similar. A drab, olive-grey bird, paler below, and with a conspicuous white eyebrow.

It inhabits the entire low country and ascends the hills to at least 3,000 feet; being common throughout its range but most abundant in the dry zone where it is one of the commonest birds. Much shyer than the Red-vented Bulbul, it loves scrub-jungle, the borders of tanks, etc., and is not rare in shrubby gardens where, however, it is more often heard than seen. The notes consist of a warning *chrr*, *chrr*, and a cry which has been well described as 'a loud rattle of sweetish notes' ('Eha', *A Naturalist on the Prowl*). This is often uttered and, being quite unmistakable, gives away the bird's whereabouts even when it cannot be seen. The 'Cinnamon Thrush'—as this bird used to be called in the 'coffee days'—feeds largely on berries of many kinds including, as that name suggests, those of the cinnamon tree. It also eats many insects, and the young are fed mainly on them, mantises and tree-crickets being much sought after.

The nest is of the usual bulbul type—a cup of small twigs, etc., lined with rootlets or other fibres—set in a bush, usually from two to four feet above the ground and often but ill-concealed. The two eggs closely resemble those of the Red-vented Bulbul, but are generally longer and narrower. They are pinkish-white, heavily spotted and streaked with varying shades of brownish red; they measure about $23 \times 15 \cdot 5$ mm. The main breeding season is in the first half of the year, February and March being the favourite months.

THE YELLOW-EARED BULBUL

Kelaartia penicillata (Blyth). Genus and species peculiar to Ceylon

Sinhalese: Galu-guduwā, Kāhā Kondayā. No Tamil name recorded

Plate 2, facing p. 25 (×one-quarter)

About the size of the Red-vented Bulbul, but fuller-plumaged. The curious head markings, and tufts of long, yellow feathers behind the eye, make it unmistakable. Sexes alike.

This bulbul is an up-country bird, seldom or never seen below 3,000 feet and not really common below 4,000 feet; in the higher hills, however, it is one of the commonest birds. It frequents jungle, wooded ravines, and well-wooded gardens, and is usually found in pairs though small flocks are not uncommon. Like other bulbuls, it feeds on both fruit and insects. In the vicinity of human habitations it is by no means shy and will often feed on berries in full view of an observer only a few yards away; but in the silence of primeval forest it seems awed by the solitude of its surroundings, and is then more shy, frequently uttering a low, warning note—*crr crr.* Another note, which seems to be a call to its mate, is a loud, but sweet-toned whistle *whēēt wit wit,* usually uttered in flight.

The nest is much more substantially built than other bulbul-nests, being a stout mass of green moss with a deep cup well lined with fine rootlets or other fibres. It is built in a fork of an upright sapling, in a bush, or on a hanging branch, and may be either well concealed or rather conspicuous. Two eggs are laid, of white or pink ground-colour, and sub-markings of purplish grey with spots, freckles and blotches of crimson-brown, usually more concentrated at the large end; they measure about 23·4 × 16·7 mm. There are two breeding seasons, viz. February–May, and August–October.

THE CHATS, ROBINS, AND THRUSHES
Family TURDIDAE

These are small to medium-sized perching birds (up to the size of the Common Mynah, in Ceylon species), of terrestrial and arboreal habits. In many respects they resemble the babblers but their plumage is less full and lax, their wings longer and, unlike the babblers, the young of these birds differ in coloration from their parents—mainly in being more or less spotted or scale-marked on back, wings and breast; in this, they resemble their near relatives, the flycatchers. The legs are rather long and strong; on the ground they generally proceed by hopping. The wings are fairly long, giving good powers of flight; many species are migratory, breeding sometimes thousands of miles away from their winter quarters. The tail is generally of moderate length and square at the tip, though in some species (e.g. the shama) it is long and graduated. The distribution of this family is almost world-wide, though the majority of species are found in Europe and Asia. They are all insectivorous, but many eat fruit as well.

The nests are of various types, though usually open at the top, not domed over; they may be situated on the ground; among foliage in trees and bushes; or in tree-holes and the like. The eggs are usually spotted.

THE INDIAN BLUE CHAT

Luscinia brunnea brunnea (Hodgson). A winter visitor

No Sinhalese or Tamil names recorded

Plate 1, facing p. 24 (male left, female right; × one-third)

Sparrow-sized, but with longer legs. Sexes differing as shown on the plate. The male somewhat resembles the Orange-breasted Blue Flycatcher in size and coloration, but it may at once be distinguished by the conspicuous white supercilium. The female might be confused with the female Kashmir Red-breasted Flycatcher, but it has no white in its tail, its legs are much longer, and its habits are quite different.

It arrives in Ceylon in October–November and immediately makes its way to the hills, where, at elevations above 1500 feet, it is fairly common in most years, though its numbers fluctuate. A jungle lover, it should be looked for in forests or shola ravines. In such places, it hops about the undergrowth, turning over the dead leaves, etc., in its search for the insects which form its food. Both sexes constantly move the short tail up and down. The alarm note is a soft *chuk*—like the sound produced by striking two pebbles together. On arrival in the Island, and also shortly before departing again in March or April, the male frequently sings a little ditty, *cheek cheek, teedleedleedlee*—whistled rapidly; it is rather like the song of the Orange-breasted Blue Flycatcher.

The breeding range of this bird is in the Himalayas. The nest is sited on the ground, well concealed among jungle herbage, and the eggs are described as unspotted, pale blue.

THE CEYLON PIED BUSH CHAT

Saxicola caprata atrata (Blyth). Race peculiar to Ceylon

No Sinhalese or Tamil names recorded

Sparrow-sized. The male is sooty black (without any bluish sheen) with white markings as shown in the figure. The female is mottled brown with a rusty red rump and upper tail-coverts. From the Black Robin both sexes may readily be distinguished because they do not habitually carry the tail elevated, as that species does.

Indian races of this chat inhabit plains as well as hills, but in Ceylon it is purely a hill bird, and does not occur below 3,500 feet. It is almost confined to the drier (Uva) side of the hills, but ascends to Nuwara Eliya and the Horton Plains. Within its range, it is common in open grassy districts, avoiding forested areas. It lives in pairs, and has a

PLATE 1

1. Velvet-fronted Blue Nuthatch. 2. Gold-fronted Chloropsis. 3. Jerdon's Chloropsis. 4. Ceylon Blue Magpie. 5. Indian Blue Chat. 6. Ceylon Iora

PLATE 2

1. Yellow-browed Bulbul.   2. Black-capped Bulbul.   3. Yellow-eared
Bulbul.   4. Ceylon White-browed Bulbul.   5. Ceylon Black Bulbul.
6. Red-vented Bulbul

characteristic habit of sitting on top of a bush or other little eminence, from which it darts down on any small insect that shows itself. In the breeding season, the male keeps very careful watch from his look-out bush for the approach of any suspicious characters, and warns his little mate, sitting on her eggs, by a monotonously repeated, plaintive *chep, chep-hēē*

—each utterance being accompanied by a jerk of the tail. As the enemy draws nearer, the little bird flits anxiously from bush to bush, adding a sharp, scolding note *chuh*—like scraping a quill against sandpaper. His 'song' is a brisk little whistle *chip chepēē-chewēēchu.* The young, when beginning to fend for themselves, utter a curious, rasping chirp—*creek, creek.*

The nest is a stout mass of dry grass-blades, etc., with a neat, deep cup lined with fine rootlets; it is built in a cavity in the ground under the shelter of a tuft of grass or weeds, often on a hill slope or near the top of a

Female lower, male upper;
× one-quarter

bank, and is well concealed. The two to four eggs vary in ground-colour, but are commonly sea-green, diffusely freckled or shaded, mainly in a zone around the large end, with pale sienna red. They measure about 19·5 × 15·2 mm. The breeding season is February–May.

A wheatear, almost certainly the PIED WHEATEAR *Oenanthe leucomela* [*leucomela* (Pallas)], was seen by me in Colombo on 16 November 1943 in a garden. It had obviously just arrived in Ceylon, presumably from India, and was exhausted by its journey—squatting on garden seats, etc.—though it showed no signs of illness. It permitted approach to within three or four yards, and the notes and sketches made during many minutes of observation enabled me to identify it by the aid of literature at the time, and later to confirm these conclusions by comparison with specimens at the British Museum (Natural History). It appeared to be a female in winter plumage.

It is a robin-like bird of greyish-buff general coloration, grizzled greyish on face and throat, with blackish wings; its most characteristic feature is the tail, which is white with the centre pair of feathers and tips of all the others black. This brief description is of the winter plumage, which my bird was wearing; in summer, the male is a strikingly white-and-black bird.

This wheatear is a bird of open, stony country where it perches on stones, clods and the like, and flits low over the ground. The tail is often oscillated up and down, showing off the white and black pattern abovementioned. It feeds on small ground insects. Its summer habitat is from south-east Europe, across Asia to Mongolia, and it winters mostly in Africa. Several species of wheatear visit north-west India in winter, and they are difficult to discriminate in winter plumage under field conditions.

The Pied Wheatear nests in holes in banks or under boulders.

Layard, about a hundred years ago, collected a few specimens of the BLUETHROAT *Cyanosylvia svecica* (Linnaeus) (subspecies?) in a south-western district of the Central Province in March. It has not been recorded in the Island since, but as it winters over much of India it is likely to occur in Ceylon from time to time. It is a slim, robin-like bird, about the size of a sparrow. Upper parts brown; conspicuous buff supercilium; sides of base of tail bright chestnut—very noticeable in flight; underparts buff-white with a black gorget surrounding the breast. The male in summer plumage has this gorget filled in with bright cobalt blue including in the middle a large spot either of white or bright chestnut (according to race); below the gorget there is a chestnut band. These blue and chestnut breast markings are more or less replaced by buff-white in winter plumage, and females and juveniles have only traces of them. Bill dark brown; irides dark brown; legs—which are rather long—yellowish-brown.

The bluethroat is a lively, rather skulking bird which hops about the ground amongst shrubbery and rank herbage, generally in damp places but not in forest. When put up it flies low and dives into cover as quickly as possible. Small insects comprise its diet. In summer it has a very sweet song.

It has two principal forms, distinguished by the colour of the spot in the middle of the blue breast-patch; they are the White-spotted Bluethroat and the Red-spotted Bluethroat. It is not known to which of these Layard's birds belonged, but most likely to the red-spotted form (*C. svecica svecica*). The species breeds in Europe and western Asia, and winters in Africa and southern Asia.

THE CEYLON BLACK ROBIN

Saxicoloides fulicata leucoptera (Lesson). Race peculiar to Ceylon

Sinhalese: Kalu-polkichchā. Tamil: Kāri-kuruvi, Kaddukari-kuruvi

Sparrow-sized, but with fuller plumage than a sparrow. Male, glossy blue-black, with white lesser wing-coverts (usually concealed by the mantle feathers), and chestnut under tail-coverts. The female is dark greyish brown, with chestnut under tail-coverts, and no white in the wing.

A very common bird throughout the low country and hills, ascending the latter to 5,000 feet on the drier, north-easterly aspect; less high in damper districts. It prefers open scrub-land or gardens, and eschews heavy forest. This merry little bird spends most of its time on the ground where it runs actively, searching for small insects, amongst which it shows a marked preference for termites. It carries its tail cocked up at an acute angle with the back, and is much given to flipping that expressive organ about, the while it frequently

Male; × one-quarter

utters its merry call *cheery-wee*. Any prowling cat, snake, or hiding owl is scolded with a harsh note *cheeee*.

In asserting territorial rights against a rival robin, the male adopts a remarkable attitude; he stretches his neck, pointing the bill vertically up, puffs out the breast feathers, white wing-coverts and chestnut under tail-coverts, and elevates the tail until it touches the back of his head; the while he runs about, pouring out a flood of rather creaky, squeaky song. This 'showing of the flag' generally seems to suffice for the establishment of his claims, as resort to fisticuffs is rare. The breeding season lasts from March till September, several broods being reared each year. The nest is rather an untidy mass of dry grass, fibres, rootlets, etc., placed in a hole in a bank or tree-trunk, or in some cavity in a building. There is almost invariably a fragment of cast slough of a snake included in the lining. The eggs number two or three; they vary considerably in size and shape, but are generally longish ovals; they are pale greenish white, freckled, especially around the large end, with spots and small blotches of reddish brown and purplish grey; they measure about 20·8 × 14·8 mm.

THE SOUTHERN MAGPIE-ROBIN

Copsychus saularis ceylonensis Sclater. Resident

Sinhalese: Polkichchā. Tamil: Vannāti-kuruvi

Bulbul-size. Glossy blue-black and white; the female has a grey head and breast and is duller than the male but otherwise resembles him in coloration.

This is the most familiar bird in Ceylon, being found in every garden, plantation, village or scrub-jungle in the Island, from sea level up to 5,500 feet, or even higher in places. It avoids heavy forest. Most of its time is spent hopping on the ground where it hunts for its food, which consists mainly of insects and other small 'creeping things' though it is not averse from a proportion of vegetable food, such as waste boiled rice or bread thrown out from houses, and fruit. Both sexes constantly indulge in a curious gesture; the black and white tail is raised in a series of

jerks until it is vertical, then suddenly depressed and spread, the wings being simultaneously expanded downwards. So ingrained in the bird's nature is this habit that it is practised even by youngsters which have just begun to grow their tails. The magpie-robin keeps late hours, often being active until well after dusk, and it is one of the first birds astir before sunrise. The ordinary call-note is a shrill, loud, four-note chirp on a descending scale; the scolding-notes are a harsh

Male; × one-quarter

chr and a spitting sound. The male has a clear, sweet, well-sustained song which is usually uttered from the top of a tall tree, or other commanding position, at the beginning of the breeding season; this song places the magpie-robin high in the ranks of bird songsters. It is a pugnacious bird in defence of territorial rights; the males show off before rivals with puffed-out breast feathers, depressed tail, and many absurd, pompous struttings and hoppings while trying to out-sing each other. Occasionally fierce combats take place.

The main breeding season lasts from about March to September, several broods being reared. The nest is an untidy mass of grass and fibres set, for preference, in a tree-hole six to thirty feet up; failing such a site, almost any dark cavity will do. The two or three eggs are generally pale prussian blue or sea-green in ground-colour, heavily freckled all over with brown; they measure about 23·1 × 17·3 mm.

THE CEYLON SHAMA, or
LONG-TAILED JUNGLE ROBIN

Kittacincla malabarica leggei Whistler. Race peculiar to Ceylon

Sinhalese: Wăl-polkichchā. No Tamil name recorded

Plate 3, facing p. 40 (male; × one-quarter)

Size of the magpie-robin, but with a much longer tail. The lack of white in the wings, white rump, chestnut underparts, flesh-coloured legs, as well as the long tail, distinguish it from the magpie-robin, with which, alone, it might be confused. Sexes nearly alike.

It is widely distributed in the low country and lower hills, up to about 3,000 feet; but it is rare and local in the wet zone and much prefers the dry zone forests for its habitat. In these it is very common, though, owing to its retiring habits and the density of the undergrowth, it is far more often heard than seen. It is not, however, really shy, and is easily 'called up' by even a clumsily-whistled imitation of its song. This song is among the finest of bird-voices; it is rich, varied and mellow. The bird often sings at dusk—like the magpie-robin it keeps late hours—and at such a time its clear yet somewhat melancholy notes seem to enhance the feeling of loneliness, mystery, and even menace, that the jungle holds as night descends. A harsh, spitting, scold-note is also uttered when the bird discovers some lurking enemy. The shama feeds largely on insects, but doubtless takes toll of jungle berries as well.

The breeding season is mainly in March to May. The nest is placed in a tree-hole or a hollow stump, and is composed of fibres, rootlets, skeleton leaves and the like. The eggs number three normally, but occasionally four. They resemble those of the magpie-robin, but are shorter ovals as a rule; they are pale sea-green in ground-colour, heavily blotched all over with brown; average measurements about 22·5 × 16·2 mm.

THE CEYLON BLACKBIRD

Turdus simillimus kinnisii (Blyth). Race peculiar to Ceylon

Sinhalese: Kalu-kurullā. Tamil: Kari-kuruvi

Mynah-sized. A dark bluish-grey bird, with bright orange bill, eye-lids and legs; sexes alike; the young are dull grey-brown, with yellow ochre spots on the breast. The shape, longer legs, and quite different habits distinguish it from the Black Bulbul, which has a somewhat similar colour-scheme and is sometimes confused with it.

It inhabits the higher hills of Ceylon, above about 3,000 feet up-wards, becoming commoner in the higher parts of its range. Primarily a forest bird, it has taken kindly to tea estates and gardens, especially well-wooded ones. Much of its time is spent on the ground, among shrubbery or jungle undergrowth, searching for insects among the dead leaves. It feeds also freely on various berries. When alarmed, it flies up into a tree, uttering a sharp *chuk, chuk, chukchuk*. The song of the male is very fine—very like the song of the British blackbird; it is commonly uttered in early morning and again towards dusk, and the performer likes to sing from some high point of vantage, such as the top of a tree.

× one-fifth

The main breeding season is in March and April, but a second brood is often reared in September–August, or even later. The nest is a large mass of green moss, with a neat, rather deep cup in the top, lined with fine rootlets or other fibres; it is placed, usually, in a well-concealed fork of a tree—preferably in forest, but not seldom in the midst of a tea estate. Other sites, such as the top of a stump, under the eaves of a building, etc., are often selected. The two or three eggs are generally pale bluish, or greenish in ground-colour, rather evenly speckled all over with some shade of reddish brown; they measure about 26·6 × 20·6 mm.

THE PIED GROUND THRUSH

Geokichla wardii (Blyth). Winter visitor

No Sinhalese or Tamil names recorded

Plate 3, facing p. 40 (male left, female right; × one-quarter)

Between the bulbul and the mynah in size. The male cannot be mis-taken for any other species, but the female may be confused with the young of the Spotted-winged Thrush.

This handsome thrush is a winter visitor to Ceylon, arriving in October–November and leaving again in March. During the whole of its stay it inhabits the hills between about 2,500 and 5,000 feet, though it is rare at the latter elevation. It favours certain localities, and its numbers fluctuate widely in different years. Mainly a forest bird, it is not uncommon in well-wooded gardens and jungly ravines. In such places it hops about among the dead leaves beneath the undergrowth, turning over the leaves in search of its insect prey; it also ascends tall trees, when they are in fruit, to feast on the berries.

On leaving Ceylon, about March, it betakes itself to its breeding grounds in the Himalayas.

THE NORTHERN ORANGE-HEADED GROUND THRUSH

Geokichla citrina citrina (Latham). Rare winter visitor

No Sinhalese or Tamil names

Plate 3, facing p. 40 (male; × one-quarter)

Between the bulbul and the mynah in size. The female is much duller-coloured than the male (figured in the Plate), and has the back suffused with greenish brown.

This beautiful thrush has been obtained in Ceylon only three or four times, mostly in the dry zone, low-country forests; a pair were reported in December 1947 at Hambantota and, as it is a shy jungle dweller and therefore easily overlooked, it is probable that it visits the Island more often than the records show. Its visits occur during the north-east monsoon. The southern race of this bird (*G. citrina cyanotus*) is resident in South India; it differs in having the face and throat white, marked with black in a pattern resembling the facial markings of the Spotted-winged Thrush. Our visiting examples all belong to the northern race, which breeds in the Himalayas, migrating southwards in winter.

THE CEYLON SCALY THRUSH
(Ceylon Thrush, or Ceylon Mountain Thrush, of some authors)

Oreocincla dauma imbricata (Layard). Race peculiar to Ceylon

Sinhalese: Wăl Avichchiyā. No Tamil name

Mynah-sized. Sexes alike. Olive-brown above, buff below, with crescentic black tips to the feathers. Unless a good view of this bird is obtained and its scaly markings seen, it might be mistaken, in the dim forest undergrowth which both inhabit, for the much commoner Spotted-winged Thrush; but the buff underparts, absence of white spots in the wing, and larger size, should make identification easy.

It is a rare, shy, forest-loving bird, confined to the hills above 2,000 feet—though it seems to prefer higher elevations, from 3,000 to 5,000 feet. Like most thrushes, it spends most of its time on the ground, turning over the dead leaves in its search for insect food.

× one-quarter

The nest has only seldom been found, but the available evidence seems to show that—like so many other Ceylon birds—this thrush is double-brooded; nesting about March–April, and again in August–September. The nest is normally built in a well-foliaged sapling, from twelve to twenty feet from the ground, in dense forest; but some nests are placed in shade-trees growing in tea estates near the border of jungle. They are large masses of green moss, with a neat cup at the top, lined with fine fern roots, etc. The two eggs are described as long, blunt ovals; they are pale olive-green, sparsely peppered with faint reddish markings all over; they measure about 30·5 × 21·2 mm.

THE SPOTTED-WINGED THRUSH

Oreocincla spiloptera Blyth. Species peculiar to Ceylon

Sinhalese: Wăl Avichchiyā, Gomā Avichchiyā. No Tamil name recorded

Plate 3, facing p. 40 (× one-quarter)

Between the bulbul and the mynah in size. Sexes alike. The young rather closely resemble the female Pied Ground Thrush, but may be distinguished by the characteristic facial pattern of white and black, which is similar to that of the adult.

This thrush is found throughout the hills, ascending to 6,000 feet; throughout the low-country wet zone; and in scattered localities in the dry zone, but its main habitat seems to lie between the 2,000 and 4,000 feet contours. It is a bird of forest, or well-wooded country (e.g. cardamom jungles, cacao estates, etc.), and is rather shy but also inquisitive; a singing male is easily decoyed within sight by whistling an imitation of its song, which is a rich, varied and sweet-toned performance, usually uttered from a perch in the lower branches of the tree-canopy. It feeds on insects, worms, etc., and probably also on berries.

In search of prey it vigorously turns over the dead leaves on the forest floor.

It is double-brooded, nesting both in March–April and again in August–November. The nest is placed in a fork of a sapling; balanced on cardamom-fronds; or in the crown of a tree-fern, etc., in forest. Though usually rather conspicuous, it is frequently so untidy a collection of rubbish that it escapes recognition as a nest; the cup, however, is well formed and lined with fine fibres, black rootlets and the like. The two eggs are either pale buff or pale greenish in ground-colour, heavily speckled with reddish brown. They measure about $26 \cdot 8 \times 19 \cdot 7$ mm.

THE INDIAN BLUE ROCK THRUSH

Monticola solitaria pandoo (Sykes). Scarce winter visitor

No Sinhalese or Tamil names

Plate 3, facing p. 40 (male; × one quarter)

Between the bulbul and the mynah in size. The female differs from the male (figured) in being dull greyish brown, with the face and breast mottled with pale buff. A slim, neat-plumaged bird, the male suggests a large edition of the Dusky-blue Flycatcher as its coloration is somewhat similar; but it is of a different shape and, of course, much larger.

This thrush visits Ceylon in small and fluctuating numbers each winter (north-east monsoon), and takes up residence wherever open boulder-strewn hills give it the conditions it likes—particularly in the dry zone, or drier parts of the hill zone. Such places as the slopes around Sigiriya Rock suit it admirably, and here it may be seen perching on top of the huge boulders, ever and anon diving down to pick some insect off the ground. It has a curious habit of frequently dipping forward, as if in a courtly bow. In March or April it leaves the Island to return to its breeding-grounds in the Himalayas. Almost silent during its winter sojourn with us, it develops a melodious song in its breeding range.

The nest is built in a cranny of a boulder, or among the stones of a boundary wall, etc., and the three or four eggs are pale blue, usually with a few sienna spots here and there.

33

THE CEYLON ARRENGA, or CEYLON WHISTLING THRUSH

Arrenga blighi Holdsworth. Species peculiar to Ceylon

No Sinhalese or Tamil names recorded

Between the bulbul and the mynah in size. A shorter, stouter-looking bird than the Ceylon blackbird, from which the male may be distinguished by his black beak and legs; the female is brown, paler on the underparts. Both sexes have a bright blue patch on the lesser wing-coverts, which is hardly ever visible, because hidden by the scapular and breast feathers, except in flight.

This is a scarce and shy mountain bird which does not occur below about 3,000 feet and is most likely to be seen between the 4,000 and 6,000 feet contours. Strictly a forest dweller, it loves densely wooded, ferny ravines and gorges, especially those that have a rapid torrent running through them, for it is seldom seen far from a stream. In such places, in the evening, the male flies restlessly to and fro, every now and then uttering his shrill, sibilant whistle, *srēeē . . . rēē*, which is much more often heard than its author is seen. The female seems to be more retiring than her mate, and is seldom seen. The arrenga is a lively bird, never still for long; it runs very rapidly and has a habit of fre-

Male; × one-quarter

quently opening and shutting the tail with a spasmodic action. It keeps late hours, and I have often watched one actively hopping about in the evening until the gloom of night made it almost indistinguishable. It feeds mainly on insects but does not despise small frogs, geckos, etc.; doubtless, it also partakes of fruit to some extent.

The breeding season is January to May, and it does not seem to indulge in a secondary season in August–September, as so many birds do. The nest is a large mass of green moss, mixed with twigs and dead leaves, with a neat and rather deep cup lined with fine rootlets, black fibres, etc. It is generally placed on a ledge or in a crevice of a rock beside a torrent or waterfall, but occasionally in a fork of a tree, or on a stump; but always in forest or on its borders. Sometimes the nest is very well concealed, but not seldom it is easily visible—though not necessarily accessible. The one or two eggs are very pale greenish with a few light reddish-brown markings around the larger end. They measure about 30·8 × 21·8 mm.

THE FLYCATCHERS

Family Muscicapidae

Small, thrush-like birds, confined to the Old World.[1] Their food consists almost entirely of small insects which they capture on the wing, and their form and structure are modified in accordance with this habit of life. The wings are fairly long, giving good powers of flight; the legs and feet, which are used for little besides perching, are small and weak; the beak, though small, is flattened, and broad at the base; the rictal bristles, fringing the upper mandible at the sides, are long and strong, assisting in the capture of flying insects. The tail is usually of medium length, and square, or slightly forked, at the tip; but in some forms (e.g. the Paradise Flycatcher) it is long and graduated. The coloration of flycatchers varies from dull browns and greys to brilliant colours. Many forms are migratory. In general, they are birds of solitary habits. They mostly take their small prey in quick sallies from a perch not, as swallows do, in continuous flight.

As with thrushes, the young are nearly always spotted, differing from the adults. The nests are open at the top, placed either in tree-cavities, holes in banks and the like, or in trees. The eggs are spotted.

THE KASHMIR RED-BREASTED FLYCATCHER

Siphia hyperythra Cabanis. Regular winter visitor to Ceylon

No Sinhalese or Tamil names

Plate 4, facing p. 41 (female left, male right; × one-quarter)

About sparrow-sized. This interesting little bird breeds in Kashmir and adjoining districts of India, and winters in Ceylon; it has very seldom been seen in any intermediate part of India. On arriving in the Island it betakes itself at once to the hills above about 2,500 feet. There it settles down in gardens, tea estates, the borders of forest, etc., each bird apparently choosing a territory of its own where it may be found day after day, until the time comes, in March or April, for its long return journey back to Kashmir. Unlike most flycatchers, it spends a good deal of time on the ground, hopping about in a search for insects. It has a habit of jerking the tail well above the back, in a spasmodic manner, at the same time flicking the wings, and uttering a curious little

---

[1] American 'flycatchers' belong to quite a different family, the *Tyrannidae* or 'Tyrant-birds'.

creaking rattle. Its song, which it utters quite freely in Ceylon, consists of a single whistled note *chip, chip, chip*—followed by the rattling note.

THE BLUE-THROATED FLYCATCHER

Muscicapa rubeculoides rubeculoides (Vigors). Very rare winter visitor

No Sinhalese or Tamil names

Sparrow-sized. The male might easily be mistaken for the next species (*M. tickelliae nesaea*), but its throat, as well as the upper plumage, is deep indigo blue. The female is olive-brown, with paler, rufous throat and breast, white abdomen and the upper tail-coverts and tail rufous-brown.

This is a Himalaya-breeding flycatcher which winters in India; an occasional, odd straggler reaches Ceylon where it seems to confine itself to the northern half of the Island. Described as a skulking, forest bird, it should be looked for, during the north-east monsoon, in the dry-zone forests. In all probability it is sometimes overlooked owing to its resemblance to the next species (male), or to the female Blue Chat (female).

THE CEYLON ORANGE-BREASTED BLUE FLYCATCHER

Muscicapa tickelliae nesaea (Oberholser). Race peculiar to Ceylon

Sinhalese: Kopi-kurullā, Mārāwā. Tamil: Kopi-kuruvi

Plate 4, facing p. 41 (male; × one-quarter)

Sparrow-sized. The female is paler coloured than the male and has whitish lores, but otherwise resembles him; young birds are browner, streaked with pale buff on the upper plumage and spotted with brown on the buff breast.

Found almost everywhere in the Island, up to about 4,000 feet, in jungle or shady types of cultivation, being particularly fond of the banks of wooded streams. In such places it flits about among the undergrowth, revealing its presence by its characteristic little warble, a quaint, rapid little jingle of about six notes. It is not shy, and is rather inquisitive towards human intruders in its haunts. Its food, like that of all flycatchers, consists mainly, if not entirely, of small insects, often captured on the wing.

The breeding season is from February to June, with April as the favourite month. The nest, composed of moss, leaf-stalks, skeleton leaves, etc., with a neat cup lined with fine fibres, is placed in a hole in a bank, or in a low stump, etc., usually within three feet of the ground. The two, or more usually three, eggs are olive brown in appearance, this being due to the density of the speckling of that colour on a lighter ground. They measure about 19·5 × 14·8 mm.

THE DUSKY-BLUE FLYCATCHER

Muscicapa sordida (Walden). Species peculiar to Ceylon

Sinhalese: Gini-kurullā (a name applied to several small birds of bright plumage). No Tamil name recorded

Plate 4, facing p. 41 (×one-quarter)

Sparrow-sized. Sexes similar, but the juveniles are brown, heavily spotted on head, back, wing-coverts and breast with pale buff; the flight-feathers are broadly margined with blue-grey.

This flycatcher is confined to the hills above 2,000 feet, but is not common below 3,000 feet. It inhabits forest or well-wooded ravines on estates, gardens, etc., where plenty of shady trees give it the seclusion it loves; in such places it is a familiar bird, not at all shy. It feeds mainly on flying insects, beetles, caterpillars and the like, but also eats berries such as the wild yellow raspberry, lantana, etc. It has a sweet, rather loud song, consisting of five or six notes in a cadence, repeated over and over again. This it utters from a fairly high perch in a tree, during the courting season. The same notes, and cadence, are used in a sub-song so low and clear that it is often hard to realize that the performer is close at hand; it suggests a much louder song being delivered fifty yards or more away. This sub-song is used by the male as a warning to his mate, or young, that an enemy is approaching.

The main breeding season is in the first half of the year, March and April being the favourite months; but a second—or third—brood is often reared in August–September. The nest is a compact mass of green moss, with a neat, rather deep cup in the top, lined with fine black fibres, probably fern roots. It is placed in a cavity of suitable size and depth, for preference in a road bank; failing such a site, in any hole in a tree, usually at no great height—three to six feet—but sometimes twenty or thirty feet above the ground. The site is always well shaded, but not always well concealed, and the bird often reveals its nest by flying out a few yards in front of one. The normal clutch is two, but occasionally three eggs are laid. They are pale pink, freckled all over with pale burnt sienna, which often forms a zone, or cap, at the large end. They measure about 20·5 × 14·8 mm.

THE BROWN FLYCATCHER

Muscicapa latirostris Raffles. Winter visitor to Ceylon

No Sinhalese or Tamil names

Plate 4, facing p. 41 (× one-quarter)

Rather smaller than a sparrow. A pale, brownish-grey bird, with a large dark eye surrounded by a whitish ring.

On its arrival in Ceylon in September–October it spreads all over the low country and ascends the hills to 4,000 feet, though it is not common above 3,000 feet. A solitary bird, it chooses shady gardens, and the like, rather than forest. It sits quietly on a twig, every now and then darting after some small flying insect which it captures with a loud snap of its bill, and then returns, as often as not, to the same perch. Frequently it depresses its tail and then jerks it back into normal position. The only note I have heard it utter is *chik, chik r r,* which is accompanied by quivering the tail.

It leaves Ceylon in March or April, and migrates to its breeding grounds in the Himalayas and northwards of them.

LAYARD'S FLYCATCHER

Muscicapa muttui muttui (Layard). Scarce winter visitor

No Sinhalese or Tamil names

Plate 4, facing p. 41 (× one-quarter)

Sparrow-size. In general shape this is very like the last species, but it is a trifle larger, darker, and more richly coloured. The eye is large and dark, with a dark supercilium above it and a fairly conspicuous white half-ring behind and below it. The white throat has a dusky moustachial stripe proceeding from the base of the lower jaw, and the breast is dusky too.

This bird, though often considered rare, probably visits Ceylon in some numbers in most years, but its manners are so retiring that it is overlooked. It loves the banks of rivers running through forest, and in such places it chooses shady recesses where it sits on twigs usually only three to six feet above the ground. It flies out after small flying insects, gnats and the like, and returns to the same perch, or a neighbouring one, and appears to be very attached to its territory. It has been met with in all zones of the Island, and occurs up to at least 5,000 feet. One that I watched maintained its active hunting until well after sunset, when dusk was well advanced. I have not heard it utter any note.

In March or April it leaves the Island on return migration to the eastern Himalayas, where it breeds.

THE CEYLON GREY-HEADED FLYCATCHER

Culicicapa ceylonensis ceylonensis (Swainson). Race peculiar to Ceylon, but almost indistinguishable races are found in many parts of India

No Sinhalese or Tamil names

Plate 4, facing p. 41 (×one-quarter)

About the size of the Large White-eye. The olive-green and yellow plumage, with slightly crested, grey head, and the habits, make this little bird quite unmistakable. Sexes alike.

It is common above 3,000 feet, and descends lower in the south-western wet zone, but prefers elevations above 4,000 feet, where it is one of the commonest and most familiar of birds. It inhabits forest, wooded ravines, gardens, and any locality where plenty of trees supply the shelter and insect food that it requires. It is remarkably tame, and will fearlessly perch and flit about within a few yards of a human. It is nearly always found in pairs, which seem very attached to each other. A lively little bird, it is always on the move, turning this way and that on its perch, dashing after some minute gnat or midge—which, in typical flycatcher fashion, it seizes with a loud snap of its bill—and frequently uttering its call-note *tweety-weety*—which, with other twittering notes, seem to comprise its only song.

The breeding season is February–May. The nest is a beautiful little pocket-shaped structure, composed almost entirely of green moss of the type that grows abundantly on tree trunks in its haunts, bound and felted with cobwebs. It is generally unlined. The nest is placed against a tree-trunk, on thè side of a boulder, or in a recess in a mossy bank. It resembles its surroundings so closely that it is usually found only by watching the birds' behaviour. The two or three eggs are dull white or buffish, peppered with grey and pale brown, mainly in a large-end zone. They measure about 15·1 × 12 mm.

THE PARADISE FLYCATCHER

Tchitrea paradisi paradisi (Linnaeus). Winter visitor to Ceylon
Tchitrea paradisi ceylonensis Zarudny & Härms. Race peculiar to Ceylon

Sinhalese: Redi-horā, Lainsu-horā (white males); Gini-horā (red males and females)
Tamil: Vedi-vāt-kuruvi (Wait); Pirāmana-kuruvi (Phillips)

Plate 4, facing p. 41, fig. 4 (left female, right male; × one-quarter); fig. 5 (male; × one-quarter)

Bulbul-sized, but with a longer tail; full-plumaged males of both races have the middle tail feathers very long, forming ribbon-like streamers. The blue-black head, with jaunty crest, and either snowy white, or bright chestnut back, wings and tail, make this bird unmistakable even in the females and young, which lack the long tail of the males.

In the north-east monsoon, it may be seen almost anywhere in the Island, up to—occasionally—5,000 feet, though normally not much above 3,000 feet; but in the south-west monsoon, which is the breeding season, it is seldom seen except in the low-country dry zone. The beautiful white-phase males are now believed to be all winter visitors from India, while the Ceylonese race appears never to develop white plumage. This very vivacious bird moves about a good deal, and must cover a large extent of country in the course of a day's hunting. Always active, it appears fully aware of its beauty, and the males whisk their long tail-streamers about with every appearance of pride. The food consists entirely of insects, which are captured on the wing. Both sexes frequently utter a loud, rather harsh note—*chreech*—and the male has also a musical little warbling song. Towards evening, the Paradise Flycatcher takes its regular bath by plunging into a pool, from a convenient perch, almost after the manner of a fishing kingfisher.

About March or April the migrant race returns to India, and about the same time our resident birds repair to the dry zone for breeding, which takes place in the months April–July. The nest is a beautiful little cup, composed of fine fibres, bast, etc., bound around with cobweb, and decorated on the sides with spider's egg-cocoons. It is placed on a downward-hanging, more or less bare branch or liana, or in a fork of a slender bough, generally with no attempt at concealment. The site may be at any height from a few feet to thirty or more above the ground. The two or three eggs are glossy, pinkish white with sienna spots mostly collected in a large-end zone but sparsely scattered elsewhere. They measure about 20·2 × 15·3 mm.

PLATE 3

1. Orange Minivet.   2. Ceylon Little Minivet.   3. Ceylon Shama.
4. Ceylon Scimitar Babbler.   5. Indian Blue Rock-Thrush.   6. Pied
Ground-Thrush. 7. Northern Orange-headed Ground-Thrush. 8. Spotted-
winged Thrush

Plate 4

1. Ceylon Grey-headed Flycatcher. 2. Ceylon Azure Flycatcher. 3. Dusky-blue Flycatcher.   4. Indian Paradise Flycatcher.   5. Ceylon Paradise Flycatcher.   6. Brown Flycatcher.   7. Layard's Flycatcher.   8. Ceylon Orange-breasted Blue Flycatcher.   9. White-browed Fantail Flycatcher. 10. Kashmir Red-breasted Flycatcher

THE CEYLON AZURE FLYCATCHER
(Ceylon Black-naped Flycatcher of many authors)

Hypothymis azurea ceylonensis Sharpe. Race peculiar to Ceylon

Sinhalese: Nil-kurullā. No Tamil name recorded

Plate 4, facing p. 41 (male; × one-quarter)

Sparrow-sized, but with a relatively long tail. The lovely, azure-blue coloration makes this bird unmistakable, provided it can be seen in a good light. Its shape, lively manners, and sharp note, in combination, however, make its identification easy. The females and young are duller and greyer than the full-plumaged males.

This is a forest bird, and is found, in suitable country, almost throughout the Island, though nowhere very numerous; it ascends the hills to 5,000 feet, on the drier (Uva) side, but probably seldom breeds much above 3,000 feet. Except in the breeding season, it is usually solitary. A most active little bird, never still for long, it travels about constantly, making its presence known by its call, which is much like that of the Paradise Flycatcher, a rasping *tchreet*. It feeds on small flying insects. Bathing is performed by plunging from an overhanging twig into some forest pool.

The breeding season is in March–May. The nest is a small, deep cup, neatly finished around the rim, composed of soft bast and other fine fibres, and lined with finer fibres still; the outside is decorated with moss or spider's egg-capsules, and often there is a ragged 'tail' below the nest. It is situated in forest, generally a few feet from the ground, in a fork of a small sapling, and is not at all well concealed; some nests, however, are built at higher levels in the forest canopy, up to twenty feet or more. The two or three eggs are pale pinkish-white, sparingly speckled with sienna which tends to form a ring around the large end. They measure about 17·2 × 13·2 mm.

THE WHITE-BROWED FANTAIL FLYCATCHER, or 'DRUNKEN PIPER'

Leucocirca aureola compressirostris Blyth. Resident

Sinhalese: Endēra-kurullā, Mārāwā, Nătănă-kurullā
Tamil: Vali-marittan

Plate 4, facing p. 41 (× one-quarter)

Rather smaller than a sparrow, but with a long and broad tail. A dull-black and white little bird, whose manners make it quite unmistakable. Sexes alike.

It is common in most parts of Uva, up to 5,000 feet, and in the drier, eastern parts of the Southern Province and most of the Eastern Province; it also occurs in isolated spots in the Central, Sabaragamuwa, and Western Provinces. In spite of its rather drab coloration, it is a delightful little bird, being completely fearless of man and seeming rather to seek his company than to avoid it as so many birds do. Its fearlessness is not its only attraction, however, for it is an exceedingly graceful and lively bird, perpetually showing off by elevating and spreading its tail into a fan and drooping its wings, the while it pirouettes about like the vainest of ballet dancers. It has a very human-sounding little whistle of seven or eight notes, forming a quaint tune which is often left unfinished, as if the performer had forgotten the last note! It also utters a sharp alarm, or scolding note—*ch'wch*—when its eggs or young are threatened by an enemy. Like all flycatchers, it subsists on small flying insects, which are always taken on the wing, and it shows great agility in capturing them although its ordinary flight is direct and rather slow. It lives in pairs, which appear to consort together for life.

The breeding season lasts from January till July, but most eggs are laid in April and May. The nest is a tiny 'coffee-cup', composed of fine fibres, rootlets, etc., plastered with cobwebs, and very neatly finished off everywhere; the rim is thin, and forms nearly a perfect circle. As a rule, the nest is perched on a single finger-thick twig, which is enclosed in its base; but often it is partly supported by one or more subsidiary twigs. It is placed in a scantily-foliaged tree, quite exposed to view in most cases, and therefore the mortality-rate among the eggs and young is very high; crows, coucals, lizards and tree-snakes taking a heavy toll of them. The site is often within a few feet of the ground, but sometimes as high as thirty or forty feet. The birds are very naïve about their nesting arrangements and will carry on building operations unconcernedly, in full view of a human two or three yards away—merely expostulating, now and then, with their scold-note. The two or three eggs are rather dumpy ovals, pale or warm buff in colour, with a zone around the large end of greyish brown and raw sienna spots and blotches. They measure about $16 \cdot 6 \times 13 \cdot 2$ mm.

THE WARBLERS
Family SYLVIIDAE

The warblers are a large family of small birds (the largest no bigger than a bulbul, and most much smaller), confined to the

Old World except for two species found in Alaska. They are structurally related closely to both the thrushes and the fly-catchers, differing from both these families in having the young unspotted; from the thrushes (including robins and chats) they differ in having the legs and feet rather weak; and from the fly-catchers, in having the rictal bristles (fringing the beak) com-paratively few and short. The beak is small and slender; wings fairly long in the more active migratory forms, short and rounded in the others; in most species, the tail is moderately long, square or rounded at the tip, but some species have longer and graduated tails. They are seldom seen on the ground, being birds of tree-tops, bushes, or grass and reeds, etc. Many forms are migratory, breeding in temperate climates and wintering in the tropics; others are resident in their breeding-grounds all the year. Their diet is almost purely insectivorous, consisting of small flies, moths, larvae, etc., which they usually capture by searching foliage—not, as flycatchers commonly do, by aerial sallies; but there is no hard-and-fast rule about this. The colouring of warblers is, in general, of a quiet and sober sort—never vividly brilliant or metallic; they are mostly dressed in soft, but beautiful, browns, greys, greens and yellows. Many of them, especially among the migratory forms, sing delightfully in their breeding haunts; but unfortunately, the season of song does not commence until these migrants have left Ceylon, and our resident forms are by no means in the forefront of songsters.

Warblers nest in a great variety of situations—on the ground, in bushes, trees or reed-beds, etc., building open or domed nests. Their eggs are spotted.

PALLAS'S GRASSHOPPER WARBLER

Locustella certhiola (Pallas). Very rare winter visitor

No Sinhalese or Tamil names

Sparrow-sized; of much the same general appearance as Blyth's Reed Warbler, but richer coloured, with the upper parts streaked with dark brown; the tail very rounded, with all except the middle pair of feathers tipped greyish white.

This bird has not been recorded from Ceylon since February 1877, when Legge met with several examples, and collected two, in the Mutturajawella swamp, between Ja-ela and the Negombo lagoon. It inhabits tangled vegetation growing in swamps, and is a great skulker, very difficult to flush and then merely fluttering a few yards into the next cover. It breeds in Siberia, and winters in China, Malaya and India.

The BROAD-TAILED GRASS WARBLER *Schoenicola platyura* (Jerdon). The evidence of existence of this bird in Ceylon rests on a specimen labelled as from 'Ceylon ex Cuming' which Legge discovered in the British Museum (Natural History) in or before 1880. Were this the only evidence of its Ceylonese status it might be ignored, but in 1939 W. W. A. Phillips saw three birds which he believed to be this species in tall māna-grass at Gammaduwa (one) and near Madugoda, 2,500 feet, in the Rangala hills (two together). These sight records have revived hopes that the bird may be resident in Ceylon after all. It is about the size of Blyth's Reed Warbler which it appears to resemble in general shape, but it has a longer and very broad, much graduated tail —the central feathers in particular being very broad for so small a bird. It is described as rufous brown with whitish underparts shading to rufescent brownish on the sides of the fore-neck and on the flanks; a whitish streak above the brown lores. Bill horny-brown paling to horny-grey or flesh colour on the lower mandible; gape yellowish; mouth yellowish pink; iris brownish grey to olive brown; legs, feet and claws greyish brown.

Sálim Ali found it fairly common in suitable country in the Western Ghats of South India from about 3,000 to 4,000 feet. It inhabits grass-covered hill-sides, especially swampy, reedy spots, where it skulks solitarily among tangled herbage, and is hard to flush. In early morning and late evening, however, it sometimes climbs up grass stems to deliver its feeble call *pink, pink*. The flight is described as 'indirect and top-heavy like that of *Prinia* and *Cisticola*, and the broad graduated tail conspicuous on the wing'.

THE CEYLON GREAT REED WARBLER

Acrocephalus stentoreus meridionalis (Legge). Race peculiar to Ceylon

No Sinhalese or Tamil names recorded

Plate 5, facing p. 72 (× one-third)

Size of the Red-vented Bulbul. In coloration, this bird is almost a large edition of the next (Blyth's Reed Warbler), but it is more slenderly built and the gape and inside of the mouth are bright orange, whilst in that species these parts are pale yellowish fleshy.

It inhabits the low country of both wet and dry zones, but lives almost entirely in reed-beds or tangled vegetation growing in, or near, tanks and swamps. It appears to move about the country a good deal, and is by no means always to be found in likely-looking spots; for instance, it no longer frequents the reed-beds in the Jaffna Fort moat where Legge found it, and the only place where I have seen it in the Jaffna Peninsula is reed-beds in the lagoon near Maruthankerni. It is, however, a great skulker, with a rooted objection to exposing itself to view except in the breeding season, when it becomes very restless and frequently sings from the tops of reeds or rushes. During the season it is a very noisy bird, keeping up a constant flow of loud and quaint squeaks, chatterings and croaks. Its food consists of small insects.

The breeding season is the middle of the year but, as I have found singing going on vigorously in January, it is probable that some birds nest early in the year. No doubt the season varies according to the amount and distribution of the local rainfall. The nest is a fairly deep cup, placed among reed stems, to which its sides are bound by the fibres, grass-blades, etc., of which it is composed. 'The two or three eggs are of pale greenish gray, rather thickly, but irregularly, marked with blotches and spots of black, yellowish brown, and grayish purple. Average size of eight Ceylon eggs ·81 by ·6.'—Wait (=about 20·5 × 15 mm.).

BLYTH'S REED WARBLER

Acrocephalus dumetorum Blyth. Regular winter visitor

Sinhalese: Hambu-kurullā. Tamil: Tinu-kuruvi

Plate 5, facing p. 72 (× one-third)

Size of the House Sparrow, but more slenderly built. Sexes alike. In spite of its sober coloration, this is a very pretty and graceful little bird.

It visits Ceylon in large numbers each winter, arriving in October and November, and leaving again, for its breeding-grounds in eastern Europe and northern Asia, in April and May. During its stay in the Island, it may be found almost anywhere, up to at least 6,000 feet, in gardens, tea estates, scrub-land, etc., and it is by no means shy. Towards evening, it likes to repair to some dense tangle of shrubbery, or to a reed-bed in a swamp, but at other times it frequents any type of bushes or trees, hopping actively about in ceaseless search for its food, which consists entirely of small insects, of which lake-flies (*Chironomidae*) seem to be favourites. If disturbed, it utters a note like *chak*, or *crrr*, and I once heard several uttering a peevish scold *ee*. Towards the end of its stay, it begins to practise its true song—a beautiful, sustained song, very like the magpie-robin's sub-song. While singing, it hops about, and slightly expands the tail with a jerking action.

SYKES'S BOOTED WARBLER

Hippolais caligata rama (Sykes). Winter visitor

No Sinhalese or Tamil names

Slightly smaller than Blyth's Reed Warbler which it resembles very closely in general form and coloration; but it has a smaller beak, slightly paler and more rufous colouring above, and the tail is less graduated, with the outer feathers distinctly pale-edged. In hand, the first primary, which extends from 5 to 10 mm. beyond the primary coverts, at once distinguishes it from Blyth's Reed Warbler which has this feather minute, not extending beyond the primary coverts. Sexes alike.

Although it has been recorded only a few times from Ceylon—always from the Mannar district—it appears to be a regular winter visitor in small numbers, escaping notice through its resemblance, in behaviour as well as appearance, to Blyth's Reed Warbler. W. W. A. Phillips found it fairly common in acacia scrub in the neighbourhood of Mannar in December 1950, and February and March 1952. He describes its alarm-note as a double *chit-chit* and says that it occasionally utters an attractive little warbling song from a shady twig in a dense thicket, generally after 10 a.m.

A single specimen of EVERSMANN'S BOOTED WARBLER *Hippolais caligata scita* (Eversmann) was collected by W. W. A. Phillips on the coast opposite Wirawila, S.P., in January 1951. In the field it is indistinguishable from *H. c. rama*, their separation depending on slight differences in the relative lengths of some of the primaries, and on measurements of bill, wing, and tail, etc.

The Booted Warbler, in several races, breeds in eastern Europe and western Asia, and winters to the south of these countries. An allied race is said to nest on or near the ground in low willow-scrub and the like; four to six eggs are laid.

HUME'S WHITETHROAT

Sylvia althaea Hume. Regular, but local, winter visitor

No Sinhalese or Tamil names

About the size of Blyth's Reed Warbler. Sexes similar. Upper plumage rather dark, brownish grey, the head less brown; lower plumage whitish, suffused with grey on the sides of the breast and flanks; the lores, line below the eye, and ear-coverts, darker grey, contrasting with the white of the chin and throat. Outer tail-feathers white, the rest more or less white-tipped. Bill blackish; irides brown; legs and feet nearly black. For differences from the next species, the Indian Lesser Whitethroat, see that species.

This whitethroat visits Ceylon in some numbers in the winter, but seems to confine itself to the very dry strip of country along the coast from about Marichchukkaddi to the Jaffna district. It has only been collected, apparently, from Mannar, but I saw several in December 1940, at Illuppaikkadavai. Since then both W. W. A. Phillips and

× one-third

Mrs Lushington have, on several occasions, found it in considerable numbers in Mannar Island and its neighbourhood. It is a shy bird, usually seen hopping about in acacia scrub and jungle. Phillips records that occasionally one will utter a few notes of a song or a low, churring call, but it is usually silent in its winter quarters. It breeds in Kashmir.

A single specimen of the INDIAN LESSER WHITETHROAT *Sylvia curruca blythi* Ticehurst & Whistler was collected in the Eastern Province in 1897 and is in the Colombo Museum. It is a trifle smaller than the last species which it very closely resembles in general appearance, but its back, wings and tail have a distinctly browner tinge, contrasting with the paler grey head, and its beak is smaller (11-13 mm. against 14-15 mm. in Hume's Whitethroat). It is described as a very active, vivacious little bird, which frequents trees, preferring acacias and avoiding deep forest. It breeds in Siberia and Manchuria and visits the plains of India abundantly in winter.

47

THE GREEN TREE WARBLER
(Green Willow Warbler of many authors)

Phylloscopus trochiloides nitidus Blyth. Abundant winter visitor

No Sinhalese or Tamil names

Plate 5, facing p. 72 (×one-third)

About the size of Loten's Sunbird, or the Large White-eye. Sexes alike. An active, graceful little bird, which arrives in Ceylon in September–October, and leaves again in April for its breeding-range, which extends from the Caucasus to Afghanistan and Chitral. During its stay in the Island it may be found wherever there are trees, but it is probably commoner in the lower hills than elsewhere. It hops and flits ceaselessly among the foliage in its search for the small insects which form its food; I have seen one capture and eat a large stone-fly which it caught among leaves overhanging a mountain stream. In general, it prefers the tree-canopy, seldom descending into the undergrowth. It constantly utters a cheery little call, *thirririp*, but this must be merely expressive of well-being as it is solitary in its habits while in Ceylon.

THE GREENISH TREE WARBLER
(Greenish Willow Warbler of many authors)

Phylloscopus trochiloides viridanus Blyth. Rare winter visitor

No Sinhalese or Tamil names

This warbler, a subspecies of the Green Tree Warbler, is almost indistinguishable in the field from its commoner relative, but may be recognized, if a sufficiently good view be obtained, by its plainer, less green-and-yellow coloration. In habits and note it is identical, and, although only two or three specimens have been collected in Ceylon, it probably visits the Island fairly regularly in small numbers as it is a common winter visitor to the South Indian hills and Travancore. This race of *P. trochiloides* breeds from eastern Europe, through western Siberia, to Kashmir.

A single specimen of a third race of this TREE WARBLER, viz. *Phylloscopus trochiloides trochiloides* (Sundevall), collected at Matara in October 1921, was discovered by Whistler amongst a series of warblers sent to him for study from the Colombo Museum. It is described as being considerably darker on the upper parts and more olivaceous on the under parts than the Greenish Tree Warbler, and its breeding range is in the eastern Himalayas and south-west China.

THE LARGE-BILLED TREE WARBLER
(Large-billed Willow Warbler of many authors)

Phylloscopus magnirostris Blyth. Regular winter visitor

No Sinhalese or Tamil names

Plate 5, facing p. 72 (× one-third)

About the size of Loten's Sunbird, or of the Large White-eye; it is a trifle larger than the Green Tree Warbler, but this is not appreciable in the field. However, it has a somewhat stouter build than that bird, much darker coloration, eye-stripe dark and definite, and the yellowish-white supercilium is very distinct and extends farther towards the back of the head. The whitish tips of the greater coverts form a clear wing-bar, and there is a trace of a second bar on the tips of the median coverts. Sexes alike.

This little warbler visits Ceylon in fair numbers in most years, but is not nearly so numerous as the Green Tree Warbler; moreover, it does not make itself so conspicuous as that species, preferring forest to the neighbourhood of human habitations. In other respects, however, it differs little in habits from the Green except in its call, which is a clear, rather plaintive, three-note whistle on an ascending scale—*yaw-wee-wee* —which Legge justly likens to the song of the Orange-breasted Blue Flycatcher. It occurs over the greater part of the Island, both low country and hills, arriving in September–October and departing again about April for its breeding-grounds in the Himalayas.

THE CEYLON TAILOR-BIRD

Orthotomus sutorius sutorius (Pennant). Race peculiar to the low country and lower hills of Ceylon

Orthotomus sutorius fernandonis Whistler. Race peculiar to the higher hills of Ceylon

Sinhalese: Battichchā, Tawikā. Tamil: Thaiyarkāran-kuruvi, Koddia-pākkān

Plate 5, facing p. 72 (male; × one-third)

Size of the Purple-rumped Sunbird. Sexes alike, except that the male has the two middle tail-feathers much longer than the next pair, while in the female all the tail-feathers are of much the same length. The young resemble the female. The coloration, ubiquity, and loud calls, make this little bird easy to identify.

It is probably the most widespread bird in Ceylon, inhabiting alike gardens, jungle, scrub, from sea level to the tops of the highest hills, wet zone and dry zone; all it asks is reasonably profuse vegetation. The two races are indistinguishable in the field and identical in habits, and are distinguished by the montane birds being merely somewhat darker in coloration. The tailor-bird spends most of its time hopping actively about in bushes, hedgerows and trees, in a ceaseless search for the tiny insects which form its food. Lake-flies form a considerable proportion of this, and it also eats many small, soft spiders. It lives in pairs, which appear to mate for life. They keep in touch with each other by a loud and rather monotonous call which, though it has many variants, sounds, in general, something like *tiwer tiwer tiwer* . . . and is sometimes speeded up to *twik twik twik* . . .; when the pair have become separated and want to find each other, it becomes a loud *twike, twike, twike.* If danger threatens the young, the parents express their perturbation in a rapid chatter. The flight is weak and fluttering, and seldom sustained for more than a few yards. Except in flight, the tail is nearly always held erect and is constantly wagged from side to side.

Breeding goes on nearly all the year, but the main season appears to be February–May. As is well known, the nest is formed in a little pocket-shaped cavity formed by sewing together, either the sides of a single large leaf, or of two or more smaller leaves. The bird commences by selecting one or more suitable leaves in a secluded place—which may be at almost any height up to twenty feet or so but, more often than not, is two to four feet from the ground. Then, with its beak, it stabs a series of punctures near the edges, and often towards the middle as well. When the requisite number of holes are formed, strands of cottony fluff are collected and pushed through them (no knot is made, as it is sufficient to push the end of the fluff through the hole); the other end of the strand is similarly pushed through the opposite edge of the leaf, or of an adjacent leaf, if more than one is used. In this way the edges are drawn and 'sewn' loosely together with strands across the gaps to form a little pocket; into this the birds build the nest proper, composed of fibres (coconut fibres—often filched from the nearest door-mat—are much liked) and lined with cotton or similar fluff.

The two or three eggs are coloured pinkish-white, or very pale bluish, irregularly, and rather sparsely, spotted with reddish brown. They average $16 \times 11 \cdot 2$ mm.

THE CEYLON FANTAIL WARBLER

Cisticola juncidis omalura Blyth. Race peculiar to Ceylon

Sinhalese: Tanacolā-kurullā. Tamil: Tinu-kuruvi, Vayalān

Plate 5, facing p. 72 (× one-third)

Size of the tailor-bird, or of the Purple-rumped Sunbird. A tiny, streaky-brown and buff bird, always associated with tallish grasses (including paddy) especially in damp situations.

It is found, in suitable country, throughout the Island from sea level up to the Horton Plains; and is common wherever it occurs. The grasses it favours are not the broad-leaved types, such as māna or illuk, but more wiry kinds, and 'water-grass'. However, it is not confined to grass as in the Jaffna district I found it very common in areas of the salt-loving shrub *Salicornia* and similar fleshy herbage, quite unmixed with grass. It feeds on insects, such as small grasshoppers, in the search for which it threads its way with amazing rapidity through the grass stems, no matter how tangled they may be. The note is a staccato *chik . . . chik . . . chik* usually uttered while the bird is flying; the flight consists of a series of big undulating bounds in the air, each punctuated with a *chik*.

The breeding season lasts from November to June, or even later, several broods probably being reared annually. The nest is a very deep cylindrical pocket, with a small circular opening nearly at the top. It is set in the middle of a tussock of grass, with the blades of grass drawn together above it and held in place with cobwebs, so as to provide perfect camouflage. It is composed of strips of grass cunningly woven together, and lined with cottony fluff. The eggs number three or four, and are pinkish-white, with purplish-brown and purplish-grey spots arranged in a strong zone around the large end and sparsely scattered elsewhere. They measure about 15·5 × 11·5 mm.

FRANKLIN'S PRINIA, or THE GREY-BREASTED PRINIA
(Franklin's Wren-Warbler of many authors)

Prinia hodgsonii pectoralis Legge (*Franklinia gracilis pectoralis* of various authors). Race peculiar to Ceylon

Sinhalese: Hambu-kurullā. Tamil: Tinu-kuruvi

Plate 5, facing p. 72 (male; × one-third)

Size of the tailor-bird, or of the Purple-rumped Sunbird. The female differs from the male only in having the grey breast-band incomplete in the middle; but the young are olivaceous brown above and lack the breast-band. This little bird might easily be mistaken for the Ashy Prinia, which it closely resembles in general appearance and size; but its grey breast-band, whiter underparts, and habits, distinguish it.

It inhabits the south-eastern sector of the Island, from the seaboard up to about 3,000 feet, or a little higher, and may be found in scrub-land, park country and the like, preferring bushes and small trees to grass. It is more active than other prinias, less given to skulking in patches of scrub, and frequently ascending quite high in trees. Its note is a rapid chatter of three to five notes—*chchchchch*; this is less loud and less musical than a very similar note produced by the Ashy Prinia. Its food, in common with that of other prinias, consists of small insects such as moths, grasshoppers and caterpillars.

The breeding season appears to be March to June. The nest resembles that of the tailor-bird, being placed in a pocket formed by the bird's 'sewing' together either the sides of a large leaf or two or more smaller leaves, usually within two or three feet of the ground. Three eggs form the normal clutch, and they are pale blue, either unspotted or finely speckled with some shade of red, the markings tending to form a zone round the large end. They measure about $15 \times 10 \cdot 5$ mm.

THE CEYLON ASHY PRINIA
(Ashy Wren-Warbler of many authors)

Prinia socialis brevicauda Legge. Race peculiar to Ceylon

Sinhalese: Hambu-kurullā. Tamil: Tinu-kuruvi

Plate 5, facing p. 72 (male; × one-third)

Size of the tailor-bird. The sexes are similar, except that the female has a slight whitish line above the lores. This is the easiest of the prinias to identify in the field, owing to its ashy-grey upperparts, and clear, pale buff underparts. From the last species (*Prinia hodgsonii pectoralis*) it may be distinguished by lacking the grey breast-band.

It is very widespread in Ceylon wherever there is long grass, such as māna, or illuk, or paddy but, while it seems to prefer a long-grass habitat, it is not confined to such but may be found in scrub-land, or tea, as well. This is the only prinia that I have seen in the Jaffna Peninsula and it is rare and local there; but in the rest of the Island it is common in suitable country, and ascends the hills to at least 5,000 feet. An active little bird, it is much given to perching on a tall grass stem or seed-head while it utters its loud, unmusical, chirrupping song, which sounds like a ringing *thrrip, thrrip, thrrip* . . . ; the alarm-note is a nasal *cher, cher, cher* or *tewtewtewtew* rapidly uttered, and suggestive of a sewing-machine; the scolding note is a peevish *mee . . . mee.* The tail is commonly carried erect and wagged about a good deal. The ordinary flight is weak and fluttering but, when excited, the bird flies from one clump of grass to the next in a curious jerky fashion, the wings producing an audible *frap, frap,* and the tail flirted at each jerk. It feeds on small insects, spiders, etc.

The breeding season lasts most of the year, as nests have been found in every month except November and January; but most nests are built in February–June, with a secondary season in August–October. The normal type of nest is a pretty little semi-domed oval, composed of fine strips of grass or fine rootlets, woven into a fabric with cobwebs and set in a grass-clump, two or three feet from the ground; but occasionally the nest is of the tailor-bird type, sewn into one or more large leaves of a bush. The eggs number two to four (three being normal), and are polished reddish-brown, unmarked but slightly deeper-coloured at the large end. They measure about 16 × 11·8 mm.

THE CEYLON LARGE PRINIA
(Ceylon Jungle Wren-Warbler of many authors)

Prinia polychroa valida (Blyth). Race peculiar to Ceylon

Sinhalese: Hambu-kurullā. Tamil: Tinu-kuruvi

Plate 5, facing p. 72 (× one-third)

Size of the House Sparrow, but with a longer tail. It is only likely to be confused with the next species (*Prinia inornata insularis*), from which it may be distinguished by (*a*) larger size; (*b*) darker coloration; (*c*) the white supercilium confined to the loreal region. The sexes are practically indistinguishable in the field.

This bird is found throughout the low country, in suitable conditions, and ascends the hills to 5,500 feet; but it is not quite so common as the Ashy and White-browed Prinias, except in certain specially favoured localities. It inhabits scrub-land, low jungle, māna-grass patanas, etc., and its habits, in general, differ little from those of its smaller relatives aforesaid, but it is rather less lively in its ways. A noisy bird, it will often give out its loud and monotonous song for long periods, from some point of vantage in a tree growing in the midst of a tangle of scrub into which the bird can dive should an enemy approach. The notes vary, but the song commonly commences with a slow *titrr̄eer . . . titrr̄eer,* which soon becomes a loud, ringing *titireep, titireep* . . . and this again changes to *thirrlip, thirrlip, thirrlip* . . . Yet another note is very like the *tewik tewik tewik* . . . of the tailor-bird, but less musical.

The breeding season covers much of the year, but February to May are the favourite months. The nest is a rather untidy ball of grass, fibres, rootlets, etc., bound with cobwebs, with the opening at one side, and is placed, within a foot or two of the ground, in a māna-grass tussock, or in a bush. The eggs number two to four. 'The ground colour is of fairly glossy pinkish-white, finely freckled all over with pale red. These markings often concentrate into a more pronounced zone or cap at the large end. I have seen two abnormal clutches and one egg of a normal clutch, in which the ground-colour was clear white and the red freckles very faint and few.'—Wait. The eggs measure about 18 × 13 mm.

THE CEYLON WHITE-BROWED PRINIA
(Common Ceylon Wren-Warbler of many authors)

Prinia inornata insularis (Legge). Race peculiar to Ceylon

Sinhalese: Hambu-kurullā. Tamil: Tinu-kuruvi

Plate 5, facing p. 72 (× one-third)

Slightly larger than the tailor-bird, smaller than the sparrow. An undistinguished-looking little, earthy-brown and pale buff bird, with a noticeably black beak. It can be distinguished from the last species by its paler colour, smaller size, and white eyebrow, which is very distinct, especially in the young. These, in general, resemble their parents but are fresher and brighter-looking. The sexes are alike in coloration.

It is found throughout the low country, except in the northernmost parts, and in the hills up to 5,500 feet. It loves long grass and is a common bird in paddy-fields, grassy swamps, māna- and illuk-covered hillsides, and the like. In such places it often associates, through 'community of interests', with the other species of *Prinia*. Like them, it spends most of its time hopping actively about the grass-stems in search for food, which consists of insects. Like the Ashy Prinia, it commonly carries its tail erect and wags it about, and it has the same habit of singing from the top of a grass-stem or from a telegraph wire. The song is a rapid, flat jingle, with a click in it—*tliktliktliktlik*, etc.—said as quickly as one can. The alarm- or scolding-note—used by the birds when their young are threatened by an enemy—is *creak, creak, creak*— like sharply striking the point of a quill across a comb; this is a loud sound, and can be heard for a considerable distance. The flight is weak and fluttering.

The breeding season lasts almost throughout the year, June being the only month in which breeding has not been recorded. The nest is a deep oval composed of thin strips of grass, woven, often while still green, into a grass tussock, or into a small bush, at a height of one to three feet from the ground—or water, as the case may be, for it is often situated in a swamp. The opening is near the top, which is lightly domed over. Three to five eggs are laid, the latter number being rare and four the usual clutch. They are coloured a beautiful turquoise-blue, with bold spots, blotches and scribblings of deep chocolate-brown. They measure about 15·2 × 11·5 mm.

THE CEYLON WARBLER

Bradypterus palliseri (Blyth) (*Elaphrornis palliseri* of many authors)
Species peculiar to Ceylon

No Sinhalese or Tamil names recorded

Plate 5, facing p. 72 (male; × one-third)

Slightly larger than a sparrow. Sexes alike, except that the male has red irides while those of the female are pale buff.

This mouse-coloured bird is essentially an inhabitant of the dense undergrowth of mountain forests, or of thick scrub; but occasionally it will venture into tea fields where these adjoin forest. It is confined to elevations above 3,000 feet, but is common in suitable country above this height. It loves nillu (*Strobilanthes*) and elephant grass (dwarf bamboo), and may be confidently expected where these plants form dense brakes of undergrowth in the damp hill forests. It lives usually in pairs which skulk in the soggy herbage, seldom ascending more than a yard or two above ground level. As it hops and flits among the stems it might easily be mistaken for a mouse, were it not for its sharp alarm-note which is well likened by Legge to the word *quitze*—though sometimes it sounds more like *queek*. It feeds on small insects, being partial to soft-bodied green crickets (*Tettigoniidae*), which it finds hiding on the undersides of leaves. In the breeding season, the male (presumably) sings a queer little, rather squeaky song, ascending a stem, to a rather more open and commanding position than usual, for the purpose of expressing his feelings. The flight seldom amounts to more than a quick flutter from one patch of undergrowth to another.

55

The nest is large for the size of the bird, and is composed of moss, grass, scrub-bamboo leaves, etc., with a fairly deep cup lined with fine fibres. It is solid and compact, and is set in a dense shrub not more than two or three feet from the ground. The breeding season is February to May, with a secondary season in September. The two eggs, which are fragile, are described as 'oval and only slightly pointed at the small end. The colour . . . whitish-pink, thickly powdered all over with rather deeper purplish markings and with one or two long hair-lines of deep brown at the larger end. Size ·9 by ·67.'—Wait (=about 22·6 × 16·7 mm.).

THE SHRIKES
Family LANIIDAE[1]

Medium-sized, or small, perching birds, of arboreal habits, found in a large part of the temperate and tropical portions of the globe, but with their greatest concentration in Africa. They are insectivorous for the most part, though the larger forms feed to some extent upon small animals as well as insects. The beak is stout and strong, hooked at the tip of the upper mandible, and with a distinct notch and 'tooth' just behind the hooked tip. The legs are rather short, but strong; wings of moderate length; tail variable but generally of medium length, and square, rounded, or slightly graduated at the tip. The plumage is soft, but neat, and coloured (in Ceylon species, at least) soberly. Shrikes have rather big heads, which, with the strong beaks, give them a somewhat pugnacious appearance, enhanced, in the members of the genus *Lanius*, by a black band through the eye which suggests a mask. Three of our species are migrants, the other two are resident. They build open nests, in bushes and trees, and lay spotted eggs.

THE SOUTHERN RUFOUS-RUMPED SHRIKE

Lanius schach caniceps Blyth. Resident

No Sinhalese name recorded. Tamil: Kāttu-puluni, Pey-kuruvi

Slightly larger than the Red-vented Bulbul. Sexes alike. A handsome, big-headed bird of black, white, light grey and rusty coloration, with a

[1] The cuckoo-shrikes and swallow-shrikes belong to different families—see pp. 61, 71.

conspicuous black 'mask', passing from the beak, through the eye, to the ear-coverts.

Its haunts, in Ceylon, are confined to a narrow strip of coastal country in the very dry region extending from about Puttalam to Elephant Pass. During two years which I spent in the Jaffna Peninsula I never saw it, though always on the look-out for it. Within its range, it is a common bird, usually to be seen sitting on top of a thorn-bush or fence-post from which it keeps a keen look-out for prey, and also for

enemies, such as hawks; when it sees one of the latter, it voices its displeasure in a harsh, chattering note. It feeds largely on insects, such as grasshoppers and beetles, but also captures larger prey, small lizards, frogs, and an occasional nestling bird. Its flight is straight and business-like, and usually within a few feet of the ground.

The breeding season is from February to June, May being the favourite month. The nest is a large, untidy collection of grass, creeper-stems, etc., with a neat cup, lined with fine rootlets

× one-quarter

or other fine fibres. It is placed, often very conspicuously, in one of the very thorny, flat-topped acacias, which grow abundantly in that dry part of the Island; usually, it is eight to ten feet from the ground. The two to four eggs are pale greenish, or buff, in ground-colour, with markings of grey or brown which often form a zone around the large end. They measure about 23 × 17·6 mm.

The INDIAN GREAT GREY SHRIKE *Lanius excubitor lahtora* (Sykes). W. W. A. Phillips identified as this species a grey shrike which he saw in December 1940, sitting on a bush in an open paddy-field in the North Central Province, but which eluded his efforts to collect it. This shrike resembles the Rufous-rumped Shrike in general build and coloration, except that it has grey and white instead of rufous colouring on the hinder part of the body, more white in the wing, and is somewhat larger. It frequents dry and open, but bush-dotted country, and is generally seen sitting on top of a bush, looking out for prey. It is found in many parts of the plains of India, and its general habits do not greatly differ from those of the Rufous-rumped Shrike.

THE BROWN SHRIKE

Lanius cristatus cristatus Linnaeus. Regular winter visitor

No Sinhalese or Tamil names

Bulbul-sized. Sexes alike. A pale-brown and dirty-white bird with a conspicuous black mask.

It arrives in Ceylon from its central Asian breeding-grounds in September–October, and leaves again in April–May. During its stay, it is common almost all over the Island, in thinly-wooded country, gardens, tea estates, etc. Each bird, on arrival, selects a territory to which it sticks throughout its stay. Within this domain, it chooses several vantage-points which, while giving it a wide outlook, are not unduly exposed; for in spite of its bold nature towards creatures smaller than itself, it is cowardly towards humans, birds of prey, etc., and likes to be able to dodge into cover with a minimum of delay on the approach of an enemy. Its alarm-note—frequently uttered—is a loud, harsh chatter. Grasshoppers, beetles and other insects form the bulk of its

× one-quarter

prey in Ceylon, but in its breeding-grounds, when it has young to feed, it most likely captures larger prey. There seems to be no evidence of its impaling victims on thorns, as is commonly done by the larger members of its genus. Its flight is straight and direct; the bird commonly drops from its perch, flies low, and ascends again on reaching its next perch.

THE PHILIPPINE SHRIKE

Lanius cristatus lucionensis Linnaeus. Scarce winter visitor

No Sinhalese or Tamil names

This shrike closely resembles its near relation, the Brown Shrike (of which it is the eastern race), in form and size, but it may be distinguished by its much greyer coloration, especially on the head.

Reputed to be very rare in Ceylon (Whistler, in his *Avifaunal Survey of Ceylon*, lists only three recorded specimens), it has been seen of late years by several observers in up-country districts, and in January 1945 I obtained a beautiful specimen not far from Jaffna; so it appears probable that the bird is either visiting Ceylon in greater numbers than of yore or, more probably, is being noticed and recorded more frequently. Its general appearance is so like the common Brown Shrike that only keen observers are likely to discriminate between the two. So far as my observations go, its habits, behaviour and voice differ hardly at all from those of the western race.

Its breeding grounds are in far-eastern Asia, and nesting takes place in June and July. In winter, it migrates to southern Asia, the Philippine Islands (whence its English name), and the Andamans from which, no doubt, as Whistler suggests, a few stragglers reach Ceylon.

THE CEYLON PIED SHRIKE[1]

Hemipus picatus leggei Whistler. Race peculiar to Ceylon; closely allied races occur in India and other parts of southern Asia

Sinhalese: Panu-kurullā. No Tamil name recorded

Less than sparrow-sized. A dapper little black, pale grey and white bird, which, in form, size and behaviour, suggests a flycatcher rather than a shrike. The sexes are alike in the Ceylon race.

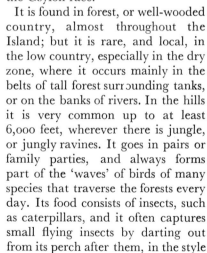

It is found in forest, or well-wooded country, almost throughout the Island; but it is rare, and local, in the low country, especially in the dry zone, where it occurs mainly in the belts of tall forest surrounding tanks, or on the banks of rivers. In the hills it is very common up to at least 6,000 feet, wherever there is jungle, or jungly ravines. It goes in pairs or family parties, and always forms part of the 'waves' of birds of many species that traverse the forests every day. Its food consists of insects, such as caterpillars, and it often captures small flying insects by darting out from its perch after them, in the style of a flycatcher. Its song sounds like *tirity tirity tirity*, and it has other little chirps besides. A bird of the tree canopy, it is never seen on the ground.

× one-half

[1] This and the next species are, by many authors, placed in the following family, *Campephagidae*.

The breeding season is in March–May, and it is apparently single-brooded. The favourite site for the nest is a dead, lichenous and gnarled branch, high up in a tree, with no foliage to hide it except the overhead leaf-canopy—and sometimes, not even that. The nest is a tiny, shallow cup, composed of bast and other fibres, perched, as it were, on the upper surface of the branch, to which it is bound by cobwebs. The outside is camouflaged with fragments of bark, lichens, etc., so that the whole resembles a mere excrescence on the bough. When the young are fledging, they, too, look like a part of the branch owing to their 'lichenous' coloration and their normal attitude, which suggests a broken-off snag. The three eggs are described as stumpy ovals, buffy-white in colour, evenly speckled all over with pale brown and grey. They measure about 15·2 × 12·3 mm.

THE CEYLON WOOD SHRIKE

Tephrodornis pondicerianus affinis Blyth. Race peculiar to Ceylon

No Sinhalese or Tamil names

A trifle larger than a sparrow. Sexes almost alike, but the female is rather duller and browner than the male. An inconspicuous grey and white bird, with a dark mask through the eye.

It is found all over the low country and hills up to at least 3,000 feet, but it prefers the drier districts, and is commonest in the dry zone. In gardens, chenas, and well-wooded country generally, but not in dense forest, it is a common bird; but owing to its unobtrusive ways and dull coloration it often escapes notice. It lives in pairs, and is arboreal, constantly searching among the branches and foliage for its prey, which consists of caterpillars, green crickets and the like. The frequently uttered call-note is a whistle *tweee twee twee twee twee*, on a descending

× one-quarter

scale, which has a peculiar, peevish quality. This note often betrays the bird's presence when, owing to the dense foliage, it cannot be seen.

The breeding season is the first half of the year, April and May being the favourite months. The nest is a very shallow saucer, composed of bast and other fibres, bound together, and fixed in a fork of a small branch, or on top of a larger one, in such a way that it appears to be a part of the branch—which is usually quite innocent of leaves in the neighbourhood of the nest. The outside of it is well camouflaged with scraps of bark, lichens, etc., so that, in spite of its exposed position, it is by no means easy to discover. The fledglings, too, when their feathers begin to grow, are so mottled in bark-like hues, and sit so still except while their parents are feeding them, that they are very difficult to recognize as birds. The nest may be at any height up to forty feet or so, but is usually much lower, from three to ten feet from the ground. The two or three eggs are buffish, or greenish white, blotched all over with purplish grey and brown. They measure about $19 \cdot 5 \times 15 \cdot 2$ mm.

THE MINIVETS AND CUCKOO-SHRIKES
Family CAMPEPHAGIDAE

These are shrike-like birds, differing from the true shrikes mainly in their lighter build and, according to Wait, in having the rump-feathers stiffened and spiny; this feature, however, does not appear on the surface. They are strictly arboreal, never descending to the ground, and they are insectivorous. Beak strong, hooked at the tip and notched just behind the tip of the upper mandible, as in shrikes; wings fairly long; tail rounded in cuckoo-shrikes, graduated in minivets; legs short, feet strong. They build open nests in trees, and lay spotted eggs.

The cuckoo-shrikes are soberly coloured in grey, black and white, but minivets are among our most colourful birds, with vivid orange and black in the males, yellow or orange and grey in the females.

THE ORANGE MINIVET

Pericrocotus flammeus Forster. Resident

Sinhalese: Gini-kurullā. Tamil: Māmpala-kuruvi

Plate 3, facing p. 40 (female left, male right; × one-quarter)

Size of the Red-vented Bulbul. The brilliant orange and black of the male, and yellow, grey and dark brown of the female, make this bird unmistakable.

It is found everywhere in the hills and also occurs, sporadically, in the low country, wherever tall forest gives it suitable conditions—particularly on the borders of tanks, or along river banks. It lives in pairs or family parties, and, as the young males resemble females until they moult into the fiery red of maturity, it was for long thought that the males were polygamous—hence the old name of 'Sultan Bird'. When the breeding season approaches, the parties break up and breeding pairs are formed. This beautiful bird loves jungle sholas, wooded gorges and the like, but it also frequents albizzia or grevillea wind-breaks on tea estates. It is arboreal in habit, seldom or never descending to ground level. The members of a flock spend their time searching foliage for prey, which consists of caterpillars, green crickets, and other insects; when one tree has been thoroughly scrutinized, the birds follow one another to the next. They cover a wide extent of country in the course of a day's hunting. The call-note, frequently uttered by each member of the party, is a sweet-toned whistle *twee twee tweetywee tweetyweetywee*, and the song of the male is merely a more elaborate version of the same sounds. The flight is direct, with the graduated tail frequently spread, and there are few more beautiful sights in the Ceylon forests than a troop of these minivets flitting 'follow-my-leader' fashion across a forest-clad gorge.

The main breeding season is in February–May, with a second brood in August–September; but an occasional occupied nest may be found in other months. The nest is a neat, small bowl composed of lichens bound together with cobweb, and lined with dead-leaf midribs, etc. It is placed in a fork, or on top of a branch, and is so well camouflaged with lichens, flakes of bark and the like, to match the branch, that it is difficult to find —especially as it is usually at a considerable height—twenty to sixty feet— from the ground. Favourite sites are a tree growing on the edge of jungle, or a tall grevillea in tea. The eggs number two, and appear to be incubated by the female only, though both sexes tend the chicks. As with many other birds, the role of the male, during the incubation period, is that of watchman and guard. In ground-colour the eggs are pale blue-green, freckled with pale yellowish brown and grey. They measure about $22 \cdot 8 \times 17$ mm.

THE CEYLON LITTLE MINIVET

Pericrocotus peregrinus ceylonensis Whistler & Kinnear. Resident

Sinhalese: Kos-kurullā. No Tamil name recorded

Plate 3, facing p. 40 (male above, female below; × one-quarter)

Size of a sparrow, but more slenderly built. The coloration and habits of this bird make it easy to recognize.

It is more of a low-country bird than its relative, the Orange Minivet, being found throughout the low country, including the Jaffna Peninsula (from which the Orange Minivet is absent), but it ascends the hills, on the drier, eastern aspect, to 5,500 feet, and is a common bird, even in the wet zone, up to 4,000 feet. In general habits it scarcely differs from its larger relative, associating in pairs or small flocks, which spend their time in diligently searching the crowns of trees for the larvae, crickets, small moths, etc., upon which they feed. The little troops move constantly over their chosen territory, flitting from one tree-clump to another in the same 'follow-my-leader' fashion as the Orange Minivet. In flight they keep in touch with their fellows by uttering a weak but sweet twitter, *wee wee wee*, etc.

The breeding season is February–May, but an occasional nest may be found outside these months. The nest is placed on a lichen-covered small branch or sometimes in a fork, at a height of twenty to fifty feet, in a forest tree or, often, in a grevillea growing in tea, or in a rubber tree. It is a beautiful, tiny cup, composed of blue-grey lichens held together, and bound to the branch, by strands of cobweb. The only lining is a rather scanty and coarse one of leaf midribs. The two or three eggs are variable in ground-colour, but most are pale greenish, and the markings consist of small blotches and freckles of various tints of brown. They measure about 16·6 × 13·4 mm.

THE BLACK-HEADED CUCKOO-SHRIKE

Coracina sykesi (Strickland) (*Lalage sykesi* of various authors). Resident

No Sinhalese or Tamil names recorded

Size of the Red-vented Bulbul. The male is a dapper, light-grey bird, with black head, wings and tail, the latter being conspicuously white-tipped on all but the middle pair of feathers. The abdomen and vent are white. Females and young are browner, with no black on the head, and the underparts buff-white, barred with dark brown except on the abdomen, vent and under tail-coverts.

This bird is found sparingly throughout the low country, and it ascends the hills to 5,500 feet on the eastern side, but less high on the wetter, western aspect. I have generally found it solitary,

Male below, female above;
× one-quarter

except during the breeding season, when mated pairs are nesting; but Legge observed females and young associating in flocks outside the breeding season. Its favourite haunts are openly-wooded, or scrub-country, but it may be found almost anywhere except in heavy forest or open country. It moves about a good deal, actively searching trees and bushes for its prey, which consists of caterpillars, green tree-crickets, small moths and the like. The male utters various loud, clear whistles, some of which sound like *twit wit wee, twy twy twy twy* and *wit wit wheet wheet wheet wheet*. It also utters a *cheer* sound.

The main breeding season is in the first half of the year, with March as the favourite month. The nest is a small, shallow saucer composed of rootlets, leaf midribs, etc., plastered with cobwebs, and placed well into a fairly stout, nearly horizontal fork of a tree, at any height from ten to forty feet from the ground. Rubber trees in the low country, and grevilleas in the hills, afford favourite sites. The two eggs are usually some shade of pale green, streaked with brown, and they measure about $22 \cdot 4 \times 16 \cdot 2$ mm.

THE CEYLON LARGE CUCKOO-SHRIKE

Coracina novaehollandiae layardi (Blyth) (*Graucalus javensis layardi* of various authors). Subspecies peculiar to Ceylon, but it differs from the South Indian race only in being a trifle smaller

No Sinhalese or Tamil names recorded

Size of the Common Mynah. A dark grey bird, with strong, black beak, and nearly black mask from the base of the beak to the ear-coverts; irides red, or brownish-red; legs black. Females are paler grey, with less pronounced mask, and the young resemble them but are barred, on the throat and breast, with dark grey on a white ground. In all, the abdomen and under tail-coverts are white.

This is rather a scarce bird, which inhabits forest or well-wooded country in the drier parts of the Island, ascending the hills on the Uva side to 2,000 feet at least. It is usually solitary, but young birds some-times associate in small flocks. A bird of the treetops, it is fond of sitting on high bare branches, but it is restless and moves about a great deal in the course of its day's hunting. The cry, frequently uttered, is a loud, harsh note well rendered by Legge as *kur-ēēch*. Its food consists mainly of insects, but I have watched one (in India) feeding on ripe banyan figs.

The nest has seldom been found. It is very small for the size of the bird, a thick-walled saucer of fine twigs and leaf-stalks, felted together

Juvenile female left, male right; × one-third

with cobwebs, and camouflaged on the outside with scraps of lichen, etc., and placed in a fork of a tree. The two eggs are described as being some shade of olive-buff or green, handsomely blotched with rich chocolate brown. They measure about 31 × 22·3 mm.

THE DRONGOS
Family DICRURIDAE

The drongos are a family of medium-sized perching birds found in Africa and southern Asia. Their most characteristic feature is the more or less glossy, black plumage, with rather long, deeply-forked tail. They are arboreal birds, of strong flight; insectivorous, taking most of their food on the wing, in quick sallies from a perch. Bill stout and strong; legs short. In perching, they usually sit very upright. Drongos are renowned for their courage and boldness in driving away marauding crows, hawks, etc., from the neighbourhood of their nests—hence the name given to some species, of 'King Crow'. They are rather noisy birds, uttering a

65

variety of more or less musical notes and calls, and many kinds are excellent mimics of the notes of other birds.

They build open, rather small nests in trees, and lay spotted eggs.

THE CEYLON BLACK DRONGO, or KING CROW

Dicrurus macrocercus minor Blyth. Race peculiar to Ceylon, but the South Indian race, *D. m. peninsularis* Ticehurst, only differs in being a trifle larger

Sinhalese: Kāudā. Tamil: Irattai-vāl-kuruvi

Size of the Ceylon Common Drongo, but its long, forked tail makes it look larger. This drongo may be distinguished in the field from the Common Drongo by its darker, coal-black plumage and longer tail which, moreover, is generally held higher. In flight, its wings look ample, and the primaries have a brownish or greyish effect, contrasting with the rest of the plumage.

× one-quarter

It is confined to the Jaffna and Mannar districts, not extending far from the coast, and, within its range, it is a common bird, to be seen everywhere where trees, hedges or palms afford it perching and nesting accommodation. It sits impartially on trees, fences, the backs of grazing animals or even on small clods of earth; and from such vantage-points it dashes after flying insects, or pounces on grasshoppers. Like other drongos, it lives in pairs, and, while it is very courageous in defence of its home, fearlessly driving off hawks, crows and other enemies from the neighbourhood of its nest, it is not generally aggressive towards smaller birds. Its notes are loud, ringing, and varied, and some of them are musical; it is a great mimic, and, particularly when excited by some enemy, such as a lurking cat or snake, it will pour forth a stream of cat-calls, alarm-notes of other birds, etc., in excellent mimicry of these sounds.

The breeding season is in March to May, but a few birds nest earlier or later than these months. The nest is a shallow cup, with thick walls but thin base, placed in a fork of a tree, from eight to twenty-five feet up, and often in very exposed situations. It is composed of fine twigs, fibres, etc., swathed with cobwebs, and with little, or no, lining. The two or three eggs vary in ground-colour from white to salmon-pink, and their markings are spots and blotches of various shades of dark brown mostly congregated at the large end. They measure about 24·2 × 18·1 mm.

THE INDIAN GREY DRONGO

Dicrurus longicaudatus longicaudatus Jerdon. Winter migrant

Sinhalese: Kāudā. Tamil: Irattai-vāl-kuruvi

Slightly larger than the Ceylon Common Drongo, which it very closely resembles in the field, being merely greyer in general effect, and with a longer tail. In stance, manners and habits it seems hardly distinguishable from its common relative.

It is a winter migrant to Ceylon, and, according to Legge, is not uncommon in the forests of the eastern side of the Island during its stay. Doubtless its numbers fluctuate widely in different years, but it does not seem to have been recorded from the Island since Legge's day. My own acquaintance with this bird is confined to several localities in South India.

THE CEYLON COMMON DRONGO, or WHITE-VENTED DRONGO

Dicrurus caerulescens leucopygialis Blyth. Race peculiar to the low-country wet zone of Ceylon

Dicrurus caerulescens insularis (Sharpe). Race peculiar to the low-country dry zone of Ceylon. In the hill zone the two races intermingle

Sinhalese: Kāudā, Kāudā-panikkiyā. Tamil: Irattai-vāl-kuruvi

Rather larger than the Red-vented Bulbul, but with a much longer, and deeply-forked tail. This feature, together with the glossy, prussian blue-black coloration, and white vent (white abdomen also, in the dry-zone race *insularis*) make it easily distinguishable from every other Ceylon bird except the drongo-cuckoo (for points of distinction from the latter, see p. 173). The sexes are alike, and the young differ from their parents only in being duller in colour. Those which inhabit the wet zone, with the adjacent hills, are altogether darker in colour and have no white on the abdomen; while dry-zone birds are paler, and have a large amount of white on the abdomen as well as on the under tail-coverts; these distinctions have led to the discrimination of two sub-species which, however, do not differ appreciably in habits.

This familiar bird is common up to at least 5,000 feet, and inhabits the low country everywhere except in the very dry districts in the north and north-west—e.g. those parts of the Island favoured by the Ceylon Black Drongo. It is found in well-wooded country, gardens, tea and rubber estates, but eschews heavy forest. Its habit is to sit on a perch, such as a fence-post or telegraph wire, from which it flies out to capture any insect or other small animal which comes within range. Frequently, it returns again and again to the same perch. Its flight is buoyant and agile, and this may be seen to great advantage when a flight of termites gives opportunity for its skill in capturing these tasty morsels. It seems to be entirely carnivorous. Like other drongos, it is quite fearless in attacking crows, hawks, etc., and driving them away from the neighbourhood of its nest, but it is not generally aggressive towards smaller birds. Its notes consist of various rather musical whistles, amongst which it includes excellent

× two-sevenths

imitations of the notes of other birds—tailor-birds, magpie-robins, the shikra, etc., and at times, the mewing of a cat.

The breeding season is rather brief, and probably a single brood only is reared in one season; it commences in February and generally ends in May. The nest is rather small and shallow, and is set in a fork of a horizontal branch, at any height from about fifteen to thirty-five feet. It is quite unconcealed, but is inconspicuous owing to its small size and the cobwebs and lichens that adorn its sides and assimilate it to its surroundings; but when the bird is sitting its head and tail projecting on either side betray the site. The two or three eggs are broad ovals, very pale cream to salmon-pink in ground-colour, with large or small specks and blotches of brown or brownish-red most numerous at the large end. They measure about 23·3 × 17·3 mm.

THE CEYLON CRESTED DRONGO
(Ceylon Black-crested Drongo of many authors)

Dissemurus paradiseus lophorhinus (Vieillot). Peculiar to the wet zone of Ceylon

Sinhalese: Māhā Kāudā, Kaputū-bālaya. Tamil: Irattai-vāl-kuruvi

Size of the Common Mynah, but with a long tail. Sexes alike, and young merely duller, and with shorter crest and tail. The slight crest, overhanging the beak; glossy black plumage; and long, deeply-forked tail, together with its manners and habitat, make this bird easy to identify.

It inhabits the tall forests of the wet zone in the south-west section of the Island, ascending the Adam's Peak range to a height of at least 5,000 feet. Mainly owing to the replacement of forest by rubber planta-

× one-sixth

tions, its range is greatly restricted from what it was in Legge's time, but it is still common wherever forest has been spared, in the wet zone. This handsome bird lives in pairs. It always forms part of the 'waves' of bird-life, composed of many species, which progress steadily through the forests in the daily hunt for food. Insectivorous, it loves to perch on some high, looping liana, from which it swoops down upon any flying insect disturbed by the busy searchers below. Often, the first sign of the approach of one of these mixed troops of small birds is a sudden, explosive medley of whistles, bell-like notes, and harsh scoldings, emanating from a pair of these drongos, where, a minute before, the solemn, mysterious silence of the jungle prevailed. The tail is frequently jerked—a common habit of all the Ceylonese drongos.

The nest of this drongo has seldom been found, but such records as exist indicate that the breeding season is in April and May. The only nest that I have seen was about thirty feet up in a tall, straight tree, growing on the edge of jungle adjoining a paddy-field. It was situated among a few leaves growing near the trunk, and these concealed it to some extent; but it was easily seen from some distance when the young had betrayed its site by moving about. It was a flimsy cup, rather small for the size of the bird, and contained—as far as could be seen from the ground—two nestlings. It was found on the 24th of May, about 20 miles east of Ja-ela, W.P. The eggs are described as broad ovals, very similar to those of the Ceylon Racquet-tailed Drongo, of which this bird is merely a race.

THE CEYLON RACQUET-TAILED DRONGO

Dissemurus paradiseus ceylonensis Sharpe. Race peculiar to the dry zone of Ceylon

Sinhalese: Māhā Kāudā, Kaputū-bālaya. Tamil: Irattai-vāl-kuruvi

Rather larger than the Common Mynah, and with a much longer tail. The large crest curving over the forehead, glossy black plumage, and especially the long, racquet-shaped outer tail-feathers, make this bird unmistakable. Sexes alike, but the young, besides having smaller crests and duller plumage, have the outer tail-feathers not fully bare-shafted above the 'racquets'. This bird is the dry-zone counterpart of the Ceylon Crested Drongo, and the two forms interbreed where their respective habitats meet—resulting in birds of inter-mediate character in respect of crest and tail development.

It inhabits the dry-zone jungles of the northern, eastern, and south-eastern portions of the Island, ascending the eastern aspect of the hills to about 2,000 feet; but it is common only in a few, scattered localities. Tall forest, such as lines the rivers of the dry zone, is its favourite habitat. In habits, it closely resembles its cousin, the Ceylon Crested Drongo, but it appears to be rather more gregarious. Its notes are loud, varied, and some of them beautifully bell-like, and it is an excellent mimic of other bird-

× one-seventh

voices. It is an active, lively bird, constantly on the move, and much given to flicking its long tail about. Like other drongos, it tolerates no nonsense from hawks, owls, crows, or other predators. Insects, almost always captured on the wing, form its food.

The breeding season is March–May. The nest is a shallow cup com-posed of twigs and stalks, bound together with cobwebs, and suspended, hammock-wise, in a horizontal fork of a slender branch, usually at a considerable height from the ground. The tree chosen is usually one growing on a river-bank, or beside a forest path or open space, and the nest is generally fairly conspicuous. The two to four eggs are described as 'pinkish-white, with a moderate amount of reddish pink markings overlying more cloudy marks of grayish purple. All the markings are inclined to be streaky, and are most numerous round the cap. Average size 1·06 by ·81.'—Wait (=about 26·7×20·5 mm.).

THE SWALLOW-SHRIKES
Family Artamidae

These are a small family of bulbul-sized birds of doubtful affinities, found principally in the Australian region; one species is found in West Africa, and one in India and Ceylon. They are strictly insectivorous; of strong flight, taking all their prey on the wing, and much given to soaring high in the heavens; and they are highly gregarious. The coloration is sober—grey, white, and black predominating. The head is rather big; beak strong and conical and pale blue in colour; wings long and pointed; legs short; tail rather short and square.

Swallow-shrikes build open, shallow nests on trees, palms, tall stumps, etc., and lay spotted eggs.

THE ASHY SWALLOW-SHRIKE

Artamus fuscus Vieillot. Resident

Sinhalese: Tal-gas-kurullā. Tamil: Mādam-pōru

Plate 7, facing p. 88 (× one-quarter)

Size of the Red-vented Bulbul, but with shorter tail and much longer wings. Sexes alike. A cobby, dark grey bird, with pale blue beak, whose distinctive habits make it easy to recognize.

It is distributed all over the low country, and ascends the hills, normally to 3,000 feet, but may occasionally be seen at much higher elevations. It moves about the country a great deal, probably in response to weather conditions, or the local abundance or otherwise of its insect food. Though sometimes occurring in pairs it is very gregarious, generally associating in flocks of a dozen or more which will often congregate in a tightly-packed row along some favourite perch. A beautiful flier, it spends much time hawking insects on the wing—all its food being obtained in flight. While gaining elevation it flutters rapidly, but it is much given to sailing, often at great heights, with motionless wings; its long pointed wings and clean-cut look then give it somewhat the appearance of a tiny falcon. It loves to perch on dead trees or palm-fronds, but while hunting in open country any little clod or stone that is available will do. Whether perched or flying, it frequently utters a quaint, wheezy *chee chee chee* which can be imitated by scraping the point of a quill across the teeth of a comb.

The breeding season is from February to June. The nest is an untidy, shallow cup of rootlets and other fibres, placed, more often than other-wise, in the angle of a palm-frond with the trunk; or sometimes on top of a dead stump. The three eggs are pale cream with specks or blotches of some shade of brown mainly distributed around the large end; they measure about 23·4 × 17·1 mm.

THE BLUEBIRDS
Family IRENIDAE

This very small family, comprising only one genus, *Irena*, is con-fined to South India and Ceylon, Assam, Indo-China, and the Malayan region. Fairy Bluebirds are of oriole-like form and size, and show some resemblance to the bulbuls in structure. They are arboreal and mainly frugivorous in habits, frequenting hill forests, where they live in pairs or small flocks. While the females and young are dull greenish-blue in coloration, the adult males are deep, velvety black on the underparts, and glistening blue on the dorsal regions. They are active, lively birds, strong on the wing.

They build open nests in forest saplings, and lay spotted eggs.

THE FAIRY BLUEBIRD

Irena puella puella (Latham). Rare and casual visitor, or possibly, extinct former resident

No authentic Sinhalese name, though Legge gives 'Nil rajah kurullā'. No Tamil name recorded

About the size of the Black-headed Oriole, or a little larger. The male is dense black on face, throat, and all underparts except the under tail-coverts, tail, and the greater part of the wings; his upperparts, from forehead to upper tail-coverts, scapulars and lesser wing-coverts and also the under tail-coverts, are beautiful, glistening lavender-blue, with a mauve sheen. The female is dull, greenish-blue everywhere, except the flight feathers, which are browner. The bill and legs in both sexes are black, and the irides crimson.

This magnificent bird has been found only very rarely in Ceylon, and

PLATE 5

1. Green Tree-Warbler.   2. Franklin's Prinia.   3. Large-billed Tree-Warbler. 4. Ceylon Ashy Prinia. 5. Ceylon White-browed Prinia. 6. Ceylon Large Prinia. 7. Ceylon Great Reed-Warbler. 8. Ceylon Tailor-bird. 9. Blyth's Reed-Warbler. 10. Ceylon Fantail Warbler. 11. Ceylon Warbler

PLATE 6

1. Indian Golden Oriole.   2. Ceylon Black-headed Oriole.   3. Common
Grackle.   4. Black-naped Oriole.   5. Ceylon Grackle

the last record appears to have been in November 1877. It delights in forest growing on the banks of mountain streams, and is a very active bird of oriole-like form, which lives usually in small parties, and feeds almost entirely on fruit; of which, wild figs—banyan, bo, etc.—are favourites. It has a loud, sharp, but pleasant-sounding, call, frequently uttered, which has been likened to *what's it* or *pee-pit*. The treetops are its normal habitat, but it will descend to ground level on occasion, e.g. for drinking or bathing.

In South India, where it is common in the forested hill ranges, up to 5,000 feet, it breeds in the first quarter of the year, building an open, rather flimsy nest of rootlets and moss, in a sapling growing in tall forest. The two eggs are described as pale greenish-white, spotted and blotched with various shades of brown. They measure about 29 × 19·25 mm.

THE ORIOLES
Family ORIOLIDAE

Orioles are medium-sized perching birds, of predominantly yellow and black coloration, found mainly in the tropics of Africa, Asia and Australia, though a single species lives in Europe.[1] They are strictly arboreal, and their diet consists of both insects and fruit. They have strong flight, and some species are migratory. They live usually solitary, or in pairs. Few birds surpass them in ornamental value, as their splendid plumage is commonly to be seen in gardens and parks, as well as in wilder, forested country.

Orioles build hammock-like nests among foliage of trees, and lay spotted eggs.

THE INDIAN GOLDEN ORIOLE

Oriolus oriolus kundoo Sykes. Winter visitor, in small numbers but probably regular

The Sinhalese and Tamil names would be the same as for the common Black-headed Oriole

Plate 6, facing p. 73 (male left, female right; × one-quarter)

About the size of the Black-headed Oriole, but it is a slimmer bird, with longer wings in proportion to their breadth. The sexes differ as shown in the Plate, and the young of both sexes resemble the female. (The

---

[1] American 'orioles' belong to a different family—*Icteridae*.

8ʙ

majority of Ceylon individuals appear to be either females or juveniles.)

This beautiful bird has only been discovered in Ceylon of recent years, but during three seasons in Jaffna I found it to be a regular winter visitor in the Peninsula. No doubt it has escaped notice owing to its resemblance to the common species of oriole, but as long ago as March 1921 I observed and sketched one (female or young male) which frequented a garden at Kotte, near Colombo, for a few days. This is a more active, lively bird than the familiar Black-headed Oriole; it is given to making dashing sallies from its perch in a tree and will playfully chase birds of different kinds, sometimes driving them off their perches—apparently from pure *joie de vivre*. Its flight is swift and powerful, and it seldom remains long in one tree. It feeds on fruit—banyan figs are favourites—and insects, of which hairy caterpillars are freely taken. The notes somewhat resemble those of the Black-headed Oriole, but are less loud—*yo-hee-hee-yu-he-yu* (the *yos* and *yus* being lower in the scale than the *hees*). It also utters a harsh scold-note, this with the beak wide open. My records seem to show that the Golden Oriole arrives in Ceylon in December, and leaves again in February and March; this limited sojourn in the Island helps to account for the failure to add it to the Ceylon list earlier.

It breeds in parts of India, including the Himalayas, and its nesting arrangements appear to resemble those of the Black-headed Oriole.

A specimen of the EUROPEAN GOLDEN ORIOLE *Oriolus oriolus oriolus* (Linnaeus) was collected for W. W. A. Phillips by E. C. Fernando at Hambantota, on 10 November 1942. It was labelled by the collector as a juvenile male but was more probably an adult female, and was at first thought to be a young Black-naped Oriole (see Whistler, *Avifaunal Survey of Ceylon*, p. 181). The European race is a trifle larger than the Indian, and its adult males lack the small black triangle behind the eye; there are other small differences, but in the field the two races are practically indistinguishable.

THE BLACK-NAPED ORIOLE

Oriolus chinensis diffusus Sharpe. Very rare winter straggler

No Sinhalese or Tamil names, but the same names would be used as for the Black-headed Oriole

Plate 6, facing p. 73 (×one-quarter)

About the size of the mynah—a trifle larger than the Black-headed Oriole. The Plate shows an immature individual, and the fully adult bird is coloured much like the Indian Golden Oriole except for a black band passing from eye to eye around the back of the head, and much less black in the wing.

This beautiful oriole has been recorded from Ceylon only once—by Layard, about a hundred years ago—but as it appears to be a shy, forest-loving species, it has probably been overlooked since Layard's time. It breeds in China, migrating in small numbers to India in winter.

THE CEYLON BLACK-HEADED ORIOLE

Oriolus xanthornus ceylonensis Bonaparte. Race peculiar to Ceylon

Sinhalese: Kāhā-kurullā, Woraka-maddula. Tamil: Māmpala-kuruvi

Plate 6, facing p. 73 (male; × one-quarter)

Size of the mynah. Sexes alike, but the female is duller in coloration than the male. Young birds of both sexes, besides being duller and somewhat greener than adults, have the black of the throat streaked with white, and some yellow on the forehead.

This gorgeous bird is found all over the low country, and ascends the hills to 6,000 feet, but it is not really common, and probably does not breed, above 4,000 feet. Except while nesting, it is usually solitary; and it is arboreal in habits, not descending, normally, to the ground. It travels about a good deal in the course of its day's hunting, and it is by no means shy, displaying its beauty freely as it flies from tree to tree; one of the finest sights to be seen in Ceylon is that of a splendid oriole winging its way across a wooded gorge, its yellow plumage contrasting with the sombre woods with superb effect. It feeds on various insects and on fruit, especially wild figs of various species (banyan, bo, nuga, etc.). Among insects, it is partial to hairy caterpillars of the kind whose hairs cause a painful rash on human skin. The notes consist of loud melodious flutings—*h'yaw haw whēēyo*, the *whēē* much higher in the scale than the rest. Besides these flute-like notes, it frequently utters a harsh *kuwak*, with a 'throat-clearing' effect.

The breeding season lasts from October to May. The nest is composed of tow-like bast and dead leaves, and is slung, hammock-wise, between two twigs of a fork among foliage; it is very deep, and rather small for the size of the bird. The two, or sometimes three, eggs are creamy white, sparsely spotted and blotched with some shade of brown or purplish black. They measure about 28 × 20 mm.

THE GRACKLES

Family Eulabetidae

These are a group of starling-like birds, of arboreal habits, found in Africa, India, Burma and Malaya, through the Moluccan Islands to Australia. They mostly have dark plumage, highly glossed with metallic colours. Their diet is mainly fruit. They nest in tree-holes, laying spotted eggs.

The members of the genus *Eulabes* (*Gracula* of many authors), of which Ceylon has two species, are glossy black birds, with a large white patch on the primaries; their most obvious characteristic, however, is the presence of rich yellow, fleshy wattles on the head. The beak is strong, slightly curved, with the margins obtusely angulated near the gape; the wings are long and broad, giving good powers of flight; the legs and feet are strong; the tail rather short and square. They are strictly arboreal, never normally descending to the ground. They feed on wild fruits. Their notes are shrill whistles and craking sounds, but they are well known in captivity as good imitators of the human voice; this, with their handsome appearance, makes them much sought after as pets.

THE COMMON GRACKLE

Eulabes religiosa indica Cuvier. Resident: found also in South India

Sinhalese: Sela-lihiniyā. Tamil: Malai-nākanam-patchi

Plate 6, facing p. 73 (×one-quarter)

About the size of the Common Mynah, but its glossy black plumage makes it look larger. From the next species—the only Ceylon bird with which it can be confused—it is easily distinguished by the much more extensive yellow wattling on the head and by the absence of black at the base of the beak.

It occurs in colonies scattered throughout the wet-zone low country, the hills up to about 3,500 feet, and about hilly areas in the North Western and Eastern Provinces. It lives in pairs or small flocks, and is partial to the borders of forests, well-wooded types of cultivation, etc. It is arboreal, inhabiting the treetops, and is an active bird, rather shy but by no means skulking in its manners. In flight, which is direct and powerful and often at a high level, the rapidly beating wings produce a pleasant, musical hum, audible for a considerable distance. The birds of a flock keep in touch by uttering piercing but musical whistles, interspersed with harsh, guttural noises. The food consists mainly, if not entirely, of fruit, such as wild figs, other berries, and the seeds of the sapu tree (*Michelia champaca*).

The breeding season is from May to August. The favourite site for the nest is in a deep cavity in a tree, the higher the better, and the birds like the entrance-hole to be just large enough to admit them. Tree-holes of this type are greatly in demand as nesting sites by parakeets, mynahs, hornbills and other birds, so competition for them is keen. The actual nest is merely a few dead leaves, straws, etc. Two eggs form the clutch, and they are pale greenish-blue with brown spots. They measure about 33 × 22·5 mm.

THE CEYLON GRACKLE

Eulabes ptilogenys (Blyth). Peculiar to Ceylon

Sinhalese: Sela-lihiniyā, Mal-kawadiyā, Kampatiyā. Tamil: Malai-nākanam-patchi

Plate 6, facing p. 73 (× one-quarter)

Rather larger than the Common Mynah; larger than the last species but very similar to it except in having only one pair of wattles, those at the back of the head, and some black at the base of the beak. Sexes alike, and the young differ only in being duller, and having smaller wattles.

This grackle inhabits the forests and well-wooded country of the wet zone, ascending the hills, in the wetter districts of the south and west, to at least 6,000 feet. Occasionally it strays into the drier, eastern slopes of the main range, but it is essentially a bird of the wet-zone hills. Like the last species, it lives in scattered colonies, but it does not seem to be quite so gregarious as *E. religiosa indica*, usually occurring in pairs. It loves high trees, and may be found in the heart of tall forests, as well as on estates and village gardens in their neighbourhood. A restless bird, a pair probably cover a large extent of country in the course of a day's wanderings. In flight, the wings produce a steady, musical hum, audible for a considerable distance. The call-notes consist of various piercing whistles, one of which sounds like a whistled *h'yu*. It also utters sundry craking and guttural conversational notes. The food consists of wild fruits such as banyan, bo and nuga figs, wild nutmegs, and sapu seeds.

The breeding season is February–May, and sometimes again in August–September. The nest is made in a cavity in a tree-bole or large branch, frequently at a great height, but the chosen tree may be in the depths of forest or in cultivated country. As both this and the Common Grackle are favourite cage birds—probably because they may be taught, if trained while young, to imitate human speech—their nests are frequently robbed by village boys for the sake of the young birds. The two eggs are pale prussian blue, blotched with purplish brown, and they measure about 33 × 25 mm.

THE STARLINGS AND MYNAHS
Family STURNIDAE

A large family of Old World perching birds, of both arboreal and terrestrial habits and insectivorous and frugivorous diet. Their plumage is sleek, giving them a peculiarly neat and dapper appearance; on the ground they walk with a characteristic air of self-assurance; some forms, however, are almost entirely arboreal in habits (e.g. the White-headed Starling). The beak in most starlings is rather slender, though strong, with the line of the mouth distinctly bent downwards near the gape; the wings are long and pointed; the tarsus rather long and stout, the feet large. Some forms are migratory, others are sedentary, and most are more or less gregarious.

The members of this family nest in holes—in trees, or in banks or buildings, etc.—and lay unspotted eggs.

THE ROSE-COLOURED STARLING, or ROSY PASTOR

Pastor roseus (Linnaeus). Irregular winter visitor

No Sinhalese name. Tamil: Soorai-kuruvi

Rather smaller than the Common Mynah. In full breeding plumage —of delicate rose-pink, with glossy black head, wings and tail—this beautiful bird is unmistakable; but in winter plumage, in which it visits Ceylon, the pink and black are much sullied with grey and brown; moreover, most of the birds which visit the Island appear to be in immature plumage in which greyish-brown predominates and the crest is not developed. In shape and general deportment it resembles the Common Mynah, but adults have a long, silky, drooping crest on the back of the head, very similar to the crest of the Brahminy Mynah.

It is highly gregarious, noisy, and spends much time on the ground, where it walks well, with a jaunty, mynah-like action. It visits Ceylon in large flocks, but very erratically, being common some years and almost or quite absent for, perhaps, several years running. During its immigrations, it generally seems to prefer the coastal areas of the dry zone, but occasionally visits other parts of the Island though it has not been recorded from the hills. It is a regular winter migrant to India, arriving early from its breeding-grounds in western Asia; and is regarded there as somewhat of a pest, owing to its depredations among ripening crops of grain, especially *jowari* or sorghum. However, it counterbalances this damage by the enormous quantities of grasshoppers and locusts which it eats. It also partakes of fruit, berries, etc., and visits certain flowers, notably the red cotton (*Bombax malabaricum*), for the sake of the nectar. The notes are described as noisy chattering and warbling.

× one-quarter

The Rosy Pastor nests in colonies, building an untidy nest of straws, feathers, etc., in a hole in a stone wall or ruined building, or even in the ground.

THE BRAHMINY MYNAH

Temenuchus pagodarum (Gmelin). Resident. Found also in India

Sinhalese: Mynah. Tamil: Nākanam-patchi

Plate 10, facing p. 121 (×one-quarter)

Size, between the Red-vented Bulbul and the Common Mynah. Sexes alike; the young are brownish-grey and buff, and lack the crest. This small, brightly coloured mynah resembles its larger relative in its general deportment, dapper appearance, and jaunty walk.

In Ceylon, it keeps to the coastal districts of the north-west, north, east and south-east, occasionally straying to other coastal areas (e.g. I have seen it in Colombo), but it never seems to go very far inland. It lives usually in small flocks, and frequents open or scrub-country and cultivated fields, eschewing forest. Much of its time is spent on the ground, hunting for insects, of which grasshoppers form a favourite food; but it also eats fruit—banyan figs and the like—and drinks nectar

79

from certain flowers. In Ceylon, it is rather shy of man; but in India, where it occurs everywhere in suitable country, it is said to nest in crannies in human dwellings as well as in more usual types of habitat. It utters various chattering notes and has a squeaky little song, in delivering which the performer nods its head and raises its crest in a quaint manner. Legge describes the ordinary call as a pleasing whistle, uttered both while perched and on the wing. The flight is performed with regular and strong beats of the wings, and the white tips of the tail-feathers (except the middle pair) show up well.

It is said to breed in July and August, but Ceylon records of nesting appear to be few. The nest is placed in a hole in a tree; the three to five eggs are very pale prussian blue, unmarked. They measure about 24·5 × 19 mm.

THE WHITE-HEADED STARLING

Sturnia senex (Bonaparte). Species peculiar to Ceylon

No authentic Sinhalese or Tamil names; (the 'Māyinā' given by Wait is merely a general term in Sinhalese for any member of the family
Sturnidae)

Size, between the Red-vented Bulbul and the Common Mynah. Sexes similar; the young are duller, and have less white on the head.

× one-third

This is a sleek, slenderly-built bird, with white forehead, face, throat and under tail-coverts; the white of the head merges streakily into the greenish-grey-black of the back, wings and tail; and the white throat shades into the smoky-grey of the breast and underparts, which are streaked with white. The beak is pale greyish-green, shading to dull blue at the base, and the legs are bluish grey. The iris is given by Legge as whitish, with a narrow brown inner circle; but one (sex?) which I collected in the Opanake district had the irides brown; it appeared to be fully adult. The orbital skin is dull bluish.

This is a rare bird, confined to the tall forests, and their adjacent patanas and clearings, of the wet zone, including the Adam's Peak range up to 4,000 feet or perhaps higher. Personally, I have seen it only at Opanake, Kitulgala, and Deniyaya. It is strictly arboreal, frequenting the tops of tall trees, and commonly associates in small flocks. Its food consists largely of wild fruits, such as cinnamon berries and the figs of several species of *Ficus*, but it doubtless eats insects; and, like many other birds, it is very fond of the nectar of the red cotton tree; one of these trees, flowering in its haunts, affords the best means of seeing the bird. Legge describes the note as a starling-like chirp, but it is generally rather silent.

The nest appears to have been discovered only once—in April, by Frederick Lewis, many years ago. It was in a tree-hole, and the two eggs were lying on bare wood. They were pale blue, and measured about 25·6 × 20 mm.

THE CEYLON COMMON MYNAH

Acridotheres tristis melanosternus Legge. Race peculiar to Ceylon

Sinhalese: Mynah, Gon-kawadiyā. Tamil: Nākanam-patchi

Slightly larger than the Common Babbler. Sexes alike; the young differ only in being duller, crestless, and anaemic-looking about the beak and facial skin. A dapper, dark-brown bird, with black head, yellow beak and facial skin, and yellow legs; in flight, a round white patch on the primaries and white tips to most of the tail-feathers are conspicuous.

This mynah is one of the commonest birds in Ceylon, and is found everywhere, except in heavy forest, up to about 5,000 feet. For habitat it prefers fields and gardens, and is much given to attending on cattle and buffalos, for the sake of the ticks which infest them, and the insects which are disturbed by their feet as they graze. It lives largely on grasshoppers, in searching for which it walks jauntily, with an amusing air of self-possession.

× one-fifth

It feeds also on fruit, mostly wild berries and small figs of banyan, bo and the like. It appears to pair for life, but the pairs, out of the breeding season, unite to form flocks, sometimes of large numbers. Mynahs, in common with many other members of the starling family, roost (out of the breeding season) in flocks, which gather towards evening at favourite roosts, often from considerable distances; reed-beds, or patches of scrub in swamps, are frequently selected. The notes of this mynah consist of various squeaks and chattering noises which do not lend themselves to transliteration; the scold-note is a loud, harsh, rasping sound. In the courting season, the male produces a ludicrous series of unmusical jingles and creaks, which he accompanies by fluffing out his plumage, raising his sketchy-looking crest, jerking his beak towards his toes, and ending the performance by saying *kok kok kok*. It is a favourite cage-bird and, if taken young, becomes very tame and sometimes learns to imitate human speech fairly well; people who make pets of mynahs should remember that a daily supply of insects, in addition to the usual diet supplied, of curry-and-rice, plantain and pawpaw, is essential to their well-being. Grasshoppers are particularly acceptable.

The breeding season commences in March, and lasts until August or September, but sporadic breeding takes place at other times. The nest is a mass of sticks, straws, feathers, etc., placed in a hole in a tree or cranny in a building. The three or four eggs are unmarked, pale prussian blue. They measure about 29·3 × 21·2 mm.

THE WEAVERS, MUNIAS, AND SPARROWS
Family PLOCEIDAE

These are an Old World family of small birds closely related to the finches (*Fringillidae*), with which the sparrows have, until recently, been included; but though in some respects they are intermediate in structure they are better placed among the *Ploceidae*. The birds of this family have the beak short, stout and conical, adapted primarily for cracking hard seeds, such as grain, which forms their main food. They are nearly all highly gregarious, and are both arboreal and terrestrial—finding most of their food on or near the ground, but also spending much of their time in trees and bushes. Most of them are non-migratory, but some forms move about a good deal, according to the availability, or otherwise, of food-supplies.

The weavers are noted for their wonderful and elaborate nests, woven of strips of grass and the like, and placed in trees. Their eggs are unspotted white. The munias build large, ball-shaped nests in trees, the entrance being in the side; their eggs, too, are unspotted white. Sparrows build domed nests in cavities of trees or of buildings, and lay spotted eggs.

THE BAYA WEAVER

Ploceus philippinus philippinus (Linnaeus). Resident

Sinhalese: Wadu-kurullā, Goiyan-kurullā. Tamil: Thūkanān-kuruvi, Manja-kuruvi

Plate 7, facing p. 88 (female left, male right; × one-quarter)

Slightly larger than the House Sparrow. The male in breeding plumage, with his yellow cap and breast, and dark brown face and throat, is unmistakable; but the female and non-breeding male might be mistaken for the female House Sparrow, from which they can readily be distinguished by the clearer buff ground-colour, slightly larger size, larger beak and, especially, different habits. The young resemble the female.

The Baya occurs locally throughout the low country and lower hills up to about 1600 feet, but it prefers the dry zone. It moves about a good deal, appearing in a locality and disappearing again in a sporadic manner. It lives in large flocks, and a colony betrays its presence by the constant chattering and rather raucous, jingling song of the birds, especially the males. It feeds on cultivated grains—paddy, kurrakan, etc.—and also eats insects to some extent.

Breeding takes place, in different localities, over most of the year. The Baya breeds in colonies, a number of nests being usually built in a single tree or palm, or in a small clump of these; the nest may be at any height from ten feet or so upwards. It is a long, hanging affair—two to four feet long, or even more—consisting of three parts; the uppermost, which is attached to an outer branch of a tree or to a palm-frond, is a narrow 'stalk' of varying length; this widens into a large bulge which contains the nest chamber; and the lowest portion is a long, pendulous, cylindrical 'sleeve', open at the bottom, up which the birds run to reach the nest-chamber. The whole is composed of narrow strips torn from palm-*pinnae* or large grass-blades. In obtaining these, the bird nicks the edge of the pinna or blade near the base, tears a short length and then flies away with the end in its beak, dragging a long strip from the edge. The inside of the nest bulge is often plastered with lumps of mud—probably, by its weight, to steady the long nest in high winds. The two to four eggs are pure white and measure about 20 × 14·5 mm.

THE STRIATED WEAVER

Ploceus manyar flaviceps Lesson. Resident

Sinhalese: Wadu-kurullā. Tamil: Thūkanān-kuruvi, Manja-kuruvi

Plate 7, facing p. 88 (male; × one-quarter)

Sparrow-sized. This is a much darker, more streaky-looking bird than the Baya, the underparts, especially, being streaked with dark brown in both sexes, and the male in breeding plumage has no yellow on the breast. Females and non-breeding males have a well-marked whitish supercilium, white spot below the eye, and an oblique pale stripe behind the ear-coverts.

It is very local in Ceylon, being confined, so far as is known at present, to coastal districts of the southern half of the Island. Its favourite haunts are beds of tall reeds and bulrushes growing in tanks or swamps; apart from this love for reeds and rushes, its habits resemble those of the Baya in most respects; it has the same gregarious nature and feeds on the same seeds and grains, being, like the Baya, somewhat of a pest in ripening paddy. A flock maintains a constant chattering and whistling.

Breeding takes place from about February to October. The nest is built of similar materials to that of the Baya, and its construction follows the same essential lines as that of the better-known species; but it is simpler, being suspended from a number of reed or bulrush leaves, without the long 'stalk' of the Baya's nest; and the tubular entrance is very short. The nests are quite exposed to view and are only two to six feet above water level. The two to four eggs are pure white and measure about $20 \cdot 5 \times 13 \cdot 7$ mm.

THE BLACK-HEADED MUNIA

Munia malacca (Linnaeus). Resident

Sinhalese: Wee-kurullā. Tamil: Nellu-kuruvi

Plate 7, facing p. 88 (× one-quarter)

Smaller than the House Sparrow. Sexes alike, but young birds are very different in coloration from adults; they are brown all over, with pale whitish heads. The distinctive coloration of this handsome little bird—the 'Nun', or 'Three-coloured Manakin' of cage-bird fanciers—makes it quite unmistakable among Ceylon birds.

It is found in the south and east of the Island, but appears to move about the country to some extent, as I once met with a flock of two adults and six or seven juveniles in the Jaffna Peninsula in the month of February. It inhabits swamps, reed-beds, and māna-grass patanas; and ascends the hills on the drier, eastern aspect, to about 6,000 feet, being common on the Uva hills. It occurs, usually, in small flocks and, like other munias, it is a pest to paddy cultivators, eagerly robbing the ripening grain. Besides paddy, it feeds on a variety of grass-seeds. The note is a reedy chirp, and the flight is undulating.

The principal breeding season, in both low country and hills, is from March to August. The nest is a ball of grass-blades, six or seven inches in diameter, with an untidy entrance-hole in the side, set in a reed-bed, grass-clump, bracken or bush, often quite near the ground. The four to six white eggs measure about $16 \cdot 2 \times 11 \cdot 8$ mm.

The well-known cage-bird known as the JAVA SPARROW *Munia oryzivora* (Linnaeus), which is a native of Malaysia, is occasionally found living wild in Colombo and other parts of the Island, the birds having originally escaped from captivity. In spite of the fact that it has been known in Ceylon since Legge's time, it shows no sign of increasing and, although it breeds freely—nesting commonly under the eaves of houses, etc.—it seems unable to establish itself in Ceylon; this is probably fortunate, as it is a notorious pest of paddy. It is a beautifully dapper, clear bluish-grey bird, with black head, rump and tail, white cheek-patch, and rose-pink bill.

THE WHITE-BACKED MUNIA

Uroloncha striata striata (Linnaeus). Resident

Sinhalese: Wee-kurullā. Tamil: Nellu-kuruvi, Tinayan, Tinai-kuruvi

About the size of the Purple Sunbird. Sexes alike, and the young are merely somewhat duller and paler than their parents. The small size, short, stout beak, and nearly-black and white plumage, together with its gregarious habits, make this bird easy to recognize. The white back shows conspicuously in flight.

It is common throughout the low country—except in the Jaffna Peninsula, where I never saw it—and occurs on the drier (Uva) side of the hills up to 5,000 feet. It inhabits gardens, cultivated country, scrub and open types of jungle, and is nearly always found in close flocks of six to ten birds. The food consists of seeds of grasses, including paddy. The birds keep close together, and it is interesting to watch a flock feeding from the heads of grasses growing on an ill-mown lawn; as the seed is consumed, the flock moves onward by the hindermost birds flying over the heads of their companions to get the richer supplies in front or, perhaps, merely to avoid getting left too far behind. The notes consist of squeaky, reedy little chirps. The flight resembles that of other munias—

× one-third

while the flock, as a whole, maintains a fairly even course, each bird in it undulates up and down independently of its fellows.

The breeding season extends more or less all the year round, but the majority of nests are made in February–May. The nest is of the usual munia type, viz. an untidy ball of grass-blades, smaller than a football, with the entrance-hole in the side, placed in a rather close-foliaged and twiggy tree (lime and orange trees are much favoured), often within hand-reach. The nest is used as a dormitory long after the family is reared, and it is amusing to watch the members of the little troop squeezing into an overcrowded nest at nightfall, with much quarrelling and argument, until at last all are packed in. The four to six eggs are pure white, and measure about $15 \cdot 3 \times 10 \cdot 8$ mm.

THE CEYLON HILL MUNIA

Uroloncha kelaarti kelaarti (Jerdon). Race peculiar to Ceylon

Sinhalese: Wee-kurullā. Tamil: Nellu-kuruvi

Plate 7, facing p. 88 (× one-quarter)

Smaller than the House Sparrow. Sexes alike, and the young are similar but duller and more uniformly coloured. The black face and throat, brown back, and pale pinkish-fawn patch on the side of the neck suffice to distinguish this from the other Ceylon munias.

It is a mountain bird, common in most districts above 2,000 feet, but in the wet zone it descends as low as 700 feet, at which height I saw one near Opanake in September; it was in jungle, searching among the leaves of a creeper growing on a tall stump. This munia frequents tea estates, gardens, etc., but may also be found in forest and in māna-grass and lantana scrub. It associates usually in pairs or small family parties, and travels about more than other munias, being often seen flying at a considerable height; the flight is undulating. The call-note is the usual munia type of reedy chirp, but a funny little song of five notes is uttered at times; this is audible only for a few yards. The food consists of seeds and grain.

The breeding season lasts nearly all the year, but April–September seems to be the favourite period. When courting, the male jerks up and down in a quaint manner on the perch before his lady-love. The nest resembles that of other munias, being an untidy ball of grass set in a densely-foliaged tree or creeper; besides grass, moss and maidenhair-fronds also frequently enter into its composition. The site chosen is often among the creepers growing on a bungalow wall. Four or five eggs form the normal clutch. They are pure white, and measure about $16 \cdot 5 \times 11 \cdot 1$ mm. As with all munias, the young deposit their droppings inside the nest, which soon becomes very dirty.

THE SPOTTED MUNIA

Uroloncha punctulata lineoventer (Hodgson). Resident

Sinhalese: Wee-kurullā. Tamil: Nellu-kuruvi

Plate 7, facing p. 88 (× one-quarter)

Smaller than the House Sparrow. Sexes alike; the young are brown all over except the head, which is pale buff; they look quite different from their parents but, as adults and young are usually in the same flock, their relationship is easy to observe.

This is a common bird throughout the low country, and it ascends the hills to about 5,000 feet. It is probably the most familiar of the munias, being very common in gardens and other cultivation. It occurs in flocks, usually up to a dozen birds, but when paddy is ripening it will form very large flocks which work considerable havoc on the crops; normally, however, its food consists of grass-seeds. The flight, usually in a close flock, is undulating—each bird rhythmically rising and falling. The call-note is a reedy chirp very similar to that of the other Ceylon munias, but the courting song of the male is a remarkable performance; raising his head-feathers and standing very erect, he pours out his soul in ecstatic melody, with quivering throat and oscillating beak; but— to human ears at least—not a sound is audible! No doubt the ears of his little love are tuned to hear music that our gross ears cannot detect.

The breeding season extends almost throughout the year, but most nests are made in the period October–May. When nest-building, the bird tears off a long grass-blade and, holding it in its beak by one end, flies off to the site trailing it; this habit makes it easy to find the nest. Lime or orange trees are much favoured as sites, but not infrequently a large clump of parasitic loranthus is selected, and sometimes a bunch of areca palm flowers. The nest is a ball of grass-blades as big as a foot-ball, and the entrance, in one side, is generally fringed with grass seed-heeds projecting outwards. The four to six white eggs measure about 16·7 × 11·3 mm.

THE WHITE-THROATED MUNIA

Uroloncha malabarica (Linnaeus). Resident

Sinhalese: Wee-kurullā. Tamil: Nellu-kuruvi

Size of other Ceylon munias (smaller than the House Sparrow), but its slender build and rather long, pointed tail, make it look smaller than them. The drab brown and dull white coloration is distinctive.

This is a dry-zone bird, confined, in Ceylon, to the coastal tracts of the Mannar, Jaffna, and Hambantota districts. In habits, it scarcely

differs from the other Ceylon munias, having very similar call-notes, flight, gregariousness, etc., and similarly feeding on grass-seeds, paddy and millet. It commonly associates in flocks of ten to twelve, but sometimes larger numbers.

The breeding season is from December to March. In Jaffna, where it is the commonest munia, I found the usual site for the nest to be in the crown of a screw-pine, but some nests were in thickly foliaged, twiggy trees. In a screw-pine the nest

× two-fifths

is fairly safe from most marauders because of the spiny leaves. The nest is of the same type as that of other munias, viz. a ball of grass with lateral entrance-hole; but it is usually small and rather skimpily built. The four to six eggs are pure white and measure about 15·2 × 11·8 mm.

THE YELLOW-THROATED SPARROW

Gymnorhis xanthocollis (Burton). Very rare winter visitor, only once recorded from Ceylon

No Sinhalese or Tamil names recorded

Size of the House Sparrow, but more slenderly built, and with more acute beak. This sparrow is a brownish-grey bird with whitish

PLATE 7

1. East Asian Swallow.   2. Hill Swallow.   3. Ceylon Swallow.   4. Ashy Swallow-Shrike.   5. Baya Weaver.   6. Striated Weaver.   7. Black-headed Munia.   8. Ceylon Hill Munia.   9. Spotted Munia

PLATE 8

1. Purple-rumped Sunbird.   2. Purple Sunbird.   3. Loten's Sunbird.
4. Legge's Flowerpecker.   5. Ceylon Hill White-eye.   6. Ceylon Small White-eye.   7. Grey Wagtail.   8. Grey-headed Yellow Wagtail.
9. Forest Wagtail

underparts, a white wing-bar on the median coverts and a less-pronounced one on the greater coverts; the lesser coverts are chestnut; on the lower throat there is a small patch of bright lemon yellow.

Females differ from males only in being paler and duller in coloration.

This sparrow has only once been recorded from Ceylon; Legge collected two specimens out of a flock which he met with a few miles south of Chilaw, in October 1876; they were associating with weaver-birds in openly wooded grass-land, near the sea. In India, where it is common and widespread, it frequents open jungle, gardens and cultivated country, associating in large flocks except in the breeding season. It feeds mainly on seeds of various grasses and weeds. The usual note is a chirp, very like that of the House Sparrow.

× two-fifths

The nest is an untidy mass of straws, feathers, etc., placed in a hole in a tree or similar site.

THE CEYLON HOUSE SPARROW

Passer domesticus soror Ripley. Resident

Sinhalese: Gé-kurullā. Tamil: Adaikalān-kuruvi, Oor-kuruvi

'Too familiar to need description'; it may, however, be well to point out that the male sparrow looks very different when newly moulted from its appearance a few months later, owing to the gradual wearing off of fringes of grey or buff which the new feathers possess; the conspicuous black bib shown at some seasons is merely grizzled-grey immediately after the moult; at the same time the grey and chocolate of the head are suffused with a buffish tinge. The grey-and-buff suffused individuals are commoner in August–September than at other periods.

The House Sparrow is distributed almost throughout the Island, wherever human communities exist. A notorious hanger-on of man, its food is anything in the way of waste grain or other farinaceous food to be found near human dwellings. It also eats seeds of various weeds and grasses, and consumes many insects such as small grasshoppers and moths. The notes are various chirps and chatters and the song of the male—uttered, while courting, with much ridiculous attitudinizing before his lady-love, and later, while she is incubating, from a nearby perch—is an endless repetition of *phillip, phillip, phillip*.

The House Sparrow breeds almost all the year round (though any particular pair will, of course, take time off from the task of increasing the sparrow population for several months in the year). The nest is a huge, untidy mass of grass, straw, etc., lined with feathers, crammed into any suitable cavity about a building; very commonly in the earthenware 'chatties' put up on the walls of houses by the inhabitants for the accommodation of these avian guests. The four or five eggs are usually greyish, finely or coarsely peppered with greenish-grey or purplish-brown, thicker in a zone around the large end. They measure about $20 \cdot 2 \times 14 \cdot 6$ mm.

THE LARKS
Family ALAUDIDAE

Small terrestrial birds of dull coloration, characteristic of open grass-land or thin scrub; on the ground, they walk or run but do not hop. Their principal anatomical distinction from other *Passeriformes* lies in the structure of the tarsus, which has the hinder aspect covered with a series of horny, overlapping scutes on each side, instead of a single long, horny lamina, as in the other families of this Order. Other features, of less importance, are found in the elongated inner secondaries which, in the folded wing, reach nearly as far back as the tips of the primaries; and in the hind claw, which is but little curved and usually very long. Larks feed both on insects and on seeds. They spend most of their time on the ground, where they find all their food, roost at night, and also nest; some species, however, perch on trees or stumps to some extent. Many forms are gregarious, others live in pairs. Their eggs are spotted.

In many respects, larks resemble the next family (pipits and wagtails), but they are heavier-built birds, with a more crouching attitude. Many species of them are renowned songsters. With the exception of a single genus, each, in America and Australia, they are confined to Europe, Africa and Asia—though the English sky-lark has now been artificially introduced into America, Australia, and New Zealand.

THE INDIAN SKYLARK

Alauda gulgula gulgula Franklin.[1] Resident, low-country dry zone
Alauda gulgula australis Brooks. Resident, Uva 4,000 to 5,000 feet

Sinhalese: Gomarittā. Tamil: Vānampādi-pullu

Size of the Indian Pipit, but a thicker-set bird. Sexes alike. In general appearance it is somewhat similar to the next species (Ceylon Bush-Lark), but is slightly smaller, greyer in tone, with a conspicuous, greyish collar behind the ear-coverts; the breast-streaks are less pronounced in the middle; both sexes have a crest which is only noticeable when it is raised in excitement.

The skylark is found in pairs or small flocks in open country in the dry zone, and in the Uva patanas which it ascends to between 4,000 and

Female left, male right, with crest erected; × one-half

5,000 feet; in the wet-zone low country it occurs only occasionally, during the north-east monsoon. It inhabits pastures, coastal flats, dry fields and the like, eschewing forest or well-wooded areas and even the coarse scrub beloved of the next species. It lives on the ground, never perching in trees though it will perch on low stumps, stone walls, etc. It feeds upon insects, such as grasshoppers, and also on seeds of grasses and weeds. Feeding skylarks do not run in little spurts, as the pipits do, but walk methodically, in a rather horizontal attitude; on the approach

[1] Since this was written, a series of skylarks collected by W. W. A. Phillips in various parts of the Island, and deposited by him in the British Museum (Natural History), has established the fact that two races of *Alauda gulgula* inhabit the Island. Low-country birds are *A. g. gulgula* Franklin, but those from the uplands of Uva prove to be the larger, richer-coloured *A. gulgula australis* Brooks, a race which is found also in the hills of South India. The habits of the two races do not differ appreciably.

of danger, they tend first to seek safety by crouching close to the ground
—when their colour and streaky pattern give good concealment—
rather than in immediate flight. The song of the skylark is world-
famed, and owes some of its reputation to the fact of its being rendered
from high above the ground by the hovering bird. It is often sustained
for several minutes as the male flutters at heights up to two or three
hundred feet. As the performance draws to a close, the bird nearly
closes its wings and descends to the ground in a steep dive. The real purpose of the song appears to be (*a*) belligerent, a warning to other male
skylarks to keep off the performer's territory; and (*b*) cautionary,
notifying the female, incubating her eggs, of the approach of an enemy.
In Jaffna, I found that, while singing went on to some extent for most
of the year, it reached its climax between February and July and died
out altogether in August. These periods agree with the nesting and
moulting periods respectively.

The skylark nests on the ground, building rather a skimpy little nest
of grass and fibres in a small hollow, usually under a small tuft of grass
or other herbage. The nest is hard to find unless the bird is watched
going to it, or else put up from it accidentally; its skimpy nature and
the inadequate-looking cover help to protect it. From one to three eggs
are laid; they are dirty-white or greenish in ground-colour, thickly
blotched and speckled all over, but most closely at the big end, with
grey and yellow-brown freckles. They measure about $21 \cdot 3 \times 15 \cdot 2$ mm.

THE CEYLON BUSH-LARK

Mirafra affinis ceylonensis Whistler. Resident; this race is found also in
Travancore, and closely related forms inhabit other parts of India

Sinhalese: Gomarittā. Tamil: Vānampādi-pullu

Rather larger than the Indian Pipit. Sexes alike. In general appearance and coloration it resembles the pipit, and also the Indian Skylark,
with both of which it may often be seen in the same habitat. From the
pipit it may easily be distinguished by its stouter build, crouching
stance, much heavier beak, and stronger dark streaking on the breast;
from the skylark, by its more ochreous colour, heavier beak, and
different habits.

This lark is found commonly throughout the low-country dry zone,
and in the less damp parts of the wet zone, but it does not ascend the
hills to any height. It likes open, scrub-covered country, and lives in
pairs. While walking, or singing, it often carries the tail elevated, as
depicted in the illustration. Unlike the skylark, it frequently perches on

bushes, fences, dead trees and the like, and it is generally from such elevations that the male utters his unmusical and monotonous song— sometimes for minutes on end; it is a high-pitched, thin, rolling, rather cricket-like note—*tilee, tilee, tilee . . .*—which has considerable carrying

power. When courting, he frequently rises in the air to a height of twenty or thirty feet, and then parachutes down, with open wings and legs dangling, singing all the while. This song is uttered with the beak open, but with no noticeable movement of the mandibles. The bush-lark feeds on grasshoppers and other ground insects and probably on weed and grass-seeds of various kinds.

The breeding season is from March to July. The nest is built in a small hollow at the base of a tussock

× one-third

of grass; it is usually more or less domed over with grass, and is well concealed although the cover is often rather scanty. Two or three eggs form the clutch. They are dirty white in ground-colour, rather liberally speckled with shades of brown overlaying grey undermarkings. They measure about 21·3 × 15·8 mm.

THE CEYLON FINCH-LARK
(Ashy-crowned Finch-Lark of many authors)

Eremopterix grisea ceylonensis Whistler. Resident. Race peculiar to Ceylon

Sinhalese: Gomarittā. Tamil: Vānampādi-pullu

Smaller than a sparrow, but of very much the same build. The male is pale grey marked with dark brown on cap, back and wings; white on cheeks and sides of breast; and deep brownish-black in a line through the eyes, another below the white cheek-patches, chin, breast and abdomen. The female and young are coloured very much like a hen sparrow, but greyer. This quaint little lark, with its short, conical beak and compact form, would be taken for a kind of sparrow were external features only to be considered, but its anatomy shows it to be a true lark.

It is abundant in the coastal areas of the dry-zone low country, wherever suitable country is found; but it avoids the wet zone and does not ascend the hills. It loves arid open country, dry fields, borders of salt-pans, etc., and is a ground dweller, never perching in trees, though it likes clods of earth, low mounds, and the like, as look-out points. Outside the breeding season (when each pair jealously guard their nesting territory), it forms large flocks whose members hop about, picking up the small seeds which form their main food and crouching close to the ground whenever there is any suspicion of danger; while so crouching, they are almost invisible. Besides seeds, insects are eaten, and the young are fed largely on them. At times they are tame, allowing one to watch them from a very short distance; but when nesting they become wary. When singing, the male flies around his territory, up to a

Male left, female right; × one-half

height of thirty or forty feet, in a series of steep ascents with wings fluttering, and deep dips with them closed. The song, a quaint *jingly jingly jingly eeee*, is uttered during the downward stoop. This song is often used as a warning to his mate that an enemy is approaching the nest.

The breeding season is from mid-March to mid-July. The nest is situated on open ground, with little or no cover, and occupies a small hole dug by the female. It is composed of soft fibres, such as disintegrating grass, and is neatly finished off at the margins, flush with the soil. Sometimes the bird decorates the nest environs with small stones, lumps of clay, etc. The two eggs are pale greenish-white, freckled all over but most thickly in a zone around the large end, with yellowish brown and purplish grey. They measure about 19·5 × 13·6 mm.

THE PIPITS AND WAGTAILS
Family Motacillidae

A nearly cosmopolitan family of small birds of graceful form, mainly terrestrial in habits and insectivorous in diet. They have slender, straight bills; longish wings, with the inner secondaries much elongated—extending nearly or quite to the tip of the closed primaries; fairly long, or long tails, not graduated; rather long, slender tarsi. In many, especially pipits, the hind claw is long and curved. They live either solitary, in pairs, or in scattered flocks, and spend most of their time on the ground, where they find all their food. Like larks, they walk or run, but do not hop, and many species, especially among the wagtails, have a habit of constantly oscillating the hinder part of the body up and down, or, in some, from side to side. Many of them are migratory (all of the Ceylon forms except one species). Pipits are mostly dull-coloured; they roost on the ground, among grass, etc., and nest also on the ground, under the shelter of grass-tussocks. Wagtails are of more slim form than pipits; generally of brighter colours, or more contrasting patterns; they commonly roost in trees or in reed-beds, etc.— often in large flocks; and they nest in cavities in rocks, banks or buildings, generally near water. The eggs of all species are spotted.

RICHARD'S PIPIT

Anthus richardi richardi Vieillot. Regular winter visitor

Sinhalese: Gomarittā. Tamil: Nettai-kāli

About the size of the Red-vented Bulbul. Sexes alike. In general appearance and coloration it is a large edition of the Indian Pipit, having exactly the same pattern of markings, and its behaviour, too, is very similar. It is, however, much larger, has a very long hind claw ($\frac{3}{4}$ inch long), and tends to bear itself with a bolder, more upright carriage. Its flight-note, too, is deeper, *twert* rather than *twit*. In spite of these differences, however, it is often difficult to discriminate from its smaller relative, unless, as frequently happens, both species are together in the same field so that the difference in size is apparent.

This large pipit is a winter visitor to Ceylon, arriving about October and leaving again in March or April. It takes up its quarters on open grass-lands in the low country, especially favouring those within a few miles of the coast, and it prefers the dry zone. It runs rapidly on the grass, frequently stopping and raising its head to look for a grasshopper or other small insect. It seldom or never perches on trees—while in Ceylon, at any rate—but is always seen on the ground unless in flight. The flight is strong and dipping, and as the bird rises it utters the flight-note described above.

Richard's Pipit breeds in central Asia and Siberia, nesting on the ground under cover of a grass-tussock, etc.

BLYTH'S PIPIT *Anthus campestris thermophilus* (Jerdon), a large pipit of very similar appearance to Richard's Pipit, was once obtained by Legge on some grassy flats south of Trincomalee. It differs from Richard's Pipit in being slightly smaller, with shorter legs, and much shorter and more curved hind claw; its plumage is more uniform, less streaky, and the breast is almost unspotted in adults. Its habits are, in general, very similar to those of our other two pipits, and it should be looked for during the north-east monsoon in places similar to those favoured by them.

Richard's Pipit left, Indian Pipit right; × two-fifths

THE INDIAN PIPIT

Anthus rufulus malayensis Eyton. Common resident

Sinhalese: Gomarittā, Panu-kurullā. Tamil: Nettai-kāli

Illustrated with Richard's Pipit, above

Between the sparrow and the Red-vented Bulbul in size. Sexes alike. A longish-legged, streaky yellowish-brown bird, very common on grass-land or low scrub everywhere in the Island. From the skylark and bush-lark, which somewhat resemble it in coloration and inhabit similar ground, it is easily distinguished by its more slender form, longer tail, and more upright stance. From its near relation Richard's Pipit, with which it often associates, it is distinguished by its smaller size and shorter—though still long, half an inch—hind claw.

This pipit lives in pairs and appears to mate for life though, out of the breeding season, it sometimes occurs in scattered flocks. It runs swiftly over the grass, frequently standing erect to 'view the landscape o'er', and has a habit of jerking its hinder-parts now and then. It is fond of dusting itself in soft sand, and sometimes bathes in shallow water. Its ablutions—dry or wet—over, it will perch on a boulder, stump or other elevation while it preens its plumage. Occasionally it will perch in a tree, but the ground is its normal habitat, and it roosts there at night. The food consists of grasshoppers, ground beetles and other insects. The flight is bounding and, while flying, the birds (for the pair usually rise together) frequently utter their sharp call *twit, twit-tit*.

The breeding season is in March to July, but an odd nest may be found in other seasons of the year. The nest is placed on the ground under the shelter of a grass-tussock or the like, and is a pad of grass, fine rootlets, etc., with a deep cup, and usually, a thickened and neatly finished 'threshold' on the side where the bird enters. Three eggs form the normal clutch; they are greyish-white, speckled with purplish grey and sepia, the markings being most concentrated in a ring around the big end. They measure about 20·2 × 15·2 mm.

THE INDIAN WHITE WAGTAIL

Motacilla alba dukhunensis Sykes. Rare winter visitor

No Sinhalese or Tamil names

Size of the well-known Grey Wagtail, but with a shorter tail. From the other wagtails that visit Ceylon, except the Large Pied Wagtail, it

× one-quarter

may be distinguished by having no yellow in its plumage; from the Large Pied Wagtail its pale grey back and mainly white head separate it.

Since Wait recorded it at Puttalam in November 1917 it has been seen several times in Ceylon. In February 1946 a pair frequented a Lake-side warehouse in Colombo, where I was able to watch and sketch them at very close quarters. They ran about actively, snapping up lake-flies, and were shy and inclined to be suspicious. The tail was wagged up and down, in typical wagtail fashion but not so incessantly as in the Grey Wagtail. This wagtail is usually to be seen on the ground, often in

97

the neighbourhood of water; it frequents open or cultivated country—never forest—and often associates with other species of wagtails. Its food consists entirely of small insects. The flight is a series of long bounding curves due to the alternate fluttering and closing of the wings, and is accompanied by frequent repetition of the flight-note *chiz-zit*. As with other wagtails, this species commonly roosts in large flocks, which congregate in a reed-bed or similar situation.

This race of the White Wagtail breeds in western Siberia.

The White Wagtail has several geographical races, four of which occur in India in winter, and it is not unlikely that Ceylon may be visited at times by other forms of this very variable species. The plumage phases—of age and season as well as sex—are complicated, and persons interested in this bird are recommended to consult H. Whistler's *Popular Handbook of Indian Birds*, where these matters are ably discussed.

The LARGE PIED WAGTAIL *Motacilla maderaspatensis* Gmelin. The inclusion of this species in the Ceylon list rests on a somewhat doubtful record of a single specimen collected in the Jaffna district over a hundred years ago. It is at least an inch longer than any other Ceylon wagtail. Sexes almost alike. This large wagtail has very much the colour-scheme of the magpie-robin, with the exception that it has a broad white eyebrow extending from the nostril to the nape.

It is widespread and common in India, and is the only wagtail which breeds south of the Himalayas. It is always found in the neighbourhood of water—river, lake or pond—and its general habits do not differ from those of other wagtails. Its nesting habits, however, are very irregular, as almost any hole, niche or crevice near water will do for a site, while the nest itself may vary from practically nothing to a fairly well-built cup of miscellaneous materials. Three to five eggs are laid.

The YELLOW-HEADED WAGTAIL *Motacilla citreola* (subspecies?). This wagtail has not yet been collected in Ceylon, but, 'About December 17th, 1940, and frequently afterwards until February, a wagtail with a conspicuously bright yellow head and lower plumage was often seen on the maidan at Trincomalee by Major G. L. Lushington. He examined it through high-powered field-glasses at from twenty to thirty yards distance and identified it as a Yellow-headed Wagtail; his identification was confirmed by C. E. Norris, H. Doudney and H. Goodfellow. Part of the time, this wagtail associated with a flock of Grey-headed

Yellow Wagtails (*Motacilla flava thunbergi*) but generally it was alone. This bird was seen again by Major Lushington on the 22nd April; it had then assumed full breeding plumage.'—W. W. A. Phillips in *Loris*, June 1941.

This seems conclusive that this wagtail occasionally visits Ceylon, and a look-out for it should be kept. It is about the size of the Grey-headed Yellow Wagtail. The adult male in breeding plumage is unmistakable, with its bright yellow head, black back, and black and white wings and tail; but females, wintering males, and juveniles are much less easy to identify. According to Whistler (*Popular Handbook of Indian Birds*) 'at all ages and seasons the Yellow-headed Wagtails may be distinguished from the Yellow Wagtails by a broad yellow superciliary streak and by a certain amount of yellow on the forehead'.

Three races of the Yellow-headed Wagtail occur in India, one of which breeds regularly in the Himalayas.

THE GREY WAGTAIL

Motacilla cinerea melanope Pallas. Regular and common winter visitor

No Sinhalese or Tamil names recorded

Plate 8, facing p. 89 (Winter plumage; × one-third)

Sparrow-sized, but with a much longer tail. In winter plumage the sexes are indistinguishable; in summer plumage, which some birds assume before leaving Ceylon in April or May, the male develops a black throat-patch, separated by a white stripe from the grey ear-coverts; this dark throat-patch is only slightly developed in the female. From other wagtails, this may be distinguished by its very long tail, grey back and greenish rump.

This graceful bird arrives in the Island from its breeding haunts in central Asia, in late August and September, and departs again in April and early May. It is pre-eminently a bird of rivers and streams, and prefers rocky mountain torrents; accordingly, soon after its arrival most birds desert the low country for the mountains, where it is one of the most familiar species on tea estates and jungle streams. Its long tail is continually oscillated up and down, either moderately, when the bird is quietly resting or preening, or vigorously, in moments of excitement. It trips lightly about the boulders, beside or in the midst of the stream, wades in the shallows, and snaps at the gnats and small insects that rise before it. If disturbed, it flies up or down the stream in a series of long bounds, the wings alternately fluttered and closed; at each bound, its flight-note *twit-it-it* is uttered. In the evenings it assembles in large flocks for roosting in some favourite spot—often a large tree overhanging water, or else in a swampy thicket. This nocturnal gregariousness contrasts with its unsociable nature during the day; each bird jealously guards its chosen territory from other wagtails.

This race of the Grey Wagtail breeds in a large part of the Asian continent south to the Himalayas. The nest is built in some hole or cavity among riverside rocks and boulders. It is a cup composed of dry grass, fibres, etc., lined with cow-hair and the like, and usually contains four or five eggs which are buff-white, uniformly mottled with shades of ochre; they measure about 17·5 × 13·7 mm.

THE GREY-HEADED YELLOW WAGTAIL

Motacilla flava thunbergi Billberg. Regular and common winter visitor

No Sinhalese or Tamil names recorded

Plate 8, facing p. 89 (× one-third)

Same size as the last species, but with a shorter tail which it does not wag so continuously or so vigorously. From the Grey Wagtail, it may be distinguished by its olivaceous back, brighter yellow underparts, and darker head with, usually, only a trace of a pale eyebrow. The Plate represents an adult male in breeding plumage; winter-plumage birds generally show a good deal of patchy dark speckling on the breast, and females and juveniles appear in a bewildering variety of plumage phases.

This wagtail is mainly a low-country bird, though it sometimes appears as high as Nuwara Eliya or the Horton Plains while on passage. It is a field wagtail, delighting in damp meadows, and is very sociable with its kind, usually associating in scattered flocks, often accompanying feeding cattle. As it runs briskly amongst the animals, it darts here and there, snapping up insects as they leap out of the way of their hooves. As with other wagtails, its flight is performed in a series of big undulations, due to the alternate fluttering and closing of the wings; a twittering flight-note accompanies each dip. As evening approaches, multitudes of these birds will congregate in some swamp or reed-bed in which to spend the night.

The Yellow Wagtail has a very wide range in the Old World, and has developed a number of races, each with its own breeding area. These races are characterized by more or less distinct colour features, which are easily recognizable in adult breeding birds, but tend to disappear in winter and are often indistinct in the young. Moreover, birds from different breeding ranges often have a common winter habitat.

These facts make the correct identification of individual wagtails a complicated business such as is best left to the experts. It is quite likely that stray members of some of the other races may visit Ceylon from time to time, as three of them are commonly found in India during the north-east monsoon.

The present race nests in north Scandinavia, Russia and Siberia. The nest is on the ground, concealed among herbage, grass, etc., in damp meadows and the like.

THE FOREST WAGTAIL

Dendronanthus indicus (Gmelin). Regular winter visitor

No Sinhalese or Tamil names recorded

Plate 8, facing p. 89 (×one-third)

Sparrow-sized, but more gracefully built than a sparrow. Sexes alike. This bird's striking colour pattern rather suggests some small game-bird than a wagtail, as it trips over the fallen leaves in its favourite, dry-zone jungle haunts.

It arrives in Ceylon about September and October and, while most take up quarters in the jungles of the northern half of the Island, a few find their way up-country, occurring at times as high as Nuwara Eliya. Unlike other wagtails, it wags its tail from side to side, not up and down, and does it with a rather deliberate motion. Its normal gait, too, is a sedate walk, unlike the lively actions of the Grey and Grey-headed Yellow Wagtails. It is solitary during the day, but flocks to some favourite roost in the evening. When disturbed in the jungle it flies up into a tree, uttering a loud *spink, spink*. One which I collected contained, in its gizzard, a number of small weevils. Its coloration camouflages it very effectively so long as it keeps still on the forest floor—rendering it almost impossible to detect; it is not shy, however, and visitors to its dry-zone haunts have little difficulty in watching its habits.

The Forest Wagtail leaves Ceylon rather early—about March, as a rule—for its distant nesting-grounds in the north-eastern parts of Asia.

THE SWALLOWS
Family HIRUNDINIDAE

The swallows are a very distinctive family of passeriform birds only confusable with the swifts, with which, however, they have no real relationship. They are small birds adapted for an aerial life of pursuing winged insects in the air—not by quick sallies from a perch, as flycatchers and drongos do, but in continuous flight. In adaptation to this role in life they have long, pointed, narrow wings, giving both speed and staying-power; the tail is forked, often deeply so, presumably for some streamlining effect; the gape is wide, but the bill is small, flattened and, as seen from above, triangular; the legs and feet are small and weak, used for perching, scarcely at all for locomotion. Many species are migratory, travelling, perhaps, thousands of miles twice a year, between their summer breeding homes and their winter quarters. Swallows perch readily, but usually on thin bare twigs, or telegraph wires, not among foliage. Most of them build nests of mud pellets, which they stick to the underside of rock caves, or under eaves of buildings, etc., lining them with straws and feathers. The family is of almost cosmopolitan distribution.

Swallows on the wing may always be distinguished from swifts by the shape of their wings, which are much broader in the secondary portion than those of swifts; moreover their wings are worked in a different manner which, though difficult to describe, is easily recognized once it has been learnt. Briefly, while swifts tend to beat their wings from the shoulder, keeping them fully extended in the form of a bow, swallows tend to work their wings in an 'opening and shutting' manner. Swifts also do far more gliding, with steady wings, than do swallows.

THE SWALLOW

Hirundo rustica rustica Linnaeus—European race. Rare winter visitor
Hirundo rustica gutturalis Scopoli—east Asian race. Abundant winter visitor

Sinhalese: Wéhi-lihiniyā. Tamil: Tām-pādi, Tarai-illātha-kuruvi

Plate 7, facing p. 88 (east Asian race; × one-quarter)

Sparrow-sized, but much more gracefully built and with long wings and long, deeply-forked tail. From the Hill Swallow, both races may be distinguished by the brighter chestnut forehead and throat, whiter underparts, and much longer outer tail-feathers; they are also larger, more metallic blue above, and have longer wings and a more dashing style of flight. From the Ceylon Swallow, they are readily separated by the chestnut underparts and rump of the latter.

The two races of the swallow which visit Ceylon are so similar that they can be distinguished only in the hand, or at very close quarters. In the east Asian race, which comprises the vast majority of our swallows, the glossy black chest-band, separating the chestnut throat from the white underparts, is incomplete in the middle; while in the European race this band is continuous across the chest, and the underparts are more suffused with rufous; also, it is larger.

Swallows arive in Ceylon at the beginning of the north-east monsoon, and leave in April for their breeding haunts, which extend from Britain, across Europe and northern Asia, to Japan. During most of their stay in the Island they are in heavy moult and present rather a ragged and moth-eaten appearance; but about April they are in beautiful, glossy, breeding plumage. They spread all over the Island, and are the commonest of the swallow-tribe during their stay. The flight is very rapid, dashing and skilful, with an 'opening and shutting' action of the wings which enables them to be distinguished from swifts very readily. While much of their time is spent on the wing—capturing the small flying insects that comprise their food—they perch readily on telegraph wires, small bare twigs, or even on clods of earth. They are very sociable with their kind, and it is a common sight to see twenty or thirty closely packed along a favourite portion of telegraph wire. They are rather silent during their sojourn, but occasionally utter a short twitter, becoming more talkative towards the time of their departure for the north.

Breeding commences soon after they arrive in their summer home. The nest is a mass of mud pellets with a hollow at the top lined with straws and feathers. It is placed on a beam, or the like, under the eaves of a building, or often inside. The four or five eggs are white, spotted with reddish-brown and grey.

THE HILL SWALLOW
(Nilgiri House Swallow of many authors)

Hirundo javanica domicola Jerdon. Resident

Sinhalese: Wéhi-lihiniyā. Tamil: Tām-pādi, Tarai-illātha-kuruvi

Plate 7, facing p. 88 (×one-quarter)

Smaller than a sparrow, but with much longer wings. Sexes alike.

This little swallow seldom descends below 3,000 feet, though I have seen it at Kitulgala—only about 600 feet. In the higher districts it is a familiar favourite, owing to its complete fearlessness of man and readiness to accept the hospitality of his verandas, etc., as a site for its nest.

Its flight is less dashing than that of the migrant swallow, and this, with the smaller size, darker underparts, and much shorter tail, make it easy to distinguish. Its note is a quaint twitter, sometimes prolonged into a few bars of a rapid little song. Like other swallows, most of its time is spent in capturing, on the wing, the small gnats and midges that compose its food. It is fond of beating to and fro along the face of a road bank, often not more than a couple of feet above the ground; no doubt such a beat provides a plentiful supply of small flies rising from the roadside drain. Like its larger relative, it perches readily on telegraph wires, or, failing these man-made resting places, on thin, leafless twigs, usually not far from the ground.

The breeding season is in February–May, and often again in September. The nest is a little 'wall-bracket' composed of lumps of mud, reinforced, like Pharaoh's bricks, with shreds of straw, and lined with feathers; when collecting these wherewith to line their cradle the birds will sometimes take feathers proffered to them from one's hands—so fearless are they. The natural site for the nest is at the top of a bare bank, e.g. a road-bank or earth-slip, where overhanging grass forms a sheltering eave. Many nests are built in such situations but, since man has come on the scene, his buildings have offered such excellent, safe sites that most nests are now to be found in planters' houses, tea-factories, etc.—under the eaves, at the top of a veranda wall or, not seldom, inside a room. Two or three eggs are laid; they are white, with brownish and purplish spots, and measure about $16 \cdot 7 \times 12 \cdot 6$ mm.

THE CEYLON SWALLOW

Hirundo daurica hyperythra Blyth. Race peculiar to Ceylon

Sinhalese: Wéhi-lihiniyā. Tamil: Tām-pādi, Tarai-illātha-kuruvi

Plate 7, facing p. 88 (× one-quarter)

Sparrow-sized, but with much longer wings and tail. Sexes alike. From the Common Swallow and the Hill Swallow it is readily distinguished by its chestnut underparts and rump, rather heavy build, and slower, more sailing style of flight.

It is found, in suitable country, almost throughout the low country except the Jaffna Peninsula and islands—where I have never seen it—and it ascends the hills to 3,000 or 4,000 feet (higher on the dry, Uva side). It loves open grassy country, paddy-fields, and grass-covered hillsides, and in such places it may be seen in pairs or small scattered flocks, flying to and fro with, for a swallow, a rather slow, steady flight, with frequent sailing, and usually at no great height from the ground. In flight, it often utters its rather loud, musical call-note, which has a distinctive quality, easily recognized when once heard. Like all swallows, its food consists of small insects, captured on the wing.

The main breeding season is in April–July, but eggs are sometimes laid in other months. The nest, made of mud pellets, is a bottle-gourd-shaped structure plastered to the roof of a rock cave, or to the underside of a bridge or culvert, etc. The entrance is the mouth of the 'bottle', and the nest proper, composed of feathers, is in the globular portion. Two or three pure white eggs form the clutch, and they measure about 24 × 14·5 mm.

The Ceylon Swallow is a local race of the Red-rumped Swallow, *Hirundo daurica*, a species with a very wide distribution in southern Europe, Africa and Asia. Within this great area it forms many races which are distinguished by variations in size, depth of colouring, striation of the lower plumage, etc. The South Indian race, SYKES'S STRIATED SWALLOW *H. d. erythropygia* Sykes, has twice been collected in Ceylon— by Layard, at Point Pedro, and by Bligh, near Haputale; both about a hundred years ago. These records show that the race is likely to visit Ceylon from time to time, and students of birds should be on the look-out for it. It resembles the Ceylon Swallow in size, general shape, and style of flight, but may be distinguished from it by (*a*) a broken chestnut collar on the hind neck; (*b*) its *pale* rufous (nearly white) underparts with brown shaft streaks. The ear-coverts and rump are chestnut as in the Ceylon race. While watching a scattered flock hawking over fields at Kotagiri in the Nilgiri Hills, South India, in December 1945, I noticed that the call-note uttered by them was quite different from that of *H. d. hyperythra*.

Sykes's Striated Swallow is common in a great part of peninsular India.

The INDIAN CLIFF SWALLOW *Hirundo fluvicola* Jerdon. In the *Journal of the Bombay Natural History Society*, vol. 47, 1948, p. 740, W. W. A. Phillips records having seen one of this species on the Sita Eliya patanas (5,500 feet), between Nuwara Eliya and Hakgala, on 8 February 1948. It was in immature plumage and was associating with Hill Swallows. In general colour-scheme this bird resembles the European and east Asian Swallows in having the upperparts glossy blue-black, duller and brownish on flight-feathers, rump and tail; but its throat and breast and entire underparts are buff-white, heavily streaked on the chin and throat, more lightly elsewhere, with brown; the top of the head is dull chestnut; the tail only slightly forked. It inhabits the plains of India, dwelling near rivers and lakes, and nests in huge colonies, building mud nests on the walls of large buildings, cliffs, etc.

It must not be confused with the Indian Wire-tailed Swallow (*Hirundo smithii filifera*), should this turn up in Ceylon at any time. It is of somewhat similar coloration to the Indian Cliff Swallow, having a chestnut cap and glossy blue-black upperparts; but its throat and entire underparts are pure white, and the tail is very short except for the two outer feathers which are enormously long and thin—really wire-like.

THE WHITE-EYES

Family ZOSTEROPIDAE

The white-eyes are a large family of very small perching birds, found in Africa and southern Asia to Japan, and through the Malayan region and Polynesia to Australia and New Zealand. The great majority of them are coloured in shades of yellowish green, bright yellow and white, though some species are more greyish; but their chief distinguishing feature lies in a ring of tiny, pure-white feathers around the eye, which gives them a very characteristic appearance. All the species of the family possess this feature, and in some of the African forms the white ring is greatly enlarged, occupying much of the face. In general form they resemble the tree warblers, but their structure shows that they are not closely related to them. The beak is small, tapering, gently curved, and acute; the tongue is rather long and extensible, brush-like at the tip, adapted for sucking nectar from flowers; wings of ordinary form; tail of moderate length, even at the tip; the legs and feet are of ordinary perching-bird type. White-eyes are arboreal, though they will descend to the ground for bathing, etc. Their diet consists largely of nectar from flowers, but they also eat many berries and small insects. They are very active and sociable little birds, frequenting gardens as well as forests; they do not migrate.

The nests of these birds are neat little open baskets made of small twigs, moss and fibres, placed among the foliage of bushes and trees. The eggs of the two Ceylon species, at least, are unspotted, pale blue.

THE CEYLON SMALL WHITE-EYE

Zosterops palpebrosa egregia Madarasz. Race peculiar to Ceylon, but closely allied races are found in the greater part of India

Sinhalese: Măl-kurullā. Tamil: Pū-kuruvi

Plate 8, facing p. 89 (× one-third)

Smaller than the sparrow; about the size of the Purple-rumped Sunbird. Sexes alike. The only bird with which it might be confused is the next species (Ceylon Hill White-eye), but it is smaller, and yellower in coloration.

It is common all over the low country, except in the northern districts; and ascends the hills to heights of from 4,000 feet in the wetter districts, to 6,000 feet on the drier, Uva side. It goes in pairs or small flocks, and is very active, constantly searching foliage for insects, and flying from tree to tree in 'follow-my-leader' fashion; each bird constantly uttering a reedy little chirp, well likened by Whistler to *tseer tseer*. It probes flowers for nectar, and also eats small berries. It is arboreal, only descending to ground level for the purpose of bathing—which it loves to do in the sunlit shallows of some small stream running through shrubbery.

The breeding season is about April and May, but some birds breed earlier in the year and it is probable that second broods are reared in some cases, as nests have been found in September. The nest is a small, neat little cup of fine fibres, cotton, moss, etc., slung between two or more leafy twigs at heights varying from a few feet to twenty or thirty. There are two (occasionally three or four) pale blue eggs without markings. They measure about 15·5 × 11·6 mm.

THE CEYLON HILL WHITE-EYE

Zosterops ceylonensis Holdsworth. Species peculiar to Ceylon

Sinhalese: Măl-kurullā. Tamil: Pū-kuruvi

Plate 8, facing p. 89 (× one-third)

Size of Loten's Sunbird—i.e. smaller than the sparrow, but noticeably larger than the last species, from which it is readily distinguished by its darker green plumage. Sexes alike.

It is found only in the Ceylon mountains above 3,000 feet; at the higher elevations, above about 5,000 feet, it is, I think unquestionably, the commonest bird. It is even more sociable than the last, forming very large, scattered flocks except in the breeding season, when the birds pair off. Always on the move, it spends its waking hours in an almost ceaseless search for small caterpillars (the tea tortrix, *Homona coffearia*, being a special favourite), tiny moths, etc., and in visiting nectar-producing blossoms and berry-bearing shrubs. Flocks of these little birds travel steadily through the mountain forests, in company with many other small birds, enlivening the sombre solitudes with their cheery twittering, the while they search almost every leaf for their small prey. It is also quite at home in flower gardens, and, being quite fearless of man, it is a great favourite with human dwellers in the hills. Probably no bird is so important as a destroyer of caterpillar pests as this. The ordinary call-note, constantly uttered, is a reedy chirp, very like that of the last species (which often associates with it, where their ranges overlap), but stronger, and deeper in tone; but in the courting season, the male sings a jingling song, suggestive of shaking a bunch of keys repeatedly, eight or nine times. I have heard this song only in the morning, before sunrise.

The usual breeding season is from March to May, but many pairs rear a second brood in August–September, and an occasional nest may be found at other times of the year. The nest is like that of the last species, but is a trifle larger and not quite so solidly built; a neat little cup, composed of fine fibres, moss and fluff, slung hammock-wise in a fork of a leafy twig. It is often placed in a comparatively low tree or shrub, growing in the open. The two eggs are very pale prussian blue in colour, unmarked, and measure about $16 \cdot 2 \times 11 \cdot 3$ mm.

THE SUNBIRDS
Family NECTARINIIDAE

The sunbirds are a large tropical family of very small birds, confined to the Old World, and ranging from Africa, through southern Asia, to New Guinea and Australia. In appearance and habits they somewhat resemble the well-known humming-birds which, however, are confined to the New World; there is no real relationship between them as the humming-birds are not *Passeriformes*, but belong to quite a different order related to the swifts. In the sunbirds (or 'honeysuckers' as they are often called), the males are brilliantly metallic in parts of their plumage; the females being usually much duller in coloration. They are strictly arboreal birds, never normally descending to the ground, and they live, mostly, in pairs, being unsociable with their kind. They are non-migratory, though they move about locally a good deal, in response to weather conditions, etc. Sunbirds feed largely on nectar and, to enable them to obtain this food, their bills are long, slender, curved, and acutely pointed, adapted for probing the corollas of flowers; the tongue is very long, tubular, and extensible far beyond the beak, used for sucking nectar. Besides this liquid food, they eat many small spiders and insects. The wings, and the legs and feet, are of the usual perching-bird type; in all Ceylon species, the tail is of moderate length and even at the tip; but some foreign species have the central pair of feathers greatly elongated.

Many sunbirds build hanging, bag-like nests, with the entrance in the side, near the top. They lay spotted eggs.

LOTEN'S SUNBIRD

Cinnyris lotenia lotenia (Linnaeus). Race peculiar to Ceylon

Sinhalese: Ran Sūtikkā. Tamil: Thēn-kudi, Pū-kudichān

Plate 8, facing p. 89 (male left, female right; × one-third)

Smaller than the House Sparrow. This is the largest of the Ceylon sunbirds, and is easily distinguished, when adult, from all the others by its very long, rather ungainly beak; apart from this feature, it closely resembles the Purple Sunbird. The male, however, has its abdomen dark, sooty brown (blue-black in the Purple Sunbird) and the female lacks the whitish eyebrow found in that species. About August to October, the males assume a plumage like that of the female except that they retain a line of metallic feathers from the chin to the abdomen, and the lesser wing-coverts are also metallic. From this 'eclipse' plumage[1] they gradually moult into full breeding plumage.

This is a common bird throughout the low country, especially the wet zone, and it ascends the hills to at least 6,000 feet. A lively and joyous bird, it spends its waking hours flitting from flower to flower, probing the blossoms with its long beak and sucking their nectar through its long, protrusible, tubular tongue; large flowers, such as hibiscus or canna, are pierced near the base, but otherwise the bird is content to use the natural opening, sometimes hovering for a few seconds while it probes the corolla. Besides nectar, it eats numbers of small insects, soft

---

[1] According to Whistler (*Journal of the Bombay Natural History Society*, vol. 38, 1936, p. 772) Loten's Sunbird has no eclipse plumage. If this be so, the birds seen in female plumage but with a metallic blue and black stripe down the middle of the underparts must be juvenile males moulting into adult plumage. The question requires further examination.

caterpillars, and especially enjoys small spiders, for which it searches cobwebby tree-trunks, etc. It has a habit of continually jerking the head to and fro. The ordinary flight-note, uttered by both sexes, is *twit* or *chit* but, in the breeding season, the male sings a very pleasing and lively song which may be rendered somewhat as *titti-titu-weechi weechi weechi*. In the fervour of courting, the male sometimes displays in a remarkable manner. He tightens all his feathers, looking strangely slim, while his gorgeous colours gleam and scintillate; the fiery yellow and red lateral breast-tufts—which are normally hidden under the closed wings—are puffed out, and he flies about in a series of deep loops, all the while singing in an ecstasy of love.

The breeding season lasts from February to May, and sometimes later. The type of nest varies; in the wet zone, it is usually a pear-shaped structure composed of fine fibres bound and felted together with cobwebs, with the entrance in the side, near the top, and overshadowed by a ragged little porch. The inside is lined with soft cottony substances, and the outside is camouflaged with all manner of rubbish—flakes of bark, discarded spiders' egg-bags, caterpillar frass, etc.—and generally there is a long, untidy tail of similar materials hanging below the nest. The whole structure is hung by the top from a drooping twig or the like. For sites, the birds show a preference for shady and secluded places— e.g. a gloomy tunnel between a hedge and a building—and often the nest is only two or three feet from the ground.

In the dry zone, wherever the gregarious spider *Stegodyphus sarasi- norum* makes its large communal nests of greyish cobweb in bushes, Loten's Sunbird saves itself a lot of work by simply pressing a cavity into the side of one of these masses of cobweb, and lining it with vegetable down. (Does it deal with its spider-landlords by eating them?) Two, or occasionally three, eggs are laid; they are dirty white in ground-colour, peppered all over with rather ill-defined small spots of brownish-grey, sometimes more concentrated in a ring around the big end. They measure about $17 \cdot 2 \times 11 \cdot 7$ mm.

THE PURPLE SUNBIRD

Cinnyris asiatica asiatica (Latham). Resident

Sinhalese: Sūtikkā. Tamil: Thēn-kudi, Pū-kudichān

Plate 8, facing p. 89 (female left, male right; $\times$ one-third)

About the size of the tailor-bird. It closely resembles Loten's Sun-bird in coloration, but is easily distinguished by its much shorter beak. For other differences, of both sexes, see that species.

It is a common bird throughout the low-country dry zone and drier hill districts, and occurs, but not very commonly, in parts of the wet zone. In general habits it behaves very much like Loten's Sunbird, and most of what is written of that species applies equally to this. It feeds on nectar from flowers, on small caterpillars and other insects, and is partial to spiders. Like all sunbirds, it is very active, never still for long, and it is strictly arboreal, inhabiting trees and bushes up to any height, but seldom descending to the ground. I have not noticed in this bird the habit, so characteristic of Loten's, of constantly thrusting the head forward and retracting it. The calls and flight-note are not very different from those of Loten's, a *chip* and, frequently-uttered, loud *chweet*. In the courting season, and sometimes out of it, the male sings a very lively and sweet song not unlike that of a canary. The flame-coloured breast-tufts shown in the Plate are only displayed in courtship.

The breeding season is from February to May; from July to September the males go into an 'eclipse' phase of plumage very like that of Loten's Sunbird; they then resemble the females except for a broad stripe of metallic blue feathers down the middle of the underparts, from chin to abdomen, and a patch on the lesser wing-coverts. From this phase they gradually moult, patchily, into the full breeding plumage.

The nesting habits resemble those of Loten's, except that the 'hanging-pear' type of nest is much neater, lacking most of the untidy decoration; and it is not sited in the dark, secluded corners so beloved by Loten's, but in open places. The majority of nests, however, are made in the cobweb-masses of the gregarious spider, *Stegodyphus sarasinorum*, and these exactly resemble those made by the last species in similar situations. The female alone does the work of nest-building and incubation, the role of the male during this period—as with many other birds— being that of watchman and defender; he warns his mate by breaking into song on the approach of any suspicious character. The two eggs are pale greenish-grey, blotched and speckled all over with small purplish-brown flecks. They measure about 17 × 12 mm.

THE PURPLE-RUMPED SUNBIRD

Cinnyris zeylonica zeylonica (Linnaeus). Race peculiar to Ceylon, but the
Indian race differs only in being a trifle larger on the average

Sinhalese: Măl Sūtikkā. Tamil: Thēn-kudi, Pū-kudichān

Plate 8, facing p. 89 (female left, male right; × one-third)

Size of the tailor-bird. The coloration of the male is quite distinctive; the female has a paler face, warmer brown wings, and clearer yellow and white underparts than the female Purple Sunbird. The young resemble the female, and this species has no 'eclipse' phase of plumage in the male.

This charming little bird is found throughout the Island, except the highest hills, in gardens, cultivated country, and open jungle, and is one of our commonest and most familiar birds. It lives in pairs all the year round, and each pair jealously guards its chosen territory from others of the same species; like other sunbirds, it is pugnacious, and the males fight intruding sunbirds with great energy. They will even fight their own reflection in window-panes, chromium plating on stationary cars, etc. This sunbird appears to be even more addicted to nectar than the other species and, although it eats many small insects—soft caterpillars and the like—it visits flowers all day long. As it hops and flits about, both sexes constantly utter a chirp which, though quite musical, sounds like the opening and shutting of a large rusty pair of scissors: *sweety-swee, sweety sweety-swee*. At the same time, the closed wings are flirted upwards and the tail opened and shut. After rain, it delights to bathe in the rain-drops which spangle large leaves, scrabbling about the wet surface until it is thoroughly bedraggled.

The main breeding season is from February to June, but many birds raise a second brood in August–September. The nest is a small hanging structure suspended from the end of a leafy twig, generally within hand-reach. A common site is a lantana branch overhanging a footpath. Its entrance is in the side near the top, and it is shaded by a little porch. It is composed of soft fibres and cottony down, bound with cobweb, and decorated on the outside with scraps of lichen, brown frass of wood-boring caterpillars, etc. Internally it is very soft and warm. The hen alone builds and incubates, but the male keeps vigilant guard and warns her of the approach of any intruder. There are two eggs; they are pale greenish-grey, covered all over with tiny freckles of dull greenish-brown, and with a big-end zone of the same. They measure about $16 \cdot 6 \times 11 \cdot 2$ mm.

The SMALL SUNBIRD *Cinnyris minima* Sykes. The inclusion of this sunbird rests on statements by Layard and Holdsworth, but no specimen seems to have been procured in Ceylon and it is very doubtful whether it has ever occurred here. Its habitat is in the Western Ghats of South India.

This tiny sunbird, very little larger than the Ceylon Small Flowerpecker, closely resembles, in pattern and general coloration, the Purple-rumped Sunbird; apart, however, from its distinctly smaller size, it may be distinguished, in the male, by its richer colour and nearly white underparts; in the female, by the metallic copper-colour of the rump. Its habits differ little from its larger relative, but its ordinary notes are less musical, more 'chittering' than those of the Purple-rumped Sunbird.

THE FLOWERPECKERS
Family DICAEIDAE

This family consists of very small birds closely related to the sunbirds, from which they differ mainly in the form of the beak, which is short. They are found mainly from the Indian and Malayan regions to Australia, though a few forms occur in West Africa. They are strictly arboreal, never descending to the ground, and they feed mainly on soft fruits and berries, on nectar, and also on small insects and spiders. They are active little birds, living in pairs or solitary, and they do not migrate. In many foreign species the males are brilliantly coloured, but the three Ceylon species are comparatively dull-coloured—two of them distinctly so. They inhabit forests and wooded country.

The oriental forms build beautiful little hanging nests of plant down, felted with cobweb, suspending them from leafy twigs. Their eggs are either plain white, or spotted.

THE CEYLON SMALL FLOWERPECKER
(Tickell's Flowerpecker of some authors)

Dicaeum erythrorhynchos ceylonensis Babault. Race peculiar to Ceylon

Sinhalese: Pililer-geddi Sūtikkā. No Tamil name recorded

The smallest Ceylon bird—over an inch shorter than the Purple-rumped Sunbird. Sexes alike. The tiny size, drab greyish-olive coloration, and curved, acute beak, make it easy to identify.

It is a common bird everywhere in Ceylon, the presence of trees being, apparently, the only essential for its existence. It is very active, generally solitary or in pairs, and always makes its presence known by a constantly uttered *tlik, tlik*. It is a good flier, and must cover tremendous distances in the course of a day as it flies from one feeding-ground to another, often, in up-country districts, across deep valleys. The flight is in a series of great bounds and dips. It feeds on juicy fruit of many kinds but, notoriously, its favourite food is the berries of the parasite of trees, loranthus. The seeds of this plant are very sticky and, when voided by

the bird, they adhere to the branches of trees, germinate, and in due course a new loranthus clump is started. Besides fruit, it eats many small insects, especially spiders. It is strictly arboreal.

The breeding season lasts from January to August. The nest is not easy to find, probably because it is often placed among large leaves high up in a tree. It is a small bag of cotton and bast fibres bound together

$\times$ one-half

with cobweb, suspended beneath a thin, leafy twig; the entrance is in the side near the top beneath the twig; the outside is decorated, rather sparsely, with the sawdust-like frass produced by wood-boring caterpillars. The two eggs are unmarked white, and measure about 14·4 × 10·3 mm.

THE CEYLON THICK-BILLED FLOWERPECKER

Dicaeum agile zeylonicum (Whistler). Race peculiar to Ceylon

No Sinhalese or Tamil names recorded

A little smaller than the Purple-rumped Sunbird, and slightly larger than the Small Flowerpecker. It is of much the same drab olive-grey coloration as the latter, but has a diffuse, brownish streak down the

sides of the throat, white-tipped tail-feathers, and a shorter, stout beak; the irides are reddish-brown, with a narrow inner ring of buff; these give the little bird, in combination with the short, stout beak, a curiously pugnacious look.

This flowerpecker inhabits the North Central Province, Uva, parts of the Eastern and Central Provinces, but it is nowhere very numerous. In the drier parts of the hills it ascends

$\times$ two-fifths

to about 4,000 feet, but probably does not breed above 3,000 feet. In general habits it is very similar to the Small Flowerpecker, having the same restless ways, and its constantly repeated note *chip, chip* is very like that of its small relative. It has a habit of jerking the tail laterally while feeding or hopping about. Juicy fruit of many sorts, loranthus berries, the nectar of flowers, and small insects and spiders comprise its food.

The breeding season appears to be from March to July, but the nest is seldom found—probably because it is often placed at a great height from the ground. It is a little felted bag, composed of reddish plant down mixed with cobweb, hung from a leafy twig; the entrance is immediately below the twig, and the whole top of the bag envelops it. So well is the felting done that the nest resembles flannel in texture. The eggs number two, and are white, speckled with reddish-brown spots. They measure about 15·8 × 11·3 mm.

LEGGE'S FLOWERPECKER

Dicaeum vincens (Sclater) (*Acmonorhynchus vincens* of some authors).
Species peculiar to Ceylon

No Sinhalese or Tamil names recorded

Plate 8, facing p. 89 (left female, right male; × one-third)

About the size of the Purple-rumped Sunbird, which it somewhat resembles at a distance; the male is at once distinguished, however, by its pure-white throat and dark bluish-grey back, while both sexes have the beak short and stout—very different from the sunbird's.

This scarce little bird is found only in the rain forests of the south-western parts of the wet zone, including the neighbouring hills up to 3,000 feet. It lives either solitary, in pairs, or in little family parties, and is not easy to meet with because it keeps mainly to the tops of tall trees, either in forest or on its outskirts. However, it is very fond of the nectar of the red cotton tree and when these trees are in flower—about Christmas time in its range—it may be found fairly easily. The red cotton is a tall tree, and a good pair of field-glasses is essential if the bird is to be studied. Besides nectar, it eats fruit of many kinds, including wild figs, and it is partial to the fruit of the climbing screw-pine which covers the trunks of many forest trees. The call-notes, which I have not heard myself, are described by Mrs Lushington as *tchip, tchip-twee-see-see*, and she describes also two types of song, one of which, the breeding song, is uttered, often during stormy south-west monsoon weather, from exposed twigs high up in tall trees.

The breeding season is from January to August. The nest, which was first discovered by Mrs Lushington in 1940, is of the same type as the nests of the other two Ceylonese flowerpeckers, viz. a little hanging pocket of felted plant down, with the entrance at the top, just below the supporting twig. The outside is camouflaged with leaf-bud sheaths. The site of the nest is among leaves, often of the hora tree (*Dipterocarpus zeylanicus*), and it is placed high above the ground. The female alone builds, the male keeping guard close by. The two eggs are dull white, irregularly spotted with purplish red, the spots tending to form a zone around the large end. They measure about 16 × 12 mm.

THE PITTAS
Family PITTIDAE

Pittas belong to a section of the perching birds (*Passeriformes*) separate from all other Ceylon birds, and nearly all their relations are found in the New World. Except for three species found in Africa they are confined to the oriental and Australian regions, and their family headquarters are in the Malayan Archipelago; India has only a few species and Ceylon but one, which is a winter migrant from India and does not breed in the Island. Pittas are of thrush-like size and form, but their tails are very short and square; their legs are comparatively long, and the wings ample. They are birds of very beautiful plumage. Mainly terrestrial, they perch freely in trees on occasion and roost in them at night. On the ground, their gait consists of vigorous hops. They are forest birds, spending most of their time searching for insects on the forest floor, turning over dead leaves, etc., in a very thrush-like manner; besides insects they eat other small animals, and are partial to snails. They live usually solitary, outside the breeding season, being pugnacious with others of their own kind.

Pittas build large, globular nests in bushes and trees, or sometimes on the ground. Their eggs are spotted.

THE INDIAN PITTA

Pitta brachyura (Linnaeus). Regular winter visitor

Sinhalese: Avichchiyā. Tamil: Āru-mani-kuruvi, Thōtta-kallan

Plate 10, facing p. 121 (×one-quarter)

Slightly larger than the magpie-robin, but with a very short tail. Sexes alike. This beautiful bird cannot be mistaken for any other Ceylonese species.

It arrives from India in large numbers in September–October, spreads all over the Island up to at least 6,000 feet, and departs again in April and May. On first arrival, many fly into human habitations—especially on misty nights, up-country—and not a few come to grief by crashing into window-panes at night. Each survivor stakes its claim to some copse, shola, portion of jungle or well-wooded compound, and remains there for the rest of its stay. It will tolerate no intrusion on its territory by any other pitta. On catching sight of a rival, or when startled, or even when it sees some specially delectable item of food, it has a pretty habit of momentarily expanding its wings and tail, displaying the gorgeous colour-scheme, which includes large white patches, usually concealed, on the primaries. The pitta spends most of its time on the ground, hopping sturdily about, and turning over the dead leaves for the insects hiding beneath them. While at ease, it constantly moves the short tail up and down in the same manner as the Indian Blue Chat. Although it is of retiring nature, always skulking in undergrowth, it is not really shy, and is easily decoyed within view by whistling its characteristic call; this is a loud whistle suggesting the words *quite clear*. On fine days, this call—or challenge—is always uttered about sunrise and sunset (hence the Tamil name 'Āru-mani-kuruvi'—'six o'clock bird') and, as soon as one pitta calls, it is promptly answered by the bird in the next territory. In dull weather, this calling often goes on sporadically all day. It has also a scold-note which sounds like a harsh *chēēr*. The pitta feeds on worms and insects—particularly termites—and is partial to small snails. At night it flies up to a branch, usually within hand-reach, to roost, and makes little attempt to conceal itself. It is easily tamed, but must be given a daily ration of insects or it will not thrive.

The pitta breeds in the Himalayan foot-hills, and in Central India, making a large, globular nest in bushes or trees. It lays four or five eggs, of very globular shape, glossy pure white with spots of purplish brown of various shades. They measure about 23×22 mm.

WOODPECKERS, BARBETS, AND THEIR ALLIES

Order PICIFORMES

THIS order comprises six families of zygodactyle birds (see Glossary) divided into two sub-orders, one of which the *Galbulae* (jacamars and puff-birds), is purely South American and does not concern us here. The other sub-order, *Pici*, includes the woodpeckers, barbets, toucans, and honey-guides. Toucans are confined to central and South America, and honey-guides to Africa, the Himalayas, Malaya and Borneo. The remaining two families, *Picidae*— woodpeckers, and *Capitonidae*—barbets, are represented in Ceylon.

THE WOODPECKERS
Family PICIDAE

This family comprises birds highly specialized for a life spent mainly in climbing tree-trunks and feeding on the insect inhabitants of rotten wood. The legs are short and the feet zygodactyle, with very strong, compressed, semicircularly curved claws, which are always very sharp. The tail (in all Ceylonese species) has the shafts of at least the two middle pairs of feathers thick and flexible, resembling whalebone, used by the bird as a prop. The beak is straight, hard, and wedge-shaped at the tip for hewing into wood to obtain larvae, etc., as well as to cut a nest cavity. The tongue is very long and worm-like but hard, acutely pointed, and barbed at the tip; it is protrusible to a considerable distance beyond the beak, and, being covered with sticky saliva, is used to extract grubs from their holes in the wood and to collect mouthfuls of small insects such as ants and termites. The neck, though thin in many forms, is provided with very strong muscles to give force to the hewing work of the beak.

Woodpeckers have no down, and their plumage is coarse and hard though often brightly coloured. The following general tendencies in the family may be noted: the head is often more or less crested; males generally have more red areas on the head than females but otherwise the sexes are similar; the flight feathers in most are spotted with white, or some other light colour, on a dark ground. Woodpeckers are not migratory and they generally live in pairs, though family parties are not uncommon for some time after nesting. The flight tends to be in bounding undulations, owing to the alternate fluttering and closing of the wings. They climb trees in series of jerky runs, generally starting low and working up, head nearly always upward and tail pressing on the bark. Ants form a considerable part of their food. The eggs are white and are laid, usually without any 'nest', on the bare wood of a cavity excavated by the birds in dead tree-trunks or branches. Many species have a habit, whose function is not thoroughly understood, of drumming with the beak on hollow wood; this produces a loud, rapid rattle of considerable carrying power.

THE SMALL SCALY-BELLIED GREEN WOODPECKER

('Small' in relation to the Scaly-bellied Woodpecker, *Picus squamatus*, a Himalayan bird not found in Ceylon)

Picus xanthopygaeus (Gray). Resident

Sinhalese: Kêrellā. Tamil: Maram-kotti, Thachchan-kuruvi. (These vernacular names are generally applied to all woodpeckers)

Plate 9, facing p. 120 (male; × one-quarter)

About the size of the Brown-headed Barbet, or of the Red-backed Woodpecker. The crown and nape in the female are black, without any red; otherwise the sexes are similar. It is paler and greyer than the Yellow-naped Woodpecker, which is the only species with which it is likely to be confused.

This woodpecker is rather rare in Ceylon, and is restricted to the drier, eastern aspect of the main mountain massif, from about 1000 to 5,000 feet. Here it is found in sparsely-wooded, park-like country, and tea or rubber estates adjoining such, as it eschews heavy forest. The great Uva patana basin appears to be its headquarters. It is generally solitary and, unlike most woodpeckers, is rather given to climbing about the huge rock boulders that bestrew the hill-sides. Its cry is a sharp, single yelp, *queep*, which often reveals its whereabouts. In flight, the bright yellow rump-patch shows up conspicuously.

The breeding season appears to be during the south-west monsoon. As with most woodpeckers, the nest is a hole cut in the trunk, or a suitable branch, of a tree; the entrance is about two inches in diameter, leading into a downwardly-directed cavity about a foot deep, at the bottom of which the eggs are laid on the bare wood. The hole may be at any height, from two to twelve or more feet above the ground. The three white eggs measure about $26 \cdot 5 \times 20 \cdot 3$ mm.

THE CEYLON YELLOW-NAPED WOODPECKER

Picus chlorolophus wellsi Meinertzhagen. Race peculiar to Ceylon

Sinhalese: Kondé-kāhā Kêrellā. Tamil: Maram-kotti, Thachchan-kuruvi

Plate 9, facing p. 120 (male; × one-quarter)

Size of the Common Mynah. The female resembles the male, except that the fore-part of her head is greenish-grey and she lacks the crimson moustachial stripe; young birds are duller.

This woodpecker is found in the central mountain massif, and in the low-country wet zone, but it does not appear to occur in the northern forests. It ascends the hills to at least 6,000 feet, but is commonest in the foot-hills of the wet zone. It inhabits jungle and well-wooded village gardens, living in pairs, and it likes the company of other birds, being frequently found among the troops of birds of many species that daily traverse the forests, hunting for food. It descends to the ground more freely than other woodpeckers, and breaks up fallen logs, or dry cow-pats, for the insects they contain. Like all woodpeckers, its food consists of wood-boring insects and their larvae, termites, and especially ants, of which it eats large numbers. Its call is a loud, harsh scream, *quēēēr*, very reminiscent of one of the notes of the Indian Pitta; but it is not a very noisy bird. Its flight, if any distance is to be covered, is performed in a series of bounding undulations, the wings being alternately fluttered and closed; but generally it contents itself with fluttering from one tree to the next. It is not very shy of man.

The breeding season is from February to May. The nest is a cavity dug in a tree, either trunk or branch, and its height varies greatly; 2 feet 9 inches from the ground has been recorded, but most nests are from ten to twenty feet up. One or two white eggs are laid; they measure about 24·7 × 17·2 mm.

THE YELLOW-FRONTED PIED WOODPECKER

Dryobates mahrattensis mahrattensis (Latham). Resident

Sinhalese: Kêrellā. Tamil: Maram-kotti, Thachchan-kuruvi

Plate 9, facing p. 120 (male; × one-quarter)

Size of the Red-vented Bulbul. The sexes are alike, except that the female has no red on her head, her crown being straw yellow through-out. The pale coloration, especially of the head, distinguishes this from

PLATE 9

1. Small Scaly-bellied Green Woodpecker. 2. Ceylon Pygmy Woodpecker.
3. Crimson-backed Woodpecker.   4. Black-backed Yellow Woodpecker.
5. Rufous Woodpecker. 6. Ceylon Golden-backed Woodpecker. 7. Ceylon
Red-backed Woodpecker. 8. Ceylon Yellow-naped Woodpecker. 9. Yellow-
fronted Pied Woodpecker

1. Ceylon Small Barbet.   2. Crimson-breasted Barbet.   3. Yellow-fronted
Barbet.   4. Brown-headed Barbet.   5. Indian Pitta.   6. Brahminy Mynah

all other Ceylon woodpeckers; moreover, it is much smaller than all but the still smaller Pygmy Woodpecker.

This woodpecker inhabits the dry zone, ascending the hills, on the eastern aspect, to about 3,000 feet. It is commonest in the strip of very dry country along the north-west coast from about Marichchukkaddi to Pallavarayankaddu, and in the Hambantota district; but it also occurs in the foot-hills of Uva and the Central Province. It prefers rather open, scrub-jungle or park-country to dense forest, and shows a predilection for the big 'candelabra plants' (*Euphorbia antiquorum*), which are abundant in dry districts. Owing to its small size and broken coloration it is not easy to see unless one's attention is drawn to it by its flight, or by the sound of its tapping wood for insects. It is active, and commonly goes in pairs or small family parties. Ants form a large proportion of its food. I have not heard it utter any note, but Mrs Lushington describes its usual note as a sharp *chik*, and says that it also utters a *chik-urr*.

The breeding season appears to be from May to July, but the nest is not often found. It is of the usual woodpecker type—a hole dug by the birds in a tree-trunk or branch; in the latter case, the lower surface is selected for the entrance-hole, which is about $1\frac{3}{4}$ inches in diameter. The two or three white eggs measure about 22 × 16·4 mm.

THE CEYLON PYGMY WOODPECKER

Dryobates hardwickii gymnophthalmos (Blyth). Race peculiar to Ceylon

Sinhalese: Măl Kêrellā, Chuti Kêrellā. Tamil: Siru Maram-kotti

Plate 9, facing p. 120 (male; × one-quarter)

Size of the House Sparrow. Sexes alike, except that the female lacks the little red tuft on the side of the head, and is duller than the male.

This quaint little woodpecker is widely distributed in the low country, both wet and dry zones, and in the hills up to 4,000 feet; but, although fairly common in most parts of its range, it eludes observation by its habit of working at a considerable height on trees, where its tiny, speckled form does not attract attention. It is a fascinating little bird to watch, as it hammers vigorously on dead twigs, woody knots, etc., every now and then calling to its mate in a tinkling trill rather like the call-note of the Crimson-backed Woodpecker in miniature. Neglected estates with plenty of dead dadap trees (*Erythrina lithosperma*), old chenas, etc., are its favourite resorts; but it also loves openly-wooded park-country, and may be found in forest. It specializes in the smaller branches of trees, leaving the stout trunks to its larger relatives. Like other woodpeckers, it feeds on ants, termites, and bark-frequenting insects; the Travancore race is recorded as drinking nectar from dadap shade-trees, and doubtless the Ceylon bird does the same.

The breeding season appears to be from February to July. The nest-hole closely resembles that of the smaller barbets. It is hewn on the lower surface of a dead branch or stump, often a surprisingly thin one two inches or so in diameter, and may be from nine to seventy feet or more from the ground. The two or three white eggs measure about 15·8 × 13·5 mm.

THE RUFOUS WOODPECKER

Micropternus brachyurus jerdonii (Malherbe). Resident

Sinhalese: Dŭmburu Kêrellã. Tamil: Maram-kotti, Thachchan-kuruvi

Plate 9, facing p. 120 (male; × one-quarter)

Size of the Common Mynah. The female lacks the small crimson patch below the eye and her colours are paler than the male's, but otherwise the sexes are similar. This woodpecker cannot be mistaken for any other owing to its dark-chestnut coloration.

It is found sparingly throughout the low country, and in the hills up to about 2,000 feet, occasionally higher, but is nowhere common. The rather dry expanse of country to the east of the main mountain massif appears to be its headquarters in Ceylon. A shy bird, it prefers open forest well away from human habitations, but may sometimes be seen near jungle villages. It lives in pairs, which keep in touch with each other by frequently uttering a loud cry which Legge renders as *quēemp-queep*. It not unfrequently descends to the ground, where it breaks into cow-pats or small termite-hills in search of insects. The flight is usually a short flutter from tree to tree, but when any distance has to be covered it proceeds in the usual woodpecker fashion of alternate flutter-ing and closing the wings. A noisy rustling sound accompanies the fluttering; this is probably due to the harsh nature of this bird's plumage. Its food is mainly ants of various kinds.

The breeding season is probably from March to June, though there is little information on this point; I have found birds in post-nuptial moult in July. The nest is remarkable in that it is commonly, if not in-variably, a cavity dug by the birds in a nest of black, or brown, tree-ants of the genus *Crematogaster*. These are small but viciously-stinging ants, which may easily be recognized by their habit, when annoyed, of carrying the abdomen elevated over the back; they build large black nests, up to the size of a football, of a tough papier-mâché, with a cellular appearance suggestive of a sponge. These nests are common objects in trees, and the woodpecker has discovered that they may easily be excavated for nesting purposes. Apparently the ants and woodpeckers maintain armistice conditions during the nesting period. The eggs are white and hard, mat-surfaced, but so translucent that the yolk can almost be distinguished through the shell; they measure about 28 × 18·1 mm.

THE CEYLON GOLDEN-BACKED WOODPECKER

Brachypternus benghalensis jaffnensis Whistler. Race peculiar to northern Ceylon

Sinhalese: Pita-răng Kêrellā. Tamil: Maram-kotti, Thachchan-kuruvi

Plate 9, facing p. 120 (female; × one-quarter)

About the size of the Common Mynah. Sexes alike, except that the female has the forehead and crown black, speckled with white (see Plate, where the female is represented; the male's head is like that of the Red-backed Woodpecker).

This woodpecker is the northern form of the next sub-species, the Ceylon Red-backed Woodpecker, with which it freely interbreeds in the country where their respective ranges meet, viz. in the inland areas of the Northern and North Central Provinces. The Golden-backed race is found in the coastal areas from Puttalam, through Mannar and Jaffna, to Trincomalee. It is common in palmyra and coconut plantations, scrub-jungle and the like, throughout this area. In habits, notes, and nesting arrangements it is indistinguishable from the red-backed form.

THE CEYLON RED-BACKED WOODPECKER

Brachypternus benghalensis erithronotus (Vieillot). Race peculiar to Ceylon

Sinhalese: Pita-rătu Kêrellā. Tamil: Maram-kotti, Thachchan-kuruvi

Plate 9, facing p. 120 (male; × one-quarter)

Somewhat larger than the Common Mynah. The female has the fore-head and fore-crown black, speckled with white (like the head of the Ceylon Golden-backed Woodpecker female—see Plate). From the

Crimson-backed Woodpecker this is distinguished by its slightly smaller size, shorter, darker-coloured beak, brighter red back, and quite different notes.

It is a common bird everywhere in the low country (wet and dry zones) but is replaced in the northern coastal districts of the Island by the preceding subspecies; the two races freely interbreed in the northern forest tract, where hybrids between them are common—showing backs of intermediate shades between red and yellow. In the hills it ascends to over 4,000 feet, but probably does not breed above 3,000 feet. This is the commonest of the Ceylon woodpeckers, and is a familiar bird in Colombo, Kandy and other towns, as it is less shy than most woodpeckers. It frequents coconut plantations, well-wooded gardens, open types of jungle, etc., but avoids heavy forest. It lives in pairs, which keep in touch with each other by a frequently-uttered loud, rattling scream; when feeding, they give vent to curious squeaks, chuckles, and squawks. Its favourite food is ants, including the vicious red ant (*Oecophylla smaragdina*), whose large leaf-nests are broken into by the woodpecker to get at the larvae and pupae; but many other insects contribute to the diet. Like other woodpeckers, it works up a tree or palm in a series of jerky runs, and sometimes it jerks downwards for a short distance, but always with its head upwards. The flight consists of a series of bounds— wings alternately fluttered and closed—and is generally accompanied by the call-scream.

The breeding season is from March to June, with a secondary season about August–September. The nest is a hole, with entrance about two inches in diameter, dug in a tree-bole, or palm trunk. The three eggs are glossy white, and measure about $28 \times 20 \cdot 2$ mm.

THE BLACK-BACKED YELLOW WOODPECKER

Chrysocolaptes festivus tantus Ripley. Race peculiar to Ceylon

Sinhalese: Māhā-răng Kêrellā. Tamil: Maram-kotti, Thachchan-kuruvi

Plate 9, facing p. 120 (male; × one-quarter)

Between the Mynah and the House Crow in size; our largest woodpecker. The female has the fore-crown speckled black and white, and the crest golden yellow; otherwise she resembles the male. The only other woodpecker with which it could be confused is the Golden-backed Woodpecker, and from this it can be distinguished by its longer bill and by a conspicuous white patch on the upper back.

This handsome woodpecker is confined to a few localities in the dry-zone low country in the northern half of the Island—particularly on the western side—and the south-eastern sector, near Hambantota and Wirawila; it is rare even in these restricted areas, tending to form small colonies in the coconut groves that surround jungle villages. Very little is on record about its habits, but Legge describes its call as a weaker trill than that of the Crimson-backed Woodpecker, and very like that of the Yellow-fronted Pied Woodpecker. According to Parker (quoted by Legge) it has great difficulty in maintaining its status against competition for nesting sites with the smaller, but more aggressive, Red-backed Woodpecker. It is described as a very active and shy bird, and its food consists of wood-boring insects and seeds (most likely swallowed in fruit).

The breeding season appears to be from January to March, and probably again in August. The nest-hole, which is often hewn in the trunk of a coconut palm, is from fifteen to thirty feet from the ground; the entrance is higher than wide, and measures about $4\frac{1}{2} \times 3$ inches. The two eggs measure about 29×22 mm., and their texture, according to Wait, resembles celluloid.

THE CRIMSON-BACKED WOODPECKER, or LAYARD'S WOODPECKER

Chrysocolaptes guttacristatus stricklandi (Layard). Race peculiar to Ceylon

Sinhalese: Mūkalăng Kêrellā. Tamil: Maram-kotti, Thachchan-kuruvi

Plate 9, facing p. 120 (male; × one-quarter)

Slightly larger than the Common Mynah. The female differs from the male in having the whole crown of the head black, with round white spots. Although practically the same size as the Red-backed Woodpecker, it looks a bigger bird and is easily distinguished from that species by its deeper red—really crimson—back and wings, much longer and paler-coloured beak, and the different call-note.

This handsome woodpecker—whose Indian representative, Malherbe's Woodpecker, has the back and wings (but not the rump, which is crimson, as in our bird) golden yellow—is a forest-loving species, widely distributed almost throughout the forested parts of the Island. It has a distinct preference, however, for the wet zone and the mountains, which it ascends to all elevations. It is a mighty worker, and must play no small part in prospering Ceylon's forests by destroying the boring insects which cause disease in trees, as well as by hastening the disintegration of rotten trees and their return to the soil. It is usually found in pairs, but family parties are often met with. A family is most amusing to watch as its members fly from tree to tree, jerking themselves up the trunks and gesticulating ludicrously while they tap for rotten spots, keeping up a weird conversation of squeaks and sucking noises. Occasionally, one will find a hollow bough and, bracing himself, will play a resounding tattoo on it with his powerful beak. The rattle so produced is amazingly loud, and, while delivering it, the bird's head and neck vibrate so rapidly as to look a mere blur. Opinions differ as to the purpose of this drumming (which is performed, in differing degrees of vigour, by most kinds of woodpeckers)—whether it be a courtship gesture, an expression of *joie de vivre*, or merely a method of driving larvae from their tunnels. The call-note of this woodpecker, usually uttered by both sexes whenever they fly—presumably to acquaint the partner of a change of locality—is a high-pitched, tinny trill, not at all commensurate with the bird's imposing presence; it has considerable carrying power, however.

The breeding season is from October to March, and sometimes again in August–September. The nest-hole is of the usual type, its entrance measuring about 4×3 inches, and is hewn in a dead tree or large branch at heights of ten to forty feet from the ground. From one to three white eggs are laid. They measure about $29 \cdot 2 \times 22$ mm.

THE BARBETS
Family CAPITONIDAE

Barbets are small to medium-sized birds of stout, heavy-looking build, and with gaudily-coloured, rather coarse plumage in which green predominates. They have thick, heavy beaks which are fringed around the gape and chin with long bristles. The feet are zygodactyle. Barbets are, in the main, fruit eaters. They nest in neatly-shaped cavities which they dig for themselves in soft, dead wood. To facilitate stowage, in the confined limits of the nest-cavity, they are able to double back the tail so that it lies flat on the back. They are strictly arboreal, and are noisy birds, with monotonous call-notes.

They are distributed in the tropical parts of America, Africa and Asia. Ceylon has four species, of which one, the Yellow-fronted Barbet, is peculiar to the Island.

THE BROWN-HEADED BARBET
(Green Barbet of various authors)

Thereiceryx zeylanicus zeylanicus (Gmelin). Resident

Sinhalese: Pollos Kottōruwā, Găbbăl Kottèruwā. Tamil: Kūtur, Kukkuruvān

Plate 10, facing p. 121 (× one-quarter)

Size of the Common Mynah. Sexes alike. The brown head and breast; yellow, naked face; and heavy, reddish-coloured bill, distinguish this from the Yellow-fronted Barbet.

It is found all over the Island in cultivated country and jungle, up to about 3,000 feet in the wet-zone hills and about 4,000 feet in the drier, eastern aspect; but it is commoner at lower elevations. It is not so fond of heavy forest as the next species, preferring village gardens, open woods and the like, and is not rare in towns. It lives in pairs which, however, do not associate very closely but keep in touch by means of their loud and frequently-uttered call, a monotonous *kuk'rā, kuk'rā, kuk'rā* (which has several variant renderings); the bird commences its call with a rolling *krrrr-r-r* on an ascending scale until it reaches its pitch, when the *kuk'rā* begins and continues for many seconds, to be answered by its mate, from a distance, in similar tones. While producing these sounds the beak is closed, and the head quivers strongly at each enunciation. The scold-note—usually uttered in concert with other small birds, when mobbing an owl, cat, or tree-snake—is a loud, coarse-sounding guffaw *quo-ho-ho* (o's short, as in ox). When flying for any distance, it proceeds very direct in a series of big bounds, alternately fluttering and sailing with outspread wings. The Brown-headed Barbet feeds on a large variety of berries and other fruit; mā-dun (*Syzygium jambolana*), and various wild figs (banyan, bo, nuga, etc.) being favourites; the young are fed on insects, such as green mantises, as well as on fruit. It is strictly arboreal, never descending to the ground.

The main breeding season is in February to July, with a secondary season in August–September. The bird, working solitarily, hammers and pecks out a hole in a soft-wooded dead stump or branch, seeming to prefer those that are nearly vertical. The entrance-hole—always on the lower aspect of the branch, etc., if there be one—is about 2½ inches in diameter, and is nearly circular, and neatly rounded. Inside, the cavity widens somewhat, and is oval in shape, and small for the size of the bird. The three or four dull white eggs measure about 31 × 22 mm.

THE YELLOW-FRONTED BARBET

Cyanops flavifrons (Cuvier). Species peculiar to Ceylon

Sinhalese: Mūkalăng Kottŏruwā. Tamil: Kūtur, Kukkuruvān

Plate 10, facing p. 121 (×one-quarter)

Between the Red-vented Bulbul and the Common Mynah in size. Sexes alike. The yellow forehead, blue face, and comparatively small beak, distinguish this bird from the last.

It is mainly a bird of the hills which it ascends to at least 6,500 feet, but it is found in many parts of the low-country wet zone, and in scattered colonies in some dry-zone districts to the east of the mountains. In many of its habits it resembles the Brown-headed Barbet, but is more partial to heavy forest although by no means confined to it. Throughout its range it is a common bird, not shy, and well known for its resounding calls, which form a pleasant feature of its haunts. The call commences with a rolling and ascending *kowowowowow* and changes to *kuiār, kuiār, kuiār* . . . repeated many times; it is always answered by the performer's mate from perhaps a hundred yards away. The Yellow-fronted Barbet feeds on numerous kinds of berries, wild figs, and cultivated fruits such as guavas and pawpaws—being rather a pest in orchards. It feeds its young mainly on fruit, but also on some animal food as W. W. A. Phillips has published a photograph of one at its nest-hole with a gecko in its beak.

The breeding season is in February to May, with a secondary season in August–September; but an occasional nest may be found at other times of the year. The nest-hole is very similar to that of the Brown-headed Barbet but slightly smaller—about two inches in diameter. The cavity inside is oval and, if a new one, is about eight inches deep; but sometimes the birds use a nest for several years running, digging it deeper each year until it may be two feet or more deep. The height from the ground varies greatly, but is usually from six to ten feet. The two or three white, and smooth but not glossy, eggs measure about 28 × 21 mm. They are evidently sometimes laid at intervals of several days, as there is often a great disparity in the size of the young. The latter commence to practise their calls before their eyes are open, and the location of the nest may often be discovered by hearing their infant voices monotonously trolling.

THE CRIMSON-BREASTED BARBET, or 'COPPERSMITH'

Xantholaema haemacephala indica (Latham). Resident

Sinhalese: Măl Kottŏruwă. Tamil: Sinna Kukkuruvān

Plate 10, facing p. 121 (×one-quarter)

Slightly larger than a sparrow. Sexes alike. The large scarlet breast-patch, pale *lemon-yellow* face and throat markings, and rather dusky green general coloration, distinguish this bird from the next species. Its note also differs, being a slow *wonk, wonk, wonk* . . . and it never produces the throbbing notes of the Ceylon Coppersmith.

It is a bird of the dry zone, and does not penetrate far into the districts which receive the south-west monsoon; it seems, however, to be gradually extending its range into the damper districts. Throughout the dry zone and in the drier, eastern aspect of the hills, up to about 4,000 feet, it is a common bird. In flight, food, and general habits it is very similar to the next species.

The breeding season is from November to May, and again in July to September. The nest-hole is cut in a dead branch or upright post, etc., and its entrance is a neat, nearly circular, hole about 1½ inches in diameter; the inside cavity is usually about six inches deep by 2¼ inches in diameter. The nest-hole may be any height from four feet to thirty feet or more from the ground. Three dull-white eggs are laid; they measure about 25 × 17·5 mm.

THE CEYLON SMALL BARBET, or 'CEYLON COPPERSMITH'

Xantholaema rubricapilla rubricapilla (Gmelin). Race peculiar to Ceylon

Sinhalese: Măl Kottŏruwă. Tamil: Sinna Kukkuruvān

Plate 10, facing p. 121 (×one-quarter)

Slightly larger than a sparrow. Sexes alike. The bright green upper-parts, orange-yellow face- and throat-patches, and very small scarlet breast-spot, distinguish it from the Crimson-breasted Barbet. The South Indian race of this Barbet, *X. rubricapilla malabarica*, has the whole front of the head, including the face and throat, bright scarlet; otherwise it resembles the Ceylon bird.

The note of the Ceylon Coppersmith is sometimes a slow *wok, wok, wok* . . ., but more often a rapid, throbbing *pop op op op op op, pop op op op op op* . . . , usually in six-syllabled beats, but sometimes in four or five syllables. This song, which is often sustained monotonously for long periods, is frequently performed from a bare twig at the top of a tree; it is somewhat ventriloquistic in character, because the performer has a habit of turning its head from side to side while singing. The beak is kept shut, and a patch of bare skin on each side of the throat is inflated into a round protuberance.

This is a very common bird in cultivated or openly-wooded country throughout the wet zone up to about 3,000 feet, and in scattered colonies in parts of the dry zone; it does not now occur, I believe, in the Jaffna Peninsula, although Legge states that it was found there in his day. Out of the breeding season it is very gregarious, forming large, scattered flocks especially in the neighbourhood of fruiting trees, such as banyan, bo, and other wild figs; like all barbets, it is predominantly a fruit eater. After gorging themselves, they repair to the top branches and indulge in their hobby of vocal music, making the air pulsate with the chorus of *pop op op*ing—to the distraction of their human audience. The flight is straight and direct, performed with rapid, steady wing-beats.

The breeding season is from January to June. The nest-hole is indistinguishable from that of the Crimson-breasted Barbet, but is more often, I think, dug into the lower surface of a sloping branch rather than into an upright post, and is usually higher in a tree than with that species. Dead branches of breadfruit, dadap, and flamboyant are much favoured as nesting sites by both species. Two or three white eggs are laid on the bare wood at the bottom of the cavity; they measure about $25 \cdot 5 \times 18 \cdot 2$ mm.

ROLLERS, BEE-EATERS, KINGFISHERS, HORNBILLS, AND HOOPOES

Order CORACIIFORMES

THIS order is somewhat of a 'waste-paper basket' in bird classification, comprising a number of sub-orders of very diverse appearance and structure yet with certain similarities which seem to indicate relationship. Without recourse to osteological and anatomical characters it is impossible to give a concise definition that will cover all the birds in this order, but the most important feature is the structure of the foot, which has the forwardly-directed toes (numbers 2, 3, and 4) in greater or less degree united at the base (syndactyle—see Glossary). The tarsi are short or very short.

All lay white eggs, in holes in trees or banks etc., with little or no nest. The young are hatched blind and naked. In many forms the feather sheaths persist until the feathers are almost full grown and are then rapidly shed, producing a most remarkable and sudden change in the young birds' appearance. They fly at once on leaving the nest.

Nearly all *Coraciiformes* are carnivorous, but the hornbills are only partly so.

Each sub-order having but one family represented in Ceylon, the family characters alone are given below.

THE ROLLERS

Family CORACIIDAE

Rollers are medium-sized birds, confined to the Old World and with their headquarters in Africa; they are characterized by brilliant coloration, syndactyle feet, rather big heads and strong beaks. They owe their popular name to a curious habit, developed most strongly in the courting season, of tumbling or 'rolling' in the air somewhat after the manner of a tumbler pigeon. They are mainly insectivorous; inclined to be noisy; and nest in cavities in trees (or in banks, etc.). They lay white eggs, and the young are blind and naked at birth. Their growing feathers retain their sheaths until they are nearly full grown, so that the young look something like miniature porcupines.

Ceylon has two species of rollers, one a common resident (the Indian Roller), the other (Broad-billed Roller) either a very rare but occasionally-breeding visitor or a nearly-extinct resident.

THE INDIAN ROLLER
(often miscalled 'Blue Jay')

Coracias benghalensis indica Linnaeus. Resident

Sinhalese: Dŭnkāwa, Dŭnkāwuluwā, Dumbonā. Tamil: Panan-kādai, Kōttai-kili

Plate 11, facing p. 136 ($\times$ one-quarter)

Between the mynah and the House Crow in size. Sexes alike. The brilliant blue coloration, especially as seen in flight, might suggest a large kingfisher but the beak is not long and heavy as is a kingfisher's. There is no other Ceylon bird for which it can be mistaken.

This is a dry-zone, low-country bird; it is common in coconut or palmyra groves, chenas, and open places in the northern half, the east and south-east of the Island; but is only an occasional straggler to the damp south-western sector. It spends much of its time sitting on posts, telegraph wires, or even on clods and stones; from such vantage-points it flies down to capture its prey, which consists of grasshoppers, beetles, small lizards, or other little animals. It keeps late hours, and may often be seen hawking flying insects—especially termites—until dusk is well advanced. The flight, though really rather fast, seems slow and soft-looking, being performed with rather heavy flaps of the broad, gorgeously-banded wings. When the courting season arrives, the roller indulges in strange aerobatics, tumbling and rolling in the air, and uttering its raucous cries the while. Its notes consist of various croaks, suggestive of a heron; a loud, coarse-sounding chatter *quak quak quak quak*, and a staccato *k'yow . . . k'yow . . .* with an explosive quality as if the bird were clearing its throat. When perched, it frequently oscillates the tail slowly up and down.

The roller nests during the first half of the year, laying its two to four pure white eggs on a pad of rubbish in a hole in a dead tree, or in a rotten palm trunk, usually at some height from the ground. The eggs are nearly spherical, and measure about 35 $\times$ 28 mm.

THE BROAD-BILLED ROLLER

Eurystomus orientalis (Linnaeus). Rare, occasionally-breeding visitor? or
nearly extinct resident?

No Sinhalese name. Wait gives the Tamil name as 'Pulupporukki'

Plate 11, facing p. 136 (× one-quarter)

Smaller than the last species, but larger than a mynah. Sexes alike.
The short, broad, orange beak, and dusky, bluish-green plumage, with
bright blue wings which show a large, round whitish patch on the
primaries in flight, serve to distinguish this bird from all other Ceylonese species.

It is extremely rare in the Island and, until very recently, no specimen
had been recorded since the 1890s; in February 1950, however, a pair
were found about to breed by W. W. A. Phillips near Maha Oya in the
Eastern Province. He had hopes of photographing them when the
young hatched, but before this happened, they were both collected by
the Museums Department. All records of this species have been from the
southern half of the Island. It is a forest-loving bird, very different in its
habits from the Indian Roller as it habitually frequents the tops of tall
trees, either those which are dead, or else have leafless branches at the
top. From such look-outs, it flies out after flying beetles and other
insects. As it sits on its perch, it presents a similar silhouette to that of
the Ashy Swallow-Shrike, though it is, of course, a much bigger bird.
The tail is frequently oscillated up and down, and every now and then
a harsh *chack-chack* or a quicker repeated *chuck-chuck-chuck-chuck* is
uttered. It is generally solitary or in pairs.

In spite of the above-mentioned instance of the bird's preparing to
breed in Ceylon, I incline to the belief that it is an occasional visitor
rather than a resident; in parts of its range, at least, it is known to be
migratory. The breeding season would appear to be February to April.
The nest is made in a cavity in a dead tree—often a deserted woodpecker's hole which the rollers enlarge to suit their needs—at a considerable height from the ground. Three or four eggs are laid; they are
white, and measure about 35 × 29·5 mm.

THE BEE-EATERS

Family MEROPIDAE

Bee-eaters are slenderly-built birds with rather large but graceful heads, rather long, gently-curved and evenly tapering beaks.

Their legs are very short, and their feet syndactyle and small. The colouring is rich, but not gaudy, and the plumage is very sleek; green predominates in most species (all the Ceylon ones). The wings are long and pointed, and the flight is strong and rapid, though, except on migration, not usually very long-sustained. The food consists entirely of insects, which are captured on the wing. In many species, the two middle tail-feathers are produced beyond the others to form narrow streamers. Bee-eaters lay their eggs on bare ground in a chamber at the end of a long tunnel, dug by the birds themselves, in a bank or, if no bank be available, in an earth-mound however slight. They lay pure-white eggs. The young are born blind and naked and their growing feathers retain the sheaths until nearly full grown.

THE CEYLON GREEN BEE-EATER

Merops orientalis ceylonicus Whistler. Race peculiar to Ceylon

Sinhalese: Kurumini-kurullā. Tamil: Kattālan-kuruvi, Panchānkam

Plate 11, facing p. 136 (× one-quarter)

Sparrow-sized, but much longer than a sparrow owing to the long tail. Sexes alike. The blue throat, and small size, distinguish this from the other Ceylonese bee-eaters.

It is a very common bird almost everywhere in the dry-zone low country, but is not normally found in the wet zone; it ascends the eastern slopes of the hills to about 2,000 feet. In the Jaffna Peninsula its distribution is curiously patchy. This lovely little bird lives in pairs, and delights to perch on telegraph wires, tops of thorny bushes, etc., from which it darts out to capture, with an audible snap of its bill, the flies, small beetles, bees and wasps, which form its food; when a capture has been made the bird returns, with a graceful sweep, to its perch and proceeds to batter the insect to death preparatory to swallowing it. This bee-eater likes cultivated country, open spaces in forest, and the like; in many parts of the dry zone, a pair will be found decorating the road-side telegraph wires every hundred yards or so. Its notes are a mellow, rolling trill very frequently uttered; they greatly resemble those of the next species, but are higher pitched. At dusk, large numbers assemble at some favourite bushy tree and, after a good deal of excitement and chirrupping, settle down to roost in company.

The breeding season is from April to August. The nesting burrow is dug into the side of a bank or, quite often, into almost flat ground, and is from two to four feet in length. The three to five pure-white, glossy eggs measure about 20 × 18 mm.

THE BLUE-TAILED BEE-EATER

Merops superciliosus philippinus Linnaeus. Abundant winter visitor

Sinhálese: Kurumini-kurullā, Natthāl-kurullā (Phillips gives Ranillā or Ambeyā). Tamil: Kattālan-kuruvi, Panchānkam

Plate 11, facing p. 136 (× one-quarter)

Size of the Red-vented Bulbul, but longer and slimmer. Sexes alike.

This bird arrives in Ceylon from India in August and September, and quickly spreads all over the Island except areas of heavy forest, leaving again in April and May. It associates in small flocks which commonly perch on leafless twigs at the top of tall trees; from these vantage-points the birds sally out after flying insects, returning again and again to the same perch. The flight is easy and graceful; when hunting it consists of a series of rapid flutters alternating with glides with outspread wings. When travelling the wings are closed between the periods of fluttering. Although a lofty perch is usually chosen, it also settles quite readily on small bushes, or even on clods and stones on the ground. Whether perched or flying, the birds constantly utter their loud and pleasant-sounding *chirrup, chirrup, chirrup*. The food consists of flying insects of many kinds including bees and wasps, and it is partial to dragon-flies, of which I have seen it capture large species of the genus *Anax*; they were snapped up near the surface of sheets of water, carried, with some embarrassment due to their big wings, to a perch, battered to death, and swallowed wings and all. This bee-eater delights in the neighbourhood of rivers and lakes, and frequently bathes by rapidly plunging into the water while on the wing. Like other bee-eaters, it roosts in flocks, often choosing a waterside clump of trees for the purpose; towards evening, parties fly great distances to join these nightly gatherings.

This race of the Blue-tailed Bee-eater nests in many parts of India. It is said to breed in colonies, a number of pairs digging their nesting tunnels in the same bank. It lays four or five pure-white, glossy eggs, which measure about 22·7 × 19 mm.

THE CHESTNUT-HEADED BEE-EATER

Merops leschenaulti leschenaulti Vieillot. Resident

Sinhalese: Kurumini-kurullā. Tamil: Kattālan-kuruvi, Panchānkam

Plate 11, facing p. 136 (×one-quarter)

Size of the Red-vented Bulbul. Sexes alike. The chestnut head and upper back, pale yellow throat, and lack of long streamers to the middle tail-feathers, readily distinguish this from the other Ceylonese bee-eaters.

It is a bird of wide but local distribution in Ceylon, being found in scattered colonies in both the wet and dry zones, and in the drier parts of the hills up to about 4,000 feet. It is more partial to forest than the other bee-eaters, but is by no means confined to it, frequenting openly-wooded country, river banks, etc., impartially. In general behaviour, flight and notes, it is somewhat intermediate between the two preceding species. I have seen it capture dragon-flies and butterflies; among the latter, the gorgeous blue and green swallowtail, *Papilio crino*. Although usually in pairs, it assembles in large flocks for roosting in some favourite site, and out of the breeding season it occurs in scattered flocks. It has been recorded as diving into water, like a kingfisher, for small fish or insects; but probably the bird observed doing this was merely taking a 'plunge bath'.

The breeding season is March–May; the birds dig a burrow, varying in length from $2\frac{1}{2}$ to six feet or more, into an earth bank; the end is enlarged into a spherical chamber in which the three or four pure-white, glossy eggs are laid on the bare earth; they measure about 22 × 19·2 mm.

THE KINGFISHERS

Family ALCEDINIDAE

Like their relatives, the rollers, bee-eaters, hornbills and hoopoes, kingfishers have their three front toes (two in the Three-toed Kingfisher) more or less united (syndactyle). They are large-headed birds with long, straight and powerful beaks, very short legs, and small, weak feet. Most species are notable for their beautiful colouring, in which various shades of glistening blue tend to predominate. They are all carnivorous and many species live mainly on fish, which are captured by plunging, either from a perch or while hovering above water; but others subsist

PLATE 11

1. Indian Crested Swift.   2. Ceylon Green Bee-eater.   3. Chestnut-headed
Bee-eater.   4. Blue-tailed Bee-eater.   5. Broad-billed Roller.   6. Indian Roller

Plate 12

1. Ceylon White-breasted Kingfisher.   2. Three-toed Kingfisher.   3. Stork-billed Kingfisher.   4. Ceylon Blue-eared Kingfisher.   5. Ceylon Common Kingfisher. 6. Black-capped Purple Kingfisher

largely on insects or other small animals. They mostly nest in burrows which they dig into river banks or the like. The eggs are nearly spherical, white and glossy. The young are blind and naked at birth; their developing feathers retain their horny sheaths until nearly fully grown, and then shed them all at once—producing, in a few hours, a most remarkable change from ugly, spiny-looking creatures to gorgeous young kingfishers.

Ceylon has seven species, one of which, the Black-capped Purple Kingfisher, is a rare vagrant, and another, the Blue-eared Kingfisher, is exceedingly rare although probably a resident.

THE INDIAN PIED KINGFISHER

Ceryle rudis leucomelanura Reichenbach. Resident

Sinhalese: Kallapu Pilihuduwā, Gōmera Pilihuduwā.
Tamil: Mīn-kutti

Size of the White-breasted Kingfisher. Sexes alike, except that the female has only the upper one of the black breast-bands, and has it broken in the middle. The speckled black-and-white plumage, combined with the obvious kingfisher-build and distinctive habits, make this bird unmistakable.

It is mainly a bird of river estuaries, but frequents almost any type of water within about ten miles of the coast, provided sufficient small fish are present; it is found also on some of the larger tanks inland, but does not ascend the hills to any height. Apart from its 'half-mourning' coloration, it is a typical kingfisher, living almost exclusively on fish and other small aquatic animals. These it prefers to capture, not, as most kingfishers do, from a fixed perch, but by hovering, with rapidly-fluttering

Male; × one-third

wings, some six to twenty feet above the water which it eagerly cons for small fish. When one comes within range the bird drops vertically upon it, plunging beneath the surface, to emerge with its quarry a moment later. It flies to a near-by perch, batters the luckless fish to death, and swallows it head first. It lives in pairs which, while proceeding methodically up the water and hovering every few yards to look for fish, call to each other continually in a rather mellow and pleasing jingling chatter. When fed, they sit together on the bank, or on an overhanging branch, and preen themselves.

The breeding season is from March to May. The nesting burrow is dug into the bank of a river, or into a saltern-bund, etc., and, this kingfisher being more sociable with its kind than others of the family, several nest-holes may often be seen, in suitable sites, within short distances of each other. The three or four pure-white, glossy eggs measure about 29·5 × 24 mm.

THE CEYLON COMMON KINGFISHER

Alcedo atthis taprobana Kleinschmidt. Resident

Sinhalese: Măl Pilihuduwā. Tamil: Mīn-kutti

Plate 12, facing p. 137 (× one-third)

Slightly larger than a sparrow. Sexes alike. The brilliant blue upperparts and chestnut underparts distinguish it from all other Ceylon kingfishers except the very rare Blue-eared Kingfisher, which has much deeper blue upperparts, deeper chestnut underparts, and deep blue— not chestnut—ear-coverts.

This lovely little bird is one of the most pleasing adjuncts of every river, canal, reservoir or lake in the Island. It is abundant everywhere in the low country, and ascends the hills to 6,000 feet at least, though it is scarce at the higher elevations. Its normal method of fishing is to sit quietly on some stick, stone, or branch, giving a good view of the water beneath, and from this point of vantage to plunge after its prey; but occasionally it will hover six to twelve feet above the surface and plunge vertically, after the manner of the Pied Kingfisher. It is a most expert fisher, seldom missing its stroke. I have seen one catch a fish at least as long as itself, batter it to death and swallow it with no little difficulty —the hinder end dangling outside the beak for some time, presumably until the head was digested. While watching for prey it frequently bobs the head and jerks the tail, at the same time uttering *chik*. This kingfisher lives in pairs, but is usually seen solitary though its mate is never very far away. Each pair occupy a well-defined territory which they jealously guard from others of their species. Within this beat they work steadily, flying from one well-known perch to the next with rapid steady flight, usually only a foot or two above the water. In flight the musical, piping call-note *peep-peep* is frequently uttered. In courtship, a pair chase each other about, giving forth excited *peeps* and chittering squeaks; and indulge in quaint attitudinizings while sitting together on a twig or stone.

The usual breeding season is in the first half of the year. The nesting burrow is dug in a bank, often beside a stream or the side of a well, but not seldom at some distance from water. The only 'nest' consists of accumulated fish-bones disgorged by the birds and, as incubation proceeds, this mass becomes very insanitary, commonly crawling with fly-maggots before the young are ready to leave. The three to five eggs are glossy white and measure about $20 \cdot 5 \times 17 \cdot 5$ mm.

THE CEYLON BLUE-EARED KINGFISHER

Alcedo meninting phillipsi Stuart Baker. Very rare resident? or occasional visitor?

Sinhalese: Măl Pilihuduwā. Tamil: Mīn-kutti

Plate 12, facing p. 137 (×one-third)

Same size and general appearance as the Ceylon Common Kingfisher, from which it may be distinguished by its rich, royal blue upperparts and deeper chestnut underparts, and by its blue, not chestnut, ear-coverts. Sexes alike.

This gorgeous kingfisher is exceedingly rare, only a few specimens having been recorded from foot-hills north and east of the mountains; none appears to have been seen in the Island for over half a century[1] and, as there is no record of its nesting in Ceylon, it seems probable that it is an occasional visitor rather than a resident. It is a forest kingfisher, frequenting jungle streams, and in the deep shade of its haunts it is likely to be mistaken for the Common Kingfisher. Apart from its shy, retiring nature it behaves very much like its familiar relative. Outside our Island it occurs sparingly in Travancore and other parts of India, but seems to be rare and elusive everywhere.

Its nesting habits and eggs are very similar to those of the Common Kingfisher.

[1] While proof-correcting was in progress, news of a satisfactory sight-record of this kingfisher came to hand in *Ceylon Bird Club Notes*. C. E. Norris reports that on 9 May 1954, in a foot-hills district of Uva, he watched one through binoculars at ten yards range. He noted that it appeared heavier than the Ceylon Common Kingfisher, with much darker plumage, the breast noticeably chestnut. Its call was similar to that of the Common Kingfisher.

THE THREE-TOED KINGFISHER

Ceyx erithacus (Linnaeus). Resident

Sinhalese: Răng Pilihuduwā. Tamil: Sinna Mīn-kutti

Plate 12, facing p. 137 (×one-third)

Smaller than a sparrow. Sexes alike. The brilliant purple-shot orange-and-black plumage, vermilion beak, tiny size, and forest-loving habits, distinguish this lovely little bird from other kingfishers.

It is mainly a low-country, dry-zone species, but enters the wet zone in border areas, and ascends the hills in the north and east of its range to about 2,000 feet. It is not common anywhere, and is shy and retiring, frequenting gloomy recesses in the forested banks of rivers and small streams. In such places it sits patiently waiting for prey, every now and then bobbing its head and jerking its tail in the same manner as the Common Kingfisher. It will fly swiftly along a watercourse, skilfully dodging obstacles, and frequently uttering its shrill piping note which is very like that of the Ceylon Common Kingfisher but less loud; as it darts across a sunlit patch its plumage gleams like a gem. Besides small fishes it eats freshwater crabs and frogs, both sometimes of astonishing size for such a small bird.

The breeding season is about March and April. The nesting burrow is dug in the bank of a small jungle stream or dry watercourse, etc., and is similar to that of other kingfishers but naturally smaller, its diameter being about two inches and its length from eight inches to two feet. The inner chamber measures about five inches in diameter. The two or three eggs are pure white, and measure about 19·5×16·5 mm.

THE STORK-BILLED KINGFISHER

Pelargopsis capensis gurial (Pearson). Resident

Sinhalese: Watturā-ānduwā, Māhā Pilihuduwā. Tamil: Mīn-kutti, Kukuluppan

Plate 12, facing p. 137 (×one-third)

Between the mynah and the House Crow in size. Sexes alike. The great size, huge beak and distinctive colouring of this handsome kingfisher make it easily recognizable.

It is found throughout the low country, but seems to prefer the dry zone, and ascends the hills to about 2,000 feet. Its favourite haunts are forested banks of rivers and streams, borders of tanks, and mangrove-lined creeks near the coast. It lives in pairs, but usually hunts singly, keeping in touch with its mate by uttering a loud, laughing cry whenever it takes to wing. The flight is strong, straight and steady. The food consists mainly of fish, but frogs, crabs and other small animals are also eaten. When hunting, the bird generally sits on a branch of a shady tree overhanging water and plunges vertically upon its prey which is carried back to the perch, killed by a few vigorous whacks against it, and swallowed, head first. This is rather a sluggish kingfisher, more often heard than seen.

The breeding season appears to be early in the year, but there are very few definite records of the breeding of this bird in Ceylon. According to Legge and Wait, the nest-hole is dug in well-concealed sites on the banks of rivers or tank-bunds. I once watched a pair digging a nest-hole in the bole of a big kumbuk tree in jungle on the bank of the Kala Oya, in January. The tree had a large cavity, full of rotten wood, in its trunk, about three or four feet from the ground, and the kingfishers were excavating this. They took turns to fly at the hole from perches about four yards away, grab a bit of rotten stuff, and drop it on the way back to the perch; now and then one would cling to the tree for a few seconds while it probed into the hole as far as it could reach, no doubt loosening more rubbish. They worked assiduously for the half-hour that I watched them, each bird making one journey a minute. Unfortunately, I was unable to follow up this observation. The two to five glossy, white eggs measure about 37 × 31·5 mm.

THE CEYLON WHITE-BREASTED KINGFISHER

Halcyon smyrnensis fusca (Boddaert). Resident

Sinhalese: Pilihuduwā. Tamil: Mīn-kutti

Plate 12, facing p. 137 (× one-third)

Size of the Common Mynah. Sexes alike. This common and familiar bird cannot be mistaken for any other Ceylon species.

It is found all over the Island up to at least 5,000 feet, wherever the country suits its habits, and it is even a common—and very attractive—feature of Colombo gardens and parks. While it *can* catch fish, and occasionally keeps its beak in practice at the piscatorial art, it prefers to capture grasshoppers, frogs, small lizards, centipedes and earthworms. Its mode of hunting is to sit on some point of vantage commanding an open space, preferably grassy, and from thence to pounce upon its prey. While so waiting for something to turn up, it frequently utters a short *chik*; but its call-note, always uttered when it takes to flight, is a loud rattling scream, somewhat like the flight-note of the Red-backed Woodpecker but less high-pitched. In the courting season it becomes active and vociferous, flying around, and perching on the tops of high trees from which it sings to its beloved in a loud whinnying cry, which is apt to become rather monotonous to human ears. When the pair meet they indulge in curious antics, jerking their heads and spreading their wings butterfly-wise, to the accompaniment of much whinnying. When so displaying, or in flight, a white patch at the base of the primaries enhances the bird's beauty. Except in the breeding season it is usually solitary, each bird frequenting its own territory where it may be found every day.

The breeding season extends from December to June, but March and April are the favourite months. Normally the nesting burrow is dug in almost any bank, whether near water or not; its entrance is about $2\frac{1}{2}$ inches high by about two inches wide, and the length of the tunnel may be anything from $1\frac{1}{2}$ to five feet or more; but two or three feet is usual. This kingfisher is, however, more adaptable than most in choice of sites for its nest; several instances are on record of its selecting a hole or cavity in a tree, and on three or four occasions I have watched pairs digging their hole in walls of human habitations—mud-huts or 'cabook' (laterite stone) buildings—but of course without success; a pair, kept in an aviary in Colombo, nested and successfully reared a young one in a wooden nest-box intended for some other birds. Three to five eggs are laid; they are glossy white, but soon become stained and dull. They measure about 29 × 25 mm.

THE BLACK-CAPPED PURPLE KINGFISHER

Halcyon pileata (Boddaert). Very rare visitor

Sinhalese: Pilihuduwā. Tamil: Mīn-kutti

Plate 12, facing p. 137 (× one-third)

A trifle larger than the White-breasted Kingfisher, which it resembles in shape and proportions. Sexes alike. Its black head, white collar, purple upperparts and reddish-buff underparts distinguish it from the preceding species.

This is a very rare visitor to Ceylon, only a half-dozen or so of specimens having been recorded from the Island. It is occasionally found in South India, both on the Malabar and Carnatic coasts, but its headquarters are in Burma, Malaya, and eastwards to China. It is mainly a coastal bird, frequenting mangrove-lined estuaries and the lower reaches of jungle rivers, creeks and lagoons; and it is said to feed principally on crabs. Unlike most kingfishers, it is a great wanderer and visits many parts of the oriental region. The nest (not likely to be found in Ceylon) is the usual burrow dug in a bank, and the eggs, of the typical, nearly spherical, kingfisher type, measure about 29·2 × 25·5 mm.

THE HORNBILLS
Family BUCEROTIDAE

These extraordinary birds (which are often confused with the quite distinct toucans of South America) have several distinctive features. Of these, the enormous bill, which in many—particularly the larger species—is surmounted by a huge protuberance, the 'casque', is the most conspicuous. The plumage is soft and rather scanty, and the under wing-coverts are very ill-developed, leaving the bases of the flight feathers exposed beneath. This results in wind rushing through the bases of the quills in flight, producing a loud droning sound; in the larger species this noise is audible for great distances. Hornbills have long, stiff eyelashes; their wings are short and rounded, but broad, and their tails rather long and graduated; like kingfishers, rollers, and bee-eaters, their three front toes are more or less united at the base, producing a broad sole to the foot; the legs are short in all arboreal forms (which include all the Ceylonese and Indian representatives of the family). They are omnivorous, but feed mainly on fruit. The gait of all, except some ground-dwelling African forms, consists of ungainly hops. Most species are very noisy.

It is in their nesting arrangements, however, that hornbills are most remarkable. They nest in holes in big trees; the female enters the cavity and then walls up the entrance with a paste composed of her own droppings, leaving only a narrow, vertical slit sufficient for her beak to pass through; the paste sets into a hard cement, imprisoning the female during the period of incubation and for some time after the eggs have hatched. Throughout this incarceration the male brings food to his mate, clinging to the bark of the tree while he passes it to her through the slit. When the young have begun to fledge, the female pecks her way out, the entrance is again walled up as before, and thenceforward both parents feed the young through the slit until their feathers have grown; then they are released—and are able to fly at once, without any practice. This, with variations in different species, appears to be the typical practice in hornbill-nidification.

THE MALABAR PIED HORNBILL

Anthracoceros coronatus coronatus (Boddaert). Resident

Sinhalese: Poruwā Kandettā. Tamil: Irattai-chondu-kuruvi

Size of a hawk-eagle. Sexes alike, except that the female has the naked skin surrounding the eye white, and no black patch on the posterior end of the casque. The enormous, casqued beak, size, black-and-white plumage, and distinctive cries make this bird quite unmistakable.

× one-tenth

It is found in isolated colonies throughout the low-country dry zone wherever there are extensive forests, especially favouring the belts of tall trees that line river banks. It is a sociable bird usually found in flocks of four to six or more, whose members keep in touch by frequent loud, clanging and yelping cries, like those made by a pack of hounds but less musical. It is fond of perching in dead trees, about whose branches it hops in a ponderous and ungainly manner. It feeds mainly on wild fruit, such as banyan or nuga figs and palu berries, but also eats any small animals it can catch. The flight is undulating, performed with the wings alternately beating the air and outstretched, motionless, and the huge head extended to the length of the neck. In spite of its apparent clumsiness, the beak is not heavy as the interior of the casque is merely thin, bony cells filled with air. In Assam, where this bird also occurs, it has been observed on the ground, feeding on termites emerging from their mounds for their nuptial flight; but this habit does not appear to have been noticed in Ceylon.

There is very little on record concerning the breeding of this hornbill in Ceylon as the nest is seldom found, but the main outlines of it are as set forth in the account above of the family characteristics. The breeding season is from April to July; two or three eggs are laid; they are white, soon becoming discoloured; average size about 51 × 38 mm.

THE CEYLON GREY HORNBILL

Tockus gingalensis (Shaw). Species peculiar to Ceylon; a closely related species, the Malabar Grey Hornbill, *Tockus griseus*, is found in South India

Sinhalese: Kandettā. Tamil: Irattai-chondu-kuruvi

Size about that of the Black Crow, but with much longer bill and tail. Sexes alike, except that the bill of the female is dull black with a long cream patch on the side of the upper mandible.

Male; × one-sixth

This hornbill is common in all low-country forested areas, both wet and dry zones, and it occasionally ascends the hills to 4,000 feet though it is decidedly rare at such elevations. It lives in pairs or small flocks except when some wild fig tree is in fruit, when large numbers will assemble to feed on the fruit. In spite of its size it is often very inconspicuous as it has a habit of sitting quietly among foliage, in a very upright position, turning its head stealthily in all directions while scanning the environment for food. Anon, it startles the stillness with its loud *kāā . . . kāā . . . kā kā kā kā . . .* or sometimes *kuk . . . kuk-kuk-kuk ko ko kokoko*, which is answered by its mate in similar tones. Its favourite abode is the medium levels of tall forest, where hanging creepers and lianas supply convenient perches as well as concealment. It feeds largely on wild fruits, such as the small figs of banyan and nuga, wild nutmegs, mā-dun, etc., but it also eats any small animal it can catch—lizards, tree-frogs, and insects such as mantises. All items of food are nipped in the tips of the beak, tossed into the air, caught and swallowed whole. The flight is undulating, with the wings flapped several times and then held extended.

The breeding season is from April to August. The nest is a cavity in the bole of a large tree, usually at some height from the ground; the entrance-hole is sometimes astonishingly small for the size of the bird but, if not, its diameter is reduced by a cement composed of the bird's own droppings, until only a narrow, vertical slit is left. Within this safe, if cramped, nursery the female lays and incubates her eggs, and at the same time moults her wing- and tail-feathers; her husband visits her several times a day and feeds her through the slit with berries which he disgorges one by one from his crop. When her wings and tail are grown she pecks away the rampart of 'cement', and assists him with the feeding of the young. The eggs number one to three, are white, soon getting dirty, and measure about $41 \cdot 5 \times 33$ mm.

THE HOOPOES
Family UPUPIDAE

These are beautiful birds of rufous and boldly-banded black and white plumage, with a long, erectile, 'fore-and-aft' crest which forms an elegant crown when erect. The beak is long, slender, and gently curved, used for probing in soft soil for insects and grubs. The legs are very short and the outer front toe is united to the middle one at the base; the hind claw is long and nearly straight. The gait is a tripping walk. The wings are broad and rounded. Hoopoes nest in cavities in trees or buildings; lay whitish, unmarked eggs; and the young, though hatched blind and helpless, are clothed with down.

Ceylon has one species of hoopoe.

THE CEYLON HOOPOE

Upupa epops ceylonensis Reichenbach. Resident; this race is also found in India, south of Bombay

Sinhalese: Poruwā-kurullā. Tamil: Chāval-kuruvi

Larger than the Common Mynah. Sexes alike. There can be no mistaking this bird for any other Ceylonese species; its form, combined with the pinkish-cinnamon head, breast and upper back, and boldly-banded, black and white wings and tail, are quite distinctive.

It is rather sparsely distributed throughout the dry-zone low country, and ascends the hills on the dry, Uva side to 4,000 feet. At higher elevations it occurs as a casual straggler, and in the wet zone it is very occasionally seen as far south as Colombo, but its headquarters in the island are the Northern Province and the dry country about Hambantota. It moves about a good deal, and I suspect that some migration takes place between Ceylon and India. The hoopoe is a bird of sparsely-wooded country; it avoids both dense forest and quite treeless areas. It is not shy of man, freely resorting to town suburbs or villages, but it may also be found in places far from human habitation. It lives in pairs, which appear to consort for life. Much of its time is spent on the ground as most, if not all, of its food consists of ground-insects, such as beetles and their grubs. For these it

× one-sixth

searches diligently, tripping hither and thither on its short legs and probing every dry cow-pat, turning over leaves, etc. While hunting, the crest is depressed and sticks out behind the head, suggesting, in opposition to the long beak, a pick-axe; when the bird's suspicions are aroused, however, and always on alighting from flight, the crest is erected into the shape of a cock's comb. The flight is performed with powerful but curiously irregular beats of the broadly-rounded wings which are nearly closed after every few strokes; the bird flies in a wavering manner as if uncertain where it wants to go. The hoopoe's note is a soft *hawpawp* . . . *hawpawpawp* which it repeats monotonously, especially in the courting season, usually from the branch of a tree; it has also a feeble conversational note like *crè*, uttered by the male when courting and by both sexes when prospecting for a nesting site.

The hoopoe breeds during the north-east monsoon, and sometimes again in June and July. It makes its untidy nest of miscellaneous rubbish (or of nothing) in some cavity, either in a tree, bank, or building; the darker the hole the better. The female alone incubates; she sits very tight, being fed by her husband as is done by the hornbills, and develops a very unsavoury odour, apparently as the result of a secretion from the oil-gland, during the incubation period. The four to seven eggs are bluish or greenish-white, soon becoming stained; they measure about 24·6 × 17 mm.

SWIFTS AND HUMMING-BIRDS

Order APODIFORMES

This order includes two sub-orders, the *Apodes* or swifts, and the *Trochili* or humming-birds. The latter are confined to North and South America and their associated islands, and do not concern us here. The *Apodes* comprises two families, both represented in Ceylon: *Apodidae* with five Ceylonese species, and *Hemiprocnidae* with only one—the Indian Crested Swift, or Tree Swift.

The main features of these two families are given together below.

THE SWIFTS AND TREE SWIFTS

Families APODIDAE and HEMIPROCNIDAE

Swifts are often confused with swallows but are quite unrelated to them and their resemblance is only in superficial details, brought about, no doubt, by a common manner of life. They are aerial birds, very highly specialized for life on the wing; past masters in the arts of sail-planing and gliding, and they are amongst the speediest of birds. The wings are very long and narrow, the length being attained by the great elongation of that portion of the wing that corresponds to the human hand—the 'upper-arm' and 'forearm' being short. In consequence of this structure, the primaries in swifts are very long but the secondaries (attached to the forearm) are short and few in number. The beak is very short but the gape is very wide, enabling these birds to capture the small, flying insects which form their only food. The legs are very short, and in most species all four toes are either directed forward or else the hind toe can be directed either backward or forward; the claws are strong and sharp, enabling the birds to cling to the vertical surfaces on which they roost—no true swift ever perches on twigs or the like, though the Tree Swifts do so. The lores in swifts are modified, presumably to protect the eyes from the rush of air as they speed through it; immediately in front of the eyes they form rounded hollows, usually lined with black, velvety down. This structure would repay investigation.

Swifts use their saliva, which is copious and glutinous, to a large extent in nest building, gluing together the nesting materials with it; in the breeding season the salivary glands become greatly enlarged. Their eggs are white, and generally two in number.

THE CEYLON WHITE-BELLIED SWIFT
(Alpine Swift of many authors)

Apus melba bakeri Hartert. Resident

Sinhalese: Wéhi-lihiniyā. No Tamil name recorded

A very large swift, with exceptionally long, narrow wings. Sexes alike. From all other Ceylon swifts, it may be distinguished by its size—twice that of the Ceylon White-rumped Swift, and comparable only with the Brown-throated Spinetail—its greyish-brown coloration, and white underparts with a brown band across the breast.

× one-fifth

This fine swift inhabits the mountains and their foot-hills, but is only truly resident where great rock cliffs afford it suitable roosting and nesting places; elsewhere it may appear sporadically, from time to time, as its tremendous powers of flight enable it to visit any part of the Island in its hunting journeys. It associates in large flocks, which swoop and veer through the sky with great speed and grace, their wings producing a loud swishing sound. Its note is a shrill, rather strident twitter, very

149

like that of the little Palm Swift, but much louder; this is commonly uttered towards nightfall, when the swifts congregate about their roosting-place in the cracks and crevices of some great rock precipice. Like other swifts, they have a habit, before going to roost, of flocking into a large spherical formation, which careers up into the sky, its members screaming and twittering. This species feeds entirely on flying insects; one individual which I dissected contained beetles, moths, and a number of pentatomid bugs ('stink-bugs') of several species.

Owing to the inaccessible nature of its nesting places, there is very little authentic information about the breeding of this swift in Ceylon, but the breeding season appears to be in the first half of the year. Although the nest has not, to my knowledge, actually been taken in the Island, there is no doubt, from the behaviour of the birds, that they breed in many of the vast rock precipices that abound in the Central Province, Uva and Sabaragamuwa. The nest, on the analogy of that of other races of this swift, is a shallow cup composed of straws, feathers and other materials, collected by the birds on the wing and stuck together with their own saliva; it is affixed to the wall or a ledge of a crevice in the rock, sometimes a very narrow one, only three or four inches wide. The birds roost in the same crevices all the year round, retiring very late in the evening when dusk is well advanced, and it is amazing to see the way they will descend from the sky and, with no apparent slackening of speed, shoot up into a narrow, vertical crack, in gloom that only just permits one to see them. The eggs probably number two or three; they are white, elongated ovals measuring about $30 \cdot 7 \times 19 \cdot 3$ mm.

THE CEYLON WHITE-RUMPED SWIFT, or CEYLON HOUSE SWIFT

Apus affinis singalensis Madarasz. Race peculiar to Ceylon

Sinhalese: Wéhi-lihiniyā. No Tamil name recorded

Size of the Eastern Swallow. Sexes alike. A slim, black swift, with conspicuous white rump-patch which distinguishes it from all other Ceylonese swifts and swallows.

This swift is widespread in Ceylon, being commonest in the foot-hills, or in the neighbourhood of big rock-masses in the low country; but it may be seen, occasionally, almost anywhere in the Island. It usually associates in large scattered flocks which spend their time, often in company with other species of swifts or swallows, speeding through the air in search of the small, flying insects which form their food. The height at which they fly seems to depend largely on the weather (probably it is the effect of the weather on the flying insects rather than directly on the birds themselves that determines this); in settled, fine weather they will often hawk their prey at a great height, but when rain threatens they will hunt within a few feet of the ground. The flight is swift and graceful, a few rapid strokes of the wings followed by a long glide with the wings held in the shape of a bow. The note is a shrill, twittering scream, uttered very freely at the roosting and nesting places but only seldom away from them.

× one-quarter

The breeding season is difficult to determine, as the birds frequent their nesting places all the year round—using the nests for roosting in, as well as for incubation. They nest in large or small colonies, building in rock caves, under bridges and culverts, or under the eaves, veranda roofs, etc., of buildings. The great rock of Sigiriya is a well-known nesting-site. The nests, composed of grass, straws and feathers glued together with the birds' saliva, are more or less large, cup-shaped structures stuck, often in contiguous masses, to the roof of a cave, underside of a bridge or the like. The eggs, like those of most swifts, are long ellipses with hardly any indication of the larger end; they number two to four, are pure white, and measure about 23·5 × 15 mm.

THE PALM SWIFT

Cypsiurus parvus batassiensis (Griffith). Resident

Sinhalese: Wéhi-lihiniyā. Tamil: Ulavāra-kuruvi

Not bulkier than the Purple-rumped Sunbird, but with much longer wings and tail. Sexes alike. A tiny, frail-looking swift which can be distinguished from the Edible-nest Swift—the only bird with which it is likely to be confused—by its narrower wings and comparatively long, deeply-forked tail (the forked character of the tail, however, is only noticeable when the bird momentarily spreads it).

This little swift may be seen almost anywhere in the Island below about 3,000 feet, but is only common where there are fan-palms, such as palmyras or talipots; in the neigh-bourhood of these it is always to be found. It is very gregarious and in palmyra palm country, such as the Jaffna Peninsula, it forms one of the most familiar features of the landscape, being, I think without fear of contradiction, the commonest bird in that district. It spends most of its time flitting about, at no great height, in its search for the small, flying insects on which it feeds. Constantly it utters its shrill,

× one-quarter

three-note twitter *tittyree*, especially while playing with its friends near the nesting colonies. For a swift, the flight is rather slow and fluttering, but it sails a good deal with wings in the shape of a bow—hence the name, sometimes applied to it, of 'Bow-and-arrow Bird'.

Breeding appears to go on over much of the year. The nest is a little untidy cup or pocket of feathers and cotton, fastened together, and to the underside of a fan-palm leaf, by means of agglutinated saliva. The leaves selected for nest-building are those that hang down, past their prime. Occasionally the fronds of the areca, or betel-nut, palm are used, but only if no fan-palm is available. The two or three white eggs measure about 18·2 × 11·8 mm.

THE BROWN-THROATED SPINETAIL SWIFT

Chaetura gigantea indica Hume. Resident

Sinhalese: Wéhi-lihiniyā. No Tamil name recorded

Larger and stouter in body than the White-bellied Swift, but with slightly shorter and broader wings. Sexes alike. From the White-bellied

Swift—the only Ceylonese species with which it might be confused—it may be distinguished on the wing by the following features: (*a*) the stout, fusiform body; (*b*) dark coloration of body and wings, contrasting with the white under tail-coverts and flank-stripes; (*c*) pointed, wedge-shaped tail; (*d*) shorter, broader wings, which are commonly held less bow-shaped than those of the White-bellied Swift.

× two-ninths

This magnificent swift is really a montane species in Ceylon though it is liable to turn up almost anywhere in the Island, its enormous powers of flight enabling it to traverse great distances in a very short time. Though sometimes solitary, it usually lives in large, very scattered flocks which move about a great deal, frequenting a district for a month or so and then disappearing, perhaps for long periods. While hawking, the Spinetail sails lazily about with steady wings stretched rather straight out from the body; when the bird is directly approaching, or receding, the wings show a very slight downward tilt and dorsal concavity; the tail is generally closed. When travelling at speed, the wings are more sloped back, look narrower, and are rapidly fluttered after the manner of other swifts; the tail is often half opened, and is fully expanded when the bird banks in a quick turn—showing the projecting, spiny shafts of the feathers. Flying past, within twenty-five yards or so, a vibrant swish is heard. A flock which I watched on several occasions in upper Maskeliya in August showed a marked preference for hawking over forest, although at times they flew over tea fields. One was seen to scratch its head while in flight—doing a brief tumble in the process—and, after recovering itself, clapped its wings together over the back with a click. Courtship appeared to be in progress, as numerous parties, from pairs to seven or eight birds, were seen chasing each other, mounting into the sky and swooping down in close formation. Three passed within twenty-five yards, uttering sharp squeaks *eek eek . . . eek eek eek*. In Malabar, I watched a small flock of this species bathing in a quietly-flowing reach of a river; they flew up and down it, just before dusk, swooping down to splash momentarily into the water.

While the Spinetail has not definitely been recorded as breeding in Ceylon, I have little doubt that the birds observed by me in upper Maskeliya in August and September were either already breeding or were preparing to do so, as their behaviour closely resembled that of courting swifts of other species. In Travancore, they have been found breeding in big, hollow forest trees; the birds enter by a hole near the top of the trunk and deposit their eggs, without any nest, in a hollow in the rubbish at the bottom of the cavity—often at, or even below, ground level. The eggs soon become very dirty and if a hole be cut into the cavity a peculiar smell emanates if breeding is going on. The three to five eggs are described as broad ovals, with stout, strong shells, white when new-laid, and measuring about $30 \cdot 7 \times 22 \cdot 2$ mm.

THE INDIAN EDIBLE-NEST SWIFT

Collocalia fuciphaga unicolor (Jerdon). Resident

Sinhalese: Wéhi-lihiniyā. Veddah: Kudukaraya (Spittel). No Tamil
name recorded

Larger and heavier-built than the Palm Swift; smaller than the Ceylon White-rumped Swift, from which its comparatively short wings and mouse-brown coloration easily distinguish it. Sexes alike.

Although it may be seen in any part of the Island, except perhaps the Jaffna Peninsula, it is really a hill species and throughout the mountain zone it is one of the commonest birds; it is numerous, also, in the low country, wherever there are rocky hills to accommodate it with suitable nesting caves. For a swift, its flight is not very speedy but it is performed in the usual swift-fashion—a few rapid strokes of the wings, to gain momentum, followed by a long glide in which the bird veers from side to side with the wings somewhat down-curved. While hunting for food, which consists of small flying insects, it is usually silent; but in and about its nesting caves it utters a short chirp such as may be imitated by sharply striking a small quill point against three or four teeth of a comb; inside the nesting caves a clicking sound is produced.

The main interest of this bird lies in its nesting habits. The breeding season is difficult to determine accurately because the birds frequent the same caves for roosting as they nest in; but the main season appears

× one-third

to be in the first half of the year, with a second brood in August–September. Breeding takes place in a deep rock cave, railway tunnel, culvert or the like, and the darkest part is always chosen for the nest. This is a shallow cup or basin affixed, like a bracket, to the sloping roof; it is very stout at the base where it adjoins the rock, but tapers to an edge at the free margin. It is composed of the bird's own saliva, more or less mixed with moss and other fibrous materials. The saliva is applied in glutinous threads, sticking to the rock surface, and it dries into a firm, horny-white substance resembling gelatine or isinglass. Almost pure saliva forms the foundation of the nest, but the cup portion is frequently composed of moss with only sufficient saliva to consolidate it. In search of moss the birds will descend into forest—which, ordinarily, they never do—and snatch shreds of it from the branches and hanging lianas. This swift nests in large colonies and, in a well-populated cave, competition for nesting sites is keen, every suitable part of the roof being crowded with them. Two white, long-elliptical eggs are laid, which measure about 21·5 × 13·5 mm. When half-grown, the young birds seem to prefer clinging to the outside of the nest. They are much bothered by parasites—wingless, blood-sucking flies, of revolting appearance—which infest the nests.

THE INDIAN CRESTED SWIFT, or TREE SWIFT

Hemiprocne longipennis coronata (Tickell). Resident

Sinhalese: Wéhi-lihiniyā. No Tamil name recorded

Plate 11, facing p. 136 (male; × one-quarter)

Larger than the Eastern Swallow, and with a long, deeply-forked tail and long, narrow wings. The female differs from the male only in having the head markings ashy-white (throat), and ashy-black (ear-coverts). The young are beautifully mottled with black, brown and white on a grey ground. The crest arises from the forehead, and is only erected when the bird is perched. The forked character of the tail is seen when the bird momentarily expands it in flight; generally it is closed, and looks like the tail of a parakeet. From all other Ceylon swifts this bird may be distinguished by its pale blue-grey back, contrasting with the dark greenish-black wings and tail, and by its habit of perching on twigs or branches (no other Ceylon swift does this).

This beautiful swift—the most graceful of all our swifts—is a common bird throughout the low country except the most northern districts, and ascends the hills, as a breeding resident, to at least 3,000 feet —though it frequently goes much higher in its hunting flights. Though it may be seen almost anywhere, it prefers well-wooded but open country, particularly the grassy hill-sides of the Central Province, Uva and Sabaragamuwa. Compared with the White-bellied and Spinetail Swifts its flight is not particularly speedy, but gives an impression of effortless grace, which is partly due to the fact that it seems able to sail almost indefinitely with steady wings, which are held sloping slightly downward. Both in flight and perched, it frequently utters its loud call *keek-ko . . . keek-ko*. It perches readily on trees, generally choosing a more or less bare twig near the top; dead trees are much favoured. While perched, its long wings cross each other at a wide angle producing, with the long tail, a 'broad-arrow' effect, and the crest is raised and lowered, cockatoo-wise. It drinks frequently, gliding down to a sheet of water, sipping from the surface, and rising again on its course. Like all swifts, its food consists of small, flying insects.

The breeding season is from March to May, with an occasional late, or second, brood in July–August, April being the favourite month. The nest is built on the side of a slender branch, generally one bare of leaves. It is a tiny, shallow basin composed of bark-flakes, lichen, etc., glued together with saliva, and is just large enough to contain one egg; seen from below, it looks like a mere knot on the branch. The parents take it in turns to incubate, practically concealing the nest by their fluffed-out belly feathers. When fledging, the young bird, with its mottled plumage, is almost indistinguishable from the knots and lichens of its branch. The egg measures about 24 × 17 mm.

NIGHTJARS AND FROGMOUTHS

Order CAPRIMULGIFORMES

THIS order, so far as Ceylon is concerned, comprises two families of nocturnal birds, the *Caprimulgidae* or nightjars, and the *Podargidae* or frogmouths. The characters of each of these is given in the family descriptions.

Ceylon has three nightjars and one frogmouth. All are resident in the Island and the same, or very closely related, races of each are found on the Indian mainland.

THE NIGHTJARS

Family CAPRIMULGIDAE

Nightjars are nocturnal, insectivorous birds, with owl-like, soft, and beautifully mottled plumage. They have long wings and tails, and silent, wheeling and gliding flight. All their food, which consists of flying insects such as moths and beetles, is captured on the wing. The beak is small and weak but the mouth is enormously wide, with gape extending to below the middle of the eyes; to increase the effectiveness of this wide mouth in engulfing insects, the sides of the upper mandible, below the lores, are fringed with long, stiff bristles projecting outwards and downwards. The nostrils (in Ceylonese species, at least) are upstanding and tubular. The eyes are large. The legs are short and weak, more or less clothed with feathers down to the feet. The hind toe and the two lateral toes are short, but the middle toe is long and, in all Ceylon species, its claw has a comb-like flange on the inner side similar to that found in herons, some owls, and a few other birds. Probably owing to this structure of the foot, nightjars perch along a branch, not across it in the usual manner. They have peculiar notes, which give excellent aid in identification of each species. They usually roost, and always nest, on the ground, where their colour schemes give perfect camouflage. No nest is made, the mottled eggs being laid on the soil. The young are clothed with long down, but are helpless for some time after hatching.

THE SOUTHERN COMMON INDIAN NIGHTJAR

Caprimulgus asiaticus eidos Peters. Resident

Sinhalese: Bin-bassā. Tamil: Pāthekai-kuruvi, Kuruttu-pakkul

Plate 13, facing p. 168 (×one-quarter)

Our smallest nightjar; about the size of the Red-vented Bulbul, but with much longer wings and tail. Sexes alike. The rather buff or sandy coloration of this bird, as well as its smaller size, distinguish it from the other Ceylonese nightjars.

It is widely distributed in the low country, but avoids the wetter districts, and ascends the drier, Uva side of the hills to about 4,000 feet. It likes open or thinly-wooded country, scrub-land, and sand-dunes. During the day it lies up, usually under the shade of a small bush but often quite in the open, trusting for safety, while it sleeps, to the concealing effect of its marvellously mottled and ochre-striped plumage among the gravel, twiglets, dry grass-blades, etc., of its resting-place. This concealment is so effective that the bird is seldom noticed until one nearly treads upon it, when it springs into the air and flies rapidly to a fresh roost a few yards away. About dusk, it flies to some bare patch of ground such as the middle of a road, or a bare branch, and commences to utter its extraordinary song *tuk tuk tuk tuk tuk tuk rrrk*, which sounds like the scudding of a stone flung along the ice on a frozen pond, or like the tapping of a glass marble dropped from a height of a yard or so on to a cement floor; hence its popular names of 'Ice Bird' and 'Marble-dropper'. In the breeding season it will keep up this song, monotonously repeated, for long periods, especially at dusk and again before dawn. It has also another note *bub-bub-bub-bubbubbub*, etc., suggestive of the sounds produced by blowing bubbles through a tube into water. Its serenade finished, it takes wing after flying beetles and moths, flapping its long, shapely wings in a curiously stiff manner but quite noiselessly, and then sailing with them held at a considerable upward angle with the body; it rises and falls, swerves and veers, in a ghostly manner through the gloom.

The breeding season is from February to July, and often again in September. The two eggs (sometimes only one) are laid on the bare ground, usually under a thin bush but frequently quite in the open. The brooding bird sits very close. The eggs are pinkish-white mottled with various shades of brown and grey, and they measure about 27 × 20 mm.

HORSFIELD'S JUNGLE NIGHTJAR, or
LONG-TAILED NIGHTJAR

Caprimulgus macrurus aequabilis Ripley. Resident

Sinhalese: Bin-bassā. Tamil: Pāthekai-kuruvi, Kuruttu-pakkul

Plate 13, facing p. 168 (male; ×one-quarter)

About the size of the Common Babbler, but with much longer wings and tail. The female differs from the male in having the pale spots on throat and wing-quills buff instead of white, and the black blotches on scapulars smaller.

This nightjar is found in jungle, chena, and well-wooded areas in most parts of the low country, but it distinctly prefers the dry zone and in the wettest districts is rare if not absent; it ascends the hills on the drier side to about 3,000 feet. Though still a common bird, especially in the dry-zone forests, its numbers in the south and west appear to be greatly reduced since Legge's time—doubtless owing to the great increase of the human population in those parts. Like other nightjars, it roosts on the ground during the day, occupying the same 'form' day after day for long periods—as is evidenced by the accumulation of droppings, castings, shed feathers, etc.—unless it be disturbed. It chooses a shady spot where dead leaves and twigs match its beautifully marbled and streaked plumage, giving perfect concealment. To motorists, travelling at night through the jungle districts, it is a familiar bird, owing to its habit—which it shares with the last species—of sitting in the middle of the road, its eyes gleaming red in the glare of the headlights, until the vehicle is nearly upon it; then it leaps into the air just in time to avoid being run over. It generally sits on a low stump or bare bough while uttering its curious call *grog, groggrog* which sounds as if the bird emitted it with an effort. The 'song' consists of a loud, coughing bark *quŏffrr . . . quŏffrr* which it will repeat at intervals throughout the night, especially in moonlight. The flight resembles that of other nightjars—an easy sailing, alternating with a few powerful strokes of its long wings. It feeds on various flying insects, of which beetles comprise the majority except when a flight of termites is in progress.

The breeding season is from February to May, with a secondary season in August–September. The two eggs are buff, sparingly spotted with dark brown, and are deposited on the ground among fallen leaves, etc., often at the side of a jungle path. They measure about 29·2 × 22·3 mm.

THE CEYLON HIGHLAND NIGHTJAR
(Ceylon Jungle Nightjar of Wait, Kelaart's Nightjar of Legge)

Caprimulgus indicus kelaarti Blyth. Race peculiar to Ceylon

Sinhalese: Bīn-bassā. Tamil: Pāthekai-kuruvi

Plate 13, facing p. 168 (male; ×one-quarter)

About the size of the Common Mynah, but with longer wings and tail. The female lacks the white tips to the outer tail-feathers and has the spots on the primaries buff, not white, and smaller than in the male. The young are very rufous or brownish in general tone.

This nightjar is mainly confined to the hills above about 3,000 feet, but Legge found it in the Eastern Province at the base of the Friar's Hood range of hills, and I have heard its unmistakable note at Dambulla (500 feet) in April. It loves grassy hill-sides, particularly the quartzy patanas of the Uva hills, and it seldom or never enters jungle. It sometimes spends the day perching along a large branch of a tree at some height, but usually it roosts on the ground in the shade of a thin bush or grass-tussock and, like other nightjars, it will allow itself almost to be trodden upon before it springs into the air and flies off to a new roost. The same form is occupied for many days in succession, but when once disturbed it usually deserts the spot. Its mottled grey, black, white and ochreous colour-scheme assimilate perfectly with the lichenous quartz or pebbly gneiss amongst which it sits. On the approach of an intruder, it crouches, tightens its feathers, and points the bill upwards so that it looks like anything except a bird. About dusk, it flies up to a branch, commanding boulder, or stump, and commences its weird song, which reminds one of the exhaust note of a small gas-engine *chuk'm chuk'm chuk'm chuk'm* . . . repeated for many minutes at a time during the courting season. At close quarters, this song has a curious resonant quality, the *chuk* being superimposed, as it were, upon a throbbing drone represented by the *m*; it carries for a great distance. The courting male has also another note which sounds like *hōō hōō hōō hōōteter hōōteter* . . . This is uttered in flight with wings held high and steady, and tail widely expanded and canted to one side or the other, exposing the white tips of the four outer feathers. The food consists mainly of beetles and moths, which are swallowed whole. The flight is of the usual nightjar type, a few rapid, rather stiff and jerky strokes of the wings, followed by a long graceful glide with the wings held at a considerable dihedral.

The breeding season is from February to June. The two eggs are laid on bare soil, without any shelter or concealment, and often on a steep, quartzy ridge. They are pinkish-white with rather sparse brown spots, and measure about 28·5 × 19·3 mm.

THE FROGMOUTHS

Family PODARGIDAE

These are weird, nocturnal birds which in some ways resemble owls, in others, nightjars; their structural characters relate them to the latter. Their most striking feature is the enormously wide, short and stout beak, with the gape extending back almost to behind the eye. The legs are very short and the feet small as in the nightjars, but without a 'comb' on the middle claw. The wings are short and rounded, the tail fairly long and strongly graduated; in the Ceylon frogmouth, at least, the two middle feathers are much curved—semicylindrical—in transverse section. The plumage is soft, but dry and dusty-looking. The coloration is grey or brown, mottled and marbled with black and white in a manner suggestive of the lichen-covered branches on which these birds roost and nest. Frogmouths feed largely on insects, but some forms eat fruits as well. The headquarters of the family are in Australia and the associated islands, and its most western extension is in South India, where the same race as our bird occurs.

THE CEYLON FROGMOUTH

Batrachostomus moniliger Blyth. Resident

Sinhalese: Gembi-kata-bassā. No Tamil name recorded

Plate 13, facing p. 168 (male left, female right; × one-quarter)

Size of the Common Babbler. The male is mottled grey, black and white; the female is brown or rufous, spotted with black and white. This extraordinary bird, with its enormously wide beak and large yellow eyes, cannot be mistaken for any other Ceylon bird.

It is rare but widely distributed in the Island, apparently at all but the highest elevations. An inhabitant of the densest forests, and strictly nocturnal, it is very seldom seen and its habits are largely matters of conjecture. One which I met beside a jungle path at Niroddumunai, near Trincomalee, in February 1914, attracted attention at dusk by darting at something and then sat on a bare stick about five yards away, enabling me to watch it for some minutes before it flew silently round a tree and disappeared. It sat transversely to the branch—not along it, as a nightjar would have done—and rotated its head like an owl, presumably to see me better. The only other occasion when I have seen the species was at Labugama, while collecting insects at dusk along a jungle path strewn with great boulders; passing one of these, arm's length away, a small stone poised on its summit suddenly took wing and flew to another boulder about fifteen yards ahead—and proved to be a frogmouth. During the day it sleeps on a branch with beak pointing upwards and the curious plumes on its lores erected forwards. In this position its lichen-like plumage suggests a dead snag on the branch. It sleeps soundly and may sometimes almost be seized in the hand before it wakes. Insects, such as beetles, comprise its food; they are swallowed whole. A bird which was kept under observation by C. E. Norris uttered a call resembling the screech of a fishing reel running out fairly slowly.

Breeding takes place in February, March, and September. The nest, which has been described and photographed by W. W. A. Phillips, is a circular pad of felt composed of the bird's own down, measuring about $2\frac{1}{4}$ inches in diameter by about half an inch deep; it is placed on a horizontal branch, and is camouflaged on the outside with flakes of lichen and bark. The top is slightly concave and supports a single egg which is brooded during the day by the male bird; probably the female broods at night. The egg is pure white and measures about $30 \times 20 \cdot 5$ mm.

TROGONS

THIS order contains a single, but very distinct, family: the *Trogonidae*. The forests of South and Central America are the headquarters of the order, but a few species inhabit Africa and the Indian and Indo-Malayan regions; Ceylon has a single species which is found also in South India.

The general characters of the order are given under the family description.

THE TROGONS
Family TROGONIDAE

Trogons are distinguished from all other families of birds by the structure of the foot, which is zygodactyle as in woodpeckers, parrots, cuckoos, etc., but differs from all these in that the second, or *inner* toe is turned backwards in addition to the hallux, or hind toe proper (in other zygodactyle birds, the fourth, or *outer* toe is turned backwards). Trogons have soft, voluminous plumage, and very thin and delicate skins. The wings are short, narrow and rounded, and the tail long, much graduated, and broad at the base; in the only Ceylon species, the tail-feathers are square-cut at the tip, especially in adults. The beak is rather short, but strong and wide, with the gape opening far back. The legs are short and weak, and the feet small, used only for perching, not locomotion. Trogons are forest birds, arboreal, and they feed mostly on the wing. They nest in holes in trees, and lay white or pale buff eggs. Their coloration is notably beautiful. The gorgeous and much-publicized quetzal (*Pharomacrus mocinno*), of Central America, is a trogon.

THE CEYLON TROGON

Harpactes fasciatus fasciatus (Pennant). Race peculiar to Ceylon

Sinhalese: Gini-kurullā. No Tamil name recorded

Plate 13, facing p. 168

(male left, ×one-quarter; female right, ×one-fifth)

Size of the Common Mynah, but with a long, graduated tail. The female lacks the white necklace, has the head and breast greyish-brown, and the wings barred with yellow ochre; the young male resembles the female.

This beautiful and interesting bird is widespread in the forested portions of the Island, both wet and dry zones, and at all elevations up to about 6,000 feet, but is not very common anywhere; it seems to favour especially the intermediate belt of country between the wet and dry zones. It loves the recesses of deep forest, and lives in pairs—which do not associate very closely—or sometimes in small flocks. The flight is rapid and adroit, with nimble dodging among the tangled branches and lianas of its haunts, but is seldom sustained for more than a few yards at a time; the wings produce a loud fluttering sound. The trogon perches very upright with its long, square-cut tail hanging straight down, and it usually keeps very still except for a slow, furtive motion of the head as it peers in all directions for insect-prey. Occasionally it raises and expands its beautiful broad tail, at the same time uttering, with the mouth open, a curious whinnying chatter *ihiiiii, ihiiiii* (i as in 'it'). Another note, which often betrays its presence, is a chuckling churr *krrrk* (high pitched in the beginning). The call-note is a whistled *h'yoch, h'yoch, h'yoch* (y as in 'you', and each syllable cut off sharp at the end), which is uttered from three to twelve times or so, with the beak shut. This call is easily imitated by whistling, and is an almost infallible lure for a trogon of either sex which may be within sound of it. All these notes are produced by both sexes, but the birds are only really talkative in the breeding season. The trogon feeds on small flying insects, beetles, moths, etc., and I once saw one snatch a stick-insect from a leaf and devour it. Related species of trogon have been recorded, in Burma, as feeding on berries and certain leaves, and it is probable that our Ceylon bird does the same.

The breeding season is from February to June. The eggs are laid on the floor of a cavity in a tree-trunk, generally a rotten dead one, and the hole appears to be, sometimes at least, pecked out by the birds themselves. Both sexes incubate. The two or three eggs are pale buff, unmarked, glossy, and measure about 24·2 × 21 mm.

CUCKOOS AND THEIR ALLIES
Order CUCULIFORMES

This order includes two families, the *Cuculidae* which are distributed throughout the temperate and tropical regions of the globe, and the *Musophagidae*—touracos, or plantain-eaters—which are confined to Africa. The *Cuculidae* are well represented in Ceylon, with sixteen species, two of which, however, are mere casual strays. Two species and two subspecies are peculiar to the Island, and five species are wholly or partially migrants in winter from the mainland of India.

The general characters of the order (apart from anatomical details, which do not come into the scope of this work) are given under the family heading.

THE CUCKOOS, MALKOHAS, AND COUCALS
Family CUCULIDAE

This family comprises—so far as Ceylon is concerned—three sub-families of diverse appearance and habits. They are zygodactyle birds, with plumage rather soft and lax, though the coloration of many is very beautiful. The true cuckoos (sub-family *Cuculinae*), are mostly migratory birds with long, pointed but narrow wings (the secondaries being short), and short, weak legs with the tarsus more or less feathered at the base. The bill is rather small, tapering, and gently curved, with the nostrils circular and having a raised rim. The tail is fairly long, and graduated. These birds, in their breeding habits, are all parasitic on other birds—foisting their eggs into the nests of various passerine species which incubate them and foster the young cuckoos. The koel is included in this sub-family, although it is in some ways intermediate between this and the next.

The second sub-family, *Phaenicophaeinae*, contains the sirkeer and the malkohas. These are non-parasitic cuckoos with strong, unfeathered tarsi, very short, rounded wings, and long much-graduated tails. They build rather flimsy saucer-shaped nests in trees, and lay chalky-white eggs.

The third sub-family, *Centropinae*, consists of the coucals—non-parasitic cuckoos of mainly terrestrial habits; they are remarkable for the long, nearly straight claw on the inner (true) hind toe. They have short rounded wings, and long, broad tails. They build large, globular nests in trees, and are noted for their deep, sonorous calls.

THE ASIATIC COMMON CUCKOO

Cuculus canorus telephonus Heine. Rare and casual winter visitor; the eastern race of the well-known Common Cuckoo of Europe, including Britain

Sinhalese: Kōhā. Tamil: Kuyil, Kusil. (These vernacular names are applied indiscriminately to all members of the true cuckoos)

About the size of a domestic pigeon but more slenderly built, and with proportionately longer tail. The male is grey on head, breast, and back; darker, brownish grey on wings and tail; and white on the underparts, narrowly and neatly barred with black. The under-wing is largely white, spotted and barred with black, and the tail, which is long and graduated, has white tips and a variable amount of spotting and barring with white, especially on the edges and shafts of the feathers. The adult female is similar, but browner, and she has a rufous, ill-defined band across the breast; some females are rufous brown, barred with black, throughout the head, back, wings and tail. Irides, base of beak, and feet, chrome yellow in both sexes. This cuckoo may easily be mistaken for a small hawk, e.g. the shikra, which it closely resembles in general appearance and coloration. Its small, pointed beak, smaller head, graduated tail, and zygodactyle feet at once reveal its true nature.

It is a very rare winter visitor to Ceylon, only four or five specimens having been recorded from the Island. As it is silent except in the breeding season, its well-publicized cry, *kuk-oo, kuk-oo*, so familiar in Britain in the spring, is unlikely to be heard in Ceylon. Its flight is swift and very hawk-like. Insects, especially hairy caterpillars, form its food. This race breeds from the Himalayas northwards, and eastwards to Japan, victimizing various small birds—pipits, chats and the like—into whose nests it insinuates its eggs in the manner so well known.

THE SMALL CUCKOO

Cuculus poliocephalus poliocephalus Latham. Scarce and irregular winter visitor

Sinhalese: Kōhā. Tamil: Kuyil, Kusil

Size of the Common Babbler, but more slenderly built and with much longer wings and tail. Sexes nearly alike. Young birds have a good deal of brown and rufous in their plumage, and the throat and upper breast are barred grey, or black, and white. This cuckoo is practically a miniature of the last species, having the same coloration, but the black bars on the underparts are broader. It has the same hawk-like appearance and flight, but its small size distinguishes it both from its large relative and from any hawk found in Ceylon.

× one-fifth

It visits Ceylon in small but variable numbers during the north-east monsoon; most of the specimens which have been collected in the Island have been immature. It appears to be silent during its stay, but in its breeding-range—from the Himalayas to north China—it is said, by Whistler, to utter a wild, screaming note suggesting the words *that's your smoky paper*. It frequents gardens and openly-wooded country and, according to Legge, is a tame and stupid bird, easily approached. It feeds on insects, including hairy caterpillars in its diet. Like other parasitic cuckoos, it delegates its family responsibilities to various small passerine birds.

THE INDIAN CUCKOO

Cuculus micropterus micropterus Gould. Resident, but probably partly a winter visitor

Sinhalese: Kōhā. Tamil: Kuyil, Kusil

About the size of a domestic pigeon, but more slenderly built. Sexes nearly alike, but the female is browner than the male. From the Common Cuckoo it may at once be distinguished by the blackish band near the tip of the tail. In general appearance and flight it strongly

PLATE 13

1. Ceylon Trogon.   2. Ceylon Frogmouth.   3. Ceylon Highland Nightjar.
4. Horsfield's Jungle Nightjar.   5. Southern Common Indian Nightjar

PLATE 14

1. Red-winged Crested Cuckoo.   2. Koel.   3. Indian Plaintive Cuckoo.
4. Red-faced Malkoha.   5. Ceylon Bay-banded Cuckoo.   6. Blue-faced
Malkoha

suggests a small hawk of the shikra type, but the weak bill and short legs—not to mention the zygodactyle feet—readily distinguish it.

The status of this cuckoo in Ceylon is somewhat doubtful; while nearly all specimens hitherto procured in the Island have been taken during the north-east monsoon—probably indicating winter migration —there is evidence that, occasionally at least, it breeds in the Island. It frequents high forest, principally in the east and south of the Island, and has seldom been collected, mainly owing to its wariness and habit

× one-third

of keeping to the tops of tall trees in forest. Nevertheless, it is not extremely rare, as is evidenced by its loud but musical whistle— usually likened to *Captain Philpotts*, but which sounds to me more like *wheewhee-h'yar-ho*—frequently repeated; the first two syllables are on the same note, the following ones descending (the Pied Crested Cuckoo has a somewhat similar, but distinct, cry). This call is constantly uttered during the early months of the year.

It is very desirable that definite information on the breeding of this cuckoo in Ceylon should be obtained; its eggs are likely to be deposited in the nests of drongos, flycatchers, or Black-headed Orioles, and any instance of these birds feeding young not of their own species should be carefully investigated and recorded. According to Phillips (*Checklist*, p. 56) it is known to victimize the Black-headed Oriole, and its young have been observed in June. It seems, however, very probable that most of these cuckoos seen in the Island are winter visitors.

THE CEYLON HAWK-CUCKOO or 'BRAIN-FEVER BIRD'

Hierococcyx varius ciceliae Phillips. Race peculiar to Ceylon

Sinhalese: Kōhā. Tamil: Kuyil, Kusil

About the size of a domestic pigeon, though more slenderly built. Sexes alike. This bird very closely resembles the shikra, in both adult and juvenile plumages, and the likeness extends to its habitual posture, style of flight, etc., as well as to size and coloration. However, the narrow, pointed beak, very short legs, peculiarly barred tail and zygodactyle feet make confusion impossible.

Left, adult; right, juvenile; × one-quarter

Until recently, this cuckoo was considered to be a winter migrant to Ceylon, but it is now known to breed regularly in the hills, and Ceylonese specimens have been found to be slightly darker in coloration than their continental representatives. It is probable, however, that a proportion of hawk-cuckoos in Ceylon are winter visitors from India. Its breeding range in the Island is restricted to the hills and it prefers the wetter districts though, out of the season, a few birds spread into the low-country wet zone and into the drier Uva hills. The hawk-cuckoo is notorious in India for its irritatingly monotonous reiteration, during the hottest weather, of a cry which suggests the words *brain-fever*—but which Mrs Lushington likens rather to *too-trrroo-yer*. This call is repeated on an ascending scale, getting more and more excited, until it suddenly stops—only to begin at the bottom of the scale again, a few moments later. Mrs Lushington says that the females and young have a strident, trilling scream, and call much less than the males. This cuckoo inhabits well-wooded country, such as tea estates, gardens and the like, but appears to avoid deep forest. Like most of the parasitic cuckoos, it feeds on insects, including hairy caterpillars; but it is said to eat also some berries and wild figs.

The breeding season is in the first three or four months of the year, and this is also the season of maximum calling. The eggs have not yet been found in Ceylon but, on the analogy of the Indian race, they will be found to be coloured a rich turquoise blue—matching closely the eggs of the favourite host, the Common Babbler, in whose nests they are laid. Indian eggs measure about 25 × 19 mm.

THE INDIAN PLAINTIVE CUCKOO

Cacomantis merulinus passerinus (Vahl). Regular winter visitor

Sinhalese: Kōhā. Tamil: Kuyil, Kusil

Plate 14, facing p. 169
(left, adult male; right, red form of female; ×one-fifth)

About the size of the Red-vented Bulbul, but with a longer tail. The female exists in two colour-phases: one, the red or 'hepatic' phase, is as shown in the Plate, a chestnut bird with white underparts, barred with black; the other phase resembles the male.

This little cuckoo arrives in Ceylon with the advent of the north-east monsoon, and leaves again about April. During its stay, it is very common in the dry zone, rather rare in the wet zone, and only a casual straggler in the hills. It moves about a good deal, seldom staying more than a few days in one place. Gardens, scrub-jungle, park-country and the like are its favourite haunts, and it is not very shy except, according to Legge, when it associates in flocks; it is, however, usually seen solitary. Its flight is rapid and adroit, suggestive of the hunting flight of a small hawk. It feeds on insects, being very partial to the hairy, gregarious caterpillars of the moth *Eupterote mollifera*; the hairs of these caterpillars are intensely irritating to human skin, but some birds eat them with impunity. While in Ceylon, this cuckoo is silent, but in India, during the breeding season, it constantly utters a plaintive, clear whistle likened to *ka-veer*, which is said to have a ventriloquistic quality, due to the bird's turning its head this way and that while calling.

So far, it has not been found to breed in Ceylon; in many parts of

India the breeding season is from July to October. It lays its eggs in the nests of small warblers, such as various species of prinia and the tailor-bird, and the eggs have a superficial resemblance to those of the host-species. When hatched, the young cuckoo instinctively ejects any other eggs or young birds from the nest in order that it may have the undivided attention and food brought by the small foster-parents. The eggs measure about 19 × 14 mm.

THE CEYLON BAY-BANDED CUCKOO

Penthoceryx sonneratii waiti Stuart Baker. Race peculiar to Ceylon

Sinhalese: Kōhā. Tamil: Kuyil, Kusil

Plate 14, facing p. 169 (× one-fifth)

Rather smaller than the Common Mynah, more slender, and with a longer tail. Sexes alike. This cuckoo may be confused with the red-phase females of the Plaintive Cuckoo, but it has some white about the face, and the entire underparts, from chin to vent, are white, with narrow, dark-brown, wavy bars; the back and wings are dark brown, plentifully banded with light chestnut—giving a darker effect than the other bird.

It is widespread in the low country but, except in a few restricted localities, is not at all common, and appears to have diminished in numbers since Legge's day. It seems to prefer the intermediate belt of country, between wet and dry zones, and is fairly numerous in the Eastern Province and the eastern foot-hills of the main range. In the north-east monsoon it ascends the hills, on the drier, eastern side, to about 4,000 feet. It favours the borders of forest, chenas, and open jungle, and is fond of the upper branches of dead trees and such-like high vantage-points from which it utters its loud whistle, which Legge syllabifies as *whī-whip, whiwhip—whī-whip, whiwhip*. In the breeding season it utters a different note, a whistled *whew, whew, whu-u-u, whu-u-u, whu-u-u*—each stanza higher pitched than the last, and the call ending abruptly as if the bird had reached the top of its compass—or run out of breath. It is most noisy in the mornings and evenings, and calls vociferously during the first quarter of the year when, presumably, breeding is going on. It feeds on insects, such as beetles, mantises and caterpillars.

The egg of this cuckoo has not yet been taken in Ceylon, but it is known to parasitize the Orange Minivet, as Mrs Lushington, in September 1940, watched a female of that bird feeding a fledgling of this cuckoo. The Indian race cuckolds various bulbuls and babblers, so most likely these birds will prove to be the normal fosterers of the Ceylon race. The eggs vary greatly in coloration and measure about 20·5 × 15·8 mm.

The tiny EMERALD CUCKOO *Chalcites maculatus* (Gmelin)—no bigger than a sparrow—was originally described from a published illustration of a specimen sent to England by the Dutch governor, Gideon Loten, nearly two hundred years ago. Gmelin, who described it, thought it to be a trogon, and as the illustration was of a juvenile with spotted wing-coverts, he named it *Trogon maculatus*. As Whistler points out (*Avifaunal Survey of Ceylon*, p. 214), cuckoos are noted wanderers and this species has since turned up near Madras, so it is quite feasible that Loten's specimen was indeed collected in Ceylon; it has not, however, been recorded in the Island since his time. Its normal habitat is in the eastern Himalayas, through Burma and Siam to Hainan. A forest bird, it frequents the tops of trees, feeds on insects, and cuckolds the beautiful, long-tailed sunbirds of the genus *Aethopyga* (not found in Ceylon).

In case it should again visit Ceylon, a brief description follows: sexes alike; head, upperparts, wings and tail brilliant, metallic, emerald green, with a coppery lustre; underparts white, boldly barred with metallic green bands; outer tail-feathers tipped and banded with white, and there is a white patch on the underwing at the bases of the primaries. Young birds are duller green, with some rufous on hind neck, wings and tail.

THE DRONGO-CUCKOO

Surniculus lugubris lugubris (Horsfield). Resident

Sinhalese: Kāudā Kōhā. Tamil: Irattai-vālang Kuyil

Slightly larger than the Ceylon Common Drongo, which it closely resembles in appearance. Sexes alike. The young are speckled all over with white, and some traces of white spotting are retained until full maturity is reached. In spite of its resemblance to a drongo, the critical observer will easily detect a certain characteristic slovenliness, such as marks all the parasitic cuckoos, in its appearance and deportment, and which distinguishes it from the smart and dapper drongo. Its head and beak are smaller, and the tail broader at the end, less deeply forked;

while its style of flight is direct, silent and 'soft' as compared with the energetic style of the drongo.

This cuckoo inhabits the low-country dry zone and parts of the wet zone, and ascends the hills, out of the breeding season, to about 4,000 feet—occasionally higher. It is primarily a forest bird but frequents the more open types of forest for preference, and in the hills it is often to be

× one-quarter

seen in wind-belts of trees, and the like, on tea estates. In my experience it is rather rare, except in a few areas, but W. W. A. Phillips and Mrs Lushington have found it abundant in parts of the low country; I believe, however, that its numbers have diminished since Legge's day. It is not shy, permitting a near approach. In the foothills, when not breeding, it sometimes associates in small, scattered flocks. It has a very characteristic call, to be heard during the first quarter of the year when, presumably, courting is proceeding; it consists of four to eight whistled notes evenly ascending, as if the bird were practising the musical scale. Its food, like that of most parasitic cuckoos, consists of various insects—caterpillars, beetles, etc.—but it probably eats some fruit, as Legge records seeds found in its stomach.

There is very little on record concerning the breeding of this cuckoo in Ceylon, but such evidence as exists points to its cuckolding the Ceylon Iora, and small babblers, such as the Black-fronted Babbler.

THE PIED CRESTED CUCKOO

Clamator jacobinus jacobinus (Boddaert). Resident

Sinhalese: Kondé Kōhā. Tamil: Kondé Kuyil

Size of the Common Mynah, but with a long, graduated tail. Sexes alike. The black and white plumage and jaunty crest render this bird unmistakable. It is widely distributed throughout the low country, but is most numerous in the dry zone; in the hills, it ascends to at least 3,000 feet on the drier, eastern side, but probably only as a winter visitor. It commonly associates in pairs or in small flocks, and is a restless bird, moving about a good deal, seldom remaining more than a few days in one spot. It favours open, scrub-country, avoiding forest, and often frequents herbage-covered swamps or reed-beds. It perches on the tops of bushes while scrutinizing their foliage for the insects on which it feeds or, in the case of the female, while looking for nests into which it can foist its eggs. A conspicuous bird, it is not at all shy, and a flock working systematically over a bush-covered area forms a pleasing adjunct to the scenery. Insects of many kinds—tree-crickets, beetles, etc. —form its diet and, like many other cuckoos, it is very partial to hairy caterpillars. In the breeding season it is noisy, frequently uttering a loud, musical, four- or five-note whistle on a descending scale—*pee-pee pew pew pew* which somewhat resembles the *Captain Philpotts* of the Indian Cuckoo. Its flight is direct and rather laboured.

× one-sixth

This cuckoo always lays its eggs in the nests of the Common Babbler, whose eggs they very closely resemble, being similar both in size and in their beautiful turquoise blue colour; they are indistinguishable, also, from the eggs of the hawk-cuckoo—which victimizes the same babbler. They measure about 24 × 19 mm.

THE RED-WINGED CRESTED CUCKOO

Clamator coromandus (Linnaeus). Regular, but scarce, winter visitor

Sinhalese: Ratu Kondé Kōhā. Tamil: Kondé Kuyil

Plate 14, facing p. 169 (× one-fifth)

Rather larger than the Common Mynah, and with a much longer, broader tail. Sexes alike. The pointed crest, distinctive coloration, and long tail, combined, make it unmistakable among Ceylon birds; in flight, with crest depressed, however, its rufous wings contrasting with the black body and tail make it look somewhat like a coucal, but the buff and white underparts and white collar should prevent any confusion.

This handsome cuckoo is a regular but uncommon winter visitor to the Island, arriving about October and departing in April. Its main habitat during its stay is in the low-country dry zone, but a few stray into the wet zone, and an occasional individual is seen in the hills up to

5,000 feet. It is a shy, forest-loving species, most often seen as it flies across a jungle road, and although sometimes ascending into the tree canopy, it appears to prefer the lower levels of forest growth for its hunting-grounds. The food consists of foliage-frequenting insects, such as tree-crickets, mantises, beetles and the like, and doubtless caterpillars form a considerable proportion. Though it is said to be noisy· in its breeding haunts, it is silent while sojourning in Ceylon. A captive which I watched for a short time constantly jerked its wings and tail in a quick, nervous manner.

In its breeding range in northern India this cuckoo parasitizes various small babblers. Its eggs are said to resemble those of the Pied Crested Cuckoo but to be larger and paler blue in colour.

THE KOEL

Eudynamys scolopaceus scolopaceus (Linnaeus). Resident

Sinhalese: Kōhā, Gōmerā Kōhā. Tamil: Kuyil, Kusil

Plate 14, facing p. 169 (male lower, female upper; ×one-fifth)

Between the Common Mynah and the House Crow in size, but with a long tail. The sexes differ as shown in the Plate, but nestlings of both sexes—contrary to the usual rule among birds—resemble the male; immature females have their speckling more or less rufous.

The koel is widely distributed throughout the low country, both wet and dry zones, and ascends the hills to at least 1600 feet. Its distribution is largely governed by that of the two species of crows—where crows are numerous, there will koels be numerous too. It loves large gardens, parks, and well-wooded country generally, but not dense forest; and is strictly arboreal, spending most of its time in the canopy of large trees, especially those in fruit. Its diet consists almost entirely of small fruits of various kinds, amongst which may be mentioned the various wild figs, mā-dun, and the berries of several kinds of ornamental garden palms. During the breeding season it is an excessively noisy bird, its rolling whistle *kuil kuil kuil*, and the monotonously reiterated *huēeyo, huēeyo, huēeyo*, ascending the scale, being heard, *ad nauseam*, throughout the day and often far into the night. At times, also, it gives vent to agonized shrieks and yelps, suggestive of the bird's being tortured, though merely expressing *joie de vivre*. These noises, coming in the hottest weather, make the bird anything but a favourite with nervy humans. The flight of the koel is swift and direct—as it has need to be, for it is much persecuted by crows, apparently in retaliation for its cuckolding them. When not feeding, it usually keeps out of sight in dense foliage, but it is fond of sunning itself at the top of a tree in the early morning.

The breeding season corresponds with that of the two crows, in whose nests it lays its eggs, viz. about April to August. It seems probable that the two sexes collaborate in the delicate business of introducing their eggs into the nests of their mortal enemies; the male koel, shrieking insults, dashes off, hotly pursued by the outraged crows. When they get back to their nest, an extra egg, very similar in general appearance to their own, has mysteriously arrived! The eggs of the koel are greyish-green, spotted with reddish-brown, and measure about 30·6 × 22·9 mm.

THE BLUE-FACED MALKOHA

(Small Green Malkoha of Wait, Green-billed Malkoha of Legge and other authors; as the bird is not conspicuously green, and as most species of malkohas have green bills, neither of these names seems very appropriate, so I propose the name **Blue-faced Malkoha)**

Rhopodytes viridirostris (Jerdon). Resident

Sinhalese: Kalahā Kōhā, Pǔnchi Mǎl Kōhā. Tamil: Kuyil, Kusil

Plate 14, facing p. 169 (× one-fifth)

Size of the Common Mynah, but with a long, much-graduated tail. Sexes alike. The pale-green beak, blue face, dark, greenish-grey plumage and long, white-tipped tail make this bird unmistakable. It is found throughout the low country, wherever conditions are suitable, but it prefers the dry zone, and ascends the hills on eastern and northern slopes to about 1200 feet. Scrub-jungle, especially of the thorny type, or places where *Euphorbia antiquorum* flourishes, form its favourite habitat, and it is not often seen in either cultivation or deep forest. It is clever in threading its way through tangled herbage, and when disturbed, usually clambers through the twigs and foliage, making off from the opposite side of the tree. While descending to the ground on occasion, most of its time is spent among the branches of trees and bushes, diligently scrutinizing the leaves for the crickets, mantises, etc., on which it feeds (according to Legge, however, it is exceptional for it to eat anything but fruit). Usually silent, it sometimes utters a low *kraa* as it flutters off if suddenly alarmed. The flight is slow, direct and laboured, as one would expect from its short, rounded wings.

The breeding season appears to last almost throughout the year. The nest is a flimsy, open saucer of twigs, lined with a few green leaves, and is placed in the middle of a small tree. The two eggs are white, covered with a chalky deposit; they measure about 31 × 24·5 mm.

THE RED-FACED MALKOHA

Phaenicophaeus pyrrhocephalus (Pennant). Species peculiar to Ceylon

Sinhalese: Măl Kōhā, Măl Kandettā. No Tamil name recorded

Plate 14, facing p. 169 (male; × one-fifth)

About the length of the Common Coucal, but more slenderly built and with, proportionally, a much longer tail. Sexes alike, except that the female has white irides—those of the male being brown. This handsome bird cannot be mistaken for any other species on the Ceylon list.

It is nowadays found mainly in the few remaining forests of the wet zone, and the adjoining hills, but a few scattered colonies exist in the dry-zone forests as well. In Legge's time it occurred as high as Haputale, but there is no doubt that, owing to the extension of cultivation, and through shooting, its numbers have seriously declined throughout its former haunts, and it must now be considered definitely a scarce bird. Unless it is protected by the enforcement of legislation, education of the people, and provision of extensive forest sanctuaries, I greatly fear that this beautiful bird will be exterminated in the not-distant future. It inhabits tall forest, and lives either solitary, in pairs, or in small flocks. It is shy and restless, a dweller in the tree canopy, where, like the last species, it cleverly threads its way through tangled twigs, creepers and foliage. Owing to the short, rounded wings, its flight is feeble, slow and direct and, if it has any distance to cover, it commonly prefers to hop from branch to branch until it reaches the top of a tree, and then to flutter and volplane from that vantage-point; in flight, the wings produce a musical hum. It is usually silent, but I have heard it utter short, single-note, yelping whistles; a note like *kok*—imitated by a sucking action of the tongue; and a low, petulant-sounding *krā*. It feeds mainly on berries of forest trees.

The breeding season is in the first half of the year and probably again in August–September. The nest is described as a shallow saucer of grass, roots and twigs, very carelessly put together, and placed in high bushes in forest with thick undergrowth. The two or three eggs are white, with a chalky surface, and they measure about 35·8 × 27 mm.

178

THE SOUTHERN SIRKEER

Taccocua leschenaultii leschenaultii Lesson. Resident

Sinhalese: Pătthăng Atti-kukkulā: No Tamil name recorded

Smaller than the Common Coucal, but of much the same shape and proportions. Sexes alike. Its coucal-like shape and sandy coloration, combined with bright red beak and white-tipped lateral tail-feathers, should make this bird easy to recognize.

× one-quarter

It is rare and shy, and there is little doubt that its range, particularly in the hills, has become much restricted since Legge's time. Nowadays, its headquarters in the Island lie in the park-like, patana, and scrub-jungle country to the east and south-east of the main mountain massif, and in the adjoining foot-hills up to the level where tea and rubber have replaced the jungle of former days. Its favourite haunts are thinly-wooded areas with undergrowth of lantana, māna-grass and illuk. It feeds mainly on the ground, capturing insects of various kinds—grasshoppers, mantises, beetles, etc., and also eats lizards; and, according to Whistler, berries and fruit. It runs quickly, and is loath to take wing, preferring to run for the nearest cover, through which, when disturbed, it adroitly threads its way to safety. A laboured flapping into a tree, or from one tree to the next, is normally the extent of its flying abilities. Silent as a rule, it is said to make a clicking sound when court-ing. Sálim Ali describes the courtship display as being performed mainly by the female, and to consist of 'bowing (or bobbing) and posturing in ludicrous fashion, tail spread out and partly cocked, before the other of the pair'.

The first nest of this species recorded from Ceylon was found by C. E. Norris in April 1940, in the Maturata district. It contained three eggs. The nest is a shallow saucer of twigs, lined with green leaves, and is placed in a fork of a bushy tree or *Euphorbia antiquorum*, from six to ten feet from the ground. The eggs are chalky white and measure about 35·5 × 26 mm.

THE COMMON COUCAL

(Southern Crow-Pheasant of Wait; commonly miscalled Jungle Crow in Ceylon)

Centropus sinensis parroti Stresemann. Resident

Sinhalese: Atti-kukkulā, Bū-kukkulā. Tamil: Chempakam

Size of the House Crow, but with a long and broad tail. Sexes alike. The only Ceylon bird with which this can be confused is the next species, but its black bill and brighter chestnut wings distinguish it from the Green-billed Coucal.

Distributed almost everywhere in the Island up to 6,500 feet, its principal haunts are in well-wooded cultivation or scrub-jungle, and it is common in towns and villages. Much of its time is spent on the ground, walking slowly along hedge-bottoms and the like, its crimson eye taking in everything that has a bearing on the problem of food-getting. In pursuit of prey it hops and runs actively. A furtive bird, it creeps through shrubbery with quiet stealth, and few are the small birds' nests that escape its baleful attentions; for it is a notorious robber of eggs and young birds. On the credit side of its balance-sheet, however, must be put the many harmful insects that it devours. It

× one-ninth

will eat almost any animal small enough to tackle: lizards, small snakes, frogs, mice, the fat, white larvae of the rhinoceros beetle, and even snails—all are grist to its mill; but it does not appear to take vegetable food. The flight is slow and laboured and, if any distance has to be covered, the bird usually hops from branch to branch to the top of a tree, taking off from there and proceeding in an alternating series of rapid flutterings and long glides with outspread wings. On alighting, the broad tail is generally spread and erected vertically as if to act as a brake and prevent the bird from toppling forward. This coucal usually hunts solitarily, but its mate is never far off, and every now and then the pair ascertain each other's whereabouts by uttering one of the best-known bird-sounds in Ceylon—a far-sounding *hoop oop oop oop oop*, which is answered by the partner in a higher key. This call is produced with the beak shut, or nearly so, and pointing down. The scold-note, used when the bird mobs a lurking snake or owl, etc., is an explosive *k'wisss*; and, in courtship, a curious sound is produced—*djoonk*—like a stone dropped into deep water, or a tight cork drawn from an empty bottle. The bird appears to pair for life, and a pair are very jealous of any encroachment on their territory by other coucals.

The breeding season lasts from February to September, and again from October to December; March and April appear to be the favourite months. The nest is a globular mass of creeper-stems, leafy twigs, etc., lined with green leaves, and with the entrance in the side. It is well concealed in dense hanging creepers, thorny bushes, or sometimes in the crown of a palm. The two or three eggs are dull, chalky white, and measure about 33·6 × 29 mm.

THE GREEN-BILLED COUCAL
(Ceylon Crow-Pheasant of some authors)

Centropus chlororhynchus Blyth. Species peculiar to Ceylon

Sinhalese: Băttā Atti-kukkulā, Wăl Atti-kukkulā. Tamil: Chempakam

Slightly smaller than the Common Coucal, from which it may at once be distinguished by its big, light-green beak; its wings, too, are much darker chestnut, and the sheen on the head and neck is purple, not blue. Sexes alike.

This coucal is found only in the forests of the wet zone, west, south-west and south of the main mountain massif, which it ascends to 2,500 feet, or perhaps higher. A very shy and elusive bird, it is far better known by its calls than by sight but, wherever the wet-zone forests have been spared the axe, it is still fairly common; its range, however, is rapidly dwindling and, as it shows no sign of being able to adjust itself to new conditions, there can be no doubt that its days will soon be numbered—with those of several other endemic forest birds—unless wise foresight reserves extensive forest sanctuaries in the wet zone. It inhabits high forest with dense undergrowth of dwarf bamboo (Sinhalese, *băttā*), or other luxuriant herbage, and the best chance of seeing it is in the early morning, when it emerges from the jungle to seek for food on roadsides or such-like open spaces or, if the night has been rainy, hops up to an exposed branch to sun itself for a few moments before descending into the soggy undergrowth again. I once watched one feeding on termites on an open grassy patch at dawn, but it never moves far from cover. Like the Common Coucal, it eats any small animal it can catch. Its flight usually consists of little more than flapping from one tree to the next. The call is of similar character to that of the Common Coucal, but is usually only two- or three-syllabled and is deeper, with a sonorous, mournful quality— *hooo-poop*, *hooo-poo-poop*—the *poop* being lower-pitched than the *hooo*. This call enables its distribution to be accurately mapped even if the bird is

× one-ninth

not seen, as it is quite distinctive and carries for a great distance. It is generally uttered, and answered by the performer's mate, in the morning and evening. A courting-note, like that of the Common Coucal but perhaps a trifle sharper, is uttered—*chewkk*.

The breeding season appears to be in the first half of the year. The nest is described by Jenkins, one of Stuart Baker's collectors, as being domed, made of sticks, twigs, roots and grass, lined with green leaves and supple green twigs. It is placed in thorny bushes about four or five feet from the ground, in deep, evergreen forest. The eggs number two or three, are chalky-white, and measure about 34·7 × 27 mm.

PARROTS
Order PSITTACIFORMES

Parrots are among the best known of birds, mainly owing to the ease with which many species may be kept in captivity, combined with their beautiful colours and the readiness with which some of the larger species will learn to imitate human speech. In consequence of this popularity, the general characteristics of the family are well known—the stout, hooked beak, zygodactyle feet, noisy habits, etc. Parrots form one of the most distinct orders of birds, having few connecting links with other orders; their nearest relatives appear to be the owls. The following features may be noted: the beak is very stout, short and strong, with the upper mandible strongly curved downward from the base; it is articulated with the skull so as to be movable up and down; and the nostrils are placed in an area of soft skin (cere) at its base. The lower mandible is small and strongly convex. The brain is large, indicating great intelligence. The tarsi are very short, and the zygodactyle feet have great power of prehension, being used by the birds for conveying food to the mouth as well as for perching and climbing; in the latter operation, the upper mandible takes a great part, being used like a grappling-hook. The flight in most parrots is swift and powerful, though, generally speaking, they do not migrate, being birds of stationary habitat. For the most part, they nest in holes in trees, generally utilizing natural cavities which they enlarge by gnawing to suit their purpose. They lay white, unmarked eggs, and the young are at first naked and blind, later developing a coat of grey down; they are fed by the parents regurgitating partly digested food. Parrots are almost entirely vegetarian, feeding on grain, nuts, buds, fruit and nectar. Many species are highly gregarious, and they are inclined to be noisy.

The order comprises two families which (apart from anatomical features) may be distinguished by their tongues:

Psittacidae—dry-mouthed parrots, with the tongue somewhat finger-shaped.

Loriidae—wet-mouthed parrots, with the tongue brush-like, adapted for feeding on liquid food such as nectar or fruit juices.

Only the *Psittacidae* are represented in Ceylon, though the lorikeet is in some respects intermediate between the two families.

PARAKEETS AND THE LORIKEET
Family PSITTACIDAE

Ceylon possesses five species of this family. Four of them belong to the long-tailed type of true parrots known as parakeets (genus *Psittacula*), and one (genus *Loriculus*) to the group of small, short-tailed parrots known variously as lorikeets, hanging parrots or bat-parrots (the last two names refer to their habit of hanging head downwards when sleeping).

Of the five species, three are widely distributed outside the Island while one species of parakeet and the lorikeet are peculiar to Ceylon, though closely related to South Indian species.

THE CEYLON LARGE PARAKEET, or
ALEXANDRINE PARAKEET

Psittacula eupatria eupatria (Linnaeus). Resident

Sinhalese: Labu Girawā. Tamil: Periya Kili

Plate 15, facing p. 184 (male; ×one-quarter)

Between the mynah and House Crow in size, but with a very long, much-graduated tail; our largest parakeet. The female lacks the black half-collar in front and the salmon-pink collar behind, but otherwise resembles the male; young birds are like the female. From the Rose-ringed Parakeet, this species is easily distinguished by its much larger beak, longer tail, and a dark red patch on the wing-coverts, present in both sexes.

This handsome parakeet is a dry-zone, low-country bird, seldom seen in the wet zone,[1] and not ascending the hills to any great height. Though its range has dwindled greatly of recent years, and it is now rare and a casual visitor in many places where it was common in Legge's

[1] Although it is not uncommon about Colombo, I believe such birds have escaped from captivity; this and the next species are frequently purchased by certain people in order to be released as a pious act.

PLATE 15

1. Blossom-headed Parakeet.   2. Emerald-collared Parakeet.   3. Rose-ringed Parakeet.   4. Ceylon Large Parakeet.   5. Ceylon Lorikeet

PLATE 16

1. Collared Scops Owl. 2. Ceylon Little Scops Owl. 3. Ceylon Bay Owl.
4. Brown Wood-Owl. 5. Jungle Owlet. 6. Eastern Barn-Owl. 7. Ceylon
Fish-Owl. 8. Forest Eagle-Owl

time, it is still numerous in jungle districts, especially to the east and south of the mountains. The dwindling of its numbers is due partly, no doubt, to the extension of cultivation, but also, I believe, to constant raiding of its nests by villagers, who take the young to be sold for pets; for it is a favourite cage bird. It lives in small flocks, principally in the neighbourhood of jungle tanks and chenas, and moves about a good deal. The flight is straight and swift, and the heavy head and long tail give it a very distinctive appearance on the wing. In flight, a harsh, loud scream *kee-arr* is constantly uttered. Outside the breeding season, it roosts in large flocks in coconut topes and the like, the birds collecting in small parties from great distances as the evening draws on. It feeds on a large variety of fruits, seeds, and grain, for which it raids villagers' chenas and paddy-fields; but it does comparatively little damage owing to its small numbers.

The breeding season is from November to May. The birds are believed to pair for life, and are very affectionate towards their mates. The nest-hole is situated in a large dead or living tree, and is generally a natural cavity or an old woodpecker's hole, which the parakeets enlarge, by gnawing, to suit their own needs. The only 'nest' is the chips and fragments of wood which happen to accumulate in the hole during the excavating process. The two to four white eggs measure about 31 × 24·3 mm.

THE ROSE-RINGED PARAKEET

Psittacula krameri manillensis (Bechstein). Resident

Sinhalese: Rannā Girawā. Tamil: Kili

Plate 15, facing p. 184 (male; ×one-quarter)

Size of the Common Mynah, but with a long and much-graduated tail. The female lacks the black and rose-pink neck-ring, and the delicate blue bloom which adorns the head of the male; young birds resemble the female. From the Ceylon Large Parakeet, which it somewhat resembles in colour-scheme, it may easily be distinguished by its smaller beak, brighter colours, shorter tail and lack of a red patch on the wing-coverts.

This parakeet is a common bird throughout the low-country dry zone, especially in coastal districts, but it avoids the hills. In the wet zone it is scarce and sporadic but common in Colombo, where small flocks may be seen in the evening flying towards their roosting place

(I believe, however, that most Colombo birds are escapes from captivity, as I have caught many of them and nearly all showed signs of former cage-life). This parakeet lives in flocks of various sizes, up to a hundred or more. The flocks move about the country a good deal, flying at a considerable height and circling down to investigate any tree in fruit; or to visit caged *confrères*, being attracted by the screams of the captives. Its scream is shriller and less harsh than that of the Large Parakeet, but is far more frequently uttered. The flight is swift and graceful, performed with quick beating of the shapely wings, and it is always punctuated by screaming. This parakeet feeds on a large variety of buds, fruit and seeds, and is partial to ripening paddy, to which it does considerable damage, biting off whole ears and wasting far more than it consumes.

The breeding season lasts from November till June, or even later. Courtship is a remarkable performance; the male, dapper in his breeding plumage, struts, with a most pompous, aldermanic air, along a perch towards his love. Then he feeds her (by regurgitation), between whiles drawing himself up to his full height and repeatedly raising one foot as high as it can reach, in a kind of 'sergeant-major salute'. This performance goes on for several minutes at a time, and gives an impression of most ardent passion combined with gentlemanly decorum. The nest-hole is generally in a dead tree or decaying palm trunk; a disused woodpecker hole is often deepened by the birds and adapted to their purpose. Two or three white eggs are laid; they measure about 29·5 × 24·3 mm.

THE BLOSSOM-HEADED PARAKEET

Psittacula cyanocephala cyanocephala (Linnaeus). Resident

Sinhalese: Pannu Girawā, Rosa Girawā. Tamil: Kili

Plate 15, facing p. 184 (male; × one-quarter)

Rather smaller than the Common Mynah, but with a long, slender tail; our smallest parakeet. The female has the head bluish-grey above a yellowish collar, and she lacks the red blotch on the wing-coverts. The adult male, with his lovely scarlet and blue-suffused head, is unmistakable; the female is readily distinguished from the Emerald-collared Parakeet by her brighter green coloration, yellow beak, and longer, conspicuously white-tipped tail. Young birds are green all over.

This is the common parakeet of the lower hill zone up to about 3,500 feet, or somewhat higher on the eastern aspect of the mountain massif. It may occur in scattered colonies in the dry zone—probably where isolated, wooded hills occur—but I believe that, as with the Large Parakeet, its range is greatly restricted since Legge's time. It lives in small flocks and travels about a good deal, though probably only within a circumscribed area. The flight is swift, performed by rapid wing-strokes, and as it flies it constantly utters a musical, single-note scream, which is quite distinct from the cries of the other parakeets; it also has more squeaky, but still musical, notes which it utters when excited, e.g. over the choice, or defence from other birds, of a desirable nesting site. Like other parakeets, it feeds on fruit, buds, seeds and grain; in respect of the latter item it is rather a pest to the cultivator, whether of paddy or kurrakan—descending in flocks upon the ripening grain, and devouring some but wasting far more. It is also very fond of the nectar of dadap, red cotton, etc.

The breeding season is from February to May, and often again in August–September. The nest-hole, which is often an adapted barbet's or woodpecker's hole or else a natural cavity, is commonly in a dead tree. The birds prefer a high site but sometimes nest in a suitable hole within hand-reach; aviary-confined birds will dig holes for nesting in the ground—loosening the soil with their beaks and kicking it out backwards with their feet—but it is doubtful if they ever do this under natural conditions. The two to four eggs are dull white, and measure about $25 \cdot 5 \times 21$ mm.

THE EMERALD-COLLARED PARAKEET, or
LAYARD'S PARAKEET

Psittacula calthorpae Blyth. Species peculiar to Ceylon

Sinhalese: Alu Girawā. Tamil: Kili

Plate 15, facing p. 184 (male; ×one-quarter)

Between the Rose-ringed Parakeet and the Blossom-headed Parakeet in size. The female is duller than the male, and has the beak black. Young birds are green, with the head darker, and the lower back and rump cobalt-blue; their beaks are at first dull orange, later black, from which colour that of the male gradually changes to the bright scarlet of the adult. The dark grey head (green around the eye), pale grey back, and comparatively short, deep-blue tail distinguish this from the other Ceylonese parakeets; its cry is quite distinctive.

This is pre-eminently the hill parakeet of Ceylon, and although it descends nearly to sea level in parts of the wet zone its main habitat is in the hills, from their bases to about 5,000 feet; at times it ascends to

6,000 feet, but it is doubtful if it breeds at such high altitudes. Over much of its range it overlaps the territory of the Blossom-head, with which it often disputes for the possession of coveted nesting-holes. Its very beautiful plumage assorts rather ill with its voice, which is a loud, harsh, chattering scream *ak ak ak ak ak ak*—interesting enough when heard in its natural setting of forested hills, valleys and streams, but rather overpowering at close quarters. This parakeet associates in pairs or small flocks. Its flight is swift and dashing, and is always accompanied by screaming; the birds are very adept in dodging at full speed through the trees of their forest home. It is, however, by no means confined to forest but frequents any kind of well-wooded country. Like other parakeets, it feeds on a large variety of fruits, flowers, buds, nectar, etc., but it is less destructive in grain fields than the Blossom-headed or Rose-ringed Parakeets, being more definitely arboreal than they.

The breeding season is from January to May, and often again in July–September. The favourite site for the nest is a hole high in the trunk of a tall tree; but as such sites are in great demand by other birds, especially mynahs, grackles, and other parakeets, many have to content themselves with lower sites. A dead softwood tree, such as dadap, will often have nest-holes occupied by several species breeding in close proximity. The two or three dull-white eggs measure about 25 × 20 mm.

THE CEYLON LORIKEET

Loriculus beryllinus (Forster). Species peculiar to Ceylon

Sinhalese: Girā̄ Malichchā, Pol Girawā. Tamil: Kanni-kili,
Thennang-kili

Plate 15, facing p. 184 (male; ×one-quarter)

Size of the House Sparrow. Sexes alike, but the female is duller-coloured than the male, and has only a trace of the pale-blue throat-patch; young birds have the head all green, but otherwise resemble their parents.

This brilliantly-coloured little parrot is found everywhere in the hills up to 4,000 feet, and in the north-east monsoon it ascends a thousand feet higher; it also inhabits the low-country wet zone and parts of the dry zone to the south of the Northern Province. Although very common in most parts of its range, it often escapes observation owing to its green plumage harmonizing with the leaves of the trees which it frequents; for it is strictly arboreal, never descending to the ground. Although often solitary, companions are never far away, and it keeps them informed of its movements by constantly uttering, while on the wing, a sharp three-syllabled whistle *twitwitwit . . . twitwitwit*. The flight is swift and is performed by alternate fluttering of the wings—during which the flight-note is uttered—and near closing of them; this results in the bird's proceeding in a series of big undulations. While perched, it converses with its fellows in queer little squeaky warblings, often uttered from a bare twig at the top of a tree. The lorikeet is a convivial little bird, delighting in juicy fruits, the nectar of flowers (especially dadap and red cotton), and the juice of palms collected in toddy-drawers' pots; imbibing the latter item is said to lead to its easy capture through intoxication. It eats also small seeds such as those of *Casuarina*, which I have watched it extracting from the cones. While feeding, it is most amusing to watch as it scampers along the twigs 'hand-over-hand' or hangs at all sorts of angles, ever reaching for some more succulent item. A restless little bird, it must cover great distances in the course of a day's wanderings. It sleeps bat-wise, hanging head downwards from a slender, leafy twig.

The lorikeet breeds in the first half of the year, and sometimes again in July–September. Its breeding habits are highly remarkable; the courting male attitudinizes before his lady in a ridiculous fashion, strutting along the perch with jerky gait and short hops, beak held high, blue throat-feathers puffed out, tail spread, and the scarlet rump-feathers raised and spread—altogether the embodiment of conceit and self-importance; all the while, he utters the little squeaky warble above-mentioned, interspersed with *twit*s. When nesting time arrives, a hollow tree or branch is chosen—preferably one with a long, narrow, nearly vertical cavity, and a narrow entrance at the top. Then the female builds her nest, which consists of strips nibbled from the edges of green leaves. Having cut a strip, she inserts one end of it under her scarlet rump-feathers, apparently digging it well into the skin; this does not, however, prevent a large proportion of the strips from falling out. When a rumpful of strips is collected, she flies off to her nest-hole and deposits them, accumulating a large mass, on top of which the eggs, two or three in number, are laid. The hen appears to do all the nest building and incubation, but the male takes a great interest in her doings. She sits very close and, if interfered with, voices her displeasure in angry screechings and, in some mysterious way, produces an extraordinary, heavy, thumping sound, suggestive of pounding the inside of the hollow with a sledge-hammer. The eggs are white and nearly spherical, measuring about $19 \cdot 3 \times 16$ mm. At the time of leaving the nest the young bird, though fully fledged, has the whole forehead and face naked—an adaptation which prevents the soiling of the face with liquid food.

OWLS

Order STRIGIFORMES

Owls are carnivorous, mainly nocturnal birds of very distinctive appearance and habits. They have strong, hooked beaks, with the nostrils set in a cere or saddle-shaped area of soft skin at the base of the upper mandible. Their legs and feet are powerful, with strong, curved claws, and the outer toe reversible, directed either forward or backward at will—though it is nearly always in the backward position when the bird is perched. The head is large, flat-faced, and full plumaged, never crested but in many forms furnished with a tuft of elongated feathers above and behind each eye; these tufts, which are variously called 'horns', 'aigrettes' or 'ear-tufts', are more or less erectile, their position indicating the bird's emotions—they are generally laid flat when it is at rest but erected in times of excitement, anger or fear; they have nothing to do with the ears. The latter are large openings on the sides of the head, often of complicated structure and, in many species, differently shaped on the two sides of the head; the hearing is very acute. The eyes are large, forwardly directed, their sides internally strengthened by a cylinder of small, flat bones; in consequence of this structure they are almost immobile, and the whole head must therefore be turned when the bird wishes to change the direction of its gaze. This fixity of the eyes doubtless accounts for the strange habit most owls have, especially when young, of swaying the head from side to side and rotating it, when regarding something that takes their interest. In closing the eyes, owls, unlike most birds, move mainly the upper eyelid, not the lower. The feathering of the face radiates away from the orbits, forming the 'facial disk' which, in most owls, is bounded by a 'ruff' of short, recurved, stiff feathers; these features, together with the large, forward-looking eyes, give the characteristic expression to an owl's face. The gape and base of the beak are concealed by bristly, forwardly-directed feathers. The plumage of owls is very voluminous and soft. The wings are long and broad, rounded at the tips, with the quills flexible; the leading edge of the first (functional) primary is furnished with soft, recurved filaments, whose function is to muffle the sound of the bird's flight. The tail is short in most forms, moderately long in a few; it is rounded, never forked or much graduated.

The coloration is always sober, with grey, brown, ochre, black and white predominating, the markings arranged in softly mottled, barred, or streaked patterns. Many species have two colour varieties—some individuals tending towards a reddish tint, others towards grey. Owls, in general, show a tendency for the outer scapulars and the outer median and lesser wing-coverts to be marked with pale spots, streaks or bars, often accentuated by adjacent dark patches. These markings form 'disruptive' patterns, helping to disguise the bird when, as most owls do, it draws itself up, compressing the plumage and erecting the ear-tufts (if any), on the approach of an enemy; the effect of this instinctive action is to give the bird the semblance of a stub branch, or some such item in its normal environment. When seriously frightened or annoyed, these birds have a habit of snapping the beak by pressing the tips of the two mandibles together until the lower mandible suddenly snaps into its closed position.

Owls are well known for their weird cries which, being uttered mostly at night, have made them, in conjunction with their strange facial expressions, objects of superstitious dread among all primitive peoples. The larger forms feed on small mammals—up to rabbit-size—and birds, but the smaller ones prey mainly on mice, geckos, and insects such as beetles and grasshoppers. The prey is always swallowed whole unless its size makes this impossible. Some hours after a meal the indigestible portions—fur, feathers, bones, wing-cases, etc.—are voided through the mouth in a compact pellet. Examination of these pellets (which accumulate beneath the roosting perch, or in the nesting cavity) gives a good indication of the food of each species. Most owls are highly beneficial to man owing to the enormous numbers of noxious rodents and insects they destroy.

They lay white eggs, depositing them either in the deserted nests of other birds or, more often, without any nest-lining, in cavities in trees, cliffs, or buildings. The young are hatched help-less, blind, and covered with white down, which gives place to a suit of fluffy, downy feathers; from the latter they moult into adult plumage. Owls are among the most courageous of birds in defence of their young.

The classification of owls is subject to divergencies of scientific opinion, but for the purpose of this work they are considered to form but a single family—*Strigidae*—with two sub-families, *Tytoninae* and *Striginae*. The first species on our list, the Eastern Barn Owl, alone represents the *Tytoninae*, all the rest being *Striginae*.

THE EASTERN BARN OWL

Tyto alba stertens Hartert. Resident

Sinhalese: Bakamunā. Tamil: Chavu-kuruvi

Plate 16, facing p. 185 (×one-seventh)

About the size of the House Crow. Sexes alike. The pale ochre and mottled grey of the upperparts and wings, and white face and under-parts, suffice to distinguish this owl from all other Ceylonese species. It is rather a slender owl; the legs are comparatively long, and the wings too are long, extending when folded to about two inches beyond the tail.

In Ceylon, it is rare and very restricted in range, being confined to the Jaffna Peninsula and the north-west strip of coast down to Put-talam; and even in this limited area it seems to be scarce except in Jaffna itself. However, its distribution in the Island requires investiga-tion; being strictly a nocturnal species, and secretive in its ways, it is not easily observed. Dark crannies and holes, in old buildings or gnarled old trees, provide its day-time retreats; it commonly lives near human habitations, probably because man's granaries and warehouses attract its favourite prey, rats and mice. Being intolerant of sunlight, it does not usually emerge from its hiding-place until dusk is well established; then it issues forth, perches for a short time on some near-by vantage-point while it preens its plumage and scans the outlook; and then, with slow-flapping and gliding flight, repairs to its hunting-ground. Before dawn it returns to its roost. Like all birds of prey, it regularly dis-gorges the indigestible portions of its prey (fur, feathers, bones, etc.) in the form of a rounded pellet or 'casting', and by examining these castings, accumulated beneath its perch, an accurate idea of its food may be obtained; destructive rodents form a high proportion of it.

The breeding season is in February and March and, as it approaches, the Barn Owl becomes noisy; it utters a harsh, high-pitched scream *eeee* or *wheech*, which has a hoarse quality as if the bird were straining its throat. A more wheezy version of the same sound is the hunger-cry of the young. The two or three white eggs are laid on the bare floor of the nesting cavity; as incubation proceeds, however, a layer of castings accumulates, forming a bed for the eggs and young. The eggs measure about 43 × 32·8 mm.

THE CEYLON BAY OWL

Phodilus badius assimilis Hume. Race peculiar to Ceylon

Sinhalese: Bassā (a general term for all small owls). Tamil: Āndai

Plate 16, facing p. 185 (× one-seventh)

About the size of a domestic pigeon. Sexes alike. The rich chestnut and buff back and wings, and pinkish-buff underparts, distinguish this owl from other Ceylonese species.

It is one of our rarest birds, under a dozen specimens having been recorded; such evidence as exists shows that it inhabits the hills from the base up to about 4,000 feet, and parts of the wet zone. It is a shy, forest bird, strictly nocturnal and apparently almost blind in daylight. It spends the day, and also nests, in hollow trees.

Young birds have been taken from the nest in November. They were three in number, and showed great discrepancy in size—indicating that, as with some other owls, this species probably lays its eggs at intervals of several days but commences incubation as soon as the first is laid—resulting in the hatching period being extended.

Persons who come into possession, or have opportunities for observing the habits, of this rare owl, are urged to do all they can to note and record permanently every detail about it.

THE SHORT-EARED OWL

Asio flammeus flammeus (Pontoppidan). Irregular winter visitor

Sinhalese: Bassā. Tamil: Āndai

About the size of the Black Crow, but with fuller plumage and longer, narrower wings. Sexes alike. The general colour is ochreous or buff, streaked and mottled with dark brown and black. Its ear-tufts are very small and inconspicuous, situated close together above the eyes. The wing lining is whitish, with a dark crescent on the under primary-coverts, dark bars at the tips of the primaries, and slight dusky bars on the quills. Irides yellow; beak black; legs and feet fully feathered.

The Short-eared Owl, which is a migratory species and a great traveller, has a very wide distribution almost throughout the temperate and tropical regions of the world. It visits Ceylon at irregular intervals; some years in considerable numbers, in others not at all, or in very small numbers. Its habits differ from those of all our other owls in that it nearly always perches on the ground, and frequents open scrub-land, swamps and marshes, etc. Moreover, it flies readily, and often hunts, in the day-time, when its

× one-ninth

long, narrow wings and slow, easy, sailing style of flight may cause it to be mistaken for a harrier; the big, round head, short tail, and under-wing pattern, however, help in identifying it. Small mammals, birds and reptiles, especially swamp-frequenting kinds, comprise its food. It sleeps on the ground among bushes or grass-tussocks, where its streaked 'dry-grass' coloration gives it good concealment.

The Short-eared Owl breeds in temperate climates, nesting on the ground among heather or swamp vegetation. The nest is a mere scrape. Four to seven white eggs are laid; they measure about 40 × 32 mm. (British eggs).

THE BROWN WOOD OWL

Strix leptogrammica ochrogenys (Hume). Race peculiar to Ceylon

Sinhalese: Ulamā. Tamil: Āndai

Plate 16, facing p. 185 (×one-seventh)

About the size of the Brahminy Kite, but much fuller-plumaged. Sexes alike, except that the female is somewhat larger than the male. The light-chestnut facial disk, brown eyes, white-barred outer

194

scapulars, and closely barred, ochreous underparts, distinguish this beautiful owl, which has no ear-tufts.

It is fairly common in most parts of the Island, up to a height of at least 7,000 feet; but being strictly a forest bird and nocturnal, never flying by day unless disturbed, it is not often seen. It spends the day perching in a dark, close-foliaged tree, and if intruded upon seeks to elude observation by compressing itself into the semblance of a stub of wood, while watching the intruder through half-closed eyelids. If this ruse fails, it flies silently off, threading its way cleverly between the tree-trunks. It apparently pairs for life, but a pair are seldom seen together in the day-time. At dusk they call to each other in a sonorous hoot *hŭhŭ-hooo*—calling and answering each other for some time before flying off on their night's hunting. The food consists almost entirely of small mammals, such as rats, mice and shrews, with an occasional small bird or lizard; and the service this owl renders to mankind in destroying vermin entitles it to complete protection. Besides the call above-mentioned, it utters various other notes under stress of emotion, especially when its young are threatened by an enemy. One, which I watched driving a troop of macaques away from its baby, flapped its wings violently against foliage, giving vent at the same time to a curious whistle or scream; later, when I approached its chick, it menaced me with beak-snapping, growls, hoarse hoots—*huh huh huh*—and a short bark, *wow wow wow*. The hunger-note of the young is a hoarse, wheezing sound, quavering at the end—*eeeeerrrr*.

The breeding season is in the first half of the year. The eggs are deposited on the touchwood and rubbish at the bottom of a large cavity in a big forest tree. As a rule, only one egg appears to be laid—at any rate, a single young bird per brood is reared. The eggs are white and measure about $48 \cdot 7 \times 42 \cdot 5$ mm. This owl is very courageous in defence of its young. If reared from the nest, it makes a nice pet; I once had an albino which lived for several years in an aviary with a normally-coloured specimen. It occasionally laid an egg, but the eggs were all infertile.

THE CEYLON FISH OWL

Ketupa zeylonensis zeylonensis (Gmelin). Race peculiar to Ceylon

Sinhalese: Bakamūnā. Tamil: Periya Āndai, Ūmatan-kuruvi

Plate 16, facing p. 185 (×one-seventh)

About the size of the Serpent Eagle. Sexes alike. This is the only *large* Ceylon owl with yellow irides, and the only one that has quite unfeathered tarsi; these features, and its much shorter ear-tufts, readily distinguish it from the Forest Eagle-Owl, the only species with which it might be confused.

It is a common bird and is widely distributed throughout the low country and in the hills up to at least 6,000 feet, wherever forest borders a stream—large or small—or a lake; for it is seldom found far from water. Even a narrow strip of forest will do, provided it includes some large trees for hiding in by day. Like most owls, it lives in pairs, which roost separately. As dusk falls, they fly from their hiding-places to some stump or dead branch and commence to call to each other in doleful, and most human-sounding moans; *oomp-ōō-oo* says one, to be answered by its mate with an assenting *oo*. This dismal concert goes on for some time before the birds decide that hunger as well as music has claims, and proceed to hunt for food. In producing these moans, the throat swells into a large, white bulge. The Fish Owl, as its name implies, lives largely on fish, but it is by no means confined to a fish diet and many live permanently along up-country streams where no fishes exist; it eats many freshwater crabs, large insects, lizards and snakes, and such small mammals as it can catch.

The breeding season is from January to May. The nest is in a cavity in a big tree; on a ledge of rock, or small cave in a stream-side cliff; or in the hollow at the junction of several large branches. The clutch comprises one, or sometimes two eggs; they are white and measure about 59×45 mm. In 1942, a pair bred in an aviary at the Colombo Museum, laying a single egg on the ground; they successfully raised a chick to maturity in spite of the fact that three other Fish Owls shared the aviary.

THE FOREST EAGLE-OWL

Bubo nipalensis blighi Legge. Resident

Sinhalese: Loku Bakamūnā. Tamil: Periya Āndai

Plate 16, facing p. 185 (×one-ninth)

About the size of the Serpent Eagle, but fuller-plumaged and heavier built; our largest owl. Sexes alike, but the female slightly larger than the male. The young are pale buff-white, barred on back and wing-coverts with black, and with faint grey bars on back of head, ear-tufts and breast. This fine owl may easily be distinguished from the Fish Owl by its deep brown eyes,[1] very stout, *feathered* legs, and its much longer, black and white barred ear-tufts.

[1] There is some evidence that in very old birds the irides tend to become yellowish-brown.

It is rare, but appears to be widely distributed, wherever forest is extensive, both in the hills and the low country; but it probably does not occur in the Northern Province, and its headquarters are undoubtedly in the lower hills of the mountain zone. As it is strictly a forest bird, and nocturnal, it is seldom seen and most specimens that have been collected have been shot while raiding fowls or pigeons at lonely dwellings near jungle. It spends the day hiding amongst foliage in a tall tree, and sallies forth at dusk. Like other owls, it is fond of bathing and, if the behaviour of a tame one is a reliable guide to its habits in the wild state, it generally takes a bath—in some shallow pool or jungle stream—before beginning its night's hunting. Small mammals, birds up to the size of junglefowl and, doubtless, lizards and snakes, comprise its prey. One, which I came upon in a tree in precipitous jungle on the slopes of the Nilgiri Hills in South India, had been feeding on a large flying squirrel, whose remains were draped across the branch on which the owl was sitting.

All real evidence of the identity of the 'Devil Bird' in Ceylon points to this owl as the author of the dreadful shrieks and strangulating noises. It is probable that other owls, at times, produce some of the various cries attributed to the Devil Bird, but I believe that the authentic gurgling shrieks, etc., are nothing more than the mating love-song of the Forest Eagle-Owl; this would account for the rare and sporadic occurrence of these cries. As to its ordinary call, a deep, human-sounding snore, which I have heard at night in the Ceylon jungles, was probably uttered by this bird. The only note the tame one above-mentioned produced, was a weak, chittering squeak, uttered in protest at being disturbed.

The breeding season appears to be about April and May. A single egg is laid, without any true nest, in such a site as the hollow at the junction of several large boughs of a big tree growing in deep forest. Indian eggs measure about 62 × 50·2 mm. They are white.

THE CEYLON LITTLE SCOPS OWL

Otus scops leggei Ticehurst. Race peculiar to Ceylon

Sinhalese: Pŭnchi Bassā. Tamil: Sinna Āndai, Nattu

Plate 16, facing p. 185
(left, rufous form; right, greyish-brown form; ×one-sixth)

About the size of the Red-vented Bulbul, but with short tail and fuller plumage; much smaller than the Collared Scops Owl. Sexes alike. Like many other owls, this bird has two colour-forms, both of which are figured on the Plate; one is dark brown and grey, heavily marbled, mottled and streaked with black, and with a white stripe on the outer scapulars; the other is bright chestnut, much less heavily marked. Between these two forms intermediates occur. This tiny owl may be at once distinguished from the next species by its yellow irides; it might, conceivably, be mistaken for the frogmouth—which has a somewhat owlish look, not very dissimilar coloration, and yellow irides —but its small, narrow beak, ear-tufts, facial disk and raptorial feet should make such a blunder impossible. From the Jungle Owlet and the Chestnut-backed Owlet—both of which have yellow irides—it may be distinguished by its small size, shorter tail, and ear-tufts; the latter, however, are only conspicuous when the bird erects them under the influence of fear or excitement.

It is a rare bird, seldom seen; but its wide distribution in both low country and hills up to 5,000 feet is evidenced by its very distinctive call; this is a loud, monotonously repeated, *tuk, tok torok . . . tuk, tok torok*, etc. (the first syllable *tuk* being much less loud than the others), which continues for long periods at night. (I have heard exactly the same note in the forests of Travancore—evidently produced by the Travancore race of this owl.) It is strictly a forest bird, spending the day roosting in some dense tangle of creepers, dark foliage, etc. If alarmed by the approach of an intruder, it erects its ear-tufts, contracts its plumage until it assumes the semblance of a snag of wood, and watches the enemy through nearly-closed eyes; in this pose it is almost indistinguishable as an animate object. It feeds mainly on insects—principally beetles—though doubtless geckos and other small animals are eaten; Legge's correspondent who informed him that it devoured numbers of small birds, leaving their remains on his veranda, was unquestionably blaming the malign work of the oriental vampire bats (*Megaderma spasma ceylonense* and *Lyraderma lyra lyra*) on this harmless little owl.

The eggs do not appear to have been recorded from Ceylon, but W. W. A. Phillips had a fledgling, just able to fly, brought to him on 7 May, in the West Matale district; so the breeding season is probably in the first half of the year. No doubt the eggs are laid in holes in trees, probably at a considerable height.

THE COLLARED SCOPS OWL

Otus bakkamoena bakkamoena Pennant. Resident

Sinhalese: Pŭnchi Bassā. Tamil: Sinna Āndai, Nattu

Plate 16, facing p. 185 (×one-sixth)

Size of the Common Mynah, but with fuller plumage. Sexes alike. The size, combined with the possession of ear-tufts and *brown* irides suffice to distinguish this small owl from its relatives. The Plate shows the commonest type of coloration, but more rufous, and also greyer, forms occur.

This is quite the commonest and most familiar of the small owls of Ceylon. It is widely distributed in the low country, both wet and dry zones, and ascends the hills to about 3,000 feet. Unlike most owls, it does not shun human society but frequents gardens, even in the midst of towns, and often chooses a roosting-place under the eaves of houses; but it also dwells in jungle, far from human habitations. Soon after dusk has fallen it issues from its hiding-place—under eaves, in dark and tangled foliage, or a hollow tree, etc.—and commences to call to its mate in a quaint, monosyllabic note resembling the word *what* with the *t* omitted; this is repeated at intervals of two to three seconds for several minutes, and is answered by its mate in similar tones. On their meeting, the call gives place to a loud *wā wā wā wā wā*, descending in scale, and often followed by a shrill, chittering squeal. A pair will call to each other several times during the night, especially during the courting season. The principal food, as proved by examination of castings beneath its roosts, consists of beetles and grasshoppers; but it is fond of geckos—which it not infrequently snatches from the walls of lighted verandas—and it also occasionally captures a mouse or small shrew. Its flight is rapid and silent, performed by quick beating of the wings; on reaching its perch it is able to check its flight, however fast, with no appreciable slowing-up. If raised from the nest this little owl makes a most delightful pet. The young are very amusing as, in studying anything that interests them, they oscillate their bodies from side to side through a very wide arc and rotate their heads in a ludicrous manner. Their diet, however, must include a high proportion of insects, geckos, mice, etc., or they will not thrive.

The breeding season is from February to May. The two or three eggs are laid in a tree-cavity, hollow dead palm, or suitable nook in the eaves of a building; usually no nest is made. The eggs are white, and measure about 32×27·8 mm. This owl is very bold in defence of its young, and will fearlessly attack with its claws anyone who attempts to capture them.

THE JUNGLE OWLET

Glaucidium radiatum radiatum (Tickell). Resident

Sinhalese: Pŭnchi Bassā. Tamil: Sinna Āndai

Plate 16, facing p. 185 (×one-sixth)

About the size of the Collared Scops Owl. Sexes alike. From the next species, this may be distinguished by its dark-brown and white-barred back and underparts, and the absence of blackish shaft-streaks on the latter; from the two scops owls by the barred coloration of head, back and breast, and the absence of ear-tufts.

Although probably not uncommon in the dense forests of the south and east of the mountain zone, it is seldom seen, and very few specimens have been collected since Legge first met with it in 1873. Although he obtained only one specimen, it enabled him to identify the author of a strange cry, through which he was enabled to trace the bird's distribution. Legge describes this note as: 'The syllable *kaōw*, slowly repeated and gradually accelerated until changed to *kaōw-whap*, *kaōw-whap*, which increases in loudness until suddenly stopped.' This owl is very diurnal, calling frequently in broad daylight, and also hunting well before dusk and again after dawn. It feeds mainly on insects—beetles and the like—but it also kills small birds, mice and lizards. Its flight is swift and direct, rather like that of a small hawk.

The nest does not appear to have been found in Ceylon, but in India it is in tree-holes, the three or four eggs being laid on the floor of the cavity, without any lining. They are, as usual in owls, white, and measure about 32·3 × 27 mm.

THE CHESTNUT-BACKED OWLET

Glaucidium cuculoides castanonotum (Blyth). Race peculiar to Ceylon

Sinhalese: Pŭnchi Bassā. Tamil: Sinna Āndai

About the size of the Collared Scops Owl. Sexes alike. This little owl is very like the last species in shape, size, and general appearance, but it is chestnut on back, scapulars, and wing-coverts, and has white underparts marked with blackish shaft-streaks, and bars on the flanks. Some specimens have white spots on the outer scapulars. Irides bright yellow; feet pale yellow.

This owl appears to have been fairly common in Legge's time in many parts of the southern half of the Island, especially the hills and the wet-zone low country extending to the outskirts of Colombo; but its range has undoubtedly shrunk very greatly since then, and it is now found sparingly in the remaining forests of the wet zone and the adjoining hills up to 6,500 feet. It is shy and wary, and as it frequents the tops of tall trees, usually on steep hill-sides, it is seldom seen. It is very diurnal in habits, often hunting and calling in broad daylight. The call is a curious note, like *kraw kraw kraw kraw kraw* (the *r* accentuated), which carries for a long distance. The Chestnut-backed Owlet feeds mainly on insects, such as beetles, but also captures mice, small lizards, and small birds, on occasion; most likely, the larger vertebrate forms of prey are taken only when young are being fed.

According to Legge, the breeding season is from March to May, the eggs being laid on the bare wood in a hole in the trunk or limb of a tree. The two glossy white eggs measure about 35 × 28·2 mm.

THE BROWN HAWK-OWL

Ninox scutulata hirsuta (Temminck). Resident

Sinhalese: Pŭnchi Bassā. Tamil: Sinna Āndai

Smaller than the House Crow, but larger, and with longer wings and tail, than the Collared Scops Owl. Sexes alike. The rather slender build, long wings, coloration, and lack of ear-tufts, distinguish this from all other Ceylon owls. Its head is ashy brown, with some white on the face,

and yellow irides; the entire upperparts are dark brown, with some half-concealed white spots on the outer scapulars and inner secondaries; the breast is dark brown, streaked with yellow, and the rest of the underparts are white, heavily blotched and streaked with dark brown. The legs are feathered and the toes, which are dusky yellow, are clothed with sparse bristles, and are prickly beneath.

The Brown Hawk-Owl is widely distributed in well-wooded—though not necessarily forested—parts of the low country, and ascends the hills to about 6,000 feet; but nowadays it is not common anywhere. Its favourite haunts are in the belts of forest lining the banks

× one-quarter

of rivers or around tanks, but it sometimes occurs in the outskirts of Colombo and other populous areas. Its method of hunting differs from that of the scops owls, as it does not generally pounce from a perch on its prey, but spends much time on the wing, chasing flying beetles and other insects, which form its food. The flight is quick and adroit, and its long wings give it somewhat the appearance of a nightjar. It moves about a good deal, being less sedentary than most owls. At evening and early morning, and at intervals throughout the night, especially when the moon shines brightly, it utters its musical call, which sounds like a mellow *kŏŏ-ook*, *kŏŏ-ook* . . ., etc. (the *ook* being lower in the scale than the first syllable). This call may be heard for a considerable distance on a still night. It roosts, during the heat of the day, concealed among the dark tangle of foliage, creepers, etc., at the top of a jungle tree; but it sees well by daylight and sometimes, on gloomy days, hunts until morning is well advanced.

It breeds during the first quarter of the year, laying its two or three white, very round eggs on the bare wood at the bottom of a cavity in a tree; they measure about $37 \times 32 \cdot 2$ mm.

RAPTORS, OR DIURNAL BIRDS OF PREY

ORDER FALCONIFORMES

THE *Falconiformes,* or raptorial birds, include two sub-orders, the *Cathartae* and the *Falcones.* The former, comprising the New World vultures (of which the famous condor is a member), are confined to the Americas and do not come within the scope of this book. They are quite distinct, except for some similarity in feeding-habits, from the Old World or true vultures. The *Falcones* include all remaining birds of prey and, so far as Ceylon is concerned, comprise three families, as follows:

Pandionidae—the osprey.
Accipitridae—vultures, eagles, kites, harriers, hawks,[1] buzzards, and bazas.
Falconidae—falcons.

The distinctive features (apart from purely anatomical characters) of each of these families are given at the head of each. In addition, general accounts of certain well-defined groups (harriers, short-winged hawks, etc.) are given, to assist in field identification of these somewhat puzzling birds.

THE OSPREY

Family PANDIONIDAE

The osprey which, in three races, exists almost throughout the temperate and warmer regions of the world, forms a family of its own differing in many anatomical features from all other hawks. For the purposes of this work, however, these structural details are unimportant and the main features of the bird are those concerned with its specialization for an exclusively fish diet. The osprey lives on fish which it captures by plunging from a height while on the wing, submerging itself more or less completely, and seizing its prey in its claws; it then flies with the fish to some convenient

---

[1] The term 'hawk' is loosely applied to most raptors; in its special sense it applies to the short-winged hawks belonging to the genus *Accipiter.*

perch to devour it. In accordance with this habit, its plumage is hard and close, wings long and powerful, legs stout and strong with the feathering of the tibia short and close unlike most hawks, which have the feathers of this part lengthened; the tarsus unfeathered; toes strong, with the outer one reversible as in owls; the soles are covered with sharp prickles, to give a good grip of slippery prey; the claws are strong and much curved.

THE OSPREY

Pandion haliaetus haliaetus (Linnaeus). Winter visitor

No Sinhalese name recorded. Tamil: Viral-addippān

Between the Brahminy Kite and the Sea Eagle in size. Sexes alike in coloration, but the female is slightly larger than the male. The dark brown upperparts, white head with black markings as shown in the figure, white underparts with brown band across the breast, long, narrow wings, and the distinctive habits, make the osprey easy to recognize.

It is a fairly common winter visitor to the coastal lagoons and

× one-tenth

estuaries of Ceylon, particularly those of the dry zone, and it occasionally travels inland, having been seen as high as Nuwara Eliya Lake. It is fond of perching on posts or other commanding objects in the midst of the waters it frequents. While doing so, it looks a heavy, dark-coloured hawk, with mainly white head and underparts. It has, however, graceful, easy, and powerful flight, with the long wings often slightly bent in the middle. When hunting, it flies at a height of fifty to a hundred feet or so, diligently scanning the water beneath. On spying a fish of suitable size it hovers for a moment—like an ungainly kestrel—and then, half-closing its wings, descends into the water with a mighty splash to emerge a moment later, with powerful flappings, holding (usually) a struggling fish in its talons. In bearing its capture to a perch, it carries it head foremost, presumably to reduce wind-resistance. It is usually silent while in Ceylon.

The osprey breeds in temperate regions, building a large nest of sticks, etc., in a tree, or sometimes on the ground, near water. The two to four eggs are white, handsomely marked with reddish-brown, and measure about 62 × 46 mm.

THE VULTURES, EAGLES, HAWKS, AND THEIR ALLIES

Family ACCIPITRIDAE

These are medium-sized to very large birds, characterized by diurnal, carnivorous habits, and structure adapted for the pursuit and capture of living vertebrate prey. Their principal features are: strong, hooked beak, with the nostrils situated in a soft, waxy area of skin (cere) at the base of the upper mandible; strong feet, with toes arranged three in front and one behind, bearing sharp, powerful claws; large wings, giving great powers of flight; highly efficient eyes, which are much more mobile than those of owls, but are not directed so much to the front. Their coloration is generally sober, with greys, browns, black and white predominating. They have much white under-down beneath the contour feathers. In habits and nidification they vary greatly. The young are blind and helpless on hatching, but covered with white down. In most forms, the female is considerably larger than the male.

Except the vultures, which feed on carrion and do not kill prey for themselves, the members of this family normally slay their victims by the tremendous grip of their feet driving home the sharp claws; this method is different from that of the falcons (family *Falconidae*), which typically kill by a blow with the hind claw delivered in flight with the force of a tremendous downward stoop. Correlated with these distinct methods of killing there is a difference in the structure of the feet in the two families; in the *Accipitridae*, the claws of the hind and the inner toes are always the largest and provide most of the gripping force; next in size comes the middle front claw, while the outer claw is comparatively small and weak. In *Falconidae* this divergence in size of the claws is much less pronounced.

A single specimen, in juvenile plumage, of the SMALLER WHITE SCAVENGER VULTURE or NEOPHRON *Neophron percnopterus ginginianus* (Latham) was collected at Nuwara Eliya in March 1874; it was for many years exhibited in the Colombo Museum. Phillips (*Checklist*, p. 23) states that one was believed to have been seen in the Jaffna Peninsula in January 1950. These are the only records of this bird in Ceylon but, as it is extremely common throughout India and is a bird of powerful flight, this is surprising, and it seems probable that it will in time establish itself in the dry zone, at least, of Ceylon.

It is about the size of a large domestic cock. Sexes alike. The adult is dirty white, with black primaries; there is a dark line at the base of the secondaries; the tail is wedge-shaped. The wings are broad and long, extending well beyond the tail when closed. The naked, yellow face is surrounded by a ruff of hackle-shaped feathers; beak long and slender for a vulture's, hooked at the tip, yellow; legs and feet dirty yellow. Young birds are dark brown mottled with buff, and have the head and beak greyish. The whole appearance is slovenly, bedraggled, and repulsive, in keeping with the bird's filthy habits. It frequents the precincts of towns and villages, subsisting on garbage and filth and performing a useful function in the absence of sanitation. It walks with a waddling gait, the body rather horizontal. As some compensation for its unprepossessing appearance on the ground, the flight is easy and graceful. It is generally solitary or in small parties, and is silent as a rule.

The nest is a large, untidy, and filthy collection of all manner of rubbish, placed in a tree, or on some ledge or cornice of a building or cliff. The two or three eggs are white, handsomely marked with various shades of reddish brown; they measure about $66 \cdot 7 \times 51$ mm.

THE BOOTED EAGLE

Hieraaetus pennatus (Gmelin). Occasional winter visitor

Sinhalese: Rājāliya. Tamil: Rāsāli, Kalugu

Plate 18, facing p. 217 (×approx. one-twentieth)

Slightly smaller than the Serpent Eagle. Sexes alike. This eagle has two colour forms: the commonest is brown above, buff-white below, with fawn-coloured head, and pale buff areas in the pattern shown on the Plate. The underwing is buff-white, with subterminal black spots on the greater coverts; quills dark brown, spotted with buff-white towards their bases, especially on the inner primaries, which are paler than the rest. Irides rich brown; cere and gape chrome yellow; beak bluish, darkening to black at the tip. The tibial feathers are long, tarsus feathered down to the foot. Feet chrome yellow, claws black. The other form is similar in pattern to the first, but very much darker, a brown and black bird.

This small eagle, which is a winter visitor to India, has a wide range in Europe, Africa, and Asia, but visits Ceylon very seldom, only about half a dozen specimens having been recorded hitherto; doubtless it occurs in the Island more frequently than the records suggest. Most specimens have been collected in the north, and in the neighbourhood of Colombo. It is a daring and predatory bird which hunts on the wing, capturing birds, rats, and, no doubt, lizards. One which I met with in Jaffna, in December 1944, sailed easily, with little flapping, a few feet above treetop level, accompanied by a raucously cawing mob of crows and a few Brahminy and Pariah Kites; it took no notice of the crows, but once or twice feinted at a Brahminy. It caught a Brown-headed Barbet, which it carried into a tree and proceeded to pluck. I noted that, in flight, it had much the same silhouette as a Brahminy Kite, but it was half as large again and, of course, quite different in coloration. It uttered no sound.

A single specimen of BONELLI'S EAGLE *Hieraaetus fasciatus* (Vieillot) was collected in Ceylon over a hundred years ago, but the locality and sex are unknown. It is considerably larger than the Booted Eagle and Serpent Eagle; a powerfully built bird, with no crest, feathered tarsi, yellow irides, cere and gape, and black beak, bluish near the cere. The upperparts are dark brown, the throat, lower face and breast white with black shaft-streaks and drop-shaped markings. The tail is greyish-brown above, with a broad, blackish band at the tip.

THE RUFOUS-BELLIED HAWK-EAGLE

Hieraaetus kienerii kienerii (E. Geoffroy) (*Lophotriorchis kienerii* [de Sparre] of many authors). Resident

Sinhalese: Rājāliya. Tamil: Rāsāli, Kalugu

Plate 17, facing p. 216 (× one-ninth)
Plate 18, facing p. 217 (× approx. one-twentieth)

About the size of the Serpent Eagle. Sexes alike, but the female is slightly larger than the male. Head with a short, triangular crest on the back of the head but this is generally inconspicuous, being depressed down the back of the neck. When adult, this eagle is easily recognized by its black upperparts, chestnut underparts and under wing-coverts, and white throat and breast. Young birds are mottled brown above, pure white beneath and on the under wing-coverts; they have a whitish supercilium, black lores and region round the eye. In this phase, they may easily be mistaken for the young of the Ceylon Hawk-Eagle and for one variety of the young of the Serpent Eagle; however, their wings are longer and their tails shorter than either of these, and the under-wing looks white, shading to a dark border all round, and with a band of black spots on the greater coverts; the under-surface of the tail is pale grey with a number of narrow dark bars, of which the subterminal one is the darkest.

When perched, this handsome little eagle has a cobby, compact appearance which distinguishes it from the comparatively slender Ceylon Hawk-Eagle. It is rare but widely distributed in the Island, favouring patana woods and the like in the medium elevations of the hill zone from about 1,000 to 4,000 feet, though it may be seen, at times, at other elevations. It has a fine style of flight, soaring and circling in a lively manner; and it is a bold and skilful hunter, feeding largely on birds which it captures on the wing by stooping from a height, with wings nearly closed and winglets elevated, after the manner of a falcon. It also captures small mammals and, no doubt, lizards, but its favourite prey appears to be birds, of which doves and pigeons come in for a considerable share of its attentions; several specimens known to me have been shot while harrying domestic pigeons. I have never heard it utter any note.

The breeding season seems to be from December to March. The nest is a large one of sticks, etc., lined with green leaves, placed in a forest tree. A single egg is laid; it is white, speckled and blotched with various shades of brown and red, and measures about $58 \cdot 7 \times 47$ mm.

THE BLACK EAGLE

Ictinaetus malayensis perniger (Hodgson). Resident

Sinhalese: Kalu Rājāliya. Tamil: Karuppu Rāsāli

Plate 18, facing p. 217 (×approx. one-twentieth)

Between the Serpent Eagle and the Ceylon Mountain Hawk-Eagle in size, but its very long wings and tail make it look larger than it really is; the closed wings reach to the end of the tail. Sexes alike; young birds are browner and somewhat mottled in appearance. The black plumage, and very long wings, with widely-separated primaries strongly up-curved in flight, and the slow, sailing character of the latter, make this grand eagle easy to recognize. Irides brown; cere and gape chrome yellow; beak bluish at the base, black at the tip; lores and eyebrow greyish; legs feathered to the feet, which are chrome yellow, and have the claws much less curved than those of most eagles. It has no crest.

This is a fairly common bird throughout the mountain zone, and may also be met with about forested hills in the low country. It prefers a mixture of forest and patana or scrub to dense forest, and where such country is combined with rugged crags and precipices it is sure to be found. Its flight is magnificent but is normally slow, though it can stoop with great speed when occasion demands. While hunting, it sails slowly along a hill-side only a few yards above the treetops, its keen eyes scanning every tree for prey; the wings are seldom flapped and the bird shows marvellous skill in circling in and out of small hollows among the trees without flapping its great pinions. Presently it checks suddenly and plunges into a tree, to emerge in a few moments carrying something in its talons. The 'something' is probably a bird's nest with eggs or young, for this eagle is notorious for its un-aquiline habit of feeding largely on the eggs and chicks of small birds—bulbuls, doves, munias, etc. It preys also on adult birds up to the size of a fowl, and on small mammals; the only one I have dissected contained the remains of a large rat. While sailing, it sometimes dangles its legs (as shown in the Plate) presumably to act as an air-brake. I have never heard it utter any sound in its natural state, but a captive one became very restless in the evenings and would then utter a loud cry *ah-a* at intervals. It is seldom seen to perch.

The nest does not appear to have been found in Ceylon, but Indian nests are huge masses of sticks, lined with green leaves, and set in the crown of tall forest trees, usually growing in precipitous places. The breeding season is in December. One egg seems to be the rule; it is whitish, handsomely marked with large spots and marks of deep brown, and measures about 63×50 mm. The birds are very courageous in defence of their home.

THE CEYLON HAWK-EAGLE

Spizaetus cirrhatus ceylanensis (Gmelin). Resident

Sinhalese: Kondé Rājāliya. Tamil: Kondé Rāsāli, Kalugu

Plate 17, facing p. 216 (×one-ninth)

About the size of the Serpent Eagle but more slenderly built. Sexes alike. Juveniles are paler, with the head fawn-coloured; wing-coverts mottled with white; underparts white, almost unmarked except for a few light-brown spots on the flanks and pale fawn bars on the tibia coverts. Some adults appear to retain the juvenile type of coloration, merely becoming darker and more streaked below with brown. The underwing is white, with blackish tips to the quills and a chequered pattern of dark bars on the flight-feathers. Identification points for this eagle are: yellow irides (pale grey in the young); beak black; cere, lores and eyebrow dark grey; crest usually erect but sometimes laid flat down the neck, when it is inconspicuous; legs feathered down to the feet, which are pale yellow.

This eagle inhabits mainly the low country and medium elevations of the hills—to 5,000 feet on occasions, though it probably does not breed above 4,000 feet. It is fairly common in the dry zone, generally frequenting fairly open but well-wooded country such as chenas, the borders of tanks, etc. Much of its time is spent perching, with upright posture, in a tree, keenly looking out for prey. This consists mainly of lizards, with such small rodents and birds as wander far enough from cover to enable the eagle to pounce upon them before they can regain it. At times it indulges in a good deal of screaming, both while perched and on the wing; the cry is a loud, ringing *k'lee-kle-k*. This eagle is not much given to soaring. A tame one was fond of sun-bathing; it would sit on the ground with wings fully opened, exposing them to the midday sun for several minutes at a time. It also bathed in water, but without the vigorous splashing that most birds perform. At night it slept with the head hidden beneath the scapulars.

The breeding season appears to be usually in the early part of the year, but sometimes in June–July. The nest is a large mass of sticks with the hollow lined with green leaves, placed in the crown or in a stout fork of a tall tree, either in forest or more open country. A single egg forms the normal clutch; it is dull white, sometimes feebly streaked with reddish-brown, and measures about 68 × 52 mm.

THE MOUNTAIN HAWK-EAGLE
(Legge's Hawk-Eagle, or the Feather-toed Hawk-Eagle of some authors)

Spizaetus nipalensis kelaarti Legge. Resident

Sinhalese: Māhā Kondé Rājāliya. Tamil: Periya Kondé Rāsāli, Kalugu

Plate 17, facing p. 216 (female; ×one-ninth)
Plate 18, facing p. 217 (×approx. one-twentieth)

About the size of the Sea Eagle, but with shorter wings and longer tail. Sexes alike, but the female is larger than the male. From the preceding species, which it resembles in form, it may be distinguished by its rufous-barred underparts. The tarsi are feathered down to the feet, which are very large and powerful in this species, with enormous claws. The bird's appearance in flight as it is usually seen, from below, is shown in Plate 18, but the following points should be noted: comparatively short, broad wings, with short slots between the primaries; wing-lining mainly white, with rufous-brown lesser coverts; long tail, which is generally rather widely spread. Young birds are very pale in colour, with the head largely white, much white in the wing-coverts, and the underparts white, barred from the breast downwards with pale brown; irides pale grey.

This splendid eagle inhabits the mountain zone above 2,000 feet, confining itself as a rule to forested areas, but occasionally visiting estates and hill villages where it makes itself unpopular with humans by carrying off poultry—and too often pays the penalty by getting shot. So rare and magnificent an adornment to Ceylon's mountain scenery should surely be forgiven an occasional lapse of behaviour. On fine, sunny mornings it often soars into the sky, usually solitarily—in this differing from the Serpent Eagle which generally soars in pairs. According to Legge it utters a loud scream while soaring, but I have generally found it silent. Its hunting methods resemble those of the Ceylon Hawk-Eagle: taking up a post of vantage on a high branch, with a good background of foliage to disguise its form and with an open glade or stretch of patana in front, it waits until some small mammal or junglefowl ventures into the open and then descends upon it with a mighty stoop. It preys upon rats, hares and fowls—both tame and wild —and no doubt, like other raptors in Ceylon, finds lizards a useful standby when larger game fails; it is not generally speedy enough to capture birds on the wing.

The breeding season is said to be December–March. The nest is a large mass of sticks, lined with green leaves, placed in a tall tree generally in heavy forest. Often a pair maintain two eyries, using them alternately year after year unless they are disturbed. A single egg forms the normal clutch; it is white, sometimes marked with a few spots of yellow or red, and measures about 69·1 ×54·6 mm.

THE CEYLON SERPENT EAGLE

Spilornis cheela spilogaster (Blyth). Race peculiar to Ceylon

Sinhalese: Rājāliya. Tamil: Mullai-kuruvi, Kudumiyān

Plate 17, facing p. 216 (female; ×one-ninth)
Plate 18, facing p. 217 (×approx. one-twentieth)

Size of a large domestic cock. Sexes alike. From other hawks and eagles the following combination of features readily distinguish it: yellow cere, lores, and eye-ring; bushy, rounded crest which is usually depressed as shown in Plate 17, but is erected when the bird is excited; naked, yellow tarsi; closed wing reaching about three-quarters of the tail's length; in flight, the broadly-banded wings and tail—the latter generally closed when soaring (see Plate 18)—and habit of screaming. Juveniles are not so easily discriminated from some other birds of prey because their wing and tail pattern below is more of the 'chequerboard' type, like that of the Ceylon and Mountain Hawk-Eagles; it is, however, much bolder than in those species. Two forms of young exist —dark and light. The dark form is not very different from the adult except that the crest is buff-white, mottled with dark brown; but the light form has the underparts from chin to abdomen white, spotted and blotched with brown. Its yellow cere and lores, bushy crest, and naked tarsi, prevent confusion with the Ceylon Hawk-Eagle which, in this plumage, it somewhat resembles. Both forms of young have the irides grey.

This is the commonest and best known of Ceylon's eagles. It is found throughout the Island wherever sufficient jungle exists to give it sanctuary. In the tea and rubber districts it is a familiar sight, and it is also common throughout the forests of the dry zone. It makes itself conspicuous by its habit of soaring, usually in pairs, to great heights on every fine day, circling up into the blue on motionless wings which are held at considerable dihedral. While soaring the pair call frequently to each other in a loud, ringing cry, audible at a great distance and quite distinctive; it sounds something like *kuk kuk quēēr, queer, queer*—the *kuk kuk* suggesting a preliminary throat-clearing, and the first *quēēr* strongly accentuated and higher pitched than the others. This cry is always uttered on the wing; when perched the bird utters a scream like an abbreviated version of the first *quēer*. As its name implies, this eagle feeds largely on snakes of various kinds, pouncing upon them from a look-out on a high branch. It feeds also on lizards, frogs, and probably rodents, but it appears to be quite harmless to birds and poultry— though, doubtless, a sick or wounded one would be taken if opportunity offered. Except when soaring, it is rather a dull, sluggish bird, content to sit for long periods on its look-out points, of which it has several in its chosen beats. In the courting season it indulges in curious aerobatics, stooping and rolling on the wing, with tail raised and wings half closed and 'shivering'.

The breeding season is from February to May. The nest is a mass of sticks and twigs, not very large, placed in a tree in jungle, usually in a well concealed position; it is lined with green leaves. One egg forms the normal clutch but occasionally two are laid; they are dull white with rufous markings, and measure about 64 × 50 mm. The young are fed mainly on snakes, the common green whipsnake being a favourite.

THE WHITE-BELLIED SEA EAGLE

Haliaeetus leucogaster (Gmelin). Resident

Sinhalese: Muhudu Rājāliya. Tamil: Kadal Āli

Size of a turkey-cock. Sexes alike. Adults are white with dark ashy grey back and wings; the tips of the primaries above, all the quills and their greater coverts on the underside of the wing, and the base of the tail are black. Irides light brown; beak, cere, lores and gape dark grey; tarsi unfeathered, yellowish-white, stout and strong but rather short. Young birds are streaky pale yellowish-grey on head and underparts, mottled dark brown on back and wings; tail white, with a dark-brown subterminal band.

This fine eagle is common all round the coasts of the dry zone and in the neighbourhood of the larger tanks; it also occurs about lagoons and estuaries on the south-western coast, but in the hills it is a rare visitor. On the wing, it presents a magnificent spectacle owing to its striking colour-scheme, and its long and broad wings which are held well above the level of the back, their primaries separated by long slots. When travelling, it flies in a series of powerful flaps followed by a long glide; but it is much given to soaring with motionless wings, circling up to great heights, often in pairs. When not flying, it generally perches on a dead tree or on some jutting rock, usually near the water's edge. It lives in pairs, apparently mating for life, and each pair frequents the same locality for many years if undisturbed. In the breeding season it becomes noisy, frequently calling in a loud honking cry *ah ah ah ah*; in uttering this, the head is extended with the open beak pointing skyward. The principal food of the Sea Eagle consists of fish and sea-snakes, which it

× one-twelfth

rakes with its talons from sea or lagoon when they come near enough to the surface to be seized without the eagle's getting too wet; it is not so skilful a fisher as the osprey, its stoop being more slanting, and less determined. Frequently, however, it makes up for its own lack of skill by robbing a more successful osprey of a fish—chasing it until it drops its prey.

It breeds from December to March, making a huge nest of sticks in a tall and stout tree, often on a small island, or rocky promontory. The nest is added to year by year, its bulk growing until it may contain several cartloads of sticks and branches. The lining is of green leaves. Two eggs form the normal clutch; they are dull white, rather rough, and measure about 75 × 54 mm.

THE CEYLON GREY-HEADED FISHING EAGLE, or TANK EAGLE

Ichthyophaga ichthyaetus plumbeiceps Stuart Baker. Race peculiar to Ceylon

Sinhalese: Wéwa Rājāliya, Lūl-mārā. Tamil: Vidai Āli

Between the Serpent Eagle and the Sea Eagle in size. Sexes alike. When adult, this eagle is easily recognized by the following combination of characters: ashy-grey head, brownish-grey breast; white abdomen,

tibia coverts, and base of tail; back, rump, and wings dark brown; a wide black tip to the tail; irides varying from hazel-brown in immature birds to bright yellow in fully adult individuals; beak and cere dull black, lores pale grey. The eyebrow ridge is less pronounced than in most eagles and, with the rather small head and thin neck, this gives the bird, at times, a somewhat vulturine appearance. The tibia feathers short, not 'trousered'; tarsi and feet very stout and strong, pale yellowish-grey, with the outer toe reversible; claws black, very strong and well curved; the soles of the toes are prickly.

× one-twelfth

These leg- and foot-characters resemble those of the osprey; in both birds they are adaptations to a fish-diet.

The wings are rather short—reaching only about half-way down the tail—and broadly rounded at the tip. In flight, this eagle looks brownish-black and white. The young are pale brown on back and wings, mottled with fulvous; head and breast yellowish-brown, streaked with white; white base of the tail mottled with brown.

The Tank Eagle is a low-country bird; it frequents the jungle borders of tanks, lagoons and rivers in the dry zone, being always found in the neighbourhood of water. Heavy and sluggish, it spends most of its time sitting on a branch above water, watching for a sizable fish to come near the surface, whereupon it sails down and snatches it in its talons. The end of the dry season is its happy time, for then the tanks are dried up to mere pools in which masses of fish gasp in the liquid mud, and the eagle can rake them out with a minimum of effort. It seldom or never soars and its flight generally consists of an occasional excursion around its favourite tank—affording a fine, if brief, sight during these moments of activity. In early morning and late evening and sometimes far into the night—especially in the breeding season—it utters a loud, unmusical, rather weird shout with a curious gurgling quality—*awh awhrr*, etc.

The breeding season is from December to March; the nest is a large heap of sticks and branches, set in a big tree usually fifty to sixty feet from the ground. The one or two eggs are dirty-white and measure about 69 × 53 mm.

THE BRAHMINY KITE

Haliastur indus indus (Boddaert). Resident

Sinhalese: Ukussā. Tamil: Sem-parundu

Plate 18, facing p. 217 (× approx. one-twentieth)

Between the Black Crow and the Serpent Eagle in size. Sexes alike. The adult, with its white head, neck and breast, black-tipped primaries, and chestnut plumage elsewhere, cannot be mistaken for any other Ceylon hawk. Irides dark brown; beak and cere pale greenish-grey; tarsi—which are short and bare of feathers—and feet, dull yellow. The young are mottled dark brown and fulvous on wings, back and tail; head, breast and underparts mottled and streaked fulvous and pale grey; primaries black, with a large, pale area on the underwing at their bases. In immature plumage, the shorter and rounded, not forked, tail, and much more conspicuous pale patch on the under-surface of the primaries, prevent confusion with the Pariah Kite.

The Brahminy Kite is very common throughout the dry zone and visits the hills occasionally up to about 3,000 feet; in the wet zone it is less common, but may be seen about coastal lagoons and estuaries during the north-east monsoon. At this season it is common at Colombo, especially about the harbour area, which it frequents for the sake of scraps of food thrown overboard from ships. It loves the neighbourhood of water, fresh or salt, and every tank, lagoon or coastal village in the dry zone has its

× one-seventh

PLATE 17

1. Ceylon Serpent Eagle.   2. Rufous-bellied Hawk-Eagle.   3. Shahin Falcon.
4. Legge's Baza.   5. Ceylon Hawk-Eagle.   6. Mountain Hawk-Eagle

PLATE 18

1. Pariah Kite.   2. Brahminy Kite.   3. Rufous-bellied Hawk-Eagle.
4. Ceylon Serpent Eagle.   5. Mountain Hawk-Eagle.   6. Black Eagle.
7. Booted Eagle

population of Brahminies. The flight is easy and graceful and, if wind be adequate, is performed with a minimum of flapping. As it soars, it scans the ground for any edible morsel and, on spying one, descends with a graceful swoop to snatch it up skilfully in its talons. The food consists of almost anything of an animal nature, dead or alive, which it can steal or capture; small fish, lizards, young or wounded birds, shore-crabs and grasshoppers; it will take young chickens, but only if it can catch them in circumstances which allow it to get clear away before the mother hen can defend them, for it is a cowardly bird. Small morsels of food are eaten on the wing. In the breeding season, or when disputing with other kites or crows for food, a peevish, squealing cry is frequently uttered.

The breeding season is from October to April; nest-building commences in the former month, but eggs are not usually laid until December, and the young do not leave the nest until April or May. The nest is made of sticks and twigs which the birds snatch from trees while on the wing; it is placed in the crown of a tree, at varying heights from the ground. The two or three, scantily red-speckled, white eggs measure about 50×42 mm.

THE PARIAH KITE

Milvus migrans govinda Sykes. Resident? or winter (breeding) visitor?

Sinhalese: Ukussā. Tamil: Para-parundu

Plate 18, facing p. 217 ($\times$ approx. one-twentieth)

Larger than the Brahminy Kite. Sexes alike. Coloration dark brown, streaked darker, with black tips to the primaries. The deeply-forked tail distinguishes it from all other Ceylon hawks. Irides light brown; beak black, cere yellow, lores pale grey; the ear-coverts are blackish-brown, forming a dark patch behind the eye. Tarsi, which are short and unfeathered, and feet, chrome yellow. The wings, though long, reach to only about two-thirds down the tail when closed; in flight, they look rather narrow and are usually somewhat angled at the wrist. The tail which, though forked, appears almost square at the end when fully spread, is much used as a rudder by the bird, being canted from side to side according to the needs of the moment.

In Ceylon, this kite—so very abundant in all Indian towns—is confined to the northern half of the Island, and common only in coastal districts. Even from this restricted range it seems to disappear in the south-west monsoon, and I suspect that it migrates to South India for the dry, windy months, returning to the Island about August. A hanger-on of man, it is seldom to be seen far from thickly populated areas for it is a scavenger, living mainly on scraps of food-refuse cast out

× one-ninth

from human habitations. Though bold in snatching morsels of food, even in crowded streets, it is suspicious and wary and few birds are more difficult to catch. Much of its time is spent on the wing, sailing lazily about with a peculiar, indecisive manner as it circles and veers—always on the alert for some titbit below. If this be small enough, it will be eaten on the wing; if too big it will be carried to some convenient perch. There is always, however, great competition for scraps of food, not only against its own kind but against crows and Brahminy Kites as well, and much squealing and chasing take place before any desirable item is finally disposed of. Its cry is a shrill, quavering squeal.

The Pariah Kite breeds from December to April, building a large untidy nest of sticks, rags, etc., in the canopy of a tree, or at the base of coconut-fronds. The two to four eggs are greenish-white, spotted with some shade of brown, and they measure about 53 × 40 mm.

THE BLACK-WINGED KITE

Elanus caeruleus vociferus (Latham). Resident

Sinhalese: Kurullā-goyā. Tamil: Parundu

Plate 20, facing p. 233 (×one-sixth)
Plate 21, facing p. 248 (×one-twelfth)

Rather smaller than the House Crow; similar in size to the kestrel and shikra. Sexes alike. The young are browner, somewhat mottled on scapulars and wings, and the underparts sullied with buff; their irides are hazel-brown, paling to olive-grey and then to yellow, before they become the ruby-red of the adult. This pretty little hawk, with its pearly-grey, white and black plumage, can be mistaken only for the adult male of either Pale or Pied Harrier, but a glance at the illustrations should prevent any such mistake; it is much smaller than the harriers, has a shorter tail, and its style of flight is different.

In suitable country, it is widely distributed in the Island, both low country and hills, but is not very common anywhere. Well-wooded country, parkland, patanas, scrub and the like, form its habitat but it avoids heavy forest. Nearly always solitary, it moves about a good deal, here today, gone tomorrow. The style of flight is very characteristic; it usually flies at a good height, with a mixture of slow but strong flapping, and easy sailing with the wings held at a strong dihedral. Every now and then it will turn into the wind and poise against it, like a kestrel, though with slower and heavier wing-action, while it scrutinizes the ground below for prey. Seeing something interesting, it slowly descends, parachute-wise, as if let down on an invisible thread, to inspect the object from a lower level. Should the prey be suitable, it drops on to it and either eats it on the spot or carries it off. It feeds on locusts and grasshoppers, lizards, and occasionally field-rats or young birds. A favourite perch is on the top of a solitary or dead tree; while perched, it has a curious habit of raising the tail nearly to a right angle with the back and slowly moving it up and down. It is silent as a rule, but is said to utter a shrill squeal at times; Mrs Lushington records a soft, full whistle, *wheep, wheep*, and a nasal purr.

The breeding season is from December to March, and sometimes a second brood may be reared in July to October. The nest is an untidy mass of sticks, like that of a crow, placed among foliage at the top of a tree growing in fairly open country. The two or three eggs are dull white, spotted with reddish-brown, and measure about 40 × 31 mm.

THE HARRIERS

(Genus *Circus*)

Four species of harrier occur in Ceylon—all of them winter migrants from their breeding-grounds in northern lands. They are medium-sized, slenderly-built hawks, with long wings and tails and long, slender legs with tarsi unfeathered. Their plumage is soft and silky, and they have a curious ruff, like that of an owl, consisting of short crisp feathers, surrounding the sides of the face and crossing the throat; this ruff is very conspicuous in some species, less so in others. Harriers are past masters in the art of slow flight; in this, they contrast strongly with the falcons, which are built for speed. Their characteristic style of hunting is slow, easy gliding, usually at a height of only a few yards above the ground, with just enough wing-flapping to maintain air-speed. Every yard is scanned for prey, which consists of small animals—lizards, small snakes, young or unwary birds, frogs, grasshoppers and the like. On spying prey below them, they drop quickly upon it and usually devour it on the spot; but they seldom give chase if the first pounce is unsuccessful. All the harriers love open country, particularly low-lying land such as swamps and paddy-fields; open, grassy hill-sides are also favoured by some. They normally perch on the ground, seldom on trees or other elevated objects, and they habitually roost on the ground at night. Nesting, too, is on the ground, in the midst of reedy swamps or tundras. Except in the breeding season, they are very silent birds.

Few birds give more pleasure to the bird-watcher than these graceful and beautiful masters of their particular craft.

With the exception of the largest species, the Marsh Harrier, the field identification of harriers is rather difficult, especially of females and young males, owing to great similarity of form and coloration and complicated changes of colour during growth. However, with a little close observation and attention to detail, it is possible to attain a satisfactory degree of accuracy in discriminating them in the field, provided one can get a sufficiently good view of the birds. Points to be borne in mind are given under the several species, but the following general principles should be noted: (*a*) Young birds of both sexes have brown irides, which change to golden yellow in adults. (*b*) The underparts in the young tend to be uniform rufous; in adult females the underparts become paler and more or less streaked with brown. (*c*) Young birds show a conspicuous white triangle at the back of the head; this becomes streaked with brown, or disappears, with age. (*d*) In the young, the underside of the wing is less heavily barred with dark brown than in the adult female, and the secondaries tend to be nearly uniform dark brown, which becomes broken, later, by pale bands.

THE PALE HARRIER
(Pallid Harrier of many authors)

Circus macrourus (Gmelin). Winter visitor

Sinhalese: Ukussā, Kurullā-goya. Tamil: Pūnai-parundu

Plate 19, facing p. 232
(flying, adult male; standing, juvenile male; ×one-fourteenth)

Smaller and more slenderly built than the Brahminy Kite, with proportionately narrower wings and longer tail. The adult male may easily be distinguished from that of Montagu's Harrier by the following points: paler, more silvery, grey on back and wings; face and upper breast very pale grey, nearly white; streaking on breast and flanks very narrow and inconspicuous; underwing nearly white, with very slight dark barring at the bases of the quills; black tip of the wing confined to primaries 2–6, and forming a long patch projecting towards the middle of the wing; no black band on secondaries near their bases. Females and young males are difficult to distinguish from the corresponding forms of Montagu's but, in general, they have the ruff much paler and more conspicuous, forming a white, or pale buff, curved line behind the ear-coverts; the plumage, especially of the head, has a sleeker appearance, with the white and buff facial markings clear-cut; the wings, when closed do not reach nearer to the tip of the tail than $1\frac{1}{2}$ inches or more; the adult female is paler beneath, and much less heavily streaked with brown than Montagu's. In hand, the Pale Harrier may be at once recognized by having the notch on the *leading* edge of the *second* primary level with, or concealed by, the primary coverts; in Montagu's, this notch is three-quarters of an inch beyond the primary coverts.

The Pale Harrier is probably the commonest, and certainly the best distributed, of the harriers that visit Ceylon. It arrives from August to November, and spreads all over the Island, hills and low country alike, wherever suitable conditions exist; and leaves again for its breeding-grounds in northern Asia about February to April. It frequents patana hill-sides, scrub-covered plains, paddy-fields and marshes; sailing slowly above them at a height usually of only a few feet, and adjusting its flight to the contours of the ground with amazing skill; the wings are held at a strong dihedral, and it flaps them only enough to maintain headway. It systematically quarters a hill-side or field and, on seeing prey beneath, circles quickly and plunges upon it, usually eating it on the spot. Lizards, grasshoppers, frogs, and small birds, especially ground-feeding kinds, form its food. It is usually silent during its stay in Ceylon.

Although an occasional individual loiters in the Island through the south-west monsoon, there is no evidence that it ever breeds in Ceylon; its nesting is carried out on the steppes and swamps of northern Asia and Europe. The nest, of flags, rushes, etc., is placed on the ground among concealing vegetation.

MONTAGU'S HARRIER

Circus pygargus (Linnaeus). Winter visitor

Sinhalese: Ukussā, Kurullā-goya. Tamil: Pūnai-parundu

Plate 19, facing p. 232

(female left, male right; ×one-fourteenth)

Smaller than the Brahminy Kite and more slenderly-built, with narrower wings and longer tail. Though slightly smaller than the Pale Harrier, this is not appreciable in the field. The adult male may be distinguished from that of the Pale Harrier by the following features: darker, more bluish-grey coloration; head and breast as dark grey as the back; flanks strongly streaked, and axillaries and under wing-coverts barred or spotted with chestnut; secondaries with a bold, blackish band near their bases; outer five primaries almost entirely black. Females and young males are difficult to distinguish from those of the Pale Harrier, but they have the ruff less accentuated, and the closed wings reach almost to the tip of the tail; adult females are much more heavily streaked with brown on the flanks and breast.[1]

This beautiful hawk visits Ceylon in large numbers during the north-east monsoon, but keeps more to the low country, especially the coastal districts, than the Pale Harrier, and is seldom seen in the hills; it is particularly common in the Jaffna Peninsula and similar country to the south of it. In general, its habits are almost indistinguishable from those of the Pale Harrier; it has the same style of flight, especially while hunting—a few strong but slow strokes of the wings followed by a long, easy glide with the wings held in a very open V. It sails slowly a few feet above the ground, following every slight dip and rise, canting and veering with consummate ease. When not hunting, it tends to fly higher than the Pale Harrier, occasionally soaring to a great height. Its favourite country comprises swamps and paddy-fields, but it also frequents any kind of open land or scrub. Like other harriers, it perches

---

[1] A melanistic variety of Montagu's Harrier sometimes appears, though it does not yet seem to have been recorded from Ceylon. In this form the whole plumage is dark brown, more or less washed with grey in the male, and the normal markings are obscured.

readily on the ground but only occasionally on fences, posts, etc. Being a weaker bird than the Pale, it does not often, in Ceylon, aspire to such active prey as birds, but contents itself with frogs, lizards, water-snakes and grasshoppers; when breeding, however, it is said to take a good many small birds for feeding its young. It is silent except in the breeding season.

Montagu's Harrier leaves the Island for its northern breeding-grounds about March and April. It nests on the ground amidst swamp vegetation, or on steppes in Europe and Asia, laying three to five eggs.

THE PIED HARRIER

Circus melanoleucos (Pennant). Scarce winter visitor

Sinhalese: Ukussā, Kurullā-goya. Tamil: Pūnai-parundu

Plate 19, facing p. 232
(left, male; right, female; ×one-fourteenth)

About the same size as the Pale Harrier; smaller than the Brahminy Kite, and more slenderly built, with narrower wings, and longer tail. The adult male and female are shown on the Plate; immature birds of both sexes are difficult to distinguish in the field from those of the Pale and Montagu's Harriers, but they have broader wings, especially at the tips, and a somewhat heavier style of flight, with more flapping. In hand, this harrier may be distinguished from either of the above by its fifth primary (as well as 2–4) notched (or emarginated) on the *leading* edge; the notch on 2 is like that of Montagu's, about three-quarters of an inch beyond the primary coverts.

This handsome harrier is the rarest of those that visit Ceylon, though it seems to be commoner nowadays than it was in Legge's time; during two years spent in Jaffna I saw it on at least twenty occasions, and often several individuals at a time. By far the greater number were seen in February and March—a period when harriers of all species concentrated in the Peninsula, partly to feed on the abundant frogs and grasshoppers in the paddy-fields at that time, and partly preparing for migration to the north for nesting. Although it usually frequents the coastal areas of the Island, there are several records of its occurrence inland on up-country patanas. The adult male is sometimes confused with the Black-winged Kite, but its much larger size and different pattern should obviate any such mistake. In habits it hardly differs from the Pale and Montagu's Harriers; it sails slowly over swamps, paddy-fields, and open country, a few feet above the ground, with leisurely strokes of its wings and long glides in which it will rise over a hedge or dip into a hollow with effortless ease, in a most beautiful manner. When it momentarily hovers over some likely spot, the slightly broader wings and heavier flight above-mentioned become apparent. Its prey consists of the usual harrier diet—frogs, lizards, small snakes, grasshoppers and the like; no doubt it will capture birds when opportunity offers. It perches on the ground, and roosts at night on open fields or marshes, often in loose association with other harriers of its own and other species.

This harrier breeds in the marshes and tundras of eastern Asia and its nesting-habits seem to follow the usual harrier pattern.

THE MARSH HARRIER

Circus aeruginosus aeruginosus (Linnaeus). Winter visitor

Sinhalese: Ukussā, Kurullā-goya. Tamil: Pūnai-parundu

Plate 19, facing p. 232
(male flying, female standing; ×one-fourteenth)

About the size of the Brahminy Kite, though it looks larger owing to its wings and tail being longer; it is considerably larger than the other Ceylon harriers. The adult male, with his striking colour-scheme of rufous, dark brown, black, white, and clear grey, cannot be mistaken for any other Ceylon hawk. Females and young males are dark brown almost throughout, with the entire top of the head, the chin and throat and, in adult females, a patch on the lesser wing-coverts, buff (some young males have the entire head dark brown). Adults of both sexes have the irides yellow, young birds have them brown.

This fine harrier arrives in Ceylon about November, and takes up its winter quarters mainly in the coastal districts of the Island, particularly the dry zone, though it is not uncommon in suitable places on the wet-zone seaboard and an occasional bird finds its way up-country. As its name implies, it is pre-eminently a lover of marshes, swamps and paddy-fields, seldom frequenting dry country. Like other harriers, it spends most of its time hunting over such places with a slow and sailing flight, steadily quartering the ground; a few strong strokes of its long wings give it sufficient impetus to glide for long distances by merely trimming its wings to the air-currents. Not infrequently, it flies with its legs dropped, as shown in the Plate, probably using them as an air-brake. The flight is not so light and graceful as that of our other harriers, and the primaries are more spread as a rule. On occasion, it will soar to great heights and, when doing so, the females and young, with their dark plumage, strongly suggest the Black Eagle—which, however, is unlikely to be found in the sort of country favoured by the Marsh Harrier. The food of this harrier scarcely differs from that of its smaller congeners, but it appears to concentrate more upon frogs and water-snakes than they do, and also eats fish to a considerable extent; its greater size enables it to attack such large birds as teal and water-hens, and small mammals up to the size of leverets; it does not despise grasshoppers, however. Generally it devours its capture on the spot. As with other harriers, it habitually perches on the ground—and appears always to roost there at night—but it also frequently perches in trees, particularly during the heat of the day. It has communal roosting places, in fields or swamps, to which large numbers resort towards dusk, settling in scattered formation over an area of several acres. It is quite silent while in Ceylon.

The Marsh Harrier breeds in Europe and Asia, north of the Himalayas. It nests in reedy swamps, in typical harrier-fashion.

THE DESERT BUZZARD

Buteo burmanicus burmanicus Hume. Occasional winter visitor

Sinhalese: Ukussā. Tamil: Parundu

About the size of the Brahminy Kite. Sexes alike. This bird is very variable in coloration, which is therefore an unsafe guide to identity. It has a small, black beak, yellow cere, light brown irides, and yellow tarsi and feet, the former bare of feathers for most of their length. A dark line runs from above the eye, around the lores, and is continued from the gape as a 'moustache' below the ear-coverts. Most individuals may be described as mottled dark brown on head, wings and back, with a pale supercilium and forehead. The underparts are buff-white, boldly streaked and spotted with dark brown. The tail is somewhat rufous brown, with about eight smoky-brown, narrow bars. The underwing is buff-white, with dark tips to the primaries; coverts mottled brown; primary coverts smoky, forming a dark patch on the underwing, which is succeeded by a light patch before the short, dark tips of the primaries.

In posture and silhouette this buzzard somewhat resembles the Serpent Eagle and, in flight as seen from below, it has similar, broad, rounded wings; however, it lacks the bold, dark-brown bands of the eagle, its tail is usually widely expanded while soaring, and it does not scream. In soaring, it circles quicker than the Serpent Eagle. It is an uncommon winter visitor to the Island, though less rare in some years than in others. Nearly all individuals met with have been seen in up-country districts, where they frequent patanas bordered by jungle, and the like. It is said to hunt somewhat like a harrier, but with more wing-flapping and less sailing; but it also watches for prey from the tops of bushes or dead branches, pouncing from such points of vantage upon the lizards, frogs and insects that form its main items of food.

The Desert Buzzard breeds in east Asia and Japan, making its nest of sticks, etc., lined with green leaves, either on trees, ledges of cliffs, or sometimes on the ground on steep hill-sides.

THE SHORT-WINGED HAWKS

(Sparrow-Hawks and Goshawks—Genus *Accipiter*)

These are (as found in Ceylon) small hawks, of dove- to crow-size, which inhabit either forest or well-wooded cultivation. They have the beak small but powerful, with a strong convexity or 'festoon' on the cutting edge of the upper mandible (this festoon must be distinguished from the distinct 'tooth' or angular projection on the cutting edge of a falcon's beak). The irides are grey in the young, soon turning to bright yellow and, in some species, becoming deep orange or ruby-red in old birds. The tarsi are rather long and bare of feathers; the claws very well-curved and sharp. The wings are rounded and short, reaching, when closed, only to the middle, or less, of the rather long tail. These hawks are bold hunters, capturing their prey usually by a quick dash, but seldom chasing it for any distance. They always nest in trees.

THE CEYLON SHIKRA

Accipiter badius badius (Gmelin). Resident

Sinhalese: Kobēyi-ukussā, Kurullā-goya. Tamil: Vallūru

Plate 20, facing p. 233
(left, adult male; right, juvenile female; ×one-sixth)
Plate 21, facing p. 248 (×one-twelfth)

Female about the size of a domestic pigeon, but more slender and with a longer tail; the male is considerably smaller. In adult plumage, he is darker and bluer above than his mate. This hawk may be distinguished, when adult, from the Besra Sparrow-Hawk, which it rather closely resembles, by the following features: cheeks shading gradually from the white throat to the grey ear-coverts; paler, and narrower rufous bars on the underparts; middle tail-feathers almost unbarred; some white on sides of upper tail-coverts; underwing lightly and sparsely barred with grey. In juvenile plumage: upper surface less dark, becoming greyish on secondaries and tail; upper tail-coverts with much white; tail, above, with four or five *narrow* dark bands; below, with five narrow bands; tibia-coverts with small 'drops' of brown. In hand, the two species can be distinguished at once by the legs and feet, which are stout and strong in the shikra, long and thin in the Besra.

The shikra is our commonest small hawk, and is found almost everywhere in the Island except heavy forest which it avoids, though chenas and clearings are sure to be visited by it. It prefers mixed open and wooded country, and is common on most tea estates and village cultivation and by no means rare in the outskirts of towns. It is fierce and courageous and, although its usual food consists mainly of lizards, many small birds fall victim to it when it has a young brood to feed. When hunting, it often flies swiftly behind a hedge or the like and suddenly darts over the top, taking by surprise any small bird or lizard that may be on the other side. The flight is swift and direct, performed by rapid fluttering of the wings followed by a glide. At times it indulges in soaring, ascending to a considerable height with widespread wings; it circles quickly with a curious, unsteady action, unlike the regular circling of the Serpent Eagle, and its soaring never lasts long. When courting, it performs curious aerobatics—stooping, shooting upwards, and performing other unusual antics—high in air. It has a noisy, staccato scream, frequently uttered whenever it is excited—*ihēēya, ihēēya, ihēēya*, etc. (*i* as in 'it').

The shikra breeds about March to May, and probably sometimes has a second brood in August–September. The nest is an openwork affair, of small twigs, lined with finer twigs, grass, etc.; it is placed among foliage, usually high in a big tree, not infrequently a grevillea, or a rubber tree. The eggs, two or three in number, are bluish-white, and measure about 40 × 32 mm.

THE BESRA SPARROW-HAWK

Accipiter virgatus besra Jerdon. Resident

Sinhalese: Ukussā, Kurullā-goya. Tamil: Sinna Vallūru

Plate 20, facing p. 233

(upper, juvenile female; lower, adult male; ×one-sixth)

Female about the size of the female shikra, i.e. that of a domestic pigeon, but more slender, and with longer tail; but the male is a good deal smaller than the male shikra, about the size of the Common Mynah. Although very similar in general appearance to the shikra, it is a slimmer bird, with longer and more slender legs and toes. In adult plumage, it differs from the shikra as follows: dark head-colouring meeting the white throat in a definite line; rufous colouring of the breast and underparts deeper, broken only by narrow white bars; tail longer, more square-cut at the end and the middle feathers above with four black bands; upper tail-coverts have no white; underwing boldly banded and spotted with dark grey. In juvenile plumage: upper surface (back, wings and tail), in general, dark brown throughout—no grey suffusion on secondaries and tail; upper tail-coverts have no white; tail, both above and below, has four broad dark bands; tibia-coverts boldly blotched with brown.

The Besra is scarce but, according to Legge and Wait, widely distributed in Ceylon. It is a forest hawk, seldom seen away from jungle, though it will leave it, now and then, on hunting expeditions. It is very expert in threading its way, at speed, through dense forest growth, dodging and twisting. Like the shikra, it feeds largely on lizards, but small birds come in for a share of its attentions, especially when it is feeding young. Mrs Lushington describes it as 'a noisy bird, frequently uttering its squealing cry, a rapidly repeated *tchew-tchew-tchew* . . .'

The breeding season is about April. The nest is an untidy mass of twigs, etc., placed in a tall forest tree. The two to four eggs are pale bluish-white, marked with reddish-brown, and measure about 37 × 30 mm.

THE CEYLON CRESTED GOSHAWK

Accipiter trivirgatus layardi (Whistler & Kinnear). Race peculiar to Ceylon

Sinhalese: Ukussā, Kurullā-goya. Tamil: Vallūru

Plate 20, facing p. 233 (female; ×one-sixth)

Plate 21, facing p. 248 (×one-twelfth)

About the size of the House Crow; larger than the shikra. Sexes alike, but the female is larger than the male. Young birds are marked like the juvenile shikra, but they may be distinguished by the tibia-coverts, which are boldly *barred* with black on white at all ages. The small, pointed crest is a good identification mark when it can be seen, but it is often depressed on the back of the neck, when it is inconspicuous. Other points to note are: dark-grey cheeks meeting the white throat in a blackish border; a strong, black stripe down the middle of the throat; three (visible) dark, smoky bands crossing the tail; the underside of the wing is white, with blackish spots on the coverts and bold black barring, forming a chequered pattern, on the quills.

The Crested Goshawk is sparsely distributed throughout the more densely-forested parts of the Island, but seems to be commonest in the hills, which it ascends to at least 6,000 feet. It frequents jungle and is seldom seen away from it or its outskirts and, like the Besra, it is very nimble in dodging its way through tangled forest. Its usual method of hunting is to sit quietly in a commanding, but concealed, position in a tree, scanning the surroundings keenly for any betraying movement of lizard or small bird, etc., which it captures by a lightning dash. It feeds mainly on lizards but, in the breeding season when its brood has to be fed, it captures many small birds; there seems, however, to be no factual evidence for the bad reputation for chicken-stealing given it by Layard (as quoted by Legge); Layard's account of its behaviour is clearly a mixture of poetry and mistaken identity. Its note is a shrill scream *he, he, hehehehe.*

The Crested Goshawk breeds from February to July, building a large and untidy nest of sticks in the top of a tall sapling or the crown of a tree in forest; the nest-lining, as with so many hawks and eagles, is of green leaves. The two eggs are bluish, or greenish-white, unmarked, and measure about 51 ×36 mm.

THE CRESTED HONEY BUZZARD[1]

Pernis apivorus ruficollis Lesson. Winter visitor; some birds resident

Sinhalese: Rājāliya. Tamil: Then-parundu

About the size of the Serpent Eagle or slightly larger. Sexes alike. In hand, this honey buzzard may readily be recognized by its lores which, unlike those of all other Ceylon hawks, are clothed with small, close, scale-like feathers—not mere bristles. The coloration is so variable that it is of little use in identification. Young birds tend to be light-

---

[1] The honey buzzards are not closely related to the true buzzards, of which the Desert Buzzard (see p. 225) is a representative.

coloured, with dark brown back and wings mottled with white; under-parts whitish, variously streaked or spotted, and barred on the flanks, with dark brown; tail irregularly barred and mottled with dark brown on a paler ground. Adults are generally dark brown throughout, mottled with white on the underparts, and with a broad, pale band across the middle of the tail. Beak rather small and weak, black, with the large cere greenish in the young, dark grey in adults. Irides brown in juveniles, yellow in adults, sometimes becoming deep orange or red

Head, showing closely
feathered lore;
× one-quarter

× one-ninth

in very old birds. Tarsi and feet dull yellow; the tarsi are very short and the tibia-coverts long, tending to hide the legs when the bird is resting. The head is comparatively small and sleek, in adults generally greyish, projecting well forward in flight; the small, pointed crest is usually inconspicuous, being depressed down the back of the neck except under excitement. The wings are long, rounded, with short slots between the primaries and a pale area at their bases. The tail is long, usually well expanded in flight.

The majority of our honey buzzards appear to be winter visitors to the Island, arriving about November and December, and leaving again about April; but as a few may be seen up-country in every month, and pairs have been observed mating and performing courting flights, it seems certain that it breeds in Ceylon to some extent. It is a forest bird, but occasionally ventures away from the jungle for brief periods. When flying from tree to tree it proceeds rapidly, with regular wing-beats, but when travelling it gives four or five rapid flaps, followed by a short glide. At times it soars, sailing easily, with little wing-flapping, the wings held nearly level with the back. This large hawk has the strange habit of feeding largely on wild bees and wasps, raiding the nests of these insects to get the larvae. It eats other insects also, and sometimes captures lizards and small mammals. Though usually silent, it occasionally utters a scream very like one of the Serpent Eagle's notes—a loud, clear *wheew* or *queer*.

In India, it builds its nest of sticks and twigs, lined with green leaves, in a forest tree. The two eggs are white or pale buff, heavily marked with some shade of red or brown; they measure about 52 × 44 mm.

A specimen of the SIBERIAN HONEY BUZZARD *Pernis apivorus orientalis* Taczanowski was collected by W. W. A. Phillips near Mannar in December 1943 and deposited by him in the British Museum (Natural History). This race breeds in east Siberia and Japan. It lacks the crest, but otherwise is practically indistinguishable in the field from the Crested Honey Buzzard.

THE BAZAS
(Genus *Aviceda*)

These are small to medium-sized hawks whose main characteristic is the possession of *two* tooth-like projections on each margin of the upper mandible in adults (compare with falcons, which have a single 'tooth'; and with other hawks, which have, at most, a 'festoon', or slight convexity of the margin in this position). Bazas have a long slender crest consisting of a few, narrow feathers, on the back of the head; this is usually worn erect, pointing straight upwards, except during flight. They have very short legs, with the tarsus feathered for the upper half of its length. The wings are fairly long, rounded at the tip. Bazas are forest hawks; they feed mainly on large insects, lizards and the like, and are not known to capture birds.

Ceylon has two species, Legge's Baza being a scarce resident, and the Black Baza a very rare and occasional winter visitor, which has not been recorded from the Island for many years.

THE BLACK BAZA
(Black-crested Baza of many authors)

Aviceda leuphotes leuphotes (Dumont). Very rare winter visitor

No Sinhalese or Tamil names

About the size of the kestrel or female shikra. Sexes alike. This beautiful little hawk is mainly glossy greenish-black, with bold white and chestnut blotches on scapulars, inner secondaries and greater secondary-coverts; the lower parts, from the breast downwards, are white, with a broad chestnut and black band across the lower breast and wide chestnut bars across the flanks; the abdomen is black. Underwing: lesser and median coverts black; greater coverts, primaries and secondaries, pale grey, tips of flight-feathers black. The underside of the tail is pale grey, with a diffuse, black spot on outer webs.

Head, showing double-
toothed beak;
× one-half

× one-fifth

This baza is a rare straggler to Ceylon from its haunts in the eastern Himalayas and Assam; it is said to breed in Travancore also. Less than a dozen individuals have been recorded in the Island in the last hundred years. It is a forest hawk, and most specimens have been taken in the low-country dry zone. According to Legge, it is inclined to be gregarious, going in small parties, and behaving more like a pigeon than a hawk. The long, elegant crest is frequently raised and lowered. It is said to be somewhat crepuscular, hunting until dusk is well established.

PLATE 19

1. Montagu's Harrier.   2. Pied Harrier.   3. Marsh Harrier.   4. Pale Harrier

PLATE 20

1. Black-winged Kite.   2. European Kestrel.   3. Besra Sparrow-Hawk.
4. Ceylon Shikra. 5. Ceylon Crested Goshawk

Its prey consists largely of insects, such as cicadas and beetles, but it also eats lizards.

The breeding season in Travancore is said to be from February to April. The nest, which resembles that of a crow, is placed in a high forest tree, and contains two or three chalky-white eggs.

LEGGE'S BAZA, or CEYLON BROWN BAZA

Aviceda jerdoni ceylonensis (Legge). Resident; found also in the hills of South India

Sinhalese: Kurullā-goya. Tamil: Parundu

Plate 17, facing p. 216 (male; ×one-ninth)

About the size of the Black Crow, or between the shikra and the Brahminy Kite. Sexes alike in coloration, but the female is slightly larger than the male and has a longer crest; young birds are paler, especially on the head and breast. The crest is usually worn erect as shown in the Plate, except in flight.

This handsome hawk inhabits the hill zone, in which it is widely distributed though nowhere common; however, it now seems to be less rare and elusive than it was in Legge's day. It is a forest hawk, but strays, at times, into tea estates, etc., bordering its jungle haunts. It generally lives in pairs, which show considerable affection for each other, even outside the breeding season. Rather a sluggish bird, much of its time is spent sitting in a tree, on the look-out for the lizards and other small animals which form its food; but it is given to soaring in pairs especially as the breeding season approaches, circling to considerable heights. In flight, the wings appear broad and rounded, whitish, with some rufous barring on the lesser underwing-coverts and dark bars on the quills towards the tips; the underside of the tail shows a dark subterminal bar and two or three narrow ones before it, on the whitish ground-colour. The male performs aerobatics while soaring during the period of courtship; he alternately stoops and throws up, high in air, at the same time uttering a loud note *chip, chip, chip* or *kit, kit, kit*. The usual call, uttered by both sexes, is described as a loud mew *pee-ow* (W. W. A. Phillips) or *ker-chew* (Mrs Lushington).

The breeding season is during the north-east monsoon, from about November to May. The nest is composed of leafy twigs broken off by the birds and carried in the talons to the chosen site, which is in a fork, more or less hidden among foliage, in the crown of a tall tree; it is usually situated in forest, but several nests found by Mrs Lushington and Phillips, of recent years, have been in trees growing in tea. The nest is somewhat like that of a crow, but is lined with green leaves. The two eggs are white, with a faint grey tinge, quickly becoming stained. They measure about 44·9×33·6 mm.

THE FALCONS

Family FALCONIDAE

In the falcons, the raptors, or birds of prey, reach their highest degree of specialization. They are characterized by long, pointed, but rather narrow wings which give them both speed and staying-power in flight. The beak is short, stout, and strongly hooked, with a well-marked 'tooth' on the edge of the upper mandible, and a corresponding notch on the lower mandible. The nostrils are circular, with a small tubercle in the centre. The tibia is well feathered; the tarsus rather short, naked; the feet strong, with the claws well-curved and sharp, but not very different in size on the four toes (in all raptors, the hind claw is longest, the inner front claw next in size, and the outer claw smallest). Falcons all have dark-brown irides—never yellow or red. They nearly all have, variously developed, a dark line proceeding downwards from below the lore, past the gape, to the sides of the throat; this, with a somewhat spectacle-like, pale eye-rim, gives them a very characteristic appearance. When folded, the wing-tips reach well beyond the middle of the tail, and in some species extend slightly beyond its tip. The second or second and third primaries are the longest. Falcons' forms are stout and compact, their usual posture very erect, their plumage crisp, the flight-feathers stiff and strong. They are of small to medium size. They generally capture their prey on the wing; in the case of the typical falcons, this consists principally of birds, which are pursued in the air, out-manœuvred, and finally cut down by a lightning stoop from above, the hind claw being the instrument of execution. The more slack-mettled kinds, such as kestrels and hobbies, feed largely on insects and small mammals.

Falcons are poor nest-builders. Many kinds lay their eggs, without any nest, on ledges of cliffs or the like, while those that nest in trees generally make use of the abandoned nests of other birds, such as crows. Their eggs, generally three in number, are white, handsomely spotted with various shades of brown or brick-red.

THE EASTERN PEREGRINE

Falco peregrinus calidus Latham. Scarce, but regular, winter visitor

Sinhalese: Kurullā-goya. Tamil: Vallūru

Plate 21, facing p. 248 (male; ×one-twelfth)

Female about the size of the Brahminy Kite; male about that of the House Crow. Sexes alike. The adult Peregrine is dark grey above, heavily spotted and barred with darker grey; nearly black on head, quills and tail, pale grey on lower back and rump. Underparts, from chin to under tail-coverts, white, suffused with pinkish-buff and pale grey from the breast downwards, and flecked on breast, barred on flanks and lowerparts, with black; black 'moustaches' on sides of throat. Wing-lining whitish, heavily spotted and barred with dark grey as shown in the Plate. Bill black at tip, bluish at base; cere, eye-rim and legs rich yellow; irides dark brown. Juveniles are dark brown above, buff below, with brown longitudinal streaks (not bars) on breast and flanks; cere, eye-rim and legs pale greenish-grey. From the Shahin Falcon, which is another race of the Peregrine and of the same size and build, this race may be distinguished by its paler, more speckled upperparts, and whitish, or very pale rufous underparts; both races vary in colour and marking to a considerable extent.

Head; × one-third

This splendid falcon is found, in numerous local races, almost throughout the world. The eastern race breeds in northern Asia, and winters in India and Ceylon, visiting the Island in small numbers but fairly regularly, from about October till April. It prefers the dry zone, usually frequenting the coasts and the larger tanks, but occasionally strays up-country—probably on passage. In some years, one or two will take up residence in Colombo, making their headquarters on some lofty building. The Peregrine has very regular habits; it generally sallies forth from its roosting place—generally a high ledge of a cliff, lofty and sheltered cornice of a building, or even the crown of a palm—shortly before sunrise, to hunt for its breakfast. Having killed some luckless pigeon or other bird—for it feeds almost exclusively on birds—it either eats it where it falls or else carries it back to its favourite perch. Hunger assuaged, it spends the day quietly preening itself and 'viewing the landscape o'er', with an occasional fly around to exercise its wings, sometimes stooping into the middle of a flock of birds, scaring and scattering them, apparently merely for fun, for it seldom kills unless hungry; towards evening it again flies forth in search of prey. This routine depends, of course, on its success in the hunt. The ordinary flight consists of spells of rapid fanning of the shapely wings alternating with short glides with them held level with the back; the tail is usually closed. This style of flight is not particularly swift or remarkable, but when pursuing a bird—especially a speedy one, such as a pigeon or shore-bird—the falcon draws in its wings a little, the strokes become deep and powerful, and it hurls itself through the air at its victim. The final stoop, which the falcon always endeavours to effect from a height above its quarry, is breath-taking in its speed, skill and style; the wings are almost closed and the whistling of the wind through them may be heard for a great distance. The back or head of the prey is ripped with the powerful hind claw, usually killing it instantaneously; the falcon checks its rush by swooping up and then descends to pick up its victim. On sunny days the Peregrine is fond of circling up into the heavens on ascending air-currents, with the wings more fully expanded than usual and the tail also expanded. In its winter quarters it is usually silent, but in the breeding season it utters a variety of sharp notes, of which the commonest is a shrill *kek kek kek kek*. It enjoys bathing in shallow water.

The Peregrine generally lays its eggs, without any nest, on a ledge or small cave in the face of a rock-cliff; but it is adaptable and, in Siberia, where the race *calidus* breeds, it will nest on the ground in tundras, or will make use of the nest of some other bird—e.g. raven—in a tree. The two to four eggs are white, more or less heavily marked with some shade of reddish-brown; they measure about 56×43 mm. Layard, about a hundred years ago, claimed to have found a pair of Peregrines nesting on the leaf-bases of a palmyra palm near Point Pedro; but apparently he did not take the eggs and it is probable that he made some mistake as this race is most unlikely to nest in Ceylon; the possibility of its occasionally doing so should, however, be borne in mind.

THE SHAHIN FALCON, or INDIAN PEREGRINE

Falco peregrinus peregrinator Sundevall. Scarce resident

Sinhalese: Kurullā-goya. Tamil: Vallūru

Plate 17, facing p. 216 (male; ×one-ninth)
Plate 21, facing p. 248 (female; ×one-twelfth)

Female rather smaller than the Brahminy Kite; male about the size of the House Crow. Sexes alike in coloration. Juveniles are brownish-black above, and paler rufous below than adults, with blackish flecks and streaks on breast and flanks; they have the cere, eye-rims and legs pale yellowish-grey, gradually changing to the rich chrome yellow of the adult. The colour scheme of this handsome falcon is very similar to that of the Rufous-bellied Hawk-Eagle, and also to that of the Indian Hobby; from the first it may be distinguished by its smaller size, pointed wings, and white patch behind the cheeks; from the latter, it differs in being much larger but with relatively shorter wings. Though in form and silhouette it resembles its migratory relation, the Eastern Peregrine, it differs by its very dark upper plumage and deep chestnut underparts.

The Shahin is found in both low country and hills, though it does not reside permanently much above 4,000 feet. Its favourite haunts are isolated, precipitous hills surrounded by mixed woodland and fairly open country. In such places the Shahin may be found, sitting during the heat of the day on a shaded ledge or a branch of an out-jutting tree, or flying around with inimitable style and dash. In most of its habits it closely resembles the Eastern Peregrine, but is more partial to well-wooded country, and commonly hunts smaller birds. In chasing these it is very adept in following every turn and twist until it can seize the quarry in its talons. It is not at all averse, however, to larger prey, such as pigeons and parakeets, and in pursuing them displays all the skill and power of the Peregrine, stooping upon them from a height with terrific force. I have personal knowledge of its capturing the Ceylon White-rumped Swift, Ceylon Lorikeet, Wood Shrike, Green Fruit-Pigeon, and domestic pigeon. As it generally captures only flying quarry, poultry are normally safe from attack. When excited or annoyed the Shahin utters a loud scream—*hehehehe*—and also a shrill chatter.

The breeding season appears to be from December to April, but the eyrie has very seldom been found in Ceylon. It is situated on a ledge or in a small cave in the face of a high cliff, usually in an inaccessible position. Two or three eggs are laid, as a rule on bare ground or with only such bedding as naturally accumulates. They are yellowish- or pinkish-white variously blotched with reddish-brown, and measure about 52 × 43 mm.

THE INDIAN HOBBY

Falco severus rufipedoides Hodgson. Very rare straggler to Ceylon
No Sinhalese or Tamil names

About the size of the kestrel but with the tail much shorter. The female is larger than the male, but otherwise the sexes are alike. Head black; back and wings dark ashy-grey, paling on rump and upper tail-coverts, and darkening to black towards the tail-tip; throat, cheek-patch, and upper breast white, shading to deep chestnut on the rest of the underparts; cere, eye-rims and legs yellow; irides deep brown; beak bluish, darkening to black at the tip. Young birds are browner above, paler rufous below, with black streaks and spots on the underparts.

This beautiful little falcon is almost a miniature of the Shahin in general form and coloration; but, as it is only about two-thirds the Shahin's size and has relatively longer and narrower wings, there should be no difficulty in distinguishing between the two. The wings when closed extend beyond the tip of the tail, and in flight they give the bird somewhat the appearance of a large swift. The normal habitat of this falcon is in the eastern Himalayas, from which it spreads in winter throughout the Indian peninsula; but its visits to Ceylon are very few and far between, only three or four specimens, and a few sight-records, having been recorded. The hobbies, including this species, are among the most graceful of the raptors, and the speediest in flight. They feed mainly on insects, such as dragon-flies, locusts and grasshoppers, but capture small birds on occasion. Their favourite haunts are in well-wooded country, and they usually perch on trees, not on rocks and cliffs as their larger relatives the Peregrines normally do. They nest in trees, generally making use of the discarded nest of some other bird, such as a crow or magpie.

THE EASTERN RED-LEGGED FALCON

Falco vespertinus amurensis Radde. Very rare straggler to Ceylon

No Sinhalese or Tamil names

Slightly smaller than the kestrel, which it resembles in shape, but it has relatively longer wings and shorter tail. The sexes in this little falcon differ strongly; adult male: dark slaty-grey, darker on head and back, paler on wings and breast; tibia-coverts, abdomen, and under tail-coverts deep chestnut; axillaries and under wing-coverts white. Adult female: grey, barred with black, on back, wing-coverts and tail; head and upper back rufous brown; moustachial streak, and region round the eye, black; underparts rufous or buff, with black streaks and spots on breast and flanks, and paling to whitish on throat and face; under-wing white, with brown spots. Adults of both sexes have cere, eye-rims and feet orange; irides dark brown. Immature birds are dark brown; wing-quills and tail greyish, the latter barred with black; face and throat whitish, with brown lores and slight moustachial streak; underparts white, streaked with brownish black on breast; buff or pale rufous on tibia and under tail-coverts.

This race of the Red-legged Falcon breeds in eastern Asia and winters in eastern Africa, a few visiting India. It has been recorded only two or three times from Ceylon, all records being of immature birds. Legge obtained one at Trincomalee in December 1872, and in March 1932 one frequented the Colombo Racecourse, where I watched it on many occasions. It hunted grasshoppers in the evenings, in company with several kestrels, and was very tame, permitting a close approach. Although, at times, it hovered like a kestrel, its usual method of hunting was from the top of a fence or post, and sometimes it would run and hop along the ground after its prey. When chased by a kestrel, its long wings —which extended beyond the tail when closed—enabled it to escape without difficulty. It would continue to hunt until late dusk, long after the kestrels had retired to roost.

This falcon breeds in China and adjacent countries. It nests gregariously, and generally uses an abandoned nest of crow or magpie.

THE KESTREL

Falco tinnunculus tinnunculus Linnaeus. The European and west Asian race; abundant winter visitor—by far the commonest kestrel to be seen in Ceylon

Falco tinnunculus interstinctus McClelland. The north China and Japanese race; a heavily-marked form which sometimes visits Ceylon in winter

Falco tinnunculus objurgatus (Stuart Baker). A small, richly-coloured race which breeds on the hills of South India and Ceylon

All these races of the kestrel are practically indistinguishable in the field

Sinhalese: Kurullā-goya. Tamil: Vallūru

Plate 20, facing p. 233 (male European Kestrel; ×one-sixth)
Plate 21, facing p. 248 (female European Kestrel; ×one-twelfth)

About the size of the domestic pigeon, but with longer tail. The female and young male differ from the adult male as follows: head rufous, streaked with dark brown; back and wing-coverts paler rufous, strongly barred with brown; rump and tail rufous, the latter with many narrow bars besides the subterminal broad one; underparts heavily streaked with brown. The sexes do not differ greatly in size.

Apart from a few pairs of race *objurgatus* which inhabit the mountains of Ceylon all the year round, the kestrel is a common winter visitor, arriving about September and October, and leaving in April. During its sojourn it spreads all over the Island, in much greater numbers in some years than in others. It loves open or sparsely wooded country, patana hill-sides, etc., and in such places it may be seen industriously quartering the ground, every few minutes performing its well-known feat of hovering, with body motionless but wings and tail continually adjusted to the strength of the breeze. Where a gale blows up a hill-side, the bird does not need to fan its wings, or spread its tail, but remains poised for long periods 'with no visible means of support'—a most fascinating sight. Its keen eyes scan the ground below for prey which, in Ceylon, consists mainly of grasshoppers and other insects, and lizards; it does no harm to adult birds, though it will take nestlings of ground-nesting birds when it can find them. On spying some quarry it drops upon it and either eats it on the spot or, if small enough, flies away with it in its foot, daintily picking it to pieces and devouring it in the air. When annoyed—e.g. by mobbing crows—it utters a shrill, angry *kekekeke*. In addition to bathing, the kestrel will dust itself in sandy soil, though it does this much less efficiently than a hen would.

Tame kestrels which I have kept would carefully hide surplus food under shrubs and the like, and search for it next day, showing obvious disappointment on discovering that ants had made away with the cache—as invariably happened. The kestrel prefers dead stumps, cliffs, buildings, etc., rather than leafy trees, as resting places.

The breeding season of the resident race is from March to June. It breeds in small numbers on rocky precipices in the drier, eastern aspect of the mountain zone, at elevations of about 3,000 to 5,000 feet. The eggs do not appear to have been collected yet in Ceylon, but young birds being fed by their parents have been observed, and several eyries are known. Following the behaviour of other races, it is probable that no nest is built, the eggs being deposited on a ledge of rock on the face of some inaccessible cliff. They number two or three, and are rich, mottled brick-red in colour, and measure about 40×31 mm. The hunger cry of the young is a weak *kirri kirri kirri*.

PIGEONS AND SAND GROUSE

Order COLUMBIFORMES

THIS order includes two sub-orders, as follows:

Pterocletes—sand grouse. These are birds of somewhat partridge-like appearance but with short legs, long wings, and very swift, powerful flight, which inhabit desert or dry, open country in Europe, Africa and Asia. They live and nest entirely on the ground, never perching, and their young are clothed with down and are able to run soon after hatching. Although several species are found in India (mainly in the north-west) no sand grouse occurs in Ceylon.

Columbae—comprising two families: (*a*) *Raphidae*—the dodo and solitaire, of the Mauritius and Rodriguez Islands in the Indian Ocean; both of these have long been extinct; (*b*) *Columbidae* —including all pigeons and doves.

Only the *Columbidae* are found in Ceylon.

THE PIGEONS AND DOVES

Family COLUMBIDAE

This is a very distinctive group of birds, marked by several peculiar features which, in conjunction, make them easily recognizable. They have rather small heads and heavy bodies; usually strong wings, which give them great powers of flight; and well-developed tails, which are capable of being very widely expanded. The beak is straight, with only the terminal half hard and horny; the basal part (of the upper mandible) is swollen and fleshy, with the nostrils situated in it in the form of slits. The gape is capable of wide expansion, enabling these birds to swallow large morsels of food. The contour plumage is of peculiar character; it has a dry and powdery appearance and, though soft, is crisp and stiff, due to the structure of the shafts of the feathers which are broad and flattened in the basal part, fine and flexible distally; these feathers are loosely attached to the skin. The wings, though comparatively short, are pointed, with the secondaries long. The legs are short but strong, with the toes arranged three in front and one behind, the hinder toe, which is well developed, being set on the same level as the front ones. Pigeons are almost entirely vegetarian, feeding on seeds, fruit, buds, etc. The flight of most species is powerful and swift, usually with the head well advanced, and the tail, at least when taking off and alighting, widely spread. In drinking, these birds immerse the entire beak, and gulp water—not taking little sips and raising the beak after each, as most birds do. All species are monogamous.

They nest either in holes in trees or rocks, or among twigs and foliage; those that nest in the latter situations generally make very scanty, flimsy nests. They seldom or never lay more than two eggs to the clutch and some kinds lay only one. Both sexes incubate the eggs and tend the young, which are hatched blind and helpless. Their parents feed them by regurgitation—at first of a milky secretion ('pigeon's milk') from the crop, and later with partially digested food.

As a family, the *Columbidae* are inclined to be wanderers, and to this propensity Ceylon owes no less than three of the species on our list. They are: the Purple Wood Pigeon, of which a single specimen was collected by Layard about a hundred years ago; the Rufous Turtle Dove, recorded three times; and the Indian Red Turtle Dove, which was found in a small breeding colony by Layard, and has recently turned up again in the Island. Another pigeon that may visit Ceylon from time to time is Jerdon's Imperial Pigeon, a lilac-grey and olive-brown bird larger than the Green Imperial Pigeon. It was reported by Stuart Baker to have been found nesting in the Ratnapura district some years ago, but the record is considered insufficiently substantiated for the bird to be accepted on the Ceylon list until corroborative evidence is obtained.

No real distinction exists between pigeons and doves; the latter are merely small pigeons.

THE CEYLON YELLOW-LEGGED GREEN PIGEON

Treron phoenicoptera phillipsi Ripley. Race peculiar to Ceylon; almost indistinguishable races inhabit India

Sinhalese: Bata-goya, Sipaduwā. Tamil: Pachchai Purā

Plate 22, facing p. 249 (male; ×one-fifth)

About the size of the domestic pigeon; larger than the Pompadour or Orange-breasted Green Pigeons. Sexes alike, but the female is duller than the male. From either of the two Green Pigeons above-mentioned it may at once be distinguished by its legs which are chrome yellow, not dull purplish-red. Other points of distinction are the pale purplish-grey patch on the lesser wing-coverts, and the acutely-pointed tips of the longest primaries.

This handsome pigeon was first recorded from Ceylon by Layard followed by Holdsworth, who found it in the Jaffna Peninsula and at Aripu respectively, about a hundred years ago. Since then it has not been recorded in the Island until 1947, when W. W. A. Phillips discovered a colony in the Bibile district (Uva foot-hills), and collected specimens; these have been pronounced by Dr Dillon Ripley to represent a local race of a species of wide distribution in India and neighbouring countries. In view of the large number of Green Pigeons that are shot in Ceylon every year it is extraordinary that so distinct a species should have eluded recognition so long. Possibly it is not a permanent resident of the Island but a visitor from the mainland which has founded a small breeding colony in the Bibile jungles—perhaps to disappear again after a few years. In general habits, this pigeon does not greatly differ from the better-known 'bata-goyas'. It has the same habit of flocking to fruiting trees, especially of the genus *Ficus*, and gorging itself on the ripe fruit which it swallows whole; it utters a whistle which, according to Phillips, is very similar to the call of the Orange-breasted Green Pigeon but louder and pitched in a rather lower key. The same observer states that the clatter made by its wings, as it suddenly dashes out of a tree, is loud, and has a somewhat hollow note. Like other Green Pigeons, it is adept at concealing itself among foliage when apprehensive of danger. It is arboreal, descending to the ground only for the purpose of quenching its thirst at some stream or water-hole, and perhaps to pick up grains of gravel for the grinding of food in its gizzard. The flight is swift and direct.

The nest does not appear to have been found in Ceylon, but the Indian races build flimsy platform-nests among foliage in moderate-sized trees. The two eggs are glossy white and measure about 32 × 24 mm.

THE POMPADOUR GREEN PIGEON

Treron pompadora pompadora (Gmelin). Race peculiar to Ceylon, but closely allied races are found in India

Sinhalese: Bata-goya, Sipaduwā. Tamil: Pachchai Purā

Plate 22, facing p. 249 (female left, male right; × one-fifth)

Between the Spotted Dove and the domestic pigeon in size. The sexes differ as shown in the Plate. The adult male, with his maroon back, cannot be confused with the Orange-breasted Green Pigeon, but the female is very similar to the same sex of that species; the best distinction is in the tail: in the Pompadour, the two middle tail-feathers are olive-green above and the under tail-coverts are yellowish-white, somewhat mottled with greyish-green; in the female Orange-breasted, the middle tail-feathers are bluish-grey above and the under tail-coverts are cinnamon-red on their inner webs.

This cobby and beautiful little pigeon is found almost throughout the low country and ascends the hills to 3,000 feet, or even higher on occasion; it is not so fond of coastal districts as the next species. It inhabits both forest and well-wooded cultivation, and moves about a good deal, living in small flocks. The flight is swift and direct, and is performed by rapid fluttering of the wings; these produce a loud clapping sound—presumably by being beaten together over the back—when the bird is frightened out of a tree. It feeds exclusively on small fruits such as it can swallow entire; wild figs (banyan, bo, nuga, etc.) are favourites, and it also delights in the berries of mā-dun, and palu. A fruiting tree attracts the pigeons from miles around. Amongst foliage they are extraordinarily hard to detect and a tree may be full of them without one's knowledge, as they 'freeze' on the approach of a human; they are very quarrelsome, however, and sooner or later are sure to betray their presence by fighting. The strong feet enable them to clamber about the twigs very actively, and to reach out for tempting fruit. In the intervals of feeding they utter a beautifully modulated, mellow whistle; this is often uttered from a bare branch at the top of a tree. Like other Green Pigeons, the Pompadour is arboreal, seldom descending to the ground.

The breeding season is from December to June and sometimes in August–September. The nest is a slight, nearly flat platform of small twigs, unlined, and is placed in a small bushy tree growing on the outskirts of jungle or in scrub-land; it is generally well concealed among foliage. Both sexes incubate the two eggs, which are pure white and smooth, and measure about 29 × 23 mm.

THE CEYLON ORANGE-BREASTED GREEN PIGEON

Treron bicincta leggei Hartert. Race peculiar to Ceylon; closely related races inhabit India

Sinhalese: Bata-goya, Sipaduwā. Tamil: Pachchai Purā

Plate 22, facing p. 249 (female behind, male in front; × one-fifth)

Between the Spotted Dove and the domestic pigeon in size. The female lacks the purple and orange breast-band of the male; for points

244

of distinction between the females of this and the Pompadour Pigeon, see the account of the latter.

This pigeon is common in most parts of the low country, but does not ascend the hills to any height. While its general behaviour is very similar to that of the Pompadour Pigeon it is less fond of tall forest than the latter, being generally found in scrub-jungle, patches of trees in swamps, and the like, and it will descend into low bushes in search of fruit. Lantana and cinnamon berries, the fruit of the small wild date-palm, wild figs, and other small fruits, are eaten. It lives in small flocks which travel about the country a good deal and unite into large ones where food is plentiful—for instance, when a big banyan tree is fruiting. In such circumstances it associates freely with other species of Green Pigeons congregating to feast on the figs. Although sociable it is very quarrelsome, scrapping over fruit and expressing annoyance by a sound like *kek kek kek*, and by a chuckling sound which is accompanied by much head-jerking. The call is a beautifully modulated, mellow whistle. When perched, the bird often waves its tail up and down. The flight is swift, performed by rapid beating of the wings. According to Legge, it drinks regularly at about seven in the morning and four in the afternoon, descending to the margin of a stream or water-hole for this purpose. On the ground it walks rather clumsily, with the tail held high.

The breeding season is from December to May, and again in August–September. The nest, a skimpy platform of small twigs, is placed in a small tree beside a jungle path or in the open, at heights of from eight to fifteen feet from the ground; it is generally well hidden among foliage. Both parents take turns to incubate and they sit very close. The two glossy-white eggs measure about $28 \times 22 \cdot 5$ mm.

THE GREEN IMPERIAL PIGEON

Ducula aenea pusilla (Blyth). Resident

Sinhalese: Māila-goya, Māhā-nila-goya. Tamil: Periya Purā, Maruttan Purā

Plate 22, facing p. 249 (×one-fifth)

Our largest pigeon; considerably larger than the domestic pigeon. Sexes alike.

This splendid pigeon is mainly a low-country bird, ascending the hills only to about 1500 feet. It is found throughout the low country wherever heavy forest exists, but not in cultivated districts as it is shy of man. There can be no doubt that its numbers have been severely reduced through shooting since Legge's time, even in the wilder jungle districts of the Island. In the dry zone, it frequents the belts of tall forest that line river banks, living usually in pairs and forming small flocks only when favourite trees are fruiting heavily. At such times it associates with other fruit-pigeons, hornbills, grackles, and other fruit-eating birds. It eats wild figs, palu berries, and many other wild fruits, including wild nutmegs which, though larger than the pigeon's head, are swallowed whole; when the flesh has been digested the nut is disgorged. The flight is straight and powerful, performed with rather slow strokes of the wings, and often at a considerable height when the bird is travelling to its feeding-grounds. The ordinary call-note is a deep *wuk-wooor*; when courting, it utters frog-like croaks, and an extraordinary mixture of coos and loud roars rather suggestive of a bear. Like other fruit-pigeons it has very strong feet with broad soles, which enable it to clamber about the twigs and branches and to reach for outlying fruit. It feeds mainly in the early mornings and evenings and sits sluggishly, hidden in a tree canopy, during the heat of the day. It is arboreal, descending to the ground only for quenching its thirst at some water-hole.

The breeding season is from December to May. The nest is placed in a smallish tree in jungle, at a height of about fifteen to twenty feet; it is a scanty saucer of twigs. The single egg is white and smooth and measures about 42 × 33 mm.

THE CEYLON BRONZE-WING PIGEON, or EMERALD DOVE

Chalcophaps indica robinsoni Stuart Baker. Race peculiar to Ceylon

Sinhalese: Nil-kobēyiyā. Tamil: Pāthekai Purā, Thamil Purā

Plate 22, facing p. 249 (male; × one-fifth)

Between the Spotted Dove and the domestic pigeon in size. The female differs only slightly from the male but her colouring is duller, with only a slight indication of the white forehead and blue-grey crown and upper neck, and her lateral tail-feathers are largely rufous.

This beautiful little pigeon cannot be mistaken for any other bird. It is found, in jungle and well-wooded country, almost everywhere in the Island and is common in most parts of its range but avoids very dry areas. The highest elevations are visited only when nillu is seeding up-country (about once in eleven years), when it migrates to exceptional heights to feast on the seeds. It spends much time on the ground, where it obtains practically all its food, consisting of various seeds, grains, berries, etc. Carters' bivouacking places on jungle roads are much frequented for the sake of waste grain from the bullocks' fodder. In such places it may be seen, generally solitary, walking with pretty, tripping gait, head jerking forward at every step after the manner of the domestic pigeon, and pecking here and there as it spies some titbit. Although essentially a jungle bird it is not shy and where human dwellings are in well-wooded surroundings it will freely associate with man; the candle-nut tree *Sapium sebiferum* and the castor-oil plant *Ricinus communis* are great attractions, for it is very fond of their seeds. Its flight is very swift, usually only a few feet from the ground. In the open it is direct, but in jungle, obstacles are dodged with great adroitness; nevertheless, where human buildings, wire fences, etc., intrude in its jungle haunts, it is very apt to kill or injure itself by dashing into windows, wire-netting, or even whitewashed walls. When courting, the male utters a deep, mournful, booming note like *tk-hoon . . . tk-hoon*; this is somewhat ventriloquistic in quality and is generally uttered from a branch in a big, shady tree. While producing it his crop inflates like that of a Pouter Pigeon.

The main breeding season is during February to May with another brood in September, but breeding occurs to some extent all the year. The nest is generally rather better built than most doves', and is placed in a small tree, or on a cardamon or tree-fern-frond, in jungle, at no great height from the ground. The two eggs are pale buff, and measure about $27 \times 21 \cdot 5$ mm.

THE INDIAN BLUE ROCK PIGEON

Columba livia intermedia Strickland. Resident

Sinhalese: Gal-parēyiyā. Tamil: Māda Purā, Malai Purā

In size and form identical with the domestic pigeon of the Blue Rock type. It has darker-grey mantle and wings than the European Blue Rock Pigeon (from which all the domestic breeds of pigeon have been derived), and the lower back and rump, instead of being white as in the latter, are darker grey than the wings; in other respects the wild bird is indistinguishable from tame ones.

This pigeon is rare and very local in Ceylon; this is surprising, as on the neighbouring continent of India it is one of the commonest and most familiar of birds. In the Island, it is confined to two or three small colonies which roost and breed on rocky islets off the coast on the south and east, visiting the mainland daily for food. In Legge's time there were several other colonies in various inland districts in the northern half of the Island, but these seem to have disappeared. No doubt many of the pigeons which frequent bazaars, warehouses, railway stations, and the like, have some admixture of wild blood, but genuine wild birds are confined to the islets above-mentioned. They flight, twice a day as a rule, to the cultivated country on the mainland, where they feed on waste grain and various seeds and herbs, returning to their fastness for the heat of the day and for roosting at night. This pigeon does not normally perch on trees but on rocks, cliffs and the like. Its flight is swift and direct; the white wing-lining is conspicuous, especially in the display-flight of the courting male when he sails around with wings held stiffly, high above the back. The ordinary note of this pigeon is the familiar *coo, cooo* of the domestic bird, and the courting note of the male, too, is the throaty *wop, wop, woppera-woo-oo*—accompanied by bowing, crop-inflation, and circling gait—which may be observed at any pigeon-cote; at the height of his excitement, the male hops towards his love and scrapes the ground with his partly-expanded tail.

The main breeding season seems to be from February to June, but sporadic nesting probably goes on all the year. The nest is a scanty pad of twigs, dry grass, etc., placed in a deep cleft or cave among the piled rocks of the islets. The two white eggs measure about 37 × 29 mm.

THE CEYLON WOOD PIGEON, or
LADY TORRINGTON'S PIGEON

Columba torringtoni Bonaparte. Species peculiar to Ceylon; a closely related species inhabits the South Indian hills

Sinhalese: Māila-goya. Tamil: Karuppu Purā

Plate 22, facing p. 249 (× one-fifth)

About the size of the domestic pigeon, but with a longer tail. Sexes alike. Young birds are duller, and have only a trace of the black and white 'chess-board' patch on the side of the neck. This handsome pigeon is confined to the hill forests of Ceylon, though it has a close relation (the Nilgiri Wood Pigeon), of very similar appearance and habits, in the hills of South India. Its normal range is from 3,000 feet upwards to the highest elevations, but it wanders about a great deal and sometimes descends as low as 1000 feet in the damp forests of the wet zone. Exclusively a forest dweller, it lives in pairs though small

PLATE 21

1. Eastern Peregrine.   2. Ceylon Crested Goshawk.   3. Ceylon Shikra.
4. Shahin Falcon.   5. European Kestrel.   6. Black-winged Kite

PLATE 22

1. Pompadour Green Pigeon.   2. Ceylon Orange-breasted Green Pigeon.
3. Green Imperial Pigeon.   4. Ceylon Spotted Dove.   5. Ceylon Wood-
Pigeon.   6. Ceylon Yellow-legged Green Pigeon.   7. Indian Ring-Dove.
8. Ceylon Bronze-wing Pigeon

flocks will form where food is abundant. It is strictly arboreal, feeding on a variety of small jungle fruits and berries, among which the fruits of the wild cinnamon are much liked. Shy and wary, it usually keeps well concealed in the forest canopy, from which it dashes out, with loud clapping of wings, on the approach of a human. The flight is speedy and powerful, with rather leisurely wing-beats, and often at a considerable height, the long and broad tail giving it a characteristic appearance as it passes overhead.

Except when courting, when it utters a deep and rather owl-like *hoo*, it is rather a silent bird.

The breeding season is from February to May, and again from August to October. The nest is the usual pigeon-type, scanty platform of twigs; it is placed among foliage and twiggery in the canopy of a forest tree, or in the top of a tall sapling, usually at a height of fifteen to twenty feet. The single, white egg measures about 38·5 × 28·2 mm.

A single specimen of the PURPLE WOOD PIGEON *Columba punicea* Blyth was collected by Layard somewhere in Ceylon about a hundred years ago; this is the only definite record, but Legge saw some brown pigeons, which he suspected to be this species, frequenting cinnamon bushes near Borella (Colombo) in 1869. The following description is given to assist in identifying this species if it should turn up again in the Island.

Slightly larger than the Ceylon Wood Pigeon, which it closely resembles in shape and proportions. From that species, it may be distinguished by its chocolate-brown general coloration, shot with metallic purplish-pink on back, scapulars, and wing-coverts, and shading into dark grey on the rump, and ashy-black on the tail. The underparts are paler and greyer chocolate. The neck-patch, though present in the form of rows of small feathers, is the same colour as the upper back and is therefore inconspicuous. In the male, the entire cap and a narrow line below the eye are greyish-white; in the female, the cap is purplish-ashy. The edge of wing, primaries and secondaries are dull black. Irides yellow or orange; beak white at the tip, purple at the base; legs dull purple. This handsome pigeon inhabits eastern Bengal, eastwards to Indo-China, and southwards to Malaya. It is said to be a shy, forest-haunting bird, and its general habits are very similar to those of the Ceylon Wood Pigeon except that it is more of a lowland species, and feeds on grain as well as on wild fruits.

THE RUFOUS TURTLE DOVE

Streptopelia orientalis meena (Sykes). Very rare straggler from northern India

No Sinhalese or Tamil names

Nearly the size of the domestic pigeon—larger than the Spotted Dove, which it resembles in shape. Sexes alike. It may be described as a light brown dove, with grey forehead, grey and black 'chess-board' patches on the sides of the neck, and grey outer wing-coverts; scapulars and inner wing-coverts bright ferruginous, with the centres of the feathers dark brown—giving a scaly effect; lower back and rump bluish-grey, shading into the blackish-brown tail which has conspicuous greyish-white tips; abdomen whitish, under tail-coverts white; flight-feathers dark brown above, underwing bluish-grey; beak black, irides orange, feet purplish-red. In flight, the grey rump and white-tipped, dark-coloured tail contrast strikingly with the ferruginous scapulars and wing-coverts.

This large turtle dove is a migratory bird which breeds in the Himalayas and central Asia and winters in India, very occasionally straying as far as Ceylon; there are only two records of its occurrence in the Island—both over eighty years ago.[1] It is said to be rather shy but, in general, its habits differ but little from those of other turtle doves; it feeds on the ground, gleaning waste grain in stubble-fields, beside roads, etc.; and flies up into trees when disturbed. In its winter quarters, it associates in loose flocks. The note is described as 'a dull, sleepy drone, *cooo-cooo-kakour*' (Whistler), and it is said to drink frequently.

It nests in forests but, out of the breeding season, frequents cultivated but well-wooded country.

THE CEYLON SPOTTED DOVE, or ASH DOVE

Streptopelia chinensis ceylonensis (Reichenbach). Race peculiar to Ceylon

Sinhalese: Alu-kobēyiyā. Tamil: Mani Purā, Ūmi Purā

Plate 22, facing p. 249 (×one-fifth)

About the size of the Common Mynah, but of stouter build and with a longer tail. Sexes alike. This small dove is by far the commonest and most generally-distributed of the pigeon tribe in Ceylon. It is common

---

[1] Since this was written, a specimen of this turtle dove was shot by B. Gordon-Graham in the jungle between Telulla and Hambegamuwa (southern part of Uva) in November 1953. The wings and legs were sent to W. W. A. Phillips, who reports that it was a bird in its first year.

almost everywhere up to 4,000 feet, and is gradually extending its range up-country, especially on the eastern aspect of the hills where the climate is drier than in the west; it is now common near Hakgala at over 5,000 feet, where a few years ago it was unknown. Its main headquarters are, however, in the dry jungles of the low country, in the eastern and northern parts of the Island. It frequents both cultivation and the more open types of forest, but, as it obtains all its food on the ground, some open spaces are essential in its habitat. It lives in pairs which are very faithful to each other but, where food is plentiful—for instance, in newly-reaped paddy-fields or kurakkan chenas—large numbers collect to feed on the waste grain. Besides grain, it eats the seeds of many grasses and weeds, and also devours much green-stuff. The gait is a tripping walk. When disturbed, it flutters up with a great clatter of wings and flies off to some near-by tree with peculiar, jerky, yet powerful wing action; the tail is widely spread, displaying the white tips of the outer feathers, until the bird is well under way. In the courting season the male performs a pretty evolution; he flies steeply up to a height of a hundred feet or so with much wing-clapping, and then parachutes down in a spiral, wings and tail fully spread, to alight beside his modest little mate awaiting him on a branch. The male's courting note is *kookerāu, kookerāu, kookerāu*, uttered briskly with inflated crop, and a bow at each *kookerāu*; the ordinary call-note of both sexes is a rather drowsy-sounding coo—*kookoo krrōō, kroo, kroo, kroo, kroo.*

The breeding season lasts practically throughout the year, each pair probably nesting several times annually; but February to June, and August–September are the main seasons. The nest is a scanty, shallow saucer of small twigs, grass-roots, etc., placed in a small tree or bush, or balanced on a cactus branch or the base of a palm-frond. It is generally fairly well concealed, but the sitting bird often betrays its site by the foolish way it flies off on one's approach. The two white eggs measure about 26 × 21 mm.

THE INDIAN RING DOVE

Streptopelia decaocto decaocto (Frivaldsky). Resident

Sinhalese: Māhā-kobēyiyā. Tamil: Kalli Purā, Sāmbal Purā

Plate 22, facing p. 249 (× one-fifth)

Between the Spotted Dove and the domestic pigeon in size. Sexes alike.

This dove, which is common over most of India, is confined in Ceylon to the coastal strip of very dry country extending from Puttalam in the south to the Jaffna Peninsula in the north. In most parts of this limited range it is abundant, but in the Jaffna Peninsula it is not nearly so numerous as it was in the days of Legge, and there is little doubt that incessant pot-hunting is responsible for this diminution. It frequents scrub-covered or cultivated land, and is never seen in forest. In most of its habits it resembles the Spotted Dove, but it is much shyer of man. Much of its time is spent on the ground, picking up the grain, grass-seeds, and green-stuff on which it feeds; if disturbed, it rises with rapid wing-strokes, producing a loud clatter, and decamps with strong and swift flight. It lives in pairs, but sometimes these unite into a small, scattered flock. The call-note of this dove is a loud *kookoo-koo*, or sometimes *kawkaw-kaw*; this is uttered principally at dawn and in the evening. The courting male expresses his feelings in a vibrant *hŭ hōō hŭhŭ*; a bird which I startled as it came in to its nest gave vent to a loud bark, *wow wow*, as it veered off. The display-flight of the male is similar to that of the Spotted Dove—a steep ascent with clapping wings to a hundred feet or so, and then a graceful glide down in a spiral with wings and tail fully spread.

The breeding season appears to be mainly during the south-west monsoon, commencing in April or May. The nest, which is of the typical dove-type—a flimsy platform of small sticks and grass-stalks, etc.—is placed in a *Euphorbia* bush, a thorny tree, or, as I found in Jaffna, in dense mangrove bushes growing in a saline swamp. The two eggs are white, and measure about 29 × 23 mm.

It is interesting to know that this dove, of recent years, has steadily been extending its breeding range westward from the Balkans until it now nests in much of southern Europe and, as a summer migrant, has even reached Britain though in very small numbers at present.

THE INDIAN RED TURTLE DOVE

Streptopelia tranquebarica tranquebarica (Hermann). Only twice recorded from Ceylon

No Sinhalese or Tamil names

Considerably smaller than the Spotted Dove. The sexes differ in this species; the male has the head grey, paling to white on the chin; there is a neat black half-collar on the hind-neck; the upper plumage, except the lower back, rump and upper tail-coverts—which are dark grey—is pinkish brick-red, and the underparts are a paler shade of the same; flight-feathers dark brown; underwing pale grey; tail brown on the centre feathers, dark grey and white on the rest. The female is duller and browner, with brown upperparts. Irides dark brown; bill black; legs reddish-brown.

The only Ceylon record of this pretty little dove, which is widely distributed in India, was made by Layard about a hundred years ago; he found a small colony in an isolated coconut and palmyra tope situated in a parched plain between Point Pedro and Chavakachcheri. Strange to say, they were nesting, and he collected both birds and eggs—and, from his own account, seems to have done his best to exterminate the colony! It has never been recorded from the Island since.[1] In general habits it does not differ from the other doves above-described, but is less familiar with man, preferring to keep away from human habitations though frequenting cultivated country. It feeds on the ground, on grain, weed-seeds, etc. The flight is swift, and it is said to fly quite away on being disturbed, instead of taking refuge in a near-by tree as the Spotted Dove does. The note is described by Sálim Ali as 'a harsh rolling *groo-gurr-goo, groo-gurr-goo,* repeated several times quickly'.

In India it breeds practically throughout the year, making the usual type of dove's nest on an out-spreading branch of a big tree. It lays two eggs, of a slightly creamy-white colour, which measure about 26×21 mm.

---

[1] Since this was written, W. W. A. Phillips collected a specimen of this dove near Panama, Eastern Province, in November 1951. It was a male in full plumage.

GAME BIRDS

Order GALLIFORMES—Cock-like Birds

THIS order comprises seven families of birds found in most parts of the world, and characterized mainly, from the human point of view, by their edibility; nearly all of them are sought after for their flesh, and for the pleasure of hunting them.

The families are as follows:

Opisthocomidae—the hoatzin, a strange South American bird which has a sub-order all to itself.

Megapodiidae—megapodes; a small group of fowl-like birds distributed from the Nicobar Islands to Australia. They incubate their eggs as reptiles do, by burying them in mounds of decaying vegetation, or in moist sand.

Cracidae—curassows and guans, South American birds.

Tetraonidae—grouse and ptarmigans, etc.; found in North America, Europe and Asia.

Numididae—guineafowls; an African family.

Meleagridae—turkeys; found in North and Central America.

Phasianidae—pheasants, peafowl, quails, partridges, etc.

Only the *Phasianidae* are found naturally in Ceylon.

THE PEAFOWL, JUNGLEFOWL, SPURFOWL, QUAILS, AND PARTRIDGES

Family PHASIANIDAE

Small to fairly large birds, of mainly terrestrial habits, characterized by their compact, plump form, rather small heads, short, rounded wings, and bare tarsi; with four toes, of which the hinder one is small and is set at a higher level on the leg than the three front ones; the claws are blunt, curved and strong, adapted for scratching the surface of the soil; in many species, the tarsus is armed in the male (and sometimes in the female too) with a sharp, horn-covered, bony spur, placed above the hind toe; its purpose is for fighting rivals. The beak is short and strong, used for picking up grain, seeds and other food from the ground. The females, and in many forms the males also, are coloured in sombre, mottled shades of brown, ochre and grey, adapted for concealment amongst ground herbage, etc.; but the males of many game birds are noted for their highly-developed secondary sexual characters, such as gaudy combs and wattles, and brilliantly coloured and extravagantly developed plumage. Nesting nearly always takes place in slight scrapes on the ground. The young are clothed with down when hatched, and are able to run with their mother almost immediately. Their flight-feathers develop very quickly so that they are able to fly at an early age. All game birds are good walkers and runners; their short, concave wings enable them to 'get off the mark' very quickly and to fly rapidly for short distances, but not to soar, or, except in the case of migratory quails, to maintain extended flights. All are edible, and have numerous enemies among carnivorous beasts and birds as well as man. They have developed keen faculties of sight and hearing and a wary nature, to meet the constant danger that surrounds them; but their 'intelligence' and adaptability to unusual circumstances are of a low order.

Probably no other birds are so directly important to man; domestic fowls, all derived from the Indian Red Junglefowl, belong to this family.

THE INDIAN PEAFOWL

Pavo cristatus Linnaeus. Resident

Sinhalese: Monarā. Tamil: Māyil

Plate 23, facing p. 264
(female left, male right; ×one-twentieth)

Size of the domestic turkey. The sexes differ as shown on the Plate. The peafowl inhabits the low-country dry zone, being commonest in the wilder, coastal districts of the north-west, east, and south-east; but it is found also inland in scattered colonies, especially around the larger tanks. It avoids dense forest but delights in a mixture of jungle with open country, scrub-land, chena, etc., and the grassy borders of tanks. A very wary bird, endowed with keen sight and hearing, it is not easily approached, usually running for cover at the first suspicion of danger from man; but towards carnivorous mammals, snakes, etc., it shows considerable curiosity. When suspicious, peahens will erect the feathers of the neck, bottle-brush fashion, and raise the crest, as they peer in the direction of the enemy.

The peafowl is a great walker, wandering over a large area in the course of a day; the male carries his long train—which is surprisingly light—well above the ground and level with his body. The ample wings are used mainly for flying up to, and down from, the nightly roost, and for escaping from sudden attack; but the bird flies readily when it wishes to cross some obstacle, such as a river. In flight, the tail is widely spread, fan-wise, with the train (comprising the rump-feathers and upper tail-coverts) compressed into a narrow bundle. On taking flight, a loud *kok kok kok* is uttered. The call-note is the familiar loud, trumpet-like *pehawn, pehawn*; this is produced by both sexes but especially by the male, who utters it most frequently during the breeding season, and even at night if he becomes suspicious. The true alarm-note is an extraordinary, loud, hollow grunt preceded by a squawk. Loneliness is expressed by a mournful cry *aw-h aw-h*. Chicks, until half grown, utter a whistling cheep like that of turkey poults.

The food of the peafowl consists of a variety of vegetable and animal substances—grain, grass-blades, leaves of certain plants, termites, grasshoppers, small reptiles, etc. It cleverly strips the seeds from grass-heads by drawing the stem through its beak. As a scratcher of the soil it is by no means efficient. The principal feeding times are in the early morning and for an hour or so before sunset; at these periods the birds leave the shelter of the jungle and visit open plains or scrub-land. After feeding, they repair to some stream or water-hole to drink, and then, in the day-time, return to the jungle to preen or dust-bathe in sandy soil. About sunset they fly into some tall tree which gives an uninterrupted view of the countryside, to roost; not infrequently a top branch of a dead tree is chosen, where they are exposed to all the vicissitudes of the weather. These they do not seem to mind, and the only effect a night of rain seems to have upon them is that the cocks delay their descent in the morning until their trains have dried sufficiently to be manageable.

The breeding season in Ceylon is from December to May; it commences soon after the cocks have grown their trains after the autumn moult. In courtship display the cock erects the train vertically and spreads it into a great semicircular fan, in the centre of which the head, with beak open and pointed downwards, forms the focal point. The wings are drooped and constantly 'waggled' behind the train, and frequent gusts of vibration cause the many-eyed and multi-hued apparition to shimmer and scintillate in marvellous fashion. It is difficult to discover whether the main biological purpose of this amazing performance is to excite the jealousy of other cocks or to excite sexual desire in the hen—often she appears to be utterly indifferent to it. The instinct for displaying is very strongly developed in the peafowl; not only cocks but young hens, and even quarter-grown chicks, will go through all the motions of display before almost anything that excites them; I have seen one do it to a tortoise!

The peahen lays her eggs in a slight hollow scraped in the ground in a well-hidden situation in dense shrubbery; often in an isolated patch of bushes growing among long grass. The three to five eggs are glossy, pale buff, thick-shelled and pitted, and they measure about 69 × 55 mm. The chicks are at first clothed in greyish-yellow down; their wing-feathers soon grow, and the crest begins to appear when they are about a month old. Development is slow, and the cocks do not acquire their full trains until they are nearly three years old.

THE CEYLON JUNGLEFOWL

Gallus lafayettii Lesson. Species peculiar to Ceylon

Sinhalese: Weli-kukkulā, cock; Weli-kikkili, hen. Tamil: Kāttu-kōli

Plate 23, facing p. 264 (hen left, cock right; × one-seventh)

Size of a small, but not bantam, breed of domestic fowl. The jungle-fowl is distributed throughout the Island, wherever jungle or dense scrub of any extent is to be found, but it is nowadays common only in the wilder parts of the dry zone. In the neighbourhood of villages and roads it is shy and wary, but in remote jungles it is sometimes very tame and will strut about and crow in full view, like a village fowl. A slight acquaintance with man and his ways, however, quickly changes it into the embodiment of caution. It spends its life in forest or its outskirts, never venturing far from cover, though, especially in wet weather, it likes to frequent open places, such as roadsides or glades, for the purpose of feeding free from drippings from the trees. Most of the hours of daylight are spent on the ground, where it walks with a jaunty carriage though with the tail less elevated than in domestic fowls. If disturbed by human approach it generally runs for cover unless come upon suddenly when, with a great flurry of wings, it flies off to a distance; but if put up by a dog or other carnivore it almost invariably flies up to a branch of the nearest tree, from which it peers at its enemy, with tail elevated, cackling its alarm for some time before flying off to a safer area.

The hen's cackle is a high-pitched, metallic *kwikkuk, kwikkukkuk* . . . Her desire-note, uttered when, for instance, she is about to lay an egg, is a *krā, krārk* very like that of the domestic hen but higher pitched. She calls her chicks with a rather shrill cluck. The cock's crow, which appears to be basically an assertion of territorial claims, is a staccato, musical, ringing *chiok, chaw-choyik*—the terminal '*ik*' being higher in the scale than the rest; this crow is uttered with the head somewhat depressed and the beak jerked sharply up at each syllable. In early morning the cock will crow for several minutes while strutting up and down a branch of his roosting tree, before fluttering down to begin his morning feed. When challenging a rival, the crow is generally preceded by vigorous clapping of the wings together above the back, from three to six claps. Unfortunately for the cock, the sound of this clapping is very easily imitated, and numbers are thus lured within gunshot by this means. Although the cocks are very pugnacious, evidence of actual fighting is rare, crowing being normally sufficient for the maintenance of territorial rights; when a fight does occur, however, it is fierce and bloody.

The food of the junglefowl consists of grain, weed-seeds, berries, various succulent leaves and buds, and a large proportion of small animals, such as crickets, centipedes and termites; the latter form the main food of the chicks. When nillu flowers and seeds in up-country jungles, junglefowl migrate to these areas in large numbers to fatten on the abundant seed. They are also very fond of the seeds of the small hill-bamboo which, like nillu, seeds only at long intervals. The hens are very industrious scratchers, particularly when they have a brood of chicks. Early in the evening, junglefowl fly up into trees to roost—usually singly, but sometimes in pairs or family parties. Unless disturbed they will use the same perch night after night for considerable periods. The perch chosen is generally high, well screened with foliage, and not much thicker than a man's thumb.

The main breeding season is in the first quarter of the year, but often a second clutch is laid in August–September, and breeding may go on throughout the year. The courtship display of the male is very similar to that of a domestic cock; it consists of running closely round the hen with his body canted towards her so as to display as much as possible of his plumage, and especially the metallic purple rump-feathers; at the same time, the wing nearest to her is drooped and its primaries scraped with the foot. The nest is often a shallow scrape in the ground, concealed by herbage, at the foot of a tree or beside a dead log; but many nests are above ground level, on top of dead stumps or on a platform of rubbish caught up in a tangle of creepers, etc. The hen sits very close, and leaves her eggs only at intervals of several days. She approaches and leaves the nest very stealthily. The eggs number two to four; they are creamy-white, some very finely peppered, others more boldly but sparingly speckled with brown. They measure about 48×35 mm. The chicks are very precocious, learning to scratch as soon as they leave the nest.

At the mother's alarm-call they instantly scatter and disappear in an amazing way under dead leaves, etc.—remaining motionless until her little metallic cluck reassures them. Their wing feathers grow rapidly, and in a week they are able to fly into trees to roost, which they do covered by the mother's wings, or even snuggled between her legs on the perch.

THE CEYLON SPURFOWL

Galloperdix bicalcarata (Forster). Species peculiar to Ceylon

Sinhalese: Haban-kukkulā. Tamil: Sinna Kāttu-kōli

Plate 23, facing p. 264 (female left, male right; ×one-seventh)

Size of a partridge, or of a half-grown village fowl. The hen resembles a small, brown village chicken; the cock, with his white-spangled black foreparts and dark chestnut hinderparts, is unmistakable.

The spurfowl, a rotund, full-plumaged little bird, is widely distributed in the southern half of the Island, both in the hills, up to 6,000 feet, and in the low country; but is commonest in the damp rainforests of the wet zone. Strictly a forest bird, it is so shy and wary that its presence in a district would often pass quite unknown were it not for its unmistakable cry; this reveals that it is not uncommon in much of the more densely forested parts of its range. The cry is a peculiar, ringing cackle, consisting of series of three-syllabled whistles, each series on a higher note than the preceding one and the last dropping suddenly to the starting note: *yŭhŭhŭ, yŭhŭhŭ, yŭhŭhŭ, yŭhŭhŭ, yŭhŭhŭ, yŭhŭheeyŭ*. This cackle is uttered by the male and is replied to by other males in the neighbourhood in similar strains, so that for some minutes at a time, and several times during the morning, the welkin rings with their music.

Distinctly a ground bird, it normally flies only when ascending trees for roosting but, if compelled to use its wings, it flies in a whirring, partridge-like manner and loses no time in dropping into the nearest cover. The normal gait is a high-stepping strut, but it runs very swiftly when alarmed. The food consists of various seeds, fallen berries, termites and other insects, and it scratches vigorously for them amongst the dead leaves, etc., of the forest floor. Like the junglefowl, its numbers increase greatly up-country in nillu-flowering years.

I believe the spurfowl pairs for life, as captive pairs show a close attachment to each other and will not tolerate others, of either sex, in their aviary—even killing their own offspring when these become three-quarters grown. The little cock is very attentive to his hen at all times, running to her with little titbits, which he proffers uttering a low mewing note suggestive of the whimpering of a very young puppy. On approaching each other, both expand the tail and whimper a little lovesong, but I have never observed any definite courtship display. The breeding season is in the north-east monsoon, and sometimes a second brood is raised in July–September. The nest is a slight scrape in the ground in the shelter of a rock, bush, etc. Two eggs form the normal clutch, but up to five have been recorded; they are cream or warm buff in colour, and exactly resemble miniature hens' eggs in appearance. They measure about 43×31 mm. The chick is clothed in rather uniform, dark brown down. Each sex quickly develops its distinctive plumage, but the white streaks and spots of the young male are relatively fewer and larger than in the adult.

THE BLUE-BREASTED QUAIL

Excalfactoria chinensis chinensis (Linnaeus). Resident

Sinhalese: Pandara-watuwā, Wil-watuwā. Tamil: Kādai

Plate 24, facing p. 265 (male left, female right; ×one-quarter)

A tiny quail, not much bigger than a sparrow, but much more rotund in figure. The dark bluish-grey and maroon coloration of the male, with white and black throat, make him unmistakable; but the female is to be distinguished from other quails mainly by her small size.

Although widely distributed in the low country, and in the hills up to about 6,000 feet, it appears to have diminished somewhat in numbers since Legge's time. It usually lives in pairs or small bevies, and frequents damp, grassy situations such as swamps, paddy-fields, the margins of weedy tanks, etc. Like other quails, it is hard to flush without a dog, but when flushed it flies rapidly in a straight line for a few yards and then drops into the herbage; it is difficult to flush a second time. According to Mrs Lushington, 'both sexes have a sweet, rather plaintive whistle, which sounds like *tee-tee-tew*, the last syllable being lower than the others'. Its food consists of small seeds, insects, etc.

The breeding season appears to be mainly in the first half of the year with a second brood in August and September. The nest is in a small cavity in the ground amongst damp herbage, lined with dry grass, roots, etc. The eggs number four to seven, and are described by Wait as 'dumpy ovals of olive brown thinly speckled with very dark brown dots'; they measure about $25 \times 19 \cdot 5$ mm.

THE BLACK-BREASTED QUAIL, or RAIN QUAIL

Coturnix coromandelica (Gmelin). Occasional (rather doubtful) straggler
to Ceylon

Sinhalese: Wil-watuwā, Pun-watuwā. Tamil: Kādai

Plate 24, facing p. 265 (female left, male right; ×one-quarter)

Size of a fortnight-old domestic chicken, but shorter in the leg and
very rotund in figure. This quail, which is common in many parts of
India, and resident though locally migratory there, is at best a rare
visitor to Ceylon; it is sometimes imported in large numbers for food
and the few records of its occurrence—all, apparently from the environs
of Colombo—are open to the question whether these birds were
humanly introduced. It lives in small bevies in grass-land, scrub, and
dry cultivation, dwelling on the ground, where it seeks its food of grain,
weed-seeds, termites, etc. Like other quails, it trusts as long as possible
for safety to its concealing coloration amongst herbage but, when an
enemy approaches too close, it springs into the air and flies with rapidly
whirring wings for a short distance before dropping into cover again.
Its call is described by Sálim Ali as a disyllabic musical whistle—*which-
which . . . which-which*, constantly repeated, chiefly in the mornings and
evenings.

In India, the breeding season is said to be during the south-west
monsoon; the nest is a shallow scrape in the ground, lined with grass,
and well concealed among herbage. The six to eight eggs are various
shades of buff, speckled with brown, and they measure about 27·8 ×
21·5 mm.

THE CEYLON JUNGLE BUSH QUAIL

Perdicula asiatica ceylonensis Whistler & Kinnear. Race peculiar to
Ceylon; closely related races are found in India

Sinhalese: Pandara-watuwā, Wil-watuwā. Tamil: Kādai

Plate 24, facing p. 265 (male left, female right; ×one-quarter)

About the size of a fortnight-old domestic chicken, but shorter in the
leg. The sexes differ as shown in the Plate. From all other Ceylon
quails this may be distinguished by its deep brick-red colouring, curious
head-markings and, in the male, the black-and-white barred breast
and underparts. From the bustard-quail it can at once be distinguished,
in the hand, by the presence of a hind toe.

This handsome quail is confined, in Ceylon, to the park-country of the Eastern Province and eastern portion of Uva. It inhabits thinly-forested grassy country and scrub, avoiding both dense forest and quite open areas; and lives in bevies of from five to ten birds which keep closely together except in the breeding season, when they pair off. Acquaintance with it is usually made by walking into a bevy, hiding in the grass or scrub, which 'explodes' almost beneath one's feet, its members flying off in all directions; after a short flight, they drop to the ground, commence calling to each other, and run together until the little family is reunited. It has a piping call, and a low chuckling cry when flushed. Legge found it remarkably tame for a game bird, feeding freely along roadsides and about carters' camping places. Like all quails it is strictly a ground bird, never perching in trees but spending most of its life under the cover of grass and herbage. The bevies roost at night in a little circle on the ground, all heads pointing outwards. The food consists of grass-seeds, grain, termites, grasshoppers, and the like.

The nidification of the Ceylon race does not appear to have been observed but, in India, the breeding season is said to be between August and April. The nest is composed of grass and small rootlets, placed in a little hollow scratched in the ground in the shelter of a small bush or tuft of grass. The five to seven eggs are various shades of cream or buff, unmarked, and they measure about $26 \times 21 \cdot 5$ mm.

THE CEYLON PAINTED PARTRIDGE

Francolinus pictus watsoni Legge. Race peculiar to Ceylon

Sinhalese: Ussa-watuwā, Pun-kukkulā. Tamil: Kauthāri

Plate 24, facing p. 265 (male; ×one-quarter)

Size of a domestic pigeon, but with shorter wings and tail, and a more rotund figure. The female is somewhat duller in coloration than the male, and has the underparts marked rather differently.

This partridge occurs in Ceylon only in the dry patana and park-country of Uva, inhabiting the foot-hills and mountains up to about 4,500 feet. It loves hills covered with māna-grass, scrub and bracken, and is a great skulker, very hard to flush without a dog; but in the early morning, and again in the evening, it emerges from cover to feed. At the same times of day the cocks, in the breeding season, perch on the tops of termite hills, boulders and the like, and utter their loud challenge, a rasping cackle which is well likened by Legge to the words *quserk-quserk-quserk*. The flight is of the usual partridge type—a rapid whirring a few feet from the ground, to which the bird drops after covering a short distance, to continue its progress by running under cover of the long grass. Legge found black ants in the crops of his specimens, but the bird doubtless feeds on other insects also, such as grasshoppers and termites, and on grass-seeds and lantana berries, etc.

The nest does not appear to have been found in Ceylon, but the Indian race breeds from the middle of June till September; I have put up â hen with two or three young chicks (just able to fly) in May. The nest is a slight hollow in the ground under a bush or grass-tussock, lined with a little grass. Indian birds are said to lay four to eight eggs in a clutch, but it is probable that Ceylon clutches are smaller. The eggs are pale cream or buff, and measure about 38 × 30 mm. The hen is a close sitter.

There is no doubt that this partridge is steadily losing ground in Ceylon, and it is now very rare in most parts of the Uva patana basin where it used to be fairly common; it is still holding its ground in the eastern—and wilder—parts of its very limited range. This decrease in much of its former territory needs no other explanation than the constant shooting to which it is subjected, combined with the custom, so rife in Ceylon, of indiscriminate firing of the patana hills whenever the weather is dry; these patana fires undoubtedly destroy multitudes of nests.

THE CEYLON GREY PARTRIDGE

Francolinus pondicerianus ceylonensis Whistler. Race peculiar to Ceylon, but scarcely distinguishable from the South Indian race

Sinhalese: Ussa-watuwā. Tamil: Kauthāri

Plate 24, facing p. 265 (× one-quarter)

About the size of a large domestic pigeon, but with shorter tail and wings. Sexes alike. The Ceylon race of this partridge is confined to the coastal strip of very dry country extending from Puttalam to the Jaffna Peninsula, together with the adjacent islands. It frequents scrub-lands, hedgerows, pastures dotted with clumps of bushes, etc., and lives in small covies which break up into pairs in the breeding season. It is a great walker and runner, seldom flying except to escape from an enemy when suddenly startled; then it rises with a loud whirr, and skims rapidly, a few feet from the ground, dropping when out of danger. Usually it continues to make good its escape by running, which it does with great speed. Danger over, the members of the covey reunite, calling to learn each other's whereabouts. It is a noisy bird, especially in the early morning and evening, when it utters a loud cackle, likened by Legge to *ka-tēē klar-ka, ka-tēē klar-ka*; a variation of this is *kēēyekok kēēyekok kēeyekokee*; another note sounds like *kito kito kito*. Pairs converse with each other in a quaint, whimpering sound, and a covey sometimes produces a noisy rattle, quite unlike the usual cackle. The Grey Partridge feeds on a variety of grass- and weed-seeds, grain, ants, termites, grasshoppers and such-like. It is said to perch readily in trees, but I have never observed this.

The breeding season is from May to August; the nest is a scrape in the ground in the midst of a small bush, grass-tussock, or spinifex clump, often away from other cover. The scrape is lined with grass, roots, etc. The four to eight eggs are pale buff, usually unmarked, and measure about $33 \cdot 2 \times 25 \cdot 6$ mm.

Plate 23

1. Indian Peafowl.   2. Ceylon Spurfowl.   3. Ceylon Junglefowl

PLATE 24

1. Blue-breasted Quail. 2. Ceylon Bustard-Quail. 3. Ceylon Jungle Bush-Quail. 4. Black-breasted Quail. 5. Ceylon Painted Partridge. 6. Ceylon Grey Partridge

WADERS AND THEIR ALLIES

ORDER CHARADRIIFORMES—PLOVER-LIKE BIRDS

THIS order comprises a number of families of terrestrial and water-birds which, though shown by osteological and anatomical structure to be related to each other, are of such diverse form and habits that it is difficult to give a concise definition applicable to all of them. The order includes such large birds as the cranes and bustards, but neither of these occur in Ceylon and, for the purposes of this work, the birds included in it are all of small or medium size (up to that of a domestic cock). While practically every characteristic mentioned below has exceptions, the following hold good for nearly all Ceylonese species in the order:

(*a*) Colouring sober—white, black, grey, brown, buff, etc.

(*b*) Food mainly of an animal nature—insects, crustaceans, molluscs and fish.

(*c*) Either waders or swimmers, or both; legs in the former generally long, and toes not, or only slightly, webbed; in the latter, legs shorter, with three front toes generally webbed more or less fully.

(*d*) Wings well developed in all, long in most, flight powerful.

(*e*) Nest on the ground; eggs camouflage-coloured.

(*f*) Young downy when hatched, and able to run soon after.

Members of the following families of *Charadriiformes* are found in Ceylon:

Turnicidae—bustard-quails.

Jaçanidae—jaçanas.

Burhinidae—stone curlews and stone plovers.

Glareolidae—coursers and pratincoles.

Dromadidae—crab plover.

Charadriidae—plovers, lapwings, and their allies.

Scolopacidae—sandpipers, snipes, and their allies.

Rostratulidae—painted snipes.

Laridae—terns and gulls.

Stercorariidae—skuas.

The main general features of these families are briefly described at the head of each.

THE BUSTARD-QUAILS OR HEMIPODES
Family TURNICIDAE

Although they are so similar to the true quails in form and general behaviour, these birds are considered, on anatomical grounds, to be more nearly related to the cranes and bustards (*Grues*, a sub-order of the *Charadriiformes*) than to the game birds (*Galliformes*) to which the true quails belong. The sole Ceylon representative of this small family may at once be distinguished from any true quail by its lack of a hind toe. In the bustard-quails, the female is larger and more handsomely coloured than the male, and usurps the masculine functions of fighting rivals (of her own sex), and courting the male, to whom she leaves the duties of incubation and rearing of the young.

THE CEYLON BUSTARD-QUAIL

Turnix suscitator leggei Stuart Baker. Race peculiar to Ceylon

Sinhalese: Bola-watuwā. Tamil: Kādai

Plate 24, facing p. 265 (male left, female right; ×one quarter)

Size of a week-old domestic chicken. In this bird, the usual order of the sexes is reversed in that the female is larger than the male, and she alone has the throat and middle of the upper breast black.

This is the only really common and well-distributed 'quail' in Ceylon. It inhabits suitable country everywhere in the Island from sea level up to about 5,000 feet, but seems to prefer the drier districts. Scrub-land, māna-grass patanas, park-country and the like, form its habitat. It lives in pairs or solitary, but never in bevies like the true quails. The usual view of it that one gets is when, in the above types of country, a small, round brownish bird springs up almost at one's feet, flies rapidly, with a whirr of wings, for twenty yards or so, and drops abruptly into the shrubbery; it is difficult to put up a second time. In the morning and evening, a cautious observer may watch it at the edge of some patch of scrub as it trips along, picking up the seeds, termites, etc., which form its food. If suspicious, but not really alarmed, it will slink off through the grass in a curious fashion—in a series of jerks, with a motionless pause after every step. Several which I kept as pets proved very wild and untamable, never voluntarily showing themselves even after a year's aviary life.

The domestic economy of this bird is very remarkable. The female is an Amazon, and lives up to her larger size and handsomer coloration by usurping the prerogatives normally belonging to the male. She is very pugnacious with her own sex, challenging rival females to fight by means of a loud, but low-pitched, purring call, *krrrrrrrr . . .*, sustained for several seconds, which sounds much farther off than it really is. She courts the males, with whom she practises polyandry. Having laid a clutch of eggs, she leaves her mate to incubate them and bring up the chicks while she sets about a fresh orgy of fighting and courting. The breeding season appears to last for most of the year. The nest is composed of dry grass, rootlets, etc.; it is placed in a hollow at the base of a small shrub or tussock of grass, and is usually well concealed. It contains two to four eggs, which vary greatly in colour and marking but are generally greenish grey, very thickly peppered with darker specks. They measure about 23 × 18 mm. The chicks resemble tiny domestic chickens, and are clothed with brown down with darker brown marblings. Their father is most solicitous for their safety and tends them very assiduously.

THE JAÇANAS

Family JACANIDAE

These are a small family of tropical marsh-birds, somewhat like waterhens but more nearly related to the plovers. Their chief feature is the very long, slender, unwebbed toes with long, nearly straight claws; these enable them to walk on floating vegetation by distributing the weight over a large area. Like certain plovers and some other birds, they have a sharp tubercle or bony spur on the bend of the wing; this is used in fighting, and becomes enlarged in the breeding season. The Pheasant-tailed Jaçana, or 'Tank Pheasant', is the only Ceylonese representative of this family. Its wings show a remarkable feature in that the first primary has its shaft prolonged beyond the vanes into a slender, lance-like process about an inch long; the next two primaries have the shafts slightly projecting beyond the vanes; and the fourth and, to a lesser degree, the fifth, have the tips very long and narrow. The function of these curious features, which are found in both sexes, is unknown.

THE PHEASANT-TAILED JAÇANA

Hydrophasianus chirurgus (Scopoli). Resident

Sinhalese: Pān-kukkulā, Ballal-sēru, (Vil-giravā *or* Gnāvvā—
Phillips). Tamil: Mīwa, Manal Purā

Plate 28, facing p. 313 (×one-fifth)

Rather larger than the domestic pigeon but, in the breeding season, with a long, slender, gracefully curved tail. Sexes alike, but the female is slightly larger than the male. In non-breeding plumage the underparts become white, the upperparts olive brown; a dark-brown line passes from the beak, through the eye and ear-coverts, down the side of the neck and across the breast, forming a gorget; the glistening yellow neck-patch becomes paler, and divided by a brown line down the back of the neck; the wings develop an olive-brown patch on the median and greater secondary coverts; and the tail becomes much shorter, and white on the outer feathers, olive-brown on the median ones.

This very beautiful and graceful bird, with its predominantly white and black plumage and distinctive habits, cannot be mistaken for any other species. It inhabits the low country wherever suitable waters exist, but does not ascend the hills. Weedy, lotus-covered lakes and large ponds supply the necessary conditions for its life, and in such places it lives in scattered flocks which spend their time walking or resting on the floating vegetation, supported by the enormously long toes and claws which distribute the bird's weight over a large area. It swims well, floating lightly like a gull, but it seldom leaves the water-weeds and lotus leaves which are its true habitat. Amongst such vegetation it is very inconspicuous, but when it flies, which it does freely, its black-edged, white wings, contrasting with the black body and long tail, make a striking sight. The style of flight is somewhat like that of a pigeon. It freely utters a loud nasal *tew, tew* . . . , and a cat-like, high-pitched *miuu*. Seeds of various water-plants, grain, green-stuff, and small aquatic animals such as insects and shrimps, comprise its diet. In the breeding season it fights, striking with a sharp tubercle on the bend of the wing; but most of the fighting is mere demonstration, little harm being done.

The breeding season is in the first half of the year. The nest is usually a small waterlogged accumulation of weeds, either floating or almost so, amongst the lotus leaves; but sometimes the eggs are laid, without even an apology for a nest, on a floating lotus leaf. Three or four eggs are laid; they are peg-top shaped, bronze-brown in colour and are arranged with the small ends pointing inwards; they measure about 37 × 27 mm.

THE STONE CURLEWS AND STONE PLOVERS
Family BURHINIDAE

These are a small family of long-legged, big-headed, plover-like birds which are believed to be related to the bustards (the latter are absent from Ceylon, though several species are found in India). They are of dull-coloured, rather harsh plumage, with long pointed wings and strong flight, and are strictly terrestrial in habits. As might be guessed from their very large eyes, they are mainly nocturnal. Their feet have but three toes which are rather thick and are only slightly webbed at the base. The sexes are alike. They frequent either open, stony, or scrub-country, or the shores of lagoons and tanks, and prefer dry climatic conditions. Their diet consists of insects, crabs, molluscs, and other small animals. Their coloration assimilates to the ground which they inhabit, and they take advantage of this, especially when young, by crouching on the soil with head and neck laid flat along the ground when an enemy approaches; in this posture, they are indistinguishable from the small hummocks, stones, etc., lying around.

The one or two eggs, which are heavily spotted and blotched in soil-like colours, are laid on the bare ground without any nest. The chicks are clothed with soil-coloured down, and are able to follow their parents soon after hatching.

THE INDIAN STONE CURLEW, or INDIAN THICK-KNEE

Burhinus oedicnemus indicus (Salvadori). Resident

Sinhalese: Gōlu-kiraluwā, Gōlu-kiralā. Tamil: Musal-kinändi

Size of the whimbrel; slightly larger than the Red-wattled Lapwing. Sexes alike. The following features make this bird easy to recognize: streaky, drab plumage, with a conspicuous band of white running through the median wing-coverts, and a parallel one at the tips of the greater coverts; white head-markings, as shown in the figure; very large, yellow eyes with pronounced eyebrow; beak yellow at the base, black at the tip; pale greenish legs, with only three toes. In flight, the black primaries show a white patch on the first two, and a large white blotch in the middle of the inner ones, producing a striking pattern. From the next species, the Great Stone Plover, it may be distinguished by its smaller size, much smaller beak, and heavily streaked plumage.

In Ceylon this bird ,which in several races has a very wide distribution in Europe, Africa and Asia, is mainly a dry-zone coastal species, seldom appearing far inland, and never in the hills. It usually frequents sandy pastures, scrub-land dotted with bushes, open palm plantations and the like, and lives in pairs or, at times, small flocks. It is mainly nocturnal, spending the day squatting on the ground in the shade of a small bush; but it is very wary, and on the approach of a human it

× one-eighth

either runs rapidly, with head low and furtive air, or crouches with its head laid flat on the ground and trusts to its concealing coloration. If this ruse should fail, it rises, runs a few paces and takes wing, flying low with curious stiff wing-strokes, to a distance. As dusk descends it becomes lively, flying about and calling to its mate in a loud, wailing but musical cry, something like the call of the curlew; another note,

probably connected with courtship, is a piping whistle on a descending scale, *whe, whe, whe, whe, whew whew whew whew*; these notes, once heard, are unmistakable, and often reveal the bird's presence in a locality. The food of the Stone Curlew consists mainly of ground-insects— beetles, grasshoppers, termites and bugs—and other small animals.

The breeding season is during the south-west monsoon. Two eggs are laid in a shallow scrape, without any nest, on the ground; sometimes under a small bush, but often with no shelter at all. The eggs are well hidden by their colour, which is buff, mottled all over with dull black spots and blotches; they measure about 49 × 34 mm.

THE GREAT STONE PLOVER

Esacus recurvirostris (Cuvier). Resident

Sinhalese: Gōlu-kiraluwā, Gōlu-kiralā. Tamil: Musal-kināndi

About the size of the curlew or of a village hen, but more slender and longer in the leg than the latter. Sexes alike. Upper plumage drab grey, under plumage white; eyes very large and yellow; long, heavy beak, which is slightly up-curved—suggesting that it has been attached upside down—pale yellow at base, black for the rest of its length; legs pale, whitish green. The primaries are black, with a white band across the first three and a large blotch on the bases of the inner—forming a distinctive pattern in flight.

This strange-looking bird inhabits the coastal districts of the entire dry zone and also ventures inland to the shores of the larger tanks; but it avoids the wet zone, and does not ascend the hills. Its favourite haunts are the sandy or muddy shores of lagoons, estuaries and tanks, and even the seashore where this is free from human disturbance, for it is a

× one-tenth

very wary bird, difficult to approach within gunshot. It lives in pairs, probably mating for life, but after the breeding season small flocks up to fourteen or so are formed. It is mainly nocturnal, feeding at night and spending the day resting and preening, usually close to the water's edge, with its mate. On the approach of a human, they fly to a safe distance from which they watch the intruder's movements, and warn each other in a clear, shrill whistle of rather plaintive tone, *chēēp* . . .

chēēp . . . *chēēpchēēpchēēp* . . ., which carries a long way. In flight, the neck is stretched forward, and this, with the stout beak, gives somewhat the impression of a flying duck; the wings are flapped through a shallow arc in a stiff, jerky manner. When alarmed or suspicious the bird has a curious way of jerking, first its head, then its tail, as if pivoting on the legs. The male of a tame pair, on seeing a tortoise walking, elevated and expanded the tail, at the same time uttering a hoarse *errrr*. These birds, which were most engaging pets, frequently rested by squatting on the hock-joints. The food of the Great Stone Plover consists of ground-frequenting insects, crabs and molluscs, worms and other small animals.

The breeding season lasts from January to August. One or two eggs are laid, usually without any pretence of a nest, on a shingle bank, stony islet, or thinly-grassed lagoon-margin, generally not far from water. They are dark greyish-buff, thickly blotched and streaked with dark brown and black. In spite of their exposed situation, they are hard to find owing to their camouflage coloration. It is not known whether both sexes incubate, but whichever partner is off duty keeps a most vigilant watch for enemies, warning its mate by the shrill whistle above-mentioned; the sitting bird leaves its eggs by a stealthy, crouching walk for some distance and then flies to join its mate, perhaps a quarter of a mile away. Danger over, the bird returns to her eggs in a similarly cautious, stealthy way—running hither and thither and pretending to feed in a nonchalant manner, as if eggs were the last things in her mind. The hatchlings are quaint little creatures, clothed in short woolly, drab down, spotted and streaked with black. During the day they squat prone on the ground with head and beak laid flat along it, and in this position they are almost impossible to distinguish among the clods, stones, etc., about them. At night they follow their parents in their hunt for food. The eggs measure about 59×43 mm.

THE COURSERS AND PRATINCOLES
Family GLAREOLIDAE

A small family of somewhat plover-like, small to medium-sized birds, with headquarters in Africa and Asia, a few species extending to Europe and Australia; they inhabit mainly open country, and prefer dry climates. Though of diverse appearance and habits their anatomy shows them to be nearly related. None of them perch, nor do they ordinarily swim. All have strong flight but, while the pratincoles spend much time on the wing and take their food mainly in flight, the coursers are terrestrial in habits, feeding on the ground. The eggs are laid on the ground, in slight scrapes; they are coloured like their normal surroundings. The chicks are downy and can run soon after hatching.

Coursers have the legs long and slender, with only three rather thick toes, the middle one much longer than the other two. The bill is slender, slightly curved. They frequent open, dry country, on which they run speedily. Their diet consists of various ground-insects and other small animals.

Pratincoles have comparatively short legs, and hind toe well-developed; their wings are very long and pointed, and the tail is more or less forked. In general appearance, and style of flight, they resemble swallows—hence the name, sometimes given to them, of 'Swallow-Plovers'. They feed mainly on flying insects, which are captured in swift and sustained flight; but they rest on the ground.

THE INDIAN COURSER

Cursorius coromandelicus coromandelicus (Gmelin). Resident

Sinhalese: Weli-kiralā. Tamil: Āl-kātti

Plate 25, facing p. 296 ($\times$ one-sixth)

About the size of the Common Mynah, but with short tail and long legs. Sexes alike.

This interesting plover-like bird has a very small range in Ceylon, though it is widespread in India. It is confined to the narrow, coastal strip of very dry, sparsely-populated country extending from about Marichchukkaddi to the Jaffna Peninsula, and even in this restricted range it is only found on open, arid plains within a few miles of the sea. In the Jaffna Peninsula it is probably only an occasional visitor, as during two years' residence there I never saw it. Sun-baked fields and stony pastures, with scanty covering of grass and herbs, suit it best; in such places it may be seen in pairs or, out of the breeding season, in small, scattered flocks. It runs about in a curiously aimless fashion, in little spurts, every now and then bending stiffly forward to pick up some insect from the ground. Although it can run very fast, it seldom does so for any distance without stopping and standing erect for a few moments to survey the scene. It flies readily, sometimes mounting high into the air; the flight is performed with strong but rather slow flaps of the wings, and the bird is capable of considerable speed on occasion. The courser feeds on small ground insects—beetles, grasshoppers, termites and the like. It is silent as a rule, but is said to utter a peculiar note on taking to wing.

The breeding season is in May and June. Two eggs are laid on the bare ground, quite in the open; they are broadly oval in shape, pale yellowish-buff, mottled all over with purplish-grey and black specks and blotches. The female alone broods but the male remains in attendance and assists in tending the chicks. On the approach of an intruder, the birds silently abandon both eggs and chicks to the safety afforded by their concealing coloration until the danger is past; in this, the courser contrasts strongly with the Red- and Yellow-wattled Lapwings. The eggs measure about 30·5 × 24·5 mm.

THE INDIAN LARGE PRATINCOLE

Glareola pratincola maldivarum Forster. Resident

No Sinhalese or Tamil names recorded

Plate 25, facing p. 296 (× one-sixth)

About the size of the Common Mynah, but with long wings which project well beyond the tail when folded. Sexes alike. The usual appearance and posture of this bird, as seen on the ground, are shown on the Plate; on the wing, its style of flight is very swallow-like while hawking for insects but at other times it is more suggestive of a sandpiper or a tern.

Its distribution in Ceylon is very local; it occurs in some numbers in the Hambantota district, and small colonies sometimes frequent the margins of the larger dry-zone tanks—Minneriya, Kantalai, and perhaps others—but its visits to these seem to be irregular. Low-lying pastures in the neighbourhood of water form its favourite habitat. It associates in scattered flocks and is crepuscular in habits, spending the day resting on the ground or running here and there in a plover-like manner; but in early morning and evening the flock take to the air, dashing about, wheeling and veering as they chase flying insects—beetles, moths, termites, etc.—which form their food. In turning, the forked tail is momentarily spread and the chestnut under wing-coverts show up. One note of this pratincole is a grating *krrrè krrrè*, but it probably has others, and it is said to be noisy when its breeding colonies are invaded.

The breeding season is from March to July. Two eggs are laid on the ground, without any nest but often in the middle of a dry, disintegrated cow-pat. The eggs are greyish-yellow, mottled and blotched with shades of dark brown and grey; they measure about 31×24 mm.

THE INDIAN LITTLE PRATINCOLE

Glareola lactea Temminck. Resident

No Sinhalese or Tamil names recorded

Plate 25, facing p. 296 ($\times$ one-sixth)

About the size of the Little Ringed Plover, or the Kentish Plover. Sexes alike.

This small, drab-grey pratincole is found in scattered colonies about sandy beaches along the eastern seaboard, and around some of the larger dry-zone tanks. It is very gregarious, associating in large flocks. On the wing, the black axillaries and under wing-coverts, contrasting with the white bases of the primaries and secondaries, are distinctive aids to identification; and the black-tipped, white tail, which is slightly forked, is also helpful. In general, its habits resemble those of its larger relative, the Large Pratincole, but it is more partial to bare sandy ground, is more gregarious, and hawks even later in the evening than the latter species. Its flight is swift, graceful and swallow-like, but on the ground it stands higher on the legs than any swallow, and has a plover-like way of running in little spurts with halts between. It feeds on the wing, swooping and careering after flying insects such as beetles, plant-bugs, termites, etc.

The breeding season is from about March to June. The two to four eggs are laid in a shallow scrape in sand or gravel with little or no shade from the sun. They are pale sandy brown, lightly speckled with flecks of grey and light brown which make them hard to distinguish from their surroundings; they measure about 26×21 mm.

THE CRAB PLOVER
Family DROMADIDAE

The family *Dromadidae* contains only a single genus and species, the crab plover. Its nearest relations appear to be the coursers and pratincoles (family *Glareolidae*), and a sub-antarctic family of shore-birds, the sheath-bills (family *Chionididae*); but in many respects the crab plover is unique. It is a medium-sized shore-bird of black-and-white plumage, with a long, heavy black bill, shaped somewhat like that of a tern; the legs are long, with the three front toes webbed together and the hind toe fairly well-developed; the wings are long and pointed; the tail short and square. In habits, the crab plover resembles the oyster-catcher, frequenting sea-beaches and reefs and feeding on crabs and other marine organisms, which it captures in shallow water or between tide-marks. It is gregarious. In its nesting-habits, it resembles the petrels—laying a single white egg in a chamber at the end of a burrow which it digs in a sandbank.

The crab plover is confined to the shores of the Indian Ocean.

THE CRAB PLOVER

Dromas ardeola Paykull. Status doubtful; probably resident

No Sinhalese or Tamil names recorded

About the size of the whimbrel, but with longer legs. Sexes alike; young birds have the mantle pale grey, and the back of the crown streaked with dark grey; otherwise they resemble adults. These are white and black, with black beak, dark brown irides, and lavender blue legs and feet; the feet are webbed, but not fully so, and the hind toe is well developed.

This large-headed shore-bird, with its heavy black beak, pied plumage, and long, blue legs, cannot be mistaken for any other on the Ceylon list. It is a rare bird, evidently much scarcer now than it was in Legge's day, and it is confined to the coasts of the northern part of the Island, from Puttalam, through Mannar and Jaffna Peninsula, to Trincomalee. It frequents secluded sea-beaches, sandbanks, and coral reefs, and is particularly partial to the shores of lagoon estuaries and the like. Outside Ceylon, it is found sparingly and locally on most of the shores of the

× one-quarter

Indian Ocean. It lives solitary, in pairs, or small flocks, and, when not feeding, spends its time resting, often in a close flock, on some coastal rock, reef or sand-spit. It walks, runs, and also swims well, and flies with somewhat tern-like action, the long legs extended behind the short tail. A flock commonly flies in close formation and, according to Legge, its members utter a loud, not unmusical note, in consonance. As its name implies, the main food consists of crabs, which it captures while wading between tide-marks on the seashore or in the shallow water of salt lagoons; it beats them to death and swallows small ones whole, larger ones piecemeal after dismembering them. No doubt it partakes also of other small marine forms of life, such as sand-worms and molluscs.

The breeding season is about May–June. The nesting-habits of this strange bird are very abnormal for a shore-bird; on lonely beaches, it selects a sandbank on the shoreward side of the strand and digs a tunnel into it—or perhaps utilizes one already dug by a crab—and at the end hollows out a small chamber in which it lays a single egg, usually without any nest; the tunnel, which is from two to four feet long, curves, so that the egg-chamber is in darkness. The egg is white, and measures about 65×45 mm. The chicks are clothed with down, and are able to run at an early age, but they appear to remain in the nest-burrow until they are well advanced in growth.

THE PLOVERS, LAPWINGS, AND THEIR ALLIES
Family CHARADRIIDAE

This family comprises small to medium-sized wading-birds found almost throughout the globe. While the three sub-families (described below) are diverse in some respects, the following features are common to all: (*a*) they are all ground-birds, never perching on trees; (*b*) they feed on insects, crustaceans, molluscs and other small animals—not on vegetable substances; (*c*) they all nest on the ground, laying eggs of spotted and mottled coloration adapted to concealment among their surroundings; (*d*) their young are downy, and can walk and run soon after hatching; (*e*) their wings are long, usually pointed, and with the inner secondaries elongated; the tail is short and even, or rounded, at the tip; (*f*) the great majority lack a hind toe, but some forms possess a small one; the legs are fairly long, or very long in some, and are extended under or behind the tail in flight; (*g*) the gait is a walk or run; most forms can swim, on occasion, but few do so normally; (*h*) all have strong flight, and the great majority (of Ceylon species at least) are migratory, breeding in northern lands and spending the winter in warmer countries. Most species are more or less gregarious.

This large family is divided into three sub-families, each of which is represented in Ceylon though only one has many representatives in the Island.

Haematopodinae—the oyster-catchers. Rather large and stoutly-built shore-birds of pied black and white plumage, with the bill long, straight, and compressed laterally towards the tip, which is not pointed; the legs are comparatively short and stout, and the three toes are broad and somewhat flattened. Oyster-catchers feed mainly on molluscs, which they find on sea-rocks, etc. One oyster-catcher is a rare winter visitor to Ceylon.

Charadriinae—the plovers and lapwings. Shore-birds with the head rather large and round, the bill somewhat short, straight, pointed, and slightly constricted in the middle. The legs are fairly long; most forms have only three toes which are, at most, webbed only at the base; but a few have a small hind toe as well. Plovers have sharply-pointed wings and swift flight; Lapwings have broader and more rounded wings and the flight is slower. The birds of this sub-family make up a large proportion of the small waders and shore-birds that abound on our lagoon shores and mud-flats.

Recurvirostrinae—the avocets and stilts. Long-legged wading birds, generally of black-and-white coloration. The bill is long, slender, and tapering; in the avocets, it is strongly curved upwards in the forward half; in the stilts, it is nearly straight. Avocets have a minute hind toe, and the three front toes rather fully webbed; stilts have no hind toe, and the webbing of the front toes is very slight; their legs are enormously long. One avocet is a rare visitor to Ceylon; the stilt is a resident subspecies.

THE OYSTER-CATCHER

Haematopus ostralegus Linnaeus. Rare winter visitor

No Sinhalese or Tamil names

Nearly the size of the whimbrel, but shorter in the leg. Sexes alike. In winter plumage, which most birds wear during their stay in Ceylon, there is a white band across the throat, but otherwise the coloration is similar to the summer plumage; a few birds don the latter before leaving the Island, in February or March. This handsome shore-bird, with its deep-black and snowy-white plumage, long, straight, orange-red beak, and pink legs, cannot be mistaken for any other bird.

In several racial forms it is found almost world-wide, but it visits Ceylon only in small numbers during the winter; the particular race that occurs in the Island is not certainly known but is probably *H. o. osculans*, which breeds in northern Asia. Normally its range in Ceylon is confined to the coasts of the northern half of the Island where, in favourable years, it may be seen in twos or threes frequenting coastal reefs and sand-spits, usually in or near the mouths of rivers or lagoons. It is an exceedingly wary bird, very difficult to approach. On the wing it presents a beautiful sight, especially in a flock, as its wings are shapely and have a broad, white wing-bar through the middle of the primaries and secondaries. In its summer haunts it is highly gregarious except when paired off for breeding. Regarding its feeding-habits, it will at times eat young oysters, but feeds mainly on smaller molluscs such as mussels and limpets; the former are opened by a smart blow with the

Left, winter plumage; right, summer plumage; × one-fifth

point of the beak between the valves, levered open, and the flesh devoured; limpets are dislodged from their emplacements on sea-rocks by inserting the wedge-like tip of the beak under the shell and turning the mollusc over. Besides shellfish, it eats marine worms and crustaceans. In its winter quarters—e.g. in Ceylon—it appears to be mostly silent, but on its breeding-ranges it frequently utters a loud, clear, piping call *klee-eep* as well as other notes. Normally a bird of the seashore, and particularly of rocky coasts, it will sometimes during the summer months move inland to breed on the shingly shores of moorland streams; more commonly, however, it breeds near the coast. The nest consists merely of a slight cavity scraped by the birds in a shingle-bank or on a sand-dune. The two to four eggs are stone-colour, spotted and blotched with brown and black, and they measure about 57 × 40 mm.

THE RED-WATTLED LAPWING, or 'DID-HE-DO-IT'

Lobivanellus indicus indicus (Boddaert). Resident

Sinhalese: Kiraluwā, Kiralā. Tamil: Āl-kātti

Plate 25, facing p. 296 (× one-sixth)

About the size of a domestic pigeon, but with long legs. Sexes alike. The striking black, white, and drab coloration, with red wattles and beak and long, slender, yellow legs, together with its obtrusive habits, prevent confusion with any other bird.

It is found throughout the low country but is commonest in the dry zone, where it is generally distributed; in the hills it occurs only as a casual straggler. Its favourite haunts are the grassy borders of tanks, fallow paddy-fields and, in general, any flat ground near water. In such places it lives in pairs or small family parties, spending its time walking hither and thither in little spurts, every now and then stooping to pick up some small insect or other titbit; all the time keeping a watch for any approaching enemy. Though not shy, it is a most vigilant bird, and clever indeed must be the predator—human or otherwise—that can circumvent it. At ordinary times it contents itself with keeping at a safe distance but, when a pair has eggs or young, they take to wing, with a preliminary yell, and fly around the disturber of their peace with an incessant, and most irritating, scream of *did-he-do-it?* . . . *pity-to-do-it!* until the marauder has withdrawn. The flight is usually slow and of flapping character but the bird can develop a surprising turn of speed on occasion. The food of the Red-wattled Lapwing consists of ground-dwelling insects such as beetles, grasshoppers, termites, etc. It is never found far from water but, although it wades quite freely, it takes most of its food on dry ground.

The breeding season is during the south-west monsoon, June being the favourite month. Four eggs are laid in a shallow scrape on the ground, usually among stones or debris but quite unsheltered by vegetation; they are arranged in the form of a cross, the small ends pointing inwards. They are greyish ochreous, mottled and blotched all over with sepia and black, and measure about 43 × 31 mm. The young chicks are quaint little creatures, with very large head and long legs, and just enough body to hold head and legs together. They are clothed in black, white, and mottled-drab down, arranged much as in the adult pattern. At their parents' warning, they crouch, with head laid along the ground, and are almost impossible to distinguish from their surroundings.

THE YELLOW-WATTLED LAPWING

Lobipluvia malabarica (Boddaert). Resident

Sinhalese: Kiraluwā, Kiralā. Tamil: Āl-kātti

Plate 25, facing p. 296 (×one-sixth)

About the size of a small domestic pigeon, but with long legs; smaller than the Red-wattled Lapwing. Sexes alike. The yellow lappets hanging on each side of the gape distinguish this bird from all other Ceylonese species, but care must be taken not to confuse it with the Indian Courser, which somewhat resembles it in colour and shape and inhabits similar types of country.

This bird is commonest in the coastal belt between Puttalam and the Jaffna Peninsula, and in the Hambantota district; it also occurs sparingly in the Eastern Province. Unlike the Red-wattled Lapwing, it likes very dry conditions, being found in arid waste-land, fallow fields, stony pastures and the like. It lives in small flocks except when breeding, when pairs separate—although several will nest within a single field. When standing motionless the birds are hard to detect as they merge into their surroundings in a wonderful way, often escaping notice until they take to wing. Like other plovers, they have a habit of running a few paces, stopping for a second or two, then running a few paces in another direction; every now and then stooping to pick up an ant, termite, grasshopper or beetle. The flight is easy and generally rather low; the wings show a conspicuous white wing-bar, and the feet project beyond the tail. Although this bird has not so loud a scream as the Red-wattled Lapwing, it is equally demonstrative when its eggs or young are threatened, and a pair will fly around, agitatedly crying *tee-ēe* and a sharp *kit, kit, kit* until the intruder has taken himself off.

The breeding season is from May to July. The four pear-shaped eggs are arranged in cross-formation in a shallow scrape in open ground, usually among clods, stones, etc.; often the scrape and an inch or two around it are decorated with small stones or lumps of soil. The eggs are greyish-buff, mottled with sepia and grey; in their normal surroundings they are hard to detect. They measure about 37 × 27 mm.

THE SOCIABLE PLOVER

Chettusia gregaria (Pallas). Rare winter visitor

No Sinhalese or Tamil names

About the size of the Red-wattled Lapwing. Sexes alike. In winter plumage, which this bird wears during its stay in Ceylon, its general colour is light, drab brown. The following parts are white: a broad supercilium extending from the forehead, over the eye, to the back of the head; throat; underparts from the breast downwards, including the flanks; secondaries and their greater coverts; underwing; upper and under tail-coverts and most of the tail. Black parts are: a conspicuous band from the lores, through the eye, to the back of the ear-coverts; the primaries; a broad subterminal band on the tail, disappearing on the outer feathers. Irides dark brown; bill and legs black. In summer, the crown becomes black, sides of the head buff, back and breast purer grey, shading into chestnut and black on the lower parts. In general shape this bird resembles the Red-wattled Lapwing, but it lacks wattles. In flight, the black primaries, white secondaries, and white and black tail are conspicuous identification marks.

This plover breeds in eastern Europe and central Asia, and winters from north Africa to India, where it occurs mainly in the northern parts; but a few straggle down through the Peninsula, and some reach Ceylon. It seems to be a fairly regular visitor in small numbers to the Western Province where I have seen it, in October and November of several years, on the Colombo racecourse. Flocks of eight and nine associated with Asiatic Golden Plovers on the wide expanse of grass, and spent their time in feeding on the grasshoppers and other insects which abounded there. When put up, they flew low, in a compact flock, and alighted simultaneously. They uttered no note, but a shrill whistle is recorded for the species.

In its breeding habits, this plover appears to differ but little from its relations, the lapwings.

THE GREY PLOVER

Squatarola squatarola (Linnaeus). Regular winter visitor

Sinhalese: Oléyiyā. Tamil: Kōttān

About the size of the Red-wattled Lapwing, but with shorter neck and legs. Sexes alike. In winter plumage, which it wears during most of its stay in Ceylon, it is mottled, brownish-grey, with face and underparts white; bill black, ochreous at base of lower mandible; irides dark brown; legs grey; the wing quills are black, with a white bar, conspicuous in flight, running through their bases; the underwing is white, but the *axillaries are black*, forming a definite black patch at the base of the underwing; this patch is an excellent identification mark; the upper tail-coverts and tail are white, barred, especially on the tail, with blackish. In summer plumage, in which some birds arrive in August and which some begin to assume before they leave in April, the back and wing-coverts are more definitely spangled dark grey and white, and the entire underparts, from the beak to the abdomen (which remains white), are deep black, separated by a white band from the

upper part of the head and neck. While, in general, this plover resembles the Golden Plover, it is a larger and thicker-set bird, generally solitary or in twos or threes. It may always be distinguished by its black axillaries and, in hand, by the possession of a minute hind toe—which most plovers completely lack.

The Grey Plover breeds in the far northern regions of Europe, Asia, and America, and spreads southwards in winter to almost the whole world. It visits Ceylon regularly but in rather small numbers, and takes

Winter plumage; × one-seventh

up its winter quarters along the coasts of the dry zone, being commonest in the north, but also occurring in the Hambantota district. Unlike the Golden Plover, it seldom goes any distance from salt or brackish water, and is nearly always seen within a yard or two of it, if not actually wading. It loves the shores of lagoons, muddy estuaries, creeks, and tidal flats, and in such places it finds its food, which consists of small animals such as marine worms, molluscs and crustaceans. Rather a sluggish bird, it is usually seen resting on a mud-bank, with head drawn in and one leg drawn up to the body; or else running a few steps, halting, picking up some small creature, running a few more steps in another direction—and so on. It is very wary, taking wing as soon as it sees a human approaching, and uttering its alarm-note, a loud, clear whistle, *klee*. Though frequently solitary, it sometimes associates in scattered flocks of up to twenty birds. The flight is swift and graceful, with the long, pointed wings well bent at the 'wrist'.

The Grey Plover nests on open tundras within the Arctic Circle. It lays its four mottled eggs in a slight scrape among peat-moss, etc., often on a bank or small cliff.

THE ASIATIC GOLDEN PLOVER

Pluvialis dominica fulva (Gmelin). Winter visitor

Sinhalese: Oléyiyā, Rana-watuwā. Tamil: Kōttān

About the size of the Pintail Snipe, but with much shorter beak and longer legs. Sexes alike. In winter plumage, this is a brown and buff bird, spangled with bright yellow on back and scapulars, with a good deal of buff-white about the face, and white underparts; there is a dark

spot on the ear-coverts; the quills are dark brown above; underwing and axillaries pale smoky brown; bill purplish brown; eye large, and dark brown; legs deep blue-grey, darker on the feet. In summer plumage, which many birds assume just before they leave the Island in April, the back and wing-coverts are spangled black and bright yellow, and the face, throat, and breast become deep black, separated by a white band from the upperparts. So great is the difference between the summer and winter plumages— owing mainly to the development of the black face, breast, etc.—that it is

Winter plumage; × one-fifth

difficult to recognize birds in the two plumages as the same species.

The Asiatic Golden Plover breeds in northern Siberia and Alaska, and migrates in winter to the countries south of these regions, including Ceylon which it visits in large numbers. It usually arrives in September and October, and spreads throughout the low country; in the hills, up to 4,000 feet, it occurs occasionally, but probably only on passage. Its favourite haunts are open pastures near water, but it also frequents mud-flats, the shores of coastal lagoons, the grassy margins of tanks, dry paddy-fields, and the like. It associates in flocks, of varying size but usually large, which feed in scattered company; if disturbed, all unite into a compact flock as they fly away. When feeding, it has the typical plover habit of running in short spurts, with halts in between while it stands erect, and every now and then stoops to pick up some insect. It feeds on grasshoppers, ground-beetles and other insects, and also marine worms and crustaceans. The flight is very swift and graceful, performed with sharp strokes of the wings, which are pointed, and usually well angled at the 'wrist' bend; a flock will twist and turn in unison, in a very pretty manner. It often flies high. The flight-note, frequently uttered by each member of a flock, is a musical piping, likened by Legge to *til-wee*.

In its northern breeding-grounds, this plover nests on the ground, making a shallow scrape, in which four eggs are laid, in tundra herbage.

THE LARGE SAND PLOVER

Charadrius leschenaultii leschenaultii Lesson. Winter visitor; a few, in non-breeding plumage, loiter throughout the summer

Sinhalese: Oléyiyā. Tamil: Kōttān

Between the Asiatic Golden Plover and the Lesser Sand Plover in size. Sexes alike. In winter plumage, this plover is almost indistinguishable in coloration from the much commoner Lesser Sand Plover in a similar phase of plumage; however, it may be recognized by its larger size and longer beak (about one against three-quarters of an inch); unless, however, both species are in view at the same time and in favourable conditions for comparison, it is often very difficult to distinguish from its smaller relative. In summer plumage, which a few birds assume before leaving the Island in April, it develops a definite.black band from the side of the beak, through the lore and eye to the ear-coverts, and another, incomplete one, across the forehead; the crown, sides of neck, and a broad band across the chest become pale rufous. Bill black; irides dark brown; legs slaty-bluish, paling to olive-grey. In flight, it shows a white wing-bar, comprising the tips of the greater coverts and bases of the inner primaries; the underwing is white; the rump, in a band down the middle, is greyish-brown, and the same colour extends to the upper tail-coverts and tail—both more or less edged with white.

The Large Sand Plover breeds in far-eastern Asia and Japan, and winters all around the coasts of the Indian Ocean. It visits Ceylon regularly but in comparatively small numbers, frequenting the coasts of the dry zone from about Puttalam in the west, around by the Jaffna Peninsula to the Hambantota district in the south-east. It inhabits the seashore, coastal lagoons, mud-flats, and the shores of estuaries; but does not go inland to any extent. In general behaviour it is similar to the Lesser Sand Plover, but is often solitary or in small parties of three or four, never in large flocks, though it mingles in those of the smaller bird to some extent. It is shyer than the Lesser Sand Plover, and less active. The flight is swift, and performed with rapid strokes of the pointed wings, which are well angled. The food consists of small ground-insects, crustaceans and worms.

THE LESSER SAND PLOVER

Charadrius mongolus atrifrons Wagler. Abundant winter visitor; many, in
non-breeding plumage, loiter throughout the summer

Sinhalese: Oléyiyā. Tamil: Kōttān

About the size of the Common Sandpiper, but with shorter beak,
plumper form, and big, round head. Sexes alike. In winter plumage,
which most wear throughout their sojourn in Ceylon, drab greyish-

Left, winter plumage; right, summer
plumage; × one-sixth

brown, with white face, underparts
and wing-bar; a dark brown mark
on lore, below eye, and on ear-
coverts. Beak black; irides dark
brown; legs dark grey, or greenish-
grey. In summer plumage, which
some partly or wholly assume before
leaving Ceylon in April and May,
the forehead, lores, line under the
eye and ear-coverts are black, the
forehead more or less mixed with
white in the middle; top and sides of head, and broad band across breast
light chestnut.

This plover arrives in Ceylon in large numbers in September and
October from its breeding-grounds in central Asia. It spreads throughout the coastal districts of the dry zone and, more sparingly and locally,
of the wet zone as well, but does not penetrate far inland. It frequents,
with about equal favour, the seashore, mud-flats, salt marshes, and
open pastures. Flocks numbering up to hundreds feed in scattered
formation but mass into compact flights when disturbed. As with many
other small waders, a large flock on the wing presents a beautiful
spectacle as they swerve and veer simultaneously, now all showing the
white undersides of bodies and wings, then turning the dark uppersides.
The flight is swift, performed with rapid and regular strokes of the
sharply pointed and well angled wings. As they fly, a flock keeps up a
continuous musical piping. The food consists of various ground-insects,
such as grasshoppers and beetles, and crustaceans. I have seen several
capture astonishingly large crabs which were vigorously shaken to
dislodge their limbs; these, and the dismembered torso, were swallowed
seriatim with no little difficulty, but the birds were obliged to abandon
some of the more unwieldy morsels such as large claws.

This plover breeds during the south-west monsoon in parts of central
Asia north of the Himalayas. Its eggs are laid in a scrape on the ground
in usual plover manner.

THE LITTLE RINGED PLOVER

Charadrius dubius curonicus Gmelin. European race—winter visitor
Charadrius dubius jerdoni (Legge). Ceylon and Indian race—resident

Sinhalese: Punchi-oléyiyā. Tamil: Sinna-kōttān

Size of the Ceylon Kentish Plover or the Little Stint, or a little larger
according to race. Sexes alike. In winter plumage, the black band
across the fore-crown disappears; the black marks on face and black

collar become duller, and the forehead
becomes pale buff; in this phase of
plumage, the two races are indistinguishable except by size, which is
unreliable as a means of identification
in the field. In summer (breeding)
plumage, the small resident race
jerdoni has a larger white patch on the
forehead than *curonicus*, and its eye-
ring becomes very swollen, yellow,

Left, young; right, adult *jerdoni*;
× one-fifth

and conspicuous. In both races, the beak is black, with the basal
half, or less, of the lower mandible yellow-ochre; irides dark brown;
legs dull ochreous in winter, greenish-yellow or fleshy-pink in summer.
The crown, back, wings and centre portion of tail are olive brown, sides
of the tail and all the underparts white; the first primary has the shaft
white, all the others brown; there is no white wing-bar (compare with
next species).

The migrant race arrives in Ceylon in September and October, begins
to assume breeding plumage by the end of January, and leaves the
Island in April. Both races mingle freely during the north-east monsoon, when they are found in large or small flocks in the coastal districts
of the dry zone and occasionally south as far as Colombo in the wet
zone. This pretty little plover frequents open pastures, mud-flats, semi-
dry paddy-fields and the like, but it is not so fond of sandy beaches as
either the Kentish Plover or the Sand Plovers; grassy plains, particularly somewhat marshy ones, appear to suit it best. While feeding, a
flock scatter widely but, when put up on the wing, they mass together
and fly in a swift and dashing manner, turning and canting in unison,
usually only a few yards above the ground. Each bird frequently utters
its flight-note, a plaintive little whistle, *hwee*—producing a pleasant
twittering effect when many utter it. It has the quaint plover-habit,
when feeding, of running a few paces, bobbing down to pick up some
small insect, running a few more paces in another direction, etc. When
feeding in wet mud it will rapidly vibrate, first one foot then the other,
on the mud—presumably to drive small prey to the surface; the taps

are given at about five to a second. Its food consists of a variety of small animals, taken both on dry ground and in shallow water.

The resident race of the Little Ringed Plover breeds from May to July on the gravelly shores and islets of some of the large tanks, and among coastal sand-dunes; the three eggs are laid in a small hollow scraped in a gravel bank or among scanty grass or low herbage. The birds are very solicitous for their young, flying around an intruder with anxious pipings, and attempting to decoy him away from the neighbourhood by fluttering about on the ground as if disabled—but taking care, when he follows, always to flutter a few yards in a direction away from the young. These, meanwhile, will be crouching amongst debris where their mottled brownish-grey down makes them indistinguishable. As soon as the enemy has been lured to a sufficient distance, the 'wounded' bird takes to its wings and flies off—mysteriously cured. The eggs are stone-coloured, blotched and spotted with dull black, and they look so much like the pebbles or rubbish among which they lie that they are very difficult to detect; they measure about $29 \times 21 \cdot 5$ mm.

The RINGED PLOVER *Charadrius hiaticula* (*tundrae* Lowe). The inclusion of this species in the Ceylon list rests upon a field observation by Rev. S. K. Bunker and myself, on 4 January 1944 on a mud-flat near Punnalai, Jaffna. We saw a Ringed Plover associating with Lesser Sand Plovers and Little Ringed Plovers—both of which approached it within two or three feet, giving excellent opportunities for comparison—and watched it for about eight minutes with binoculars at twenty to twenty-five yards range under favourable lighting conditions; this observation left us in no doubt of its identity.

It is about the size of the Lesser Sand Plover—distinctly larger than the Little Ringed Plover. Sexes alike. In general appearance and coloration it closely resembles the Little Ringed Plover, from which it may be distinguished by the following features: (*a*) larger size; (*b*) well-marked *white wing-bar* comprising the bases of the secondaries and inner primaries; the shafts of all primaries are partly white; (*c*) bill, in adult, orange in basal half of both mandibles (our bird was probably sub-adult as its beak appeared black throughout); (*d*) legs bright orange.

The Ringed Plover is more of a coastal strand-loving bird than its small relative, but otherwise the habits of the two are very similar. It breeds on the beaches and tundras of Europe and Asia, laying its eggs in scrapes on shingle-beds and the like.

The CASPIAN PLOVER *Eupoda asiatica* (Pallas). A female specimen of this was collected by W. W. A. Phillips on 25 February 1951, at Bundala Lagoon, Southern Province. It was moulting into breeding plumage and was a solitary bird frequenting short grass on the lagoon shore. Its skin is now in the British Museum (Natural History), where I have examined it.

This bird is of the size and general appearance of the Large Sand Plover, and appears to have much the same habits and behaviour. In winter plumage it would be very hard to distinguish from that species in the field; but its beak is altogether smaller—about 19–23 mm. long (forehead feathers to tip) by about 5 mm. deep at base, as against corresponding measurements in the Large Sand Plover of 26 mm. long by 8–9 mm. deep. In flight, its wings would show only a small patch of white at the base of the inner primaries instead of the long white wing-bar of the Large Sand Plover. In breeding plumage, the Caspian Plover has no black or rufous on the head, but across the chest it wears a band, about 1½ inches wide, of light chestnut which shades into a smoky-brown band, concave behind, on the lower breast. Irides dark brown; beak black; legs dark greenish-brown.

The Caspian Plover breeds in south-east Russia and parts of central Asia and winters mainly in Africa and Arabia. According to Stuart Baker (*Fauna of British India, Birds*, 2nd ed.) a single specimen was obtained in the former Bombay Presidency near Ratnagiri many years ago; but it is evidently only a rare straggler to India as well as to Ceylon.

THE CEYLON KENTISH PLOVER

Leucopolius alexandrinus seebohmi (Hartert & Jackson). Race peculiar to Ceylon

Sinhalese: Punchi-oléyiyā. Tamil: Sinna-kōttān

About the size of the Little Stint, or the Indian Pipit. Sexes nearly alike, but the head markings of the female are paler and browner than those of the male, especially in breeding plumage. A dumpy, big-headed little plover, drab-grey, snowy-white, and with black markings on head and sides of breast as shown in the figure; in flight, a narrow white wing-bar is seen, and the middle line of rump and tail show dark blackish-brown against the white sides. Bill black; irides dark brown; legs very dark grey.

This plover is common on the coasts of the dry zone, from about Negombo on the west, northward to the Jaffna Peninsula, and thence down the east coast to the Hambantota district; it is also common on the shores and islets of the larger tanks in the interior of the northern half of the Island. It frequents sandy and muddy beaches, salt-flats near the sea, margins of lagoons and tanks, etc. In such places it lives in pairs or scattered flocks, often associating with other small waders, and is not at all shy, allowing a reasonably near approach at most times. It is very

Left, female; right, male; × two fifths

active, running with legs moving so fast that they appear to twinkle and covering great distances in this manner. The head is generally carried low, but every now and then the bird halts and raises it in a characteristic manner. When feeding, it runs in little spurts, bobs down stiffly to pick up an insect, then off again in another direction. The food is small insects, sand-hoppers, and the like. The flight is swift and graceful, generally accompanied by a call-note, *twit, twirit,* and an occasional higher *tweet.* When courting, the male expresses his feelings to his lady-love by running around her with head held low, throat and crop inflated, and singing a quaint little song—*crwair, crwair-a-wair* (said quickly).

The breeding season lasts from about March till August, but June and July appear to be the favourite months. The two or three eggs are laid in a little depression made by the birds, usually among thin, short grass or other herbage, on dry mud or sand above high-water mark near a lagoon or tank. They are placed sloping steeply with big ends upward, and the hollow is then partly filled in with shell-fragments, crumbs of dry mud, etc., so that only the tops of the eggs are exposed. As they are coloured and mottled exactly like their surroundings they are almost invisible. On the approach of an enemy, the bird leaves her eggs stealthily and runs some distance in a crouching manner before she takes to wing; then she flies around the intruder, anxiously *twit-twirit*-ing; often her mate joins her in this. If the eggs are well advanced in incubation, or the young have hatched, the mother runs before the enemy at a short distance, with wings and tail drooping in a peculiar manner, trying to decoy him away from her offspring. Meanwhile, the chicks crouch and trust to their concealing coloration to escape notice; if this fails, they run, almost from birth, with amazing speed, turning and dodging so that it is difficult to catch them. The eggs are greenish-grey, without gloss, and marked all over with blotches and spots of dull black; they tend to get bleached at the exposed end, and it is doubtful if the mother turns them in the usual way; probably their up-ended position obviates the necessity for this operation. They measure about 30×22 mm.

It is probable that a migratory race of the Kentish Plover *Leucopolius alexandrinus alexandrinus* (Linnaeus), which has a very wide range in Europe, Africa and Asia, and winters, amongst other countries, in India, visits Ceylon occasionally during the north-east monsoon; it is said to do so by Wait. It differs from our bird merely in being a trifle larger, and in the males showing a distinct rufous tinge on the crown in breeding plumage. In general appearance and habits it is indistinguishable from the Ceylon race.

THE AVOCET

Recurvirostra avosetta Linnaeus. Rare winter visitor, and occasional summer loiterer

No Sinhalese or Tamil names

Slightly larger than the whimbrel, and with much longer legs. Sexes alike. The avocet is a graceful wading bird of striking white and black plumage, with long, pale bluish legs and the feet webbed though not fully so. Its most characteristic feature is the beak which is long, thin, and tapering to a fine point; straight in the basal half, thence gracefully and strongly curving upwards to the tip; it is black. The plumage is pure white with the following black markings: entire top of the head and back of the neck; greater part of the primaries; a broad band through the wing-coverts, joining, when the wing is closed, with a similar broad band on each side of the back, formed by the inner scapulars.

This beautiful bird is a rare straggler to Ceylon, having been recorded only four or five times from the Jaffna Peninsula, Elephant Pass, Minneriya and Hambantota. There is a faint possibility that it might occasionally breed in Ceylon as Phillips found a flock at Minneriya tank in July 1935. Its normal breeding-range is in Europe and central Asia and it has recently been found nesting in the Rann of Kutch. It is highly gregarious. The avocet frequents open marshes, tidal flats, the shores of lagoons and tanks, etc., and obtains its food, which consists of small aquatic insects, crustaceans, molluscs, worms and the like, by wading in shallow water and passing its up-curving beak from side to side through the surface of the mud to seize any small creature that is disturbed by this action. It swims well and freely, but wading is its normal habit.

It breeds in colonies. The four eggs are laid in a shallow scrape on a dry mud-flat or sand-dune. When breeding, the birds are very demonstrative against intruders, flying around with loud screams of *kleet, kleet, kleet,* and endeavouring to lure the enemy away from their eggs or young by pretending to be mortally wounded—fluttering on the ground in well-simulated agony. The eggs are ochreous, speckled with black, and measure about 49·2 × 35 mm.

THE CEYLON BLACK-WINGED STILT

Himantopus himantopus ceylonensis Whistler. Race peculiar to Ceylon

Sinhalese: Kalapu-kiralā. Tamil: Pavala-kāli

Somewhat larger than the Red-wattled Lapwing, and standing much higher owing to its enormously long legs. Sexes in general alike, but the female is browner on the back than the male. This graceful wader, with its white head, underparts, lower back; glossy, green-black scapulars and wings; slender, tapering, nearly straight beak; and above all, its very long, slender, vermilion-pink legs, cannot be mistaken for any other bird.

As a species, it is almost cosmopolitan, forming a number of races in different parts of the world. The stilt inhabits the coastal districts of the dry zone, from about Chilaw, around the north and east, to the Hambantota district in the south; it also frequents the larger tanks in the northern half of the Island. A gregarious bird, it lives in flocks up to a dozen or so, which feed in scattered company but unite into a compact flock when disturbed. It haunts freshwater or brackish shallow lagoons, marshes and tanks, wading to the depth of its long legs, though usually not much deeper than the hock-joint. It walks deliberately, lifting its legs clear of the water at each stride, and pecks hither and thither at the small aquatic insects, molluscs, crustaceans and worms which form its food. The flight is performed with regular, rather slow flaps of the wings, and is not very fast; the long legs project far beyond the tail and appear to make the bird 'tail-heavy'—producing a slight seesaw motion at every stroke. In flight, the white back may be seen to extend nearly up to shoulder-level.

× one-fifth

The breeding season is in June and July, but occasionally a pair will breed earlier or later than these months. The nesting site is on the margin of a tank or lagoon, or on a small islet. The birds nest in scattered company, laying their eggs in slight scrapes in the ground amongst flood-wrack, short herbage, or in the midst of desiccated cow-pats. They are very demonstrative when nesting, flying around an intruder with an incessant cry *ik ik ik ik . . .*; another note is likened by Legge to a brassy-toned *gnrnēēt, gnrnēēt gnrnēēt.* Both sexes incubate and tend the young, which are able to run soon after hatching. The four eggs are greyish-buff, mottled and blotched with sepia and black; they measure about 44 × 31 mm.

293

THE SANDPIPERS, SNIPES, AND THEIR ALLIES
Family SCOLOPACIDAE

These are wading- and shore-birds, of small or medium size (up to that of a hen), of practically global distribution. The vast majority of them are migratory (including all the Ceylon forms), breeding in northern, temperate or Arctic regions, and wintering in warmer countries to the south. Many species fly enormous distances—many thousands of miles, in some cases—twice a year, between their breeding- and wintering-ranges. They are all associated with water, fresh or salt, and most of them are strictly terrestrial, though a few forms perch on stumps and trees when courting and nesting; one or two species actually nest in trees, using discarded nests of other birds; but in their winter quarters—including Ceylon—they never perch. Probably all can swim well, and some do so freely but, as a rule, they content themselves with wading in shallow water. Their diet consists mainly of small aquatic animals, but many sandpipers eat quantities of berries in their northern, moorland breeding-grounds. Their plumage is always coloured in sober tints of grey, brown, chestnut, black and white; but many moult in spring into a breeding plumage which is strikingly different from the winter one. This breeding-garb is often characterized by chestnut or russet colouring on various parts of the body. All are birds of strong flight, capable of great speed. Most species are more or less gregarious, some highly so.

As regards physical features, the birds of this family differ from the plovers mainly in the more slender and graceful form, with smaller head and longer neck. The bill is of various shapes, but usually at least as long as the head, and in many much longer; it is always slender and tapering, without the constriction in the middle that marks the bill of a plover. The nostrils, near the base, are situated in a longitudinal groove of varying length. The legs are long and slender, the three front toes not, or only slightly, webbed at the base; nearly all have a small hind toe which is set on the leg at a higher level than the three front toes; in all, except the woodcocks, the tibia is partly bare. The wings are always long and pointed, with the inner secondaries elongated; the tail is always short, and nearly square at the tip; in flight, the legs are extended under it, in many projecting more or less beyond it.

This large family is divided into six sub-families, as follows, all of them are represented in Ceylon:

Arenariinae—turnstones.
Phalaropodinae—phalaropes.

Limosinae—godwits, curlews, and whimbrels.

Tringinae—typical sandpipers (here, Terek Sandpiper to Common Sandpiper, pp. 302-10).

Calidridinae—stints (here, Ruff and Reeve to Broad-billed Sandpiper, pp. 311-18).

Scolopacinae—woodcocks and snipes.

THE TURNSTONE

Arenaria interpres interpres (Linnaeus). Common winter visitor and occasional summer loiterer

Sinhalese: Oléyiyā. Tamil: Kōttān

Plate 26, facing p. 297 (×one-ninth)

About the size of the Wood Sandpiper, but more stoutly built and with shorter legs. Sexes nearly alike but the female is duller coloured than the male, especially in breeding plumage. In winter plumage, the turnstone is mottled dark brown above, white below, with wings and back boldly patterned with white as shown in the Plate; a black band across the chest is deeply indented with white in the middle, and encloses on each side a diffuse white spot, as shown in the text-figure. Bill short, tapering, black; irides dark brown; legs and feet bright orange, or sometimes pinkish-red, with the joints dusky. In summer plumage, the head is white, with a black pattern as shown in the figure, and the back and scapulars are chestnut; many birds assume this plumage before they leave Ceylon in April and May.

This handsome shore-bird arrives in the Island in August and September and occupies the entire dry-zone coast, wherever conditions are suited to its requirements; in the wet zone it is rare and local. Besides the coasts, it frequents lagoons and estuaries but never goes far inland. Rocky islets and promontories afford favourite haunts, but it may also be found on open beaches, tidal flats, and the like. Although not seldom solitary, it usually associates in compact flocks up to a dozen or so. Not very shy, it is most interesting to watch owing to its habit of flipping over small objects, such as pebbles and shells, to capture the sand-hoppers and other creatures that hide beneath them. In spite of

Left, winter plumage; right, summer plumage; × one-seventh

its striking colour-scheme—or perhaps because of it—it is very inconspicuous when quietly resting among tide-wrack. When disturbed, a flock
fly in a close bunch, usually at no great height; their boldly-pied
plumage gives them a very beautiful appearance as they all turn and
twist in unison. The flight-note is a musical whistle *yuhuhuhuhu.*

The turnstone breeds in northern lands all around the Arctic Circle.
It nests on the ground, in very diverse situations but generally on
islands. The four eggs are some shade of greyish- or olive-green, spotted
and streaked with brown.

The RED-NECKED PHALAROPE *Phalaropus lobatus* (Linnaeus) must be
included in the list of Ceylon birds on the strength of an excellent view
which I had of one on 1 January 1944 at Koppai, four miles north-east of
Jaffna. It was in a wet, ploughed paddy-field near a lagoon, and was
associating with a flock of Wood Sandpipers, remaining behind when
they decamped at my approach. For a quarter of an hour I had good
opportunities for watching and sketching the little bird with the aid of
binoculars, though, owing to its extreme tameness, the latter were often
unnecessary as it came several times within five or six yards. It fluttered
from puddle to puddle, pecking hither and thither at small insects, and
several times uttered a sandpiperish twitter. A certain weakness about
its actions soon led to the discovery that it had lost the greater part of
one leg and the foot of the other—possibly bitten off by some underwater predator.

The small sub-family *Phalaropodinae* are sandpipers modified in structure to fit them for oceanic life. Except when breeding, they live in
flocks far out on the ocean, on which they swim habitually, feeding on
small, surface organisms. In accordance with this mode of life, their
plumage is thick and dense and their feet are unique among sandpipers
in that each toe is fringed with web—somewhat after the manner of the
toes of the coot and the Little Grebe. The three species are all northern
birds, breeding in swamps in circum-polar lands. The Red-necked
Phalarope may be described as a small, very neat-looking sandpiper,
about the size of the Common Sandpiper, with a straight, fine bill about
the length of the head. In winter plumage, which my bird was wearing,
the greater part of the head, all the underparts, and a conspicuous wing-
bar, are pure white; a patch on the crown, extending down the hind
neck, is black or dark grey, and an elongated black mark on the side of
the head extends from just in front of the eye to the end of the ear-
coverts. *This black eye-patch is distinctive,* as no other Ceylonese sandpiper
has such a mark. The back, scapulars and wing-coverts are grey,
streaked and mottled with white. A band down the middle of lower

PLATE 25

1. Pintail Snipe.   2. Indian Little Pratincole.   3. Indian Courser.   4. Indian Large Pratincole.   5. Terek Sandpiper.   6. Painted Snipe.   7. Yellow-wattled Lapwing.   8. Red-wattled Lapwing

PLATE 26

1. Turnstone.   2. Curlew-Sandpiper.   3. Long-toed Stint.   4. Fantail
Snipe.   5. Pintail Snipe.   6. Greenshank.   7. Whimbrel.   8. Eastern
Redshank.   9. Eastern Curlew.   10. Wood Sandpiper.   11. Terek
Sandpiper.   12. Green Sandpiper.   13. Common Sandpiper

back and rump, expanding over most of the tail, dark grey. Flight-feathers mostly blackish. Irides nearly black; bill black; legs and feet dark blue-grey. In summer the upperparts become dark slaty-grey with some buff streaks, and a bright rufous band develops on the sides and front of the neck below the white throat. The male is smaller and less brightly coloured than the female.

It is likely that the Grey Phalarope, *Phalaropus fulicarius*, may turn up in Ceylon some day. In winter plumage it is very similar to the Red-necked Phalarope but is slightly larger, and has a comparatively thick, somewhat yellow bill.

THE BAR-TAILED GODWIT

Limosa lapponica lapponica (Linnaeus). Rare winter visitor

No Sinhalese or Tamil names

Nearly as big as the whimbrel which, in winter plumage, both sexes somewhat resemble in coloration; considerably larger than the green-shank with which, amongst other waders, it is often seen associating. In summer plumage (not worn while in Ceylon), the male becomes bright chestnut on head and entire underparts, and suffused with rufous on the back; the female merely becomes tinged with rufous. Bill pink in the basal half, shading to black at the tip; irides dark brown; legs and feet greenish-grey. From the Black-tailed Godwit, this bird may be distinguished by its shorter legs, more distinctly up-curved beak, and numerous, narrow dark bars on the white tail; it is also more streaky on back and wing-coverts, and lacks a white wing-bar. From other waders, its size, and long, up-curving beak, readily distinguish it.

This godwit is a recent addition to the Ceylon list, three specimens having been collected by the Avifaunal Survey of Ceylon in November 1937, on the north-west coast. Since then, however, it has often been seen in lagoons and mud-flats of the Jaffna Peninsula, and it is probably a regular, though rare, visitor to the north of the Island during the north-east monsoon. In Ceylon it usually frequents tidal waters, favouring lagoon estuaries and shallow creeks, and it is generally seen solitary or in twos and threes; but in northern lands, in spring and autumn,

× one-eighth

it forms very large flocks. It wades in shallow water, probing the mud deeply with its long beak in search of the worms, crabs and other small animals which form its food; at times it will immerse the whole head while probing. In flight, the neck is drawn in and the long bill pointed somewhat downwards, giving much the silhouette of a flying snipe; the toes only project beyond the tail.

The Bar-tailed Godwit breeds in the north of Europe and north-west Asia, nesting on the ground in swamps, usually on slight hillocks or ridges. It lays three or four eggs which are coloured olive-brownish, or greenish, and spotted with dark brown.

THE BLACK-TAILED GODWIT

Limosa limosa limosa (Linnaeus). Rare winter visitor

No Sinhalese or Tamil names

About the size of the whimbrel, but with longer, straight or very slightly up-curved beak, and longer legs. Sexes alike. The only bird with which it might be confused is the Bar-tailed Godwit; from this it

× one-fifth

298

may be distinguished by (*a*) much longer legs; (*b*) more uniform, smoky-grey plumage in winter; (*c*) a very well-marked white wing-bar; (*d*) a single, broad black band across the tip of the white tail; the entire feet and part of the tarsi project beyond the tail in flight. In summer plumage (not worn while in Ceylon) it becomes rich rufous throughout the anterior half of the body, and head.

This tall, handsome wader is a rare winter visitor to Ceylon, having been recorded less than a dozen times, though its visits are doubtless more frequént than the published records suggest and in some years it arrives in considerable numbers. For instance, in October 1944 W. W. A. Phillips saw two to three hundred feeding in the shallow water of the lagoon at Mullaitivu, and in the same year, in December, I put up a party of four at a place about twelve miles ESE of Jaffna. Since then it has been recorded several times from the Eastern Province and the Hambantota district. It is more of a freshwater bird than the Bar-tailed Godwit, being found at times on inland waters although it also frequents shallow coastal lagoons, mud-flats, and estuaries; in such places it wades, stalking along with a dignified gait and probing in the mud for worms, insects and crustaceans, etc. It is shy and wary.

This godwit[1] breeds in Europe and western Asia, making a nest of dry grass, etc., in a hollow in the ground among grasses in a bog or damp meadow. The four eggs are of various shades of olive-green or brown, more or less speckled with dark brown.

THE EASTERN CURLEW

Numenius arquata orientalis Brehm. Regular winter visitor, and summer loiterer

Sinhalese: Māhā-watuwā. Tamil: Kuthirai-mālai-kōttān

Plate 26, facing p. 297 (×one-ninth)

Size of a domestic hen. Sexes alike. This species is the largest of the shore-birds and can only be mistaken for the whimbrel; but the latter is smaller, has a shorter beak, and can always be distinguished, in the hand at least, by its dark crown, divided by a median, broken, pale line. In the field the two species are not always easy to discriminate, mainly

[1] Phillips (*Checklist*, p. 36) reports that recently collected birds have shown that, in addition to the typical race described above, the Eastern form of this godwit, *L. l. melanuroides*, sometimes visits Ceylon. It appears to differ only in having shorter bill and wing, and would be indistinguishable in the field. It breeds in eastern Siberia, Mongolia and Kamchatka, and normally winters from east Asia to north Australia.

owing to the variation in length of the beak in both—that of the curlew varying from four to seven inches, that of the whimbrel three to nearly four inches; the curlew is, however, a heavier-looking bird, with a more stately walk. Both species are often seen together.

This fine wader arrives in Ceylon in large numbers in September and October, leaving again in March and April, but considerable numbers

× one-sixth (The tertials are shown blown up by the wind)

remain throughout the south-west monsoon. It is common, in suitable localities, throughout the northern coastal districts and down the east coast, but is only occasionally seen on the coasts of the wet zone. During its stay it frequents the muddy or stony shores of lagoons, creeks, estuaries, tidal flats and low pastures, etc., and a few visit the shores of some of the large, inland tanks. It may be seen either solitary, in small parties, or in large flocks; often in company with other shore-birds, gulls, terns and the like. A very wary bird, it usually keeps well out in the open away from cover, so that it is not easy to approach. Like other waders, its favourite feeding times are when the tide has begun to ebb, exposing areas of mud or sand; the curlew stalks about with a dignified pace, probing the mud for the marine worms, shellfish and crustaceans upon which it feeds. On some item of prey being captured it is jerked up the long bill into the mouth, in a very characteristic way. The flight of the curlew is swift but is performed with rather slow strokes of the ample wings; it is often accompanied, especially on taking off, by the wild musical cry which gives the bird its name—a loud *crrr-lēē*—which is a sure pointer to its identity. It often flies high and a flock, travelling some distance, will string out into a long, wavering line, or Λ-shaped formation.

The breeding-range of the Eastern Curlew is in central and northern Asia. The nest is a hollow in the ground lined with dry grass, etc., and hidden amongst rough grass or heather; often at considerable heights on mountain moors and bogs. Four eggs form the normal clutch; they are of various shades of olive green or brown, marked with spots of dark brown.

THE WHIMBREL

Numenius phaeopus phaeopus (Linnaeus). Regular winter visitor, and summer loiterer

Sinhalese: Māhā-watuwā. Tamil: Kuthirai-mālai-kōttān

Plate 26, facing p. 297 (×one-ninth)

Between the greenshank and the Eastern Curlew in size. Sexes alike. From the curlew—the only species with which it can be confused—it may be distinguished by its smaller size, shorter beak and, at close quarters, by the top of its head which is blackish with a buff line down the middle; from all other shore-birds, this and the curlew are at once distinguished by their long, slender, down-curving beaks combined with large size.

The whimbrel arrives in Ceylon in September and October and leaves again in April, but a good number loiter in the Island throughout the south-west monsoon. It frequents estuaries, lagoons, and salt flats, all round the coast, but is not common in the wet zone. It prefers salt or brackish waters to fresh, and does not normally range inland to any distance. In general, its habits are very similar to those of the curlew but it is quicker in its movements and is less averse from the neighbourhood of trees, bushes and other cover; nevertheless, it is exceedingly wary. Favourite haunts are mangrove-fringed, muddy creeks, and rocky islets. In such places it finds an abundance of the crabs, molluscs and worms that form its food. When disturbed, it is noisy, flying off with loud cries which sound like *hihihihihihi* (*i* as in hill). Although gregarious it does not form such large flocks as the curlew, being generally seen in small parties of four or five birds. Its flight is swift, performed with regular strokes of the wings.

× one-fifth

This race[1] of the whimbrel nests in the northern parts of Europe and western Asia. The nest is a hollow in the ground, on a moor or heath, lined with grass. The four eggs are olive green or brown, spotted and blotched with dark brown.

THE TEREK SANDPIPER

Xenus cinereus (Güldenstädt). Regular winter visitor in small numbers

No Sinhalese or Tamil names

Plate 25, facing p. 296 (× one-sixth)
Plate 26, facing p. 297 (× one-ninth)

Size of the curlew-sandpiper, but with shorter legs; slightly larger than the Common Sandpiper. Sexes alike. The long, distinctly up-curving beak combined with the uniform, pale smoky-grey upperparts, and rather short, orange legs, make this sandpiper unmistakable. In

[1] Phillips (*Checklist*, p. 35) says that a specimen collected near Mannar, in February 1952, has been identified as belonging to the eastern race of whimbrel, *N. ph. variegatus*, which breeds in eastern Siberia and Japan, and normally winters in south-east Asia and Australia. This subspecies differs from the typical race in having the back, rump, and underwing more boldly marked with brown.

flight it suggests a small redshank, having a similar broad white band at the trailing edge of the secondaries and inner primaries.

This sandpiper, which was long considered to be a very rare straggler to Ceylon, has of recent years been found to be a regular visitor in small numbers to the north-west and north coasts from Puttalam to the Jaffna Peninsula, and the Hambantota district, Southern Province. It frequents the shores of shallow lagoons, tidal creeks, and estuaries; and is usually seen either solitary or, more often, in small flocks of five or six—often associating with other sandpipers and small plovers. The Terek Sandpiper is most amusing to watch while feeding as it is very active, running hither and thither with the head held low, turning and pecking, and sometimes probing into a crab-hole. It is apt to be irascible with its neighbours, chasing them, and on one occasion I saw one run up to a sand plover which was innocently feeding, and give it a heavy dig in the ribs. It feeds on various small shore-line animals and has a habit of carrying them to the water's edge and washing them before swallowing them. I have seen one catch and swallow—apparently whole—a calling-crab which seemed to be of enormous size for so small a bird to swallow. When put up on the wing it utters a mellow whistle *tweeweewit*—uttered rather rapidly.

The Terek Sandpiper breeds in the high north of Europe and Asia, nesting on the ground near the margins of rivers and lakes. It lays four eggs, which are of various shades of buff, blotched with sepia, etc.

THE GREEN SANDPIPER

Tringa ochropus Linnaeus. Regular, but uncommon winter visitor

Sinhalese: Sili-watuwā. Tamil: Kōttān

Plate 26, facing p. 297 (× one-ninth)

About the size of the Pintail Snipe, but more lightly built and with much shorter beak; larger than the Wood Sandpiper. Sexes alike. This is a plump-looking sandpiper which may be recognized in the field by the following combination of characters: (*a*) the dark, greenish-brown back and wings, marked only with small whitish flecks; the lower back is black, faintly barred with white; (*b*) the pure white rump, upper tail-coverts, and tail, contrasting strongly, in flight, with the dark wings and back; the tail is marked towards the end, except on the outer feathers, with a few, bold black bars; (*c*) the underwing is black, with fine, regular white bars on coverts and axillaries—except at very close quarters, these bars are not distinguishable and the underwing looks black. Beak dusky-olive; irides dark brown; legs and feet olive-green.

This sandpiper arrives in Ceylon, from August to October, in comparatively small numbers, and takes up its winter quarters principally in the northern half of the Island; it occurs also in the wet zone and sometimes ascends the hills as high as the Horton Plains and Nuwara Eliya. Its favourite haunts are pools in well-wooded places, riversides, and the like, and it generally avoids both the wet paddy-fields so beloved of the Wood Sandpiper, and coastal waters such as lagoons and tidal flats. Less gregarious than many sandpipers, it is usually single or in loose association with one or two of its own species. It is apt to frequent the same pool or puddle day after day. In many of its habits it resembles the Common Sandpiper, having a similar way of walking and wading sedately, pecking here and there at small insects, and swinging its tail-end up and down. It is generally shy and wary, flying off on the approach of a human intruder with rapid and swerving flight accompanied by its sweet, rather plaintive whistle, *che wer chēē, chwee chwit* (with variations). Usually, when disturbed, it goes clear away but soon returns when the coast is clear.

× one-fifth

The Green Sandpiper breeds in Europe and Central Asia. It chooses for the purpose swampy woods, and has the habit—strange for a sandpiper—of nesting in trees; it does not, however, build its own nests but utilizes old nests of other birds—thrushes, wood pigeons and the like. The four eggs are some shade of green or olive-buff, sparingly spotted with purplish-brown.

THE WOOD SANDPIPER

Tringa glareola Linnaeus. Abundant winter visitor

Sinhalese: Sili-watuwā. Tamil: Kōttān

Plate 26, facing p. 297 (×one-ninth)

Slightly larger than the Common Sandpiper, and with much longer legs; smaller than the Green Sandpiper. Sexes alike. From other sandpipers this is distinguished by the following combination of characters: (*a*) bronzy greyish-brown back and wings, much speckled with white flecks; (*b*) no white wing-bar; (*c*) underwing pale smoky grey, with faint, darker markings; (*d*) white rump and underparts; (*e*) tail mainly white, but barred throughout with blackish. Bill olivaceous black; irides dark brown; legs olive-yellow or olive-green.

This is by far the commonest sandpiper in Ceylon from August or September till April. It spreads throughout the low country and lower hills, and occurs occasionally as high as Nuwara Eliya (6,000 feet). It is mainly a freshwater bird, seldom frequenting salt water, though it is common in marshes and paddy-fields near the coast as well as inland. This is the paddy-field 'snippet' *par excellence*, delighting in the wide stretches of oozy mud resulting from the ploughing operations of the

× one-fifth

cultivator; in these it finds an abundance of the small aquatic insects that form its food—beetles, bugs, larvae, etc. In such good feeding-grounds it associates in large flocks, but on the margins of shallow weedy ponds, and the like, it is more inclined to be territorially-minded, each bird claiming a length of shore-line which it defends vigorously from other sandpipers. Although by no means shy or wary it is an excitable little bird, always ready to take wing with shrill pipings on the approach of an intruder. The flight is very swift, performed with rapid strokes of the well-angled wings, and is always accompanied by the loud but musical flight-note which has been likened to *chiff-iff-iff*; when uttered by a flock, this sounds like a continuous twitter. Other notes are uttered, one of which is a miniature yelp *yep yep yep yep*. When undisturbed it walks quietly about, pecking on this side and that, and swinging its tail-end up and down like a wagtail; though it does not indulge in this habit to the extent that the Common Sandpiper does.

The Wood Sandpiper breeds in northern Europe and Asia, nesting on the ground in tundras, open places in woods, etc. Sometimes it lays its eggs in deserted nests of other birds, in bushes and trees. Like many other sandpipers, it perches freely on trees and the like in the breeding season, though it never does so in its winter habitat. The four eggs are very variable in colour, from pale olive to buff, and they are speckled with various shades of brown, mainly in a big-end zone.

THE MARSH SANDPIPER

Tringa stagnatilis (Bechstein). Abundant winter visitor and occasional summer loiterer

Sinhalese: Sili-watuwā. Tamil: Kōttān

Smaller than the Pintail Snipe, but with much longer legs and shorter beak. Sexes alike. From other sandpipers of comparable size it may be distinguished by the following combination of characters:

× one-sixth

(*a*) general coloration very white and grey; (*b*) beak long, thin, and *very* slightly up-curved; (*c*) neck and legs long and slender, giving it a more graceful appearance than most sandpipers; (*d*) no white wing-bar; (*e*) the entire lower back, rump and most of the tail are pure white; the latter has some dark-grey broken bars; (*f*) the face, fore-neck, and entire underparts are pure white. Bill black, greenish at base of lower mandible; irides dark brown; legs olive-green. These points suffice to distinguish it from all sandpipers except the greenshank which, in winter plumage, it very closely resembles; but it is much smaller (ten inches long, against fourteen inches in the greenshank). The above description applies to the winter plumage, which it wears through most of its sojourn in Ceylon; in breeding plumage, the grey of head, scapulars, and tertials becomes spotted and blotched with black.

This sandpiper visits Ceylon in large but fluctuating numbers, arriving about September and departing again in April and May. It is mainly a dry-zone coastal bird, though a few stray inland to visit the large tanks. Its favourite haunts are shallow lagoons and salt-pans, but it also frequents swamps, flooded fields, and marshes. Though not infrequently solitary, it usually associates in flocks of varying size. Like its large relative the greenshank, it is much given to wading far from cover on tidal flats, where it finds the small crustaceans, worms and the like, on which it feeds. While feeding, its actions are very brisk and alert. A wary bird, it seldom permits of a very near approach. The flight is very swift, with the head drawn in, wings angled, and feet projecting beyond the tail; the white of the back is seen to extend forward like a narrow Λ almost up to the shoulders. As it flies, and particularly when disturbed by a human, it utters loud, piping cries.

The Marsh Sandpiper breeds in southern Russia and central Asia, nesting on the ground in grassy flats near lakes, etc. It sometimes breeds in colonies. The four eggs are cream or buff, variously marked with purplish-brown and ashy-grey.

THE GREENSHANK

Tringa nebularia (Gunnerus). Abundant winter visitor and fairly common summer loiterer

Sinhalese: Māhā-watuwā. Tamil: Periya-kōttān

Plate 26, facing p. 297 (×one-ninth)

Larger than the Eastern Redshank, smaller than the whimbrel. Sexes alike. In winter plumage, the greenshank is streaky grey on head, hind-neck and scapulars; face, fore-neck and entire underparts pure white; wing-coverts mottled grey, quills blackish; beak grey at base, shading to black at the tip; it is slightly but distinctly up-curved; irides nearly black; legs and feet pale greenish grey (hardly 'green'). From all other Ceylonese sandpipers, except the Marsh Sandpiper, it is distinguished by the following combination: (*a*) size; (*b*) greyish upperparts; (*c*) pure white lower back, rump, and greater part of the tail; (*d*) dark wings with no white in them; (*e*) slightly up-curved beak; (*f*) long, greenish-grey legs. From its small relative, the Marsh Sandpiper, it may be distinguished by its size, coarser build, and heavier beak. In summer plumage, the head and neck are much streaked with dark grey and the scapular feathers develop black centres with pale, indented edges.

This large sandpiper arrives in Ceylon in large numbers in August and September, departing in April and May, but a good many loiter throughout the south-west monsoon. It is common in all the coastal districts of the dry zone, from Negombo to Jaffna, thence down the east coast to the Hambantota district, and also around the larger tanks in the northern half of the Island; but it is rare and local in the wet zone. It frequents almost any

× one-seventh

307

kind of waters but prefers tidal flats, creeks, estuaries, lagoon shores and salt-pans; in such places it associates in flocks of varying size, though solitary individuals are common. Its long legs enable it to wade in deeper water than most sandpipers, and it may commonly be seen far out on a tidal flat, probing the mud or sand and picking up the small crabs, worms and molluscs that form much of its food; it eats also many aquatic insects, which it finds in freshwater pools. Though always alert, it is not as a rule difficult to approach to within satisfactory range for observation. When put up, it flies off with rapid and twisting flight, uttering its loud, musical pipe *tew tew tew*.

The greenshank breeds in the north of Europe and in northern and central Asia; its nest is a hollow in the ground in moorland or heath, often on mountains near lochs or tarns. While breeding, it perches freely on trees, stumps, fences, etc.; this it never does in its winter habitat. The four eggs are of varying shades of buff, pale green or olive, marked with spots or flecks of reddish-brown.

THE EASTERN REDSHANK

Tringa totanus eurhinus (Oberholser). Winter visitor and occasional summer loiterer

Sinhalese: Māhā-watuwā. Tamil: Mālai-kōttān

Plate 26, facing p. 297 (×one-ninth)

Larger than the Wood Sandpiper but smaller than the greenshank. Sexes alike. This sandpiper is easily recognized in the field by the following features: (*a*) basal half of the beak, and the legs, orange-red; (*b*) head, hind-neck, upper back, scapulars and wing-coverts, brownish-grey—browner than in the green-shank; (*c*) lower back pure white, rump and tail white, barred with black; (*d*) entire secondaries and tips of inner primaries pure white—producing a distinctive white crescent, very noticeable in flight, at the trailing edge of the wing; this is a good recognition-mark.

The redshank is fairly common during the north-east monsoon in all coastal districts of the dry zone, but is scarce and local in the wet

× one-sixth

zone; it does not venture far inland. Salt or brackish creeks, mangrove-fringed estuaries, tidal runnels and the like, are its favourite resorts. In Ceylon, it seems less sociable than many of its congeners and is usually solitary or in small, scattered parties. An exceedingly shy and wary bird, it takes wing at the first sign of danger, dashing off with swift and erratic flight, swerving from side to side. As it flies it utters loud, piping cries which put every bird in the neighbourhood on the *qui vive*. When suspicious, it has a habit of jerking up first the head, then the tail, pivoting on the legs in a characteristic gesture. The redshank swims well on occasion, but normally wades, down to belly-depth, in its search for food which consists of small crabs, molluscs, worms and other aquatic animals.

This race of the redshank breeds in central Asia, nesting on the ground in swamps and marshes, riverside meadows, etc. The nest is concealed in a tuft of grass or the like. Four eggs form the normal clutch.

The SPOTTED REDSHANK *Tringa erythropus* (Pallas) has twice been recorded from Ceylon; it was obtained in the Jaffna district by Layard about a hundred years ago, and a specimen was collected by W. W. A. Phillips on the shores of a small tank in the North Central Province, in December 1942. It is between the redshank and the greenshank in size. Sexes alike. In winter plumage, which is worn while in Ceylon, this bird resembles the Eastern Redshank in many respects, but it is larger, more ashy-grey on the upperparts, and has a much longer bill (2½ as against almost two inches), and longer legs. In flight, it may at once be distinguished by the secondaries which, instead of being pure white are heavily barred with dark grey—looking but little lighter than the coverts. In breeding plumage, the bird is black throughout, except for white mottlings on the back and wings, and white rump and tail-bars. Beak black, orange-red on basal half of lower mandible; irides dark brown; legs orange-red in winter, dark red in summer.

Undoubtedly this handsome wader visits the Island more frequently than the records suggest, but is overlooked or mistaken for the common Eastern Redshank. In general habits, gait and flight it differs but little from the latter, but it has a distinctive flight-note which is described as a disyllabic *tchuet* or *tchueet*. In flight, the whole foot projects behind the tail—in the Eastern Redshank only the front toes do so.

The Spotted Redshank breeds in northern Europe and Asia, nesting on the ground in open spaces in woods. The nest is a hollow in a grass-tussock or the like, on either swampy or dry ground. Four olive-buff or greenish eggs, boldly blotched with reddish-brown, are laid.

THE COMMON SANDPIPER

Actitis hypoleucos (Linnaeus). Abundant winter visitor

Sinhalese: Sili-watuwā. Tamil: Kōttān

Plate 26, facing p. 297 (×one-ninth)

Smaller than the Common Mynah. Sexes alike. From other small sandpipers it may easily be distinguished by the following combination of characters: (*a*) comparatively short legs, which vary in colour from greenish-ochreous to greenish-grey; (*b*) olive-brown back, wing-

× one-fifth

coverts, rump, and central two or three pairs of tail-feathers; the outer tail-feathers are white, barred with black; (*c*) with wings closed it invariably shows a definite white, vertical band on the side of the breast, between the wrist-bend of the wing and the greyish-brown lateral breast-patch— this is a good recognition-character in the field; (*d*) in flight, a distinct white wing-bar shows, formed by the white bases of the secondaries and inner primaries; (*e*) its distinctive habits. Beak olive-brown, paler at the base; irides dark brown. In summer plumage the head and neck are streaked with dark brown, and the feathers of the back and wing-coverts are barred with black near the tips.

This attractive little sandpiper arrives in Ceylon in large numbers in August and September and departs in April and May. During its stay it may be seen, in suitable places, almost anywhere in the Island—wet and dry zones, low country and hills alike. In spite of its name it is seldom seen on *sandy* shores, but wherever rocks and water exist together it is sure to be found. In default of rocks it will frequent places where fallen tree-trunks, mud-banks, or the like, adjoin the water of streams, lakes or the sea; but rock-masses arising from water are definitely its favourite habitat. It is a solitary species, never seen in flocks though several may, at times, be seen together; when this happens, however, they are generally quarrelling as the species has strong territorial instincts, each bird choosing its own stretch of shore-line which it jealously guards from other sandpipers—by vigorous fighting if necessary. It trips daintily over the rocks and wades in shallows, picking at the small aquatic creatures that form its food, and perpetually swinging the tail up and down after the manner of a wagtail. Its flight is generally low over the water with wings bowed downwards, and vibrated in a curious, stiff manner, unlike any other sandpiper. While so flying, it frequently utters a shrill, piping cry *twee-wee-wee*.

The Common Sandpiper breeds over much of Europe, and Asia as far south as the Himalayas. It nests on the ground, usually near water and often high on mountains, laying four eggs which are buff or pale greyish, spotted with dark brown.

THE RUFF (male) and REEVE (female)

Philomachus pugnax (Linnaeus). Scarce winter visitor

No Sinhalese or Tamil names

Male slightly larger than the Eastern Redshank, female slightly smaller. In winter plumage, which is worn while in Ceylon, the sexes are much alike though the male is larger than the female. Head, back, and wing-coverts brownish-grey, each feather edged paler giving a scaly effect; lower back, rump and upper tail-coverts (the latter very long, reaching nearly to the end of the tail) white, with a dark brown band down the middle, dividing the white area into two oval patches— this is a good recognition-mark in the flying bird; throat and underparts white, breast more or less suffused with brown or greyish-brown; in flight, a narrow white wing-bar shows on the tips of the greater coverts. Bill brownish-black; irides dark brown; legs and feet very variable— greenish, yellow, orange, brownish-yellow, or flesh-colour. The bill is rather short (female $1\frac{1}{4}$ inches, male $1\frac{1}{2}$ inches), nearly straight but very slightly down-curved at the tip. In summer plumage, the male develops an extraordinary ruff of feathers around the neck, and two great 'ear'-tufts on the back of the head; the feathers of the face are shed, and in their place the skin becomes covered with yellow or brown tubercles; the coloration of the ruff and ear-tufts is very variable, from purplish-black, through brown and chestnut, to white, in infinite variations of pattern. The female in summer plumage merely becomes darker and more mottled, especially on the breast.

This remarkable sandpiper is a rare and irregular winter visitor to Ceylon, specimens having been procured in the Island perhaps twenty times since Legge first recorded it. It breeds in a great part of Europe and Asia, and winters in Africa and southern Asia. Its favourite haunts are freshwater marshes, flooded meadows, paddy-fields and the like; though it also frequents tidal creeks and estuaries at times. In general behaviour and flight it resembles the redshank except that it is generally silent, and is said to stand more erect except when walking or feeding. Its food consists mainly of insects but it also eats grain, such as paddy.

The breeding behaviour of the ruff is very interesting; the males assemble in regular resorts where they indulge in curious displays, and fight with much show of fierceness but little actual damage; the females resort to the 'parade grounds' and select their mates from among the combatants. The nest is placed among rank grass, and is well hidden. The four eggs are varying shades of pale blue, green or ochreous, spotted and blotched with sepia and grey.

THE SANDERLING

Crocethia alba (Pallas). Scarce winter visitor

No Sinhalese or Tamil names

Size of the Lesser Sand Plover, which it somewhat resembles in form; but it is a much paler-grey bird, and its actions are those of a stint, not those of a plover. Sexes alike. In summer plumage the head, breast and upperparts are mottled rufous brown, but in winter plumage, which it wears in Ceylon, it is very pale grey, more or less mottled with black on head and upperparts; white on face, breast and underparts; the bend of the wing shows dark against the white breast-feathers; wing quills black, with white shafts; a broad white wing-bar is conspicuous in flight. There is a dark, blackish-grey band down the middle of the lower back, rump and upper tail-coverts. Bill black; irides dark brown; legs black; there is *no hind toe*.

The sanderling, which breeds in the far north of Europe, Asia and America, spreads in winter almost throughout the coasts of the world. In Ceylon it is scarce, though probably more regular in its visits than the published records suggest. It occurs on the coasts of the dry zone but has not, so far, been found in the wet zone. As its name suggests, its favourite haunt is the edge of sandy beaches, where it follows the waves

Winter plumage; × one-quarter

as they advance and recede, picking up the small organisms that are exposed to view at each ebb. It is a most active little bird, nearly always rushing along as if actuated by machinery. In Ceylon, it is usually solitary or in small parties, but when migrating it forms very large flocks. It is not very shy, and often prefers to run ahead of one for considerable distances along a beach, rather than to take wing; but when

PLATE 27

G.M.Henry

1. Large Crested Tern. 2. White-shafted Little Tern. 3. Eastern Roseate Tern. 4. Great Black-headed Gull.
5. Brown-headed Gull. 6. Caspian Tern

PLATE 28

1. Banded Crake.   2. Blue-breasted Banded Rail.   3. Baillon's Crake.
4. Pheasant-tailed Jaçana.   5. Purple Coot.   6. Ruddy Crake

put up, it flies swiftly, uttering a squeaking flight-note *cheep cheep cheep*, and usually alights a hundred yards or so ahead of, or behind, the disturber of its peace.

The sanderling nests on tundras in the far north, choosing stony or gravelly sites with scanty vegetation, usually near the coast. The four eggs are greenish olive, sparsely spotted with brown.

A single specimen of the KNOT *Calidris canutus canutus* (Linnaeus) was shot by T. H. Haddon near Mannar in December 1923, as recorded by Wait (*Manual*, 1925, p. 374). It is a large, plump-looking, short-necked stint, about the size of the Asiatic Golden Plover but with shorter legs. In winter plumage, which it is sure to wear while in Ceylon, it is a grey and white bird of similar general pattern to the Grey Plover (in winter plumage), which it somewhat resembles in shape. However, its head is smaller, eye much smaller, beak longer, upperparts less mottled than those of the Grey Plover, and its axillaries are not black. In breeding plumage the knot is mainly bright chestnut, with grey wings.

Its favourite haunts are sand and mud-flats, borders of lagoons and estuaries, etc., and it is generally very gregarious, packing, both while feeding and in flight, into close flocks; but in Ceylon it will most likely be found solitary, or in parties of two or three. Its flight is swift and strong, and is punctuated by the note that probably gave the bird its name—*knut, knut*. Its method of feeding is similar to that of other stints, quick picking here and there, with head down, as the bird walks along on wet sand or mud.

The knot breeds in the far north of both hemispheres, and winters on the coasts of all the great oceans and the Mediterranean Sea. It is a rare visitor to India.

THE CURLEW-SANDPIPER, or CURLEW-STINT

Calidris testacea (Pallas). Abundant winter visitor and fairly common summer loiterer

Sinhalese: Pŭnchi-watuwā. Tamil: Kallu-porukki

Plate 26, facing p. 297 (× one-ninth)

Size of the Wood Sandpiper. Sexes alike. In winter plumage, brownish-grey and white; wing-quills dark brown; greater secondary coverts with white tips, showing as a wing-bar in flight; lower back, centre of rump, and tail, ashy-brown; but the sides of rump and all the upper tail-coverts are white—producing a pattern which is a useful identification-mark in flight; another feature useful in identification is the rather long, slightly down-curving bill, which is purplish-black; irides dark brown; legs black. In summer plumage—which many birds are still wearing on their arrival in Ceylon in August, and which they begin to assume before departing in April—the head, breast, and

Left, winter plumage; right, summer plumage; × one-third

underparts down to the upper abdomen are bright chestnut, and the back and scapulars are mottled chestnut, black and white; but the front of the face and the chin remain white as in winter plumage.

This sandpiper arrives in Ceylon in large numbers in August and September, leaving again in April and May; but a considerable number, retaining their winter plumage, loiter throughout the south-west monsoon. It frequents the coastal districts of the dry zone, but seldom goes inland and is rare in the wet zone. It usually lives in flocks of varying size—up to several hundreds—but is sometimes seen solitary, or associating with other kinds of stints and sandpipers. Its favourite haunts are the margins of shallow lagoons, salt flats, tidal mud-banks and the like, where it forms a large proportion of the swarms of small waders that frequent such places. When the tide is running out, exposing large areas of mud or sand, the birds find multitudes of small organisms, worms, molluscs, crustaceans, etc., on which they feed. Like other stints, it is very active while feeding, running over the mud with head down, picking and probing for its prey. During tide-flow, it generally rests, standing on one leg with the bill hidden under the scapulars. The chosen resting-place is often some tiny islet or sand-spit. The birds will mass in very close formation on a suitable spot; I have seen a flock estimated at over a hundred resting on a space of about four square yards. Every now and then one will stretch its wings, raising them vertically for a second or two in a graceful gesture. The flight is swift, and is often in a close flock which will twist and turn in unison, showing now the dark upperparts, then the white underparts, alternately. It is not a noisy bird, but a chirruping flight-note is uttered.

The curlew-sandpiper nests on tundras in arctic eastern Asia, and winters over a large part of the eastern hemisphere.

THE LITTLE STINT

Calidris minuta (Leisler). Abundant winter visitor and occasional summer loiterer

Sinhalese: Pǔnchi-watuwā. Tamil: Kallu-porukki

About the size of the House Sparrow but with longer wings and legs. Sexes alike. In winter plumage, brownish-grey with pale edges to the feathers, giving a somewhat scaly appearance especially to the back and scapulars; forehead, eyebrow and eye-ring, throat, middle of breast, and underparts, pure white; middle of lower back, rump, and tail-coverts, dark brown, the sides white; tail dark brown on the centre feathers, pale greyish-brown on the lateral ones; the primary shafts are white, and there is a broad, white wing-bar formed by the tips of the greater secondary coverts and bases of the secondaries. Bill olive-black; irides black; legs greyish-black. In summer plumage, which some birds begin to assume before leaving the Island in May, the head, sides of breast, scapulars and wing-coverts become mottled with rufous. This stint is difficult to distinguish from the Long-toed and Temminck's Stints, as all three are much of a size and not conspicuously different in coloration or habits; from the Long-toed Stint it may be distinguished by its white forehead and centre of breast, greyer upperparts, broader wing-bar, and blackish legs; from Temminck's Stint, by its much whiter face and breast, greyer and more mottled scapulars, greyish-brown outer tail-feathers, and blackish legs; and, in the hand, by all the primary shafts being white.

315

This small wader is very abundant in Ceylon during the north-east monsoon, throughout the coastal districts of the dry zone wherever suitable conditions exist. It loves tidal mud-flats, the shores of coastal lagoons, etc., being much more partial to salt or brackish water than either of its congeners above-mentioned; and it is quite independent of cover, feeding normally on open flats uncovered by the ebbing tide. It

Left, Little Stint; right, Long-toed Stint; × two-fifths

lives in big flocks, which scatter over a large area while feeding but unite into compact groups when put up on the wing. The flight is very swift and is accompanied by a note like *twit twit twit*, frequently uttered. Like other small waders, a flock will turn and twist in unison, as if drilled in manœuvring. It is generally rather shy of humans, but when resting in the heat of the day a *small* flock will sometimes allow of near approach. While feeding, it runs actively on the mud with quick busyness, beak pointing downwards and incessantly picking at minute aquatic forms of life; ever and anon stopping to make sure no enemy is approaching, for it is rather a 'jumpy' little bird.

The Little Stint breeds on steppes and tundras in the far north of Europe and Asia, nesting on the ground among grass, usually near the coast.

TEMMINCK'S STINT

Calidris temminckii (Leisler). Scarce winter visitor

Sinhalese: Pŭnchi-watuwā. Tamil: Kallu-porukki

About the size of the House Sparrow but with longer wings and legs; sexes alike. Superficially, this is so much like the Little Stint in size and coloration that there is no doubt it has been overlooked, being mistaken for that species; the first specimen obtained in Ceylon was collected by Legge in the Trincomalee district, and no other specimen appears to have been procured in the Island until I collected one at Elephant Pass in February 1944; subsequently, it was found to be a regular winter visitor, in small numbers, chiefly to the north of the Island, but occasionally as far south as the Hambantota district. In winter plumage, it may easily be recognized by the following features: (*a*) general coloration of head and upperparts more uniform brownish-grey than the Little Stint; (*b*) forehead brown; supercilium softly whitish, but not so pronounced as in either the Little or Long-toed Stints; (*c*) breast uniformly greyish-brown right across the chest; (*d*) legs greenish-yellow, or pale olive; (*e*) outer tail-feathers white; (*f*) first primary shaft white, the rest brown. From the Long-toed Stint it may be distinguished by its uniform, unstreaked coloration, and the shorter middle toe (three-quarters against nine-tenths of an inch).

This stint, in its winter quarters at least, is much less gregarious than the Little Stint, being usually found in small parties of three or four; sometimes consorting with Little Stints but more often with Long-toed, or with Little Ringed Plovers, Wood Sandpipers, etc. Unlike the Little Stint, it is not fond of open mud-flats or tidal marshes, preferring the shores of shallow creeks or muddy places where grass and low herbage give it some cover. In its manner of feeding it closely resembles other stints—pattering along on the mud, with beak down, picking up tiny organisms with quick pecks. It is less nervous than the Little Stint, and will allow one to watch it at close quarters. When put up, it flies rapidly uttering its trilling flight-note *tirrirrirrirri*.

Temminck's Stint breeds in northern Europe and Asia, nesting on the ground amongst grass, etc., usually near rivers or lakes. It winters in Africa and southern Asia.

THE LONG-TOED STINT

Calidris subminuta (Middendorf). Abundant winter visitor and occasional summer loiterer

Sinhalese: Pŭnchi-watuwā. Tamil: Kallu-porukki

Plate 26, facing p. 297 (×one-ninth)
(For text illustration see Little Stint)

About the size of the House Sparrow but with longer wings and legs. Sexes alike. Although, in winter plumage, it is very like the Little Stint, it may easily be distinguished, provided a good view is obtained, by (*a*) brown, not white, forehead; (*b*) grey-brown breast; (*c*) back and scapulars boldly streaked dark brown; (*d*) its legs, which are olive-yellow, or greenish, with long middle toe (about an inch). From Temminck's Stint it differs in (*a*) longer and whiter supercilium; (*b*) breast more streaked and spotted with brown; (*c*) broad, dark brown streaks on the back and scapulars; (*d*) outer tail-feathers not white but very pale brown.

This pretty stint visits Ceylon in large numbers every year, but not in such big flocks as the Little Stint; it usually forms parties of a dozen or less. It spreads throughout the dry-zone coastal districts, but is rare in the wet zone and its favourite haunts appear to be in the north of the Island. It frequents marshes, paddy-fields, and swampy flats, near sea or lagoon, but is not fond of the bare, tidal mud-flats so beloved of the Little Stint; it often associates, however, with both that species and Temminck's Stint, and also with Wood Sandpipers and Little Ringed Plovers. It is more approachable than the Little Stint and will often, when in a mixed flock with the latter, continue feeding long after they have taken alarm and fled. Like other stints, it feeds on minute aquatic animals, for which it pecks and probes the wet mud with a very busy action as it patters along. Its flight resembles that of other stints, being very swift and dashing, twisting and erratic. The flight-note is described by Legge as a weak, trilling whistle.

This stint breeds in eastern Siberia and migrates in winter to Australia as well as to south-eastern Asia.

THE BROAD-BILLED SANDPIPER, or BROAD-BILLED STINT

Limicola falcinellus falcinellus (Pontoppidan). Rare winter visitor

No Sinhalese or Tamil names

Between the Little Stint and the curlew-sandpiper in size (length seven inches, wing $4\frac{1}{4}$ inches). Sexes alike. The coloration in winter plumage is very similar to that of other stints—brownish-grey above and white below, with broad white supercilium, blackish-brown lower back, centre of rump, tail-coverts and tail—and the only ready way to recognize it is by the bill, which is proportionately long (1¼ inches), high at the base, broad (an eighth of an inch) and flattened, curving very slightly down at the tip. Bill brownish-black; irides dark brown; legs olive-brown or greenish-black.

This stint is a rare winter visitor to Ceylon having been recorded only half a dozen times, from the North Western Province, Jaffna Peninsula, and the Hambantota district; but it is doubtless often overlooked amongst the multitudes of other small waders with which it associates. It is entirely a coastal bird, never found far from the sea, its favourite haunts being muddy, salt swamps, tidal flats, shallow creeks near lagoons, etc. It is usually solitary or in small parties, but frequently mingles in flocks of other stints and sandpipers. It is said to be rather sluggish, inclined to crouch among low herbage when approached by a human; but its flight is swift, similar to that of other stints. As it rises, it utters a short trilling note. Its food consists of small mud-living animals, and also seeds of certain swamp-plants.

The Broad-billed Sandpiper has two races, differing slightly in coloration of breeding plumage but indistinguishable in winter plumage. Ceylonese specimens have been identified as belonging to the typical, or western race (Phillips, *Checklist*, p. 42), which breeds in north-west Europe, making its nests in grass-tussocks, etc., in bogs. The eastern race (*L. f. siberica*) breeds in northern Siberia and winters from south-east Asia to Australia.

THE WOODCOCK

Scolopax rusticola Linnaeus. Rare and irregular winter visitor

Sinhalese: Māhā-keswatuwā. Tamil: Periya Ullān-kuruvi

About the size of a domestic pigeon, but with a long bill (three inches). Sexes alike. The woodcock may easily be distinguished from all snipes, which it resembles in general form, by (*a*) its beautifully mottled, grey, brown, black and rufous plumage; (*b*) forehead, to above the eyes, greyish-buff; crown, beyond the eyes to the hind neck, black, crossed *transversely* by three or four bars of rufous; (*c*) tibia feathered down to the hock (in all snipes, the tibia is bare for some distance above the hock); (*d*) underside of tail-feathers at the tips silvery white; (*e*) much larger size and heavier build. Bill fleshy at the base, darkening to blackish-brown at the tip; irides dark brown; legs greyish flesh-colour, or grey.

The woodcock breeds over a large part of Europe and Asia, as far south as the Himalayas, and winters in northern Africa and southern Asia. It is a rare and spasmodic visitor to the Ceylon hills above 5,000 feet, apparently arriving late and leaving early as it has only been recorded in January and February. Unlike most snipes, it is a woodland bird, loving boggy hollows in woods though it will sometimes lie up during the day among bracken, etc., on open hill-sides. It is mainly nocturnal, hiding amongst undergrowth during daylight and flying at dusk to its feeding-grounds in swampy places. It bores into soft soil with its long, straight beak for earth-worms, which form its main food and which it eats in enormous quantities. The tip of its beak is flexible and sensitive, enabling the bird to seize a worm at the bottom of the bore-hole and to swallow it without withdrawing the beak. The flight of the woodcock is soft and owl-like, though swift when needful, and it has the power of adroitly dodging between tree-trunks and other obstructions in its haunts. It is probably silent during its sojourn in Ceylon, but in its breeding-grounds it utters various notes, and the male in courtship indulges in curious display-flights, known as 'roding'.

The woodcock nests on the ground, amongst the dead leaves and rubbish of its woodland habitat and usually near a tree-trunk. Four eggs form the normal clutch; they are some shade of grey or buff, spotted with reddish-brown and ashy-grey. The bird sits very closely, trusting to its concealing coloration among the debris that surrounds the nest.

THE WOOD SNIPE

Capella nemoricola (Hodgson). Doubtfully, a very rare winter visitor

No Sinhalese or Tamil names

Considerably larger than the Pintail Snipe, but with no longer beak. Sexes alike. This is a large, heavy, dark-coloured snipe, of the same general colour-pattern as the Pintail; but it may at once be distinguished from all the other snipes that occur in the Island by its abdomen, which is barred throughout with brown on a white ground. Its tail contains from sixteen to eighteen feathers, none of them 'pin' feathers.

The occurrence of this snipe in Ceylon is doubtful as, although several snipe-shooters have reported having shot it on various occasions during the past century, not one of them appears to have 'produced the corpse' for scientific examination. It is probable, however, that the species visits Ceylon now and then, as it occurs fairly regularly, as a winter visitor, on the South Indian hills. Its breeding-grounds are in the Himalayas. The Wood Snipe, as its name suggests, frequents swamps in woods or on their outskirts. It is usually solitary and is said to be sluggish, rising heavily and flying comparatively slowly, without the flight-note uttered by the Fantail and Pintail Snipes.

THE FANTAIL SNIPE, or COMMON SNIPE
('Common Snipe' in Britain)

Capella gallinago gallinago (Linnaeus). Scarce winter visitor

Sinhalese: Keswatuwā. Tamil: Ullān-kuruvi

Plate 26, facing p. 297 (× one-ninth)

Size of the Pintail Snipe. Sexes alike. In the field, this snipe is almost indistinguishable from the far commoner Pintail Snipe, its form and coloration being almost identical; in the hand, the following points will enable the two species to be discriminated with certainty: (*a*) tail of fourteen to eighteen feathers, all of them of normal form; (*b*) outer edge of first primary white; (*c*) secondaries more broadly tipped with white; (*d*) under wing-coverts banded dark-grey and white, with the white bands broader than the grey and often a white patch on the middle of the series; the axillaries are less regularly barred with grey than in the Pintail, white predominating and sometimes occupying the whole of these feathers; (*e*) bill slightly longer, on the average ($2\frac{1}{4}$ to $2\frac{3}{4}$ inches), and slightly more swollen at the tip.

This snipe is generally more clearly and brightly marked, especially as regards the buff stripes on the back and scapulars, than the Pintail. It gets up, when disturbed, in a more lively manner, with a loud cry *scape, scape*, and flies with a very erratic and twisty flight, mounting high into the air as it dashes off to some more retired spot. It inhabits weedy swamps, paddy-fields, the grassy margins of tanks and the like; is usually solitary, or in very scattered 'wisps'; and is mainly nocturnal, spending the day crouching among grass-tufts, etc., in damp situations. At dusk, it sallies forth to feed in muddy ground, where it finds its favourite food—earth-worms—by probing deep into the mud with its highly sensitive bill. Besides earth-worms, it eats various insects, especially larvae.

The Fantail Snipe breeds in Europe and Asia, as far south as the Himalayas and, in another racial form, also in North America. When courting, the male performs strange evolutions in the air, and also perches freely on fence-posts, bare trees and the like—a thing he never does in his winter quarters. In his display-flight he produces a strange tremulous, bleating sound during steep descents in an undulating flight. This bleat is produced by the outermost pair of tail-feathers which are stiffly extended on each side, separate from the rest of the tail; a quivering action of the half-closed wings assists in producing the sound. The nest is on the ground among grass, usually in or near a swamp; the four eggs are of various olivaceous shades, boldly blotched and spotted with brown, and they measure about $41 \times 29 \cdot 3$ mm.

THE PINTAIL SNIPE

Capella stenura (Bonaparte). Abundant winter visitor

Sinhalese: Keswatuwā. Tamil: Ullān-kuruvi

Plate 25, facing p. 296 (×one-sixth)
Plate 26, facing p. 297 (×one-ninth)

About the size of the greenshank, but with shorter legs and longer beak. Sexes alike. The Pintail, which is by far the commonest snipe in Ceylon, is a brownish wading bird, with the upper plumage beautifully mottled and streaked with buff and rufous, giving great concealment in its normal environment of grassy swamp. Among the true[1] snipes that visit Ceylon in winter, all of which have a very similar colour-scheme and are hard to discriminate in the field, this species may be distinguished by its tail, which is of twenty-six to twenty-eight feathers, the six to eight outer ones on each side being very narrow 'pin' feathers (ranging from the width of a pin to that of an ordinary nail). These feathers, however, are concealed beneath the tail-coverts, requiring some diligence to discover them. The only other Ceylon snipe that has pin-feathers in the tail is Swinhoe's Snipe, which has only once been recorded from the Island (see next species). From the Fantail or Common Snipe—the only fairly common species of snipe with which it is likely to be confused—the Pintail may be distinguished by (*a*) outer edge of first primary, which is pale brownish, not white; (*b*) under wing-coverts and axillaries all regularly barred dark grey and white, the grey bars slightly broader than the white; other points of difference are given under the Fantail Snipe.

The Pintail arrives in Ceylon during September and October, and leaves again for its breeding-grounds, north of the Himalayas, in April. During its stay, it spreads all over the Island wherever suitable conditions exist, ascending to over 6,000 feet though it is most abundant in

---

[1] The Painted Snipe (see p. 326) is not a true snipe.

the low country. It frequents paddy-fields, weedy swamps and the like, and is not infrequently found, during the day, hiding in scrub-jungle in damp little hollows; for it is less partial to watery conditions than the Fantail Snipe. It is mainly nocturnal but, where undisturbed, it will often feed until a late hour in the morning and again in the afternoon. Its food consists of swamp insects and their larvae as well as earth-worms, but the latter form the bulk of its food. It bores into soft mud for them with its long beak, the tip of which is highly sensitive and also very flexible, enabling the bird to open its bill widely at the tip while the rest of it remains closed. The Pintail Snipe is somewhat slower on the wing than the Fantail Snipe; it does not jink and twist so much, though when disturbed it rises with a similar alarm-note, *scape*, as it rapidly decamps.

This snipe breeds in eastern Asia, nesting on the ground in similar manner to the Fantail Snipe.

SWINHOE'S SNIPE, or THE CHINESE SNIPE

Capella megala (Swinhoe). Only once recorded from Ceylon

The Sinhalese and Tamil names would not differ from those of the Pintail Snipe

Very slightly larger than the Pintail Snipe but with longer legs. In coloration it is practically indistinguishable but it may be known by the tail, which is of twenty to twenty-two feathers; the outer six or seven pairs of these are very narrow, but are not mere 'pins' as they are in the Pintail. This snipe has only once been recorded from Ceylon, a specimen having been shot in April 1934, by R. H. Spencer-Schrader, and sent by him to the Colombo Museum for identification. It doubtless visits the Island more often than the one record suggests, any individuals shot being merely lumped in the bag with Pintails. Swinhoe's Snipe breeds in north China and eastern Siberia, and normally winters in south China, Malaysia, and some of the Pacific Islands, a few finding their way to South India.

THE GREAT SNIPE

Capella media (Latham). Only twice recorded from Ceylon

No Sinhalese or Tamil names other than those used for snipe generally

Distinctly larger and heavier than the Fantail, Pintail, or Swin-hoe's Snipes, all of which it resembles in general colour-scheme. Its beak is short in proportion, no longer than a Pintail's. In tail characters it resembles the Fantail or Common Snipe more than the other species, having sixteen tail-feathers, the outer pairs not exceptionally narrowed; however, it may always be distinguished from the Fantail by the fact that the *four* outer feathers are pure white, with only a little black barring near the base (in the Fantail, only the outermost feather is white and all the feathers have a blackish bar near the tips). In addition ·to tail-characters, the flanks are more boldly barred with black, and the median wing-coverts, as well as the greater, are tipped with white. The only Ceylon record of this large snipe is one collected by E. C. Fernando near Kalutara, in December 1940.[1] The Great Snipe is heavier on the wing than the smaller species above-mentioned, and tends to go straight away when flushed, without dodging and twisting; it does not usually utter an alarm-note.

It breeds in northern Europe and Asia, nesting in similar manner to other snipes.

THE JACK SNIPE

Lymnocryptes .minimus (Brünnich). Rare winter visitor

No Sinhalese or Tamil names

A very small snipe, about the size of the Lesser Sand Plover but with longer bill and shorter legs. Sexes alike. While its coloration, in general, resembles that of the Pintail and other snipes, it may be distinguished from them all by the following points: (*a*) small size—roughly two-thirds that of the Pintail; (*b*) bill 1½ inches, or a little more; (*c*) tail wedge-shaped, of only twelve feathers which are pointed at the tips; (*d*) no buff stripe along the centre of the crown; (*e*) the broad, buff supercilium is longitudinally divided by a blackish line; (*f*) the black portion of the scapulars is glossed with green and purple. The buff stripes margining the scapular-feathers are clear and definite.

This beautiful little snipe is a rare straggler to Ceylon, having been recorded only a dozen times or so; doubtless it falls to snipe-shooters' guns more often than the published records suggest. It frequents similar localities to those favoured by Pintail Snipe, viz. weedy swamps, paddy-fields, and the like, and is usually solitary. Like other snipes, it is mainly nocturnal or crepuscular, spending the day crouching among damp herbage where its striped and mottled plumage gives it

---

[1] Since writing this I learn that Fernando shot another specimen of the Great Snipe, in a paddy-field at Nedimale, Dehiwela, near Colombo on 1 January 1950.

concealment. It is reluctant to rise, often remaining hidden until nearly trodden upon, when it springs up with startling suddenness, to drop into cover again within a short distance. It seldom utters any cry on rising, and the flight, though twisting, is slower than that of the larger snipes. It feeds on worms, insects, small molluscs, and certain seeds of swamp-plants, probing into mud for the first-named like other snipes.

× one-fifth

The Jack Snipe breeds in the more northerly parts of Europe and Asia, nesting on the ground in similar manner to other snipes. It migrates in winter to southern Europe, the northern half of Africa, and southern Asia.

THE PAINTED SNIPES
Family ROSTRATULIDAE

The painted snipes form a very small family, comprising only two species of snipe-like birds. One is confined to South America and the other—divided into two subspecies—is widely distributed in Africa, southern Asia, through the Malayan region, to Australia and Tasmania. While in general form they resemble the true snipes, on anatomical grounds they are regarded as a separate family with no very close relationship. The bill, though long and slender, is slightly curved downwards at the tip, which is hard, not soft and flexible as in the snipes; the wings are broad and ample, giving a different character to the flight, which is comparatively slow. The plumage is more colourful than snipes', and this is especially marked in the case of the female; for in these birds, as in the bustard-quails and a few other families of birds, the female is larger and more handsomely marked than the male and her behaviour is masculine. She does the fighting and courting, and leaves the male to incubate the eggs and rear the young.

In other respects—habitat, nesting, food, etc.—these birds resemble the snipes.

THE PAINTED SNIPE

Rostratula benghalensis benghalensis (Linnaeus). Resident

Sinhalese: Rājā-watuwā, Ulu-keswatuwā. Tamil: Ullān-kuruvi

Plate 25, facing p. 296
(standing, female; squatting, male; ×one-sixth)

About the size of the Pintail Snipe. The sexes differ as shown in the Plate, the female being the larger and more brightly coloured of the two sexes.

This handsome bird is found throughout the low country and the lower hills; but it moves about a good deal—sometimes common in a locality, at other times absent. It inhabits swamps, marshy ground and secluded corners of paddy-fields, specially favouring places where puddles of open water alternate with small clumps of bushes and grass-tussocks. It usually occurs in pairs, but occasionally in small wisps. In the day-time it lies close, waiting until nearly trodden upon before it springs into the air and flies, with curiously silent flapping flight, for a few yards before dropping again into cover; the flight is quite unlike that of the true snipes, and is much slower. Although mainly crepuscular or nocturnal, where it is undisturbed it will feed in the open until morning is well advanced. Its food consists of water insects, small snails, worms, and also grain, such as paddy. The call-note of the female is generally likened to the sound produced by softly blowing into the mouth of a bottle; that of the male is described as a squeak; but I have no personal experience of these notes. When cornered, the Painted Snipe displays in a remarkable manner, spreading the wings and tail forwards to form a brightly-spotted disk; at the same time a hiss is uttered. This display is also performed in courtship.

The domestic economy of this bird resembles that of the bustard-quail, in that the normal role of the sexes is largely reversed. The female, in keeping with her larger size and richer colouring, takes the active part in courtship, fighting others of her own sex for possession of the male and relegating to him all the duties of incubation and tending of the young; she is said to be polyandrous, but definite information on this point seems to be wanting. The main breeding season is from November to May. The nest is a solid pad of grass-blades, etc., placed on the ground, often in a small, more or less isolated, grass-tussock on the margin of a swamp or on a paddy-field bund. The four eggs are ochreous, thickly blotched with deep, rich brown. They measure about 35 × 24 mm.

THE TERNS AND GULLS
Family Laridae

These are water-frequenting birds, with webbed front toes, and long wings adapted for sustained and powerful flight. The great majority of them are coloured in beautiful soft greys and pure white, though many forms are predominantly brown. Most of them have distinct summer and winter plumages, and in many there is a black cap, which is more or less lost or reduced in winter; immature birds differ in coloration from adults to a greater or less extent. Their eggs are generally laid in mere scrapes, or slight nests on the ground, and are coloured and mottled to resemble their surroundings. The young are downy at first and, though they are capable of walking soon after birth, they do not follow their parents but stay in or near the nest. They are fed by regurgitation, until fledged. Many species nest in colonies.

Terns (sub-family *Sterninae*) are more slenderly built than gulls; their wings are very long, narrow, and acutely pointed, making them marvels of grace and beauty in the air, in which they spend most of their time. Their beaks are slender, acutely pointed, not at all hooked at the tip. In nearly all, the tail is more or less deeply forked and, in many species, the two outer feathers are elongated into long, tapering, narrow 'streamers', developed especially in the breeding season. The legs and feet are short and weak and, though webbed, are used very little by most species for swimming except in case of necessity. Terns mostly prefer to rest on solid objects—rocks, the seashore, or on posts, etc.—and their walk is, at best, a slow shuffle. They feed on fish and other water creatures, which they capture by swooping or plunging from the air, and swallow in flight. In strange contrast to their sylph-like forms, their voices are generally harsh and strident.

Gulls (sub-family *Larinae*) are heavier-built birds, with broader, more rounded wings, and longer and stronger legs. The beak is stout, and somewhat hooked at the tip of the upper mandible. The tail is nearly always square. Though wonderful fliers, they are less aerial than terns and frequently settle on water to rest, swimming very buoyantly. They also rest on the ground—where they walk freely and well—and some kinds habitually perch on elevated objects, such as mast-heads, etc. Gulls are less specialized feeders than terns and, though their main food is fish, they will eat carrion, scraps thrown from ships, etc. They mostly have very distinct juvenile and adult plumages, taking several years before becoming fully adult. The young are generally mottled brown.

In identifying adult gulls on the wing, the pattern of their wing-markings is of great assistance. All utter more or less harsh and raucous cries.

THE INDIAN WHISKERED TERN

Chlidonias hybrida indica (Stephens). Abundant winter visitor and summer loiterer

Sinhalese: Muhudu-lihiniyā. Tamil: Kadal-kuruvi. (These names—respectively signifying 'Sea-Swallow' and 'Sea-bird'—are generic names for all terns)

About the size of the Spotted Dove but slimmer, and with shorter tail and longer wings. Sexes alike. In winter plumage, which it wears during most of its time in Ceylon, the upperparts are very pale, ashy-grey—looking almost white in the distance—and the rest of the bird is white with a streaky, black cap on the back of the head; beak and legs reddish black, irides very dark brown. In summer plumage—which some birds begin to assume as early as the middle of February and nearly all are wearing by the time they leave the Island, in May or June—the entire cap, down to the level of the eyes, is glossy black; back, wings and tail, a deeper and purer grey than in winter; underparts, except the under tail-coverts, dark, but soft, bluish-grey—much darker than the back; chin and sides of the face to the nape, white, shading into the dark grey breast; edge of the outer tail-feathers, and the under tail- and wing-coverts white; bill and legs dark crimson. This and the next species are 'marsh-terns', frequenting mainly fresh water; they have shorter, broader wings than the salt-water terns, and their tails are only slightly forked, never developing long, narrow 'streamers'.

This is by far the commonest species of tern found in Ceylon; during the north-east monsoon it abounds at every low-country tank, swamp and paddy-field, and ascends the hills, on occasion, to at least the height of Kandy; but it is commonest near the seaboard. It lives either solitary or in flocks of varying size, preferring weedy, still, or slowly flowing waters; at times, however, it frequents sea-harbours and coastal lagoons. Over its chosen area it flies tirelessly at a height of a few feet, beating to and fro, bill pointed downward, in a lengthy search for food. This consists mainly of aquatic insects, tadpoles and small fish, which it captures, not usually by a determined plunge, as the sea-terns do, but by a graceful downward swoop, daintily picking the prey from the surface. It seldom, if ever, alights on the water but, when tired, rests

either on a paddy-field bund or the like, or perches on top of a stake. Its note, uttered very freely when it is excited—especially when a flock finds good hunting—is a shrill, craking sound; solitary birds are generally silent.

Winter plumage; × one-sixth

The Whiskered Tern is not known to breed in Ceylon, though it may yet be found to do so. This race nests freely in northern India and Kashmir, breeding in colonies on weedy or lotus-covered tanks and swamps. The nest is a rough pad of reeds, etc., more or less floating but supported by weeds. The two or three eggs are of varying tint, from pale olive, or olivaceous buff, to blue-green, marked in spots and blotches of some shade of brown; they measure about 39 × 28 mm.

THE WHITE-WINGED BLACK TERN

Chlidonias leucopterus (Temminck). Scarce winter visitor and summer loiterer

Sinhalese: Muhudu-lihiniyā. Tamil: Kadal-kuruvi

Slightly smaller than the Whiskered Tern, and with a smaller beak (1¼ against 1½ inches). Sexes alike. In winter plumage, this tern is practically indistinguishable in the field from the Whiskered Tern; though, according to Wait, its white forehead extends farther back, the black spots of the crown seldom coming farther forward than the eye, this would be impossible to assess under field conditions. In summer plumage the two are quite distinct, as this species becomes deep black throughout the head and body and the *under wing-coverts*; the rump, upper and under tail-coverts and tail are white; wings grey, paling to white on the lesser coverts which form a conspicuous white patch when the wing is folded, contrasting with the black breast and scapular-feathers. Bill black, with a crimson tinge; irides dark brown; legs orange-red.

This tern probably visits Ceylon in small numbers fairly regularly during the north-east monsoon; but, as it mingles freely in flocks of the Whiskered Tern and has almost identical habits and appearance, it escapes notice. In April or May, however, both species begin to assume their breeding dress, when the black under wing-coverts at once reveal the identity of this tern. It appears to prefer the dry zone, but otherwise its habitat coincides with that of the Whiskered Tern and it feeds in the same way, on similar prey. According to Legge its flight is swifter than that of its congener.

The White-winged Black Tern breeds in Europe and much of Asia, nesting in colonies in weedy swamps, in similar manner to the Whiskered Tern. It winters in Africa, southern Asia, and Australia.

THE GULL-BILLED TERN

Gelochelidon nilotica nilotica (Gmelin). Abundant winter visitor and summer loiterer

Sinhalese: Muhudu-lihiniyā. Tamil: Kadal-kuruvi

About the size of the Smaller Crested Tern. Sexes alike. A white tern with pale ashy-grey back and wings, comparatively short and not very deeply forked tail, and rather short and stout black bill; the legs also are black and the irides practically so. In breeding plumage, the whole cap is greenish-black; in winter plumage, it is mainly white, with a small black spot in front of the eye, another on the ear-coverts, and a variable amount of grey and black streaking on the crown and nape. Birds in winter plumage abound in Ceylon throughout the north-east monsoon and a good many loiter throughout the year; but some begin to assume the breeding dress as early as February and, by April, many are in full nuptial plumage.

This beautiful tern is very common in all the coastal districts of the dry zone but is only occasionally seen in the wet zone. Although not averse from the seashore it prefers fresh or brackish

Upper, breeding plumage; lower, winter plumage; × two-fifths

waters not far from the sea, lagoons, estuaries, tidal creeks, and wet paddy-fields. Over such places it flies, usually solitary or in small scattered flocks, with steady, direct flight, every now and then dipping, in a rather leisurely manner, to scoop up some small animal; for it seldom plunges for its prey as the more seagoing terns do. It feeds largely on such things as water insects, small prawns, crabs and frogs, as well as on small fish. By no means shy, it will often fly around one well within gunshot, scolding with cries of *wik, kuwikkeewik* or a high-pitched *hik . . . hikhikhikhikhik*; it has other notes, but on the whole is rather silent during its stay in Ceylon. When fed, it rests on sandbanks, paddy-field bunds and the like, often in company with other terns; I have never seen it perching on stakes as the Whiskered Tern commonly does.

This race of the Gull-billed Tern breeds in a great part of Europe, north Africa and central Asia; it has not yet been found breeding in Ceylon but may possibly do so. It nests in colonies on sand or mud-banks on the shores of lagoons, etc., the nest being a slight hollow in the earth, scantily lined with grass or other handy vegetation. The three eggs are buff or cream, sparsely speckled with some shade of brown, and they measure about $49 \cdot 3 \times 35 \cdot 4$ mm.

THE CASPIAN TERN

Hydroprogne caspia (Pallas). Common winter visitor, and summer resident in small numbers

Sinhalese: Mā-muhudu-lihiniyā. Tamil: Periya Kadal-kuruvi

Plate 27, facing p. 312 (breeding plumage; × one-eighth)

Rather larger than the Black Crow, and with much longer wings. Sexes alike. The bird shown in the Plate is in breeding plumage, with black cap; in winter plumage, the crown and nape are grey, streaked with black, and the lores and ear-coverts are mostly black; otherwise as in summer plumage.

This splendid bird, the largest of all terns, is common but not abundant around the coasts of the northern half of the Island, and is occasionally seen in the Hambantota district but only casually elsewhere. Its large size, combined with the strong, vermilion beak, black legs, and rather short tail, make it unmistakable. It patronizes the sea coast, being partial to estuaries and lagoons, and is usually seen flying singly or in pairs, with a stately and measured flight, a little way out from the shore-line; but where fishing is good, a number will collect, often in company with other terns and gulls, to feed. It has a habit, especially when fishing solitarily, of hovering with steadily beating wings, legs dangling, and beak pointing straight downwards, over some spot in the water which interests it. Fish, up to six or seven inches long, form its main food, and it plunges for them, sometimes completely submerging. Unlike most terns, it settles rather freely on water, but prefers resting on sandbanks, etc.; this it does often in companies of its own and other species. Though usually silent, it has a variety of notes among which I have heard: (*a*) a feeble squeak or whistle, not unlike the word *wheeze* (probably uttered by young birds); (*b*) a harsh cry *krwekiair*, repeated several times by a bird flying along a lagoon shore; (*c*) a loud squawk *kuwow, kuwow*—a startling sound which is probably an alarm, or a scolding note. Legge says that it frequently utters a harsh, loud note like *krake-krà*; I have heard one utter this while mobbing a Great Black-headed Gull which had robbed it of a fish.

The Caspian Tern has a very wide breeding-range, almost throughout the temperate and tropical regions of the world where conditions are suitable. It breeds not only on sea coasts but also on the shores of big inland lakes. A few pairs nest in May and June on sandbanks of Adam's Bridge, between Mannar Island and Rameswaram. The nest is a mere scrape made by the birds in the sand. The one to three eggs are greyish-buff, blotched and speckled sparingly with dark brown and grey, and they measure about 63 × 43·5 mm.

THE SMALLER CRESTED TERN

Thalasseus bengalensis (Lesson). Abundant winter visitor, and summer loiterer

Sinhalese: Muhudu-lihiniyā. Tamil: Kadal-kuruvi

About the size of a domestic pigeon, but with much longer wings. Sexes alike. From the Large Crested Tern (next species), which it resembles in general colour-scheme, it may easily be distinguished by: (*a*) its smaller size—roughly three-quarters; (*b*) its paler grey back and mantle; (*c*) its *orange* beak; (*d*) in summer plumage, by the black of its cap extending forwards to the base of the beak. The orange beak at once distinguishes it from the Gull-billed Tern, which is about the same size.

Throughout the north-east monsoon this is one of our commonest terns, abounding all round the coasts; but from May to September the majority disappear, though a few loiterers, in non-breeding plumage, remain throughout the south-west monsoon. It is a sea-tern, habitually fishing in salt water, though it will visit lagoons and even freshwater lakes and estuaries near the coast. It is very common in Colombo and other harbours, where it finds ideal resting-places on the mooring-buoys and breakwaters which it shares with its larger relative, the next species. A very sociable bird, it often feeds and usually rests in flocks; but in spite of this sociability it is very quarrelsome, resenting any attempt by its companions to alight on the same rock or buoy—greeting them with raucous screams and vicious pecks. Once, however, a bird has succeeded in gaining a footing among the crowd it is generally left

in peace. It is a very skilful fisher, its usual method being to fly at a height of fifteen to thirty feet above the sea until it espies a fish below; then it plunges vertically, usually submerging itself completely, to emerge in a second or two with the fish struggling in its beak. A quick shake to rid itself of moisture, and then the fish is swallowed on the wing, head first. Small herrings are a favourite prey, and when fisher-

Winter plumage; × one-third

men's seines are being drawn these terns have a royal time, screaming and plunging into the seething mass of fish, feeding until they can hold no more. They are very noisy, uttering a variety of harsh, rasping crakes. The flight is very swift and graceful, performed with regular, and rather leisurely strokes of the long, pointed, and narrow wings. When resting, the crest is raggedly erected but is depressed in flight.

The Smaller Crested Tern breeds on sandy islands and banks in the Red Sea and the Persian Gulf, and also in Australia. It is possible that, as Legge suggests, the non-breeding birds that spend the south-west monsoon in Ceylon may belong to the Australian population, and be really 'wintering' in the Island.

THE LARGE CRESTED TERN

Thalasseus bergii velox (Cretzschmar). Resident

Sinhalese: Muhudu-lihiniyā. Tamil: Kadal-kuruvi

Plate 27, facing p. 312 (breeding plumage; × one-eighth)

Between the Smaller Crested and the Caspian Terns in size. Sexes alike. Breeding plumage is shown in the Plate. In winter plumage, the front part of the crown is white, spotted with black. Beak pale *greenish-yellow*; irides nearly black; legs black, with a variable amount of yellow on the soles and hock-joint. The size, beak-colour, and darker, more smoky-grey back and wings, distinguish this from the Smaller Crested Tern with which it often associates.

333

This fine tern is common around the coasts of Ceylon, especially during the south-west monsoon. Being a true sea-tern it often fishes far from land and, though it sometimes frequents coastal lagoons and estuaries, it never goes far inland or fishes in fresh water. Its favourite haunts are the neighbourhood of rocky islets but it takes kindly to man's harbours, with their breakwaters and mooring-buoys, which, like the last species, it uses freely as resting-places, often crowding on a buoy—usually in company with the Smaller Crested Tern—until not another bird can find a foothold. Each newcomer has to fight for its right to perch, and much raucous screaming goes on. For some reason, a buoy or rock that has terns already on it appears to have greater attractions than an unoccupied one of apparently equal suitability. When fishing, however, this tern is not so gregarious as its smaller congener, often fishing in ones or twos, and its plunge is comparatively clumsy, though quite effective in catching fish. It will settle on the sea, for resting, when far from land; but not if rocks or other stable perches are available. Fish, up to six inches long, appear to form its entire diet.

The breeding season in Ceylon is in April, May and June. Breeding colonies exist on some sandbanks of Adam's Bridge and on rocky islets off the Southern Province. I believe, too, that breeding takes place on the shores of some of the Hambantota lewayas (salt-pans), as I have seen many there in full breeding plumage, in June, flying inland carrying fish in their beaks. A single egg is laid on bare sand, without any nest or even a scratched hollow. The eggs are greyish-white, blotched or speckled variously with sepia, and measure about 62×43 mm.

THE TIBETAN COMMON TERN

Sterna hirundo tibetana Saunders (probably other races of the Common Tern sometimes visit Ceylon). Occasional winter visitor

Sinhalese: Muhudu-lihiniyā. Tamil: Kadal-kuruvi

About the size of the Gull-billed Tern, but slimmer, and with much longer tail streamers. Sexes alike. A slender, graceful sea-tern, with long narrowly-tapering outer tail-feathers. In size, build, and general coloration, it closely resembles the Roseate Tern (next species), from which, in winter plumage, it would be very difficult to distinguish in the field; it is, however, somewhat deeper grey on the upperparts, and the outer web of the tail-streamers is grey, not white as in the Roseate. In breeding plumage, the entire cap is black (white on the forehead in winter), and the underparts from the breast downwards are very delicate grey. Bill scarlet with black tip in summer, nearly all black in winter; irides dark brown; legs vermilion-red.

This tern is an irregular winter visitor to the coasts of Ceylon, arriving in considerable numbers in some years, but in most being absent. So far, it appears to have been collected only on the north-west and north-east coasts, but I have seen what I believe was this species at Mount Lavinia, seven miles south of Colombo. In general, its habits resemble those of the Lesser Crested Tern; it is sociable with its kind, given to resting in companies on sea-rocks, and fishes in the same manner, plunging vertically with half-closed wings from heights of fifteen to thirty feet and almost, or quite, submerging itself in the process. It is noisy, uttering a large variety of more or less harsh cries, especially when fishing in company; one of these cries, by which, according to Legge, the species may always be identified from other terns when fishing in a mixed flock, is a piping, metallic-sounding *twink*. Although partial to estuaries, it does not normally visit inland waters while in its winter range. Its food consists entirely of marine life, mostly fish, though it will eat crustaceans and molluscs as well.

The Common Tern breeds in many parts of Europe, Asia, and North America, not only in coastal areas but also about great inland lakes; the present subspecies repairs to Tibet and Turkestan for this purpose. It nests in large colonies, laying its eggs on sand, gravel, or dry mud, with a variable amount of nest-material. The two to four eggs are stone-colour, grey or brown, spotted and blotched with dark brown and grey, and they measure about 41 × 30 mm. The birds are very noisy and demonstrative at their breeding colonies, and they will attack marauding animals, birds and even humans with great courage, diving upon them with stabbing beaks.

THE EASTERN ROSEATE TERN

Sterna dougallii korustes (Hume). Summer (breeding) visitor

Sinhalese: Muhudu-lihiniyā. Tamil: Kadal-kuruvi

Plate 27, facing p. 312 (breeding plumage; × one-eighth)

About the same length as the Gull-billed Tern, or the Smaller Crested Tern, but more slenderly built than either. Sexes alike. This loveliest of terns may be identified by its slender, graceful form; very long and narrow, *white* tail-streamers; pale, pearly-grey back and wings; bill black, with vermilion-red at the base, varying from a mere trace to half the bill; legs scarlet or vermilion; the underparts suffused with a variable amount of delicate pink which quickly fades in preserved specimens.

The Roseate Tern, which in several racial forms inhabits the coasts of much of the globe, visits Ceylon, for the purpose of breeding, during the south-west monsoon and is seldom or never seen during the rest of the year. During its stay it seldom strays far from its nesting-places, which are rocky islets off the coasts of the Southern and Eastern Provinces, and sandbanks off Mannar Island. Essentially a marine tern, it never goes inland but is quite at home among the roaring surf of the sea coast. Like other sea-terns, it is a very expert fisher, plunging from a height upon small fishes when they come near the surface and often immersing its body, to emerge a moment later with the fish in its bill. The flight is very buoyant and graceful. While fishing, it frequently utters a musical note *chew-it*; the alarm-, or scold-note, however, is a rasping *aaak*.

On the above-mentioned islets, the Roseate Tern breeds in March to June, often in company with the Large Crested Tern, though its colonies are more or less separate from those of its big relative. The nest is a scrape in sand, or among scanty grass, etc., slightly decorated with a few scraps of grass, bits of shells, and the like. The two eggs are variable in colouring, from olive-brown to greenish-grey, speckled with dark brown and grey. They measure about $41 \times 29 \cdot 5$ mm. As usual with terns, the birds are very noisy and demonstrative at their nesting-grounds, especially when an intruder appears on the scene.

THE LITTLE TERN

Sterna albifrons sinensis Gmelin. (White-shafted Little Tern.) Resident

Sterna albifrons saundersi Hume. (Black-shafted Little Tern.) Status doubtful; see Whistler, *Spolia Zeylanica*, 23, p. 271; and Legge, p. 1023

Sinhalese: Muhudu-lihiniyā. Tamil: Kadal-kuruvi

Plate 27, facing p. 312
(White-shafted Little Tern, breeding plumage; × one-eighth)

Considerably smaller than the Whiskered Tern and more slenderly built, with narrower wings. Sexes alike. In winter plumage, the white forehead extends farther back, and its hind border is less clear-cut than in summer; the tail is shorter; the lesser wing-coverts become dark grey, forming a dark edge to the wing. In *sinensis*, the two outer primaries are blackish with white inner edges, the shaft of the first being white, that of the second partly white; in *saundersi*, the shafts of these feathers are black or dark brown. Bill yellow, with the tip black; irides nearly black; legs dusky yellow in winter, orange in breeding plumage. Immature birds have the back and wing-coverts spotted with brown, the bill brown, legs brownish-yellow.

This pretty tern, our smallest, is abundant along the coasts of the dry zone and, in the breeding season, also inland around the larger tanks; but it visits the wet zone only occasionally. It frequents lagoons, tidal creeks, lakes, etc., as well as the open seashore. An interesting bird to watch, its flight is fast and lively, performed with quick strokes of the narrow wings—quite a different style from that of the Whiskered Tern. It usually fishes solitary or in widely-scattered flocks, and is given to hovering with rapidly winnowing wings over some promising spot, after the manner of the Pied Kingfisher. When suitable prey is seen, it is captured by a brisk plunge, the bird immediately rising again to continue its hunting. It feeds mainly on small fish, but prawns are also eaten, and doubtless aquatic insects do not come amiss.

The white-shafted race breeds freely in Ceylon in small colonies on sea-beaches, dry mud-flats, gravelly shores of tanks, etc., from May to August—the former being the favourite month. When courting, the male catches a small fish which he dangles in his beak while walking around the female, turning his head from side to side to the accompaniment of much chattering by the couple (somewhat similar behaviour in courtship is common to many terns). The two to three eggs are laid in a shallow scrape, with little pretence of lining, on open ground or thin grass with no attempt at concealment; the sitting bird can be seen from afar and usually a number incubate at the same time, scattered over a space of an acre or so. The eggs are greenish or ochreous-grey, with purplish-grey clouds and dark brown blotches; they measure about $32 \cdot 7 \times 24 \cdot 3$ mm. The birds mob intruders with incessant cries of *tchik tchik tchik*.

THE BROWN-WINGED TERN, or BRIDLED TERN

Sterna anaethetus anaethetus Scopoli. Regular winter visitor

Sinhalese: Muhudu-lihiniyā. Tamil: Kadal-kuruvi

Slightly smaller than the Gull-billed and Smaller Crested Terns. Sexes alike. Forehead, supercilium passing beyond the eye, face, entire underparts, and underwing, white; the rest of the bird sooty-brown, darker on head and wings, paler and greyer on mantle. Beak black; irides black; legs black. The above description is of the winter plumage, which it wears while in Ceylon; in breeding plumage, the crown, lores and nape become deep black, sharply defined from the white portions of the head, and the hind-neck becomes a clear grey, shading into the mantle; in both phases of plumage, the outer web of the outer tail-feathers is more or less white. From the Sooty Tern (next species) this

× one-third

may be distinguished by its longer white supercilium, greyish hind collar, and greyish-brown, not black, mantle; it is also considerably smaller.

The Brown-winged Tern is a regular winter visitor to the coasts of Ceylon, arriving in September and October and leaving again—so far as my observations go—in January and February; but, being an oceanic tern which seldom comes in shore except under stress of heavy weather, it is seldom seen by landsmen. During its stay, it is, however, by no means rare from one to twenty miles off the coast. At least in winter, it is not a very sociable species, often fishing alone, though flocks of five or six are not unusual. It feeds largely on *Halobates*—a small, silvery-grey bug of the 'pond-skater' type, abounding in tropical seas, which scuds along the surface, looking like a drop of quicksilver. In addition to a mass of these, one which I dissected contained a green 'stink-bug' (*Nezara* sp.) which had doubtless been blown out to sea. In other parts of the world, it is said to feed on small, surface-swimming fish, crustaceans and molluscs. It commonly rests on floating objects—billets of wood and the like—and I have several times seen one settled on a floating mass of

Sargassum seaweed; but it readily takes advantage of the spars of boats and ships for roosting on at night. When so perched it may easily be captured by hand owing to its unfamiliarity with the ways of man. Its flight is very graceful and buoyant, but not very swift as a rule, and it usually scoops up its prey from the surface, not plunging determinedly as some terns do. The only note I have heard it utter is a harsh craking, when seized in the hand.

This tern is distributed, in several races, almost throughout the seas of the tropics. It breeds on rocky islands; our birds probably nest in the Seychelles, Maldives or Laccadives, where breeding colonies are known to exist. The single egg is laid on bare ground or rock, in a cranny, or under vegetation.

THE SOOTY TERN

Sterna fuscata fuscata Linnaeus. Rare straggler to Ceylon

Sinhalese: Muhudu-lihiniyā. Tamil: Kadal-kuruvi

About the size of the Smaller Crested Tern. Sexes alike. From the Brown-winged Tern, which it somewhat resembles in colour-scheme, it may be distinguished by its larger size; *black* upperparts, with no pale hind-collar; more obliquely descending black loreal stripe; white supercilium not passing backwards beyond the middle of the eye. Bill, irides, and legs black. In juvenile plumage, this tern is sooty brown almost throughout, with whitish tips to the scapulars, wing-coverts, and upper tail-coverts; in this plumage it might be mistaken for the Philippine Noddy (see next species), but the bill is more slender, the forehead and crown not white, and the tail is deeply forked (wedge-shaped in the noddy).

× one-third

This tern, the 'Wide-awake' of sailors, is a very occasional visitor to Ceylon,[1] although it is distributed, in several races, throughout the seas of the tropics. It is a deep-sea tern, ranging over the oceans and never, except accidentally, visiting fresh waters; but it is seldom seen at

---

[1] There are two records of this tern finding its way into the Ceylon hills, at heights of about 4,000 and 3,500 feet, in the Central and Uva Provinces respectively. See Phillips, *Checklist*, p. 49.

distances greater than a hundred miles or so from land of some kind, such as small rocky islets. It breeds in large colonies—often many thousands of pairs—on oceanic islands, coral-reefs, etc., laying its single egg on the ground, with very little attempt at a nest, in close proximity with those of its companions. A 'Wide-awake Fair', as these nesting places are called, is a noisy scene, as it is very demonstrative and aggressive at its breeding-grounds.

In general habits and behaviour it closely resembles the Brown-winged Tern, and fishes in the same way, picking its prey from the surface of the sea and seldom plunging. Most of the Ceylon records have been in the south-west monsoon, during stormy periods when the birds were doubtless forced inshore by stress of weather. The nearest breeding places to Ceylon are in the Seychelles, Maldives, Laccadives and Andaman Islands, and no doubt our birds come from one or more of these colonies.

THE PHILIPPINE NODDY

Anous stolidus pileatus (Scopoli). Very rare straggler to Ceylon

No Sinhalese or Tamil names

About the size of the Smaller Crested Tern. Sexes alike. A dark sooty-brown tern, with white forehead gradually shading into the greyish-brown of the nape; a black spot in front of the eye; tail *wedge-shaped* (in all other Ceylon terns it is forked). Bill black; irides dark brown; legs brownish-fleshy, webs paler.

This tern, which is found in several races throughout the seas of the tropics is only a casual straggler to Ceylon. It is an oceanic bird, ranging far from land except in the breeding season, when it repairs to barren rocky islands or coral reefs for nesting. According to Legge, it behaves more like a petrel

× one-eighth

than a tern, alighting on the water to feed on the marine surface organisms that form its food. Its flight is swift and enduring.

In their breeding haunts noddies congregate in large numbers and build nests of sticks, etc., either on low bushes or on the ground; or if nesting materials be absent they will lay their eggs on bare soil or rock. The nearest nesting colony to Ceylon appears to be the Cherbaniani Reef, in the Laccadive Islands.

THE GREAT BLACK-HEADED GULL

Larus ichthyaetus Pallas. Regular winter visitor

Sinhalese: Muhudu-kaputā. Tamil: Kadal-kākkai

Plate 27, facing p. 312 (breeding plumage; ×one-eighth)

Size of a large domestic cock, but much longer in the wing. Sexes alike. The breeding plumage, which is worn from January onwards, is shown on the Plate; winter plumage of adult similar, except that the black of the head is confined to a streaky patch around the eye and ear-coverts, and streaks on the crown and nape. In flight the wing shows white on both leading and trailing edges, that of the leading edge broadening to include most of the outer six primaries and their coverts; the tips of all the primaries are white, followed on the six longest by a more or less broken black band crossing the wing near the tip. In juvenile plumage the head is mottled greyish; back and wings mottled brown, darkest on the ends of the primaries and the entire secondaries; rump, upper tail-coverts, and tail white, with a broad, subterminal black band on the latter; underparts greyish-white. This plumage gradually changes to that of the adult.

This splendid big gull was long believed to be a mere occasional straggler to Ceylon but, of recent years, it has been found to be a regular winter visitor to the northern coasts and lagoons from November to April. Though usually solitary, it congregates at times, for resting and preening, in flocks up to several hundred on sand-spits or tidal flats. The flight is steady and majestic, and the bird is fond of flying along the coast above the line of breakers. On perceiving a shoal of fish, it hovers, with rather slowly beating wings and dangling legs, finally plunging like a tern—though, of course, without the airy grace of the latter. In spite of its normal leisurely style it is capable of speed and adroitness; I once watched one chase a Caspian Tern, following all its turns and twists until it compelled it to drop a fish which the gull caught before it reached the sea. Its food consists mainly of fish but, like most gulls, it will eat almost any small animal it can catch, and also carrion. At rest, it has a stout, bull-necked appearance, very different from other large gulls; the snowy white collar is conspicuous and the primaries project a comparatively short distance beyond the secondaries. When in a flock it produces loud gaggling cries suggestive of a flock of geese, and occasional yelps like the commencing notes of a jackals' chorus.

The Great Black-headed Gull breeds in south Russia and central Asia. It nests in colonies on sand-spits and islands of big rivers and lakes, laying its eggs in slight hollows scraped in the sand, without any proper nest. The two or three eggs are yellowish-grey, boldly streaked with dark brown.

THE BROWN-HEADED GULL

Larus brunneicephalus Jerdon. Abundant winter visitor

Sinhalese: Muhudu-kaputā. Tamil: Kadal-kākkai

Plate 27, facing p. 312 (breeding plumage; ×one-eighth)

About the size of the House Crow but with much longer wings. Sexes alike. The bird shown on the Plate is in summer plumage; this begins to appear by the end of March and nearly all are wearing it by the time they leave Ceylon in April and May. In winter the head is white with a black spot in front of the eye, a dark grey spot on the ear-coverts, and usually two pale grey bands crossing the crown; one from the hinder part of the eye, and the other a little farther back; otherwise as in summer. In flight, the wing shows a long black tip comprising the greater part of the outer three primaries and the tips of the next three or four, diminishing inwards; the outer two primaries each have a big white spot near the tips.

This bird, which is the only common gull in Ceylon, is abundant throughout the north-east monsoon on the coasts of the northern half of the Island; less common in the south-east, and rare in most parts of the south-west though it visits the Colombo harbour in considerable numbers at times. There it contests with House Crows and Brahminy Kites for scraps of food thrown overboard from ships. From all terns it may easily be distinguished by its broader, more rounded wings, slower flight, and habit of resting on the water, on which it swims readily, floating buoyantly. It also walks with ease. In winter quarters—e.g. Ceylon—it is strictly confined to the seaboard and adjacent lagoons and estuaries, never going far inland; this seems strange as its breeding-grounds are on the great lakes of Central Asia, thousands of miles from the sea. It is not shy and, like most gulls, is very gregarious, usually seen in flocks. It does not often plunge for fish after the manner of terns but either picks them from near the surface, or else alights on the water and immerses its head to seize its prey. Besides fish, it feeds on crabs, prawns, molluscs, etc., and on almost any animal substance it finds floating. The usual note—frequently uttered when competing with its companions for food—is a grating *krā-krāā*.

THE LESSER BLACK-BACKED GULL
(Dark-backed Herring Gull of Wait)

Larus fuscus (*taimyrensis* Buturlin). (*Larus argentatus heuglini* Bree—Phillips, *Checklist*). Very rare straggler to Ceylon

Sinhalese: Muhudu-kaputā. Tamil: Kadal-kākkai

About the size of a domestic duck but with longer legs and much longer wings. Sexes alike. In adult plumage, pure white on head, neck, entire underparts, rump and tail; the back and wings are slate-grey with bold, white, crescentic tips to the longest scapulars; all the quills white-tipped, forming a white edge to the wing in flight; bill yellow, with a red spot on the lower mandible near the tip; irides nearly white; legs pale yellow. In juvenile plumage the bird is mottled brown, paler below; beak fleshy-black; legs pale fleshy. This plumage passes into the adult phase by complicated stages, spread over several years.

The only definite records of this gull from Ceylon are those given by Wait, viz. three specimens, all immature, taken at Negombo, Hambantota and Beruwela (opposite Barberyn Island). In its habits it does not greatly differ from the Brown-headed Gull, though, being much larger, it is more aggressive and predatory, attacking terns, etc., to force them to relinquish food for it to retrieve. Its flight is easy and graceful, and it swims readily, floating high out of the water, and also walks well. In addition to fish and other marine organisms, it eats carrion and almost any garbage, being much given to following ships for the sake of the food thrown overboard. A bird of inshore waters, it seldom ventures far from land, but it will frequent coastal lagoons and the like. It utters various raucous croaks, especially when in a flock competing for food.

This race of the widely-distributed Lesser Black-backed Gull breeds in north Europe and Siberia, nesting in colonies on the ground, or on ledges of sea-cliffs, etc.

THE SKUAS
Family STERCORARIIDAE

Skuas are gull-like sea-birds, of powerful flight and savage, predatory habits; they are characteristic mainly of the high northern and southern regions of the globe, but they have a tendency to wander to warmer regions in winter. All of them have the upper plumage, at least, largely brown, but some species have a light phase in which the underparts are white. From gulls, they may be distinguished by the bill, of which the upper mandible has the tip strongly hooked and the basal half covered by a horny cere; and by the claws, which are very strong, sharp and curved. These features give a clue to the habits of skuas; they live largely by either robbing other sea-birds of their prey—chasing and harrying them relentlessly until they disgorge it—or else by stealing their eggs and young; but they also catch fish for themselves, and do not despise carrion. Two species have turned up in Ceylon as rare stragglers, one of them, in two racial forms, from the Antarctic, and a single specimen of another species from the northern regions.

THE ANTARCTIC SKUA

Stercorarius skua antarctica (Lesson). Two specimens recorded

McCORMICK'S SKUA

Stercorarius skua mccormickii Saunders. One or two specimens recorded

No Sinhalese or Tamil names

About the size of a domestic duck. Sexes alike. These two subspecies may be described as large brown birds, with webbed feet, and long, pointed wings. From immature gulls (in brown plumage) they are discriminated by bill and claw characters as given above; from any of the shearwaters, for which they might be mistaken, they can at once be distinguished by not having the nostrils in a tube on top of the bill but under the front edge of the cere; moreover, the bill is not so strongly hooked as it is in shearwaters. These two forms are southern races of the Great Skua, which has other races in the northern regions of the globe. They inhabit the coasts and islands of the southern oceans, and their appearance in Ceylon must be regarded as merely accidental.

A single specimen of the POMATORHINE SKUA *Stercorarius pomarinus* (Temminck) was captured at Colombo in 1912. This gull-like bird is about the size of the House Crow. It has two colour forms: one is dark brown throughout; the other is white on lower part of head, neck and underparts, suffused with pale yellow on sides of head and neck, and usually with brown barring across the breast in adults and throughout the underparts in juveniles. Bill yellowish-brown, tip black; irides black-brown; legs and feet black with some grey on tarsus and webs. In adults the two centre tail-feathers are twice the length of the rest, and are curiously twisted at the tips so that their vanes are vertical.

This is a northern species, breeding in the Arctic regions on tundras, and in winter ranging over the seas of the northern hemisphere. Like other skuas, it obtains much of its food by harrying other sea-birds and robbing them of their prey. Its flight is swift and powerful, and very adroit when it is chasing a victim.

RAILS, CRAKES, WATERHENS, AND COOTS

Order RALLIFORMES

THIS order comprises small or medium-sized water-birds, characterized by their soft, rather loose plumage, hen-like build, long legs and toes; the latter four in number, with the hind one well developed. The wings are short and rounded, in most species used but little, though some undertake long, migratory flights. The tail is short and is often cocked and flirted. They can all swim well, though usually rather slowly owing to the absence of webs between the toes; but they are typically birds of reedy swamps, adapted for threading their way through tangled vegetation. Most of them are excessively shy and wary, largely nocturnal, and spend most of their time skulking about in cover; in consequence of this secretive nature many species are among the most difficult of birds to make acquaintance with. They are generally omnivorous in diet, feeding on both animal and vegetable substances. In general, they are inclined to be noisy, uttering a variety of strange cackles and roars, grunts, etc., whereby their presence in a swamp is often betrayed, even though the birds themselves may seldom be seen. They nest in reed-beds and the like, building large nests of reeds, etc., often in very damp situations. The young are clothed in black down and can walk and swim almost as soon as they are hatched.

The Ceylon list includes ten species of these birds, but one of these is rather doubtful, and the status of some others is uncertain.

THE INDIAN WATER RAIL

Rallus aquaticus indicus Blyth. Only once recorded

No Sinhalese or Tamil names

Slightly smaller than the White-breasted Waterhen, of more slender build, and with longer, slimmer bill, but otherwise of similar shape. The upperparts (head, neck, back, rump, tail and wings) are olivaceous-brown, with centres of feathers dark sooty-brown, giving a spotted and streaked effect; the lores, face, supercilium, sides of head and neck, and the under surface from chin to lower breast, pale, bluish-grey; abdomen and flanks sooty-black with narrow, white cross-bands; centre of lower abdomen and sides of under tail-coverts biscuit-colour; rest of under tail-coverts white; irides red; bill brown, with the basal half of the lower mandible bright red; legs and feet fleshy-brown.

This rail, the eastern race of the European Water Rail, breeds in eastern Asia, and winters in India. The only record of its occurrence in Ceylon is one by Layard, about a hundred years ago; he was given a few specimens which had been shot in the Ja-ela paddy-fields. Since then the species has never turned up, so it must be regarded as the merest straggler to Ceylon. It is a very shy, skulking bird which dwells in dense reed-beds or the like, and seldom shows itself for more than a second or so, as it darts across some open gap in the reeds. It would probably be silent while wintering in the Island, but in its breeding-grounds it is a noisy bird, producing a large assortment of weird grunts, groans and squeals from the depths of its reedy haunts. It should be looked for during the north-east monsoon, in swamps and paddy-fields.

THE BLUE-BREASTED BANDED RAIL

Hypotaenidia striata gularis (Horsfield). Resident

Sinhalese: Kiri-meti Korowakā. Tamil: Kānān-koli

Plate 28, facing p. 313 (×one-fifth)

About the size of the Common Mynah, or of the better-known Banded Crake. Sexes alike.

This rail appears to be less of a skulker than some of its family. It is probably partly resident and partly a winter visitor from India, but its status and movements require a great deal of study before they will be satisfactorily known. Such records as exist indicate that it occurs in all zones of the Island up to 6,000 feet. Legge found it inhabiting dense herbage on the shores of small islets in the Negombo Lagoon and observed that it would feed along the edge of tidal water, allowing approach to within gunshot before running for cover. Up-country, it frequents swamps and paddy-fields. Mrs Lushington records its notes as a staccato cluck, and it also utters a grunting sound. Its food consists of small insects, molluscs, etc., and doubtless, also seeds and grain.

Wait obtained its eggs in December in the North Western Province, and in August and September in the Galle district. He describes the nest as 'a pad of flattened down grass-stalks on the edge of a paddy-field'. The five to eight eggs are 'pinky white, rather sparingly spotted, chiefly at the larger end, with reddish brown and pale greyish purple. Average size 1·35 by 1·02' (=about 34·8×26 mm.).

BAILLON'S CRAKE

Porzana pusilla pusilla (Pallas). Rare winter visitor

Sinhalese: Punchi-korowakā. Tamil: Sinna Kānān-kōli

Plate 28, facing p. 313 (×one-fifth)

Size of a quail. Sexes alike. This small crake has been recorded from Ceylon only on a few occasions in the last hundred years. It probably visits the Island much more frequently than the records suggest but is overlooked owing to its secretive habits and the difficulty of penetrating the densely tangled and boggy swamps that it favours as a habitat. Possibly some birds may be resident. It is hard to put up, but when it can be induced to fly it does so very much after the manner of a quail—springing into the air, flying a few yards and dropping again into the reeds. Like all rails and crakes, it can thread its way through close vegetation with great skill and speed. It feeds on various swamp insects and on seeds and other vegetable substances. It is said to produce a grunting sound.

The nest is made of rushes, etc., and is well hidden among grass-tussocks and the like, in very swampy ground or sometimes actually floating on water. Five to eight eggs are laid; they are pale olive, marked with dark brown, and measure about 29·5×22·3 mm.

THE BANDED CRAKE

Rallina eurizonoides nigrolineata (Gray). Regular winter visitor

Sinhalese: Kiri-meti Korowakā. Tamil: Kānān-kōli

Plate 28, facing p. 313 (male; ×one-fifth)

About the size of the Spotted Dove, but with a short tail and long legs and toes. Sexes much alike but the female has the top of the head and back of the neck brown, like the back, and her face and breast are paler chestnut.

348

This crake arrives on the west coast of Ceylon from India about October and November, and leaves again before April. It is probably the best known of the Ceylon crakes and rails owing to its propensity for blundering into human dwellings along the sea front on its arrival; exhausted by its long flight across the sea, it takes refuge in the first place that offers shelter, and often gets captured in consequence. Those that avoid this fate promptly disappear up-country, where they take up residence in swampy jungles and thickets at any elevation up to 5,000 feet. Once settled, they are seldom seen, being skulking birds of mainly nocturnal habits. This crake runs well, but its ordinary gait is a jerky, high-stepping walk, with the short tail erected and jerked at every step; at night it becomes active, flying and clambering about bushes and trees. It feeds on earth-worms, grasshoppers and other insects, and also grain and seeds. Mrs Lushington describes the call-note as 'a long, drumming croak, *krrrrrrrrr-ar-kraa-kraa-kraa-kraa*' uttered just before dusk; I have not heard this, but captive birds have uttered a low churr and, at night when alarmed, a subdued *kok kok*.

The nest, as found in India, is described as a 'fairly large structure of dead leaves and sticks placed in bushes in scrub-jungle. Four to eight eggs are laid. The colour is a creamy white and the texture close. Average size 1·35 by 1·03.'—Wait ($=34 \times 26 \cdot 2$ mm.).

THE RUDDY CRAKE

Amaurornis fuscus fuscus (Linnaeus). Status uncertain; probably mainly a winter migrant, but partly resident in Ceylon

Sinhalese: Punchi-korowakā. Tamil: Kānān-kōli

Plate 28, facing p. 313 (× one-fifth)

Smaller than the Common Mynah. Sexes alike. In shape this small crake is similar to its cousin, the White-breasted Waterhen, but its coloration is very different. It may be distinguished from all other Ceylonese rails and crakes by its orange-red legs. It has been found in scattered localities both in the low country and in the hills to over 4,000 feet; but it is very little known and it seems probable that normally it is a winter migrant in small numbers with a few pairs occasionally remaining to breed. It frequents swamps and well-grown paddy-fields and, although secretive like all crakes, it is less shy than some and will walk about the edges of reed-beds, or venture short distances from dense cover, while feeding. Its flight is slow and fluttering. Nothing seems to be on record concerning its notes or its food but it is probably inclined to be noisy in the breeding season, while it doubtless eats small animals—worms, insects, etc.—and some vegetable matter; definite observations on these points are much to be desired.

The nest is generally placed in grass and herbage bordering paddy-field bunds and similar places. It is composed of reeds and grass, and is placed on the ground, or almost floating in water. The three to five eggs are whitish-buff, marked with purplish-grey and brown. They measure about 31 × 21·6 mm.

THE WHITE-BREASTED WATERHEN

Amaurornis phoenicurus phoenicurus (Pennant). Resident

Sinhalese: Korowakā. Tamil: Kānān-kōli

About the size of a half-grown domestic hen. Sexes alike. The white face, throat and breast, dark grey back and wings, and chestnut abdomen and under tail-coverts, distinguish this bird from all its relatives. It is by far the best-known of the *Ralliformes* in Ceylon, being very common throughout the low country and in the hills up to 4,000 feet or locally even higher, being sometimes seen at Nuwara Eliya (6,000 feet). It loves swamps, the borders of paddy-fields, and any place where wet and marshy ground is combined with thick, tangled shrubbery in which it can hide; for it never departs far from cover. Most of the day it lives in concealment, but in the mornings and evenings it emerges and walks about in the open, picking hither and thither at food items. While thus employed, its short tail is generally carried erect, showing the chestnut under tail-coverts, and is jerked at every step. Although the bird exposes itself freely and is easy to watch, it is very wary, running for cover at the least sign of danger and remaining hidden until the coast

× óne-sixth

is clear. It lives usually in pairs and each pair jealously guard their territory against intrusion by any other of their own species. If suddenly disturbed it flies in a laboured fashion, with its long legs dangling, but usually trusts to its legs to take it to safety. It swims well, on occasion, but does not take to the water very readily. It is also very adept at clambering about in tangles of creepers and the like, often at some height from the ground. Grasshoppers, other insects, worms, and also some grain comprise its diet. In the courting season it becomes very noisy, indulging with its mate in loud concerts which sound like *quaarr, quaarr, korowakwak, korowakwak . . .,* sustained for long periods. These weird noises are usually uttered from the depths of some tangled thicket in or near water.

The principal breeding season is during the south-west monsoon, but eggs may be found in any month. The nest is a mass of rush-leaves, etc., placed among rank vegetation growing in swampy conditions; sometimes it is placed in a small tree or bush but most nests are within a few feet of ground (or water) level. The four to seven eggs are greyish-cream, blotched and spotted with reddish-brown and greyish-purple; the markings tend to form a zone around the large end. They measure about 40·7 × 30·5 mm.

THE INDIAN WATERHEN

Gallinula chloropus indicus Blyth. Resident

Sinhalese: Wil-kukkulā. Tamil: Tannīr-kōli, Kānān-kōli

Size of the White-breasted Waterhen. Sexes alike. The Indian Waterhen, or Moorhen, is a race of a species which is very widely distributed through the globe. It is slaty-black with the back slightly greenish; a long, white stripe along the flank; white under tail-coverts, divided into two patches by a black median band. Irides red; beak yellow at the tip, remainder scarlet, prolonged on the forehead into a small, flat plate; legs and toes—the latter very long—green, with a small orange 'garter' where the feathers end on the tibia.

This waterhen is found, in pairs or small, scattered flocks, on weedy tanks and lakes, principally in the Southern Province but also in the North Central Province, and probably in other parts of the low-country dry zone. It is much more of a water-bird than the White-breasted Waterhen, spending much time swimming, though it likes to keep near to reed-beds or other forms of cover into which it can retreat on the approach of danger. It swims rather slowly because its feet are not webbed, jerking the head forward at every stroke—a habit which distinguishes it, even at a distance, from any kind of wild duck or grebe. Whether swimming or walking, the tail is generally cocked up and constantly flirted, displaying the white under tail-coverts. The waterhen dives well, generally to escape from sudden attack by a hawk, or the like, when it is surprised on open water; it will remain submerged for some time, clinging to underwater objects, with only the beak protruding above the surface. It walks, runs and climbs with equal facility, but its flight is slow and laboured, and seldom long-sustained except when the bird is changing its quarters. In taking off from water it runs and flutters for some distance, with much splashing, before it can rise clear. The food consists of water insects and other small animals, and also grain and various kinds of green-stuff. In the breeding season it is noisy, uttering a variety of loud cackles and kricking notes. In courtship, pairs indulge in strange displays and attitudinizings, and much fighting and chasing take place.

The breeding season is from March to July. The nest is a heap of rushes, etc., usually placed in a tussock growing in water. The five to eight eggs are stone-colour, variously blotched with brown and purplish markings. They measure about 42 × 29·5 mm.

THE KORA, or WATERCOCK

Gallicrex cinerea (Gmelin). Resident

Sinhalese: Wil-kukkulā. Tamil: Tannīr-kōli

Size of a small domestic hen; larger than the White-breasted Waterhen. A leggy, rather slenderly-built bird, with very long, slender toes. In the breeding season the male is slaty-black, with streaky olive back

Left, female; right, male; × one-fifth

and wings, and buff-white under tail-coverts; beak yellow, changing to red at the base, with the upper mandible prolonged on the forehead into a finger-shaped, fleshy, scarlet horn; irides red; legs dull red. Out of the breeding season he resembles the female, which is brownish-buff, with the upperparts dark brown fringed with buff, and the breast finely cross-barred with wavy black lines. Her irides are dark brown; beak olive paling to pinkish at the base of the lower mandible; legs dull green.

This bird is widely distributed throughout the low country, wherever suitable conditions exist, but it does not ascend the hills to any great height. It is a very shy, skulking bird which inhabits weedy swamps and well-grown paddy-fields, reed-beds and the like, and is very reluctant to show itself; consequently, few people except snipe-shooters ever see it. It is able to thread its way through long grass with great facility, and it prefers to escape from danger in this way rather than by flying; but when forced to fly, it does so in typical rail-fashion, with rather laboured wing-strokes and trailing legs, but nevertheless with considerable speed. It is largely nocturnal. Its food is mainly vegetable, consisting of grain, rice-blades, tender shoots, etc., but it also eats insects and molluscs.

The breeding season is in the south-west monsoon. The nest is a large mass of rushes or grass placed among reeds or floating vegetation, in dense cover. The two eggs are creamy or reddish-white, speckled, especially at the large end, with reddish-brown and greyish-purple; they measure about $43 \cdot 5 \times 32 \cdot 3$ mm. In the breeding season the cocks are pugnacious, challenging each other in deep, booming calls, and indulging in fierce fights.

THE PURPLE COOT

Porphyrio poliocephalus poliocephalus (Latham). Resident

Sinhalese: Kittalā, Kittā. Tamil: Kānān-kōli

Plate 28, facing p. 313 ($\times$ one-fifth)

Size of a village hen. Sexes alike. This bright blue and purple bird, with its red beak ascending into a flat plate on the forehead, and long, clumsy legs and feet, cannot be mistaken for any other species.

It is found, in suitable terrain, throughout the low country but does not ascend the hills. Dense reed-beds, swamps and lotus-covered tanks are its habitat. In such places it lives gregariously, clambering about among the reeds, walking on the floating vegetation, where its long toes give it support, and chasing its companions with much fluttering and splashing. If undisturbed it ventures fairly freely into the open, but, being much persecuted by shooters, it generally keeps well under cover of reeds. From these safe retreats it sends forth a chorus of noisy cacklings, hoots and grunts. When walking, the tail is generally elevated and jerked, displaying the white under tail-coverts. It swims well, but does not often do so voluntarily. The flight is laboured and generally of brief duration but, on occasion, it flies both fast and far. The toes project well beyond the tail in flight. The Purple Coot is mainly a vegetarian, feeding on the succulent stems of rushes and sedges, which it bites off and then, holding them up to the beak in one foot, parrot-fashion, nibbles off little pieces. Unfortunately it has taken very kindly to young rice plants and does a good deal of mischief to this crop. Besides vegetable matter it eats some insects, and it is under suspicion of the crime of sucking the eggs of swamp-nesting birds.

The breeding season is during the first half of the year, but March to May are the favourite months. The nest is a large heap of rushes and sedges, hollowed at the top to provide a receptacle for the eggs. It is placed in a reed-bed or lotus-swamp among lush vegetation. The four to eight eggs are greyish-buff, spotted and blotched with brown and pale purplish-grey; they measure about $50 \cdot 5 \times 35 \cdot 3$ mm. The chicks are black balls of fluff, with red legs and a red patch on the forehead; if taken young they are easily tamed and will live happily with domestic fowls; but they require certain types of aquatic vegetation for food, and their feet are apt to develop corns if they are kept on dry ground.

THE COMMON COOT

Fulica atra atra Linnaeus. Resident

No Sinhalese or Tamil names recorded

Slightly larger than the White-breasted Waterhen. Sexes alike. The entire plumage is slaty-black, darker on the head and with narrow white tips to the secondaries; the beak and a broad shield on the forehead are white—contrasting strongly with the dark head; irides red; legs and feet dull green, orange above the hock. The toes are long and each is fringed on both sides with a broad, scalloped membrane; this feature at once distinguishes this coot from all other Ceylon birds except the Little Grebe which has somewhat similar feet; but the different size and coloration prevent confusion of these two species.

This coot has but recently established itself in Ceylon, the first specimen on record having been shot at Giant's Tank in 1924; but since then the species appears to have increased in that neighbourhood though it is unknown elsewhere in the Island; in India it is widely distributed and occurs in vast numbers on some of the huge reservoirs and lakes in the north. It is definitely a swimmer, spending most of its time, in flocks of various sizes, on open water; but it prefers those lakes, etc., which are well fringed with reed-beds. When swimming it presents a thick-necked, stocky appearance, and its habit of jerking the head forward at every stroke of the feet distinguishes it, at a distance, from teal or other ducks. It dives frequently and has a habit of bringing up from the bottom masses of water-weed for its food; for it is mainly vegetarian, though small aquatic animals are also eaten. The flight is heavy and laboured and it has to run and splash along the surface of the water for some distance before it can take off; the wings are fluttered rapidly, and the large feet trail behind. Nevertheless, it is able to undertake long flights when occasion demands. It is highly gregarious, and also very pugnacious with its kind; in the courting season vigorous fights take place between rivals. It utters a variety of notes, some of them loud and trumpet-like, others like *kik*.

The breeding season in Ceylon is not known, but is most probably during the north-east monsoon when Giant's Tank is full of water. The nest is a large heap of rushes or other water-plants placed in the margin of a reed-bed. The six to ten eggs are greyish-buff, speckled and spotted all over with brown and black. They measure about 51×36 mm.

PELICANS, CORMORANTS, GANNETS, TROPIC-BIRDS, AND FRIGATE-BIRDS

Order PELICANIFORMES

This order comprises five families of aquatic birds which, though differing greatly among themselves in form and habits, have one notable feature in common, distinguishing them from all other birds: they have *all four toes united by webs*, the hind toe being somewhat turned inwards and webbed to the inner front toe (all other web-footed birds have the three front toes, only, united by webs). They are nearly all birds of powerful flight and all but one family swim well; but they are poor walkers, most of them being capable of nothing more than an awkward shuffle. Fish and, to some extent, other aquatic animals, form practically all their food, but their methods of capturing it vary greatly. They mostly nest on trees or on sea-cliffs, building large and untidy nests of sticks, etc. The young are hatched blind and naked but soon develop thick coats of down; they are fed by regurgitation of semi-digested food by the parents, and they take a long time to become fledged.

The five families, and their main characteristics, are as follows:

(*a*) *Pelicanidae*—Pelicans. Large, ungainly, swimming-birds, which have the beak long and flattened, with a strong, horny hook at the tip of the upper mandible; the lower mandible consists of two long, slender and flexible bones, united in front but with the space between them and the floor of the mouth composed of a great pouch of extensible skin, used by the bird as a scoop-net for engulfing fish. The legs, though short, are strong, and pelicans can walk better than most birds of this order though they do it with a pronounced waddle. The wings are long and powerful, the tail short and rounded. They are very gregarious birds.

(*b*) *Phalacrocoracidae*—cormorants, shags, and darters. Medium to fairly large-sized birds adapted for swimming and diving. The plumage is hard and close, with an undercoat of soft down. Wings powerful, but not exceptionally long; tail of medium length, somewhat graduated or rounded, of rather stiff, narrow feathers. In the cormorants and shags (sub-family *Phalacrocoracinae*), the bill is hooked at the tip; in the darters (sub-family *Plotinae*), the bill is straight and acutely pointed, the head small and narrow, the long, slender neck sharply kinked in the middle (giving great power to the forward thrust of the beak); the wings are more ample than in cormorants, and the rounded tail is longer.

(*c*) *Sulidae*—gannets and boobies. Large, marine birds, of very powerful and sustained flight, which capture their prey mostly by plunging from a height, on the wing, into the sea. Their wings are long and narrow; the tail more or less wedge-shaped; the beak straight, stout and pointed, with the nostrils completely closed in adults; and the legs short and strong.

(*d*) *Phaethontidae*—tropic-birds; the 'Bo'sun Birds' of seamen. Graceful, oceanic birds of somewhat tern-like appearance though the body is heavier-looking than a tern's. The wings are long and narrow and the tail, which is wedge-shaped, has the two centre feathers, in adults, greatly elongated into narrow streamers. The plumage is mostly satiny-white—often with a beautiful, golden suffusion—more or less spotted and marked with black. The beak is about as long as the head, deep, tapering to a point, nearly straight. The legs are short and weak, almost useless for locomotion on land, but useful for swimming. Tropic-birds nest on oceanic islands but, out of the breeding season, they range widely over the seas of the tropics. They feed largely on squids and flying-fish, which they capture by plunging into the water from a height while on the wing. The flight is very easy and graceful. They lay a single egg, usually in a crevice in a cliff, or in a hole in a dead tree.

(*e*) *Fregatidae*—frigate-birds. Large-sized, oceanic birds, of black, brown and white coloration, highly specialized for an aerial existence. The wings are *very long*, pointed and broad, and the tail is long and deeply forked; but the legs are very short and weak, and the webs of the feet are much reduced, so that swimming is almost or quite impossible. Walking, too, is difficult, and the feet appear to be used only for perching. The beak is fairly long and sharply hooked at the tip. At the chin there is a naked pouch of skin which is inflated by courting males into a huge, scarlet balloon. Frigate-birds spend the greater part of their time on the wing, sailing over tropical seas, often at great heights. They feed by swooping down and snatching fish, squids, etc., from the surface-water, and by robbing other sea-birds of their prey. It is doubtful if they ever settle upon the sea. They breed on oceanic islands.

THE SPOTTED-BILLED PELICAN, or GREY PELICAN

Pelicanus roseus Gmelin. Resident

Sinhalese: Pas-boruwā, Pas-bārā. Tamil: Kūlaī-kidā

Size of a large domestic goose, or of the Sea Eagle. Sexes alike. A long-necked, long-winged, short-legged bird with long, flattened bill, from the whole length of which beneath hangs a pouch of very elastic skin. Plumage somewhat sullied white, with lower back, rump, flanks, and under tail-coverts greyish-pink; primaries and their coverts brownish-black; secondaries brownish-grey. Bill pale yellowish-fleshy, with blue-black spots on each side of upper mandible; pouch pale fleshy with bluish-grey spots; bare skin around eye purplish-grey; irides pale yellow, surrounded by scarlet sclerotic membrane, giving a bloodshot appearance; legs and feet dark purplish-grey or dusky-flesh. In juveniles the wing-coverts are brownish-grey, the pinkish tinge on back, flanks, etc., is absent, and the beak, facial skin, and feet are pale yellowish-fleshy.

This large and ungainly bird cannot well be mistaken for any other species. It is distributed throughout the dry zone wherever suitable sheets of water, such as large tanks or coastal lagoons, exist; but it moves about a good deal, here today, gone tomorrow. Shallow waters are preferred to the deeper tanks. In the wet zone it occurs only occasionally, and it does not ascend the hills at all. Very sociable, it is usually seen in flocks numbering from two or three up to a hundred or more. Much of its time is spent in fishing; a number will co-operate in driving fish into a shallow backwater, from which each bird proceeds to scoop them, by a sideways action of the beak, into the enormous distensible pouch. When sated, the birds either sail about on the water, preening and sleeping, or betake themselves to some sand-spit, rock or snag projecting from the water. In swimming, the closed wings are often held well above the back, as if to keep them dry. The pelican flies well, proceeding by steady flaps of its ample wings, the head drawn back, and the long bill projecting in front. On sunny days it often circles up into the heavens, but when travelling any distance a flock usually flies in Λ formation, or in a long, wavy line. Though it is usually silent, a courting pair utter curious husky hisses—*huh huh huhhuh*. At the same time they make quaint jabs and passes with their beaks at each other, and shiver the wings as if they felt cold.

The breeding season is from March to May, or earlier in the year—depending, probably, on prevalent weather conditions. The nest, composed of sticks, is two or three feet in diameter, and is placed on lofty branches of trees growing in swamps or flooded areas. Usually several nests are grouped within a few square yards, and in more or less close proximity with the nests of various other water-birds—storks, herons, etc. The three eggs are chalky-white, and measure about 77 × 55 mm.

THE SOUTHERN CORMORANT, or INDIAN CORMORANT

Phalacrocorax carbo sinensis (Shaw). Rare resident

Sinhalese: Diya-kāwa. Tamil: Nīr-kākam

Size of a domestic Muscovy drake. Sexes alike. General shape like that of the Indian Shag, but with a slight crest on the back of the head. Greenish-black, with scapulars and wing-coverts dark brown, each feather margined black giving a scaly effect; a large white patch on the throat. In breeding plumage, a big white blotch on the lower flank; numerous white filaments on head and neck almost obscuring the black beneath them; facial skin and throat-pouch more or less yellow.

This race of the well-known cormorant of Europe and North America occurs, sometimes in large numbers, on some of the larger dry-zone tanks and coastal lagoons; but although it is now known to breed in Ceylon—at least occasionally—it is by no means common, and would appear to be in the main a winter visitor. In general habits it differs little from the Indian Shag and the Little Cormorant; like them it is an expert diver and fisher, pursuing its prey under water and usually bringing it to the surface to be swallowed. Large quantities of fish are devoured. In the water it floats low with little of the back exposed and the head generally held high, beak pointed upward; it dives constantly, often springing almost out of the water to gain impetus for its descent. Hunger satisfied, it rests in companies on shore, rocks, dead trees, etc., in or near the water, and spreads its wings to dry. The flight is strong, performed by rapid flapping of the wings; if travelling to a distance a flock will string out into long lines or Λ formation.

W. W. A. Phillips found a colony of seven pairs of this cormorant nesting, in February 1940, at a large tank near Yakalla, midway between Anuradhapura and Minneriya, N.C.P. The nests were among the branches of a small tree standing in shallow water, and each contained two young birds. The eggs of this species, which may number up to five, are pale sea-blue in colour, but so coated with a chalky deposit that the true colour is visible only when this is removed. They measure about 60 × 39·2 mm.

THE INDIAN SHAG

Phalacrocorax fuscicollis Stephens. Resident

Sinhalese: Diya-kāwa. Tamil: Nˉr-kākam

About the size of a small domestic duck. Sexes alike. Adult plumage glossy greenish-black except on the scapulars and wing-coverts, which are brownish-black, each feather margined with deep black in a scale-like pattern; wing and tail quills black. Bill dark brown; facial skin black; irides emerald green; legs and feet black. In breeding plumage, a small tuft of white feathers appears on each side of the head behind the ear-coverts; out of the breeding season these are lost, but the throat becomes speckled with white. Young birds are dark brown, with the throat, breast and underparts dirty white, shading into the surrounding brown. In the distance, this bird is difficult to distinguish from the Little Cormorant; it is, however, larger and has a sleeker appearance.

This shag is a lover of fresh water, seldom, if ever, seen on brackish lagoons or the sea. It is common on most of the larger tanks of the dry-zone low country and also frequents village tanks when these are full of water. It lives in flocks and moves about the country a good deal, its movements being governed, no doubt, by rainfall conditions and also by the fish-population of the tanks;

× one-eighth

for, like all the cormorant tribe, it is very voracious, rapidly depleting the food-supply in a small tank. It captures fish by pursuing them under water. When fed it sits in rows on the bank, or on any convenient perch in or near the water, and spreads its wings to dry.

The breeding season is during the north-east monsoon. Shags nest in colonies, building stick nests on trees standing in water. These colonies are usually situated in areas of wild, almost inaccessible jungle growing in the shallow water of overflowing tanks; such places are commonly patronized at the same time by colonies of various storks, herons, darters, etc. Three to five eggs are laid; they are pale sea-blue in colour, but are so overlaid by a chalky deposit that their colour cannot be seen without first removing the chalk. They measure about 51·3 × 33·2 mm.

THE LITTLE CORMORANT

Phalacrocorax niger (Vieillot). Resident

Sinhalese: Diya-kāwa. Tamil: Nīr-kākam

About the size of the Black Crow but with a longer neck. Sexes alike. Black, with a very slight, greenish gloss except on the scapulars, wings and tail; the scapulars and wing-coverts are dark grey, each feather

× one-fifth

margined with· black. In breeding plumage, the lores and a short supercilium become slightly mottled with white, and a few white filaments— indistinguishable at a short distance —appear on the head and neck; at the same time a short crest develops on the forehead and a small, mane-like tuft on the back of the neck, at the kink. In non-breeding plumage, a small white patch appears on the throat. Young birds are browner.

This is by far the commonest of the Ceylonese cormorants; it is widely distributed throughout the low country, though most numerous in the dry zone; and occasionally ascends the hills, though only in very small numbers, to the height of Nuwara Eliya where one or two some-

361

times sojourn for a time on the lakes. On all the larger sheets of fresh water and on many of the smaller tanks it abounds, living sometimes solitary but more often in flocks up to a hundred or more; but it moves about the country a good deal. Like all fish-eating birds it requires enormous quantities to maintain it in health, and therefore a flock will soon deplete the supply in a small piece of water. Besides fish, it eats large numbers of small prawns. On large tanks a flock will often fish in concert, spying shoals of fish from the air and then plunging among them with much splashing and diving. Like other cormorants, it swims low in the water with only the head, neck, and upper part of the back exposed, and the beak usually pointed upwards. Every few moments it dives, going under without splash, to reappear some distance away. When not fishing, it sits for long periods on banks, half-submerged rocks, or the branches of a dead, waterlogged tree, with its wings spread to catch the sun. The flight is performed with regular, rather quick flapping of the wings, the head projected forward; usually, a flock flies in mob-formation, but sometimes they string out into long, wavy lines, after the manner of many kinds of duck. It is usually silent but, when breeding, sundry croaks are produced.

The Little Cormorant breeds during the north-east monsoon rains, building stick nests, somewhat like those of crows, in colonies in trees standing in the water of tanks. Usually its breeding colonies are amongst those of many other water-birds—storks, egrets, pelicans and the like. The three to five eggs are pale blue-green, covered with a chalky deposit; they measure about $48 \cdot 8 \times 29$ mm.

THE INDIAN DARTER, or SNAKE-BIRD

Anhinga melanogaster Pennant. Resident

Sinhalese: Hanseyā. Tamil: Pāmbu-kuruvi (Wait), Nedung-kilaththi, Nedung-kaluththān

About the size of a domestic duck but with much longer neck, wings and tail. Sexes alike. The head, neck, and upper back are pale brown, with a narrow, white spectacle-mark crossing the forehead and ringing the eyes; two narrow white bands along the sides of the fore part of the neck; a brownish-buff band separating the fore-neck and sides of the chest from the black of the breast and entire underparts; wings and tail black; wing-coverts and scapulars—the latter long and lanceolate—

with broad, silvery-white shaft-streaks. Bill, upper mandible olive-brown, lower ochreous; irides yellow; legs and feet black. The bill is slightly up-curved, very acutely pointed, with the edges finely serrated to give grip upon slippery fishes. The head is small and slender—little thicker than the neck, which has a distinct kink in the middle due to the

× one-tenth

structure of the vertebrae; this gives great speed and power to the forward thrust of the bill in striking at a fish. The legs are short and the feet large.

This strange bird is distributed throughout the low-country dry zone but is a mere straggler into the wet zone and only occasionally strays into the hills—sometimes as high as Nuwara Eliya. It frequents fresh-water lakes and the larger rivers, salt or brackish waters not suiting it. It is a very expert diver, covering long distances at speed under water. On the surface it swims with only the head and neck exposed, strongly suggesting a snake—hence one of its popular names. It lives entirely on fish which it seizes, or perhaps stabs, while swimming under water, by a lightning stroke of the needle-sharp bill; this stabbing propensity makes it dangerous to handle, or to keep with other birds, as it always darts at the eyes. After fishing, it mounts some rock, snag, or dead tree standing in the water and sits for long periods, often in company with others of its own species and cormorants, with its wings spread to dry. A powerful flier, it is fond of soaring up into the sky with motionless wings, ascending on rising air-currents; the neck is fully extended, showing a curious bulge in the middle due to the above-mentioned kink. The note of the darter is a hoarse croak, but it is not a noisy bird.

The breeding season is during the north-east monsoon rains or soon after they have ceased, while the tanks are still full of water. It breeds in colonies, often in company with other swimming and wading-birds, building stick nests in trees standing in water. The three or four eggs are pale blue-green, hidden under a chalky deposit; they measure about 53 × 35·5 mm.

THE BROWN GANNET, or BOOBY

Sula leucogaster plotus (Forster). Occasional, or perhaps regular, visitor

No Sinhalese or Tamil names

About the size of a Muscovy drake. Sexes alike. In adult plumage deep brown with wing and tail quills darker; underparts, below the chest to the under tail-coverts, pure white; axillaries, and a broad band along the middle of the underwing, white. The beak, which is heavy, straight and conical, is yellowish-white, merging into the pale greenish of the bare skin of the face, which extends around the eyes and gape. This pale beak and face, contrasting with the surrounding dark brown feathering, gives the bird a most peculiar appearance and helps in its identification even at a distance. Irides pale yellow; legs and feet pale yellow or greenish. The wings are long and narrow and the tail rather long and wedge-shaped. Immature birds are lighter brown on the upper plumage than adults, and pale brownish below; the juvenile plumages of all gannets are, however, somewhat complicated, and it is advisable for the inexperienced to use caution in identifying them in the field.

This gannet is a fairly frequent, or perhaps regular, visitor, in small numbers, to the coasts of Ceylon during the north-east monsoon. In several racial forms it occurs in all tropical seas. Its flight is easy and graceful, usually low over the sea, and is very interesting to watch, especially when a high sea is running with strong wind; it swings now over the crest of a wave, then down into the trough, alternately flapping and gliding. This style of flight somewhat resembles that of shear-waters, but the booby's large size and big, pale-coloured beak prevent confusion with them. Every now and then it plunges into the sea after a fish, flying-fish being favourite quarry. It rests on the sea, swimming well, but usually roosts at night on rocks, moored buoys, etc., or on the spars of ships. In the latter situation, its unfamiliarity with man makes it stupidly tame so that it is easily caught by hand—hence the sailors' name for it, 'Booby'.

This gannet lays a single egg on the bare ground of oceanic islands, such as Christmas Island off the southern coast of Java, and some of the Mascarene Islands.

THE MASKED GANNET, or MASKED BOOBY

Sula dactylatra personata Gould. Only twice recorded from Ceylon

No Sinhalese or Tamil names

About the size of a domestic goose. Sexes alike. In adult plumage, pure white, with the wing-quills and their greater coverts and the tail-feathers black. Bill yellow or greenish-yellow; naked face dark bluish-grey; irides yellow, reddish, or greenish-yellow; legs and feet slaty grey, with darker webs. Immature birds, according to Wait, are brown, with a few paler feathers on the breast and abdomen, and the wing-lining white with some brown.

× one-sixteenth

This gannet, in several races, inhabits the tropical oceans of the globe, breeding on small oceanic islands, atolls, etc., and ranging widely over the oceans out of the breeding season. It probably visits the seas around Ceylon far more often than the few records suggest, but as it comes in shore only under stress of weather it escapes being 'collected'. It flies, in calm weather, usually at heights of thirty or forty feet above the sea, with steady, rather slow flight; five to fifteen rather shallow flaps followed by a short glide. The body looks long and cigar-shaped, with the long, pointed, and narrow wings projecting straight out from the middle of the body—giving the effect of a **+**. On spying a fish, it half closes its wings and plunges straight down upon it, submerging itself with a great splash. For rest, it floats on the sea, swimming lightly.

The breeding-place of this gannet nearest to Ceylon would appear to be Christmas Island; or the Cocos-Keeling Islands, farther west. The two eggs are laid in a shallow depression in the ground, each pair of birds claiming a small territory which they guard from their neighbours. The eggs are bluish-green, overlaid by a white, chalky deposit.

A specimen of the RED-FOOTED BOOBY *Sula sula (rubripes* Gould) was captured somewhere in Ceylon and brought to the Colombo Museum on 2 July 1936. I examined and made sketches of it but unfortunately failed to obtain the facts relating to its capture. It was a young bird, in greyish-brown plumage; bill rosy flesh-colour, black at the tip; facial skin pale blue and purple; irides chestnut; legs and feet salmon flesh-colour.

With the help of the available literature I satisfied myself of its identity, and it was then kept alive in the Museum Zoo for some months, in the hope that it would moult into adult plumage; but while in process of doing so, it died. The skin was preserved, but was never registered or added to the collection, and eventually disappeared. It is mentioned here in order to draw the attention of ornithologists to the probability of this species visiting the Ceylon coasts from time to time.

This rather small booby, in three races, frequents tropical seas almost around the globe. *S. s. rubripes* breeds on islands of the Indian, and tropical western and central Pacific Oceans, its breeding-ground nearest to Ceylon being, apparently, the Cocos-Keeling Islands in the eastern portion of the Indian Ocean, about six hundred miles south-west of Java Head.

It is very probable that ABBOTT'S BOOBY *Sula abbotti* Ridgway may visit the seas around Ceylon occasionally. It is said to breed at Assumption and Christmas Islands, and it ranges over the tropical Indian Ocean.

THE YELLOW-BILLED TROPIC-BIRD, or LONG-TAILED TROPIC-BIRD

Phaethon lepturus lepturus Daudin. Fairly frequent north-east monsoon visitor

No Sinhalese or Tamil names

Larger than the Large Crested Tern. Sexes alike. A graceful satiny-white bird with long, narrow wings pointed at the tips, and the two centre tail-feathers very narrow and twenty inches or more long. The following black markings are present: a crescentic mark passing from the gape through the eye to the back of the ear-covert; a broad band on the median wing-coverts and tertials; outer webs of the outer five or six primaries, and shafts of most of the quills and tail-feathers. Bill pale yellow; irides dark brown; legs dull yellow, feet black. Juveniles have the crown and nape spotted, and the mantle barred, with black; centre tail-feathers not elongated; bill fleshy-grey changing to yellow on the ridge and edges, and black tipped. From its near relations, the Short-tailed Tropic-bird *Phaethon aethereus indicus* and the Red-tailed Tropic-bird *Phaethon rubricauda*, both of which are not unlikely to turn up in Ceylon, adults of this species may be distinguished by the combination of yellow bill, and centre tail-feathers white and more than eighteen inches long.[1]

The Yellow-billed Tropic-bird is a fairly regular north-east monsoon visitor, in small numbers, to the Ceylon coasts. There are four specimens in the Colombo Museum, and in August 1933 I examined another, which escaped while I was drawing it; there are sight-records of many others, mostly from Colombo and the Pearl Banks. This lovely bird, whose satiny plumage often has a delicate golden suffusion, spends most of its life sailing over the open ocean, often hundreds of miles from land. It flies with easy grace, the long, narrow wings fanning through a small arc and the long, ribbon-like centre tail-feathers trailing. Every now and then it plunges vertically upon some flying-fish or surface-swimming squid, immersing itself but quickly rising into the air again. It rests on the sea, swimming lightly; but on land it is almost helpless, the weak legs being capable of only the clumsiest of shuffling gaits. While resting it has a broad, plump appearance, the large, round head drawn back upon the shoulders. The bird above-mentioned uttered the following notes while being sketched: (*a*) a rattling cackle; (*b*) a harsh *krā*; (*c*) a sound like *chik*. It was sub-adult. All tropic-birds are inquisitive towards ships, generally visiting them and flying around at close range, and sometimes resting on the spars at night—when they are easily caught, being quite fearless of man.

This race of the Yellow-billed Tropic-bird breeds on oceanic islands in the Indian Ocean, near or south of the equator. It chooses those that have a clothing of trees or palms, laying its single egg, without any nest, either in a cavity in a large tree, in a deep cavity among rocks, or under dense bushes, etc. The egg is reddish-white, heavily speckled with brownish-red stipplings.

THE GREAT FRIGATE-BIRD

Fregata minor aldabrensis Mathews. Recorded two or three times

THE SMALL FRIGATE-BIRD

Fregata ariel iredalei Mathews. A fairly frequent south-west monsoon visitor

No Sinhalese or Tamil names

Both these frigate-birds occur from time to time on the coasts of Ceylon but, as it is probable that representatives of other species or

---

[1] An interesting paper, with excellent photographs, on 'The Tropic-birds occurring in the Indian Ocean and adjacent Seas' by C. A. Gibson-Hill will be found in the *Journal of the Bombay Natural History Society*, vol. 49, 1950, p. 67.

races may visit the Island from time to time, I have decided to treat the frigate-birds as a group, rather than attempting to describe individual species. Their identification, even in the hand, is a matter for an expert, and it is almost impossible for the ordinary bird-watcher to discriminate between the several species and sub-species of these birds on the wing. They are large birds of predominantly black plumage, though females and young tend to have white underparts and collars, and brownish median-coverts. In breeding plumage males have the back strongly glossed with green. In size they are comparable with eagles, though the body is small compared with the enormous wings, which are very long, acutely pointed, and broad, and are usually well angu-lated in flight. The tail is long and very deeply forked. The beak is longer than the head, conspicuously pale in colour, nearly straight but sharply hooked downwards at the tip. The legs are very short and weak, and the feet, though feebly webbed between all four toes, are useless for either walking or swimming and are used only for perching.

Small Frigate-bird, male;
× one-sixteenth

Frigate-birds, of one species or another, are not uncommonly seen along the coasts of Ceylon—especially the west coast (? because there are more observers there)—during the south-west monsoon. They are usually solitary but sometimes in pairs. Their flight, thanks to the huge wings, is wonderfully effortless sail-planing with very little flapping, and they seem able to progress in any direction, with or against the wind at will, merely by trimming their wings to the air-currents. Usually they fly at a considerable height and, though appearing to move slowly, they cover the ground very quickly. Surface-swimming fish, molluscs, crustaceans, etc., form their food and they obtain some of it by snatching it from the water, immersing only the beak; but they are much addicted to robbing other sea-birds of fish—stooping upon them from a height and so bullying them that they drop their prey, which the frigate-bird swoops after and seizes before it reaches the water.

They build stick nests on low bushes or trees on oceanic islands, and lay two white eggs.

PETRELS AND SHEARWATERS
Order PROCELLARIIFORMES

These are oceanic birds of amazingly enduring powers of flight, most of them visiting land only during the breeding period each year; when not nesting, many species range far over the oceans. This wide ranging, however, is not promiscuous, as recent re-searches have shown that any given species has regular ocean haunts—determined by the distribution of currents, etc.—from which individuals stray only through stress of weather or other accidental cause. Nearly all the Ceylon records of these birds are due to such casual straying. As a group, they may always be recognized by the following combination of characters: (*a*) coloration always sober—brown, black, grey and white, in various patterns; (*b*) feet with three front toes fully webbed, hind toe extremely small or absent; (*c*) bill with the nostrils in a distinct short tube, or tubes; the bill itself is strong, nearly straight, but with the tip of the upper mandible sharply hooked downwards and the tip of the lower mandible downwardly curved to correspond: (*d*) the wings are long, the tail either wedge-shaped, square, or slightly forked. Their food consists of various marine surface organisms and oily substances floating on the sea, e.g. as the result of man's whaling operations. With the exception of the great albatrosses and one or two other forms, which do not occur anywhere near Ceylon, they are all birds of small to moderate size—up to that of a domestic duck. They breed on oceanic islands, cliffs, etc., and most forms are nocturnal in their nesting habits; a single egg forms the usual clutch, and it is generally laid on the ground in a burrow, or in a crevice among boulders.

The Ceylon list contains representatives of two families, as follows:

(*a*) *Hydrobatidae*—Storm petrels. These are small birds (up to the size of a mynah), with rather long slender legs, and the nostrils united into a short, *single* tube, projecting on top of the base of the beak. They have comparatively broad, rounded wings, and in many the tail is forked (Wilson's and the Ashy Storm Petrels).

(*b*) *Procellariidae*—Petrels and shearwaters. Larger than the storm petrels (up to the size of a domestic duck). The nostrils are in a short tube on the top of the bill, but the *tube is divided by a vertical septum* visible from in front. The wings are long, narrow and pointed, and the tail is either square or wedge-shaped (shearwaters and cape petrel.)

WILSON'S STORM PETREL

Oceanites oceanicus (Kuhl). Regular south-west monsoon visitor to Ceylon seas

No Sinhalese or Tamil names

Size of the magpie-robin, but with longer wings and shorter tail. Sexes alike. A sooty-black bird, with a broad, white patch at the base of the tail above, and a pale whitish or brownish band on the greater secondary coverts. Bill, irides, and legs black, but the *webs between the toes are yellow*. In appearance, this small oceanic bird somewhat suggests a swallow but its wings are broader than a swallow's and the tail is square and usually looks rather broad. It is probably the only petrel that visits Ceylon seas regularly; but as it keeps off shore, seldom approaching the coast nearer than, perhaps, a mile, it seldom comes within the landsman's purview. It is familiar enough, however, to those whose duties take them out to sea during the south-west monsoon, but in spite of this, very few specimens have been obtained in Ceylon.

This petrel is very widely distributed through the oceans of the globe, though its breeding places are all in islands, or barren, rocky coasts, in the far south. It spends most of its time fluttering along the surface of the sea, seldom rising more than a few feet above the water and often

patting it with its feet, or seeming to *stand* upon it, while, with extended wings, it picks at small organisms on the surface. It is generally seen in scattered flocks. The wake of a ship, containing many small organisms churned up and food-refuse thrown overboard, has a great attraction for this storm petrel and gives good opportunities for watching it from the taffrail, as it flutters and skips along the turbulent waters. Its food

× one-eighth

consists largely of small crustaceans but it probably eats any small marine animal it can catch; one that I picked up dead on the Galle Face beach, Colombo, had obviously died from choking caused by trying to swallow some long, spiny fish-bones which had stuck in its gullet; it was quite fresh.

The breeding season of Wilson's Storm Petrel is in December to February—the summer season in its Antarctic breeding-grounds. The single, white, finely brown-speckled egg is laid either in a crevice under tumbled rocks or in a burrow dug by the birds in peaty soil. Both incubation and the fledging period are long and the chick, being fed by its parents largely on regurgitated oil, becomes very fat; on the analogy of related species of petrels, it probably lives on its accumulated store of fat for an extended period, being abandoned by its parents long before it can fly and fend for itself. The birds visit their nest only at night.

The ASHY STORM PETREL *Oceanodroma monorhis monorhis* (Swinhoe)[1] is rather smaller than the Common Mynah. Sexes alike. This is a dark, ashy-brown petrel, very similar in general appearance to Wilson's, but paler, with no white on the rump and with the tail rather deeply forked; the greater and median wing-coverts are pale brown, forming an ill-defined light patch on the otherwise dark wing.

A single specimen of this petrel was caught in exhausted condition, at Mutwal, Colombo, on 3 July 1927, was skinned and sold to the Colombo Museum by a taxidermist; it was a male. I handled it and made drawings while the skin was still supple and fresh.

This bird breeds on islands of the north-west coast of Formosa and ranges north to Japan and south to the Philippines and the South China Sea. It is not uncommon at Singapore, but there are only two records of its straying west of the Straits of Malacca.

THE WHITE-FRONTED SHEARWATER

Puffinus leucomelas (Temminck). Only once recorded from Ceylon

No Sinhalese or Tamil names

About the size of the Whistling Teal. Sexes alike. A dusky-brown and white bird, with plumage pattern as shown in the illustration,

---

[1] Recorded by Wait, Whistler, and Phillips as the race *socorroensis* Townsend, following mis-identification of the specimen by Stuart Baker. See Gibson-Hill, *Spolia Zeylanica*, vol. 27, 1953.

× one-fifth

which was drawn from the only specimen that has been recorded from Ceylon. It was captured at Mount Lavinia in September 1884; was a male; and was for many years on exhibition in the Colombo Museum, labelled as a 'Green-billed Shearwater' (Haly, *First Report on the Collection of Birds in the Colombo Museum*, p. 69).

This species breeds at the Bonin and Pescadores Islands in the Pacific Ocean, and its normal range is from the coasts of Korea and Japan to the Malay Archipelago and New Guinea.

THE GREEN-BILLED SHEARWATER

Puffinus[1] *pacificus chlororhynchus* Lesson. Occasional straggler to Ceylon seas

No Sinhalese or Tamil names

About the size of the House Crow. Sexes alike. Dark brown above, paler brown beneath, with greyish chin and throat and an ashy suffusion on the back. Bill dusky greenish; irides very dark brown; legs and feet fleshy-white.

This shearwater appears to visit the seas off Ceylon rather more frequently than any other of its genus; it may, indeed, be a regular visitor in the south-west monsoon but, as it is strictly an oceanic bird, it

---

[1] It may be well to point out that the genus *Puffinus* has nothing to do with the well-known and much photographed puffin, *Fratercula arctica*, of northern seas, which is a sea-bird belonging to the sub-order *Alcae* (not represented in Ceylon) of the *Charadriiformes*.

is only when driven ashore by stormy weather that it is likely to be seen by the landsman. A bird of the open ocean, it flies tirelessly with the characteristic style of flight that gives these birds the name of 'Shearwater'; in calm weather, the flight is of ordinary, flapping character, much like that of a gull; but when the sea runs in high, white-crested waves, with a gale blowing, the shearwaters come into their own. They are fascinating birds to watch as they skim the waves, their long, narrow wings held stiffly extended while they swing, now low in the trough, now topping the crest, canting from side to side in their speedy progress. Shearwaters do not, as a rule, follow ships for offal as many other sea-birds do; they feed on various marine organisms—fishes, squids, etc.; alighting on the water for this purpose and swimming buoyantly.

This shearwater breeds on many islands in the Pacific, on the east and west coasts of Australia, and on the Seychelles Islands.

THE FLESH-FOOTED SHEARWATER

Puffinus carneipes Gould. Two specimens recorded from Ceylon

No Sinhalese or Tamil names

About the size of the Black Crow. Sexes alike. Sooty brown all over, with some paler feathers on the throat. Bill pale flesh-colour; irides nearly black; legs and feet flesh-colour.

A specimen of this shearwater was captured at Panadura, sixteen miles south of Colombo, on 21 June 1879, and was purchased by the Colombo Museum; it was a female; a male, in non-breeding plumage and moulting, was picked up by Y. Burn, dead but fresh, near Mount Lavinia on 26 June 1944 (*Journal of the Bombay Natural History Society*, vol. 45, 1945).

This species breeds on islands off south-western Australia; North Island, New Zealand; and at Lord Howe Island. In its general habits it doubtless differs little from other shearwaters.

The SLENDER-BILLED SHEARWATER or MUTTON BIRD *Puffinus tenuirostris* (Temminck). 'A single specimen was found dead by P. J. Dickson in a salt-pan near Palatupana, in the Hambantota district, on the south coast in May 1949. The head, wings and feet are in the Colombo Museum.'—Phillips, *Checklist*, p. 2.

This species frequents the seas around Japan.

A specimen of THE CAPE PETREL ('CAPE PIGEON' of sailors) *Daption capensis* (Linnaeus) was collected in the Gulf of Mannar about 1870. It is about the size of the House Crow. Sexes alike. A beautiful, pigeon-like petrel with white plumage, heavily spangled on the upperparts with black. Its normal range is throughout the southern oceans, breeding on many sub-Antarctic islands; but an occasional straggler finds its way north of the equator. It is well known to seafarers in the southern seas, owing to its habit of following ships for the sake of scraps of food, which it alights on the water to retrieve, when these are thrown overboard.

IBISES, STORKS, HERONS, AND THEIR ALLIES

ORDER CICONIIFORMES

THESE are medium-sized to very large birds, with long necks and legs, adapted to a wading life; in most forms the bill, too, is long and usually straight. The feet are webbed, at most, at the base of the three front toes; the hind toe is well-developed, and is set on the foot at practically the same level as the front toes; the tibia is generally bare of feathers for some distance above the hock-joint. All of them have well-developed wings and they are birds of powerful flight. The tail is short, and nearly always rounded. Their usual gait on land is a dignified walk; they can also swim, but few of them do so except under necessity. They perch freely on trees, or among reed-beds, etc. Swamps and marshes, the reedy margins of lakes and streams, etc., are their usual habitat. Their food consists of various small animals, mostly of an aquatic or swamp-frequenting kind. The eggs are generally unmarked, white or pale blue, and are laid in nests of sticks placed in trees, or of rushes and the like, in reed-beds. The young are hatched helpless and covered with down, and are fed by regurgitation of partially digested food by the parents. Many forms are highly gregarious, especially when nesting. (Flamingos—see below—are exceptions to many of these statements.)

So far as Ceylon is concerned, this order is divided into four families, as follows:

(a) *Threskiornithidae*—ibises and spoonbills. These, though generally smaller and more lightly-built birds, are closely related to the storks from which they differ in certain details of anatomy. Like the storks, they fly with the neck extended. Ibises have the beak long, tapering, and curved downward; spoonbills have it nearly straight, but broadened and flattened at the tip into the shape of a spatula.

(b) *Ciconiidae*—storks. Mostly very large birds, with the beak long, heavy-looking, and nearly straight. The tongue is very small.

375

They fly with the neck extended (except the Lesser Adjutant). Their wings are long and broad and they are much given to soaring into the sky. Their vocal powers are very limited, owing to their lack of voice-muscles, but many forms produce clattering noises mechanically by clapping their mandibles together.

(c) *Ardeidae*—herons, egrets, and bitterns. In spite of the three names, there are few or no structural grounds for dividing them. This family differs considerably from the above two, in the following respects: (1) the long neck is distinctly kinked in the middle owing to the structure and arrangement of the vertebrae; this enables the neck to be retracted into a very compact S, and extended with great force and suddenness for the capture of fish by the beak; in flight, the neck is nearly always retracted—a useful field character for discrimination of these birds on the wing; (2) the toes are long and thin, and the middle front claw bears a comb-like serration on its inner side; (3) on the sides of the breast and rump, the birds of this family have, concealed under the feathers, patches of peculiar, specialized feathers known as 'powder-down', which give off a powdery substance used in preening their feathers; (4) the tongue is long and thin. The heron family, though they eat a variety of small animals, are more specialized for a diet of fish than the other families. They have well-developed voice-muscles, and are inclined to be noisy at their breeding places. Though all fly well, they are less given to soaring than the Storks.

(d) *Phoenicopteridae*—flamingos. These are the most aberrant of this order of birds, and in some ways they appear to be a link between the storks, and the geese and ducks (order *Anseriformes*). Their main peculiarity is in the beak, which is bent downwards at an angle in the middle and has the edges of both mandibles laminated with rows of parallel ridges, forming a sifting apparatus like that of a duck's bill. The tongue is large and fleshy. The three front toes are webbed together and the hind toe is very small or absent. They fly with the neck fully extended and the long legs stretched out behind. They never perch, and their nests consist of low mounds of mud placed communally in saline flats. The young are able to run soon after hatching. In manner of flight, and in notes, they resemble geese.

The birds of this order are nearly all miscalled 'cranes' in Ceylon, but true cranes are not found in the Island; though superficially like the storks and herons, they are structurally very different.

THE SPOONBILL

Platalea leucorodia Linnaeus. Resident

Sinhalese: Handi-alawā. Tamil: Chappai-chondan

Nearly the size of the Large Egret. Sexes alike. Plumage white, with a pale yellow suffusion on the side of the breast in the breeding season; this, and also the crest of long, white feathers shown in the illustration, are lost in non-breeding plumage. Bill slate-grey, with black, transverse bands breaking up into spots near the tip, which is yellow; the naked skin of the throat is dull crimson at the sides, yellow between the rami of the lower jaw and on the throat; irides dark crimson; naked skin around eye, chrome yellow; legs and feet black.

This handsome but quaint-looking bird is fairly common in most of the more secluded parts of the low-country dry zone, wherever large tanks and swamps exist. It is usually found in small flocks, which spend the day resting and preening, either on the ground in the midst of a

× one-twelfth

swamp or perched on trees. Occasionally one will wade in shallow water and do a little feeding, but towards sunset the flock wake up and fly, strung out in single file, towards some favourite feeding-ground in a marsh, or the shallow margin of a tank. On arrival, they form a line and work steadily through the shallows, each bird passing its slightly-opened beak through the water with a semicircular motion from side to side; whenever some small aquatic animal—tadpole, dragon-fly larva, etc.—passes between the tips, it is seized and swallowed. A good deal of vegetable matter is eaten as well. The flight of the spoonbill is powerful, performed by steady wing-strokes, and it also soars at times, circling up on ascending air-currents to a considerable height. It is a silent bird, its only note, apparently, being a low grunt which it utters at the nest.

The breeding season in Ceylon is from December to March. The spoonbill nests in colonies, usually in association with numerous other large waders, in tree- or bush-covered swamps or mangrove-fringed lagoons, in the wilder parts of the country. The nest is of sticks, placed on top of a bush or on low branches of trees growing in water. The two to five eggs are chalky-white, with sparse brown blotches near the large end; they measure about 63·5 × 47 mm.

THE WHITE IBIS

Threskiornis melanocephala (Latham). Resident

Sinhalese: Tattu-kokkā, Dāhākatti-kokkā. Tamil: Thālkaththi-chondan

Between the Little and Large Egrets in size. Sexes alike. Plumage pure white, with the elongated tertial plumes (overhanging the tail)

× one-seventh

greyish. Bill, naked head and neck, and legs black; irides dark brown. Young birds have the head partly, and the neck fully, clothed with dark grey feathers. In non-breeding plumage, the filamentous feathers on the breast and the long, grey plumes on the tertials and longer scapulars are lost. In flight, a blood-red strip of bare skin shows between the under wing-coverts.

The White Ibis is fairly common in the wilder parts of the low-country dry zone wherever it can find the freshwater tanks, marshes and swamps that suit its habits; but it does not normally stray into the wet zone, and it leaves the hills severely alone. It lives in small flocks, frequenting weedy swamps, flooded jungle and grass-land, and is an active bird, walking briskly about in its search for food. It will eat almost any small animals it can catch—frogs, crabs, worms, grass-hoppers, etc.; these are seized between the tips of the mandibles and jerked up into the mouth. It commonly rests perched on the tops of trees, but at dusk the flock will fly, often in single file or Λ formation, to feed in some distant marsh; for it is largely nocturnal. Its flight is steady and powerful, performed with regular strokes of the ample wings. It is silent as a rule, though it is said to produce grunting sounds when breeding.

The White Ibis breeds in the early part of the year, in colonies, usually in company with numerous storks, egrets, cormorants, etc. It nests in trees or bushes growing in flooded country such as that at the back of some of the larger tanks after the north-east monsoon rains. The nests, composed of sticks, are often so crowded on favoured branches as to be almost touching each other. The three eggs are bluish- or greenish-white, sometimes spotted with brown, and they measure about 66 × 42·5 mm.

THE GLOSSY IBIS

Plegadis falcinellus falcinellus (Linnaeus). Resident in Legge's time, but present status very doubtful

Sinhalese: Ratu-dae-tuduwā. Tamil: Karuppu-kōttān

Slightly larger than the curlew; smaller than the White Ibis. Sexes alike. In breeding plumage, the lower part of the head, the neck, back, lesser wing-coverts and underparts are rich maroon-brown; cap, greater part of the wings, scapulars, and tail, black, richly glossed with green and purple. Bill dark greyish-brown; loreal skin purplish-black, or green; irides dark brown; legs and feet greenish-brown. In non-breeding plumage, the coloration is duller, more brownish-black, and the head and neck become streaked with white. The head and neck are feathered in this ibis. It looks, in the distance, like a very dark, blackish curlew, but in flight its much broader, more rounded wings readily distinguish it.

In Legge's time, this bird was widely distributed in the low-country dry zone and, though not numerous, it was evidently by no means rare. Nowadays, however, it must be considered—if present in Ceylon at all —as a very rare species in the Island;[1] I have never met with it, but it possibly occurs in some of the more remote jungle districts. As it is known to wander about a good deal, it may repopulate Ceylon in the future. It has a wide range, in two or three races, from North America, through Europe, Africa, and Asia, to Australia. In general habits it resembles the White Ibis; it is sociable, usually seen in flocks of a dozen or so; perches readily in trees; flies with quick wing-strokes producing a whizzing sound, but sometimes glides for some distance and often flies high. A flock travels either in a compact bunch or in lines of evenly-spaced birds as many other waders and swimming-birds do. It frequents weedy marshes, mangrove swamps, coastal lagoons and the like, and feeds on small animals, such as worms, crustaceans, water insects, frogs, and is said to be partial to water-leeches. The usual note it produces is likened to a harsh, crow-like croak, but it is generally silent.

Legge found a small colony of these birds nesting, in March 1872, in company with Open-billed Storks, on thorny trees growing in the half-dried bed of a small tank at Uduwila (which, from his map, appears to be the same as Wirawila), Southern Province. The nests, composed of twigs and lined with grass-roots, were rather small and were placed high in the trees. The eggs of this species are coloured deep greenish-blue, and measure about 52 × 37 mm. The normal clutch is three eggs.

THE INDIAN WHITE-NECKED STORK

Dissoura episcopus episcopus (Boddaert). Resident

Sinhalese: Pādili-kokkā. Tamil: Vannāti-nārai

About the size of the Grey Heron, but a heavier-looking bird. Sexes alike. Entire neck, abdomen, and under tail-coverts white; crown and the rest of the plumage black, glossed with green on the crown and most of the wings, and with coppery-red on the breast and median

[1] Phillips, *Checklist*, Appendix, p. 115, reports that 'two (possibly a pair) of Glossy Ibises were seen by C. E. Norris at Kalametiya lagoon, near Ambalantota, on the sea coast in the Hambantota district, S.P., on 2 November 1952'.

wing-coverts. Bill black, with red tip and margins; naked skin of the forehead and face dark grey; irides brownish-scarlet; the sclerotic membrane is white in front of the iris, chrome yellow behind it; eyelid black; legs and feet dull crimson. The structure of the tail in this bird is very peculiar and even such an acute observer as Legge has been misled by it (*Birds of Ceylon*, p. 1118). The tail itself is black, short and deeply forked; but the under tail-coverts are white, longer than the tail, and with strong shafts—giving the impression that they are the true tail.

× one-twelfth

The White-necked Stork, or 'Parson-bird', is found sparingly throughout the low-country dry zone, in the neighbourhood of tanks, swamps and flooded grass-land, etc. It is evidently much reduced in numbers since Legge's day, and this is doubtless due to the constant shooting by poachers that nowadays makes even the most remote of jungle tanks unsafe for the rapidly diminishing wild-life of the Island. However, this handsome bird may still be seen, in pairs or small parties, stalking solemnly about in open country or soaring on motionless wings up into the sky on sunny days. Its long white neck, contrasting with the black of most of the plumage, makes it impossible to mistake this stork for any other bird. When not feeding or flying, it stands on the ground in rather upright pose, the head somewhat sunk into the shoulders. Though it roosts in trees at night, it seldom perches in them in the day-time. Its food consists of fish, frogs, molluscs and water insects, and it eats many grasshoppers. The only sound it appears to produce is a clattering of the mandibles.

This stork is said to breed in February and March, nesting in trees in the heart of the jungle. Though sociable out of the breeding season, it nests in isolated pairs, not in colonies. The nest is a large mass of sticks and twigs, placed in a high tree. The four eggs are bluish-white, and measure about 64×47 mm.

THE BLACK-NECKED STORK

Xenorhynchus asiaticus asiaticus (Latham). Status uncertain; rare resident, or regular visitor in small numbers?

Sinhalese: Ali-kokkā. Tamil: Periya-nārai

Standing nearly the height of a man. Sexes alike except that the irides in the male are dark brown, in the female bright yellow. This enormous stork has the head and neck, which are fully feathered, black,

Female; × one-fifteenth

strongly glossed on the cap with crimson-purple, elsewhere with metallic prussian blue; the longer scapulars, greater and median wing-coverts, tertials, and tail, glossy green-black; the rest of the plumage, including all the flight-feathers, pure white. The very long, stout bill is black; legs and feet bright scarlet-pink. Although so big, this is by no means an ungainly bird; the head and beak seem rather disproportionately large but the body is comparatively small and slender. In flight it is a noble sight with its neck extended, its long, bright red legs projecting behind the tail, and the huge white wings marked with a broad black band formed by the greater and median coverts; this pattern is repeated on the underwing.

The Black-necked Stork, in two races, is found from India, through the countries of south-eastern Asia and the Malaysian chain of islands, to northern and eastern Australia. In Ceylon it occurs very sparingly in the low-country dry zone, mainly in the wilder parts of the Eastern and Southern Provinces. Throughout its range it is a scarce bird, living solitary or in pairs, and inhabiting wild, lowland country with forest interspersed with secluded tanks and lagoons. It is very wary, flying off with heavy flaps of its great wings at the first sign of approach of its arch-enemy, man. When well under way it sails along in easy, gliding flight. Fish, frogs, crabs and other small animals form its food. When at rest its usual posture is rather upright, often with the beak resting on the fore-neck as shown in the illustration.

Although it is usually regarded in Ceylon as a resident species there is no positive proof that this is so, as the nest has not been found in the Island up to date; but it has been seen in both monsoons, and one or two immature individuals have been recorded, so it is probable that, occasionally at least, it breeds in Ceylon. When courting, this stork, like others of its family, indulges in strange dances and antics accompanied by much clappering of the mandibles. The nest is a huge mass of sticks, with a fairly deep cavity lined with rushes, water-weeds, etc., and some-times with mud. It is placed on the top of a big tree, often a banyan or bo. The two to four faintly bluish-white eggs, which quickly become stained and dirty, measure about 75 × 54 mm.

THE OPEN-BILL

Anastomus oscitans (Boddaert). Resident

Sinhalese: Bellan-kokkā, Beli-kāvā. Tamil: Nāththai-kuththi-nārai

About the size of the Large Egret; the smallest of the Ceylon storks. Sexes alike. Plumage white or greyish-white, with the wing quills and their greater coverts, and the tail, glossy greenish-black. Bill greenish-grey, slightly reddish beneath; bare facial skin and throat blackish-blue; irides grey; legs dull pinkish-red. Young birds are sullied greyish, and they take some time to develop the strange gap between the mandibles that gives the bird its name.

This species is the commonest of our storks, but it appears to be a good deal less abundant and widely distributed than it was in Legge's day; no doubt constant shooting by irresponsible persons has reduced its numbers and driven it further from the haunts of men. In the wilder jungle areas of the low-country dry zone it is still common, living in flocks up to a hundred or more. In swamps and along the shores of tanks and lagoons it finds its favour-ite food, which consists of fresh-water snails and mussels. From these it extracts the flesh either by

× one-eleventh

383

hammering the shell with its powerful beak, or, in the case of the snails, by cutting off the operculum; small specimens are crushed between the mandibles. Besides molluscs, it eats crabs, fish and other small animals. On sunny days a flock will soar, circling up to a great height in the sky. It is probable that some migration takes place from India as I once, in July, watched a flock of about a hundred crossing the northern coast of the Jaffna Peninsula, as if arriving from the mainland. Most of them were moulting some of the flight-feathers. This species is found through-out India and extends through Burma and Siam to Cochin-China.

The breeding season is from December to March. The open-bill nests in colonies, building its nests of sticks and twigs on the tops of low trees and bushes growing in swamps or flooded jungle; the nests are often crowded together. The two to five eggs are creamy-white, but they soon get dirty and stained; they measure about 58×41 mm.

THE PAINTED STORK

Ibis leucocephalus (Pennant). Resident

Sinhalese: Dae-tuduwā. Tamil: Sangu-valai-nārai

Considerably larger and more stoutly built than the Grey or Purple Herons. Sexes alike. The plumage of adults is pure white and glossy greenish-black, in the pattern shown in the illustration; the longer scapulars, tertials, and inner greater coverts are beautiful, rich crimson, fringed with white; the long tertials almost conceal the tail, which is glossy, greenish-black; the underwing is black, with white tips to the coverts. Bill yellow ochre; naked skin of the head deep flesh pink; irides pale grey; legs flesh-pink. Juveniles are mainly patchy grey, with only traces of pink on the scapulars, etc.

This beautiful but rather grotesque-looking stork—the 'Pelican-Ibis' of Legge—is common in the northern half of the Island and down the eastern low country to about the Tangalla district, wherever tanks, large swamps, and secluded lagoons give it safe feeding-grounds. It lives in small parties but, where feeding is abundant, sometimes assembles in large flocks. In searching for food it wades slowly in shallow water with the tips of its mandibles submerged and open, feeling in the mud for prey; every now and then it uses one foot to drive some small animal between the mandibles. Few creatures small enough to be swallowed whole come amiss to its voracious appetite; fish, frogs, water-snakes, lizards, crabs, larvae—all are acceptable. When resting it stands very upright with the beak pointing steeply downwards, and often clasps the tarsus of one leg with the other foot. Another common resting posture is squatting on the hocks. In common with some other large storks, it has a strange habit of 'whitewashing' its legs, while at rest, by squirting excreta over them. The flight of the Painted Stork is easy and powerful, usually an alternation of flapping with long glides; the neck is extended and the legs trailed in the usual manner among storks. On sunny days,

× one-fifteenth

especially in the breeding season, it is much given to soaring in circles, generally in large flocks, to great heights in the sky; on one occasion I saw a soaring bird bend its head under the wing and pick a parasite off the flight-feathers. It perches readily, and generally roosts at night on the tops of large trees. Like most storks, this bird is almost voiceless when adult, but young birds constantly utter a kind of wheezy croak while begging food from their parents. They follow them about with wings half-extended and the open beak sawed up and down.

The breeding season is in the early months of the year. Courtship is attended by a good deal of attitudinizing, bill-clappering, etc., and the under tail-coverts, which are very long and fluffy, are puffed out and expanded downward under sexual excitement. Nesting is in large colonies, in association with many other kinds of water-birds, in trees growing in water, mangroves and the like. The rather small nest, composed of sticks, is placed on the top of a tree. The three or four eggs are dull white, and measure about 71 × 48 mm.

A very remarkable case of hybridization between this species and the Lesser Adjutant took place at the Dehiwela Zoo, Colombo, in the early part of 1940. Which of the pair was the male partner was not definitely ascertained, but it was believed to be the Painted Stork. Both birds were completely free and full-winged and, though tame and semi-domesticated, they ranged over neighbouring paddy-fields at will. A nest was built on top of a large, creeper-covered aviary and three or four hybrid young were successfully reared to maturity by the ill-assorted pair. The offspring, when full grown, were larger than either parent. They were coloured and patterned like the Lesser Adjutant, but browner in shade. They had enormous beaks shaped like that of the Painted Stork; the forehead and face were bare and the neck was fully, though somewhat thinly, feathered. In stance they took after the Painted Stork. For a year or more these hybrids ranged freely (they made a habit of visiting a small collection of semi-domesticated storks, of the same species as their parents, that roamed the lawns of the Colombo Museum —about five miles from their birth-place); but the war prevented further observation of them.

Sight records have been obtained in Ceylon of two large storks both belonging to the genus *Ciconia*. They are the WHITE STORK *Ciconia ciconia* (Linnaeus) and the BLACK STORK *Ciconia nigra* (Linnaeus). The White Stork is considerably larger than the Painted Stork but not so big as the Black-necked Stork. Its head, neck, body plumage, lesser and median wing-coverts, and tail are white; the longer scapulars, wing-quills and their greater coverts, black. The beak and legs are red. From the Black-necked Stork—the only species with which it might be confused—its red beak, white head, neck and tail, and black flight-feathers, clearly distinguish it.

The White Stork, in several racial forms, has a wide distribution through Europe, Asia and Africa, breeding in the northern parts of its range and wintering in the south. It is common in northern India in the winter but only a rare straggler in South India, and the only Ceylon records are of a single specimen seen near Yala, Southern Province, in 1879, by Samuel Bligh, as recorded by Legge (*Birds of Ceylon*, p. 1120); and several seen and suspected to be breeding, at Nikaweratiya, North Western Province, in 1880, by Parker, another of Legge's correspondents. It is, however, most unlikely that this species would breed in Ceylon and suspicion of mistaken identity must rest on Parker's record.

The Black Stork is about the size of the Painted Stork. Its underparts, from the lower breast to the under tail-coverts, are white; all the rest of the plumage is black, highly glossed with green, blue and purple. The bill, lores, orbital skin and legs are red. Juveniles are dark brown on head and neck and have the bill and legs greyish-green. The black or brown neck and more extensively white underparts prevent confusion with the somewhat similarly coloured White-necked Stork.

This species breeds in Europe and Asia and winters in Africa and northern India. The only Ceylon record is of a pair watched at close range by W. W. A. Phillips, at Bagura, south of Arugam Bay, Eastern Province, in March 1938. They were feeding together at the edge of a lagoon (*Loris*, December 1940).

THE LESSER ADJUTANT

Leptoptilos javanicus (Horsfield). Rare resident

Sinhalese: Māna. Tamil: Māna, Mēva-kokku

Ceylon's largest bird, though it is not quite so tall as the Black-necked Stork. Sexes alike. Plumage dirty white below, ashy greenish-black on back, wings and tail; the longer scapulars and tertials margined with white; beak and head bone-yellow, more or less sullied with brown and dull red on the sides of the beak and face; the crown of the head is bare bone; the neck, which is naked except for scanty, long, greyish down, is dirty yellow. Irides pale bluish-grey; legs and feet dark brown, but their real colour is difficult to see owing to the bird's habit of ejecting its white excreta over them. The illustration shows the bird in normal resting attitude, with head sunk into the shoulders; when alert, the neck is extended to about the same length as the beak.

× one-sixteenth

This weird-looking stork is found sparsely scattered throughout the wilder low-country jungles of the dry zone, but is common nowhere. It lives singly, as a rule, though a pair may sometimes be seen together. It frequents the loneliest of jungle tanks, water-holes, and the half-dry beds of rivers, and is a very wary bird, flapping heavily off at the first suspicion of approach of a human; this wariness is its salvation, for so large and meaty a bird could never survive in over-shot Ceylon were it not protected by constant watchfulness. Fish, frogs, crabs, small mammals, lizards, snakes and even insects, form its food, and when hunting for them it shows considerable alertness and activity in contrast with its dignified and sluggish demeanour when resting. Like other large storks, it often squats on the hock-joints with the tarsi stretched out in front—presenting a grotesque appearance. It is a silent bird and I have never even heard it clattering the mandibles together, as most storks do; but it may do so in the courting season. Its flight, though heavy and lumbering while getting under way, is easy and stately when once aloft. Unlike most storks, the head is drawn back between the shoulders when soaring, and this, with the enormous black wings and short tail, give it rather a vulturine appearance. Besides Ceylon, this stork is found in South and Central India, Burma, southern China, and through Malaya to Borneo.

That breeding takes place in Ceylon is certain, because on several occasions young birds have been brought alive to the Colombo Museum; but the nest has rarely been found in the Island. It is a huge mass of sticks placed in a big tree. The breeding season is given by Phillips as March–April and also September. The three white eggs measure about 73 × 53·5 mm.

For an account of the hybridization of this bird with the Painted Stork, see under that species.

THE EASTERN PURPLE HERON

Ardea purpurea manilensis Meyen. Resident

Sinhalese: Karawalā-kokkā, Barendi-kokkā. Tamil: Chen-nārai

About the size of the Grey Heron but more slenderly-built; slightly bigger than the Large Egret. Sexes alike. In spite of its name, there is nothing purple about this bird; its main colour is rather dark ashy-grey, darkening to nearly black on the wing-quills and tail-feathers; sides of the neck cinnamon-red, with long black streaks as shown in the illustration; a deep, maroon-red patch on the sides of the chest; lower breast, abdomen, and under tail-coverts slaty-black. Bill: upper mandible dark brown, paling to yellow on the margins; lower mandible yellow; irides bright yellow; bare, facial skin pale green; legs: tibia yellowish, tarsus and toes dark brown. Young birds are much more uniformly coloured—rufous-brown for the most part. The head and neck are very long and slender in this heron, and the toes are very long.

It is a common bird throughout the low country, wet and dry zones alike, wherever suitable conditions exist; these consist of reedy swamps, mangrove-lined lagoons and the like; for, unlike the Grey Heron, it is seldom seen away from cover. It is shy, generally solitary, and wary, spending most of its waking time stealthily wading, or creeping along the margins of small water-holes or canals among reeds or grown paddy, ever on the alert for fish, frogs, or even insects. Its long S-kinked neck gives tremendous power for its stabbing thrust, and it does not often miss its stroke. As in all the heron tribe, its gullet is highly extensible, enabling it to swallow large fish with ease. Another feature, common to all herons, is punctilious cleanliness; it gives much attention to its plumage, preening it frequently in a slow and methodical manner. When suddenly disturbed it rises with clumsy flappings, giving vent to its alarm or annoyance by a series of harsh croaks as it betakes itself to a safer spot. When travelling any distance, the head is drawn back between the shoulders with the fore-part of the neck projecting in a curve beneath the beak; the feet extend behind the tail, and the ample

× one-ninth

wings beat slowly and regularly. Although it feeds quite freely by day, it becomes most active towards dusk, flying long distances across country to some favourite feeding-ground.

The Purple Heron breeds in December to February, and again—or instead—in May and June; no doubt breeding is regulated by rainfall conditions. It nests in scattered colonies, often in company with other herons, egrets, etc., either in low trees and bushes growing in flooded ground, or in dense, tall reed-beds or screw-pine thickets. The nest is a mass of sticks or reeds, according to the surrounding vegetation. The three or four eggs are pale bluish-green in colour, unspotted, and measure about 56 × 40 mm.

THE EASTERN GREY HERON

Ardea cinerea rectirostris Gould. Resident

Sinhalese: Kalapu-kokkā. Tamil: Nārayan, Nārai-kokku

Smaller than the Painted Stork, larger than the Large Egret. Sexes alike. An ashy-grey bird, with the head, neck, and underparts pale or white in places, and marked with black as shown in the figure; wing-quills black, contrasting with the grey coverts. Bill yellow-ochre, shading on the lores into dark purplish-grey (out of the breeding season, into greenish); irides orange-ochreous; legs and feet greenish-brown. Young birds are more uniformly-coloured, rather sullied grey.

This heron, in several slightly differentiated racial forms, has a very wide distribution almost throughout Europe, Africa and Asia. In Ceylon, it is found throughout the dry zone but occurs only as a straggler in the wet zone, and does not ascend the hills to any height. It is commonest about the brackish lagoons of the northern and eastern coasts but also frequents the margins of the larger tanks, river estuaries, etc. When fishing it is usually solitary but at times associates in large flocks, presumably where the fishing is extra good. It is much less secretive than the Purple Heron, generally preferring to wade and fish in open places where it can see the approach of intruders from afar, for it is equally wary of humans. In search of fish it will wade in water up to its belly, but usually contents itself with patrolling in the shallows where it stalks along slowly, its neck stretched forward, intently peering into the water for an unwary fish within range of its lightning thrust. Large fish are carried ashore and beaten to death, but small ones are merely jerked into a head-first position and swallowed. Besides fish, it eats almost any small animal, bird or reptile that it can catch. Its flight is much like that of the Purple Heron and, like that species, it utters a series of loud complaining croaks as it flaps heavily off on being disturbed. When in full flight—which is often at a considerable height—it utters periodically a loud *kraaak* ... *kraaak*. At a heronry, a weird

× one-thirteenth

assortment of harsh croaks and chatters emanates from the inhabitants. This heron perches freely on trees; in spite of its size it is very lightly built and can poise on astonishingly small branches. It is largely crepuscular in habits, flighting at dusk for long distances to its feeding-grounds.

The breeding season is from December to April. Nesting is in colonies, usually in more or less close company with numerous other wading- and swimming-birds. The nest is a large mass of sticks placed among the branches of a tree, or on top of bushes growing in shallow water. The two or three eggs are pale bluish-green (like very dilute prussian blue), and measure about 59 × 44 mm.

THE GIANT HERON

Ardea goliath Cretzschmar. A very rare straggler to Ceylon; only four or five specimens recorded

No Sinhalese or Tamil names

Nearly twice the size of the Grey Heron. Sexes alike. Head and neck deep reddish-chestnut, with the throat white, and a white line, bordered with slaty-black spots, down the front of the neck; long plumes on the sides of the chest rufescent-white, streaked with slaty-brown; back, wings, and tail, slate grey; underparts from breast to under tail-coverts, and underwing, dark chestnut. Bill dark slate, fleshy on the lower mandible; facial skin pale slate; irides yellow; legs and feet slaty-black. Young birds are duller and paler, with the upperparts somewhat rufous.

This enormous heron normally inhabits Africa, from Senegal and the Egyptian Sudan to Cape Province; but a few individuals have found their way, from time to time, to various parts of India, and four or five have been collected in wild parts of the North Central and Eastern Provinces of Ceylon. It does not appear to have occurred in the Island— or at any rate, been collected—for the last sixty or seventy years. It frequents wild jungle tanks, river banks and lagoons, and is a very shy bird. In general, its habits and behaviour do not differ greatly from its smaller relatives, the Grey and Purple Herons, but it is, of course, able to tackle much bigger fish, etc., than they.

THE EASTERN LARGE EGRET, or GREAT WHITE HERON

Egretta alba modesta (Gray). Resident

Sinhalese: Lōku-sudu-kokkā, Badadel-kokkā. Tamil: Periya-vellai-
kokku

Smaller than the Grey and Purple Herons, but much larger than all other egrets. Sexes alike. Plumage entirely pure white. In the breeding season, the bill is black and the tibia and hock-joint are dull flesh-colour, merging into the black of the tarsus and feet; there is a long train of filamentous feathers, projecting beyond the tail. In non-breeding plumage, the bill is ochreous yellow, dusky at the tip; tibia and hock greenish-grey; and the dorsal train is lost. Its size distinguishes this egret from the Median and Little Egrets and also from the Cattle Egret.

It is common throughout the low country, frequenting the shores of lagoons, tanks and paddy-fields, and is usually solitary or in small, scattered flocks, but sometimes assembles in flocks of a dozen or more. A wary bird, usually keeping well out in the open, it is not easy to approach close enough for satisfactory observation of details; to make up for this, however, its dazzlingly white plumage makes it so conspicuous that its actions may be watched from a great distance. Its usual stance is very upright, often with the long neck extended as it stalks through shallow water or rests on sand-spits or grassy fields. It

perches freely on the tops of trees, and roosts in them at night. Fish, prawns and other aquatic animals, and grasshoppers, form its food. The flight is strong, performed with steady, rather slow beats of the wings, the head drawn back between the shoulders and the feet trailed behind the tail, in the manner common to all the heron tribe. It is generally silent but, on being suddenly disturbed, utters a low *kraa-a* as it flies off.

The breeding season is from December to May. For the purpose of breeding, Large Egrets resort to certain areas of flooded jungle at the back of some of the larger tanks, or to mangrove

× one-twelfth

392

PLATE 29

1. Chestnut Bittern. 2. Little Green Heron. 3. Yellow Bittern. 4. Black
Bittern. 5. Malay Bittern. 6. Night Heron

THE LITTLE EGRET

Egretta garzetta garzetta (Linnaeus). Resident

Sinhalese: Sudu-kokkā. Tamil: Vellai-kokku

A good deal taller and slimmer than the Pond Heron. Sexes alike. Plumage pure, snowy white. In the breeding season, the following nuptial plumes develop: (*a*) two long, tapering, narrow feathers on the nape; (*b*) a tuft of long, deli-cate, filmy feathers on the breast; (*c*) long, 'egret' plumes, extending an inch or so beyond the tail, on the back. The bill in this egret is black at all times; bare skin of the face greenish or yellowish, but in the height of breeding condition, for a brief period, it becomes crimson-pink; irides pale yellow; legs black with the feet and adjoining part of the tarsus green, yellow, or in full breeding condition, crimson-pink. This differentiation of the colour of the feet from the tarsus is the best means of distinguishing this bird from the Median Egret in the field.

This beautiful bird, in several subspecies, has a very wide range through Europe, Africa, Asia, the Malaysian groups of islands, to

× one-ninth

Australia. In Ceylon it is found in the low country, particularly the dry zone, and seems to be commonest in coastal districts. It is sociable, often forming large flocks which scatter while feeding but unite when flying to roost. It frequents swamps, paddy-fields, shallow lagoons, and even tidal mud-flats on which it may often be seen fishing in company with other wading birds. Small fish, which it captures by a very quick thrust of the beak, comprise its main food, but it also eats prawns, water-insects, grasshoppers, etc. The flight is rather slow, with steady strokes of the wings, the body slightly rising and falling at each stroke. It roosts in companies in leafy trees, and has favourite roosts to which it returns regularly. It is less shy and wary than most of its tribe.

The breeding season is from December to April and, as it approaches, the birds desert their ordinary haunts and repair to great heronries scattered about the country, most of them in flooded jungle at the back of the larger tanks or in mangrove swamps. The nest is the usual plat-form of sticks and often a number are situated in a single tree amongst the nests of a variety of other water-birds. In courtship the long, nuptial plumes are puffed out, those of the back raised fan-wise—giving a most beautiful effect as of a spray-like mist above the bird's back. The three or four pale blue eggs measure about 42 × 33 mm.

THE INDIAN REEF HERON

Demigretta asha (Sykes). Resident (probably also a winter migrant)

No Sinhalese or Tamil names recorded

Size of the Little Egret which it closely resembles in proportions, but the beak and legs are stouter. Sexes alike. This small heron exists in two colour-forms, independently of age or sex; the commonest form is dark ashy-grey throughout except the chin and throat, which are white; the other form is white, sometimes marked, here and there, with grey spots. Some individuals are parti-coloured, grey and white. Bill chrome yellow, shading into the greenish-grey of the bare facial skin; irides golden yellow; legs rather variable in coloration but usually the tibia, hock-joint, and an inch or so of the tarsus are black or dark brown; the rest of the tarsus and the feet are pale green or yellow.

As its name implies, this heron frequents reefs on the coast, but it is also found on tidal creeks and brackish lagoons, mangrove swamps, etc., though never far from the sea. It ranges along the coasts of the Indian Ocean from the Persian Gulf, west coast of India, the Laccadives, to

× one-sixth

Ceylon, where it is found from Chilaw northwards to the Jaffna Peninsula. In the latter I had frequent opportunities for watching its habits during two years, but it was present only from December to May and was seen most often in February and March. Though usually solitary or in pairs, it not infrequently associated with Little Egrets, from which even its white variety was easily distinguished by the yellow beak, stouter legs, and much more extensively green or yellow tarsi. It was always seen wading in shallow muddy creeks, lagoons, or flood-water ponds, or else flying with flocks of Little Egrets. When fishing, the Reef Herons were found to be much more lively than the egrets, running gawkily about, turning quickly, jumping, and frequently stabbing at small fish. They were less shy than Little Egrets, and would often allow approach to within thirty-five yards or so before taking wing.

Layard found the Reef Heron breeding near Chilaw in May and June, about a hundred years ago, but it does not appear to have been found breeding in Ceylon since. The nests were large masses of sticks, etc., placed in trees near the water's edge—probably in a mangrove swamp. This species is said to breed, in India, in colonies, usually apart from other species. The three or four eggs are the pale sea-green common to most of the heron tribe, and they measure about 44 × 33·5 mm.

THE CATTLE EGRET

Bubulcus ibis coromandus (Boddaert). Resident

Sinhalese: Harak-kokkā. Tamil: Unni-kokku

Size of the Little Egret. Sexes alike. In non-breeding plumage it is white throughout, though not so snowy-white as the Little and Median Egrets; a slight yellowish tinge is usually present. In breeding plumage the head, neck, chest and back are beautiful golden buff, the bushy crest somewhat lengthened, and the dorsal feathers long and narrow. Bill chrome yellow; lores greenish-yellow; irides yellow; legs black, the tibia yellow. In non-breeding plumage this bird is difficult to distinguish in the field from the Median Egret, but its shorter bill (three against 3¾ inches from gape) and less graceful form help to identify it. From the Little Egret its yellow bill distinguishes it at all times.

In two races, this egret extends from the Iberian Peninsula, tropical Africa, throughout southern Asia to Japan and many islands of the Indian and western Pacific Oceans. In Ceylon it is abundant throughout the low country and lower hills, wherever cattle graze; as its name suggests, it is always found associating with cattle or buffaloes, wild or tame. While preferring damp, swampy meadows, any open, grassy country suits it provided cattle are present. With its bovine friends it lives in great amity, walking fearlessly about their feet, picking ticks,

leeches and biting flies off their hides, and perching on their backs. The main reason for this association with cattle is probably the number of grasshoppers and other insects, frogs, and lizards, etc., that are disturbed by the beasts as they move about. It is interesting to watch one taking aim at some insect, with lateral oscillations of the retracted neck until aim and distance are correct, when the beak is shot forward as if by the release of a powerful spring. The Cattle Egret is highly gregarious. It roosts in flocks, flighting in companies to and from

× one-eighth

favourite roosting trees. The flight is similar to that of other small herons. Normally a silent bird, it utters a variety of croaks at its nesting places.

The breeding season is from December to May. Like other egrets, it breeds in colonies, placing its stick nests high up in trees growing in water. The three to five very pale, bluish-white eggs measure about 44 × 34 mm.

THE POND HERON, or PADDY BIRD

Ardeola grayii (Sykes). Resident

Sinhalese: Kana-kokkā. Tamil: Kuruttu-kokku, Nuli-madayān

Size of the White-breasted Waterhen but with a very much longer neck. Sexes alike. In non-breeding plumage, the head, neck and breast are greyish-brown, boldly streaked with buff; mantle plain greyish-brown; all the rest of the plumage, and notably the wings, white; beak blackish, with the lower mandible dull yellow; lores pale green. In breeding plumage, the head, neck and breast are soft greyish-buff, darker on the dorsal parts; the breast-feathers long and decomposed; the whole mantle deep, maroon-brown; a nuchal crest, of three or four long narrow white feathers, develops; the wings, rump and tail, and underparts remain white. Bill yellow, with the tip black and the base shading into the bluish lores; irides bright yellow; legs and feet dull green, except when the bird is in the height of breeding condition when they change to yellowish-fleshy for a short time.

This small heron is by far the commonest and most widely distributed of its family in Ceylon, being found in every paddy-field, tank-margin, pond, lagoon-shore, borrow-pit or wet ditch in the Island, up to at least 4,000 feet; and it has, of recent years, found its way up to the Nuwara Eliya lake. Throughout the low country it is one of the commonest and most familiar of birds. Outside Ceylon, it is found from the Persian Gulf, eastwards, through India and Burma, to the Malay Peninsula. It spends most of its time standing in shallow water, or by its edge, its body nearly horizontal and neck retracted, intently watching for the approach of any unwary fish, frog, or water-insect. While thus engaged it is very inconspicuous, especially in non-breeding plumage, its drab mantle concealing the white wings which flash out with startling effect when the bird flies. It is tame and unsuspicious as a rule. The flight is performed with rather rapid flaps of the rounded wings and, like all herons, with head retracted and feet projecting beyond the tail. It perches freely on stumps, fences, etc., and flights at dusk, in flocks, to favourite roosting trees where a number will collect nightly. Except when breeding it is not noisy, merely uttering a peevish-sounding *krake* as it flies off on being disturbed; but at its heronries it utters a variety of guttural and harsh notes. It is dangerous to confine in an aviary with other birds, often blinding them by stabs of its sharp beak.

The main breeding season is from December to May but some pairs nest much later than this. As the season approaches the birds betake themselves to regular heronries, where a number will nest in company, often, but not always, in association with other species of waders. The nest is an untidy platform of twigs, placed usually in the higher branches of a leafy tree, generally one that overhangs water. The three or four greenish-blue eggs measure about 39·5 × 29·5 mm.

Breeding plumage; × one-seventh

THE LITTLE GREEN HERON

Butorides striatus javanicus (Horsfield). Resident

Sinhalese: Podi-kokkā. Tamil: Thōsi-kokku

Plate 29, facing p. 392 (×one-sixth)

Smaller than the Pond Heron; scarcely as big as a domestic pigeon but with a much longer neck when extended. Sexes alike, and there is no distinctive breeding plumage in this species. Young birds are smoky-brown, with three broad, longitudinal, buff stripes on the side of the neck, a mottled black and white stripe down the middle of the fore-neck, underparts white in the middle, smoky-brown at the sides; four rows of wing-coverts have triangular buff tips to the feathers.

In some nineteen or twenty slightly differentiated racial forms this little heron has an enormous distribution, practically throughout the tropics of the world. Our subspecies is found in India, Malaya, through the Indo-Chinese region, to the Philippines, Sunda Islands, and Celebes. In Ceylon it is found in all coastal districts and along the lower reaches of the rivers to several hundred feet above sea level; and it also frequents inland tanks. Its favourite habitat is where mangroves or other forms of dense vegetation grow down to the water's edge; where this condition exists it is not uncommon on the sea-shore itself. Although it must have shady vegetation within easy reach, it is not a skulking bird and will fish in the day-time within full view of a road. It becomes more active, however, towards dusk, when it leaves its shelter and flies out on a round of visits to favourite fishing spots. Two juveniles, observed fishing in rock pools on the sea-shore, showed their excitement, while stalking small fishes, by erecting their head-feathers into bushy crests and jerking the tail from side to side in the same manner as the Yellow Bittern (see p. 402).

When suddenly disturbed, the Green Heron utters a staccato alarm-note *k'yow, k'yow* or *k'yek, k'yek* (*y* as in 'yes'), as it flies off. Its flight resembles that of other small herons, the wings being somewhat bent downwards at the wrist and flapped rather leisurely, the body rising and sinking at each flap. Small fish, prawns, and aquatic insects and their larvae form its food.

In the Jaffna district I found this little heron breeding in July, in a mangrove-covered, low islet in the midst of a lagoon. Two occupied nests and four old ones (probably the previous year's) were found within an area of about fifteen yards square, and they were from 2½ to seven feet from the ground. The nests were platforms of twigs about eight inches in diameter placed well under the tree canopies. One occupied nest contained two half-grown young, the other two small

399

babies and an addled egg; this was elliptical in shape, very pale prussian blue in colour, glossless and rather mat-surfaced, and measured 37·5 × 27·7 mm.

THE NIGHT HERON

Nycticorax nycticorax nycticorax (Linnaeus). Resident

Sinhalese: Rê-kāna-kokkā. Tamil: Vakkā

Plate 29, facing p. 392 (× one-sixth)

About the size of a village hen. Sexes alike. Young birds are ashy-brown, much streaked on head, neck and breast with pale buff and with each of the quill-feathers and wing-coverts tipped with dirty white, forming neat rows of spots. Bill in the young green, darkening to brown on the top; irides yellow; legs greyish-green. In full breeding condition, the loreal skin of adults is dark greyish-purple, and the legs, which are normally greenish-yellow or pale orange, become for a few days deep flesh-colour, or pale crimson. This is a stocky-looking heron, with comparatively short, stout beak, and short legs; its head is usually drawn close in to the shoulders, making the bird look almost neckless, but in striking at fish, etc., it can be extended to ten inches or more.

The Night Heron, in several races, ranges almost throughout the tropical and temperate regions of the globe. In Ceylon it is found in scattered colonies all over the low country. It prefers mangrove-lined lagoons or estuaries, tree-covered islands in tanks and the like, but where undisturbed it will form colonies in clumps of trees even in the midst of towns, and not necessarily very near water. A large colony took possession of some big trees at the Museum Zoo, Colombo, nesting freely. Except when feeding young—when it brings food for them all day long—it is nocturnal, spending the day roosting quietly, in companies, in densely-foliaged trees; but at dusk it flies forth, usually in small parties, to its feeding-grounds which may be a considerable distance away. It flies with steady, even strokes of the wings, the head retracted, and only the toes projecting beyond the tail. As it flies, it keeps in touch with its companions by frequently uttering a *kwak* . . . *kwak* or sometimes *quārk*. This cry is often heard from birds passing overhead when it is too dark to see them. The Night Heron appears to feed mainly on fish, but frogs and water insects are also eaten. In trees it clambers about stealthily and is usually so well concealed by the foliage that its presence may go unsuspected unless the birds are driven out, when they will flutter off to safer quarters with hoarse croaks of disapproval.

The breeding season is variable, depending on rainfall. When conditions are favourable it is probable that two or more broods are raised during the year, but December to March appear to be the favourite months. The nest is an untidy mass of sticks, placed at varying heights from the ground but generally well under the tree canopy. The three or four pale bluish eggs measure about 50·8 × 35·2 mm. The hunger-cry of the nestlings is a reiterated *clik clik clik*.

THE MALAY BITTERN

Gorsachius melanolophus melanolophus (Raffles). Winter visitor

Sinhalese: Rê-kokkā. No Tamil name recorded

Plate 29, facing p. 392 (× one-sixth)

Size of a village hen; slightly smaller than the Night Heron. Sexes alike. The bird shown on the Plate is adult but the majority of individuals that visit Ceylon are juvenile; in these the general colour is dark brown, ashy-black on crown and bushy nuchal crest; feathers of the latter each with a white spot near the tip; fore-neck and breast dull buff with a line of blackish streaks and bars down the centre.

This bittern, in several races, ranges through most of the Indo-Malayan countries and islands, to southern China, Formosa and the Philippines. In Ceylon it is a regular winter migrant, arriving on the west coast in October and November and, as soon as it has recovered from its long flight across the sea from India, leaving for the interior. It ascends to 5,000 or 6,000 feet in the hills. Being a shy jungle bird of nocturnal habits, it seldom comes under notice except on its arrival when, being more or less exhausted, many blunder into houses and gardens and are easily caught. It spends the day-time skulking beneath undergrowth in damp places, but becomes lively at night, flying into trees and clambering actively about the branches. Captive birds generally stand hunched up, now and then walking stealthily about; but when alarmed, their crests are erected, wings half expanded, and they make savage jabs with the open beak towards the object of their fear, at the same time uttering a hoarse croak. When hungry, a rasping *arh arh arh* (*a* as in 'hat') is uttered. Frogs, lizards and insects, rather than fish, seem to comprise the bird's main food—though it will doubtless eat fish when it can catch them.

In Travancore the breeding season of this bittern appears to be from May to July. It nests in trees, usually at a considerable height, but sometimes in reed-beds. The site chosen is in dense forest on the bank of a stream, and the nest is made of small branches and twigs. The four or five eggs are dead white, and measure about 46·5 × 37·5 mm.

THE YELLOW BITTERN

Ixobrychus sinensis sinensis (Gmelin). Status not quite certain; certainly partly resident, but probably also a winter migrant

Sinhalese: Meti-kokkā. Tamil: Mannal-nārai

Plate 29, facing p. 392 (male; × one-sixth)

Ceylon's smallest member of the heron tribe; hardly as bulky as a domestic pigeon though with much longer neck and legs. The female is darker than the male, and has three or four brown, longitudinal streaks down the sides of the neck; young birds appear to resemble the female, but the plumage-changes of this bird require further study before they will be properly understood. From the Chestnut Bittern, the ashy-black flight-feathers at once distinguish it at all ages.

The Yellow Bittern, in a number of doubtfully-distinct races, is found in a large part of the oriental region extending from India to Japan and including many of the associated islands. In Ceylon it appears to be mainly a winter migrant as it becomes rare except in the north-east monsoon; during which, however, it is common in the low country and ascends the hills, in places, to 4,000 feet. Its favourite haunts are reed-beds and screw-pine thickets bordering rivers, canals and lakes; and being a good deal less shy, and less nocturnal, than our other bitterns it may easily be observed within a few miles of Colombo. Its habits and behaviour make it most amusing to watch owing to the strange attitudes it adopts while fishing; it perches on reed-stems, sticks, etc., with all the adroitness of a warbler, clambering about tangled waterside vegetation with the utmost agility. When excited by the approach of prey it has a curious habit of jerking its short tail from side to side, with a downward, semicircular sweep, the terminal positions of the tail being almost at right angles with the axis of the body (the bird in the Plate is shown performing this gesture). Excitement is shown, also, by frequent raising and expanding of one wing in a spasmodic manner. When it walks about, the head-feathers are often raised as a ragged, bushy crest. On the approach of an intruder the bird will freeze into immobility and, if the danger does not pass, will slowly raise the beak and neck into a vertical line, keeping the front of the neck towards the intruder; in this posture it is almost impossible to distinguish among the surrounding reed-stems. Small fishes, frogs, water-insects, crabs and the like, form its food. The flight of this bittern is rather slow and laboured and, in the day-time at least, seldom long sustained—a flutter from one reed-bed to the next; no doubt it flies well and strongly on migration, which is probably performed at night. The breeding season appears to be from May to August. The nest is a shallow platform of reed-stems, etc., placed low down in the midst of dense reeds, or in a clump of long grass. The three to five eggs are pale greenish-white, and measure about 33·3 × 24·5 mm.

THE CHESTNUT BITTERN

Ixobrychus cinnamomeus (Gmelin). Resident

Sinhalese: Meti-kokkā. Tamil: Kuruttu-kokku

Plate 29, facing p. 392 (male; × one-sixth)

Slightly larger and heavier-built than the last; much smaller than the Pond Heron. The Plate shows the male; the female is browner, mottled with buff on the wing-coverts and streaked with dark brown on the underparts; a dark, broken streak down the centre of the throat, neck and breast; her loreal skin is yellow.

This bittern ranges from India to Manchuria, the Philippines and Celebes, etc. In Ceylon it is common throughout the low country and ascends to Nuwara Eliya. Like other bitterns, it lives solitary or in pairs, and inhabits swamps and reed-beds, and paddy-fields when the paddy is well grown. In my experience, it is a much shyer bird than the Yellow Bittern and, as a rule, all one sees of it is a bright chestnut bird flying off, with a complaining croak, when put up out of standing paddy or reeds. In general, its habits and behaviour are similar to those of the Yellow Bittern but it is more nocturnal and its flight is stronger, performed with rather slow, steady strokes of the wings which, as with most small herons, are slightly bent downwards at the wrist, giving a characteristic style to the flight; the head is, as usual in all the heron tribe, drawn back to the shoulders, the long neck being so S-bent as to seem almost non-existent, and the toes project beyond the tail. Besides the croaking flight-note above-mentioned I have heard a male uttering a low *kokokokokoko*, which was probably a courtship-note. Fish, frogs, insects and other small animals form its food.

Legge found the Chestnut Bittern breeding in June and July, in the Western Province. The nest is formed of dry grass, etc., and is placed low down in the middle of a grass-tussock growing in a swamp. The three to five eggs are white, and measure about 33 × 26 mm.

THE BLACK BITTERN

Dupetor flavicollis flavicollis (Latham). Partly resident, but probably in the main a winter migrant from India

Sinhalese: Kalu-kokkā. Tamil: Karuppu-nārai

Plate 29, facing p. 392 (male; ×one-sixth)

About the size of the House Crow, but with much longer neck and legs. The female is browner than the male but resembles him in pattern. This bittern, in some five races, has a range from India and China, through Malaya and the chain of islands extending eastwards from it, to Australia and the Solomon Islands. In Ceylon it is fairly common, in suitable places, almost throughout the low country, and is sometimes seen in the hills, though probably only on passage, up to 4,000 feet. It is mainly nocturnal, and is a shy, skulking bird, delighting in densely-tangled swamps, especially those which have open channels fringed with thickets of screw-pine and climbing fern running through them. In these impenetrable retreats it spends the day perching on some stump or snag, or occasionally visiting the water's edge, under cover of over-hanging herbage, to do a little fishing. Towards dusk it becomes lively, showing itself on top of the vegetation and flying over the swamp in search of fishing-grounds. Like other bitterns, while at rest its neck is retracted so that the head appears to grow out of the shoulders and breast; but this appearance is deceptive, as the long, sharp beak—a dangerous weapon—can be shot out to a distance of a foot or so. It climbs actively about among the twigs and creepers of its retreat, threading its way through vegetation with marvellous facility. Its ordinary flight-note is described by Legge as a loud, hoarse croak and, in the breeding season, it produces a low, deep booming sound likened to that of a small drum. Its food consists largely of fish, but frogs and insects are also eaten.

Wait, on two occasions, found the Black Bittern breeding in the North Central Province in April. The nests were small structures of twigs placed, within three feet of the water, in small, thorny trees over-hanging a tank. The three or four eggs are very pale sea-green, and measure about 42·3 × 32 mm.

THE FLAMINGO

Phoenicopterus ruber roseus Pallas. Winter visitor and summer loiterer

Sinhalese: Sīyak-kārayā. Tamil: Pū-nārai, Urian

Size of the Painted Stork but much taller, owing to the very long legs and neck. Sexes alike. Plumage white, with a pink flush more or less present; the upper and under wing-coverts rose-pink to bright scarlet, varying in intensity; all the flight-feathers black. Bill pink, black at the tip; irides pale yellow; legs and feet dull pink. Young birds are greyish, with the wing-coverts mottled brown and traces of pink here and there; bill dark grey; legs and feet grey or brown.

This very long-necked and long-legged bird, with its curiously-shaped beak and white, scarlet-pink, and black colouring, cannot be mistaken for any other bird. In three races, it occurs in the tropics and sub-tropics of both hemispheres. Our race breeds in suitable places in southern Europe, north Africa, and central Asia; recently it has been found breeding in the Rann of Cutch. In Ceylon it is mainly a winter visitor, but a good many

× one-fifteenth

loiter through the south-west monsoon and it has often been suspected of breeding on remote lagoons in the Eastern Province. Positive evidence of this is, however, lacking, and while it may have done so in times past, when the country was very much wilder, it seems improbable that it could nowadays find a sufficiently undisturbed, large area of suitable country for the purpose.

The flamingo lives in flocks of up to a thousand or more, being highly gregarious; and is shy and wary, avoiding cover, and preferring brackish or salt water to fresh. While it can swim well and its long legs allow it, on occasion, to wade in water a yard deep, it prefers depths of a few inches in which it can reach the bottom with its peculiarly-shaped beak. It sifts the mud between its mandibles, straining out the vegetable substances and small aquatic animals, such as shellfish, which form its food. Its long neck assumes a series of graceful curves, particularly when the bird is preening its plumage. It commonly sleeps standing on one leg, with the neck coiled round to bring the head between the shoulders where the bill is tucked between the scapulars; the resting leg is tucked under the flank feathers, its hock-joint projecting behind the tail. Flight is easy and sustained, with the neck and legs fully extended. The birds of a flock fly, evenly spaced, in long lines or Λ formation and, with their scarlet wing-coverts contrasting with the white plumage and black flight-feathers, they provide a magnificent spectacle. The flamingo utters a variety of goose-like, gaggling notes when feeding, and loud, honking cries on the wing; a solitary bird, which I watched in a lagoon at Jaffna, repeatedly uttered, with open beak, a croaking sound, *aaaaa*.

Nesting is in large colonies, in shallow, vast areas of muddy water, preferably brackish. Mud is scooped up from the bottom until a small hillock, from a few inches to a couple of feet high and about fifteen inches across, rises above the water; a shallow cavity is formed on the top for the eggs, and the bird incubates with its legs drawn up under the body. The two eggs are white, with a chalky outer layer; they measure about $88 \cdot 8 \times 54 \cdot 6$ mm. The young are clothed with down and are able to walk and run soon after hatching.

GEESE AND DUCKS

Order ANSERIFORMES

SWIMMING water-birds, with the bill broadened and flattened, the inside edges of both mandibles furnished with horny, comb-like ridges or serrations adapted for sifting food-particles from water; the whole bill, except the hard nail or dertrum at the tip, is covered with soft skin. Legs rather short; feet with three front toes fully webbed; hind toe small, and set higher on the leg than the front ones. Body long and boat-shaped, the sternal keel ('breastbone') rather low. Wings generally moderately long; tail short. Body plumage thick and close, with an undercoat of dense down. All the wing quills are moulted at the same time, so that flight is impossible until the new ones have grown. The young are clothed with down on hatching, and can run and swim as soon as they have dried off from the egg. Until the birds are well-grown, the wings remain in a very small and undeveloped state, but they grow rapidly after the body has reached nearly its full size. Geese and ducks nest usually on the ground, but some kinds habitually nest in hollow trees and the like. The nest is commonly lined with copious quantities of the mother's own down, which she plucks from her breast for the purpose; this down is used to cover the eggs when the bird leaves them temporarily. The eggs are white, or nearly so, and are unmarked.

So far as Ceylon is concerned, the *Anseriformes* contains a single family, *Anatidae*, which comprises swans, geese, ducks and sawbills. Swans and sawbills are absent from our fauna, geese are represented by one record of a single species, and of the ducks only three species are resident (one of these, the Comb Duck, is almost certainly now extinct in Ceylon). All the remaining ten species are winter migrants and at least half of them are mere stragglers, with only one or two records apiece. There is, however, little doubt that they visit the Island more frequently than the records indicate and, as these birds are of great interest to sportsmen, fuller accounts of them are given below than their meagre records seem to justify.

THE GREY-LAG GOOSE

Anser anser (Linnaeus). Only once recorded from Ceylon

Sinhalese: Pāteyā. Tamil: Vātthu

Smaller and more lightly-built than the common domestic goose, of which it is the wild progenitor. Sexes alike. A large, brownish-grey bird, with the upperparts much barred in neat transverse lines, with pale greyish-white; rump and lesser wing-coverts pale, clear grey; upper and under tail-coverts white; base of most of the tail-feathers dark ashy-brown, tips white. Bill orange or pink, with a large, white nail at the tip; irides dark brown; legs and feet pink. Anyone familiar with the ordinary, domestic goose (not the long-necked Chinese goose, which has a large knob on the dorsal base of the bill) will have no difficulty in recognizing this species.

It has a wide range through northern Europe and Asia and winters in southern Europe, northern Africa, and north-western India and China. A single specimen has been procured in Ceylon but sportsmen have several times reported having seen 'geese', which were probably of this species, in various parts of the Island. It should be looked for in open, grassy country, preferably not far from the sea. It is a bird of powerful flight, usually associating in flocks which travel, evenly spaced, in long lines or in ∧ formation; gaggling and honking cries, similar to those made by the domestic bird, are frequently uttered. Although it can swim well and does so freely, it spends most of its time on land, where it finds its favourite diet of grass. It is very wary and watchful, difficult to approach.

The Grey-lag Goose breeds in the northern parts of its range, nesting on the ground in moors or swamps.

THE COMB DUCK, or NUKHTA

Sarkidiornis melanota (Pennant). Formerly resident, but probably now extinct in Ceylon

Sinhalese: Kabalittiyā. Tamil: Mūkkan-tāra

Size of the domestic Muscovy duck, but standing higher on the legs. Sexes alike in coloration, but the female is smaller than the male and lacks the high, black, fleshy protuberance that adorns the top of his bill; this is most pronounced in the breeding season. Head, neck, and underparts white, the head and most of the neck being irregularly sprinkled with small, black spots which are thickest on the dorsal parts;

a white collar separates the black-spotted neck from the glossy-black back, wings and tail, which are shot with metallic green, blue and purple; lower back brownish-grey, blending into the metallic-green-black of the rump; a black band descends from the upper back down the sides of the chest, and another descends from the rump down the lower flanks; between these two marks, the flanks are greyish-brown. Bill and 'comb' black; irides dark brown; legs and feet dark leaden-grey.

Male; × one-twelfth

This large and handsome duck might be mistaken for a Muscovy, except that it has no red caruncles around the eye. It ranges through a large part of Africa, Madagascar, India, Burma, to Siam and south-eastern China. In Legge's time it was not uncommon in the wilder districts of Ceylon, but it does not appear to have been seen for many years and it is to be feared that it is now extinct in the Island. It may, however, visit us occasionally from India, and it is greatly to be hoped that, should it do so, sportsmen and poachers will restrain their natural hankering to shoot so splendid a duck, so that it may have a chance of rehabilitating itself as a resident species. It frequents weedy jungle tanks and lives in small flocks, which move about freely in the day-time—it being less nocturnal than most ducks. It feeds on various vegetable substances, being partial to paddy, and also eats a variety of aquatic animals. The flight is powerful and speedy; a flock flies in mob-formation, not in the orderly lines and Λs that many ducks and geese adopt. It perches readily, and roosts at night, on the larger boughs of trees. The ordinary note is described as a low, guttural quack-like sound, but in the breeding season it becomes a loud *honk*.

The breeding season in Ceylon was about February and March. The nest is a rough collection of grass, sticks, etc., mixed with feathers, and is usually placed in a large hollow in the trunk of a big tree growing near water. The seven to twelve or more eggs are polished ivory-colour, and they measure about 62 × 43·5 mm.

THE COTTON TEAL, or 'QUACKY-DUCK'

Nettapus coromandelianus coromandelianus (Gmelin). Resident

Sinhalese: Măl-sēruwā. Tamil: Rāja-tāra

Plate 30, facing p. 393 (female left, male right; ✕ one-tenth)

A tiny duck, no bigger than a domestic pigeon. In the Plate, the male is shown in breeding plumage; out of the breeding season he resembles the female, losing the black collar and becoming mottled on head and breast with brown, but he retains the white band on the wing, and some of his green gloss.

In two racial forms, the Cotton Teal ranges from India to southern China and the Philippines, and through Malaysia to eastern Australia. In Ceylon it is found, in suitable places, throughout the low country, but is much commoner in the dry zone than in the wet zone, where it is probably only a north-east monsoon visitor. It lives in flocks of up to thirty or so and frequents, for preference, those tanks and large ponds where patches of open water occur among weedy and lotus-covered areas. In such places, it may be seen swimming slowly about in small parties, usually keeping near the weedy parts. It feeds both on green-stuff and on water-insects, molluscs, etc. Most of its time is spent on the water and it seldom comes ashore, being a poor walker; but in the breeding season it perches freely on the larger boughs of trees. It flies well and fast with rapid fluttering of the wings, frequently uttering a curious rasping *quak, quakyduck* . . . *quak, quakyduck*—usually rendered as *fix bayonets*. When frightened, a flock generally flies around the tank but soon settles again among lotus leaves where it is practically invisible. The male looks particularly handsome on the wing.

This quaint little duck breeds from January to March, and again in August. It nests in cavities in trees growing near tanks; the cavity may be at any height, from near ground level to thirty feet or more, but usually ten or fifteen feet; it is lined with a little grass, etc., mixed with feathers. The eight to twelve eggs are ivory-white, very smooth-textured, and measure about 42 ✕ 33 mm.

THE WHISTLING TEAL, or WHISTLING TREE DUCK

Dendrocygna javanica (Horsfield). Resident

Sinhalese: Sēruwā, Thumba-sēruwā. Tamil: Chilli-tāra

Plate 30, facing p. 393 (✕ one-tenth)

About the size of a half-grown domestic duck. Sexes alike. From all other Ceylon ducks it can at once be distinguished by its broad, rounded black and maroon wings, and by its habit of uttering a clear, cackling whistle in flight.

This little duck, which has a wide distribution through the Indian, Indo-Chinese, and Malayan regions, is common throughout the low country in weedy tanks and swamps, particularly those surrounded by jungle; it does not frequent coastal lagoons, being a freshwater bird. Except when paired for breeding, it lives always in flocks—usually of a dozen or so but occasionally up to several hundreds. The day is spent swimming among lotus leaves, sleeping on some small islet or perching on the boughs of a dead tree standing in water, etc.; but as dusk approaches, the flock takes to wing and, flying in mob-formation with much musical whistling, betakes itself to some rice-field where its members spend the night devouring the cultivators' paddy, to which this bird is very partial. It is a nuisance to farmers, but as it also eats quantities of insects and small animals detrimental to paddy cultivation its influence on human agriculture is not wholly bad. Its flight is rather slow and laboured, with heavy flapping of the wings. On land it walks well though with a slight waddle, but its true home is in the water where it swims powerfully and dives readily—both in play and for food—descending to at least six or eight feet and remaining submerged for many seconds on occasion. Owing to the constant shooting to which it is subjected it is shy and wary, but it quickly becomes tame if kept in an aviary, and makes an amusing little pet.

The breeding season is in December and January, and again in July–August. The nest is either hidden in clumps of grass or the like or is placed in a cavity in a large tree up to twenty feet from the ground. The site chosen is often on an islet or a tree standing in water. The seven to twelve eggs are white and smooth but not glossy; they measure about 48 × 38 mm.

THE LARGE WHISTLING TEAL

Dendrocygna bicolor bicolor (Vieillot). Rare winter visitor

The Sinhalese and Tamil names would be the same as those of the last species

About the size of a small domestic duck; considerably larger than the common Whistling Teal. Sexes alike. In general appearance and coloration this species closely resembles the last; it may at once be distinguished from it, however, by the following features: a black line down the back of the neck; sides of the neck in the middle, pale buff longitudinally streaked with grey; less maroon-red on the wing-coverts; the *upper tail-coverts are buff-white*, not maroon.

This duck has a remarkable distribution; it is found in tropical America, Africa and Madagascar, through India to Pegu, but it has occurred only very rarely in Ceylon; according to Wait, a few specimens were once obtained near Mannar, and there is one record from the Southern Province. Very likely it visits the Island more often than these records suggest but, when shot by sportsmen, it would probably be regarded merely as a large specimen of the common species —and find its way into the pot, unrecorded! In general, its habits resemble those of its small relative.

THE RUDDY SHELDRAKE, or BRAHMINY DUCK

Casarca ferruginea (Pallas). Rare straggler

Sinhalese: Lōku-sēruwā. Tamil: Tāra

Size of a large domestic duck. Sexes nearly alike. An orange-brown duck with white wing-coverts which show more especially in flight—at rest they are mostly concealed by the scapular and flank feathers; wing-quills and tail black, the secondaries highly glossed with metallic green; the head is pale buff, paler in the female, which has the face whitish. Bill and legs black, irides dark brown. In breeding plumage, the male develops a narrow black collar on the lower neck.

This handsome duck breeds in southern Europe and central Asia, including Tibet and Mongolia, and winters to the southward of these countries. It is common in winter throughout India, in suitable places, but has been recorded in Ceylon on only a few occasions. It lives in pairs and frequents the shores or islets of spacious lagoons and tanks, always keeping well out in the open, away from cover, for it is a very wary bird. Though it swims well enough, on occasion, with the neck erect and stern held high, it is usually seen resting on rocks or sandbanks. It flies powerfully, with rather slow beats of its long wings, and often rises high in the air. Largely nocturnal, when dusk arrives it betakes itself to grass-fields and the like, where it crops grass like a goose; it is not entirely vegetarian, however, being omnivorous like most ducks. It has a loud, goose-like cry which Whistler likens to *a-onk*; this is freely uttered by both sexes.

The Brahminy Duck nests in holes in cliffs, deserted burrows of animals, or even in cavities in buildings, in the lands where it breeds; in Tibet and Ladakh it breeds at elevations of 12,000 feet or more, usually near a lake or large river but sometimes at a distance from water. The six to ten eggs are laid on a mass of down plucked by the bird from her breast. They are creamy-white and slightly glossy, and measure about 64 × 46 mm.

THE SPOTTED-BILLED DUCK

Anas poecilorhyncha poecilorhyncha Forster. Rare winter visitor

Sinhalese: Sēruwā. Tamil: Tāra

Size of a domestic duck. Sexes alike. This is a greyish-looking duck, of very similar build and appearance to the ordinary domestic duck. It can be distinguished at once from all other ducks by the bill, which is black with half an inch of the tip chrome yellow and two orange-red spots at the dorsal base of the upper mandible. The head and neck are greyish-white; dark brown on top of the head, and with a brown band from the side of the beak through the eye; back and scapulars dark brown, with pale grey edges to the feathers, giving a scaly effect; posteriorly, the colour deepens to dark brown, becoming nearly black at the tail; breast and underparts pale greyish, spotted with dark brown; primaries dark brown; secondaries rich, metallic green, forming a speculum which is bordered, in front and behind, with black and white bands; outer webs of the long and broad tertiaries white, forming a conspicuous white patch. Irides dark brown; legs and feet orange. The combination of mottled greyish coloration, red spots at the base of the bill, green speculum, and orange legs, make this duck unmistakable.

It is resident in India, making only local migrations; but though at one time fairly common in Ceylon it is now a very rare visitor in the north-east monsoon. This handsome duck is a freshwater species, frequenting jungle tanks in pairs or small flocks; it is less gregarious than many ducks. It likes weedy lakes in which it finds the vegetable substances and aquatic insects, etc., upon which it feeds; a good deal of paddy, when available, is eaten as well. Its flight is rather slow and heavy to begin with, but when properly under way it travels fast. The note is a quack, rather like that of the mallard (or its domesticated variety, the farmyard duck).

In India, this species breeds from March to December, according to rainfall conditions. The nest is well-made and compact, concealed in long grass or herbage, usually on a small islet or the margin of a tank. The eight to ten eggs are pale greyish-buff, and measure about 55·3 × 43·5 mm.

THE GADWALL

Anas strepera Linnaeus. Only one specimen recorded from Ceylon

No Sinhalese or Tamil names more specific than the 'Sēruwā' and 'Tāra', respectively, which are applied indiscriminately to all wild ducks

About the size of the Whistling Teal or a little larger. In general, this bird may be described as a brownish-grey duck very like the mottled-brown variety of the ordinary domestic duck. It is smaller, however, and has the underparts, below the breast, white, and a *white* speculum on the secondaries; the wing-coverts are more or less chestnut, shading to black against the speculum; head and neck paler and browner than the parts below, meeting these in a definite line; the breast in the male is dark brown with grey edges to the feathers, giving a scaly effect; scapulars and flanks closely vermiculated with grey; upper and under tail-coverts black. Bill in male, leaden-grey with dull orange edge; in female, blackish with dull orange sides; irides brown; legs and toes dull orange, webs dusky. Young birds are almost exactly like the domestic variety above-mentioned, except that they have the speculum white.

The gadwall ranges almost throughout the temperate parts of the northern hemisphere, breeding in the north and wintering in the south of its range. Vast numbers winter in northern India but it does not usually extend southwards of Mysore. A single specimen, shot at Palatupana in the Hambantota district about forty years ago, is the only Ceylon record up to date; but there is little doubt that it visits the Island in good migrant years amongst the thousands of garganey and pintail that winter on our dry-zone lagoons and tanks. It is mainly a freshwater bird, is a fast and lively flier, and is usually seen in flocks of twenty or thirty. The note is described as a quack (female) or a chuckling croak (male), but other sounds are also uttered. It is a shy species, generally keeping well out in the open on lagoons or tanks during the day and flighting to fields and swamps, for feeding, at night.

In its temperate-zone breeding-grounds it behaves much like other surface-feeding ducks, nesting on the ground, near water, in concealed sites among grass and herbage.

THE PINTAIL

Anas acuta acuta Linnaeus. Winter visitor

Sinhalese: Sēruwā. Tamil: Tāra

Plate 30, facing p. 393 (male left, female right; × one-tenth)

Size of a small domestic duck. The female closely resembles a dark-coloured specimen of the mottled-brown variety of the domestic duck, but she is more slender and graceful. In breeding plumage (shown on the Plate), the handsome drake is unmistakable; but when the birds arrive in Ceylon, sometimes as early as September, many of them are in process of moulting out of eclipse plumage and in this state they present a very patchy and confusing appearance. This induces many shooters to think they have obtained the mallard, but the following points will serve to prevent any confusion between the two species: (*a*) bill, in pintail, dark leaden-grey in both sexes; in mallard, it is dull yellowish-green in the drake, olive-brown and orange in the duck; (*b*) legs and feet in pintail leaden-grey, in mallard orange-red; (*c*) speculum in male pintail bronze-green, bordered cinnamon internally and white externally; in female, brown, bordered white both sides; in mallard, both sexes, rich metallic purple-blue, bordered black and white both sides. The mallard, which is the progenitor of the ordinary domestic duck (not the Muscovy), has not so far definitely been recorded from Ceylon although sportsmen often claim to have shot it; but there is no reason why it should not occasionally visit the Island in the winter, as it is common in India.

The pintail ranges throughout the northern hemisphere, breeding in temperate regions and wintering in the south of its range. It visits Ceylon in varying numbers each year during the north-east monsoon, frequenting dry-zone coastal lagoons in flocks up to a hundred or so. It is shy and watchful, spending the day on the water, or on low sand-banks, well out in the middle of a lagoon where it cannot be approached unobserved. Like other ducks, it gives much time to its toilet, preening and washing itself vigorously and frequently raising itself upright on the water while it flaps its wings. In shallow water it often 'up-ends' with the forepart of the body immersed while it searches with its beak on the bottom for food. At dusk, the flock flights to feeding-grounds, such as paddy-fields, where the birds feed on grain, other seeds and vege-table substances, and aquatic animals. The flight of the pintail is very swift, performed with rapid beating of the pointed wings; the long neck is extended, and the long, pointed tail gives a good indication of the bird's identity even at a considerable distance. The female produces a low note *quk quk*, less loud and more guttural than the quack of the mallard; but the male is silent as a rule.

The nesting of the pintail is similar to that of other species of *Anas*.

THE GARGANEY

Anas querquedula Linnaeus. Winter visitor

Sinhalese: Sēruwā. Tamil: Tāra

Plate 30, facing p. 393 (female left, male right; ✕ one tenth)

About the size of the Whistling Teal but more slenderly built, and with narrower, pointed wings. The Plate shows the difference between the sexes. From the teal, the male may readily be distinguished by (*a*) his broad, white eyebrow; (*b*) dark brown breast, mottled with buff, and sharply demarcated from the white underparts; (*c*) pale, bluish-grey wing-coverts; and (*d*) speculum, dull greyish-green, bordered with broad white bands in front and behind. The female is very much like the female teal, but may be distinguished by her pure white throat, white spot at the base of the bill, white eyebrow, and dull, brownish speculum.

The garganey breeds in many parts of Europe and Asia and winters in tropical Africa and southern Asia. It visits Ceylon in large numbers in the north-east monsoon, being the commonest of the migratory ducks in the Island; but it keeps mainly to lagoons on the coasts of the dry zone, from Mannar to Hambantota, avoiding the greater part of the west coast and seldom going inland to the tanks. It is highly gregarious, associating in large flocks often in company with other migratory ducks such as teal, pintail and shoveller. It is shy and suspicious of man and usually spends the day floating, far out from the shore, in a close flock; sometimes preening, sometimes sleeping, often rising in the water to exercise its wings by fluttering them; but always watchful for the approach of an enemy. At night, it flies to good feeding-grounds, such as paddy-fields. Although it likes grain, it is said to be more carnivorous than most ducks, eating insects, molluscs, crustaceans, etc. It is much given to feeding by 'dibbling' along the surface with its beak, sifting small food-particles from the water. The flight is very swift, performed by rapid fluttering of the wings. The female utters slight quacking sounds, and the male, in the breeding season, utters a curious crackling note.

In its breeding-grounds the garganey nests among long grass or other herbage, near water. As with other migratory ducks, the nest is lined with the mother's own downy breast-feathers. Seven to twelve creamy-buff eggs are laid; they measure about 45 ✕ 33 mm.

THE TEAL

Anas crecca crecca Linnaeus. Winter visitor

Sinhalese: Sēruwā. Tamil: Tāra

Plate 30, facing p. 393 (female left, male right; × one tenth)

A very small duck, not much bigger than a domestic pigeon. The sexes differ as shown in the Plate, but in eclipse plumage, which some birds still retain on their arrival in Ceylon, the male resembles the female. For points of difference between this bird and the garganey, see that species; here it will suffice to draw attention to the following recognition-points: small size; chestnut head of the male, with a broad, metallic-green patch on the side of the head enclosing the eye; this patch is bordered in front by a narrow, buff line; the male has a long, white stripe along the edge of the scapulars, with a black one below it; a buff triangle, surrounded by black, on each side of the posterior, under the tail; in both sexes, the speculum is brilliant metallic green on the inner secondaries, black on the outer ones.

This pretty little duck breeds from Iceland in the west, through Europe and Asia, to the Aleutian Islands in the east, and winters in the southern parts of this large area. In Ceylon, it arrives in varying numbers, being abundant in some years and scarce in others. It takes up its quarters mostly on coastal lagoons of the dry zone, though it often visits the larger tanks in the northern half of the Island. The heavy shooting to which it, in common with all ducks, is subjected, appears to be steadily reducing its numbers and it is certainly much less numerous than it was in Legge's day. It is very gregarious but, nowadays, is seldom seen in flocks of more than a dozen or so—generally associating with garganeys and other ducks. It likes shallow swamps with plenty of marsh vegetation and stretches of open water and in such places, if undisturbed, it will feed until late in the morning; but where its suspicions are aroused it keeps more out in open water and flights at night to the feeding-grounds. The teal is very agile on the wing, springing straight off the water if alarmed, and flying rapidly, with a twisty flight reminiscent of some sandpipers. On migration a flock will form lines of evenly-spaced birds, but in ordinary circumstances mob-formation is adopted. The food of this duck consists of the mixed diet of vegetable and animal substances usual among surface-feeding ducks. The note of the male is a musical *krik, krik*, that of the female a quack.

The teal breeds in the temperate zone in the spring, nesting on the ground in well-concealed sites among herbage, usually near water; the nest is lined with the breast-down of the mother. The eight to ten eggs are pale greyish-buff or greenish, and measure about 45·5 × 33·5 mm.

THE WIGEON

Anas penelope Linnaeus. Rare winter visitor

Sinhalese: Sēruwā. Tamil: Tāra

Between the Whistling Teal and the domestic duck in size. The male in breeding plumage may be recognized by the following combination of characters: head and neck chestnut, with a broad, buff band along the top of the head from beak to nape; breast pinkish-brown; back, scapulars and flanks grey, beautifully pencilled; underparts white; forepart of the wing, comprising the wing-coverts, white, and this white patch continued on the long inner secondaries, forming a long stripe on the side of the body when the wings are closed; tail pale smoky-grey; upper and under tail-coverts black; the tail is pointed, though not nearly so long as that of the male pintail; primaries and their coverts sepia-brown; speculum rich metallic green, bordered with black fore and aft. Bill rather small and tapering, greyish-blue, with the nail at the tip black; irides brown; legs and feet some shade of grey. The chestnut head with buff cap, grey body, and white wing-coverts make the male, in breeding plumage, unmistakable; but eclipse males, females, and young birds of both sexes, are difficult to describe satisfactorily for recognition purposes in the field; in general, they are mottled rufous-brown birds, with white underparts, a narrow, white wing-bar, and some metallic green on the speculum; in hand, the small grey or bluish beak will identify them.

The wigeon's breeding range is from Iceland, through the northern parts of Europe and Asia; and it winters in parts of North America, Europe, north Africa, and southern Asia. Although it is said to visit the north-western coasts of Ceylon regularly in small numbers during the north-east monsoon, the only definite record of a specimen obtained in the Island appears to be a male shot in December 1927, on a lagoon near Jaffna, the wing of which was sent to Wait for identification. In its breeding quarters it is mainly a freshwater bird, but prefers salt or brackish lagoons and estuaries in winter. It is highly gregarious, often associating in huge flocks which generally spend the day floating well away from cover. At night, it betakes itself to the shore, where it feeds on grass and other plants, a favourite being *Zostera* or 'sea-grass' which grows abundantly in many brackish lagoons; but as it does not dive for its food it can get this only where it is exposed at low tide. The wigeon flies speedily, with rapid wing-beats, and it also walks and runs well. The note of the male is a musical whistle *whee-oo*, that of the female is a purring growl.

On its northern breeding-grounds the wigeon nests among grass or heather, generally near water, and lines its nest with its own down. The six to ten eggs are creamy-white, and measure about 53·9 × 38 mm.

THE SHOVELLER

Spatula clypeata (Linnaeus). Occasional winter visitor

Sinhalese: Sēruwā. Tamil: Tāra

Plate 30, facing p. 393 (female left, male right; × one-tenth)

Slightly smaller than a domestic duck. The male in breeding plumage is shown on the Plate, but this is assumed rather late in the season and many birds, for some time after their arrival in Ceylon, wear a patchy mixture of both eclipse and breeding plumages; however, the identity of this duck need never be in doubt if the following points are borne in mind: (*a*) the big beak, which is twice as wide near the tip as at the base; no other Ceylon duck has a beak like it; (*b*) the wing-coverts are bright greyish-blue; (*c*) speculum green, with a broad white border in front; (*d*) legs orange-red.

The shoveller breeds in the temperate regions of the northern hemisphere—both Old and New Worlds—and winters to the south of these areas. Though common in northern India in winter it is only an occasional visitor in small numbers to Ceylon, where it frequents lagoons in the north and sometimes in the south-east. It is mainly a freshwater duck, delighting in shallow, weedy and muddy pools and, in India, where unmolested, it will even live on small and foul village ponds. Much of its time is spent swimming about with its head held low, diligently sieving the surface-water with its strainer-bill to extract small larvae and other items of food. It lives usually in pairs or small parties, though large flocks may form at migration time. The flight is strong with rapid wing-beats, and it springs up from water smartly, though not so quickly as the teal. It is rather a silent bird.

The shoveller breeds about April, in the countries where it nests, making the usual type of duck-nest on the ground, concealed among long grass, etc., and lining it with its own breast-down. The eight to twelve eggs are white, with a slight tinge of green or buff, and measure about 52 × 37 mm.

THE TUFTED DUCK

Aythya fuligula (Linnaeus). Only one record from Ceylon

No specific Sinhalese or Tamil names

About the size of the Whistling Teal. A tubby little duck with a slender, drooping crest (only slightly developed in the female) on the back of the head. The male has the head, neck, breast, back, most of the wing, and posterior of the body, black, glossed with purple on head and neck and green elsewhere; the flanks and belly are white and also the interior of the secondaries and inner primaries; bill pale blue-grey with the tip black; irides bright yellow; legs and feet slate-grey. The female is dark brown, with white underparts less clear-cut than those of the male, merging into the brown chest and abdomen; her bill is darker grey than the male's; speculum and inner primaries whitish. The combination of dark brown or black plumage, with white underparts and white speculum in the wing; bluish-grey bill, with black tip; and *bright yellow eyes*, contrasting with the dark head, make this duck unmistakable among Ceylonese species, even if the crest is not developed. It belongs to a section of the ducks known as 'diving ducks' because they habitually dive for their food, which they find mostly on the bottom of lakes or even, in many cases, the sea. To fit them for this diving habit they have big feet, on short legs set rather far back, and the hind toe has a lobe of skin; their plumage is closer and thicker than in the surface-feeding ducks.

The Tufted Duck is a recent addition to the Ceylon fauna; a wing of a male shot out of a flock of thirty or forty, in February 1949, at a small tank in the North Western Province, was sent by the shooter to W. W. A. Phillips, who identified it as belonging to this species. It breeds over a large part of Europe and Asia, and its winter quarters, which include much of India, lie to the south of its breeding range. It is mainly a freshwater bird, frequenting lakes, especially those which are fringed with reeds, .etc. When resting, it packs into compact flocks in open water. Being a poor walker, it seldom comes ashore. When feeding, it dives neatly, swimming along the bottom and sifting the mud with its beak for roots of water-plants, etc., and small aquatic animals; after a few seconds it pops up on the surface for a breather, then dives again, and so on. Its flight is rapid, with quickly-beating wings; but it gets off the water with some difficulty, splashing along for a few yards before it gets clear. The female utters a growling *kur-r-r, kur-r-r*, but the male is usually silent during the winter.

In temperate regions, it nests among herbage near the edge of a lake or pond, often on a small island. From six to fourteen or more eggs are laid, in a 'blanket' of the bird's down; they are greenish-grey, and measure about 58 × 41 mm.

It is probable that the RED-CRESTED POCHARD *Netta rufina* (Pallas) may occasionally visit Ceylon in the north-east monsoon; Layard, about a hundred years ago, watched two or three pairs of a duck, which he identified with this species, for several weeks on a stretch of brackish water between Jaffna and Elephant Pass; but they were too wary to allow him to collect them. This species is an abundant winter visitor to northern India, becoming scarcer towards the south. It is a large duck, nearly the size of a domestic duck. The male is easily identified by his bright scarlet-pink bill; bushily-crested chestnut head; black breast and underparts, with a large white patch on the flanks; a white crescent on the shoulder; brown back and wings, the latter with a white speculum; red legs, with blackish webs. The female is dark brown, with pale grey sides of the head and breast, a white speculum, and the bill and feet darker than in the male.

A look-out should be kept for this handsome bird on brackish lagoons near the dry-zone coasts. It is likely to occur in small flocks, which will keep well out in open water.

GREBES

Order PODICIPITIFORMES

GREBES are a highly-specialized order of swimming- and diving-birds, their whole economy being adapted to a life in water. In general, the form is duck-like but the bill is rather short, pointed and tapering, not at all like a duck's. The legs are attached to the body very far back and the tibia is almost all contained within the body-skin; this backward position makes walking difficult and compels these birds to adopt an upright posture when on land; they do not, however, normally go ashore. The large feet are not webbed in the ordinary way but each toe is separately webbed in the shape of a leaf. The tail-feathers are minute, almost indistinguishable from those surrounding them, so that the bird appears to have no tail. The body feathers are of peculiar structure, soft and close and rather furry in appearance; on the underparts they are smooth and silky. The wings are short and narrow, seemingly quite inadequate to support the plump body in flight; but, though grebes have considerable difficulty in getting off the water, when once under way they can fly quite well and often cover long distances, even ascending to high mountain-lakes. They feed on fish, prawns and water-insects, etc., and obtain nearly all their food by diving. Their nests are mere heaps of water-weeds piled up to form small islets in shallow water, and are generally very wet and soggy; the eggs, however, are resistant to damp and cold conditions and will hatch with a minimum of incubation. The chicks, which are downy, swim as soon as they have dried off after hatching.

The order contains but a single family, *Podicipitidae*.

THE LITTLE GREBE, or DABCHICK

Podiceps ruficollis capensis Salvadori. Resident

Sinhalese: Diya-sēruwā, Gembi-sērā. Tamil: Mukkuluvān, Kuluppai

A good deal smaller than the Cotton Teal—our smallest swimming-bird. Sexes alike. In the breeding season, smoky-brown, with ear-coverts and fore-neck chestnut; out of the season, paler, and whitish on the throat. Secondaries, and basal halves of primaries except the outer three or four, mostly white. Breast and underparts silky greyish-white, shading into the smoky flanks. Bill black, with whitish tip and a pale green patch around the gape; irides cinnamon; legs and feet dark olive-green.

This grebe, in several races, is found over a great part of the Old World. In Ceylon it is abundant on low-country tanks and lakes, especially in the dry zone; before Colombo became citified it was common on the Beira Lake, but it appears to have deserted this now. Legge

× one-quarter

states, on the authority of other people, that it had been seen on the Nuwara Eliya lake (6,200 feet) but it is probable that the Little Cormorant was mistaken for it. It lives in small parties or flocks of up to a dozen or so, though single birds are often seen. The dabchick is a squat little bird, which swims low in the water and constantly dives, both for feeding purposes and when alarmed. It goes under neatly, usually without any splash, to reappear many seconds later, perhaps twenty or thirty yards away from where it went under; and in an unpredictable place. In swimming, the legs, which are attached to the body almost under the tail, project laterally and work in a kind of rotary, 'twin-propeller' action. Small fish, prawns, and various water-insects and their larvae form its diet and it eats also a certain amount of vegetable matter. The waters it favours are those which combine plenty of reed-beds, lotus, etc., with areas of clear water. As breeding time approaches it indulges in playful chasing of its companions, fluttering along the surface with much splashing, and often uttering its shrill whinny, *hehehe-hehehe* . . . Every now and then it will raise itself in the water, puffing out its plumage until it looks nearly spherical. It seldom flies more than a few yards—and then with much fuss and splashing before it takes off— in the day-time; but at night it sometimes traverses great distances in search of a new home when its tank begins to dry up. Its short and narrow wings compel it to fly fast to fly at all; they are fluttered at a great rate.

The dabchick breeds in Ceylon from December to February, and again in June. The nest is a floating mass of water-weeds anchored among sedges or the like, the shallow cavity on top being an inch or so above water level. The three white eggs—quickly becoming stained— measure about 36 × 25·2 mm.

ADDITIONS AND AMENDMENTS TO THE LIST OF CEYLON BIRDS

Extracted from the following publications:

1. W. W. A. Phillips, *A (1952) Revised Checklist of the Birds of Ceylon.*
2. W. W. A. Phillips, *1956 Supplement to the (1952) Revised Checklist of the Birds of Ceylon.* Both these volumes are published by the National Museums of Ceylon. In the following pages they are given as *Checklist* and *Supplement*, respectively.
3. An unpublished *Revised and Annotated Checklist*, prepared by W. W. A. Phillips.
4. A 1966 Supplement to the last item, by the same author.
5. Sundry notes extracted from *Ceylon Bird Club Notes*, and from *Loris*, for several years up to 1968. I am very greatly indebted to Major Phillips for supplying me with all the above sources of information.
6. Edited by A. Landsborough Thompson, *A New Dictionary of Birds*, 1964.
7. Sálim Ali and S. Dillon Ripley, *Handbook of the Birds of India and Pakistan*, Vols. 1 and 2, 1968 and 1969. Subsequent volumes, still in production, will doubtless contain further changes of nomenclature.

Page

4. Ceylon Blue Magpie: the scientific name is given as *Kitta ornata* (Wagler). *Checklist*, p. 113; in *A New Dictionary of Birds*, Pl. 17, the genus is given as *Urocissa!*

9. The Ceylon Rufous Babbler is now considered to be a subspecies of the Indian Jungle Babbler, and its scientific name is therefore *Turdoides somervillei rufescens* (Blyth). *Checklist*, p. 91.

10. The Ashy-headed Babbler is restored to the genus *Garrulax*, in which Blyth placed it. *Checklist*, p. 91.

15. The Black-fronted Babbler is restored to the genus *Alcippe* in which Blyth placed it. *Checklist*, p. 91.

16–18. The Ioras and Chloropses, under the popular name 'Leafbirds', are united by J. Delacour, 1960, with the Bluebirds in the family *Irenidae* (see p. 72); see *A New Dictionary of Birds*, p. 423. In avicultural circles, the Chloropses are commonly known as 'fruit-suckers'.

424

Page

19. The scientific name of the Ceylon Black Bulbul is given as *Microscelis madagascariensis humii*, Whistler & Kinnear. *Checklist*, p. 85.

19. The generic name of the Red-vented Bulbul is changed from *Molpastes* to *Pycnonotus*. *Checklist*, p. 84.

20. The Ceylon Yellow-browed Bulbul is divided into two subspecies by S. Dillon Ripley, under the names *Iole icterica intensior* Koelz, which inhabits the Dry Zone and hills, and is found also in South India; and *Iole icterica guglielmi* (Ripley), peculiar to the Wet Zone of Ceylon. The two races appear to differ only in *guglielmi* being somewhat richer in colour than *intensior*. *Checklist*, pp. 84, 85.

22. The scientific name of the Yellow-eared Bulbul is changed from *Kelaartia penicillata* (Blyth) to *Pycnonotus penicillatus* Blyth. *Checklist*, p. 84.

24. The generic name of the Indian Blue Chat is changed from *Luscinia* to *Erithacus* in *Checklist*, p. 85, and restored to *Luscinia* in the *Supplement*, p. 190!

26. The generic name of the Bluethroat is given as *Erithacus* in *Checklist*, p. 85, and changed to *Luscinia* in the *Supplement*, p. 190, where a new record of the occurrence of the species in Ceylon is given; a male in winter plumage was collected on 30 November 1955, by E. C. Fernando Jr., in a paddy field at Boralesgamuwa, two miles east of Dehiwela, W. Province.

29. The generic name of the Ceylon Shama is changed to *Copsychus*. *Checklist*, p. 87.

29. The scientific name of the Ceylon Blackbird is given as *Turdus merula kinnisii* (Blyth). *Checklist*, p. 87.

30, 31, 32. The Pied Ground Thrush, Northern Orange-headed Ground Thrush, Ceylon Scaly Thrush, and Spotted-winged Thrush are all placed in the genus *Zoothera*; *Checklist*, pp. 87, 88. Several Orange-headed Ground Thrushes were seen by several observers in 1965 and 1966 in Wilpattu National Park, N.W.P., and at Okanda and Yalatota, S.P., in December 1966.

ADDITIONS AND AMENDMENTS

Page

34. The scientific name of the Ceylon Arrenga is given as *Myiophoneus blighi* (Holdsworth). *Checklist*, p. 88.

36. The correct scientific name of the Ceylon Orange-breasted Blue Flycatcher is *Muscicapa tickelliae jerdoni* (Holdsworth). *Supplement*, p. 192.

41. The generic name of the White-browed Fantail Flycatcher is changed to *Rhipidura*. *Checklist*, p. 101.

44. Phillips records two specimens of the Indian race of the Great Reed Warbler *Acrocephalus stentoreus brunnescens* (Jerdon), from Jaffna and the Mutturajawella Swamp, 14 miles north of Colombo, respectively; it is slightly larger and paler-coloured than the Ceylon race. *Checklist*, p. 95.

46. Phillips records that he found Sykes's Booted Warbler (Sykes's Tree-Warbler) fairly common in low, thorny acacia scrub, near Mullaitivu on the north-east coast, where he collected specimens in March 1955. *Supplement*, p. 191.

46. The name of the bird called Eversmann's Booted Warbler, *Hippolais caligata scita* (Eversmann) should be changed to Booted Warbler, *Hippolais caligata caligata* (Lichtenstein). *Supplement*, p. 192.

47. Hume's Whitethroat, *Sylvia althaea*, was found to be plentiful in acacia thorn scrub around Mullaitivu in March 1955, by Phillips, who collected specimens there. *Supplement*, p. 192.

51. Phillips has discovered that there are two races of the Fantail Warbler in Ceylon; the subspecies *omalura* Blyth, a larger, darker bird with a big bill, inhabits the Wet and Hill Zones; while the Common Indian Streaked Fantail Warbler race *cursitans* (Franklin), a smaller, paler form, occupies the low-country Dry Zone. *Supplement*, p. 191.

72. As pointed out in this Appendix (p. 424), the Ioras and Chloropses, treated in this book as a sub-family, Liotrichinae, of the Pycnonotidae, are united by J. Delacour with the Bluebirds in the family Irenidae. However, further to complicate matters, 'Wetmore places *Irena* in a special subfamily of the Oriolidae, and treats the other two genera (*Aegithina* and *Chloropsis*) as constituting a family Chloropseidae'. *A New Dictionary of Birds*, p. 424.

Page

76, 77. The Grackles are united with the Starlings and Mynahs under the family Sturnidae, and given the generic name *Gracula. Checklist*, p. 109.

78, 79, 80. The Rose-coloured Starling, Brahminy Mynah, and White-headed Starling are all placed in the genus *Sturnus. Checklist*, p. 108.

Mrs M. Stevenson has observed evidences of breeding of the White-headed Starling in the Dolosbage district, *c.* 3,000 feet, C.P., during January–March, in several years from 1962 to 1965; pairs carrying food to tree-holes, etc. *Ceylon Bird Club Notes.*

85. The Java Sparrow is placed in the genus *Padda. Checklist*, p. 105.

85–8. The White-backed, Ceylon Hill, Spotted, and White-throated Munias are placed in the genus *Lonchura* instead of *Uroloncha. Checklist*, pp. 106, 107.

95, 96. Richard's Pipit and the Indian Pipit are now regarded as races of the species *Anthus novaeseelandiae*, and their scientific names are therefore *Anthus novaeseelandiae richardi* and *Anthus novaeseelandiae malayensis* respectively. *Checklist*, p. 77.

96. Specimens of Blyth's Pipit were collected by E. C. Fernando Jr., at Boralesgamuwa, W.P., on 1 February 1953, and by W. W. A. Phillips a few miles north of Mullaitivu, N.P., on 23 March 1955. *Supplement*, p. 188. The species *Anthus campestris*, in several racial forms, has a wide breeding distribution in Europe and Asia, and, under the popular name Tawny Pipit, is a frequent passage migrant in South England.

97. Indian White Wagtail: several sight records of this species were made during the winters of 1964 and 1965 at Muwangala, Galoya Valley, E.P., and Amparai, by K. G. H. Munidasa, and at Ambalantota by Rev. G. C. Jackson. *Ceylon Bird Club Notes.*

98. The Yellow-headed Wagtail (now known as the Citrine Wagtail) *Motacilla citreola*: sight records of this species were made in January and February 1966 by Rev. G. C. Jackson at Kalametia, and by C. E. Norris at Attunagala Wewa, near Palatana, S.P. (two together). *Ceylon Bird Club Notes*, February 1966.

In a MS. diary, now in my possession, kept by the late famous artist-naturalist George Lodge, during a visit to Ceylon in 1903, the following interesting observation occurs, under date 3 April: 'at the margin of the other [a tank near Madawach-

Page

chiya] I shot a wagtail which was entirely yellow except most
of the wing feathers. The eyes normal (black). I think this
may be a sort of albino.'
There seems little doubt that the bird was in fact an individual
of the Yellow-headed Wagtail.

100. The Black-headed Wagtail, *Motacilla flava feldegg* Michahalles:
Phillips records that two individuals of this race of *Motacilla
flava* were observed at Kantalai Tank, E.P., on 27 April 1940.
They were in full breeding plumage. *Checklist*, p. 78.

103. The scientific name of the Hill Swallow is given as *Hirundo tahitica
domicola* Jerdon. *Checklist*, p. 76.

105. Hodgson's Striated Swallow, *Hirundo daurica nepalensis*: sight
records of this race of *H. daurica* were made by C. E. Norris at
Hindagalla Patana, Namunukula, in December 1965; they were
hawking for flying insects in association with Eastern Swallows
and Crested Tree Swifts. Norris states that their most noticeable
features were their pale rumps, nearly white underparts,
and describes the note as similar to that of *H. d. hyperythra*, but
more reedy and weak. *Ceylon Bird Club Notes* for December
1965.
H. G. Alexander identified one (perhaps two) of this race in
December 1957, flying amongst 30–40 *H. d. hyperythra* at
Peradeniya. *Ceylon Bird Club Notes*.

106. The Indian Wire-tailed Swallow, *Hirundo smithii filifera* Stephens:
one was observed at close range, sitting on a telegraph wire
in company with Eastern Swallows, on the road between
Poonaryn and Mannar, N.P., on 26 February 1966, by Mrs
R. Wynell-Mayow and Mrs Nugawela.

109–12. The generic name of all the Ceylon Sunbirds is given as
Nectarinia instead of *Cinnyris*. *Checklist*, pp. 103, 104.

Plate 10

fig. 5. The head of the Pitta in this illustration is too large in relation
to the rest of the bird. *Meâ culpâ!*

Page

120. The Ceylon Yellow-fronted Pied Woodpecker is given the
scientific name *Dendrocopos mahrattensis koelzi* Biswas. *Checklist*,
p. 73.

ADDITIONS AND AMENDMENTS

Page

121. The scientific name of the Ceylon Pygmy Woodpecker is given as *Dendrocopos moluccensis gymnophthalmus* (Blyth). *Checklist*, p. 73.

123. The Ceylon Golden-backed Woodpecker is given the scientific name *Dinopium benghalense jaffnense* (Whistler). *Checklist*, p. 72. The Ceylon Red-backed Woodpecker becomes *Dinopium benghalense erithronothon* (Vieillot). *Checklist*, p. 72.

125. The Crimson-backed Woodpecker is given the scientific name *Chrysocolaptes lucidus stricklandi* (Layard). *Checklist*, p. 73.

127-9. All four Ceylonese Barbets are placed in the genus *Megalaima*. *Checklist*, pp. 70, 71.

133. The Broad-billed Roller, *Eurystomus orientalis* (Linnaeus): the Ceylonese bird has been distinguished from its nearest relative, the Travancorean race *E. o. laetior* Sharpe, under the name *E. o. irisi* Deraniyagala. *Checklist*, p. 69. I have not seen the description of this subspecies, but gather that it differs from *E. o. laetior* only in having slightly shorter wings and tail. (See W. Meise, *Journal of the Bombay Natural History Society*, 49, No. 2, p. 305.)

Of recent years there have been a number of observations of this Roller by C. E. Norris, G. C. and Graham Jackson and R. McL. Cameron, all in the neighbourhood of Maha Oya; birds have been seen mating, feeding young, etc., and these observations prove that the species is truly a breeding resident of Ceylon.

After publication of the first edition of this book, I was informed by Mrs Iris Darnton that the rediscovery of this bird in Ceylon, in February 1950, must be credited to her, and not to W. W. A. Phillips, to whom, under a misapprehension, I attributed it. Mrs Darnton kindly sent me a copy of her interesting paper, published in *Spolia Zeylanica*, vol. 26, pp. 19-20, wherein she describes how she found the birds about to breed at Maha Oya, E.P., with useful descriptions of their appearance and behaviour in life.

The Broad-billed Rollers of South India and Ceylon offer a very interesting case of 'discontinuous distribution', being separated from the main range of the species *Eurystomus orientalis* by almost the whole Indian Peninsula. In view of this, it is much to be hoped that the small relict population in Ceylon will henceforth be suffered to live and breed in peace.

ADDITIONS AND AMENDMENTS

Page

135. The Blue-tailed Bee-eater is given the scientific name *Merops philippinus philippinus* Linnaeus. *Checklist*, p. 68.
C. E. Norris, in May 1962, April 1963 and May 1964, found several colonies of this bird nesting in burrows excavated in sand-dunes and banks, at, respectively, Oluvil (5 miles north of Akkaraiputtu, E.P.), Iliyagalla Lagoon, near Kumuna, E.P., and Bagura, south of Pottuvil. The Blue-tailed Bee-eater is therefore a breeding resident of Ceylon, as well as an abundant winter visitor.

145. The Ceylon Grey Hornbill is now regarded as a subspecies of the S. Indian Grey Hornbill, and its scientific name is therefore *Tockus griseus gingalensis* (Shaw). *Checklist*, p. 69.

152. The specific and subspecific names of the Brown-throated Spinetail Swift should be spelt *giganteus indicus*. *Checklist*, p. 64.

154. The scientific name of the Indian Edible-nest Swift is given as *Collocalia brevirostris unicolor* (Jerdon). *Checklist*, p. 64.

165. The Trogon found in the forests of the dry coastal plain in the north of Ceylon has been described as a smaller, lighter-coloured race than the Wet Zone form, under the name *Harpactes fasciatus parvus* Deraniyagala. *Supplement*, p. 66.

173. The Ceylon Drongo-Cuckoo is given subspecific rank under the scientific name *Surniculus lugubris stewarti* Baker, on rather flimsy grounds. *Checklist*, p. 58.

225. The Desert Buzzard, *Buteo burmanicus burmanicus* Hume: in Sálim Ali and Ripley, *Handbook of the Birds of India and Pakistan*, vol. 1 (1968), p. 255, the Buzzards that visit Ceylon belong not to the Desert Buzzard but to a race of the Common Buzzard, *Buteo buteo burmanicus* Hume. However, the identification of oriental buzzards in their winter quarters, as distinct from their breeding habitats, is exceedingly difficult because of their great variability and plumage changes. See Whistler, *Avifaunal Survey of Ceylon*, *Spolia Zeylanica*, vol. 23, p. 247.

235. The Eastern Peregrine is given the scientific name *Falco peregrinus japonensis* Gmelin in Sálim Ali and Ripley, *Handbook of the Birds of India and Pakistan*, vol. 1 (1968), p. 347.

250. Footnote. The Rufous Turtle Dove: another specimen of this species was collected by Mr Gordon Graham at Urubokka, near Deniyaya, S.P., on 19 December 1954. This specimen too was in first-year plumage. *Supplement*, p. 188.

Page

273. The Indian Large Pratincole: two Pratincoles, collected by Phillips near Ambalantota, S.P., on 25 February 1951, were identified at the Natural History Museum, London, as belonging to the race *Glareola p. pratincola* (Linnaeus), whose breeding area extends over most of Europe and North Africa; it appears to differ from *G. p. maldivarum* mainly in having a deeper fork to the tail (2 in. *v.* 1 in.), and white tips to the secondaries. *Supplement*, p. 187.

279. The heads in these figures of Oyster-catchers are too big.

280. The Ceylon Red-wattled Lapwing is regarded by Koelz and Ripley as a separate race, *Lobivanellus indicus lankae* Koelz, on the basis of trifling differences in average measurements. *Checklist*, p. 32. In the *Handbook of the Birds of India and Pakistan*, vol. 2, all lapwings and the Sociable Plover are placed in the genus *Vanellus*.

289. A Caspian Plover was observed on 5 May 1960 in Ceylon (? locality) by Lt.-Com. P. Troubridge. *Ceylon Bird Club Notes*.

289. The Kentish Plovers are placed in the genus *Charadrius* instead of *Leucopolius*, which involves the following changes in nomenclature: Ceylon Kentish Plover, *Charadrius alexandrinus seebohmi* Hartert & Jackson. Kentish Plover, *Charadrius a. alexandrinus* Linnaeus. *Checklist*, p. 34.

Plate 25

fig. 5. It has been pointed out to me that the legs in this figure of the Terek Sandpiper are too yellow. In winter plumage as shown, they should be a rather dull ochraceous orange, but in breeding plumage they become brighter. In breeding plumage the bird develops a conspicuous black streak along each side of the back, comprising the inner scapulars.

In the same Plate, fig. 7, it was pointed out to me by the Rev. S. K. Bunker, that in life, the side wattles of the Yellow-wattled Lapwing do not hang down as shown, but lie along the sides of the throat. In a dead specimen the wattles may lose their turgidity and hang down.

Page

302. The scientific name of the Terek Sandpiper is now given as *Tringa terek* (Latham). *Handbook of the Birds of India and Pakistan*, vol. 2, p. 269.

ADDITIONS AND AMENDMENTS

Page

310. The Common Sandpiper is now *Tringa hypoleucos* Linnaeus instead of *Actitis hypoleucos* (Linnaeus). *Handbook of the Birds of India and Pakistan*, vol. 2, p. 271.

318. An adult female of the Asiatic, or Siberian Pectoral Sandpiper (also called Sharp-tailed Sandpiper), *Calidris* (or *Erolia*) *acuminata* (Horsfield), was collected by Phillips at Embilikala Kalapuwa, 8 miles north-east of Hambantota, S.P., on 18 September 1955. It was feeding with various other sandpipers in shallow water. *Supplement*, p. 187. This sandpiper is about the size and general appearance of the Curlew-Sandpiper, from which, in winter plumage, it is probably difficult to distinguish in the field; but its beak is shorter and straight, it lacks a white wing-bar, and the middle of its upper tail-coverts are blackish. Its summer haunts are in north-eastern Siberia and it commonly winters in S.E. Asia to as far south as Australia and New Zealand. It is an occasional vagrant to Britain.

319. A specimen of the Buff-breasted Sandpiper, *Tryngites subruficollis* (Vieillot), was collected by Dr de Zylva at Kalametiya lagoon on 5 March 1960. *Loris* 815, pp. 330–1. This beautiful sandpiper, about the size of the Common Sandpiper, is a rich, warm buff colour throughout the head and body; the feathers of crown, back, sides of breast, with dark brown centres, giving a scaly effect; wings and tail darker above; the axillaries are white, under-wing whitish, with dark mottling on the primary coverts and secondaries, and the primaries finely barred with blackish speckling towards the dark tips. The beak is short, slender and tapering, black; irides dark brown; legs and feet dull orange.

This species is normally confined to North America in summer, wintering in South America. It is less dependent on watery situations than most sandpipers, frequenting dry prairies in America, and it breeds in tundras in the far north. It is said to be very tame, a fact which nearly caused its extermination by 'sportsmen' and market hunters a few decades ago.

323. Two specimens of Swinhoe's Snipe, *Capella megala* (Swinhoe), were shot by E. C. Fernando Jr. on 28 December 1966, at Bandaragamma paddy fields. (*Litt.* to W. W. A. Phillips.)

324. Footnote. A third example of the Great Snipe, *Capella media* (Latham) was collected by H. G. Pandithesekera in a paddy field near Chilaw, N.W.P., on 27 January 1953. *Supplement*, p. 186.

Page

337. Apparently both races of the Little Tern (*Sterna a. sinensis* and *Sterna a. saundersi*) breed in Ceylon. *Checklist*, pp. 49, 50.

344. Pomatorhine Skua, *Stercorarius pomarinus* (Temminck): 'A reliable sight record was made by Mr A. E. Butler, at Hambantota, S.P., on 27 July 1954. The skua was settled on the beach and rose on a close approach. It was of the dark form with a pale neck and dark cap.' *Supplement*, p. 187.

347. The Blue-breasted Banded Rail is given the scientific name *Rallus striatus gularis* Horsfield. *Checklist*, p. 29.

349. The Ruddy Crake is given the scientific name *Porzana fusca zeylonica* (Baker). *Checklist*, p. 29.

359. The subspecific name of the Southern or Indian Cormorant is attributed to (Blumenbach) not (Shaw). *Checklist*, p. 5.

367. The Short-tailed Tropic Bird, *Phaethon aethereus indicus* Hume: a juvenile male was captured at sea about 14 miles off the S. Indian coast not far from Cape Comorin on 3 February 1956. *Supplement*, p. 184.

380. Footnote. A Glossy Ibis was shot by M. Andrado out of a party of six in paddy fields between Kiula and Hungama, 2 December 1968. Identified by A. E. Butler. *Ceylon Bird Club Notes*, December 1968.

408. Comb Duck or Nukhta: in December 1960, two large ducks, believed to be of this species, were observed by C. E. Norris at Lahugalla, and others were seen by P. Jayawardene in the same area, on several occasions during 1961. *Ceylon Bird Club Notes*.

411. Large Whistling Teal, *Dendrocygna b. bicolor* (Vieillot): sixteen were observed by C. B. Bavinck in company with Garganeys, Pintails, and Lesser Whistling Teal, at a lagoon (near Jaffna?) in December 1968. *Ceylon Bird Club Notes*, December 1968.

412. Ruddy Sheldrake: A flock of eight was seen several times on a large lagoon near Arugam Bay in March 1948 (Phillips, *Loris* IV, p. 498), and a single one near Hambantota in 1949/50 (Norris, *Loris* V, p. 171).

Page

413. Spotted-billed Duck: a pair were seen, and the drake shot in February 1947, near Kuchchaveli, E.P. (Phillips, *Loris*, IV (1948), pp. 498, 516). One was shot and others seen at Anthananthidal, near Sarasalai, Jaffna Peninsula, on 15 April 1966. (Dr A. Gabriel, *Loris* X, p. 383.)

420. Tufted Duck: Two males were observed by R. McL. Cameron at Giants Tank on 4 February 1962. *Ceylon Bird Club Notes.*

ORDER OF FAMILIES AS USED IN THIS BOOK

Compared with the order used in

A (1952) Revised Checklist of the Birds of Ceylon

ORDER OF FAMILIES

NOTE: In the GUIDE, the Darters, *Anhingidae*, are united with the Cormorants in the Family *Phalacrocoracidae* (*Phalacrocoridae* in CHECKLIST); the Oystercatchers, *Haematopodidae*, and also the Avocet and Stilt, *Recurvirostridae*, are included in the *Charadriidae*; the Phalaropes, *Phalaropodidae*, are placed with the Sandpipers, etc., in the *Scolopacidae*; the Iora and Chloropses, *Aegithinidae*, are included with the Bulbuls in *Pycnonotidae*. In the CHECKLIST, the Grackles, *Eulabetidae*, are united with the Starlings and Mynahs in *Sturnidae*.

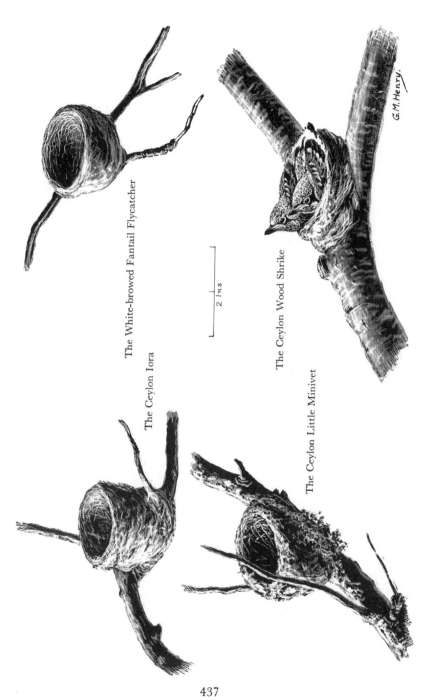

The White-browed Fantail Flycatcher

The Ceylon Iora

The Ceylon Wood Shrike

The Ceylon Little Minivet

G.M.Henry.

2 Ins

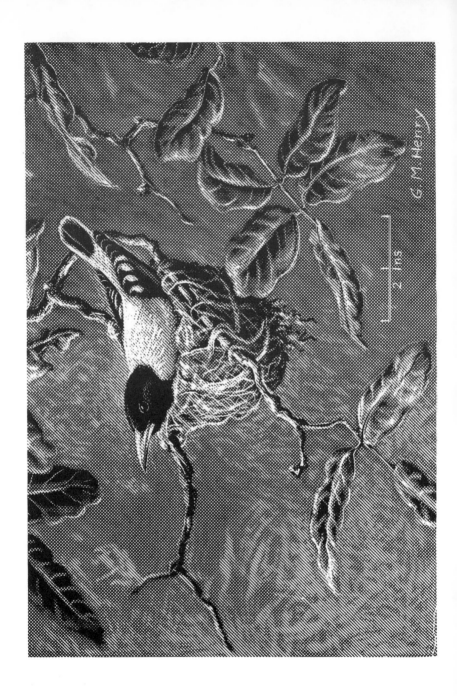

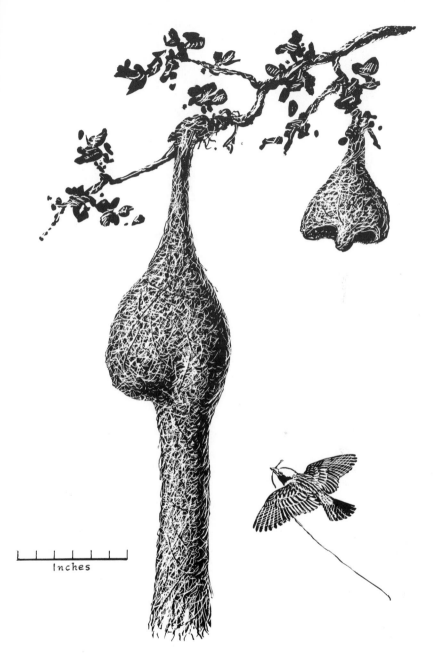

Inches

The Baya Weaver

439

The Ceylon Bush-Lark

440

The Indian Edible-nest Swift

The Purple Sunbird; nest in cobweb-mass of the spider   The Ceylon Small Flowerpecker
Stegodyphus sarasinorum

Inches

G. M. Henry

The Purple-rumped Sunbird   Loten's Sunbird

Indian Crested Swift

INCHES

Ceylon Pygmy Woodpecker

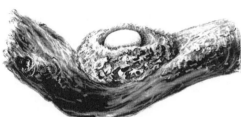

Ceylon Frogmouth

The Ceylon Small Barbet

G. M. Henry

443

G. M. Henry

The Ceylon White-breasted Kingfisher leaving nest-burrow

444

2 ins

G.M.Henry.

The Collared Scops Owl

Ceylon Junglehen and nest

The Ceylon Bustard-Quail; male approaching nest

447

The Great Stone Plover

INDEX

449

INDEX

INDEX

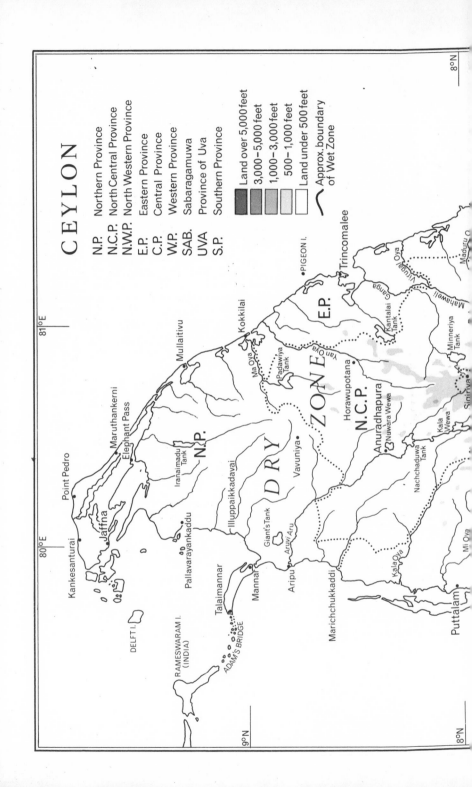